SQL for MySQL Developers

SQL for MySQL Developers

A Comprehensive Tutorial and Reference

Rick F. van der Lans
Translated by Diane Cools

Addison-Wesley

Upper Saddle River, NJ ▪ Boston ▪ Indianapolis ▪ San Francisco
New York ▪ Toronto ▪ Montreal ▪ London ▪ Munich ▪ Paris ▪ Madrid
Cape Town ▪ Sydney ▪ Tokyo ▪ Singapore ▪ Mexico City

The publisher offers excellent discounts on this book when ordered in quantity for bulk purchases or special sales, which may include electronic versions and/or custom covers and content particular to your business, training goals, marketing focus, and branding interests. For more information, please contact:

U.S. Corporate and Government Sales
(800) 382-3419
corpsales@pearsontechgroup.com

For sales outside the United States please contact:

International Sales
international@pearsoned.com

Library of Congress Cataloging-in-Publication Data

Lans, Rick F. van der.
SQL for MySQL developers : a comprehensive tutorial and reference / Rick F. van der Lans.
p. cm.
ISBN 978-0-13-149735-1 (pbk. : alk. paper) 1. SQL (Computer program language) 2. MySQL (Electronic resource) I. Title.
QA76.73.S67L345 2007
005.13'3—dc22

2007000578

ISBN 0131497359
Text printed in the United States on recycled paper at Edwards Brothers in Ann Arbor, Michigan.
Second printing, June 2007

Dedicated to Alyssa.

Contents

About the Author

Rick F. van der Lans is author of the classic *Introduction to SQL*, the definitive SQL guide that database developers have relied on for more than 20 years. This book has been translated into various languages and has sold more than 100,000 copies.

He is an independent consultant, author, and lecturer specializing in database technology, development tools, data warehousing, and XML. As managing director of the Netherlands-based R20/Consultancy, he has advised many large companies on defining their IT architectures.

Rick is an internationally acclaimed lecturer. Throughout his career, he has lectured in many European countries, South America, USA, and Australia. He chairs the European Meta Data Conference and DB2 Symposium, and writes columns for several magazines. He was a member of the Dutch ISO committee responsible for the ISO SQL Standard for seven years.

You can contact Rick via email at sql@r20.nl.

Preface

INTRODUCTION

Many books have been written about MySQL, the best-known open source database server. Then why another book? Most books about MySQL discuss a wide variety of topics, such as the installation of MySQL, using MySQL from PHP, and security. As a result, each topic cannot be explained in detail, and many questions of readers cannot be answered. This book focuses on one aspect of MySQL: the language that drives MySQL, which is *SQL* (Structured Query Language). Every developer working with MySQL should master this language thoroughly.

Especially in the more recent versions, SQL has been extended considerably. Unfortunately, many developers still limit themselves to those features that were available in the first versions. Not all the features of MySQL are fully used, which means that the product is not employed in the best way possible. The result is that complex statements and programs must be built needlessly. When you buy a house, you also do not restrict yourself to 20 percent of the rooms, do you? That is why this book contains a complete and detailed description of the SQL dialect as implemented in MySQL version 5.0.18. It should be seen primarily as a textbook rather than as a reference book; it will teach you the language, and you can complete the exercises to test your knowledge. After reading this book, you should be familiar with all the statements and features and some idiosyncrasies of MySQL's SQL, and you should be able to use it efficiently and effectively.

Topics

This book is completely devoted to the SQL dialect as implemented in MySQL. It discusses every aspect of the language thoroughly and critically. These aspects of SQL among others, are covered:

- Querying data (joins, functions, and subqueries)
- Updating data
- Creating tables and views
- Specifying primary and foreign keys and other integrity constraints
- Using indexes
- Considering data security
- Developing stored procedures and triggers
- Developing programs with PHP
- Working with transactions
- Using the catalog

For Whom Is This Book Intended?

We recommend this book on MySQL's SQL dialect to those who want to use the full power of MySQL effectively and efficiently in practice. This book is therefore suitable for the following groups of people:

- **Developers** who develop applications with the help of MySQL
- **Database managers** who have to know the possibilities and impossibilities of SQL
- **Students** in higher education, including those in technical colleges, polytechnics, universities, and sixth-form colleges
- **Designers, analysts,** and **consultants** who have to deal, directly or indirectly, with MySQL and/or SQL and want to know about its possibilities and impossibilities
- **Home students** who are interested in MySQL and/or SQL
- **Users** who have the authority to use SQL to query the MySQL database of the company or institute for which they are working

- **Web site developers** who are creating web sites with the help of MySQL and languages such as PHP and Python
- **IT hobbyists** who are interested in MySQL and want to develop an SQL application using MySQL themselves

A Practical Book

This book should be seen primarily as a *textbook* and less as a reference work. To this end, it contains many examples and exercises (with answers). Do not ignore the exercises. Experience shows that you will learn the language more thoroughly and more quickly by practicing often and doing many exercises.

The Book's Web Site

When you leaf through the book, you will come across numerous SQL statements. Sometimes these are examples, and sometimes they are answers to questions. After you have installed MySQL, you can run through these statements to see whether they work and see their effects. You could type in all the statements again like a real Spartan, but you can also make life easy for yourself by downloading all the statements from the Internet. A special web site for this book, www.r20.nl, includes all the SQL statements.

We also have used the web site for these purposes:

- The web site includes an installation process and instructions for MySQL. You will find useful tips for installing MySQL under Windows. The site also explains the installation process of the example database.
- If an error is found in the book, the web site will rectify the mistake.
- Reader comments that could be of interest to others will be added periodically to site.
- We even will consider making additional chapters available on the web site in the future.

Therefore, keep an eye on this web site.

Prerequisite Knowledge

Some general knowledge of programming languages and database servers is required.

The History of This Book

It was 1984, and the database world was under the spell of a revolution. SQL had started its triumphal procession. Vendors such as IBM and Oracle had introduced the commercial versions of their SQL database servers, and the marketing machine went at full speed. The market reacted positively to this rise of first-generation SQL database servers. Many organizations decided to buy such a database server and gradually phase out their existing products.

My employer at that time had decided to get involved in this tumult as well. The company also wanted to make money with this new database language, and the plan was to start organizing SQL courses. Because of my background knowledge, I was charged with this task. That SQL would become such a success and that my agreement to present the courses would have far- reaching consequences (personally as well as professionally) never entered my mind.

After studying SQL closely, I started to develop the material for the course. After teaching SQL for two years with great pleasure, I got an idea to write a book about SQL. It would have to be a book completely dedicated to this language, with its many possibilities and idiosyncrasies.

After producing gallons of blood, sweat, and tears, I completed the first Dutch edition in 1986, entitled *Het SQL Leerboek.* The book did not focus on a specific SQL database server, but on the SQL standard. Barely before the book was published, I was asked to write an English version. That book, *Introduction to SQL,* was published in 1987 as the first English book completely devoted to SQL. After that, I wrote versions in German and Italian. Obviously, a need existed for information about SQL. Everyone wanted to learn about SQL, but not much information was available.

Because SQL was still young, development went fast. Statements were added, extended, and improved. New implementations became available, new application areas were discovered, and new versions of the SQL standard appeared. Soon a new edition of the book had to be written. And more was to come. And this will not be the last because SQL has gloriously won the revolution in the database world, and no competition is in sight on the horizon.

Through the years, many vendors have implemented SQL. At first, all these products had much in common, but slowly the number of differences increased. For that reason, I decided in 2003 to write a book specifically dedicated to the SQL dialect of MySQL. I thought it would be a piece of cake. I would use *Introduction to SQL* as an example, add some details of MySQL, and remove a few general aspects. How long could that take? Two weeks of hard work and some speed typing, and I'd have the book ready. However, that appeared to be a serious underestimation. To give a complete view of all the features, I had to dive deeply into the SQL dialect of MySQL. This book, which definitely took more than two weeks of writing, is the result of that time-consuming effort. Obviously, it is related to the book from which it is derived; however, it contains many MySQL-related details not included in *Introduction to SQL.*

AND FINALLY...

Writing this book was not a solo project. Many people have contributed to this book or previous editions. I would like to use this preface to thank them for their help, contributions, ideas, comments, mental support, and patience.

It does not matter how many times a writer reads his own work; editors remain indispensable. A writer reads not what he has written, but what he thinks he has written. In this respect, writing is like programming. That is why I owe a great deal to the following persons for making critical comments and giving very helpful advice: Klaas Brant, Marc van Cappellen, Ian Cargill, Corine Cools, Richard van Dijk, Rose Endres, Wim Frederiks, Andrea Gray, Ed Jedeloo, Josien van der Laan, Oda van der Lans, Deborah Leendertse, Arjen Lentz, Onno de Maar, Andrea Maurino, Sandor Nieuwenhuijs, Henk Schreij, Dave Slayton, Aad Speksnijder, Nok van Veen, John Vicherek, and David van der Waaij. They all have read this manuscript (or parts of it) or the manuscript of a previous edition, a translation of it, or an adjusted version.

I would like to thank Wim Frederiks and Roland Bouman separately for all the hours they spent editing this book. Both patiently studied each page and pointed out the errors and inconsistencies. I am very grateful to them for all the work they put into this project.

I would also like to thank the thousands of students across the world whom I have taught SQL over the past years. Their comments and recommendations have been invaluable in revising this book. In addition, a large number of readers of the previous edition responded to my request to send comments and suggestions. I want to thank them for the trouble they took to put these in writing.

From the first day I started working on the project, I had the support of the MySQL organization. They helped me by making the required software available. I want to thank this group very much for the support and help.

Again, I owe Diane Cools many thanks. As an editor, she made this book readable to others. For a writer, it is also reassuring to find someone who, especially in difficult times, keeps stimulating and motivating you. Thanks, Diane!

Finally, again I would like to ask readers to send comments, opinions, ideas, and suggestions concerning the contents of the book to sql@r20.nl, referencing *SQL for MySQL Developers.* Many thanks, in anticipation of your cooperation.

Rick F. van der Lans
Den Haag, The Netherlands, March 2007

Part I

Introduction

SQL is a compact and powerful language for working with databases. Despite this compactness, it cannot be described simply in a few chapters. We would do the language no justice then. And that certainly applies to MySQL's SQL dialect, which has many, many possibilities. For this reason, we start this book with a number of introductory chapters that form the first part.

In Chapter 1, "Introduction to MySQL," we provide an overall description of SQL, including its background and history, and the history of MySQL. MySQL is *open source software;* in Section 1.8, we explain what that really means. We also describe a number of concepts in the relational model (the theory behind SQL).

This book contains many examples and exercises. So that you do not have to learn a new database for each example, we use the same database for most of these examples and exercises. This database forms the basis for the administration of an international tennis league. Chapter 2, "The Tennis Club Sample Database," describes the structure of this database. Look closely at this before you begin the exercises.

We strongly recommend that you use MySQL when doing the exercises and get some hands-on experience. For this, you have to download and install the software, and create the example database. Chapter 3, "Installing the Software," describes how to do that. Note that for several aspects, we refer to the web site of the book.

This part closes with Chapter 4, "SQL in a Nutshell," which reviews all the important SQL statements. After reading this part, you should have both a general idea of what SQL offers as a language and an overall impression of what this book discusses.

CHAPTER 1

Introduction to MySQL

1.1 Introduction

MySQL is a relational database server that supports the well-known SQL (Structured Query Language) database language. Therefore, MySQL is named after the language that developers use to store, query, and later update data in a MySQL database. In short, SQL is the native language of MySQL.

This chapter discusses the following topics. None of these topics is really important for studying MySQL's SQL. When you are familiar with these background topics, you can jump to the next chapter.

- The chapter starts with an explanation of basic subjects, such as the database, database server, and database language.
- SQL is based on theories of the *relational model.* To use SQL, some knowledge of this model is invaluable. Therefore, Section 1.3 describes the relational model.
- Section 1.4 briefly describes what SQL is, what can be done with the language, and how it differs from other languages (such as Java, Visual Basic, or PHP).
- Section 1.5 covers the history of SQL.
- Section 1.7 presents the most important current standards for SQL.
- MySQL is open source software. Section 1.8 explains what that really means.
- Section 1.9 discusses the history of MySQL and its vendors.
- The chapter closes with a description of the structure of the book. The book consists of several parts, with each part summarized in a few sentences.

1.2 Database, Database Server, and Database Language

SQL (Structured Query Language) is a database language used for formulating statements processed by a database server. In this case, the database server is MySQL. The first sentence of this paragraph contains three important concepts: *database, database server,* and *database language.* We begin with an explanation of each of these terms.

What is a *database*? This book uses a definition derived from Chris J. Date's definition (see [DATE95]):

> A **database** consists of some collection of persistent data that is used by the application systems of some given enterprise and managed by a database-management system.

Therefore, card index files do not constitute a database. On the other hand, the large files of banks, insurance companies, telephone companies, and the state transport department can be considered databases. These databases contain data about addresses, account balances, car registration plates, weights of vehicles, and so on. For example, the company you work for probably has its own computers, which are used to store salary-related data.

Data in a database becomes useful only if something is done with it. According to the definition, data in the database is managed by a separate programming system. This system is called a *database server* or *database management system (DBMS).* MySQL is such a database server. A database server enables users to process data stored in a database. Without a database server, it is impossible to look at data in the database or to update or delete obsolete data. The database server alone knows where and how data is stored. A definition of a database server appears in [ELMA06], by R. Elmasri:

> A **database server** is a collection of programs that enables users to create and maintain a database.

A database server never changes or deletes the data in a database by itself; someone or something has to give the command for this to happen. Examples of commands that a user could give to the database server are 'delete all data about the vehicle with the registration plate number DR-12-DP' or 'give the names of all the companies that haven't paid the invoices of last March.' However, users cannot communicate with the database server directly; an application must present the commands to a database server. An application always exists between the user and the database server. Section 1.4 discusses this in more detail.

The definition of the term *database* also contains the word *persistent.* This means that data in a database remains there permanently until it is changed or deleted explicitly. If you store new data in a database and the database server sends back the message that the storage operation was successful, you can be sure that the data will still be there tomorrow (even if you switch off your computer). This is unlike the data stored in the internal memory of a computer. If the computer is switched off, that data is lost forever; it is not persistent.

Commands are relayed to a database server with the help of special languages, called *database languages.* Users enter commands, also known as statements, that are formulated according to the rules of the database language, using special software; the database server then processes these commands. Every database server, regardless of manufacturer, possesses a database language. Some systems support more than one. All these languages are different, which makes it possible to divide them into groups. The *relational database languages* form one of these groups. An example of such a language is SQL.

How does a database server store data in a database? A database server uses neither a chest of drawers nor a filing cabinet to hold information; instead, computers work with storage media such as tapes, floppy disks, and magnetic and optical disks. The manner in which a database server stores information on these media is very complex and technical, and this book does not explain the details. In fact, you do not need this technical knowledge because one of the most important tasks of a database server is to offer *data independence.* This means that users do not need to know how or where data is stored. To users, a database is simply a large reservoir of information. Storage methods are also completely independent of the database language being used. In a way, this resembles the process of checking in luggage at an airport. Travelers do not care where and how the airline stores their luggage; they are interested only in whether the luggage arrives at their destinations.

Another important task of a database server is to maintain the *integrity* of the data stored in a database. This means, first, that the database server has to make sure that database data always satisfies the rules that apply in the real world. Take, for example, the case of an employee who is allowed to work for one department only. In a database managed by a database server, the database should not permit any employee to be registered as working for two or more departments. Second, integrity means that two different pieces of database data do not contradict one another. This is also known as *data consistency.* (As an example, in one place in a database, Mr. Johnson might be recorded as being born on August 4, 1964, and in another place he might have a birth date of December 14, 1946. These two pieces of data are obviously inconsistent.) Each database server is designed to recognize statements that can be used to specify *constraints*. After these rules are entered, the database server takes care of their implementation.

1.3 The Relational Model

SQL is based on a formal and mathematical theory. This theory, which consists of a set of concepts and definitions, is called the *relational model*. E. F. Codd defined the relational model in 1970 while at IBM. He introduced the relational model in the almost legendary article entitled "A Relational Model of Data for Large Shared Data Banks" (see [CODD70]). This relational model provides a theoretical basis for database languages. It consists of a small number of simple concepts for recording data in a database, together with a number of operators to manipulate the data. These concepts and operators are principally borrowed from *set theory* and *predicate logic*. Later, in 1979, Codd presented his ideas for an improved version of the model; see [CODD79] and [CODD90].

The relational model has served as an example for the development of various database languages, including QUEL (see [STON86]), SQUARE (see [BOYC73a]), and, of course, SQL. These database languages are based on the concepts and ideas of that relational model and, therefore, are called *relational database languages;* SQL is an example. The rest of this part concentrates on the following terms used in the relational model, which appear extensively in this book:

- Table
- Column
- Row
- Null value
- Constraint or integrity constraint
- Primary key
- Candidate key
- Alternate key
- Foreign key or referential key

Note that this is not a complete list of all the terms the relational model uses. Part III, "Creating Database Objects," discusses most of these terms. For more extensive descriptions, see [CODD90] and [DATE95].

1.3.1 Table, Column, and Row

Data can be stored in a relational database in only one format: in *tables*. The official name for a table is actually *relation*, and the term *relational* model stems from this name. We have chosen to use the term *table* because SQL uses that word.

Informally, a table is a set of *rows*, with each row consisting of a set of *values*. All the rows in a certain table have the same number of values. Figure 1.1 shows an example of a table called the PLAYERS table. This table contains data about five players who are members of a tennis club.

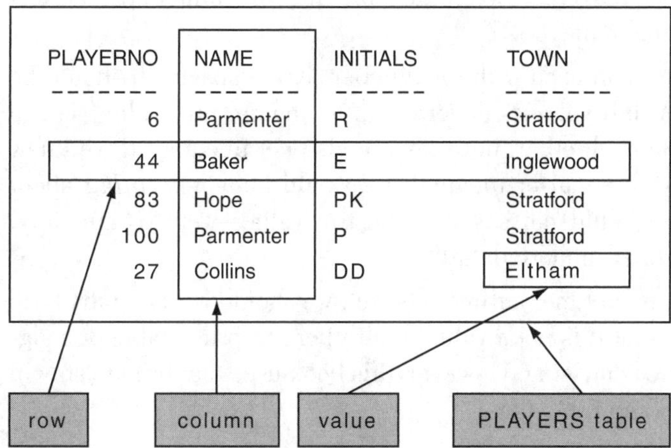

FIGURE 1.1 The concepts value, row, column, and table

This PLAYERS table has five *rows*, one for each player. A row with values can be considered a set of data elements that belong together. For example, in this table, the first row consists of the values `6`, `Parmenter`, `R`, and `Stratford`. This information tells us that there is a player with number `6`, that his last name is Parmenter and his initial is R, and that he lives in the town Stratford.

PLAYERNO, NAME, INITIALS, and TOWN are the names of the *columns* in the table. The PLAYERNO column contains the values `6`, `44`, `83`, `100`, and `27`. This set of values is also known as the *population* of the PLAYERNO column. Each row has a value for each column. Therefore, the first row contains a value for the PLAYERNO column and a value for the NAME column, and so on.

A table has two special properties:

- The intersection of a row and a column can consist of only one value, an *atomic value*. An atomic value is an indivisible unit. The database server can deal with such a value only in its entirety.

- The rows in a table have no specific order; you should not think in terms of the first row, the last three rows, or the next row. Instead, consider the contents of a table to be a *set* of rows in the true sense of the word.

1.3.2 Null Value

Columns are filled with atomic values. For example, such a value can be a number, a word, or a date. A special value is the *null value.* The null value is comparable to "value unknown" or "value not present." Consider Figure 1.1 as an example again. If we do not know the town of player 27, we could store the null value in the TOWN column for the row belonging to player 27.

A null value must not be confused with the number zero or spaces. It should be seen as a missing value. A null value is never equal to another null value, so two null values are not equal to each other, but they are also not unequal. If we knew whether two null values were equal or unequal, we would know *something* about those null values. Then we could not say that the two values were (completely) unknown. We discuss this later in more detail.

The term *null value* is, in fact, not entirely correct; we should be using the term *null* instead. The reason is that it is not a value, but rather a gap in a table or a signal indicating that the value is missing. However, this book uses that term to stay in line with various standards and products.

1.3.3 Constraints

The first section of this chapter described the integrity of the data stored in tables, the database data. The contents of a table must satisfy certain rules, the so-called *integrity constraints* (integrity rules). Two examples of integrity constraints are that the player number of a player may not be negative, and two different players may not have the same player number. Integrity constraints can be compared to road signs. They also indicate what is allowed and what is not allowed.

A relational database server should enforce integrity constraints. Each time a table is updated, the database server has to check whether the new data satisfies the relevant integrity constraints. This is a task of the database server. The integrity constraints must be specified first so that the database server knows what they are.

Integrity constraints can have several forms. Because some are used so frequently, they have special names, such as primary key, candidate key, alternate key, and foreign key. The analogy with the road signs applies here as well. Special symbols have been invented for frequently used road signs, and these also have been given names, such as a right-of-way sign or a stop sign. We explain those named integrity constraints in the following sections.

FIGURE 1.2 Integrity constraints are the road signs of a database

1.3.4 Primary Key

The *primary key* of a table is a column (or a combination of columns) used as a unique identification of rows in that table. In other words, two different rows in a table may never have the same value in their primary key, and for every row in the table, the primary key must always have one value. The PLAYERNO column in the PLAYERS table is the primary key for this table. Therefore, two players may never have the same number, and a player may never lack a number. The latter means that null values are not allowed in a primary key.

We come across primary keys everywhere. For example, the table in which a bank stores data about bank accounts has the column bank account number as primary key. Similarly, a table in which different cars are registered uses the license plate as primary key (see Figure 1.3).

FIGURE 1.3 License plate as possible primary key

1.3.5 Candidate Key

Some tables contain more than one column (or combination of columns) that can act as a primary key. These columns all possess the uniqueness property of a primary key. Here, also, null values are not allowed. These columns are called *candidate keys*. However, only one is designated as the primary key. Therefore, a table always has at least one candidate key.

If we assume that passport numbers are also included in the PLAYERS table, that column will be used as the candidate key because passport numbers are unique. Two players can never have the same passport number. This column could also be designated as the primary key.

1.3.6 Alternate Key

A candidate key that is not the primary key of a table is called an *alternate key*. Zero or more alternate keys can be defined for a specific table. The term *candidate key* is a general term for all primary and alternate keys. If every player is required to have a passport, and if we would store that passport number in the PLAYERS table, PASSPORTNO would be an alternate key.

1.3.7 Foreign Key

A *foreign key* is a column (or combination of columns) in a table in which the population is a subset of the population of the primary key of a table (this does not have to be another table). Foreign keys are sometimes called referential keys.

Imagine that, in addition to the PLAYERS table, a TEAMS table exists; see Figure 1.4. The TEAMNO column is the primary key of this table. The PLAYERNO column in this table represents the captain of each particular team. This has to be an existing player number, occurring in the PLAYERS table. The population of this column represents a subset of the population of the PLAYERNO column in the PLAYERS table. PLAYERNO in the TEAMS table is called a foreign key.

Now you can see that we can combine two tables. We do this by including the PLAYERNO column in the TEAMS table, thus establishing a link with the PLAYERNO column of the PLAYERS table.

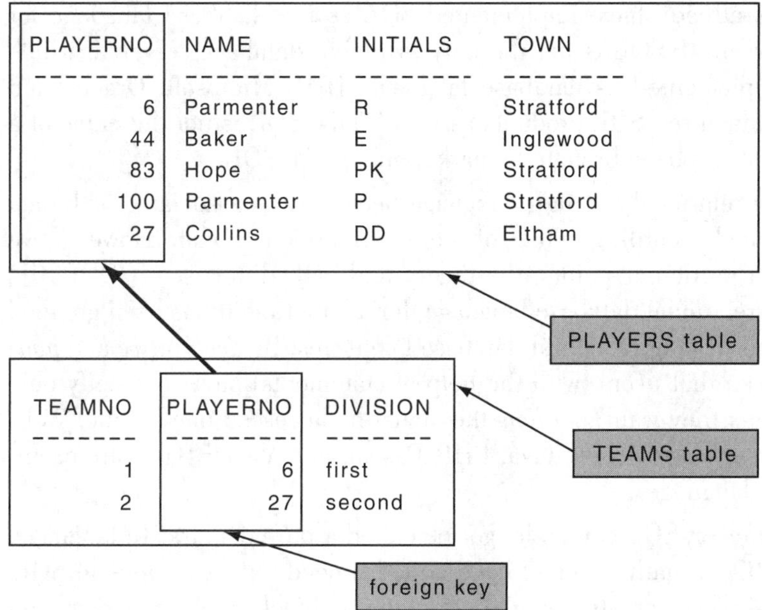

FIGURE 1.4 The foreign key

1.4 What Is SQL?

As already stated, SQL (Structured Query Language) is a *relational database language.* Among other things, the language consists of statements to insert, update, delete, query, and protect data. The following statements can be formulated with SQL:

- Insert the address of a new employee.
- Delete all the stock data for product ABC.
- Show the address of employee Johnson.
- Show the sales figures of shoes for every region and for every month.
- Show how many products have been sold in London the last three months.
- Make sure that Mr. Johnson cannot see the salary data any longer.

Many vendors already have implemented SQL as the database language for their database server. MySQL is not the only available database server in which SQL has been implemented as database language. IBM, Microsoft, Oracle, and Sybase have manufactured SQL products as well. Thus, SQL is not the name of a certain product that has been brought to market only by MySQL.

We call SQL a relational database language because it is associated with data that has been defined according to the rules of the relational model. (However, we must note that, on particular points, the theory and SQL differ; see [CODD90].) Because SQL is a relational database language, for a long time it has been grouped with the declarative or nonprocedural database languages. By *declarative* and *nonprocedural,* we mean that users (with the help of statements) have to specify only *which* data elements they want, not *how* they must be accessed one by one. Well-known languages such as C, C++, Java, PHP, Pascal, and Visual Basic are examples of procedural languages.

Nowadays, however, SQL can no longer be called a pure declarative language. Since the early 1990s, many vendors have added procedural extensions to SQL. These make it possible to create procedural database objects such as *triggers* and *stored procedures;* see Part IV, "Procedural Database Objects." Traditional statements such as `IF-THEN-ELSE` and `WHILE-DO` have also been added. Although most of the well-known SQL statements are still not procedural by nature, SQL has changed into a hybrid language consisting of procedural and nonprocedural statements. Recently, MySQL has also been extended with these procedural database objects.

SQL can be used in two ways. First, SQL can be used *interactively*. For example, a user enters an SQL statement on the spot, and the database server processes it immediately. The result is also immediately visible. Interactive SQL is intended for application developers and for end users who want to create reports themselves.

The products that support interactive SQL can be split in two groups: the somewhat old-fashioned products with a terminal-like interface and those with a modern graphical interface. MySQL includes a product with a terminal-like interface that bears the same name as the database server: mysql. Figure 1.5 shows this program. First, an SQL statement is entered (`SELECT * FROM PLAYERS`); the result is shown underneath as a table.

However, some products have a more graphical interface available for interactive use, such as MySQL Query Browser from MySQL, SQLyog from Webyog, phpMyAdmin, Navicat from PremiumSoft (see Figure 1.6), and WinSQL from Synametrics (see Figure 1.7).

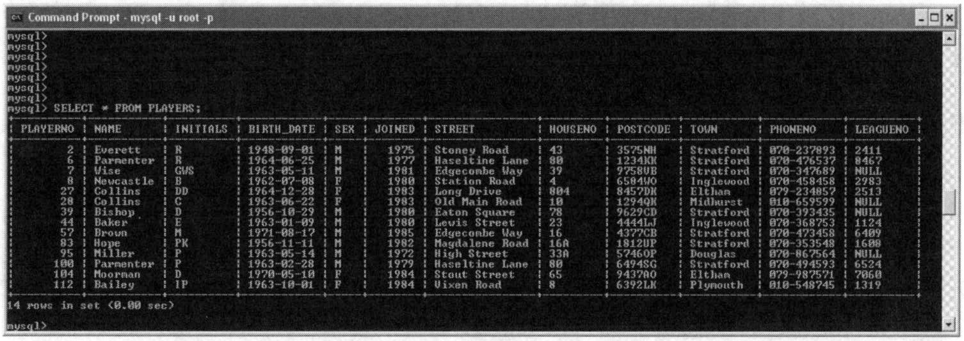

FIGURE 1.5 An example of the query program called mysql that can be used to specify the SQL statements interactively

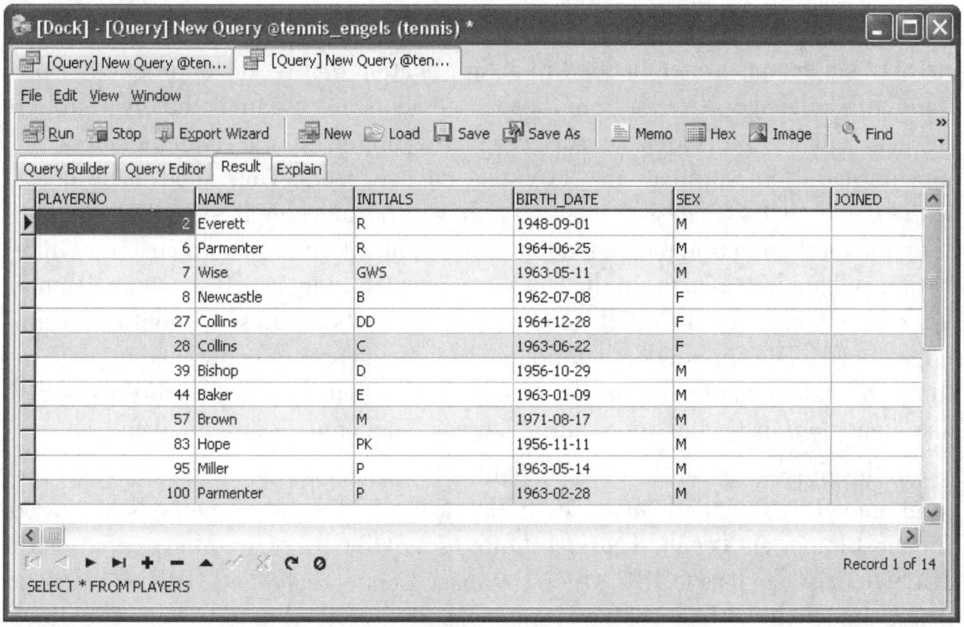

FIGURE 1.6 An example of the query program Navicat

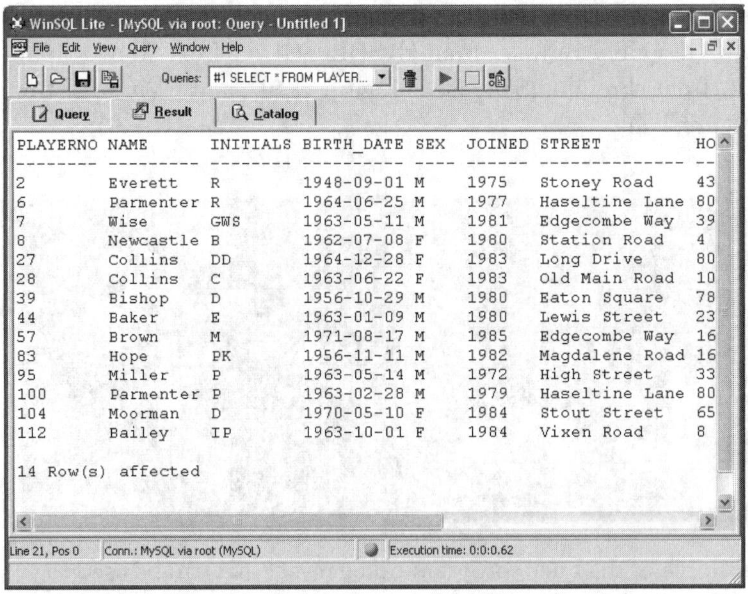

WinSQL Lite - [MySQL via root: Query - Untitled 1]

File Edit View Query Window Help

Queries: #1 SELECT * FROM PLAYER...

Query Result Catalog

PLAYERNO	NAME	INITIALS	BIRTH_DATE	SEX	JOINED	STREET	HO
2	Everett	R	1948-09-01	M	1975	Stoney Road	43
6	Parmenter	R	1964-06-25	M	1977	Haseltine Lane	80
7	Wise	GWS	1963-05-11	M	1981	Edgecombe Way	39
8	Newcastle	B	1962-07-08	F	1980	Station Road	4
27	Collins	DD	1964-12-28	F	1983	Long Drive	80
28	Collins	C	1963-06-22	F	1983	Old Main Road	10
39	Bishop	D	1956-10-29	M	1980	Eaton Square	78
44	Baker	E	1963-01-09	M	1980	Lewis Street	23
57	Brown	M	1971-08-17	M	1985	Edgecombe Way	16
83	Hope	PK	1956-11-11	M	1982	Magdalene Road	16
95	Miller	P	1963-05-14	M	1972	High Street	33
100	Parmenter	P	1963-02-28	M	1979	Haseltine Lane	80
104	Moorman	D	1970-05-10	F	1984	Stout Street	65
112	Bailey	IP	1963-10-01	F	1984	Vixen Road	8

14 Row(s) affected

Line 21, Pos 0 Conn.: MySQL via root (MySQL) Execution time: 0:0:0.62

FIGURE 1.7 An example of the query program WinSQL

The second way in which SQL can be used is called *preprogrammed* SQL. Here, the SQL statements are embedded in an application that is written in another programming language. Results from these statements are not immediately visible to the user but are processed by the *enveloping* application. Preprogrammed SQL appears mainly in applications developed for end users. These end users do not need to learn SQL to access the data, but they work from simple screens and menus designed for their applications. Examples are applications to record customer information and applications to handle stock management. Figure 1.8 shows an example of a screen with fields in which the user can enter the address without any knowledge of SQL. The application behind this screen has been programmed to pass certain SQL statements to the database server. The application therefore uses SQL statements to transfer the information that has been entered into the database.

In the early stages of the development of SQL, only one method existed for preprogrammed SQL, called *embedded* SQL. In the 1980s, other methods appeared. The most important is called *call level interface* SQL (CLI SQL). Many variations of CLI SQL exist, such as ODBC (Open Database Connectivity) and JDBC (Java Database Connectivity). The most important ones are described in this book. The different methods of preprogrammed SQL are also called the *binding styles*.

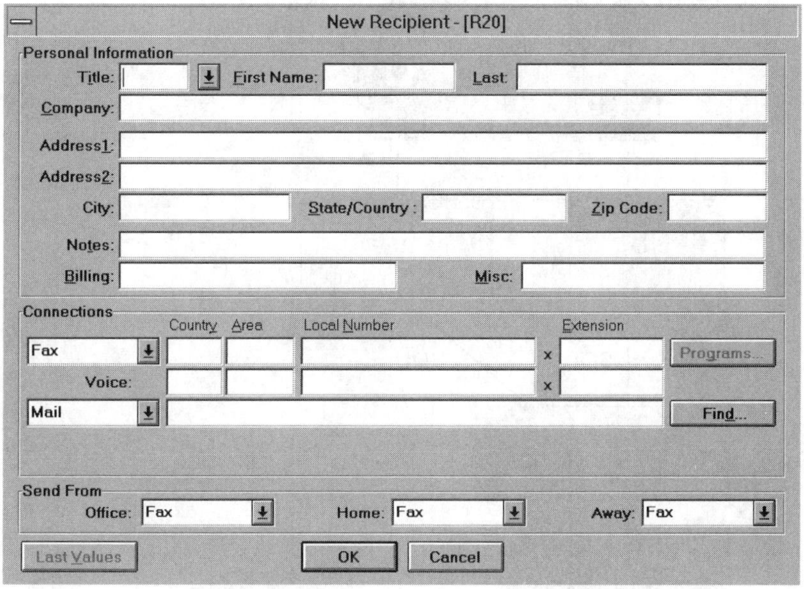

FIGURE 1.8 SQL is shielded in many applications; users can see only the input fields.

The statements and features of interactive and preprogrammed SQL are virtually the same. By this, we mean that most statements that can be entered and processed interactively can also be included (embedded) in an SQL application. Preprogrammed SQL has been extended with a number of statements that were added only to make it possible to merge the SQL statements with the non-SQL statements. This book is primarily focused on interactive SQL. Preprogrammed SQL is dealt with later in the book.

Three important components are involved in the interactive and preprogrammed processing of SQL statements: the user, the application, and the database server (see Figure 1.9). The database server is responsible for storing and accessing data on disk; the application and the user have nothing to do with this. The database server processes the SQL statements that the application delivers. In a defined way, the application and the database server can send SQL statements between them. The result of an SQL statement is then returned to the user.

MySQL does not support embedded SQL. A CLI must be used to be capable of working with preprogrammed SQL. MySQL has a CLI for all modern programming languages, such as Java, PHP, Python, Perl, Ruby, and Visual Basic. Therefore, the lack of embedded SQL is not a real problem.

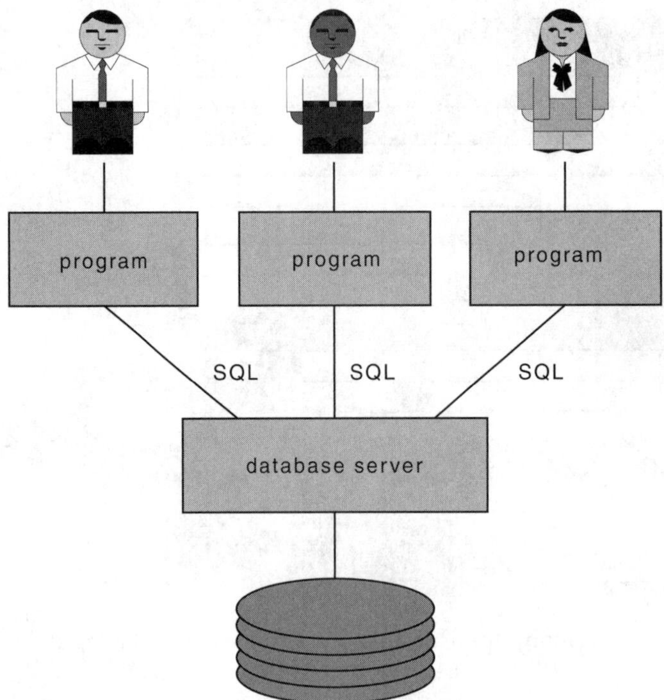

FIGURE 1.9 The user, the application, and the database server are pivotal for the processing of SQL.

1.5 The History of SQL

The history of SQL is closely tied to the history of an IBM project called *System R*. The purpose of this project was to develop an experimental relational database server that bore the same name as the project: System R. This system was built in the IBM research laboratory in San Jose, California. The project was intended to demonstrate that the positive usability features of the relational model could be implemented in a system that satisfied the demands of a modern database server.

The System R project had to solve the problem that no relational database languages existed. A language called *Sequel* was developed as the database language for System R. Designers R. F. Boyce and D. D. Chamberlin wrote the first articles about this language; see [BOYC73a] and [CHAM76]. During the project, the language was renamed SQL because the name *Sequel* conflicted with an existing trademark. (However, the language is still often pronounced as 'sequel').

FIGURE 1.10
Don Chamberlin, one of the designers of SQL

The System R project was carried out in three phases. In the first phase, phase zero (from 1974 to 1975), only a part of SQL was implemented. For example, the join (for linking data from various tables) was not implemented yet, and only a single-user version of the system was built. The purpose of this phase was to see whether implementation of such a system was possible. This phase ended successfully; see [ASTR80].

Phase 1 started in 1976. All the program code written for Phase 0 was put aside for a fresh start. Phase 1 comprised the total system. This meant, among other things, incorporating the multiuser capability and the join. Development of Phase 1 took place between 1976 and 1977.

The final phase evaluated System R. The system was installed at various places within IBM and with a large number of major IBM clients. The evaluation took place in 1978 and 1979. The results of this evaluation are described in [CHAM80], as well as in other publications. The System R project was finished in 1979.

Developers used the knowledge acquired and the technology developed in these three phases to build SQL/DS. SQL/DS was the first commercially available IBM relational database server. In 1981, SQL/DS came onto the market for the operating system DOS/VSE, and the VM/CMS version arrived in 1983. In that same year, DB2 was announced. Currently, DB2 is available for many operating systems.

IBM has published a great deal about the development of System R, which happened at a time when conferences and seminars focused greatly on relational database servers. Therefore, it is not surprising that other companies began to build relational systems as well. Some of them, such as Oracle, implemented SQL as the database language. In the last few years, many SQL products have appeared. As a result, SQL is now available for every possible system, large or small. Existing database servers have also been extended to include SQL support.

1.6 From Monolithic via Client/Server to the Internet

Section 1.4 describes the relationship between the database server MySQL and the calling application. Applications send SQL statements to MySQL to have them processed. The latter processes the statements and returns the results to the application. Finally, the results are presented to the users. It is not necessary for MySQL and the applications to run on the same machine for them to communicate with each other. Roughly, three solutions or architectures are available; among them are the client/server and Internet architectures.

The most simple architecture is the *monolithic architecture* (see Figure 1.11). In a monolithic architecture, everything runs on the same machine. This machine can be a large mainframe, a small PC, or a midrange computer with an operating system such as UNIX or Windows. Because both the application and MySQL run on the same computer, communication is possible through very fast internal communication lines. In fact, this involves two processes that communicate internally.

FIGURE 1.11 The monolithic architecture

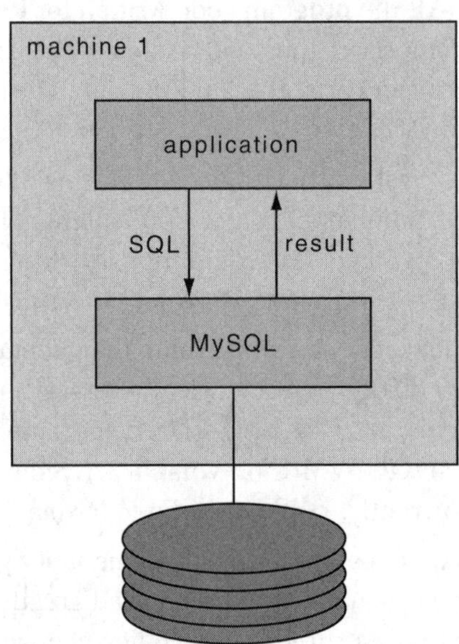

The second architecture is the *client/server architecture.* Several subforms of this architecture exists, but we will not discuss them all here. It is important to realize that in a client/server architecture, the application runs on a different machine than MySQL (see Figure 1.12). This is called working with a *remote database server.* Internal communication usually takes place through a local area network (LAN) and occasionally through a wide area network (WAN). A user could start an application on a PC in Paris and retrieve data from a database located in Sydney. Communication would then probably take place through a satellite link.

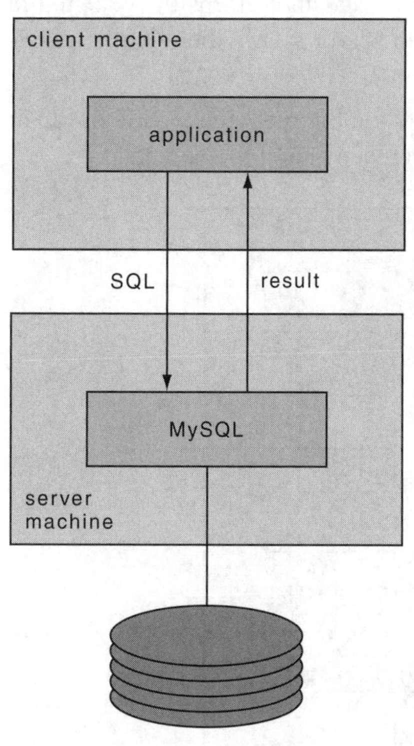

FIGURE 1.12
The client/server architecture

The third architecture is the *Internet architecture.* In this architecture, the application running in a client/server architecture on the client machine is divided into two parts (see the left part of Figure 1.13). The part that deals with the user, or the user interface, runs on the client machine. The part that communicates with the database server, also called the *application logic,* runs on the *server machine.* In this book, these two parts are called, respectively, the client and the server application.

Probably no SQL statements exist in the *client application,* but there are statements that call the server application. Languages such as HTML, JavaScript, and VBScript are often used for the client application. The call goes via the Internet or an intranet to the second machine; the well-known HyperText Transport Protocol

(HTTP) is mostly used for this. The call comes in at a *web server.* The web server acts as a kind of switchboard operator and knows which call has been sent to which server application.

Next, the call arrives at the server application. The server application sends the needed SQL statements to MySQL. Many server applications run under the supervision of Java application servers, such as WebLogic from Bea Systems and WebSphere from IBM.

MySQL returns the results of the SQL statements. In some way, the server application translates this SQL result to an HTML page and returns the page to the web server. As the switchboard operator, the web server knows the client application to which the HTML answer must be returned.

The right part of Figure 1.13 shows a variant of the Internet architecture in which the server application and MySQL have also been placed on different machines.

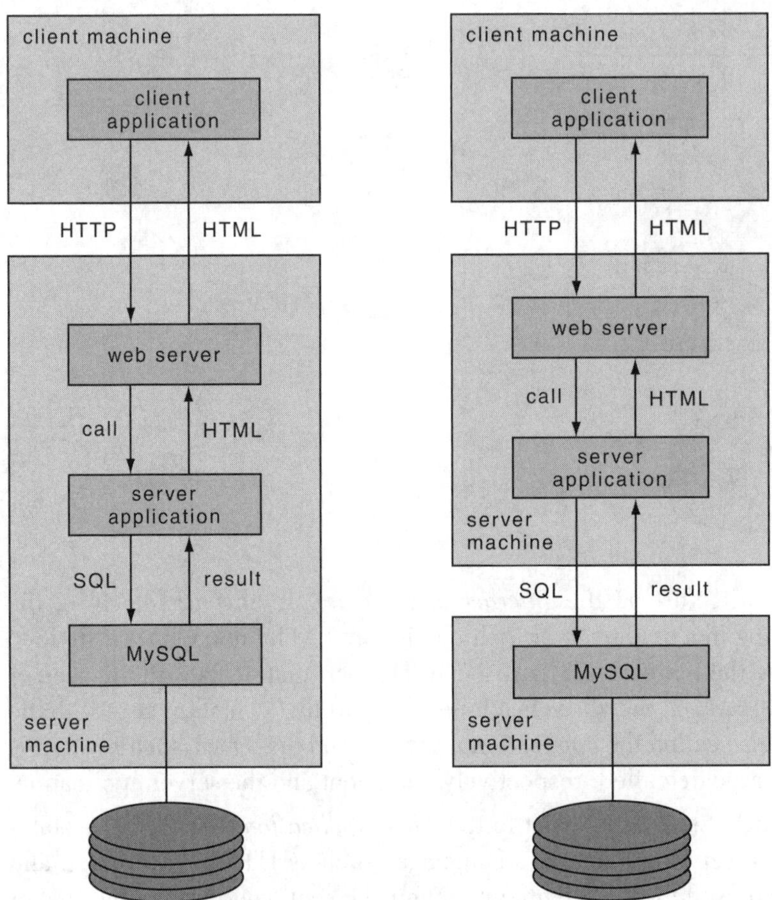

FIGURE 1.13 The Internet architecture

The fact that MySQL and the database are remote is completely transparent to the programmer who is responsible for writing the application and the SQL statements. However, it is not irrelevant. Regarding the language and efficiency aspects of SQL, it is important to know which architecture is used: monolithic, client/server, or Internet. In this book, we will use the first one, but where relevant, we discuss the effect of client/server or Internet architectures.

1.7 Standardization of SQL

As mentioned before, each SQL database server has its own dialect. All these dialects resemble each other, but they are not completely identical. They differ in the statements they support, or some products contain more SQL statements than others; the possibilities of statements can vary as well. Sometimes two products support the same statement, but the result of that statement might vary among products.

To avoid differences among the many database servers from several vendors, it was decided early to define a standard for SQL. The idea was that when the database servers grew too much apart, acceptance by the SQL market would diminish. A standard would ensure that an application with SQL statements would be easier to transfer from one database server to another.

In about 1983, the International Standardization Organization (ISO) and the American National Standards Institute (ANSI) started work on the development of an SQL standard. The ISO is the leading internationally oriented normalization and standardization organization; its objectives include the promotion of international, regional, and national normalization. Many countries have local representatives of the ISO. ANSI is the American branch of the ISO.

After many meetings and several false starts, the first ANSI edition of the SQL standard appeared in 1986. This is described in the document ANSI X3.135-1986, "Database Language SQL." This *SQL-86 standard* is unofficially called *SQL1*. One year later, the ISO edition, called ISO 9075-1987, "Database Language SQL," was completed; see [ISO87]. This report was developed under the auspices of Technical Committee TC97. The area of activity of TC97 is described as Computing and Information Processing. Its Subcommittee SC21 caused the standard to be developed. This means that the standards of ISO and ANSI for SQL1 or SQL-86 are identical.

SQL1 consists of two levels. Level 2 comprises the complete document, and Level 1 is a subset of Level 2. This implies that not all specifications of SQL1 belong to Level 1. If a vendor claims that its database server complies with the standard, the supporting level must be stated as well. This is done to improve the support and adoption of SQL1. It means that vendors can support the standard in two phases, first Level 1 and then Level 2.

The SQL1 standard is very moderate with respect to integrity. For this reason, it was extended in 1989 by including, among other things, the concepts of primary and foreign keys. This version of the SQL standard is called *SQL89*. The companion ISO document is called, appropriately, ISO 9075:1989, "Database Language SQL with Integrity Enhancements." The ANSI version was completed simultaneously.

Immediately after the completion of SQL1 in 1987, the development of a new SQL standard began; see [ISO92]. This planned successor to SQL89 was called *SQL2* because the date of publication was not known at the start. In fact, SQL89 and SQL2 were developed simultaneously. Finally, SQL2 was published in 1992 and replaced SQL89, the current standard at that time. The new SQL92 standard is an expansion of the SQL1 standard. Many new statements and extensions to existing statements have been added. For a complete description of SQL92, see [DATE97].

Just like SQL1, SQL92 has *levels*. The levels have names instead of numbers: *entry*, *intermediate*, and *full*. Full SQL is the complete standard. In terms of functionality, intermediate SQL is a subset of full SQL, and entry SQL is a subset of intermediate SQL. Entry SQL can roughly be compared to SQL1 Level 2, although with some specifications extended. All the levels together can be seen as the rings of an onion; see Figure 1.14. A ring represents a certain amount of functionality. The bigger the ring, the more functionality is defined within that level. When a ring falls within the other ring, it defines a subset of functionality.

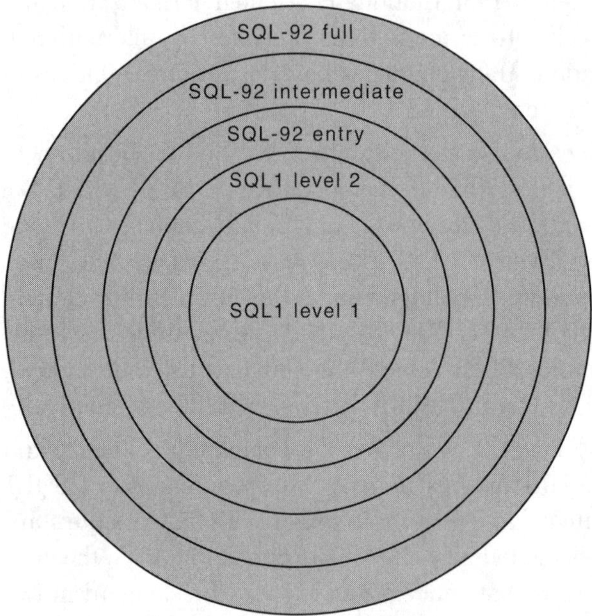

FIGURE 1.14 The various levels of SQL1 and SQL92 represented as rings

At the time of this writing, many available products support entry SQL92. Some even claim to support intermediate SQL92, but not one product supports full SQL92. Hopefully, the support of the SQL92 levels will improve in the coming years.

Since the publication of SQL92, several additional documents have been added that extend the capabilities of the language. In 1995, *SQL/CLI* (Call Level Interface) was published. Later the name was changed to CLI95; the end of this section includes more about CLI95. The following year, *SQL/PSM* (Persistent Stored Modules), or PSM-96, appeared. The most recent addition, PSM96, describes functionality for creating so-called stored procedures. Chapter 31, "Stored Procedures," deals with this concept extensively. Two years after PSM96, *SQL/OLB* (Object Language Bindings), or OLB-98, was published. This document describes how SQL statements had to be included within the programming language Java.

Even before the completion of SQL92, the development of its successor began: *SQL3*. In 1999, the standard was published and bore the name SQL:1999. To be more in line with the names of other ISO standards, the hyphen that was used in the names of the previous editions was replaced by a colon. And because of the problems around the year 2000, it was decided that 1999 would not be shortened to *99*. See [GULU99], [MELT01], and [MELT03] for more detailed descriptions of this standard.

When SQL:1999 was completed, it consisted of five parts: SQL/Framework, SQL/Foundation, SQL/CLI, SQL/PSM, and SQL/Bindings. SQL/OLAP, SQL/MED (Management of External Data), SQL/OLB, SQL/Schemata and SQL/JRT (Routines and Types using the Java Programming Language), and SQL/XML(XML-Related Specifications) were added later, among other things. Thus, the current SQL standard of ISO consists of a series of documents. They all begin with the ISO code 9075. For example, the complete designation of the SQL/Framework is ISO/IEC 9075-1:2003.

Besides the 9075 documents, another group of documents focuses on SQL. The term used for this group is usually *SQL/MM*, short for SQL Multimedia and Application Packages. All these documents bear the ISO code 13249. SQL/MM consists of five parts. SQL/MM Part 1 is the SQL/MM Framework, Part 2 focuses on text retrieval (working with text), Part 3 is dedicated to spatial applications, Part 4 involves still images (such as photos), and Part 5 deals with data mining (looking for trends and patterns in data).

In 2003, a new edition of SQL/Foundation appeared, along with new editions of some other documents, such as SQL/JRT and SQL/Schemata. At this moment, this group of documents can be seen as the most recent version of the international SQL standard. We refer to it by the abbreviation *SQL:2003*.

Other organizations previously worked on the standardization of SQL, including The Open Group (then called the X/Open Group) and the SQL Access Group. The first does not get much attention any longer, so this book does not discuss it.

In July 1989, a number of mainly American vendors of SQL database servers (among them Informix, Ingres, and Oracle) set up a committee called the *SQL Access Group*. The objective of the SQL Access Group is to define standards for the *interoperability* of SQL applications. This means that SQL applications developed using those specifications are portable between the database servers of the associated vendors and that these applications can simultaneously access a number of different database servers. At the end of 1990, the first report of the SQL Access Group was published and defined the syntax of a so-called SQL application interface. The first demonstrations in this field emerged in 1991. Eventually, the ISO adopted the resulting document, and it was published under the name SQL/CLI. This document was mentioned earlier.

The most important technology that is derived from the work of the Open SQL Access Group—and, therefore from SQL/CLI—is Open Database Connectivity (ODBC), from Microsoft.

Finally, an organization called the Object Database Management Group (ODMG) is aimed at the creation of standards for object-oriented databases; see [CATT97]. Part of these standards is a declarative language to query and update databases, called Object Query Language (OQL). It is claimed that SQL has served as a foundation for OQL and, although the languages are not the same, they have a lot in common.

It is correct to say that a lot of time and money has been invested in the standardization of SQL. But is a standard that important? The following practical advantages would accrue if all database servers supported exactly the same standardized database language.

- **Increased portability**—An application could be developed for one database server and could run at another without many changes.
- **Improved interchangeability**—Because database servers speak the same language, they could communicate internally with each other. Applications also could access different databases more simply.
- **Reduced training costs**—Programmers could switch faster from one database server to another because the language would remain the same; they would not have to learn a new database language.
- **Extended life span**—Standardized languages tend to survive longer, and this also applies to the applications written in such languages. COBOL is a good example of this.

MySQL supports a considerable part of the SQL92 standard. Especially since Version 4, MySQL has been extended considerably in this field. Currently, the objective seems to be to develop MySQL more according to the standard. In other words, when the MySQL organization wants to add something new to MySQL and something is written about it in the standard, the group keeps to that standard.

1.8 What Is Open Source Software?

MySQL is *open source software.* But what is open source software? Most software products that we buy and use could be called closed source software. The source code of this software cannot be adjusted. We do not have access to the source code; what we buy is compiled code. For example, we cannot modify the hyphenation algorithm of Microsoft Word. This code was written by a Microsoft programmer somewhere in Seattle and cannot be changed; it is blocked for everyone. When you want to change something, you have to pass on your demands to Microsoft.

The opposite applies to the source code of open source software. Open source code can actually be modified because the vendor includes the source code. This also applies to the source code of MySQL. When you think that you can improve MySQL or extend its functionality, you go ahead and try. You try to find the part in the source code that you want to improve and apply the desired changes. Next you compile and link the existing code to the code that you just wrote, and you have created an improved version. In short, the source code is open and accessible to you.

You can even go further. When you think your improved code is really good and useful, you can send it to the vendor of the open source software product. The developers then decide whether they want to add your code to the standard code. If they do, others can enjoy your work in the future. If they don't, you can become such a vendor yourself, as long as you provide your new source code publicly. So either way, an open source license ensures that open source software is improved and is spread into the world.

In short, open source software—therefore, also MySQL—is changeable. That is easy to understand. Most open source software is also free to use. However, when we talk about selling software that includes open source software, it becomes a different story. MySQL is supplied according to the use and payment rules recorded in the GNU General Public License (GPL). For details, refer to the documentation of MySQL; we recommend that you study this carefully.

1.9 The History of MySQL

At first, MySQL was not intended to be a commercial product. A new application had to be written that would access index sequential files. Normally, a programmer has to use a very simplistic interface to manipulate the data in such files. Much code has to be written, and that surely does not help the productivity of the programmers. The developers of this application wanted to use an SQL interface as interface to these files.

This need faced the final founders of MySQL: David Axmark, Allan Larsson, and Michael "Monty" Widenius. They decided to search the market for a product that already offered that SQL interface. They found a product called *Mini SQL*, often shortened to *mSQL*. This product still is supplied by the Australian Hughes Technologies.

After trying out this product, the developers felt that Mini SQL was not powerful enough for their application. They decided to develop a product comparable to Mini SQL themselves. With that, MySQL was born. However, they liked the interface of Mini SQL, which is why the interfaces of MySQL and Mini SQL still resemble each other.

Initially, the company MySQL AB was founded in Sweden, and the initial development was done there as well. Nowadays, the developers can be found all over the world, from the United States to Russia. This is an example of a modern company that relies heavily on technologies such as the Internet and e-mail and on the advantages of open source software to develop its database server.

Version 3.11.0, the first version shown to the outside world, was launched in 1996. Before that, only the developers themselves used MySQL. From the beginning, it was an open source product. Since 2000, the product has been released according to the rules specified in the GPL.

Only three years after the introduction, in 1999, the company MySQL AB was founded. Before that, a somewhat informally operating group of developers managed the software.

This book describes Version 5.0.18 of MySQL, which was released in the summer of 2006. Much has changed since that first commercial version—in particular, the SQL dialect has been extended considerably. For years, much has been done to bring MySQL more in line with the SQL92 standard. That also has increased the portability between MySQL on one hand and other SQL database servers, such as DB2 from IBM, SQL Server from Microsoft, and Oracle10*g* from Oracle, on the other hand.

Despite the extensions, many customers still use the SQL dialect of Version 3, even when they run Versions 4 or 5. The consequence of this restriction is that they do not use the full power of MySQL. Restricting yourself with respect to SQL leads to unnecessarily complex applications. Many lines of code can be reduced to one simple SQL statement.

Finally, how MySQL got its name has remained a mystery for a long time. However, Monty, one of the founders, has admitted that his eldest daughter is called My.

1.10 The Structure of This Book

This chapter concludes by describing the structure of this book. Because of the many chapters in the book, we divided it into sections.

Part I, "Introduction," consists of several introductory topics and includes this chapter. Chapter 2, "The Tennis Club Sample Database," contains a detailed description of the database used in most of the examples and exercises. This database is modeled on the administration of a tennis club's competitions. Chapter 4, "SQL in a Nutshell," gives a general overview of SQL. After reading this chapter, you should have a general overview of the capabilities of SQL and a good idea of what awaits you in the rest of this book

Part II, "Querying and Updating Data," focuses completely on querying and updating tables. It is largely devoted to the SELECT statement. Many examples illustrate all its features. We devote a great deal of space to this SELECT statement because this is the statement most often used and because many other statements are based on it. Chapter 19, "Working with XML Documents," describes how existing database data can be updated and deleted, and how new rows can be added to tables.

Part III, "Creating Database Objects," describes the creation of *database objects*. The term *database object* is the generic name for all objects from which a database is built. For instance, this chapter discusses tables; primary, alternate, and foreign keys; indexes; and views. This part also describes data security.

Part IV, "Procedural Database Objects," describes stored procedures, stored functions, triggers, and events. Stored procedures and stored functions are pieces of code stored in the database that can be called from applications. Triggers are pieces of code as well, but they are invoked by MySQL itself, for example, to perform checks or to update data automatically. Informally, events are triggers that are automatically started on a certain time of the day.

Part V, "Programming with SQL," deals with programming in SQL. MySQL can be called from many programming languages; those used most are PHP, Python, and Perl. This part uses PHP to illustrate how SQL statements are embedded inside a programming language. The following concepts are explained in this part: transaction, savepoint, rollback of transactions, isolation level, and repeatable read.

The book ends with a number of appendices and an index. Appendix A, "Syntax of SQL," contains the definitions of all the SQL statements discussed in the book. Appendix B, "Scalar Functions," describes all the functions that SQL supports. Appendix C, "System Variables," lists all the system variables, and Appendix D, "Bibliography," contains a list of references.

CHAPTER 2

The Tennis Club Sample Database

2.1 Introduction

This chapter describes a database that a tennis club could use to record its players' progress in a competition. Most of the examples and exercises in this book are based on this database, so you should study it carefully.

2.2 Description of the Tennis Club

The tennis club was founded in 1970. From the beginning, some administrative data was stored in a database. This database consists of the following tables:

- PLAYERS
- TEAMS
- MATCHES
- PENALTIES
- COMMITTEE_MEMBERS

The PLAYERS table contains data about players who are members of the club, such as names, addresses, and dates of birth. Players can join the club only at the first of January of a year. Players cannot join the club in the middle of the year.

The PLAYERS table contains no historical data. Any player who gives up membership disappears from the table. If a player moves, the new address overwrites the old address. In other words, the old address is not retained anywhere.

The tennis club has two types of members: *recreational players* and *competition players*. The first group plays matches only among themselves (that is, no matches against players from other clubs). The results of these friendly matches are not recorded. Competition players play in teams against other clubs, and the results of these matches are recorded. Regardless of whether he or she plays competitively, each player has a unique number assigned by the club. Each competition player must also be registered with the tennis league, and this national organization gives each player a unique *league number.* This league number usually contains digits, but it can also consist of letters. If a competition player stops playing in the competition and becomes a recreational player, his or her league number correspondingly disappears. Therefore, recreational players have no league number, but they do have a player number.

The club has a number of teams taking part in competitions. The captain of each team and the division in which it is currently competing are recorded. It is not necessary for the captain to have played a match for the team. It is possible for a certain player to be a captain of two or more teams at a certain time. Again, this table records no historical data. If a team is promoted or relegated to another division, the new information simply overwrites the record. The same goes for the captain of the team; when a new captain is appointed, the number of the former captain is overwritten.

A team consists of a number of players. When a team plays against a team from another tennis club, each player of that team plays against a player of the opposing team (for the sake of simplicity, assume that matches in which couples play against each other, the so-called doubles and mixes, do not occur). The team for which the most players win their matches is the winner.

A team does not always consist of the same people, and reserves are sometimes needed when the regular players are sick or on vacation. A player can play matches for several teams. So when we say "the players of a team," we mean the players who have played at least one match in that team. Again, only players with league numbers are allowed to play official matches.

Each match consists of a number of *sets.* The player who wins the most sets is the winner. Before the match begins, it is agreed how many sets must be won to win the match. Generally, the match stops after one of the two players has won two or three sets. Possible end results of a tennis match are 2–1 or 2–0 if play continues until one player wins two sets (best of three), or 3–2, 3–1, or 3–0 if three sets need to be won (best of five). A player either wins or loses a match; a draw is not possible. The MATCHES table records for each match separately which player was in the match and for which team he played. In addition, it records how many *sets* the player won and lost. From this, we can conclude whether the player won the match.

If a player behaves badly (arrives late, behaves aggressively, or does not show up) the league imposes a penalty in the form of a fine. The club pays these fines and records them in a PENALTIES table. As long as the player continues to play competitively, the record of all his or her penalties remains in this table.

If a player leaves the club, all his or her data in the five tables is destroyed. If the club withdraws a team, all data for that team is removed from the TEAMS and MATCHES tables. If a competition player stops playing matches and becomes a recreational player again, all matches and penalty data is deleted from the relevant tables.

Since January 1, 1990, a COMMITTEE_MEMBERS table has kept information about who is on the committee. Four positions exist: chairman, treasurer, secretary, and general member. On January 1 of each year, a new committee is elected. If a player is on the committee, the beginning and ending dates of his or her committee are recorded. If someone is still active, the end date remains open. Figure 2.1 shows which player was on the committee in which period.

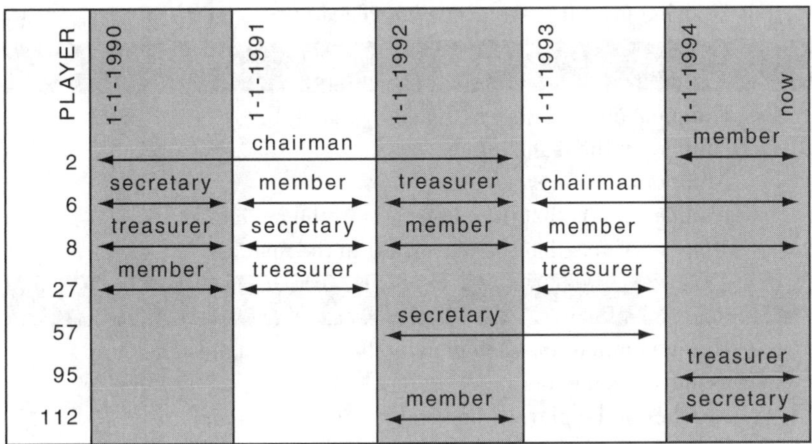

FIGURE 2.1 Which player occupied which position on the committee in which period?

Following is a description of the columns in each of the tables.

PLAYERS	
PLAYERNO	Unique player number assigned by the club.
NAME	Surname of the player, without initials.
INITIALS	Initials of the player. (No full stops or spaces are used.)
BIRTH_DATE	Date on which the player was born.
SEX	Sex of the player: M(ale) or F(emale).

continues

JOINED	Year in which the player joined the club. (This value cannot be smaller than 1970, the year in which the club was founded.)
STREET	Name of the street on which the player lives.
HOUSENO	Number of the house.
POSTCODE	Postcode.
TOWN	Town or city in which the player lives. Assume in this example that place-names are unique for town or cities; in other words, there can never be two towns with the same name.
PHONENO	Area code followed by a hyphen and then the subscriber's number.
LEAGUENO	League number assigned by the league; a league number is unique.
TEAMS	
TEAMNO	Unique team number assigned by the club.
PLAYERNO	Player number of the player who captains the team. In principle a player may captain several teams.
DIVISION	Division in which the league has placed the team.
MATCHES	
MATCHNO	Unique match number assigned by the club.
TEAMNO	Number of the team.
PLAYERNO	Number of the player.
WON	Number of sets that the player won in the match.
LOST	Number of sets that the player lost in the match.
PENALTIES	
PAYMENTNO	Unique number for each penalty the club has paid. The club assigns this number.
PLAYERNO	Number of the player who has incurred the penalty.
PAYMENT_DATE	Date on which the penalty was paid. The year of this date should not be earlier than 1970, the year in which the club was founded.
AMOUNT	Amount in dollars incurred for the penalty.
COMMITTEE_MEMBERS	
PLAYERNO	Number of the player.
BEGIN_DATE	Date on which the player became an active member of the committee. This date should not be earlier than January 1, 1990, because this is the date on which the club started to record this data.
END_DATE	Date on which the player resigned his position in the committee. This date should not be earlier than the BEGIN_DATE but can be absent.
POSITION	Name of the position.

2.3 The Contents of the Tables

The contents of the tables are shown here. These rows of data form the basis of most of the examples and exercises. Some of the column names in the PLAYERS table have been shortened because of space constraints.

The PLAYERS table:

PLAYERNO	NAME	INIT	BIRTH_DATE	SEX	JOINED	STREET	...
2	Everett	R	1948-09-01	M	1975	Stoney Road	...
6	Parmenter	R	1964-06-25	M	1977	Haseltine Lane	...
7	Wise	GWS	1963-05-11	M	1981	Edgecombe Way	...
8	Newcastle	B	1962-07-08	F	1980	Station Road	...
27	Collins	DD	1964-12-28	F	1983	Long Drive	...
28	Collins	C	1963-06-22	F	1983	Old Main Road	...
39	Bishop	D	1956-10-29	M	1980	Eaton Square	...
44	Baker	E	1963-01-09	M	1980	Lewis Street	...
57	Brown	M	1971-08-17	M	1985	Edgecombe Way	...
83	Hope	PK	1956-11-11	M	1982	Magdalene Road	...
95	Miller	P	1963-05-14	M	1972	High Street	...
100	Parmenter	P	1963-02-28	M	1979	Haseltine Lane	...
104	Moorman	D	1970-05-10	F	1984	Stout Street	...
112	Bailey	IP	1963-10-01	F	1984	Vixen Road	...

The PLAYERS table (continued):

PLAYERNO	...	HOUSENO	POSTCODE	TOWN	PHONENO	LEAGUENO
2	...	43	3575NH	Stratford	070-237893	2411
6	...	80	1234KK	Stratford	070-476537	8467
7	...	39	9758VB	Stratford	070-347689	?
8	...	4	6584RO	Inglewood	070-458458	2983
27	...	804	8457DK	Eltham	079-234857	2513
28	...	10	1294QK	Midhurst	071-659599	?
39	...	78	9629CD	Stratford	070-393435	?
44	...	23	4444LJ	Inglewood	070-368753	1124
57	...	16	4377CB	Stratford	070-473458	6409
83	...	16A	1812UP	Stratford	070-353548	1608
95	...	33A	57460P	Douglas	070-867564	?
100	...	80	1234KK	Stratford	070-494593	6524
104	...	65	9437AO	Eltham	079-987571	7060
112	...	8	6392LK	Plymouth	010-548745	1319

The TEAMS table:

TEAMNO	PLAYERNO	DIVISION
1	6	first
2	27	second

The MATCHES table:

MATCHNO	TEAMNO	PLAYERNO	WON	LOST
1	1	6	3	1
2	1	6	2	3
3	1	6	3	0
4	1	44	3	2
5	1	83	0	3
6	1	2	1	3
7	1	57	3	0
8	1	8	0	3
9	2	27	3	2
10	2	104	3	2
11	2	112	2	3
12	2	112	1	3
13	2	8	0	3

The PENALTIES table:

PAYMENTNO	PLAYERNO	PAYMENT_DATE	AMOUNT
1	6	1980-12-08	100.00
2	44	1981-05-05	75.00
3	27	1983-09-10	100.00
4	104	1984-12-08	50.00
5	44	1980-12-08	25.00
6	8	1980-12-08	25.00
7	44	1982-12-30	30.00
8	27	1984-11-12	75.00

The COMMITTEE_MEMBERS table:

PLAYERNO	BEGIN_DATE	END_DATE	POSITION
2	1990-01-01	1992-12-31	Chairman
2	1994-01-01	?	Member
6	1990-01-01	1990-12-31	Secretary
6	1991-01-01	1992-12-31	Member
6	1992-01-01	1993-12-31	Treasurer
6	1993-01-01	?	Chairman
8	1990-01-01	1990-12-31	Treasurer
8	1991-01-01	1991-12-31	Secretary
8	1993-01-01	1993-12-31	Member
8	1994-01-01	?	Member
27	1990-01-01	1990-12-31	Member
27	1991-01-01	1991-12-31	Treasurer
27	1993-01-01	1993-12-31	Treasurer
57	1992-01-01	1992-12-31	Secretary
95	1994-01-01	?	Treasurer
112	1992-01-01	1992-12-31	Member
112	1994-01-01	?	Secretary

2.4 Integrity Constraints

Of course, the contents of the tables must satisfy a number of integrity constraints. For example, two players may not have the same player number, and every player number in the PENALTIES table must also appear in the MATCHES table. This section lists all the applicable integrity constraints.

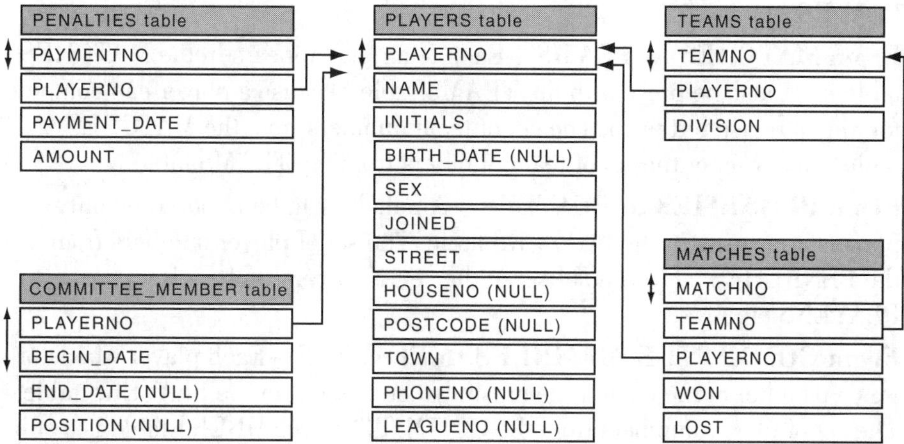

FIGURE 2.2 Diagram of the relationships between the tennis club database tables

A primary key has been defined for each table. The following columns are the primary keys for their respective tables. Figure 2.2 contains a diagram of the database. A double-headed arrow at the side of a column (or combination of columns) indicates the primary key of a table:

- PLAYERNO of PLAYERS
- TEAMNO of TEAMS
- MATCHNO of MATCHES
- PAYMENTNO of PENALTIES
- PLAYERNO plus BEGIN_DATE of COMMITTEE_MEMBERS

The example database has no alternate keys. The LEAGUENO column in the PLAYERS table looks like one but isn't. All the values are unique, but the column also allows null values and, therefore, can be no alternate key.

The database supports five foreign keys. In Figure 2.2, single-headed arrows show the foreign keys; these run from one table to another (this notation, in which the arrows point to the primary key, is used in [DATE95] and elsewhere). The foreign keys are as follows:

- **From TEAMS to PLAYERS**—Each captain of a team is also a player. The set of player numbers from the TEAMS table is a subset of the set of player numbers from the PLAYERS table.
- **From MATCHES to PLAYERS**—Each player who competes for a particular team must appear in the PLAYERS table. The set of player numbers from the MATCHES table is a subset of the set of player numbers from the PLAYERS table.
- **From MATCHES to TEAMS**—Each team that appears in the MATCHES table must also be present in the TEAMS table because a player can compete for only a registered team. The set of team numbers from the MATCHES table is a subset of the set of team numbers from the TEAMS table.
- **From PENALTIES to PLAYERS**—A penalty can be imposed on only players appearing in the PLAYERS table. The set of player numbers from the PENALTIES table is a subset of the set of player numbers from the PLAYERS table.
- **From COMMITTEE_MEMBERS to PLAYERS**—Each player who is or was a member of the committee must also be present in the PLAYERS table. The set of player numbers from the COMMITTEE_MEMBERS table is a subset of the set of player numbers from the PLAYERS table.

The following integrity constraints also hold:

- Two players cannot have identical league numbers.
- The year of birth of a player must be earlier than the year in which he or she joined the club.
- The sex of a player should always be `M` or `F`.
- The year in which the player joined the club should be greater than 1969 because the tennis club was founded in 1970.
- The postcode must always be a code of six characters.
- The division of a team can be nothing but first or second.
- Both the columns WON and LOST must have a value between `0` and `3`.
- The payment date should be January 1, 1970, or later.
- Each penalty amount must always be greater than zero.
- The begin date in the COMMITTEE_MEMBERS table should always be later than or equal to January 1, 1990, because recording of this data was started on that day.
- The end date on which the player ended service as a committee member must always be later than the begin date.

CHAPTER 3

Installing the Software

3.1 Introduction

As already mentioned in the preface, we advise that you replay the examples in this book and do the exercises. This will definitely improve your knowledge of MySQL and pleasure in reading this book.

This chapter describes where to find the required software and the information needed to install all the software necessary. It also indicates how to download the code for the many examples. For practical reasons, we refer frequently to the book's web site. Here you will find useful information.

3.2 Downloading MySQL

You can download MySQL free from the web site of the vendor, www.mysql.com, where you will find the software for many different operating systems. Choose the version that suits you best. This book assumes that you will be using Version 5.0 or higher. Of course, you can also process the SQL statements in this book with newer versions of MySQL.

This book deliberately does not indicate where on the web site you can find the software and the documentation. The structure of this web site changes rather frequently, so this book would contain out-of-date descriptions too quickly.

3.3 Installation of MySQL

On the vendor's web site, you will find documentation describing how to install MySQL. You can use this documentation or visit the book's web site: www.r20.nl. Here you will find a detailed plan that describes the installation step by step, including many screen shots. This plan might be easier to understand than the vendor's documentation.

If you have comments on the installation description, please let me know so we can improve the web site if necessary.

NOTE

We have deliberately chosen not to include the installation process in this book because it differs for each operating system and can change with every new version of MySQL.

3.4 Installing a Query Tool

This book assumes that you will use a query tool such as MySQL Query Browser, SQLyog, or WinSQL to process your SQL statements. However, these are not database servers, but programs that enable you to simply enter SQL statements interactively under Windows or Linux. They work together with MySQL and most other database servers. You also can download most of these query tools for free from the vendor's web site. Again, as with MySQL, we strongly recommend that you install one of those query tools.

3.5 Downloading SQL Statements from the Web Site

As mentioned in the preface, the accompanying web site contains all the SQL statements used in this book. This section briefly describes how you can download them. This is a good time to do so because you'll need these statements to create the sample database.

The URL of the book's web site is www.r20.nl. The statements are stored in simple text files; by cutting and pasting, you can easily copy them to any product. You can open them with any text editor.

A separate file exists for each chapter, as clearly indicated on the web site. In the file, you will find in front of each SQL statement an identification to help you search for them. For example, Example 7.1 (the first example in Chapter 7, "SELECT Statement: The FROM Clause,") has this as its identification:

```
Example 7.1:
```

Likewise, the following text is included to find Answer 12.6:

```
Answer 12.6:
```

3.6 READY?

If all went well, you have now installed MySQL and a query tool. If you want, you can start to play with SQL. However, the sample database is missing. The next chapter describes how to create that database.

CHAPTER 4

SQL in a Nutshell

4.1 Introduction

This chapter uses examples to illustrate the capabilities of the database language SQL. We discuss most SQL statements briefly; other chapters describe the details and all the features. The purpose of this chapter is to give you a feeling of what SQL looks like and what this book covers.

The first sections also explain how to create the sample database. Be sure to execute the statements from these sections because almost all the examples and exercises in the rest of this book are based upon this database.

4.2 Logging On to the MySQL Database Server

To do anything with SQL (this applies to creating the sample database as well), you must log on to the MySQL database server. MySQL requires that applications identify themselves before manipulating the data in the database. In other words, the user needs to *log on* by using an application. Identification is done with the help of a *user name* and a *password*. Therefore, this chapter begins by describing how to log on to MySQL.

First, you need a user name. However, to create a user (with a name and password), you must log on first—a classic example of a chicken-and-egg problem. To end this deadlock, most database servers create several users during the installation procedure. Otherwise, it would be impossible to log on after the installation. One of these users is called *root* and has an identical password (if you have followed the installation procedure described in the previous chapter).

How logging on really takes place depends on the application that is used. For example, with the query tool WinSQL, the logon screen looks similar to Figure 4.1.

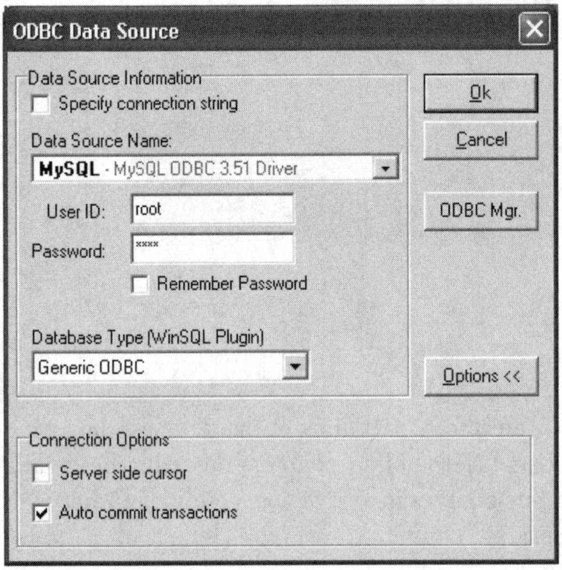

FIGURE 4.1 The logon screen of WinSQL

The user name is entered in the User ID text box, and the password in the Password text box. In both cases, you type *root*. For security reasons, the password characters appear as asterisks. User names and passwords are case sensitive, so be sure you type them correctly—not with capitals. After you enter the name and password, you can log on and start entering SQL statements.

When you use the client application called mysql that is included with MySQL, the process of logging on looks different but is still comparable (see Figure 4.2). The code `-u` stands for *user*, behind which the user name (root) is specified, followed by the code `-p`. Next the application wants to know the password. Later sections explain this in more detail.

The web site of this book contains detailed information about how to log on with different programs.

After you have logged on successfully with the users that are created during the installation procedure, you can introduce new users and create new tables.

```
Command Prompt - mysql -u root -p
Microsoft Windows XP [Version 5.1.2600]
(C) Copyright 1985-2001 Microsoft Corp.

C:\Documents and Settings\Rick van der Lans>cd\

C:\>cd\program files\mysql\mysql server 5.0\bin

C:\Program Files\MySQL\MySQL Server 5.0\bin>mysql -u root -p
Enter password: ****
Welcome to the MySQL monitor.  Commands end with ; or \g.
Your MySQL connection id is 1 to server version: 5.0.7-beta-nt

Type 'help;' or '\h' for help. Type '\c' to clear the buffer.

mysql> _
```

FIGURE 4.2 Logging on with mysql

4.3 Creating New SQL Users

Section 1.4 described the concept of a user and also mentioned briefly the respective roles of users and applications. A user starts up an application. This application passes SQL statements to MySQL that processes them. A user can enter these SQL statements "live" (interactive SQL), or they can be included in the application code (preprogrammed SQL).

A clear distinction should be made between the real, *human* user and the user name used to log on. To avoid confusion, we call the latter the *SQL user.* SQL users can be granted *privileges.* A privilege is a specification indicating what a certain SQL user can do. For example, one user might be allowed to create new tables, another might be authorized to update existing tables, and a third might be able to only query tables.The relationship between human users and SQL users can be one-to-one, but that is not required. A human user is allowed to log on under different SQL user names with different privileges. Additionally, an entire group of human users is allowed to use the same SQL user name with the same privileges. Therefore, the relationship between users and SQL users is a many-to-many relationship. You need to define these relationships.

So to be able to log on, you need to have an SQL user. Several SQL users have already been created during the installation procedure, to prevent the chicken-and-egg problem. Therefore, you do not need to create one. However, if you want to create your own SQL users, you can do that with a special SQL statement.

Imagine that we log on with the SQL user called root. Next, we can use the *CREATE USER statement* to create our own new SQL users. We give a new SQL user a name and also a password.

Example 4.1: Introduce a new user called BOOKSQL with the password BOOKSQLPW.

```
CREATE USER 'BOOKSQL'@'localhost' IDENTIFIED BY 'BOOKSQLPW'
```

Explanation: The name of the new SQL user is created with the specification `'BOOKSQL'@'localhost'`. Another chapter explains the meaning of `localhost`. The statement ends with the password, which, in this case, is BOOKSQLPW. Make sure that quotation marks surround the user name, the term `localhost`, and the password.

When an application logs on to MySQL with an SQL user name, a so-called *connection* is started. A connection is a unique link between the application and the MySQL database server for the specific SQL user. It is like a telephone cable between that application and MySQL. The privileges of the SQL user determine what the user is allowed to send over the cable. Through the connection, the user has access to all the databases that the database server manages. A new SQL user is allowed to log on, but this user does not have any other privileges yet. We need to grant those privileges to BOOKSQL first with the *GRANT statement*.

The GRANT statement has extensive features. Chapter 28, "Users and Data Security," discusses this statement and related topics." However, to get you started, the next example contains the statement that grants the new SQL user called BOOKSQL enough privileges to create tables and manipulate them afterward.

Example 4.2: Give the SQL user BOOKSQL the privileges to create and manipulate tables.

```
GRANT ALL PRIVILEGES
ON    *.*
TO    'BOOKSQL'@'localhost'
WITH  GRANT OPTION
```

BOOKSQL now can log on and execute all the statements in the following chapters.

Note: The rest of the book assumes that you log on as user BOOKSQL with the password BOOKSQLPW and that you have sufficient privileges.

4.4 Creating Databases

Section 1.2 defined the concept of a database. Using this definition, a database acts as a container for a set of tables. For MySQL, each table must also be created within an existing database. Therefore, when you want to build a table, you first need to create a database.

Example 4.3: Create a database with the name TENNIS for the tables of the tennis club.

```
CREATE DATABASE TENNIS
```

Explanation: After this CREATE DATABASE *statement* is processed, the database exists but is still empty. This book assumes that you have logged on as BOOKSQL before you enter this statement.

4.5 Selecting the Current Database

A MySQL database server can offer access to more than one database. When a user has opened a connection with MySQL and wants, for example, to create new tables or query existing tables, the user must specify the database he wants to work with. This is called the *current database.* Only one current database can exist, and

If no current database has been specified, you still can manipulate tables. In addition, you can access tables from a database other than the current database. For both situations, you must explicitly specify the database in which those tables reside.

To make a specific database current, MySQL supports the USE *statement.*

Example 4.4: Make TENNIS the current database.

```
USE TENNIS
```

Explanation: This statement can also be used to "jump" from one database to another.

After processing a CREATE DATABASE statement (see the earlier section), the created database does *not* automatically become the current database—an extra USE statement is needed for that.

No database is current when you log on using the technique described earlier. As an alternative to the USE *statement*, you can make a database current by specifying it when you log on.

```
mysql -u BOOKSQL -p TENNIS
```

The rest of the book assumes that you log on as user BOOKSQL with the password BOOKSQLPW, that you have sufficient privileges, and that the TENNIS database is the current database.

4.6 Creating Tables

Databases in MySQL are made up of database objects. The best-known and most important database object is probably the table. The CREATE TABLE statement is used to develop new tables. The next example contains the CREATE TABLE statements that are needed to create the tables from the sample database.

Example 4.5: Create the five tables that form the sample database.

```
CREATE   TABLE PLAYERS
        (PLAYERNO       INTEGER       NOT NULL,
         NAME           CHAR(15)      NOT NULL,
         INITIALS       CHAR(3)       NOT NULL,
         BIRTH_DATE     DATE                  ,
         SEX            CHAR(1)       NOT NULL,
         JOINED         SMALLINT      NOT NULL,
         STREET         VARCHAR(30)   NOT NULL,
         HOUSENO        CHAR(4)               ,
         POSTCODE       CHAR(6)               ,
         TOWN           VARCHAR(30)   NOT NULL,
         PHONENO        CHAR(13)              ,
         LEAGUENO       CHAR(4)               ,
         PRIMARY KEY    (PLAYERNO)            )

CREATE   TABLE TEAMS
        (TEAMNO         INTEGER       NOT NULL,
         PLAYERNO       INTEGER       NOT NULL,
         DIVISION       CHAR(6)       NOT NULL,
         PRIMARY KEY    (TEAMNO)              )

CREATE   TABLE MATCHES
        (MATCHNO        INTEGER       NOT NULL,
         TEAMNO         INTEGER       NOT NULL,
         PLAYERNO       INTEGER       NOT NULL,
         WON            SMALLINT      NOT NULL,
         LOST           SMALLINT      NOT NULL,
         PRIMARY KEY    (MATCHNO)             )
```

```
CREATE   TABLE PENALTIES
        (PAYMENTNO      INTEGER      NOT NULL,
         PLAYERNO       INTEGER      NOT NULL,
         PAYMENT_DATE   DATE         NOT NULL,
         AMOUNT         DECIMAL(7,2) NOT NULL,
         PRIMARY KEY    (PAYMENTNO)          )

CREATE   TABLE COMMITTEE_MEMBERS
        (PLAYERNO       INTEGER      NOT NULL,
         BEGIN_DATE     DATE         NOT NULL,
         END_DATE       DATE                 ,
         POSITION       CHAR(20)             ,
         PRIMARY KEY    (PLAYERNO, BEGIN_DATE))
```

Explanation: MySQL does not require the statements to be entered in this exact way. This book uses a certain layout style for all SQL statements, to make them easier to read. However, MySQL does not care whether everything is written neatly in a row (still separated by spaces or commas, of course) or nicely below each other.

As indicated in Chapter 2, "The Tennis Club Sample Database," several integrity constraints apply for these tables. We excluded most of them here because we do not need them in the first two parts of this book. Chapter 21, "Specifying Integrity Constraints," explains all the integrity rules in SQL.

With a CREATE TABLE statement, several properties are defined, including the name of the table, the columns of the table, and the primary key. The name of the table is specified first: CREATE TABLE PLAYERS. The columns of a table are listed between brackets. For each column name, a data type is specified, as in CHAR, SMALLINT, INTEGER, DECIMAL, or DATE. The data type defines the type of value that may be entered into the specific column. The next section explains the specification NOT NULL.

Figure 2.2 shows the primary key of the tables, among other things. A primary key of a table is a column (or combination of columns) in which every value can appear only once. By defining the primary key in the PLAYERS table, we indicate that each player number can appear only once in the PLAYERNO column. A primary key is a certain type of integrity constraint. In SQL, primary keys are specified within the CREATE TABLE statement with the words PRIMARY KEY. This is one of two ways to specify a primary key. After listing all the columns, PRIMARY KEY is specified followed by the column or columns belonging to that primary key. Chapter 21 discusses the other way to specify a primary key.

It is not always necessary to specify primary keys for a table, but it is important. Chapter 21 explains why. For now, we advise you to define a primary key for each table you create.

In the definition of a column, you are allowed to specify NOT NULL. This means that every row of the column *must* be filled. In other words, null values are not allowed in a NOT NULL column. For example, each player must have a NAME, but a LEAGUENO is not required.

4.7 Populating Tables with Data

The tables have been created and can now be filled with data. For this, we use INSERT statements.

Example 4.6: Fill all tables from the sample database with data. See Section 2.3 for a listing of all data.

For the sake of convenience, only two examples of INSERT statements are given for each table. At the web site of the book, you will find all the INSERT statements.

```
INSERT INTO PLAYERS VALUES
   (6, 'Parmenter', 'R', '1964-06-25', 'M', 1977,
   'Haseltine Lane', '80', '1234KK', 'Stratford',
   '070-476537', '8467')

INSERT INTO PLAYERS VALUES
   (7, 'Wise', 'GWS', '1963-05-11', 'M', 1981,
   'Edgecombe Way', '39', '9758VB', 'Stratford',
   '070-347689', NULL)

INSERT INTO TEAMS VALUES (1, 6, 'first')

INSERT INTO TEAMS VALUES (2, 27, 'second')

INSERT INTO MATCHES VALUES (1, 1, 6, 3, 1)

INSERT INTO MATCHES VALUES (4, 1, 44, 3, 2)

INSERT INTO PENALTIES VALUES (1, 6, '1980-12-08', 100)

INSERT INTO PENALTIES VALUES (2, 44, '1981-05-05', 75)

INSERT INTO COMMITTEE_MEMBERS VALUES
   (6, '1990-01-01', '1990-12-31', 'Secretary')

INSERT INTO COMMITTEE_MEMBERS VALUES
   (6, '1991-01-01', '1992-12-31', 'Member')
```

Explanation: Each statement corresponds to one (new) row in a table. After the term INSERT INTO, the table name is specified, and the values for the new row come after VALUES. Each row consists of one or more values. Different kinds of values may be used. For example, numeric and alphanumeric values, dates, and times exist.

Each alphanumeric value, such as Parmenter and Stratford (see the first INSERT statement), must be enclosed in single quotation marks. The (column) values are separated by commas. Because MySQL remembers the sequence in which the columns were specified in the CREATE TABLE statement, the system also knows the column to which every value corresponds. For the PLAYERS table, therefore, the first value is PLAYERNO, the second value is NAME, and the last value is LEAGUENO.

Specifying dates and times is more difficult than specifying numeric and alphanumeric values because they have to adhere to certain rules. A date such as December 8, 1980, must be specified as '1980-12-08'. This form of expression, described in detail in Section 5.2.5, turns an alphanumeric value into a correct date. However, the alphanumeric value must be written correctly. A date consists of three components: year, month, and day. Hyphens separate the components.

In the second INSERT statement, the word NULL is specified as the twelfth value. This enables us to enter a null value explicitly. In this case, it means that the league number of player number 7 is unknown.

4.8 Querying Tables

SELECT statements are used to retrieve data from tables. A number of examples illustrate the diverse features of this statement.

Example 4.7: Get the number, name, and date of birth of each player resident in Stratford; sort the result in alphabetical order of name (note that Stratford starts with a capital letter).

```
SELECT    PLAYERNO, NAME, BIRTH_DATE
FROM      PLAYERS
WHERE     TOWN = 'Stratford'
ORDER BY NAME
```

The result is:

```
PLAYERNO  NAME             BIRTH_DATE
--------  ---------------  ----------
      39  Bishop           1956-10-29
      57  Brown            1971-08-17
       2  Everett          1948-09-01
      83  Hope             1956-11-11
       6  Parmenter        1964-06-25
     100  Parmenter        1963-02-28
       7  Wise             1963-05-11
```

Explanation: This SELECT statement should be read as follows: Get the number, name, and date of birth (SELECT PLAYERNO, NAME, BIRTH_DATE) of each player (FROM PLAYERS) resident in Stratford (WHERE TOWN = 'Stratford'); sort the result in alphabetical order of name (ORDER BY NAME). After FROM, we specify which table we want to query. The condition that the requested data must satisfy comes after WHERE. SELECT enables us to choose which columns we want to see. Figure 4.3 illustrates this in a graphical way. And after ORDER BY, we specify the column names on which the final result should be sorted.

FIGURE 4.3 An illustration of a SELECT statement

This book presents the result of a SELECT statement somewhat differently from the way MySQL does. The "default" layout used throughout this book is as follows.

First, the width of a column is determined by the width of the data type of the column. Second, the name of a column heading is equal to the name of the column in the SELECT statement. Third, the values in columns with an alphanumeric data type are left-justified and those in numeric columns are right-justified. Fourth, two spaces separate two columns. Fifth, a null value is displayed as a question mark. Finally, if a result is very long, some rows are left out and colons are presented.

Example 4.8: Get the number of each player who joined the club after 1980 and is resident in Stratford; order the result by player number.

```
SELECT   PLAYERNO
FROM     PLAYERS
WHERE    JOINED > 1980
AND      TOWN = 'Stratford'
ORDER BY PLAYERNO
```

The result is:

```
PLAYERNO
--------
       7
      57
      83
```

Explanation: Get the number (SELECT PLAYERNO) of each player (FROM PLAYERS) who joined the club after 1980 (WHERE JOINED > 1980) and is resident in Stratford (AND TOWN = 'Stratford'); sort the result by player number (ORDER BY PLAYERNO).

Example 4.9: Get all the information about each penalty.

```
SELECT   *
FROM     PENALTIES
```

The result is:

```
PAYMENTNO  PLAYERNO  PAYMENT_DATE  AMOUNT
---------  --------  ------------  ------
        1         6  1980-12-08    100.00
        2        44  1981-05-05     75.00
        3        27  1983-09-10    100.00
        4       104  1984-12-08     50.00
        5        44  1980-12-08     25.00
        6         8  1980-12-08     25.00
        7        44  1982-12-30     30.00
        8        27  1984-11-12     75.00
```

Explanation: Get all column values (SELECT *) for each penalty (FROM PENALTIES). This statement returns the whole PENALTIES table. The * character is a shorthand notation for "all columns." In this result, you can also see how dates are presented in this book.

Example 4.10: How much is 33 times 121?

```
SELECT   33 * 121
```

The result is:

```
33 * 121
--------
    3993
```

Explanation: This example shows that a SELECT statement does not always have to retrieve data from tables; it can also be used to perform straightforward calculations. If no tables are specified, the statement returns one row as result. This row contains the answers to the calculations.

4.9 Updating and Deleting Rows

Section 4.7 described how to add new rows to a table. This section covers updating and deleting existing rows.

A warning in advance: If you execute the statements described in this section, you will change the contents of the database. The subsequent sections assume that the original contents of the database are intact. You can restore the values by rerunning statements found at www.r20.nl.

The UPDATE *statement* is used to change values in rows, and the DELETE *statement* is used to remove complete rows from a table. Let us look at examples of both statements.

Example 4.11: Change the amount of each penalty incurred by player 44 to $200.

```
UPDATE   PENALTIES
SET      AMOUNT = 200
WHERE    PLAYERNO = 44
```

Explanation: For each penalty (UPDATE PENALTIES) incurred by player 44 (WHERE PLAYERNO = 44), change the amount to $200 (SET AMOUNT = 200). So the use of the WHERE clause in the UPDATE statement is equivalent to that of the SELECT statement—it indicates which rows must be changed. After the word SET, the columns that will have a new value are specified. The change is executed regardless of the existing value.

Issuing a SELECT statement can show the effect of the change. Before the update, the next SELECT statement

```
SELECT    PLAYERNO, AMOUNT
FROM      PENALTIES
WHERE     PLAYERNO = 44
```

gave the following result:

```
PLAYERNO  AMOUNT
--------  ------
      44   75.00
      44   25.00
      44   30.00
```

After the change with the UPDATE statement, the result of the previous SELECT statement is different:

```
PLAYERNO  AMOUNT
--------  ------
      44  200.00
      44  200.00
      44  200.00
```

Example 4.12: Remove each penalty with an amount greater than $100 (we assume the changed contents of the PENALTIES table).

```
DELETE
FROM      PENALTIES
WHERE     AMOUNT > 100
```

Explanation: Remove the penalties (DELETE FROM PENALTIES) with an amount greater than $100 (WHERE AMOUNT > 100). Again, the use of the WHERE clause is equivalent to that in the SELECT and UPDATE statements.

After this statement, the PENALTIES table looks as follows (shown by issuing a SELECT statement):

```
PAYMENTNO  PLAYERNO  PAYMENT_DATE  AMOUNT
---------  --------  ------------  ------
        1         6  1980-12-08    100.00
        3        27  1983-09-10    100.00
        4       104  1984-12-08     50.00
        6         8  1980-12-08     25.00
        8        27  1984-11-12     75.00
```

4.10 Optimizing Query Processing with Indexes

We now look at how SELECT statements are processed—how MySQL arrives at the correct answer. The following SELECT statement illustrates this (assume the original contents of the PENALTIES table).

```
SELECT   *
FROM     PENALTIES
WHERE    AMOUNT = 25
```

To process this statement, MySQL scans the entire PENALTIES table row by row. If the value of AMOUNT equals 25, that row is included in the result. As in this example, if the table contains only a few rows, MySQL can work quickly. However, if a table has thousands of rows and each must be checked, this could take a great deal of time. In such a case, defining an *index* can speed up the processing. For now, think of an index created with MySQL as similar to the index of a book. Chapter 25, "Using Indexes," discusses this topic in more detail.

An index is defined on a column or combination of columns. See the following example.

Example 4.13: Create an index on the AMOUNT column of the PENALTIES table.

```
CREATE   INDEX PENALTIES_AMOUNT ON
         PENALTIES (AMOUNT)
```

Explanation: This statement defines an index called PENALTIES_AMOUNT for the AMOUNT column in the PENALTIES table.

This index ensures that in the earlier example, MySQL needs to look at only rows in the database that satisfy the WHERE condition. Therefore, it is quicker to produce an answer. The index PENALTIES_AMOUNT provides direct access to these rows. Keep in mind the following points:

- Indexes are defined to optimize the processing of SELECT statements.
- An index is never explicitly referenced in a SELECT statement; the syntax of SQL does not allow this.
- During the processing of a statement, the database server itself determines whether an existing index will be used.
- An index may be created or deleted at any time.
- When updating, inserting, or deleting rows, MySQL also maintains the indexes on the impacted tables. This means that, on one hand, the processing time for SELECT statements is reduced; on the other hand, the processing time for update statements (such as INSERT, UPDATE, and DELETE) can increase.
- An index is also a database object.

A special type of index is the *unique* index. SQL also uses unique indexes to optimize the processing of statements. Unique indexes have another function as well: They guarantee that a particular column or combination of columns contains no duplicate values. A unique index is created by placing the word UNIQUE between the words CREATE and INDEX.

4.11 Views

In a table, rows with data are actually stored. This means that a table occupies a particular amount of storage space—the more rows, the more storage space is required. *Views* are tables visible to users, but they do not occupy any storage space. A view, therefore, can also be referred to as a *virtual* or *derived* table. A view behaves as though it contains actual rows of data, but it contains none.

Example 4.14: Create a view in which the difference between the number of sets won and the number of sets lost are recorded for each match.

```
CREATE   VIEW NUMBER_SETS (MATCHNO, DIFFERENCE) AS
SELECT   MATCHNO, ABS(WON - LOST)
FROM     MATCHES
```

Explanation: The previous statement defines a view with the name NUMBER_SETS. A SELECT statement is used to define the contents of the view. This view has only two columns: MATCHNO and DIFFERENCE. The value of the second column is determined by subtracting the number of sets lost from the number of sets won. The ABS function makes the value positive (Appendix B, "Scalar Functions," discusses the precise meaning of ABS).

By using the SELECT statement shown here, you can see the (virtual) contents of the view:

```
SELECT    *
FROM      NUMBER_SETS
```

The result is:

```
MATCHNO  DIFFERENCE
-------  ----------
      1           2
      2           1
      3           3
      4           1
      5           3
      6           2
      7           3
      8           3
      9           1
     10           1
     11           1
     12           2
     13           3
```

The contents of the NUMBER_SETS view are *not* stored in the database but are derived at the moment a SELECT statement (or another statement) is executed. The use of views, therefore, costs nothing extra in storage space because the contents of a view can include only data that is already stored in other tables. Among other things, views can be used to do the following:

- Simplify the use of routine or repetitive statements
- Restructure the way in which tables are seen
- Develop SELECT statements in several steps
- Improve the security of data

Chapter 26, "Views," looks at views more closely.

4.12 Users and Data Security

Data in a database should be protected against incorrect use and misuse. In other words, not everyone should have access to all the data in the database. As already shown in the beginning of this chapter, MySQL recognizes the concept of SQL user and privilege. Users need to make themselves known by logging on.

That same section showed an example of granting privileges to users. Here you will find more examples of the GRANT statement; assume that all the SQL users mentioned exist.

Example 4.15: Imagine that two SQL users, DIANE and PAUL, have been created. MySQL will reject most of their SQL statements as long as they have not been granted privileges. The following three statements give them the required privileges. Assume that a third SQL user, such as BOOKSQL, grants these privileges.

```
GRANT   SELECT
ON      PLAYERS
TO      DIANE

GRANT   SELECT, UPDATE
ON      PLAYERS
TO      PAUL

GRANT   SELECT, UPDATE
ON      TEAMS
TO      PAUL
```

When PAUL has logged on, he can query the TEAMS table, for example:

```
SELECT    *
FROM      TEAMS
```

4.13 Deleting Database Objects

For each type of database object for which a CREATE statement exists, a corresponding DROP statement with which the object can be deleted also exists. Consider a few examples.

Example 4.16: Delete the MATCHES table.

```
DROP TABLE MATCHES
```

Example 4.17: Delete the view NUMBER_SETS.

```
DROP VIEW NUMBER_SETS
```

Example 4.18: Delete the PENALTIES_AMOUNT index.

```
DROP INDEX PENALTIES_AMOUNT
```

Example 4.19: Delete the TENNIS database.

```
DROP DATABASE TENNIS
```

All dependent objects are also removed. For example, if the PLAYERS table is deleted, all indexes (which are defined on that table) and all privileges (which are dependent on that table) are automatically removed.

4.14 System Variables

MySQL has certain settings. When the MySQL database server is started, these settings are read to determine the next steps. For example, some settings define how data must be stored, others affect the processing speed, and still others relate to the system time and date. These settings are called *system variables*. Examples of system variables are DATADIR (the directory in which MySQL creates the databases), LOG_WARNINGS, MAX_USER_CONNECTIONS, and TIME_ZONE.

Sometimes it is important to know the value of a certain system variable. With a simple SELECT statement, you can retrieve its value.

Example 4.20: What is the most recent version of the MySQL database server that we use now?

```
SELECT @@VERSION
```

The result is:

```
@@VERSION
------------
5.0.7-beta-nt
```

Explanation: In MySQL, the value of the system variable VERSION is set to the version number. Specifying two @ symbols before the name of the system variable returns its value.

Many system variables, such as VERSION and the system date, cannot be changed. However, some, including SQL_MODE, can be. To change system variables, use the SET *statement.*

Example 4.21: Change the value of the SQL_MODE parameter to PIPES_AS_CONCAT.

```
SET @@SQL_MODE = 'PIPES_AS_CONCAT'
```

Explanation: This change applies only to the current SQL user. In other words, different users can see different values for certain system variables.

Section 5.7 discusses system variables in detail. Some system variables are also described together with the SQL statement or clause that they have a relationship with.

Because the value of the SQL_MODE system variable affects the way of processing and the features of several SQL statements, we will discuss it in more detail. The value of SQL_MODE consists of a set of zero, one, or more settings that are separated by commas. For example, a possible value of SQL_MODE with four settings is shown here:

```
REAL_AS_FLOAT,PIPES_AS_CONCAT,ANSI_QUOTES,IGNORE_SPACE
```

With a normal SET statement, we overwrite all the settings at once. If we want to add a setting, we can use the following statement.

Example 4.22: Add the setting NO_ZERO_IN_DATE to the SQL_MODE system variable.

```
SET @@SQL_MODE = CONCAT(@@SQL_MODE,
                 CASE @@SQL_MODE WHEN '' THEN '' ELSE ',' END,
                 'NO_ZERO_IN_DATE')
```

The meaning of these settings is explained later in this book.

4.15 Grouping of SQL Statements

SQL has many statements, but this chapter briefly describes only a few. In literature, it is customary to divide that large set of SQL statements into the following groups: Data Definition Language (DDL), Data Manipulation Language (DML), Data Control Language (DCL), and procedural statements.

The *Data Definition Language (DDL)* consists of all the SQL statements that affect the structure of database objects, such as tables, indexes, and views. The `CREATE TABLE` statement is a clear example of a DDL statement, but so are `CREATE INDEX` and `DROP TABLE`.

SQL statements used to query and change the contents of tables belong to the *Data Manipulation Language (DML)* group. Examples of DML statements are `SELECT`, `UPDATE`, `DELETE`, and `INSERT`.

Data Control Language (DCL) statements relate to the security of data and the revoking of privileges. This chapter has discussed the `GRANT` statement; the `REVOKE` statement is also a DCL statement.

Examples of *procedural statements* are `IF-THEN-ELSE` and `WHILE-DO`. These classical statements have been added to SQL to create relatively new database objects, such as triggers and stored procedures.

The names of these groups sometimes assume that SQL consists of several individual languages, but this is incorrect. All SQL statements are part of one language and are grouped for the sake of clarity.

Appendix A, "Syntax of SQL," which defines all SQL statements, indicates the group to which an SQL statement belongs.

4.16 The Catalog Tables

MySQL maintains lists of user names and passwords and the sequence in which columns in the `CREATE TABLE` statements have been created (see Section 4.6). However, where is all this data stored? Where does SQL keep track of all these names, passwords, tables, columns, sequence numbers, and so on? MySQL has a number of tables for its own use in which this data is stored. These tables are called *catalog tables* or *system tables;* together they form the *catalog*.

Each catalog table is an "ordinary" table that can be queried using `SELECT` statements. Querying the catalog tables can have many uses, including these:

- As a *help function* for new users to determine which tables in the database are available and which columns the tables contain
- As a *control function* so that users can see, for example, which indexes, views, and privileges would be deleted if a particular table was dropped
- As a *processing function* for MySQL itself when it executes statements (as a help function for MySQL)

Catalog tables *cannot* be accessed using statements such as `UPDATE` and `DELETE`—the SQL database server maintains these tables itself.

MySQL has two databases in which catalog tables are included. The database called MYSQL contains data on privileges, users, and tables. The structure of these tables is somewhat cryptic and is unique for MySQL. In addition, the database called INFORMATION_SCHEMA contains catalog data that partly overlaps the data in the MYSQL database. The structure of INFORMATION_SCHEMA conforms to the SQL standard and looks similar to the structure of other SQL products.

The structure of the catalog tables is not simple. We have defined several simple views on the catalog tables of MySQL. These views are partly defined on the tables of the MYSQL database and partly on those of the INFORMATION_SCHEMA database. So actually, they are not catalog tables, but catalog views. In a simple and transparent way, they give access to the actual, underlying catalog tables.

Part III, "Creating Database Objects," which discusses different database objects, such as tables and views, describes the different catalog tables that belong to the INFORMATION_SCHEMA database. In the first two parts of this book, the catalog views suffice.

If you are familiar with MySQL and have worked your way through most chapters in this book, we recommend that you look at the structure of the actual catalog tables. They are, after all, just tables that you can access with SELECT statements. Understanding the catalog will definitely increase your knowledge of MySQL.

In the rest of this book, we use these simple catalog views, so we recommend that you create these views. You can reference the web site of this book for assistance. You can adjust these catalog views later—you can add new columns and new catalog views. By studying how these views have been built makes it easier to understand the real catalog tables later.

Example 4.23: Create the following catalog views. These views must be created in the sequence specified because of interdependences.

```
CREATE   OR REPLACE VIEW USERS
        (USER_NAME) AS
SELECT   DISTINCT UPPER(CONCAT('''',USER,'''@''',HOST,''''))
FROM     MYSQL.USER

CREATE   OR REPLACE VIEW TABLES
        (TABLE_CREATOR, TABLE_NAME,
         CREATE_TIMESTAMP, COMMENT) AS
SELECT   UPPER(TABLE_SCHEMA), UPPER(TABLE_NAME),
         CREATE_TIME, TABLE_COMMENT
FROM     INFORMATION_SCHEMA.TABLES
WHERE    TABLE_TYPE IN ('BASE TABLE','TEMPORARY')
```

```
CREATE   OR REPLACE VIEW COLUMNS
        (TABLE_CREATOR, TABLE_NAME, COLUMN_NAME,
         COLUMN_NO, DATA_TYPE, CHAR_LENGTH,
        'PRECISION', SCALE, NULLABLE, COMMENT) AS
SELECT   UPPER(TABLE_SCHEMA), UPPER(TABLE_NAME),
         UPPER(COLUMN_NAME), ORDINAL_POSITION,
         UPPER(DATA_TYPE), CHARACTER_MAXIMUM_LENGTH,
         NUMERIC_PRECISION, NUMERIC_SCALE, IS_NULLABLE,
         COLUMN_COMMENT
FROM     INFORMATION_SCHEMA.COLUMNS

CREATE   OR REPLACE VIEW VIEWS
        (VIEW_CREATOR, VIEW_NAME, CREATE_TIMESTAMP,
         WITHCHECKOPT, IS_UPDATABLE, VIEWFORMULA, COMMENT) AS
SELECT   UPPER(V.TABLE_SCHEMA), UPPER(V.TABLE_NAME),
         T.CREATE_TIME,
         CASE
            WHEN V.CHECK_OPTION = 'None' THEN 'NO'
            WHEN V.CHECK_OPTION = 'Cascaded' THEN 'CASCADED'
            WHEN V.CHECK_OPTION = 'Local' THEN 'LOCAL'
            ELSE 'Yes'
         END, V.IS_UPDATABLE, V.VIEW_DEFINITION, T.TABLE_COMMENT
FROM     INFORMATION_SCHEMA.VIEWS AS V,
         INFORMATION_SCHEMA.TABLES AS T
WHERE    V.TABLE_NAME = T.TABLE_NAME
AND      V.TABLE_SCHEMA = T.TABLE_SCHEMA

CREATE   OR REPLACE VIEW INDEXES
        (INDEX_CREATOR, INDEX_NAME, CREATE_TIMESTAMP,
         TABLE_CREATOR, TABLE_NAME, UNIQUE_ID, INDEX_TYPE) AS
SELECT   DISTINCT UPPER(I.INDEX_SCHEMA), UPPER(I.INDEX_NAME),
         T.CREATE_TIME, UPPER(I.TABLE_SCHEMA),
         UPPER(I.TABLE_NAME),
         CASE
            WHEN I.NON_UNIQUE = 0 THEN 'YES'
            ELSE 'NO'
         END,
         I.INDEX_TYPE
FROM     INFORMATION_SCHEMA.STATISTICS AS I,
         INFORMATION_SCHEMA.TABLES AS T
WHERE    I.TABLE_NAME = T.TABLE_NAME
AND      I.TABLE_SCHEMA = T.TABLE_SCHEMA
```

```
CREATE   OR REPLACE VIEW COLUMNS_IN_INDEX
        (INDEX_CREATOR, INDEX_NAME,
         TABLE_CREATOR, TABLE_NAME, COLUMN_NAME,
         COLUMN_SEQ, ORDERING) AS
SELECT   UPPER(INDEX_SCHEMA), UPPER(INDEX_NAME),
         UPPER(TABLE_SCHEMA), UPPER(TABLE_NAME),
         UPPER(COLUMN_NAME), SEQ_IN_INDEX,
         CASE
            WHEN COLLATION = 'A' THEN 'ASCENDING'
            WHEN COLLATION = 'D' THEN 'DESCENDING'
            ELSE 'OTHER'
         END
FROM     INFORMATION_SCHEMA.STATISTICS

CREATE   OR REPLACE VIEW USER_AUTHS
        (GRANTOR, GRANTEE, PRIVILEGE, WITHGRANTOPT) AS
SELECT   'UNKNOWN', UPPER(GRANTEE), PRIVILEGE_TYPE, IS_GRANTABLE
FROM     INFORMATION_SCHEMA.USER_PRIVILEGES

CREATE   OR REPLACE VIEW DATABASE_AUTHS
        (GRANTOR, GRANTEE, DATABASE_NAME, PRIVILEGE,
         WITHGRANTOPT) AS
SELECT   'UNKNOWN', UPPER(GRANTEE), UPPER(TABLE_SCHEMA),
         PRIVILEGE_TYPE, IS_GRANTABLE
FROM     INFORMATION_SCHEMA.SCHEMA_PRIVILEGES

CREATE   OR REPLACE VIEW TABLE_AUTHS
        (GRANTOR, GRANTEE, TABLE_CREATOR, TABLE_NAME,
         PRIVILEGE, WITHGRANTOPT) AS
SELECT   'UNKNOWN', UPPER(GRANTEE), UPPER(TABLE_SCHEMA),
         UPPER(TABLE_NAME), PRIVILEGE_TYPE, IS_GRANTABLE
FROM     INFORMATION_SCHEMA.TABLE_PRIVILEGES

CREATE   OR REPLACE VIEW COLUMN_AUTHS
        (GRANTOR, GRANTEE, TABLE_CREATOR, TABLE_NAME,
         COLUMN_NAME, PRIVILEGE, WITHGRANTOPT) AS
SELECT   'UNKNOWN', UPPER(GRANTEE), UPPER(TABLE_SCHEMA),
         UPPER(TABLE_NAME), UPPER(COLUMN_NAME),
         PRIVILEGE_TYPE, IS_GRANTABLE
FROM     INFORMATION_SCHEMA.COLUMN_PRIVILEGES
```

Table 4.1 lists the catalog tables (catalog views) that are created.

TABLE 4.1 Examples of Catalog Views

TABLE NAME	EXPLANATION
USERS	Contains for each SQL user the names of the users who were not created during the installation procedure
TABLES	Contains for each table information such as the date and time the table was created
COLUMNS	Contains for each column (belonging to a table or view) information such as the data type, the table to which the column belongs, whether the null value is allowed, and the sequence number of the column in the table
VIEWS	Contains for each view information such as the view definition (the SELECT statement)
INDEXES	Contains for each index information such as the table and the columns on which the index is defined, and the manner in which the index is ordered
COLUMNS_IN_INDEX	Contains for each index the columns on which the index is defined
DATABASE_AUTHS	Contains the database privileges that are granted to users
TABLE_AUTHS	Contains the table privileges that are granted to users
COLUMN_AUTHS	Contains the column privileges that are granted to users

Consider the following examples of queries on the catalog table.

Example 4.24: Get the name, data type, and sequence number of each column in the PLAYERS table (which was created in the TENNIS database); order the result by sequence number.

```
SELECT   COLUMN_NAME, DATA_TYPE, COLUMN_NO
FROM     COLUMNS
WHERE    TABLE_NAME = 'PLAYERS'
AND      TABLE_CREATOR = 'TENNIS'
ORDER BY COLUMN_NO
```

The result is:

```
COLUMN_NAME  DATA_TYPE  COLUMN_NO
-----------  ---------  ---------
PLAYERNO     INT                1
NAME         CHAR               2
INITIALS     CHAR               3
BIRTH_DATE   DATE               4
SEX          CHAR               5
JOINED       SMALLINT           6
STREET       VARCHAR            7
HOUSENO      CHAR               8
POSTCODE     CHAR               9
TOWN         VARCHAR           10
PHONONO      CHAR              11
LEAGUENO     CHAR              12
```

Explanation: Get the name, data type, and sequence number (`SELECT COLUMN_NAME, DATA_TYPE, COLUMN_NO`) of each column (`FROM COLUMNS`) in the PLAYERS table (`WHERE TABLE_NAME = 'PLAYERS'`) that is created in the TENNIS database (`AND TABLE_CREATOR = 'TENNIS'`); order the result by sequence number (`ORDER BY COLUMN_NO`).

Example 4.25: Get the names of the indexes defined on the PENALTIES table.

```
SELECT   INDEX_NAME
FROM     INDEXES
WHERE    TABLE_NAME = 'PENALTIES'
AND      TABLE_CREATOR = 'TENNIS'
```

Result (for example):

```
INDEX_NAME
----------------
PRIMARY
PENALTIES_AMOUNT
```

Explanation: MySQL created the index that is mentioned first, with the name PRIMARY, because a primary key was specified on the PLAYERS table. Chapter 25 returns to this topic. The second index was created in Example 4.13.

Other chapters describe the effect that processing particular statements can have on the contents of the catalog tables. The catalog tables are an integral part of SQL.

You can find the original catalog tables that MySQL created in two different databases, called MYSQL and INFORMATION_SCHEMA. Both were created during MySQL installation. You can access the tables of the databases directly, without the intervention of the catalog views (see the following example).

Example 4.26: Get the names of the indexes that have been defined on the PENALTIES table.

```
USE INFORMATION_SCHEMA

SELECT   DISTINCT INDEX_NAME
FROM     STATISTICS
WHERE    TABLE_NAME = 'PENALTIES'
```

The result is:

```
INDEX_NAME
----------------
PRIMARY
PENALTIES_AMOUNT
```

Explanation: With the USE statement, we make INFORMATION_SCHEMA the current database. Then all the tables of the catalog can be accessed.

Example 4.27: Show the names of the tables that are stored in the INFORMATION_SCHEMA database.

```
SELECT   TABLE_NAME
FROM     TABLES
WHERE    TABLE_SCHEMA = 'INFORMATION_SCHEMA'
ORDER BY TABLE_NAME
```

The result is:

```
TABLE_NAME
-------------------------------------
CHARACTER_SETS
COLLATIONS
COLLATION_CHARACTER_SET_APPLICABILITY
COLUMNS
COLUMN_PRIVILEGES
ENGINES
EVENTS
FILES
```

```
KEY_COLUMN_USAGE
PARTITIONS
PLUGINS
PROCESSLIST
REFERENTIAL_CONSTRAINTS
ROUTINES
SCHEMATA
SCHEMA_PRIVILEGES
STATISTICS
TABLES
TABLE_CONSTRAINTS
TABLE_PRIVILEGES
TRIGGERS
USER_PRIVILEGES
VIEWS
```

The special SQL statement called `SHOW` is another way to get access to all this descriptive catalog data. See the next two examples.

Example 4.28: Get the descriptive data of the columns belonging to the PLAYERS table.

```
SHOW COLUMNS FROM PLAYERS
```

And the result is:

```
Field         Type          Null  Key  Default  Extra
------------  ------------  ----  ---  -------  -----
PLAYERNO      int(11)             PRI        0
NAME          varchar(15)
INITIALS      char(3)
BIRTH_DATE    date          YES
SEX           char(1)
JOINED        smallint(6)                    0
STREET        varchar(30)
HOUSENO       varchar(4)    YES
POSTCODE      varchar(6)    YES
TOWN          varchar(30)
PHONENO       varchar(13)   YES
LEAGUENO      varchar(4)    YES
```

Example 4.29: Get the descriptive data of the indexes defined on the PENALTIES table.

```
SHOW INDEX FROM PENALTIES
```

An example result is:

```
Table      Non-unique  Key_name          Column_name  Collation
---------  ----------  ----------------  -----------  ---------
PENALTIES           0  PRIMARY           PAYMENTNO    A
PENALTIES           1  PENALTIES_AMOUNT  AMOUNT       A
```

Explanation: MySQL created the first index itself because we defined a primary key on the PENALTIES table. Chapter 25 returns to this. The second index was created in Example 4.13. This `SHOW` statement returns more than these columns, but we omitted them for the sake of convenience.

Try the next statement yourself and look at the result:

```
SHOW DATABASES
SHOW TABLES
SHOW CREATE TABLE PLAYERS
SHOW INDEX FROM PLAYERS
SHOW GRANTS FOR BOOKSQL@localhost
SHOW PRIVILEGES
```

4.17 Retrieving Errors and Warnings

Sometimes things go wrong. If we do something wrong, MySQL presents one or more error messages. For example, if we make a typo in an SQL statement, we get an error message. MySQL won't even try to process the statement. Perhaps a statement is syntactically correct, but we are trying to do something that is impossible, such as create a table with a name that already exists. In this situation, MySQL also returns an error message. However, not all the error messages are presented—it depends on the seriousness of the error message. After an SQL statement has been processed, we can request all the error messages with the `SHOW WARNINGS` *statement.*

Example 4.30: What is the result of the calculation 10 divided by 0?

```
SELECT 10 / 0
```

The result of this statement is empty because we cannot divide by zero. But no error message is given. We can ask for them as follows:

```
SHOW WARNINGS
```

The result is:

```
Level  Code  Message
-----  ----  ----------------------------------
Error  1305  FUNCTION tennis.chr does not exist
Error  1105  Unknown error
```

Before processing the next SQL statement, all these messages are deleted, and a new list is created.

With the statement SHOW COUNT(*) WARNINGS, we can ask for the number of error messages. We get the same result if we ask for the value of the system variable called WARNING_COUNT.

The statement SHOW ERRORS resembles SHOW WARNINGS. The former returns all the errors, warnings, and notes; the latter returns the errors only. And, of course, a system COLUMN_AUTHS variable called ERROR_COUNT exists.

4.18 Definitions of SQL Statements

This book uses a particular formal notation to indicate the syntax of certain SQL statements. In other words, by using this notation, we give a definition of an SQL statement. These definitions are clearly indicated by enclosing the text in boxes. For example, the following is part of the definition of the CREATE INDEX statement:

DEFINITION

```
<create index statement> ::=
   CREATE [ UNIQUE ] INDEX <index name>
   ON <table name> <column list>

<column list> ::=
   ( <column name> [ , <column name> ]... )
```

If you are not familiar with this notation, we advise that you study it before you continue with the next chapters (see Appendix A).

Because the functionality of certain SQL statements is very extensive, we do not always show the complete definition in one place, but instead extend it step by step. We omit the definitions of the syntactically simple statements. Appendix A includes the complete definitions of all SQL statements.

Part II

Querying and Updating Data

One statement in particular forms the core of SQL and clearly represents the nonprocedural nature of SQL: the SELECT statement. It is the showpiece of SQL and, consequently, MySQL. This statement is used to query data in the tables; the result is always a table. Such a result table can be used as the basis of a report, for example.

This book deals with the SELECT statement in Chapters 5–15. Each chapter is devoted to one or two clauses of this statement. Several chapters have been added to explain certain concepts in more detail.

Chapter 16, "The HANDLER Statement," is devoted to the HANDLER statement, which offers an alternative method to query data. In a more simple way, rows can be retrieved individually. The features of this statement are much more limited than those of the SELECT statement. However, for certain applications, HANDLER can be more suitable than SELECT.

Chapter 17 describes how to insert, update, and delete data. The features of these statements are strongly based upon those of the SELECT statement, which makes the latter so important to master.

With MySQL, data can be loaded from files into the database vice versa: Data can be unloaded to external files. Chapter 18, "Loading and Unloading Data," describes the statements and features to do so.

The use of XML documents has become increasingly popular. Because of this, the need to store these special documents in tables has increased. Chapter 19, "Working with XML Documents," describes the functions with which XML documents can be queried and updated.

CHAPTER 5

SELECT Statement: Common Elements

5.1 Introduction

This first chapter dealing with the SELECT statement describes a number of common elements that are important to many SQL statements and certainly crucial to the SELECT statement. Those who are familiar with programming languages and other database languages will find most of these concepts familiar.

Among others, this chapter covers the following common elements:

- Literal
- Expression
- Column specification
- User variable
- System variable
- Case expression
- Scalar function
- Null value
- Cast expression
- Compound expression
- Row expression
- Table expression
- Aggregation function

5.2 Literals and Their Data Types

The previous chapter used literals in many examples of SQL statements. A *literal* is a fixed or unchanging value. Literals are used, for example, in conditions for selecting rows in SELECT statements and for specifying the values for a new row in INSERT statements; see Figure 5.1.

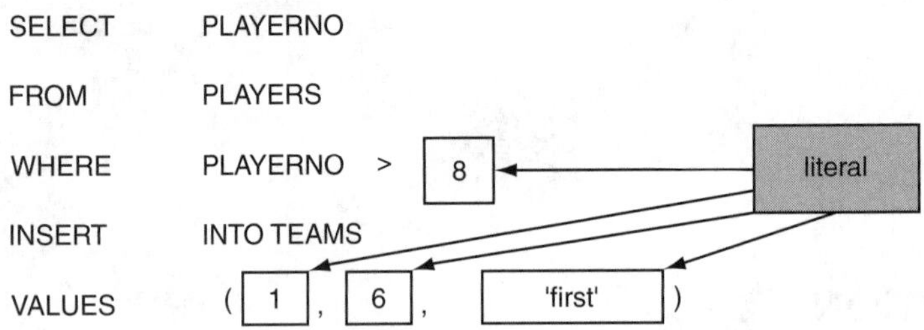

FIGURE 5.1 Literals in SQL statements

Each literal has a particular *data type*, just like a column in a table. The names of the different types of literals are derived from the names of their respective data types as we use them in the CREATE TABLE statement.

The literals are divided into several main groups: the numeric, the alphanumeric, the temporal, the Boolean, and the hexadecimal literals. They all have their own properties, idiosyncrasies, and limitations. Here you will find the definitions of all literals followed by the descriptions.

Each literal always has a *data type;* however, no literal exists for each data type. Chapter 20, "Creating Tables, discusses all data types (including the one for which no literal exists). That chapter also describes the CREATE TABLE statement in detail.

DEFINITION

```
<literal> ::=
   <numeric literal>      |
   <alphanumeric literal> |
   <temporal literal>     |
   <boolean literal>      |
   <hexadecimal literal>

<numeric literal> ::=
   <integer literal> |
   <decimal literal> |
   <float literal>   |
   <bit literal>
```

continues

```
<integer literal> ::= [ + | - ] <whole number>

<decimal literal> ::=
   [ + | - ] <whole number> [ .<whole number> ] |
   [ + | - ] <whole number>.                    |
   [ + | - ] .<whole number>

<float literal> ::=
   <mantissa> { E | e } <exponent>

<bit literal > ::=
   { b | B } ' { 0 | 1 }... '

<alphanumeric literal> ::= <character list>

<temporal literal> ::=
   <date literal>      |
   <time literal>      |
   <datetime literal>  |
   <timestamp literal> |
   <year literal>

<date literal> ::=
   { ' <years> - <months> - <days> ' } |
   { <years> <months> <days> }

<time literal> ::=
   { ' <hours> : <minutes> [ : <seconds>
        [ . <microseconds> ] ] ' }                |
   { ' [ <hours> : <minutes> : ] <seconds> ' } |
   { <hours> <minutes> <seconds> }              |
   { [ [ <hours> ] <minutes> ] <seconds> }

<datetime literal>  ;
<timestamp literal> ::=
   { ' <years> - <months> - <days> <space>
     [ <hours> [ : <minutes> [ : <seconds>
         [ . <micro seconds>] ] ] ] ' } |
   { <years> <months> <days> <hours> <minutes> <seconds> }

<year literal> ::= <year>

<hexadecimal literal> ::=
   { X | x } <hexadecimal character>... |
   0x <hexadecimal character>...

<hexadecimal character> ::=
   <digit> | A | B | C | D | E | F | a | b | c | d | e | f
```

continues

```
<years>         ;
<micro seconds> ;
<year>          ::= <whole number>

<months>  ;
<days>    ;
<hours>   ;
<minutes> ;
<seconds> ::= <digit> [ <digit> ]

<whole number> ::= <digit>...

<boolean literal> ::= TRUE | true | FALSE | false

<mantissa> ::= <decimal literal>

<exponent> ::= <integer literal>

<character list> ::= ' [ <character>... ] '

<character> ::= <digit> | <letter> | <special character> | ''

<special character> ::=
   { \ { 0 | ' | " | b | n | r | t | z | \ | % } } |
   <any other character>

<whole number> ::= <digit>...
```

5.2.1 The Integer Literal

MySQL has several types of numeric literals. The *integer literal* is used frequently. This is a whole number or integer without a decimal point, possibly preceded by a plus or minus sign. Examples are shown here:

```
   38
  +12
-3404
  016
```

The following examples are *not* correct integer literals:

```
342.16
 -14E5
   jan
```

5.2.2 The Decimal Literal

The second numeric literal is the *decimal literal.* This is a number with or without a decimal point, possibly preceded by a plus or minus sign. Each integer literal is, by definition, a decimal literal. Examples follow:

```
     49
  18.47
  -3400
    17.
0.83459
   -.47
```

The total number of digits is called the *precision*, and the number of digits after the decimal point is the *scale*. The decimal literal `123.45` has a precision of `5` and a scale of `2`. The scale of an integer literal is always `0`. The maximum range of a decimal literal is measured by the scale and the precision. The precision must be greater than `0`, and the scale must be between `0` and the precision. For example, a decimal with a precision of `8` and a scale of `2` is allowed, but not with a precision of `6` and a scale of `8`.

In the sample database of the tennis club, only one column has been defined with this data type, and that is AMOUNT in the PENALTIES table.

5.2.3 Float, Real, and Double Literals

A *float literal* is a decimal literal followed by an *exponent*. *Float* is short for *single precision floating point*. These are examples of float literals:

```
Float literal  Value
-------------  -----
        -34E2  -3400
       0.16E4   1600
         4E-3  0.004
         4e-3  0.004
```

5.2.4 The Alphanumeric Literal

An *alphanumeric literal* is a string of zero or more alphanumeric characters enclosed in quotation marks. This could be double (“) or single (‘) quotation marks. The quotation marks are not considered to be part of the literal; they define the beginning and end of the string. The following characters are permitted in an alphanumeric literal:

```
all lowercase letters      (a to z)
all uppercase              (A to Z)
all digits                 (0 to 9)
all remaining characters   (such as: ', +, -, ?, =, and _)
```

Note that an alphanumeric literal may contain quotation marks. To indicate a single quotation mark within an alphanumeric literal, two quotation marks are required. These are some examples of correct alphanumeric literals:

```
Alphanumeric literal  Value
--------------------  -------
'Collins'             Collins
"Collins"             Collins
'don''t'              don't
'!?-@'                !?-@
''
''''                  '
'""'                  ""
'1234'                1234
```

These are some examples of incorrect alphanumeric literals:

```
'Collins
''tis
'''
```

An alphanumeric literal may also contain special characters, such as a carriage return. For these special characters, rules have been laid down. They all begin with a slash followed by a character. Table 5.1 contains the explanations of all the special characters.

TABLE 5.1 Explanation of the Special Characters

SPECIAL CHARACTER	PRODUCES
\0	The ASCII 0 (zero) character
\'	The single quotation mark
\"	The double quotation mark
\b	A backspace
\n	A new line (new line)
\r	A carriage return
\t	A tab character
\z	The ASCII 26 character, or Ctrl+Z
\\	A slash

The effect of these special characters is not always visible. For example, WinSQL does not jump to the beginning of the line when an \r is used. However, an effect sometimes is apparent when using the client program mysql. In Figure 5.2, you can clearly see how a tab character is printed between the last name and the initials.

```
Command Prompt - mysql -u root -p
+------------------------------------------+
14 rows in set (0.06 sec)

mysql> SELECT CONCAT(CONCAT(NAME,'\t'),INITIALS) FROM PLAYERS;
+------------------------------------+
| CONCAT(CONCAT(NAME,'\t'),INITIALS) |
+------------------------------------+
| Everett         R                  |
| Parmenter       R                  |
| Wise    GWS                        |
| Newcastle       B                  |
| Collins         DD                 |
| Collins         C                  |
| Bishop          D                  |
| Baker   E                          |
| Brown   M                          |
| Hope    PK                         |
| Miller          P                  |
| Parmenter       P                  |
| Moorman         D                  |
| Bailey          IP                 |
+------------------------------------+
14 rows in set (0.00 sec)

mysql> _
```

FIGURE 5.2 The use of special characters

Some applications require the use of special symbols within alphanumeric literals. Therefore, MySQL supports character sets. Chapter 22, "Character Sets and Collations," extensively deals with character sets and the corresponding topic of collations. Collations have to do with the order of characters; for example, should the character æ be placed in front of or after the letter a? And is that the case in all languages?

5.2.5 The Date Literal

For working with values related to date and time, MySQL supports the *temporal literals*. Here a distinction is made among date, time, datetime, timestamp, and year literals. These temporal literals are explained in this section and the following sections.

A *date literal*, which consists of a year, a month, and a day, represents a certain date on the *Gregorian* calendar. MySQL allows this literal to be written as an alphanumeric or integer literal. When an alphanumeric literal is used, the entire value must be enclosed in quotation marks, and the three components must be separated by special characters. Usually, the hyphen is used as a character, but other characters, such as `/`, `@`, and `%`, are allowed as well. Irrelevant zeroes can be omitted in the last two components. Examples are shown here:

```
Date literal  Value
------------  ----------------
'1980-12-08'  December 8, 1980
'1991-6-19'   June 19, 1991
'1991@6@19'   June 19, 1991
```

When an integer literal is used to represent a date, the three components are written after each other, thus without hyphens. MySQL interprets the last two digits as the days component, the two digits in front of it as the months component, and everything in front of that as the year component. So be careful with omitting the zeroes. Consider these examples:

```
Date literal  Value
------------  -----------------
19801208      December 8, 1980
19910619      June 19, 1991
991111        November 11, 1999
```

In most cases, the years component is specified as a four-digit number. When diverging from this, MySQL uses several rules to determine what exactly is meant. First, when three digits are specified, a zero is placed in front of it. Second, when the year is specified as a two-digit number, it means that when that number is between 00 and 69, the value 2,000 is added, and if not 1,900 is added. Third, when the year consists of only one digit, three zeroes are placed in front of it. Several examples help illustrate these rules:

```
Date literal  Value
------------  ----------------
'999-10-11'   October 11, 0999
551011        October 11, 2055
'99-10-11'    October 11, 1999
'9-10-11'     October 11, 0009
```

So MySQL offers many features to specify a date literal. However, we recommend largely using the alphanumeric form in which the hyphen is used as the dividing character. This form is easier to read and more explicit, other SQL database servers support it, and it seldom gives unexpected results. We also advise always specifying the years component as a four-digit number and relying as little as possible on the rules of MySQL.

Date literals range from `1 January 1000` to `31 December 9999` and should also represent a date that exists in reality. Only then can MySQL guarantee that all calculations with dates are performed correctly. Calculations with dates that are not within that range could also be performed correctly, but no guarantee is given. Yet two exceptions exist. First, the date '0000-00-00' is allowed. We call this a *zero-date.* This literal is considered to be a legal date literal and can be used, for example, to indicate that a certain data is not known yet. Second, each date literal with a legal year component and with a month and/or day component equal to zero is allowed as well. For example, the literals '2006-00-00' and '2006-11-00' are both correct. Both are also called zero-dates. To summarize, the set of correct dates consists of all existing dates between 1 January 1000 and 31 December 9999, including all the zero-dates.

If an incorrect date literal is specified, it is converted into the null value during processing. The INSERT statement forms an exception to this rule. When an incorrect date is specified, it is converted to the zero-date 0000-00-00.

Example 5.1: Add an incorrect date to a special table and show the result.

```
CREATE TABLE INCORRECT_DATES (COLUMN1 DATE)

INSERT INTO INCORRECT_DATES VALUES ('2004-13-12')

SELECT   COLUMN1
FROM     INCORRECT_DATES
```

The result is:

```
COLUMN1
----------
0000-00-00
```

So the only dates allowed are those that also occur in reality, the so-called *existing* dates plus those zero-dates. We can deviate from this by turning certain settings on or off.

If we do not want MySQL to accept the zero-date '0000-00-00', we can specify that with a setting of the system variable SQL_MODE; see also Section 4.14. If SQL_MODE has NO_ZERO_DATE as the setting, '0000-00-00' cannot be used. The expression DATE('0000-00-00') would result in a null value. In this example, nothing would change. Even with NO_ZERO_DATE, a null value is stored in the K column. So with this setting, the set of correct dates becomes smaller.

Another setting is NO_ZERO_IN_DATE. If this setting is used, no zero-dates are accepted for which the month and/or day component is equal to zero. Therefore, the date literal '2006-12-00' is no longer allowed. If both the settings NO_ZERO_DATE and NO_ZERO_IN_DATE are turned on, the set of correct dates is limited to those dates that fall between 1 January 1000 and 31 December 9999.

A third important setting is ALLOW_INVALID_DATES. If we give SQL_MODE this setting, nonexisting dates can be used. For example, the date literal '2004-2-31' will be accepted even though it does not exist in reality. The only thing that MySQL checks is whether the months component is between 1 and 12 and the days component is between 1 and 31. The date literal '2006-14-14' would still not be accepted. This implies that with this setting, the set of correct dates becomes larger.

5.2.6 The Time Literal

The second temporal literal is the *time literal,* indicating a certain moment of the day. Time literals consist of four components: number of hours, number of minutes, number of seconds, and number of microseconds. An alphanumeric and an integer variant exist for this literal as well. With the alphanumeric variant, the entire value must be enclosed in quotation marks, and the first three components must be separated by special characters. Usually, the colon is used as character, but other characters, such as -, /, @, and % are allowed as well. In front of the microseconds component, we normally specify a point.

Irrelevant zeroes may be omitted for the first three components. When only two components are specified, MySQL regards them as the hours and the minutes components. When only one component is specified, it is regarded as the seconds component. Examples follow:

```
Time literal       Value
-----------------  ---------------------------------------
'23:59:59'         1 second before midnight
'12:10:00'         10 minutes past 12 in the afternoon
'14:00'            2 o'clock in the afternoon, or 14:00:00
'14'               14 seconds after midnight, or 00:00:14
'00:00:00.000013'  13 microseconds after midnight
```

When an integer is used to indicate a time literal, the first three components are written after each other without separating characters. MySQL regards the last two digits as the seconds component, the two digits in front of it as the minutes component, and everything in front of that as the hours component. So be careful with omitting the zeroes. Examples follow:

```
Time literal    Value
-------------   ---------------------------------------
235959          1 second before midnight
121000          10 minutes past 12 in the afternoon
1400            14 minutes after midnight, or 00:14:00
14              14 seconds after midnight, or 00:00:14
000000.000013   13 microseconds after midnight
```

For the same reason as for the date literal, we recommend mainly using the alphanumeric form in which the colon is used as the separating character.

When using an INSERT statement to store a time literal with a microseconds component in a table, make sure that the microseconds component is removed. For example, these statements

```
CREATE TABLE TIME_TABLE (COLUMN1 TIME)

INSERT INTO TIME_TABLE VALUES ('23:59:59.5912')

SELECT COLUMN1 FROM TIME_TABLE
```

return the following result in which the microsecond component is missing:

```
COLUMN1
--------
23:59:59
```

So far, we have assumed that a time literal represents a certain moment in time. However, a time literal can also be used to indicate a time interval: a limited number of hours, minutes, and seconds. That is why the range of a time literal is not limited from 00:00:00 to 23:59:59, but from -838:59:59 to 838:59:59. To make it easier to specify time literals with a large number of hours, you may specify a number of days before the hours. Note that this is possible only with the alphanumeric variant of the time literal. Examples follow:

```
Time literal   Value
-------------  -------------------------------------
'10 10:00:00'  ten days plus ten hours, or 250 hours
'10 10'        ten days plus ten hours, or 250 hours
```

Because the range is so wide, it is possible to store incorrect times in the database. The only check that MySQL performs is to see whether the minutes and the seconds components are between 0 and 59, and whether the hours component is between -838 and +838. This is a huge difference between MySQL and other SQL products.

For example, when an INSERT statement is used to enter a time in which the minutes component consists of the value 80, the value '00:00:00' is stored. So the INSERT statement is not rejected. Therefore, MySQL makes a distinction between correct times, incorrect times that can be stored, and incorrect times that cannot be stored.

5.2.7 The Datetime and Timestamp Literal

The value of a *datetime*, and *timestamp literal* is a combination of a date literal, a time literal, and an additional component for the microseconds.

Each datetime and timestamp literal consists of seven components: years, months, days, hours, minutes, seconds, and microseconds. Both have an alphanumeric and an integer variant. With the alphanumeric variant, hyphens separate the first three components (which indicate a date), and colons separate the next three (which indicate a time); a space comes between the date and the time, and a decimal point is placed in front of the microseconds. The microseconds component can be represented as a number consisting of six digits.

```
Timestamp literal              Value
----------------------------   ------------------------------
'1980-12-08 23:59:59.999999'   1 microsecond before midnight
                               on December 8, 1980
'1991-6-19 12:5:00'            5 minutes past 12 in the
                               afternoon of June 19, 1991
```

Most rules that apply to date and time literals also apply here.

As with time literals, when an INSERT statement is used to store a datetime or timestamp literal with a microseconds component, that microseconds component is removed. For example, these statements

```
CREATE TABLE TIMESTAMP_TABLE (COLUMN1 TIMESTAMP)

INSERT INTO TIMESTAMP_TABLE VALUES ('1980-12-08 23:59:59.59')

SELECT COLUMN1 FROM TIMESTAMP_TABLE
```

return the following result in which the microseconds are clearly missing:

```
COLUMN1
-------------------
1980-12-08 23:59:59
```

These two literals have much in common, but differences do exist. An important difference between a datetime and a timestamp literal is the range of the years component. For the timestamp literal, the year should be between 1970 and 2037; for a datetime, the year should be between 1000 and 9999.

Another difference between datetime and timestamp literals is that the latter also supports *time zones*. When MySQL starts, it looks at the time zone of the operating system. The value of the time zone is related to Universal Coordinated Time (UTC). Amsterdam is one hour ahead of the UTC, Mexico City is six hours behind, and Adelaide in Australia is 9.5 hours ahead. When a timestamp value is stored, it is first converted into the corresponding UTC time, and that result is stored in the table. Therefore, if the previous statement had been executed in Amsterdam, the value `'1980-12-08 22:59:59.59'` would have been stored. If the stored timestamp value is queried with, for example, a `SELECT` statement, it is translated to the time zone of the application. This also means that when a user who is in an entirely different time zone retrieves that same timestamp value, he sees something completely different. The timestamp then is converted into his time zone.

The system variable `TIME_ZONE` indicates the actual time zone. In most cases, the value of this variable is `SYSTEM`. This means that the time zone of the operating system is adopted. Under Windows, it is easy to retrieve the actual time zone; see Figure 5.3. This figure clearly shows that this system is one hour ahead of UTC.

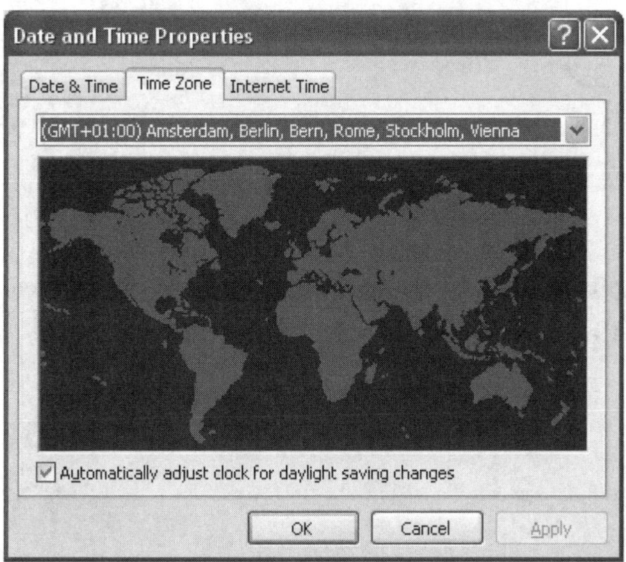

FIGURE 5.3 The actual time zone for Windows

You can adjust the time zone of the application with a `SET` statement. The following example shows the effect of this.

Example 5.2: Create a table to store timestamps, enter a timestamp, and show the contents of the table. Assume that MySQL has been started in the time zone UTC plus one hour.

```
CREATE TABLE TZ (COL1 TIMESTAMP)

INSERT INTO TZ VALUES ('2005-01-01 12:00:00')

SELECT * FROM TZ
```

The result is:

```
COL1
-------------------
2005-01-01 12:00:00
```

Note that `2005-01-01 11:00:00` has been stored in the table, not the value `2005-01-01 12:00:00`. Next, convert the time zone to that of Sydney in Australia and then show the contents of the table again:

```
SET @@TIME_ZONE = '+10:00'

SELECT * FROM TZ
```

The result is:

```
COL1
-------------------
2005-01-01 21:00:00
```

You can use the `SELECT` statement to retrieve the value of the `TIME_ZONE` system variable.

Example 5.3: Get the value of the `TIME_ZONE` system variable.

```
SELECT @@TIME_ZONE
```

The result is:

```
@@TIME_ZONE
-----------
+10:00
```

5.2.8 The Year Literal

The *year literal* is the most simple temporal literal. This digit must be between `1901` and `2155`. We can represent year literals as an alphanumeric literal consisting of four digits or as an integer literal consisting of four digits.

The benefit of having a literal with the data type `YEAR` is minimal. This data type becomes useful only when it is used for defining columns in `CREATE TABLE` statements. Chapter 20 returns to this data type and the corresponding literal.

5.2.9 The Boolean Literal

The simplest literal is the *Boolean literal* because it can consist of only two possible values: `TRUE` or `FALSE`. The numeric value of `FALSE` is `0` and that of `TRUE` is `1`.

Example 5.4: Get the values of the literals `TRUE` and `FALSE`.

```
SELECT TRUE, FALSE
```

Result:

```
TRUE  FALSE
----  -----
   1      0
```

Explanation: The values `TRUE` and `FALSE` can be written in any combination of case. In fact, you can even mix upper- and lowercase letters. Therefore, `TrUe` is allowed, too.

5.2.10 The Hexadecimal Literal

To specify values in a hexadecimal format, MySQL has the *hexadecimal literal.* This literal is specified as an alphanumeric literal in front of which the letter `X` or `x` is placed. Inside the quotation marks, only the ten digits and the letters `A` to `F` can be used. The number of characters must be an even number.

This book does not pay much attention to this data type and this literal; hexadecimal format is mainly used to store special values in the database, such as figures (in JPG or BMP formats) and movies (in AVI or MPG formats). A few examples follow:

```
Hexadecimal literal  Value
-------------------  --------
X'41'                A
X'6461746162617365'  database
X'3B'                ;
```

Specially for ODBC, MySQL also supports an alternative notation in which the `X` is replaced by `0x` and no quotation marks are used. The literal `X'41'` is therefore equal to `0x41`. Note that a lowercase letter `x` must be used.

5.2.11 The Bit Literal

A *bit literal* is a numeric literal that is specified as an alphanumeric literal with the small `b` or a capital `B` in front. Inside the quotation marks, only ones and zeroes are allowed. At most 64 digits may be specified. These are some examples of bit literals:

```
Bit literal  Value
-----------  -----
b'1001'          9
b'1111111'     127
b'0001'          1
```

Exercise 5.1: Specify which of the following literals are correct and which are incorrect; also give the data type of the literal.

1. `41.58E-8`
2. `JIM`
3. `'jim'`
4. `'A'14`
5. `'!?'`
6. `45`
7. `'14E6'`
8. `''''''`
9. `'1940-01-19'`
10. `'1992-31-12'`
11. `'1992-1-1'`
12. `'3:3:3'`
13. `'24:00:01'`
14. `'1997-31-12 12:0:0'`
15. `X'AA1'`
16. `TRUE`

5.3 Expressions

An *expression* is a combination of literals, column names, complex calculations, operators, and functions that is executed according to certain rules and that leads to one value. An expression generally *evaluates* to a value. Expressions are used, for example, in the `SELECT` and `WHERE` clauses of a `SELECT` statement.

Example 5.5: Get the match number and the difference between sets won and sets lost for each match of which the number of sets won equals the number of sets lost plus 2.

```
SELECT   MATCHNO, WON - LOST
FROM     MATCHES
WHERE    WON = LOST + 2
```

Result:

```
MATCHNO  WON - LOST
------  -----------
     1            2
```

Explanation: This SELECT statement consists of several expressions. Four expressions come after the word SELECT: the columns MATCHNO, WON, and LOST, and the calculation WON - LOST. Four expressions also come after the word WHERE: WON, LOST, 2, and LOST + 2.

An expression can be classified in three ways: by data type, by complexity of the value, and by form.

As with literals, the value of an expression always has a certain data type. Possible data types are the same as for literals—among other things, alphanumeric, numeric, date, time, or timestamp. That is why we can call them, for example, integer, alphanumeric, or date expressions. The following sections describe the various types of expressions individually.

Expressions can also be classified by the complexity of their value. So far, we have discussed only expressions that have one value as result—for example, a number, a word, or a date. These kinds of values are called *scalar values.* That's why all the previous expressions are called *scalar expressions.*

Besides the scalar expressions, MySQL supports row expressions and table expressions. The result of a *row expression* is a row consisting of a set of scalar values. This result has a *row value.* Each row expression consists of one or more scalar expressions. If PLAYERNO, 'John', and 10000 are examples of scalar expressions, this is an example of a row expression:

```
(PLAYERNO, 'John', 100 * 50)
```

Imagine that the value of the PLAYERNO column is equal to 1; then the row value of this row expression is (1, 'John', 5000).

The result of a *table expression* is a set of zero, one, or more row expressions. This result is called a *table value*. If (PLAYERNO, 'John', 100 * 50), (PLAYERNO, 'Alex', 5000), and (PLAYERNO, 'Arnold', 1000 / 20) are examples of row expressions, then this is an example of a table expression:

```
((PLAYERNO, 'John', 100 * 50),
 (PLAYERNO, 'Alex', 5000),
 (PLAYERNO, 'Arnold', 1000 / 20))
```

Imagine that the values of the three PLAYERNO columns are, respectively, 1, 2, and 3; the table value of this table expression, then, is equal to ((1, 'John', 5000), (2, 'Alex', 5000), (3, 'Arnold', 50)). Note that these examples of row and table expressions are not correct SQL statements. The way we specify these expressions depends on the SQL statements in which they are used. The most popular form of a table expression is the SELECT statement. Each SELECT statement is also a table expression because the result or the value of a SELECT statement is always a table and, therefore, a set of row values.

Sections 5.15 and 5.16 discuss row and table expressions, respectively, in more detail.

The third way to classify expressions is on the basis of form. We distinguish between singular and compound expressions. A *singular expression* consists of only one component. In the upcoming definition of *expression,* several possible forms of singular expressions are specified. You have already seen a few examples of it, such as a literal or the name of a column.

When an expression consists of operations and, thus, contains multiple singular expressions, it is called a *compound expression.* Therefore, the expressions 20 * 100 and '2002-12-12' + INTERVAL 2 MONTH are compound.

Table expressions can be compound as well. We can combine the result of two or more table expressions, which leads to one table value. Chapter 6, "SELECT Statements, Table Expressions, and Subqueries," returns to this.

An example of a compound row expression is (1, 2, 3) + (4, 5, 6). This expression would have the following row value: (5, 7, 9). A new row value is put together from multiple row expressions. MySQL does not (yet) support compound row expressions, so this book does not cover them.

DEFINITION

```
<expression> ::=
   <scalar expression> |
   <row expression>    |
   <table expression>

<scalar expression> ::=
   <singular scalar expression> |
   <compound scalar expression>

<singular scalar expression> ::=
   <literal>                  |
   <column specification>     |
   <user variable>            |
   <system variable>          |
   <cast expression>          |
   <case expression>          |
   NULL                       |
   ( <scalar expression> )    |
   <scalar function>          |
   <aggregation function>     |
   <scalar subquery>

<row expression> ::=
   <singular row expression>

<singular row expression> ::=
   ( <scalar expression> [ , <scalar expression> ]... ) |
   <row subquery>

<table expression> ::=
   <singular table expression> |
   <compound table expression>
```

Before we discuss expressions and all their different forms, we explain the assignment of names to expressions, followed by the concepts from which scalar expressions are built. We have already described literals, but we still need to discus column specifications, system variables, case expressions, and functions.

Exercise 5.2: What is the difference between a literal and an expression?

Exercise 5.3: In which three ways can expressions be classified?

5.4 Assigning Names to Result Columns

When the result of a SELECT statement is determined, MySQL must assign a name to each column of the result. If the expression in the SELECT clause consists of only a column name, the column in the result gets that name. Consider the next example.

Example 5.6: For each team, get the number and the division.

```
SELECT   TEAMNO, DIVISION
FROM     TEAMS
```

Result:

```
TEAMNO  DIVISION
------  --------
     1  first
     2  second
```

It's obvious how MySQL came up with the names of the result columns in this example. But what is the name when something else is specified instead of a simple column name, such as a literal, or a complex expression? In that case, the name is equal to the entire expression. For example, if the expression WON * LOST is used, the name of the result column is equal to WON * LOST.

Specifying an alternative name after an expression in a SELECT clause assigns a name to the matching result column. This is sometimes called a *column heading* or a *pseudonym*. This column name is placed in the heading of the result. We recommend specifying a column name when an expression in a SELECT clause is not a simple column name.

Example 5.7: For each team, get the number and the division, and use the full names.

```
SELECT   TEAMNO AS TEAM_NUMBER, DIVISION AS DIVISION_OF_TEAM
FROM     TEAMS
```

The result is:

```
TEAM_NUMBER  DIVISION_OF_TEAM
-----------  ----------------
          1  first
          2  second
```

Explanation: After the column name, we specify the word AS followed by the name of the result column. The word AS can be omitted.

Example 5.8: For each penalty, get the payment number and the penalty amount in cents.

```
SELECT    PAYMENTNO, AMOUNT * 100 AS CENTS
FROM      PENALTIES
```

The result is:

```
PAYMENTNO  CENTS
---------  -----
        1  10000
        2   7500
        3  10000
        4   5000
        :      :
```

Explanation: When you look at the result, it is clear that the word CENTS has been placed above the second column. If we had not specified a column name in this example, MySQL would have come up with a name itself.

By way of illustration, this next example has somewhat more complex expressions and assigned column names.

Example 5.9: Get some data from the MATCHES table.

```
SELECT    MATCHNO AS PRIMKEY,
          80 AS EIGHTY,
          WON - LOST AS DIFFERENCE,
          TIME('23:59:59') AS ALMOST_MIDNIGHT,
          'TEXT' AS TEXT
FROM      MATCHES
WHERE     MATCHNO <= 4
```

The result is:

```
PRIMKEY  EIGHTY  DIFFERENCE  ALMOST_MIDNIGHT  TEXT
-------  ------  ----------  ---------------  ----
      1      80           2         23:59:59  TEXT
      2      80          -1         23:59:59  TEXT
      3      80           3         23:59:59  TEXT
      4      80           1         23:59:59  TEXT
```

The examples specify only column names to make the result easier to read. The names are not mandatory in these examples. Later examples require column names; you will see that the column names can be used in other parts of the statement.

So names for columns in a result are defined in the SELECT clause. These column names can be used in most of the other clauses that are part of a select block, except for the FROM and WHERE clauses.

Example 5.10: Group all the penalties on penalty amount in cents, and order the result on that number of cents.

```
SELECT   AMOUNT * 100 AS CENTS
FROM     PENALTIES
GROUP BY CENTS
ORDER BY CENTS
```

The result is:

```
CENTS
-----
 2500
 3000
 5000
 7500
10000
```

New column names cannot be used in the same SELECT clause. Therefore, the clause SELECT WON AS W, W * 2 is not allowed.

Exercise 5.4: For each match, get the match number and the difference between the number of sets won and the number of sets lost, and name this column DIFFERENCE.

Exercise 5.5: Is the following SELECT statement correct?

```
SELECT   PLAYERNO AS X
FROM     PLAYERS
ORDER BY X
```

5.5 The Column Specification

A frequently occurring form of the scalar expression is the *column specification,* which identifies a specific column. A column specification consists of only the name of a column or the name of a column preceded by the name of the table to which the column belongs. Using the table name might be necessary to prevent misunderstandings when statements become more complex. Section 7.3 returns to this subject.

DEFINITION

```
<column specification> ::=
   [ <table specification> . ] <column name>
```

The next two scalar expressions, consisting of column specifications, are both correct: PLAYERNO and PLAYERS.PLAYERNO. When they really refer to the same column, they always have the same value. Placing the table name in front of the column name is called *qualification*.

But what is the value of a column specification? The value of a literal is easy to determine. A literal has no secrets. The value of the literal 381 is 381. However, the value of a column specification cannot be determined just like that. As it happens, the value is fetched from the database when the expression is processed.

In the SELECT statement of Example 5.6, for each team, the values of the column specifications TEAMNO and DIVISION are calculated. Those can be different for each row.

Note that the names introduced in a SELECT clause to name the columns in a result cannot be qualified. The reason is that these column names belong not to a table, but to the result of the select block.

Exercise 5.6: Rewrite the following SELECT statement in such a way that all column names are represented with their complete column specifications.

```
SELECT   PLAYERNO, NAME, INITIALS
FROM     PLAYERS
WHERE    PLAYERNO > 6
ORDER BY NAME
```

Exercise 5.7: What is wrong in the following SELECT statement?

```
SELECT   PLAYERNO.PLAYERNO, NAME, INITIALS
FROM     PLAYERS
WHERE    PLAYERS.PLAYERNO = TEAMS.PLAYERNO
```

5.6 The User Variable and the SET Statement

In MySQL, we can use *user-defined variables* within expressions. These variables can be used anywhere scalar expressions are allowed. User-defined variables are also called user variables.

```
<user variable> ::= @ <variable name>
```

It is better to define and initialize a variable before using it. Defining means that the user variable is made known to MySQL; initializing means that the variable is assigned a value. A variable that has been defined but not initialized has the null value.

The special SET *statement* can be used to define and initialize a variable.

Example 5.11: Create the user variable PLAYERNO and initialize it with the value 7.

```
SET @PLAYERNO = 7
```

Explanation: The @ symbol must always be placed in front of a user variable to distinguish it from a column name. The new value is specified after the assignment operator. This can be any scalar expression, as long as no column specifications occur in it.

The data type of the user variable is derived from the value of the scalar expression. So in the previous example, that is an integer. The data type of the variable can change later when a new value with another data type is assigned.

A defined user variable, such as PLAYERNO, can be used as a special form of an expression after it has been created in other SQL statements.

Example 5.12: Get the last name, the town, and the postcode of all players with a number less than the value of the PLAYERNO user variable that has just been created.

```
SELECT   NAME, TOWN, POSTCODE
FROM     PLAYERS
WHERE    PLAYERNO < @PLAYERNO
```

The result is:

```
NAME       TOWN       POSTCODE
---------  ---------  --------
Everett    Stratford  3575NH
Parmenter  Stratford  1234KK
```

You can retrieve the value of a user variable by using a simple SELECT statement.

Example 5.13: Find the value of PLAYERNO variable.

```
SELECT    @PLAYERNO
```

The result is:

```
@PLAYERNO
---------
        7
```

Chapter 15, "The User Variable and the SET Statement," returns to the SET statement and the possibilities of the user variables.

Exercise 5.8: Can the result of a SELECT statement be assigned to a user variable, as in this statement?

```
SET @NAME = (SELECT    NAME
             FROM      PLAYERS
             WHERE     PLAYERNO=2)
```

Exercise 5.9: What is the shortest statement to show the value of a user variable?

Exercise 5.10: What is the value of a user variable when it has not been initialized yet?

5.7 The System Variable

A simple form of an expression is the *system variable.* Section 4.14 introduced the system variable. Just as with user variables, system variables have a value and a data type. The differences with user variables is that MySQL introduces and initializes system variables.

DEFINITION

```
<system variable> ::=
   @@ [ <variable type> . ] <variable name>

<variable type> ::=
   SESSION | GLOBAL | LOCAL
```

System variables are divided into two groups: *global* system variables and *session* system variables. Global system variables are initialized when MySQL is started and apply to each session started. Some, but not all, can be changed with a SET statement. For example, the VERSION global system variable cannot be changed, whereas SQL_WARNINGS can. This system variable indicates whether MySQL should return a warning if incorrect data is added to a table with an INSERT statement. By default, this variable is off, but you can change that.

Example 5.14: Switch the SQL_WARNINGS on.

```
SET @@GLOBAL.SQL_WARNINGS = TRUE
```

Explanation: Two @ symbols and the word GLOBAL come before the system variable.

Session system variables apply only to the current session. The names of most session system variables are equal to those of the global system variables. When starting a session, each session variable receives the value of the global system variable with the same name. The value of a session system variable can be changed, but this new value applies only to the running session, not to all the other sessions. That explains the name session system variable.

Example 5.15: For the current session, set the value of the system variable SQL_SELECT_LIMIT to 10. This variable determines the maximum number of rows in the result of a SELECT statement.

```
SET @@SESSION.SQL_SELECT_LIMIT=10

SELECT @@SESSION.SQL_SELECT_LIMIT
```

The result is:

```
@@SESSION.SQL_SELECT_LIMIT
--------------------------
                        10
```

Explanation: Note that, in this example, the word SESSION is specified in front of the name of the system variable. This clearly shows that the value of the session system variable SQL_SELECT_LIMIT is in line with what the SET statement specifies. But the value of the global system variable called SQL_SELECT_LIMIT is still unchanged:

```
SELECT @@GLOBAL.SQL_SELECT_LIMIT
```

The result is:

```
@@GLOBAL.SQL_SELECT_LIMIT
-------------------------
               4294967295
```

If the terms GLOBAL and SESSION are not specified, MySQL assumes that SESSION is intended. Instead of the term SESSION, we can also use LOCAL. All three terms may be written in uppercase or lowercase letters.

MySQL has a default value for most system variables. These values are used when the database server starts. However, in the MY.INI *option file*, you can specify another value. This file is automatically read when the database server starts. A piece of this file might look like this:

```
[mysqld]
SQL_SELECT_MODE=10
```

However, a system variable can also be set with the command that starts the MySQL database server:

```
mysqld --SQL_SELECT_MODE=10
```

With a SET statement, a system variable can be returned to the default value.

Example 5.16: Set the value of SQL_SELECT_LIMIT back to the default value.

```
SET @@SESSION.SQL_SELECT_MODE = DEFAULT
```

In the SET statement, you can use an alternate formulation for system variables that omits the double @ symbols and the dot. However, we recommend using the first formulation because it can be used in every SQL statement.

DEFINITION

```
<system variable> ::=
   [ <variable type> ] <variable name>

<variable type> ::=
   SESSION | GLOBAL | LOCAL
```

The SHOW VARIABLES statement retrieves the complete list of system variables with their respective values. SHOW GLOBAL VARIABLES returns all global system variables, and SHOW SESSION VARIABLES all session versions.

Appendix C, "System Variables," describes system variables that affect the processing of SQL statements. Refer to the MySQL manuals for descriptions of all the system variables.

As already indicated, in front of each system variable, two @ symbols must be specified. However, to stay in line with several other SQL products, for some of MySQL's system variables, such as CURRENT_USER and CURRENT_DATE, those symbols can be omitted. Table 5.2 lists some of these specific system variables and gives the data type and a brief explanation.

TABLE 5.2 Examples of System Variables

System Variable	Data Type	Explanation
CURRENT_DATE	DATE	The actual system date
CURRENT_TIME	TIME	The actual system time
CURRENT_TIMESTAMP	TIMESTAMP	The actual system date and system time
CURRENT_USER	CHAR	The name of the SQL user

At a particular moment in time, the system variables might have the following values:

```
System variable  Value
---------------  ----------
CURRENT_USER     BOOKSQL
CURRENT_DATE     2003-12-08
CURRENT_TIME     17:01:23
```

Example 5.17: Get the privileges from the USER_AUTHS catalog table that have been granted to the current user.

```
SELECT   *
FROM     USER_AUTHS
WHERE    GRANTEE = CURRENT_USER
```

Example 5.18: Find the name of the current SQL user.

```
SELECT   CURRENT_USER
```

The result is:

```
CURRENT_USER
-----------------
BOOKSQL@localhost
```

Example 5.19: Show the penalties that were paid today.

```
SELECT   *
FROM     PENALTIES
WHERE    PAYMENT_DATE = CURRENT_DATE
```

Obviously, this statement has an empty result because your computer clock will undoubtedly show the present date and time, whereas most penalties were incurred before the year 2000.

Exercise 5.11: What are the differences between user and system variables?

Exercise 5.12: Find the numbers of the players who became committee members today.

5.8 The Case Expression

A special scalar expression is the *case expression*. This expression serves as a kind of IF-THEN-ELSE statement. It can be compared with the SWITCH statement in Java and the CASE statement in Pascal.

DEFINITION

```
<case expression> ::=
   CASE <when definition> [ ELSE <scalar expression> ] END

<when definition> ::= <when definition-1> | <when definition-2>

<when definition-1> ::=
   <scalar expression>
   WHEN <scalar expression> THEN <scalar expression>
   [ WHEN <scalar expression> THEN <scalar expression> ]...

<when definition-2> ::=
   WHEN <condition> THEN <scalar expression>
   [ WHEN <condition> THEN <scalar expression> ]...
```

Each case expression starts with a *when definition*. Two forms of when definitions exist. The easiest way to explain the possibilities of the first is through a few examples.

Example 5.20: Get the player number, the sex, and the name of each player who joined the club after 1980. The sex must be printed as `'Female'` or `'Male'`.

```
SELECT   PLAYERNO,
         CASE SEX
            WHEN 'F' THEN 'Female'
            ELSE 'Male' END AS SEX,
         NAME
FROM     PLAYERS
WHERE    JOINED > 1980
```

The result is:

```
PLAYERNO  SEX     NAME
--------  ------  -------
       7  Male    Wise
      27  Female  Collins
      28  Female  Collins
      57  Male    Brown
      83  Male    Hope
     104  Female  Moorman
     112  Female  Bailey
```

Explanation: This construct is equal to the following `IF-THEN-ELSE` construct:

```
IF SEX = 'F' THEN
   RETURN 'Female'
ELSE
   RETURN 'Male'
ENDIF
```

The data type of the case expression depends on the data types of the expressions that follow the words `THEN` and `ELSE`. The data types of these expressions must all be the same, or an implicit cast is performed (see Section 5.11 for an explanation of casting). An error message is returned if the data types of the values do not match.

As the definition shows, `ELSE` is not required. The previous case expression could also have been formulated as follows:

```
CASE SEX
   WHEN 'F' THEN 'Female'
   WHEN 'M' THEN 'Male'
END
```

In this case, if ELSE is omitted and the value of the SEX column is not equal to one of the scalar expressions in a when definition (which is not possible), the null value is returned.

```
SELECT   PLAYERNO,
         CASE SEX
            WHEN 'F' THEN 'Female' END AS FEMALES,
         NAME
FROM     PLAYERS
WHERE    JOINED > 1980
```

The result is:

```
PLAYERNO  FEMALES  NAME
--------  -------  -------
       7  ?        Wise
      27  Female   Collins
      28  Female   Collins
      57  ?        Brown
      83  ?        Hope
     104  Female   Moorman
     112  Female   Bailey
```

Explanation: A column name is specified to give the second result column a meaningful name.

Many when conditions can be included in a case expression.

```
CASE TOWN
   WHEN 'Stratford' THEN 0
   WHEN 'Plymouth'  THEN 1
   WHEN 'Inglewood' THEN 2
   ELSE 3
END
```

With the case expression, we can create very powerful SELECT clauses, especially, if we start to nest case expressions:

```
CASE TOWN
   WHEN 'Stratford' THEN
      CASE BIRTH_DATE
         WHEN '1948-09-01' THEN 'Old Stratforder'
         ELSE 'Young Stratforder' END
   WHEN 'Inglewood' THEN
      CASE BIRTH_DATE
         WHEN '1962-07-08' THEN 'Old Inglewooder'
         ELSE 'Young Inglewooder' END
   ELSE 'Rest' END
```

Example 5.21: Use both case expressions shown previously in a SELECT statement.

```
SELECT   PLAYERNO, TOWN, BIRTH_DATE,
         CASE TOWN
            WHEN 'Stratford' THEN 0
            WHEN 'Plymouth'  THEN 1
            WHEN 'Inglewood' THEN 2
            ELSE 3
         END AS P,
         CASE TOWN
            WHEN 'Stratford' THEN
               CASE BIRTH_DATE
                  WHEN '1948-09-01' THEN 'Old Stratforder'
                  ELSE 'Young Stratforder' END
            WHEN 'Inglewood' THEN
               CASE BIRTH_DATE
                  WHEN '1962-07-08' THEN 'Old Inglewooder'
                  ELSE 'Young Inglewooder' END
            ELSE 'Rest'
         END AS TYPE
FROM     PLAYERS
```

The result is:

```
PLAYERNO  TOWN       BIRTH_DATE  P  TYPE
--------  ---------  ----------  -  -----------------
       2  Stratford  1948-09-01  0  Old Stratforder
       6  Stratford  1964-06-25  0  Young Stratforder
       7  Stratford  1963-05-11  0  Young Stratforder
       8  Inglewood  1962-07-08  2  Old Inglewooder
      27  Eltham     1964-12-28  3  Rest
      28  Midhurst   1963-06-22  3  Rest
      39  Stratford  1956-10-29  0  Young Stratforder
      44  Inglewood  1963-01-09  2  Young Inglewooder
      57  Stratford  1971-08-17  0  Young Stratforder
      83  Stratford  1956-11-11  0  Young Stratforder
      95  Douglas    1963-05-14  3  Rest
     100  Stratford  1963-02-28  0  Young Stratforder
     104  Eltham     1970-05-10  3  Rest
     112  Plymouth   1963-10-01  1  Rest
```

So far, you have seen examples of case expressions in which just one condition within the case expression may occur. Consider some examples that show the other form.

Example 5.22: For each player, find the player number, the year in which he or she joined the club, and the player's age group.

```
SELECT   PLAYERNO, JOINED,
         CASE
            WHEN JOINED < 1980 THEN 'Seniors'
            WHEN JOINED < 1983 THEN 'Juniors'
            ELSE 'Children' END AS AGE_GROUP
FROM     PLAYERS
ORDER BY JOINED
```

The result is:

```
PLAYERNO  JOINED  AGE_GROUP
--------  ------  ---------
      95    1972  Seniors
       2    1975  Seniors
       6    1977  Seniors
     100    1979  Juniors
       8    1980  Juniors
      39    1980  Juniors
      44    1980  Juniors
       7    1981  Juniors
      83    1982  Juniors
      27    1983  Children
      28    1983  Children
     104    1984  Children
     112    1984  Children
      57    1985  Children
```

Explanation: If the first expression is not true, the next expression is evaluated, then the next, and so on. If none of them is true, the else definition applies.

The advantage of this form of the case expression is that all kinds of conditions can be mixed.

Example 5.23: For each player, find the player number, the year in which he or she joined the club, the town where he or she lives, and a classification.

```
SELECT   PLAYERNO, JOINED, TOWN,
         CASE
            WHEN JOINED >= 1980 AND JOINED <= 1982
               THEN 'Seniors'
            WHEN TOWN = 'Eltham'
               THEN 'Elthammers'
            WHEN PLAYERNO < 10
               THEN 'First members'
            ELSE 'Rest' END
FROM     PLAYERS
```

The result is:

```
PLAYERNO  JOINED  TOWN       CASE WHEN ...
--------  ------  ---------  -------------
       2    1975  Stratford  First members
       6    1977  Stratford  First members
       7    1981  Stratford  Seniors
       8    1980  Inglewood  Seniors
      27    1983  Eltham     Elthammers
      28    1983  Midhurst   Rest
      39    1980  Stratford  Seniors
      44    1980  Inglewood  Seniors
      57    1985  Stratford  Rest
      83    1982  Stratford  Seniors
      95    1972  Douglas    Rest
     100    1979  Stratford  Rest
     104    1984  Eltham     Elthammers
     112    1984  Plymouth   Rest
```

Case expressions can be used everywhere scalar expressions are allowed, including in the `WHERE` and `HAVING` clauses of the `SELECT` statement.

Exercise 5.13: Get the number and the division of each team in which the value `first` is written in full as the first division and the value `second` is written in full as the second division. If the value of the division is not `first` or `second`, display the value `unknown`.

Exercise 5.14: Imagine that the tennis club has classified all the penalties in three categories. The category `low` contains all the penalties from `0` up and to `40`, the category `moderate` contains those from `41` to `80`, and the category `high` contains all the penalties higher than `80`. Next, find for each penalty the payment number, the amount, and the matching category.

Exercise 5.15: Find the numbers of the penalties belonging to the category `low` (see the previous exercise).

5.9 The Scalar Expression Between Brackets

Each scalar expression can be placed between brackets. This does not change anything about the value of the scalar expression. Therefore, the expressions `35` and `'John'` are equal to, respectively, `(35)` and `('John')`, but also to `((35))` and `(('John'))`.

Example 5.24: For each player, find the number and name.

```
SELECT   (PLAYERNO), (((NAME)))
FROM     PLAYERS
```

It is obvious that the number of opening brackets must be equal to the number of closing brackets.

The use of brackets is redundant in the previous example. They become useful only when scalar expressions are combined. The next sections give examples of the use of brackets.

5.10 The Scalar Function

Scalar functions are used to perform calculations and transformations. A scalar function has zero, one, or more so-called *parameters.* The values of the parameters have an impact on the value of a scalar function. Consider this example of the UCASE function:

```
UCASE('database')
```

Explanation: UCASE is the name of the scalar function, and the literal 'database' is the parameter. UCASE stands for *UpperCASE*. With UCASE('database'), all letters from the word database are replaced by their respective uppercase letter. So the result (or the value) of this function is equal to 'DATABASE'.

The call of a scalar function is a scalar expression in itself; the parameters of each scalar function are scalar expressions as well.

MySQL supports tens of scalar functions. Although we could fill many pages with examples to show their possibilities, we give just a few examples of frequently used functions. Appendix B, "Scalar Functions," describes all the scalar functions in detail.

Example 5.25: Get the payment number and the year of each penalty paid after 1980.

```
SELECT   PAYMENTNO, YEAR(PAYMENT_DATE)
FROM     PENALTIES
WHERE    YEAR(PAYMENT_DATE) > 1980
```

The result is:

```
PAYMENTNO  YEAR(PAYMENT_DATE)
---------  ------------------
        2                1981
        3                1983
        4                1984
        7                1982
        8                1984
```

Explanation: The YEAR function extracts the year of any payment date and returns the year as a numeric value. As already mentioned, and as this example shows, you can use scalar functions in, among other things, the SELECT and WHERE clauses. In fact, you can use them everywhere an expression can occur.

Scalar functions can also be *nested.* This means that the result of one function acts as parameter for the other function. Thus, the expression given next is legal. First the function MOD(30, 7) is executed, which leads to a result of 2. Next, the value of SQRT(2)is calculated, and that result is passed to the ROUND function. The final answer is 1. In this example, the functions have clearly been nested.

```
ROUND(SQRT(MOD(30, 7)), 0)
```

Example 5.26: For each player whose last name starts with the capital B, get the number and the first letter of the first name, followed by a decimal and the last name.

```
SELECT   PLAYERNO, CONCAT(LEFT(INITIALS, 1), '. ', NAME)
         AS FULL_NAME
FROM     PLAYERS
WHERE    LEFT(NAME, 1) = 'B'
```

The result is:

```
PLAYERNO  FULL_NAME
--------  ---------
      39  D. Bishop
      44  E. Baker
      57  M. Brown
     112  I. Bailey
```

Explanation: For each player in the PLAYERS table, the first letter of the last name is determined with the LEFT function first LEFT(NAME, 1). When that letter is equal to the capital *B*, the nested function is calculated in the SELECT clause for each. The CONCAT function is used to concatenate three alphanumeric values.

Example 5.27: For each player living in Stratford, get the first name, the last name, and the league number. If the league number is null, give the value `1`.

```
SELECT   INITIALS, NAME, COALESCE(LEAGUENO, '1')
FROM     PLAYERS
WHERE    Town = 'Stratford'
```

The result is:

```
INITIALS  NAME       COALESCE(LEAGUENO, '1')
--------  ---------  -----------------------
R         Everett    2411
R         Parmenter  8467
GWS       Wise       1
D         Bishop     1
M         Brown      6409
PK        Hope       1608
P         Parmenter  6524
```

Explanation: The `COALESCE` function returns the values of the first parameter that is not equal to the null value. In a way, the function acts as a kind of `IF-THEN-ELSE` statement that is used in many programming languages. By using this function as shown, for each row that is printed, the following statement is executed:

```
IF LEAGUENO IS NULL THEN
   RETURN '1'
ELSE
   RETURN LEAGUENO
ENDIF
```

MySQL supports many scalar functions for the manipulation of dates and times. Several examples follow.

Example 5.28: For all players with numbers less than 10, get the player number, the name of the day and month on which they were born, and the day's sequence number within the year of the birth date.

```
SELECT   PLAYERNO, DAYNAME(BIRTH_DATE),
         MONTHNAME(BIRTH_DATE), DAYOFYEAR(BIRTH_DATE)
FROM     PLAYERS
WHERE    PLAYERNO < 10
```

The result is:

```
PLAYERNO  DAYNAME(...)  MONTHNAME(...)  DAYOFYEAR(...)
--------  ------------  --------------  --------------
       2  Wednesday     September                  245
       6  Thursday      June                       177
       7  Saturday      May                        131
       8  Sunday        July                       189
```

Explanation: The DAYNAME function determines the day of a date, MONTHNAME determines the month, and DAYOFYEAR calculates what day of the year it is.

Example 5.29: For the players who were born on a Saturday, get the number, the date of birth, and the date that comes seven days after that date of birth.

```
SELECT    PLAYERNO, BIRTH_DATE,
          ADDDATE(BIRTH_DATE, INTERVAL 7 DAY)
FROM      PLAYERS
WHERE     DAYNAME(BIRTH_DATE) = 'Saturday'
```

The result is:

```
PLAYERNO  BIRTH_DATE  ADDDATE(BIRTH_DATE, 7)
--------  ----------  ----------------------
       7  1963-05-11  1963-05-18
      28  1963-06-22  1963-06-29
```

Example 5.30: Which players have already held a certain position for more than 500 days?

```
SELECT    PLAYERNO, BEGIN_DATE, END_DATE,
          DATEDIFF(END_DATE, BEGIN_DATE)
FROM      COMMITTEE_MEMBERS
WHERE     DATEDIFF(END_DATE, BEGIN_DATE) > 500
OR       (END_DATE IS NULL AND
          DATEDIFF(CURRENT_DATE, BEGIN_DATE) > 500)
ORDER BY PLAYERNO
```

The result is:

```
PLAYERNO  BEGIN_DATE  END_DATE    DATEDIFF(...)
--------  ------- --  ----------  -------------
       2  1990-01-01  1992-12-31           1095
       2  1994-01-01  ?                       ?
       6  1991-01-01  1992-12-31            730
       6  1992-01-01  1993-12-31            730
       6  1993-01-01  ?                       ?
       8  1994-01-01  ?                       ?
      95  1994-01-01  ?                       ?
     112  1994-01-01  ?                       ?
```

Explanation: The DATEDIFF function calculates the difference in days between two dates or timestamps. The second condition has been added to find those committee members who still hold the position (the ones that have a null value as END_DATE). Every day, this statement can have another result, of course.

A more compact formulation for this statement follows. Now, the statement also calculates the number of days for the committee members who still hold their position.

```
SELECT   PLAYERNO, BEGIN_DATE, END_DATE,
         DATEDIFF(COALESCE(END_DATE, CURRENT_DATE),
         BEGIN_DATE)
FROM     COMMITTEE_MEMBERS
WHERE    DATEDIFF(COALESCE(END_DATE, CURRENT_DATE),
         BEGIN_DATE)
         > 500
ORDER BY PLAYERNO
```

Exercise 5.16: Try to calculate the values of the following expressions (refer to Appendix B for explanations).

1. `ASCII(SUBSTRING('database',1,1))`
2. `LENGTH(RTRIM(SPACE(8)))`
3. `LENGTH(CONCAT(CAST(100000 AS CHAR(6)),'000'))`
4. `LTRIM(RTRIM('   SQL   '))`
5. `REPLACE('database','a','ee')`

Exercise 5.17: Get the numbers of the penalties that were paid on a Monday.

Exercise 5.18: Get the numbers of the penalties that were paid in 1984.

5.11 Casting of Expressions

Each expression has a data type, regardless of whether this is a simple expression consisting of only one literal or a very complex one consisting of scalar functions and multiplications. If we use an INSERT statement to store a value in a column, it is obvious what the data type of that value is, namely, the data type of the column. Unfortunately, it is not always that obvious. Consider a few examples here.

If somewhere in an SQL statement the literal 'monkey' is specified, the data type is obvious. Given the possible data types, this expression can have only the data type alphanumeric. The situation is more complex when we specify the literal `'1997-01-15'`. Does this literal simply have the data type alphanumeric, or is it a date? The answer depends on the context. Even more choices arise if simply the number `3` is specified. The data type of this expression can be integer, decimal, or float.

When it is not clear what the data type of an expression is, MySQL tries to determine the data type itself. But sometimes we have to specify the data type explicitly. To this end, MySQL supports the *cast expression*. Some examples follow:

```
Cast expression                 Data type      Value
------------------------------  ------------   ----------
CAST('123' AS SIGNED INTEGER)   Integer        123
CAST(121314 AS TIME)            Time           12:13:14
CAST('1997-01-15' AS DATE)      Date           1997-01-15
CAST(123 AS CHAR)               Alphanumeric   '123'
```

Explanation: Note the use of the term `AS`, which is often forgotten. You can specify the names of the data types after `AS`. Table 5.3 indicates for each allowed data type the date type the value will have after the cast expression has been applied.

TABLE 5.3 Accepted Data Types in a Cast Expression

Data type	Results in
BINARY [(<length>)]	Decimal values
CHAR [(<length>)]	Alphanumeric values
DATE	Date values
DATETIME	Datetime values
DECIMAL [(<precision> , <scale>)]	Decimal values
SIGNED [INTEGER]	Integer values
TIME	Time values
UNSIGNED [INTEGER]	Integer values greater than zero

Chapter 20 returns to the `CREATE TABLE` statement in detail and explains the characteristics of each data type.

If MySQL cannot execute the conversion specified in a cast expression, an error message occurs. By way of illustration, the following two expressions will not be executed:

```
CAST('John' AS SIGNED INTEGER)
CAST('1997' AS DATE)
```

The expression is called cast because in literature specifying a data type or altering the data type of an expression is called *casting*. Casting has two forms: *implicit* and *explicit*. When a cast expression or function is used to specify the data type of an expression, it is explicit casting. When a data type is not specified explicitly, MySQL tries to derive one. This is called implicit casting.

Example 5.31: Get the payment numbers of the penalties that are higher than $50.

```
SELECT   PAYMENTNO
FROM     PENALTIES
WHERE    AMOUNT > 50
```

Explanation: This `SELECT` statement contains three expressions: `PAYMENTNO`, `AMOUNT`, and `50`. The data types of the first two are derived from the data types of the columns. No data type has been specified explicitly for the literal `50`. However, because the literal is compared to a column that has the data type decimal, it is assumed that `50` has the same data type. In fact, we have to conclude that the data type of `50` is integer and that MySQL implicitly executes a casting from integer to decimal.

Casting can be important when expressions with noncomparable data types are compared.

Example 5.32: For each player resident in Inglewood, get the name and the date of birth as one alphanumeric value.

```
SELECT   CONCAT(RTRIM(NAME), CAST(BIRTH_DATE AS CHAR(10)))
FROM     PLAYERS
WHERE    TOWN = 'Inglewood'
```

The result is:

```
CONCAT(...)
--------------------
Newcastle1962-07-08
Baker1963-01-09
```

Explanation: The two columns NAME and BIRTH_DATE do not have the same data types. To concatenate them, BIRTH_DATE must be cast explicitly to alphanumeric. Next, the entire expression can be executed.

With INSERT and UPDATE statements, the data types of the new values are derived from the columns in which they are stored. Implicit casting, therefore, also takes place here.

Exercise 5.19: Transform the value 12 March 2004 into a value with a data data type.

Exercise 5.20: What is the date type of the literal in the SELECT clause of the following statement?

```
SELECT   '2000-12-15'
FROM     PLAYERS
```

Exercise 5.21: Can an alphanumeric literal always be cast explicitly to a date literal, and vice versa?

5.12 The Null Value as an Expression

Section 1.3.2 discussed the null value. The specification NULL itself is also a valid scalar expression. For example, it is used in INSERT statements to enter a null value in a new row or to change an existing value of a row in an UPDATE statement to null.

Example 5.33: Change the league number of the player with number 2 to the null value.

```
UPDATE   PLAYERS
SET      LEAGUENO = NULL
WHERE    PLAYERNO = 2
```

Explanation: In this example, NULL is a singular scalar expression.

Actually, the scalar expression NULL has no data type. In no way can we derive from those four letters what it is. Is it an alphanumeric, a numeric, or a date? However, this does not cause problems in the previous UPDATE statement. MySQL assumes that the data type of this null value is equal to that of the column LEAGUENO. This way, MySQL can execute an implicit cast fairly easy, but that does not work all the time. Consider an example.

Example 5.34: For each team, get the number followed by the null value.

```
SELECT   TEAMNO, CAST(NULL AS CHAR)
FROM     TEAMS
```

The result is:

```
TEAMNO  CAST(NULL AS CHAR)
------  ------------------
     1  ?
     2  ?
```

Explanation: An explicit casting is not really required in this SELECT statement. MySQL determines that it has to be an alphanumeric value. Nevertheless, it is always better to execute an explicit cast because only then is it clear which data type the expression has.

Exercise 5.22: Does this SELECT statement return all the players without a league number?

```
SELECT   *
FROM     PLAYERS
WHERE    LEAGUENO = NULL
```

Exercise 5.23: What is the result of this SELECT statement, all the rows of the TEAMS table or not even one?

```
SELECT   *
FROM     TEAMS
WHERE    NULL = NULL
```

5.13 The Compound Scalar Expression

The scalar expressions shown so far all have consisted of one component, such as a literal, column specification, or system variable. They are all singular scalar expressions. In addition, MySQL supports compound scalar expressions; see also Section 5.3. These expressions consist of more than one component. The features of a compound expression depend on its data type.

 DEFINITION

```
<compound scalar expression> ::=
   <compound numeric expression>       |
   <compound alphanumeric expression> |
   <compound date expression>          |
   <compound time expression>          |
   <compound timestamp expression>     |
   <compound datetime expression>      |
   <compound boolean expression>       |
   <compound hexadecimal expression>
```

5.13.1 The Compound Numeric Expression

A *compound numeric expression* is a scalar expression that consists of, minimally, a singular scalar numeric expression extended with operators, brackets, and/or other scalar expressions. The result is a scalar value with a numeric data type.

DEFINITION

```
<compound numeric expression> ::=
   [ + | - ] <scalar numeric expression>                        |
   ( <scalar numeric expression> )                              |
   <compound numeric expression>
      <mathematical operator> <scalar numeric expression> |
   ~ <scalar numeric expression>                                |
   <scalar numeric expression>
      <bit operator> <scalar numeric expression>

<mathematical operator> ::= * | / | + | - | % | DIV

<bit operator> ::= "|" | & | ^ | << | >>
```

Consider some examples:

```
Compound numeric expression  Value
---------------------------  -----
14 * 8                         112
(-16 + 43) / 3                   9
5 * 4 + 2 * 10                  40
18E3 + 10E4                  118E3
12.6 / 6.3                     2.0
```

Table 5.4 lists the mathematical operators that can be used in a compound numeric expression.

TABLE 5.4 The Mathematical Operators and Their Meanings

MATHEMATICAL OPERATOR	MEANING
*	Multiply
/	Divide
+	Add
-	Subtract
%	Modulo
DIV	Divide and round off

Before reading the examples, consider the following comments:

- Non-numeric expressions can occur in a compound numeric expression. The only requirement is that the final result of the entire expression must return a numeric value.
- If required, brackets can be used in numeric compound expressions to indicate the order of execution.
- If any component of a numeric compound expression has the value null, the value of the entire expression is, by definition, null.
- The calculation of the value of a numeric compound expression is performed in keeping with the following priority rules: (1) left to right, (2) brackets, (3) multiplication and division, (4) addition and subtraction.

Some examples follow (assume that the AMOUNT column has the value 25):

```
Compound numeric expression             Value
-------------------------------------   ---------
6 + 4 * 25                                    106
6 + 4 * AMOUNT                                106
0.6E1 + 4 * AMOUNT                            106
(6 + 4) * 25                                  250
(50 / 10) * 5                                  25
50 / (10 * 5)                                   1
NULL * 30                                    NULL
18 DIV 5                                        3
16 * '5'                                       80
```

These are incorrect compound numeric expressions:

```
86 + 'Jim'
((80 + 4)
4/2 (* 3)
```

Example 5.35: Get the match number and the sets won and lost for each match in which the number of sets won is greater than or equal to the number of sets lost multiplied by 2.

```
SELECT   MATCHNO, WON, LOST
FROM     MATCHES
WHERE    WON >= LOST * 2
```

The result is:

```
MATCHNO  WON  LOST
-------  ---  ----
      1    3     1
      3    3     0
      7    3     0
```

Explanation: To be able to answer this query, we need the compound numeric expression `LOST * 2`.

What are the precision and the scale of the result of a calculation that involves two decimal values? For example, if we multiply a decimal (4,3) by a decimal (8,2), what is the precision and the scale of that result? Here we show the rules that MySQL uses to determine them. We assume that `P1` and `S1`, respectively, are the precision and the scale of the first decimal value, and that `P2` and `S2` are those of the second value. In addition, assume that there exists a function called `LARGEST` that enables you to determine the largest of two values.

- **Multiplication**—If we multiply two decimals, the scale of the result is equal to `S1` + `S2`, and its precision is equal to `P1`+ `P2`. For example, multiplying a decimal (4,3) with a decimal (5,4) returns a decimal (9,7).
- **Addition**—If we add two decimals, the scale of the result is equal to `LARGEST(S1, S2)`, and its precision is equal to `LARGEST(P1-S1, P2-S2) + LARGEST(S1, S2) + 1`. For example, adding a decimal (4,2) to a decimal (7,4) returns a decimal (8,4).
- **Subtraction**—If we subtract a decimal from another, the scale of the result is equal to `S1 + S2`, and its precision is equal to `LARGEST(P1-S1, P2-S2) + LARGEST(S1, S2) + 1`. In other words, for subtraction and addition, the same rules apply.
- **Division**—The scale of the result of a division is equal to `S1 + 4`, and the precision is equal to `P1 + 4`. For example, if we divide a decimal (4,3) by a decimal (5,4) the result is a decimal (8,6). The value `4` can be changed by changing the value of the system variable called `DIV_PRECISION_INCREMENT`.

Besides the classic mathematical operators, MySQL supports special *bit operators;* see Table 5.5. Bit operators enable you to work on data on the bit level. Note that bit operators can be used only with scalar expressions that have an integer data type.

TABLE 5.5 Overview of Bit Operators

BIT OPERATOR	MEANING
|	Binary OR
&	Binary AND
^	Binary XOR
<<	Move bits to the left
>>	Move bits to the right
~	Invert bits

Example 5.36: Move the number 50 two bits to the left.

```
SELECT 50 << 2
```

The result is:

```
50 << 2
-------
    200
```

Explanation: Bit operators work on the *binary representations* of values. The binary representation of the value 50 is 110010. With the operator <<, the bits are moved several positions to the left and zeroes are placed at the end. In the previous expression, the value 110010 is moved two bits to the left, and that gives 11001000. In the decimal system, this value is equal to 200.

Example 5.37: Move the binary value 11 three bits to the left.

```
SELECT B'11' << 3
```

The result is:

```
B'11' << 3
----------
        24
```

To be able to explain how bit operators work, we explain two scalar functions first: the *BIN* and *CONV functions*. Both enable us to get the binary representation for a decimal number.

Example 5.38: Get the binary representation of the values 6 and 10.

```
SELECT CONV(6,10,2), CONV(10,10,2), BIN(8), BIN(10)
```

The result is:

```
CONV(6,10,2)  CONV(10,10,2)  BIN(8)  BIN(10)
------------  -------------  ------  -------
110                    1010     110     1010
```

Explanation: How the BIN function works is obvious. The parameter value is converted to a binary representation. The CONV function is somewhat more complex. With this function, a value can be converted from one number base into any other. With CONV(6,10,2), we convert the value 6 (according to the decimal base—hence, the number 10) into a binary value (the number 2).

By switching the parameters 10 and 2, the CONV function can also retrieve the corresponding decimal number of a binary representation.

Example 5.39: Get the decimal values that belong to the binary representations 1001 and 111.

```
SELECT CONV(1001,2,10), CONV(111,2,10)
```

The result is:

```
CONV(1001,2,10)  CONV(111,2,10)
---------------  --------------
              9               7
```

Consider some more examples of the bit operators. For example, the expression 10 | 6 results in 14. The binary representation of 10 is 1010, and 6 becomes 110. When we use the *OR operator* or the | operator, both values are examined bit by bit. If one of the values or both values has the value 1 on a certain bit position, the resulting value also has a 1 on that same position. You could present it as follows as well:

```
1010      = 10
0110      =  6
---- |
1110      = 14
```

With the AND or the & operator, the left and right values are also compared bit by bit. Only when both values have the value 1 on a certain bit position does the resulting value have a 1 on that position. For example, the value of the expression 10 & 6 is equal to 2:

```
1010        = 10
0110        =  6
---- &
0010        =  2
```

Example 5.40: Get the odd player numbers from the PLAYERS table.

```
SELECT    PLAYERNO
FROM      PLAYERS
WHERE     PLAYERNO & 1
```

The result is:

```
PLAYERNO
--------
       7
      27
      39
      57
      83
      95
```

Explanation: A number is odd when a 1 occurs on the last position of the binary representation of that number. Applying the & operator on two odd numbers always returns a number that has a 1 on the last position of its binary representation. By definition, the result is at least 1. Therefore, the expression PLAYERNO & 1 is true if the player number is odd.

When the *XOR operator* or the ^ operator is used, the resulting value has a 1 on each position where the left or the right value has the value 1 on that same position (but not both 0 or 1). For example, the value of the expression 10 ^ 6 is equal to 12.

```
1010        = 10
0110        =  6
---- ^
1100        = 12
```

The << operator is used to move all the bits to the left. For example, in the expression `3 << 1`, we move the bits one position to the left: `11` becomes `110` then. The result of this expression is `6`. The operator >> can be used to move the bits to the right. The rightmost bit is just cut off. `7>>1` has `3` as a result because the binary representation of `7` is `111`.

When you want to convert all the zeroes to ones and the other way around, use the ~ operator. Note that this operator works on one scalar expression. The value of `~18446744073709551613` is equal to `2`. If the value that needs to be moved to the left is too large, all the `1`s are moved out of the result, and the value `0` is given. For example, the result of both the expressions `50000000000000000000 << 1` and `5 << 70` is `0`.

Consider two more examples of `SELECT` statements in which these bit operators are used.

Example 5.41: Get the number and the name of each player who has an even player number.

```
SELECT    PLAYERNO, NAME
FROM      PLAYERS
WHERE     PLAYERNO = (PLAYERNO >> 1) << 1
```

The result is:

```
PLAYERNO  NAME
--------  ---------
       2  Everett
       6  Parmenter
       8  NewCastle
      28  Collins
      44  Baker
     100  Parmenter
     104  Moorman
     112  Bailey
```

Example 5.42: Apply several binary operators to the columns of the MATCHES table.

```
SELECT    MATCHNO, TEAMNO, MATCHNO | TEAMNO,
          MATCHNO & TEAMNO, MATCHNO ^ TEAMNO
FROM      MATCHES
```

The result is:

```
MATCHNO  TEAMNO  MATCHNO | TEAMNO  MATCHNO & TEAMNO  MATCHNO ^ TEAMNO
-------  ------  ----------------  ----------------  ----------------
      1       1                 1                 1                 0
      2       1                 3                 0                 3
      3       1                 3                 1                 2
      4       1                 5                 0                 5
      5       1                 5                 1                 4
      6       1                 7                 0                 7
      7       1                 7                 1                 6
      8       1                 9                 0                 9
      9       2                11                 0                11
     10       2                10                 2                 8
     11       2                11                 2                 9
     12       2                14                 0                14
     13       2                15                 0                15
```

Exercise 5.24: Determine the values of the following numeric compound expressions:

1. `400 - (20 * 10)`
2. `(400 - 20) * 10`
3. `400 - 20 * 10`
4. `400 / 20 * 10`
5. `111.11 * 3`
6. `222.22 / 2`
7. `50.00 * 3.00`
8. `12 | 1`
9. `12 & 1`
10. `4 ^ 2`

5.13.2 The Compound Alphanumeric Expression

The value of a *compound alphanumeric expression* has an alphanumeric data type. With a compound expression, the values of alphanumeric expressions are concatenated using the `||`. operator.

If the MySQL database server is started in a standard way, the `||` operator does not lead to a concatenation of alphanumeric values, but it is seen as an `OR` operator to combine predicates. You can change this by changing the value of the system variable `SQL_MODE`. Use the following `SET` statement:

```
SET @@SQL_MODE= 'PIPES_AS_CONCAT'
```

This specification is needed for the following examples. It applies only to the current session. Specifying the term GLOBAL in front of the system variable SQL_MODE makes it a global specification that applies to all new sessions.

DEFINITION

```
<compound alphanumeric expression> ::=
   <scalar alphanumeric expression> "||"
      <scalar alphanumeric expression>
```

Two important rules apply to compound alphanumeric expressions:

- Nonalphanumeric expressions can be used in a compound alphanumeric expression as long as they are first converted into alphanumeric values with, for example, a cast expression.
- If somewhere in a compound alphanumeric expression the value null occurs, the value of the whole expression evaluates to null.

Examples:

```
Compound alphanumeric expression  Value
--------------------------------  --------
'Jim'                             Jim
'data'||'base'                    database
'da'||'ta'||'ba'||'se'            database
CAST(1234 AS CHAR(4))             1234
'Jim'||CAST(NULL AS CHAR)         NULL
```

Example 5.43: Get the player number and the address of each player who lives in Stratford.

```
SELECT   PLAYERNO, TOWN || ' ' || STREET || ' ' || HOUSENO
FROM     PLAYERS
WHERE    TOWN = 'Stratford'
```

The result is:

```
PLAYERNO  TOWN || ' ' || STREET ...
--------  ----------------------------
       2  Stratford Stoney Road 43
       6  Stratford Haseltine Lane 80
       7  Stratford Edgecombe Way 39
      39  Stratford Eaton Square 78
      57  Stratford Edgecombe Way 16
      83  Stratford Magdalene Road 16a
     100  Stratford Haseltine Lane 80
```

Exercise 5.25: For each player, get the player number followed by a concatenation of the data elements: the first initial, a full stop, a space, and the full last name.

Exercise 5.26: For each team, get the number and the division of the team followed by the word `division`.

5.13.3 The Compound Date Expression

MySQL enables you to calculate dates. For example, you can add a few days, months, or years to a date. The result of such a calculation is always a new date that is later (for addition) or earlier (for subtraction) than the original date expression.

When calculating the new date, the different number of days in the months and the leap years are taken into account. The calculation is done in a *proleptic* way, which means that no adjustment is made for the fact that, in the Gregorian calendar, the days October 5 to 14 in the year 1582 are missing completely. This also means that we can use a date such as January 1, 1000, even though this date is earlier than the point in time when the Gregorian calendar was introduced. That means that what we call January 1, 1200, according to the Gregorian calendar now, probably was called differently then.

A calculation with dates is specified with a *compound date expression.*

DEFINITION

```
<compound date expression> ::=
   <scalar date expression> [ + | - ] <date interval>

<date interval> ::=
   INTERVAL <interval length> <date interval unit>

<interval length> ::= <scalar expression>

<date interval unit> ::=
   DAY | WEEK | MONTH | QUARTER | YEAR | YEAR_MONTH
```

A compound date expression starts with a scalar expression (such as a date literal or a column specification with a date data type) followed by an *interval* that is added to or subtracted from the scalar expression.

An interval represents not a certain moment in time, but a certain period or length of time. This period is expressed in a number of days, weeks, months, quarters, or years, or a combination of these five. Interval literals help indicate how long, for example, a certain project lasted or how long a match took. Consider these examples of interval literals:

```
Interval           Value
-----------------  --------------------
INTERVAL 10 DAY    period of 10 days
INTERVAL 100 WEEK  period of 100 weeks
INTERVAL 1 MONTH   period of 1 month
INTERVAL 3 YEAR    period of 3 years
```

An interval is not a complete expression. It must always occur within a compound date expression, where it should be specified behind the + or - operators.

Example 5.44: For each penalty with a number higher than 5, get the payment number, the day on which the penalty was paid, and the date seven days after the payment date.

```
SELECT    PAYMENTNO, PAYMENT_DATE, PAYMENT_DATE + INTERVAL 7 DAY
FROM      PENALTIES
WHERE     PAYMENTNO > 5
```

The result is:

```
PAYMENTNO  PAYMENT_DATE  PAYMENT_DATE + INTERVAL 7 DAY
---------  ------------  -----------------------------
        6  1980-12-08    1980-12-15
        7  1982-12-30    1983-01-06
        8  1984-11-12    1984-11-19
```

Explanation: The SELECT clause contains the expression DATE + INTERVAL 7 DAY. The second part after the plus is the interval. The word INTERVAL precedes each interval. The word DAY is the *interval unit,* and 7 is the *interval length.* In this case, it is an interval of seven days.

As stated, an interval should always follow an expression with a date data type. The following statement, therefore, is not allowed:

```
SELECT INTERVAL 7 DAY
```

Example 5.45: Get the penalties that were paid between Christmas 1982 (December 25) and New Year's Eve.

```
SELECT    PAYMENTNO, PAYMENT_DATE
FROM      PENALTIES
WHERE     PAYMENT_DATE >= '1982-12-25'
AND       PAYMENT_DATE <= '1982-12-25' + INTERVAL 6 DAY
```

The result is:

```
PAYMENTNO  PAYMENT_DATE
---------  ------------
        7  1982-12-30
```

Explanation: In the second condition of the `WHERE` clause after the less than or equal to operator, an expression is specified that holds a calculation in which six days are added to the date of Christmas 1982.

When a compound date expression contains more than one interval, it is essential that no calculations be made with interval literals only. Interval literals can be added to dates only. For example, MySQL rejects the expression `DATE + (INTERVAL 1 YEAR + INTERVAL 20 DAY)`. The reason is that brackets are used, and they force MySQL to add the two interval literals to each other first, which is not allowed. The next two formulations cause no problems:

```
DATECOL + INTERVAL 1 YEAR + INTERVAL 20 DAY
(DATECOL + INTERVAL 1 YEAR) + INTERVAL 20 DAY
```

Instead of a literal, complex expressions can be used to specify an interval. In most cases, brackets are required. Consider a few more correct examples:

```
DATECOL + INTERVAL PLAYERNO YEAR + INTERVAL 20*16 DAY
DATECOL + INTERVAL (PLAYERNO*100) YEAR + INTERVAL LENGTH('SQL') DAY
```

The scalar expression used to indicate the interval does not have to be a value with an integer data type; decimals and floats are allowed as well. However, MySQL rounds the value first. The part after the decimal point simply is removed, and the value is rounded up or down. So the following two expressions have the same value:

```
DATECOL + INTERVAL 1.8 YEAR
DATECOL + INTERVAL 2 YEAR
```

In many of the calculations with dates and interval literals, MySQL acts as expected. For example, if we add the interval three days to the date literal `'2004-01-12'`, the value `January 15, 2004` results. But it is not always this easy. Consider the processing rules with regard to interval literals.

When a random interval is added to an incorrect date literal, MySQL returns the null value. For example, this is the case for the expression `'2004-13-12' + INTERVAL 1 DAY`. However, if this happens, MySQL does not return an error message. But if you want to see the message, you can retrieve it with `SHOW WARNINGS` statement.

Example 5.46: Add one day to the date literal `'2004-13-12'`; next show the error messages.

```
SELECT '2004-13-12' + INTERVAL 1 DAY

SHOW WARNINGS
```

The result is:

```
Level    Code  Message
-------  ----  ---------------------------------------------
Warning  1292  Truncated incorrect datetime value: '2004-13-12'
```

When an interval of several days is added to a correct date (existing or nonexisting), the new date is converted into a sequence number first. This sequence number indicates what day it is since the beginning of year 0. Next, the number of days are added or subtracted. The new sequence number is converted again to the corresponding date.

If `SQL_MODE` has the `ALLOW_INVALID_DATES` setting switched to on, MySQL can perform calculations with correct nonexisting dates. A nonexisting date such as February 31, 2004 is converted first to a sequence number that is equal to that of the date March 2, 2004. Therefore, the expression `'2004-04-31' + INTERVAL 1 DAY` returns May 2, 2004 as result because `'2004-04-31'` is converted to May 1, 2004 first. `'2004-04-31' + INTERVAL 31 DAY` gives June 1, 2004 as result.

When an interval unit of weeks is specified, the way of processing is comparable to that of the days. One week equals seven days.

When the interval unit months is used, one month does not stands for 31 days. Special rules apply when months are used for calculation. When a number of months are added to a date, the months component is increased by that number. When that date does not exist, it is rounded *down* to the last date of the corresponding month. Therefore, `'2004-01-31' + INTERVAL 1 MONTH` gives `29 February 2004` as result. If the value of the months component is greater than `12`, then 12 is subtracted, and the years component is increased by 1.

When a number of months is subtracted from a date, MySQL uses the same method of processing.

If a interval unit of quarters is specified, the processing method is comparable to that for months. With that, one quarter equals three months.

For calculations with years, certain rules apply that are comparable to those for months. With the years component, the number of years is added to or subtracted from it. If in a leap year, one year is added to February 29, it is rounded down, and the result is February 28. If one year is added to a correct but nonexisting date, the days component is not changed. The result is a correct but nonexisting date again. For example, the result of `'2004-02-31' + INTERVAL 1 YEAR` is February 31, 2004.

Because of these processing rules, using multiple interval literals in one compound date expression sometimes leads to unexpected results. See the following examples and compare examples three to four, five to six, and seven to eight. Even when the interval literals are reversed, the result is different. In these examples, assume that the setting `ALLOW_INVALID_DATES` for the variable `SQL_MODE` is turned on.

```
Compound date expression                            Value
--------------------------------------------------  ----------
'2004-02-31' + INTERVAL 1 MONTH - INTERVAL 1 MONTH  2004-02-29
'2004-02-31' + INTERVAL 1 DAY - INTERVAL 1 DAY      2004-03-02
'2004-02-31' + INTERVAL 1 YEAR + INTERVAL 1 DAY     2005-03-04
'2004-02-31' + INTERVAL 1 DAY + INTERVAL 1 YEAR     2005-03-03
'2004-02-31' + INTERVAL 1 MONTH + INTERVAL 1 DAY    2004-04-01
'2004-02-31' + INTERVAL 1 DAY + INTERVAL 1 MONTH    2004-04-03
'2000-02-29' + INTERVAL 1 YEAR - INTERVAL 1 DAY     2005-02-27
'2000-02-29' - INTERVAL 1 DAY + INTERVAL 1 YEAR     2005-02-28
```

MySQL also has a combined interval unit called `YEAR_MONTH`. For example, the expression `'2004-02-18' + INTERVAL '2-2' YEAR_MONTH` has the same result as `'2004-02-18' + INTERVAL 2 YEAR + INTERVAL 2 MONTH`. See how the two numbers are enclosed by quotation marks (so they actually form one alphanumeric expression) and separated by a hyphen.

Exercise 5.27: Determine the result of the following compound date expressions. Assume that the column DATECOL has the value `29 February 2000`.

1. `DATECOL + INTERVAL 7 DAY`
2. `DATECOL - INTERVAL 1 MONTH`
3. `(DATECOL - INTERVAL 2 MONTH) + INTERVAL 2 MONTH`
4. `CAST('2001-02-28' AS DATE) + INTERVAL 1 DAY`
5. `CAST('2001-02-28' AS DATE) + INTERVAL 2 MONTH - INTERVAL 2 MONTH`

Exercise 5.28: For each row in the COMMITTEE_MEMBERS table, get the player number, the begin date, and the begin date plus two months and three days.

5.13.4 The Compound Time Expression

As with dates, you can calculate with times. For example, you can add or subtract a number of hours, minutes, or seconds to or from a specified time. The result after the calculation is always a new time.

Calculations with times are always specified as *compound time expressions.* This type of expression identifies a certain moment of a day to a millionth of a second precisely.

MySQL does not support actual compound time expressions yet. You can use the scalar function ADDTIME instead. This book uses this function as a substitution of the compound time expression.

DEFINITION

```
<compound time expression> ::=
   ADDTIME( <scalar time expression> , <time interval> )

<time interval> ::= <scalar time expression>
```

ADDTIME has two parameters. The first is a scalar expression (such as a time literal or a column with the time data type), and the second is an *interval* that is added to or subtracted from that scalar expression.

An interval represents not a certain moment in time, but a certain period or length of time. This period is expressed in a number of hours, minutes, and seconds, or a combination of these three. Time interval literals can be used to indicate how long, for example, a match took. An interval is specified the same way as a time expression:

```
Interval     Value
----------   -------------------
'10:00:00'   period of 10 hours
'00:01:00'   period of 1 minute
'00:00:03'   period of 3 seconds
```

Because times do not occur in the sample database, we created an additional table to show some examples.

Example 5.47: Create a special variant of the MATCHES table that includes the date the match was played, the time it started, and the time it ended.

```
CREATE   TABLE MATCHES_SPECIAL
        (MATCHNO          INTEGER NOT NULL,
         TEAMNO           INTEGER NOT NULL,
         PLAYERNO         INTEGER NOT NULL,
         WON              SMALLINT NOT NULL,
         LOST             SMALLINT NOT NULL,
         START_DATE       DATE NOT NULL,
         START_TIME       TIME NOT NULL,
         END_TIME         TIME NOT NULL,
         PRIMARY KEY      (MATCHNO))

INSERT INTO MATCHES_SPECIAL VALUES
   (1, 1, 6, 3, 1, '2004-10-25', '14:10:12', '16:50:09')

INSERT INTO MATCHES_SPECIAL VALUES
   (2, 1, 44, 3, 2, '2004-10-25', '17:00:00', '17:55:48')
```

Example 5.48: For each match, get the time it starts, and get the time it starts plus eight hours.

```
SELECT   MATCHNO, START_TIME,
         ADDTIME(START_TIME, '08:00:00')
FROM     MATCHES_SPECIAL
```

The result is:

```
MATCHNO  START_TIME  ADDTIME(START_TIME, '08:00:00')
-------  ----------  -------------------------------
      1  14:10:12    22:10:12
      2  17:00:00    25:00:00
```

Example 5.49: Find the matches that ended at least 6.5 hours before midnight.

```
SELECT   MATCHNO, END_TIME
FROM     MATCHES_SPECIAL
WHERE    ADDTIME(END_TIME, '06:30:00') <= '24:00:00'
```

The result is:

```
MATCHNO  END_TIME
-------  --------
      2  16:50:09
```

Calculations with times follow predictable rules. When a few seconds are added to a certain time, the sum of the number of seconds in the seconds component of the time, and the number of seconds in the interval is calculated. For each

60 seconds that can be removed from the sum without the sum becoming less than 0, one is added to the minutes component. A comparable rule applies to the minutes component: For each 60 minutes that can be removed from the sum, 1 is added to the hours component. The hours component, however, can become greater than 24. The expression ADDTIME('10:00:00', '100:00:00') is allowed and returns the value 110:00:00.

Exercise 5.29: Show the expression for adding ten hours to the point in time 11:34:34.

Exercise 5.30: What is the result of the expression ADDTIME('11:34:34', '24:00:00')?

5.13.5 The Compound Timestamp and Datetime Expression

The value of a *compound timestamp expression* identifies a certain moment in a day in the Gregorian calendar, such as 4:00 in the afternoon on January 12, 1991.

MySQL also supports the *compound datetime expression*. The rules for both compound expressions are identical.

DEFINITION

```
<compound timestamp expression> ::=
   <scalar timestamp expression> [ + | - ] <timestamp interval>

<compound datetime expression> ::=
   <scalar datetime expression> [ + | - ] <timestamp interval>

<timestamp interval> ::=
   INTERVAL <interval length> <timestamp interval unit>

<interval length> ::= <scalar expression>

<timestamp interval unit> ::=
   MICROSECOND | SECOND | MINUTE | HOUR |
   DAY | WEEK | MONTH | QUARTER | YEAR |
   SECOND_MICROSECOND | MINUTE_MICROSECOND | MINUTE_SECOND |
   HOUR_MICROSECOND | HOUR_SECOND | HOUR_MINUTE |
   DAY_MICROSECOND | DAY_SECOND | DAY_MINUTE | DAY_HOUR |
   YEAR_MONTH
```

Just as it is possible to calculate with dates and times, it is possible to calculate with timestamps. For example, you can add or subtract a couple months, days, hours, or seconds to or from a timestamp. The rules for processing are according to those for calculating with dates and times.

If too many hours are added to a time, the surplus is simply thrown away. For a timestamp expression, this means that the days component increases. So, if 24 hours are added to something, the result would be the same as adding one day.

If a combined interval unit is specified, such as MINUTE_SECOND or DAY_SECOND, the interval length must be written as an alphanumeric literal—therefore, with quotation marks. The two values can be separated by several characters, for example, with a space, a colon, or a hyphen.

The result of using a combined interval unit is the same as writing it as two separate singular interval units. The expression X + INTERVAL '4:2' HOUR_MINUTE is therefore equal to X + INTERVAL 4 HOUR + INTERVAL 4 MINUTE.

Consider a few correct examples in which the expression E1 has the value 2006-01-01 12:12:12.089:

```
Compound expression                 Value
----------------------------------  -----------------------
E1 + INTERVAL 911000 MICROSECOND    2006-01-01 12:12:13
E1 + INTERVAL 24 HOUR               2006-01-02 12:12:12.089
E1 + INTERVAL '1:1' YEAR_MONTH      2007-02-01 12:12:12.089
```

What holds for the timestamp literal also holds for the compound timestamp expression. When the result is stored in a table, MySQL cuts off the microseconds part; see the following example:

Example 5.50: Create a table in which timestamps can be stored.

```
CREATE TABLE TSTAMP (COL1 TIMESTAMP)

SET @TIME = TIMESTAMP('1980-12-08 23:59:59.59')

INSERT INTO TSTAMP VALUES (@TIME + INTERVAL 3 MICROSECOND)

SELECT COL1, COL1 + INTERVAL 3 MICROSECOND FROM TSTAMP
```

The result is:

```
COL1                 COL1 + INTERVAL 3 MICROSECOND
-------------------  -----------------------------
1980-12-08 23:59:59  1980-12-08 23:59:59.000003
```

Explanation: Obviously, the microseconds are missing in the result of the SELECT statement, although they have been entered with an INSERT statement.

Exercise 5.31: Show the expression for adding 1,000 minutes to the timestamp 1995-12-12 11:34:34.

Exercise 5.32: For each penalty, find the payment number and the payment date, followed by that same date plus 3 hours, 50 seconds, and 99 microseconds.

5.13.6 The Compound Boolean Expression

A *compound Boolean expression* is an expression with a Boolean result. Besides the familiar scalar forms, such as the Boolean literal, the compound expression has another form: the *condition* (see the following definition). Chapter 8, "SELECT Statement: The WHERE Clause," extensively discusses conditions, so for now, we give just a few examples.

DEFINITION

```
<compound boolean expression> ::=
   <scalar boolean expression> |
   <condition>
```

Example 5.51: Get the number of each team.

```
SELECT   TEAMNO
FROM     TEAMS
WHERE    TRUE OR FALSE
```

The result is:

```
TEAMNO
------
     1
     2
```

Explanation: The WHERE clause contains a condition that is always true, which is why all the teams are displayed. However, this is not a very useful example; it just shows that this statement is allowed.

Most Boolean expressions are used in WHERE clauses. However, all the Boolean expressions—therefore, also the conditions—can be used anywhere where an expression may occur, so also within a SELECT clause.

Example 5.52: Indicate which payment numbers are greater than 4.

```
SELECT   PAYMENTNO, PAYMENTNO > 4
FROM     PENALTIES
```

The result is:

```
PAYMENTNO  PAYMENTNO > 4
---------  -------------
        1              0
        2              0
        3              0
        4              0
        5              1
        6              1
        7              1
        8              1
```

Explanation: The SELECT clause contains the compound Boolean expression PAYMENTNO > 4. If it is true, MySQL prints a 1; otherwise, it prints a 0. You can embellish the result somewhat by expanding the condition with a case expression:

```
SELECT   PAYMENTNO, CASE PAYMENTNO > 4
                       WHEN 1 THEN 'Greater than 4'
                       ELSE 'Less than 5'
                    END AS GREATER_LESS
FROM PENALTIES
```

The result is:

```
PAYMENTNO  GREATER_LESS
---------  --------------
        1  Less than 5
        2  Less than 5
        3  Less than 5
        4  Less than 5
        5  Greater than 4
        6  Greater than 4
        7  Greater than 4
        8  Greater than 4
```

Example 5.53: Find the players for whom the following two conditions are both true or both false: The player number is less than 15, and the year of joining the club is greater than 1979.

```
SELECT   PLAYERNO, JOINED, PLAYERNO < 15, JOINED > 1979
FROM     PLAYERS
WHERE    (PLAYERNO < 15) = (JOINED > 1979)
```

The result is:

```
PLAYERNO  JOINED  PLAYERNO < 15  JOINED > 1979
--------  ------  -------------  -------------
       7    1981              1              1
       8    1980              1              1
      95    1972              0              0
     100    1979              0              0
```

Explanation: The two compound expressions in the `WHERE` clause have the value `1` or `0` as result. If both are equal to `1` or `0`, the condition is `true`, and the concerned player is included in the end result.

Exercise 5.33: Show which players are resident in Inglewood. Use the values `Yes` and `No`.

Exercise 5.34: Find the penalties for which the next two conditions are both `true` or both `false`: The penalty amount is equal to 25, and the player number is equal to 44.

5.14 The Aggregation Function and the Scalar Subquery

For the sake of completeness, this section introduces the last two forms of the scalar expression: the aggregation function and the scalar subquery.

As with scalar functions, aggregation functions are used to perform calculations. They also have parameters. The big difference between these two types of functions is that a scalar function is always executed on a maximum of one row with values. An aggregation function, on the other hand, is a calculation with a set of rows as input. Table 5.6 shows the different aggregation functions that MySQL supports. Chapter 9, "SELECT Statement: SELECT Clause and Aggregation Functions," extensively discusses aggregation functions.

TABLE 5.6 Aggregation Functions in MySQL

AGGREGATION FUNCTION	MEANING
AVG	Determines the weighted average of the values in a column
BIT_AND	Executes the bit operator AND (i.e., the & operator) on all values in a column
BIT_OR	Executes the bit operator OR (i.e., the | operator) on all values in a column
BIT_XOR	Executes the bit operator XOR (i.e., the ^ operator) on all values in a column
COUNT	Determines the number of values in a column or the number of rows in a table
GROUP_CONCAT	Makes a list of all the values of a group (created with the GROUP BY clause)
MAX	Determines the largest value in a column
MIN	Determines the smallest value in a column
STDDEV (i.e., STD or STDEV_POP)	Determines the standard deviation of the values in a column
STDTEV_SAMP	Determines the sample standard deviation of the values in a column
SUM	Determines the sum of the values in a column
VARIANCE (i.e., VAR_POP)	Determines the population variance of the values in a column
VAR_SAMP	Determines the sample variance of the values in a column

The subquery enables us to include SELECT statements within expressions. With this, we can formulate very powerful statement in a compact way. Section 6.6 returns to this subject briefly; Chapter 8 discusses the subquery in great detail.

5.15 The Row Expression

Section 5.3 introduced the concept of the row expression. The value of a row expression is a row consisting of at least one value. The number of elements in a row expression is called the *degree*. Section 4.7 gave examples of rows expressions—namely, in the INSERT statement. There, a row expression is specified after the word VALUES in the INSERT statement.

Example 5.54: Add a new row to the COMMITTEE_MEMBERS table.

```
INSERT   INTO COMMITTEE_MEMBERS
VALUES   (7 + 15, CURRENT_DATE,
          CURRENT_DATE + INTERVAL 17 DAY, 'Member')
```

Explanation: This row expression has four components—in other words, the degree of this row expression is 4. First is a compound expression (7 + 15), followed by a system variable and a system variable as part of a compound date expression. A literal concludes the row expression.

Row expressions can also be used in SELECT statements, for example, to make a comparison with multiple values simultaneously.

Example 5.55: Get the numbers of the players who live on Haseltine Lane in Stratford.

```
SELECT   PLAYERNO
FROM     PLAYERS
WHERE    (TOWN, STREET) = ('Stratford', 'Haseltine Lane')
```

The result is:

```
PLAYERNO
--------
       6
     100
```

Explanation: In the condition of this statement, two row expressions are compared.

A SELECT statement with one row of values as a result can also act as a row expression.

Example 5.56: Find the numbers of the players who live on Haseltine Lane in Stratford.

```
SELECT   PLAYERNO
FROM     PLAYERS
WHERE    (TOWN, STREET) = (SELECT 'Stratford', 'Haseltine Lane')
```

Explanation: The SELECT statement in the WHERE clause returns one row with two values. We return to this specific feature later in this book.

Each expression has a data type, so that includes a row expression as well. However, a row expression does not have one data type, but it has a data type for each value from which it is built. So the previous row expression (TOWN, STREET) has the data type (alphanumeric, alphanumeric).

If row expressions are compared to each other, the respective degrees should be the same and the data types of the elements with the same order number should be comparable. "Comparable" means that both data types are identical, or that the one can be cast implicitly to the other. Therefore, the following comparisons are syntactically correct:

```
(TOWN, STREET) = (1000, 'USA')
(NAME, BIRTH_DATE, PLAYERNO) = (NULL, '1980-12-12', 1)
```

NOTE

Section 8.2 describes in detail how conditions in which row expressions are compared are evaluated.

Exercise 5.35: Get the numbers of the penalties of $25 incurred for player 44 on December 8, 1980.

Exercise 5.36: Get the numbers of the players for whom the last name is equal to the town and the initials are equal to the street name, a somewhat peculiar example.

Exercise 5.37: Get the penalties with an amount that is unequal to $25 and a player number that is equal to 44; use row expressions in the WHERE clause for this.

5.16 The Table Expression

Section 5.3 briefly discussed table expressions. The value of a table expression is a set of row values. In the INSERT statement, this expression can be used to enter not one, but multiple rows simultaneously.

Example 5.57: Add all eight penalties with just one INSERT statement.

```
INSERT INTO PENALTIES VALUES
   (1,   6, '1980-12-08', 100),
   (2,  44, '1981-05-05',  75),
   (3,  27, '1983-09-10', 100),
   (4, 104, '1984-12-08',  50),
   (5,  44, '1980-12-08',  25),
   (6,   8, '1980-12-08',  25),
   (7,  44, '1982-12-30',  30),
   (8,  27, '1984-11-12',  75)
```

Explanation: The result of this statement is the same as those of eight individual INSERT statements. However, this statement guarantees that either all the eight rows are added or none is added.

Each SELECT statement is also a valid table expression. This is obvious because the result of a SELECT statement is always a set of rows.

Table expressions have data types as well. Just as with the row expression, a table expression is a set of data types. In the earlier INSERT statement, the data type of the table expression is (integer, alphanumeric, alphanumeric, alphanumeric, integer). The rule for all row expressions within one table expression is that they must have the same degree and that they must have comparable data types.

Chapter 6 devotes more coverage to the table expression. After all, each SELECT statement is a table expression, and in several places in that same statement, table expressions can be specified.

5.17 Answers

5.1
1. Correct; float data type.
2. Incorrect; quotation marks must appear in front of and after the alphanumeric literal.
3. Correct; alphanumeric data type.
4. Incorrect, characters appear outside the quotation marks of the alphanumeric literal.
5. Correct; alphanumeric data type.
6. Correct; integer data type.
7. Correct; alphanumeric data type.
8. Correct; alphanumeric data type.

9. Correct; date data type.
10. If it is supposed to be an alphanumeric literal, it is correct. If it is supposed to be a date literal, it is incorrect because the month component is too high.
11. Correct; date data type.
12. Correct; time data type.
13. If it is supposed to be an alphanumeric literal, it is correct. If it is supposed to be a time literal, it is incorrect because if the hours component is equal to `24`, the two other components must be equal to `0`.
14. Correct; timestamp data type.
15. Incorrect; a hexadecimal data type must consist of an even number of characters.
16. Correct; Boolean data type.

5.2 The value of a literal is fixed; MySQL must determine the value of an expression.

5.3 Expressions can be grouped based on their respective data types, the complexity of their values, and their forms. Grouping based on data type refers to the data type of the value of the expression, such as integer, date, or alphanumeric. Grouping based on complexity refers to whether it is a "normal," a row, or a table expression. Grouping based on form implies whether it is a singular or compound expression.

5.4
```
SELECT   MATCHNO, WON - LOST AS DIFFERENCE
FROM     MATCHES
```

5.5 Yes, this statement is correct. It is allowed to sort on column names introduced in the `SELECT` clause.

5.6
```
SELECT   PLAYERS.PLAYERNO, PLAYERS.NAME,
                  PLAYERS.INITIALS
FROM     PLAYERS
WHERE    PLAYERS.PLAYERNO > 6
ORDER BY PLAYERS.NAME
```

5.7 This statement is incorrect because of the column specification `TEAMS.PLAYERNO`. The TEAMS table does not occur in the `FROM` clause. Therefore, the SQL statement cannot refer to columns of this table.

5.8 Yes, it is allowed.

5.9
```
SELECT @VAR
```

5.10 If a user variable has not been initialized yet, it has the value null.

5.11
1. User variables are indicated with a `@` and system variables with `@@`.
2. MySQL defines and initializes system variables; the user or programmer defines and initializes user variables.

5.12
```
SELECT    PLAYERNO
FROM      COMMITTEE_MEMBERS
WHERE     BEGIN_DATE = CURRENT_DATE
```

5.13
```
SELECT    TEAMNO,
          CASE DIVISION
             WHEN 'first' then 'first division'
             WHEN 'second' THEN 'second division'
             ELSE 'unknown'
                END AS DIVISION
FROM      TEAMS
```

5.14
```
SELECT    PAYMENTNO, AMOUNT,
          CASE
             WHEN AMOUNT >= 0 AND AMOUNT <= 40
                THEN 'low'
             WHEN AMOUNT >= 41 AND AMOUNT <= 80
                THEN 'moderate'
             WHEN AMOUNT >= 81
                THEN 'high'
             ELSE 'incorrect'
                END AS CATEGORY
FROM      PENALTIES
```

5.15
```
SELECT    PAYMENTNO, AMOUNT
FROM      PENALTIES
WHERE     CASE
             WHEN AMOUNT >= 0 AND AMOUNT <= 40
                THEN 'low'
             WHEN AMOUNT > 40 AND AMOUNT <= 80
                THEN 'moderate'
             WHEN AMOUNT > 80
                THEN 'high'
             ELSE 'incorrect'
                END = 'low'
```

5.16
1. 100
2. 0
3. 9
4. SQL
5. deeteebeese

5.17
```
SELECT   PAYMENTNO
FROM     PENALTIES
WHERE    DAYNAME(PAYMENT_DATE) = 'Monday'
```

5.18
```
SELECT   PAYMENTNO
FROM     PENALTIES
WHERE    YEAR(PAYMENT_DATE) = 1984
```

5.19 `CAST('2004-03-12' AS DATE)`

5.20 Alphanumeric literal

5.21 Not every alphanumeric literal can be converted. Conversion is possible only when the literal satisfies the requirements of a date. Converting a date literal to an alphanumeric literal always works.

5.22 No. When the null value is compared to another expression with an equal to operator, the entire condition evaluates to `unknown` and the corresponding row is not included in the end result.

5.23 Not a single row.

5.24
1. 200
2. 3800
3. 200
4. 200
5. 333.33
6. 111.11
7. 150.0000
8. 13
9. 0
10. 6

5.25
```
SELECT   PLAYERNO, SUBSTR(INITIALS,1,1) || '. ' || NAME
FROM     PLAYERS
```

5.26
```
SELECT   TEAMNO, RTRIM(DIVISION) || ' division'
FROM     TEAMS
```

5.27
1. 2000-03-07
2. 2000-01-29
3. 2000-02-29
4. 2001-03-01
5. 2001-02-28

5.28
```
SELECT    PLAYERNO, BEGIN_DATE,
          BEGIN_DATE + INTERVAL 2 MONTH + INTERVAL 3 DAY
FROM      COMMITTEE_MEMBERS
```

5.29 `ADDTIME('11:34:34', '10:00:00')`

5.30 The result is not `11:34:34`, which you might expect, but `35:34:34`.

5.31 `'1995-12-12 11:34:34' + INTERVAL 1000 MINUTE`

5.32
```
SELECT    PAYMENTNO, PAYMENT_DATE,
          PAYMENT_DATE + INTERVAL 3 HOUR +
          INTERVAL 50 SECOND + INTERVAL 99 MICROSECOND
FROM      PENALTIES
```

5.33
```
SELECT    PLAYERNO,
          CASE TOWN='Inglewood'
             WHEN 1 THEN 'Yes' ELSE 'No' END
FROM      PLAYERS
```

5.34
```
SELECT    *
FROM      PENALTIES
WHERE     (AMOUNT = 25) = (PLAYERNO = 44)
```

5.35
```
SELECT    PAYMENTNO
FROM      PENALTIES
WHERE     (AMOUNT, PLAYERNO, PAYMENT_DATE) =
          (25, 44, '1980-12-08')
```

5.36
```
SELECT    PLAYERNO
FROM      PLAYERS
WHERE     (NAME, INITIALS) = (TOWN, STREET)
```

5.37
```
SELECT    *
FROM      PENALTIES
WHERE     (AMOUNT = 25, PLAYERNO = 44) = (FALSE, TRUE
```

CHAPTER 6

SELECT Statements, Table Expressions, and Subqueries

6.1 Introduction

Earlier we introduced the SELECT statement and the table expression. You use both of these language constructs for querying data. Within SQL, a few other related constructs exist, such as the subquery and select block. All these constructs have a strong mutual relationship, which makes it difficult to keep them apart. However, the person who is programming SQL must know the differences. That is why we have devoted this entire chapter to this subject. For each construct, we describe what is meant exactly and what the mutual relationships are.

We begin with the SELECT statement. In the previous chapters, you have already seen several examples of this statement.

6.2 The Definition of the SELECT Statement

Each SELECT statement consists of a *table expression* followed by several specifications. We leave these additional specifications aside for now; they are not included in the following definition.

DEFINITION

```
<select statement> ::=
   <table expression>

<table expression> ::=
   <select block head> [ <select block tail> ]

<select block head> ::=
   <select clause>
   [ <from clause>
   [ <where clause> ]
   [ <group by clause> ]
   [ <having clause> ] ]

<select block tail> ::=
   <order by clause> |
   <limit clause>    |
   <order by clause> <limit clause>
```

This chapter is completely devoted to that table expression. The value of a table expression is always a set of rows, in which each row consists of the same number of column values.

As described in Section 5.3, two forms of the table expression exist: the singular and the compound table expressions. This section considers only the singular form.

You might wonder what the use is of introducing the concept of a table expression when every SELECT statement exists entirely of a table expression. Aren't the concepts the same? The answer is that every SELECT statement is built from a table expression, but not every table expression is part of a SELECT statement. Table expressions are also used within other SQL statements, such as the CREATE VIEW statement. For example, in Figure 6.1, a table expression appears twice, the first time as part of a SELECT statement and the next as part of a CREATE VIEW statement.

A table expression consists of one or more *select blocks*. A select block is a set of clauses, such as SELECT, FROM, and ORDER BY. The clauses of a select block are divided into two groups: the *head part* and the *tail part*.

Again, you could wonder why it is useful to make a distinction between table expressions and select blocks. A select block always consists of only one group of clauses—thus, one SELECT clause and one FROM clause—whereas a table expression, as you will see later, can consist of multiple select blocks and, thus, can also contain multiple SELECT and FROM clauses.

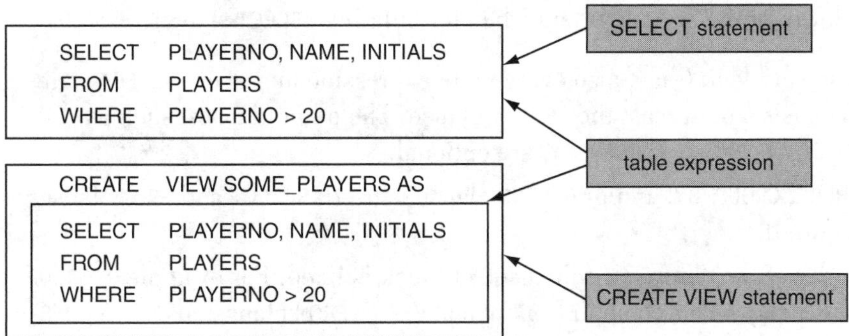

FIGURE 6.1 Table expressions as part of various statements

Figure 6.2 shows a graphical representation of the different constructs and their relationships that have been introduced in this section. An arrow indicates which concept has been built from which other concepts. The arrow head points to the concept that forms a part.

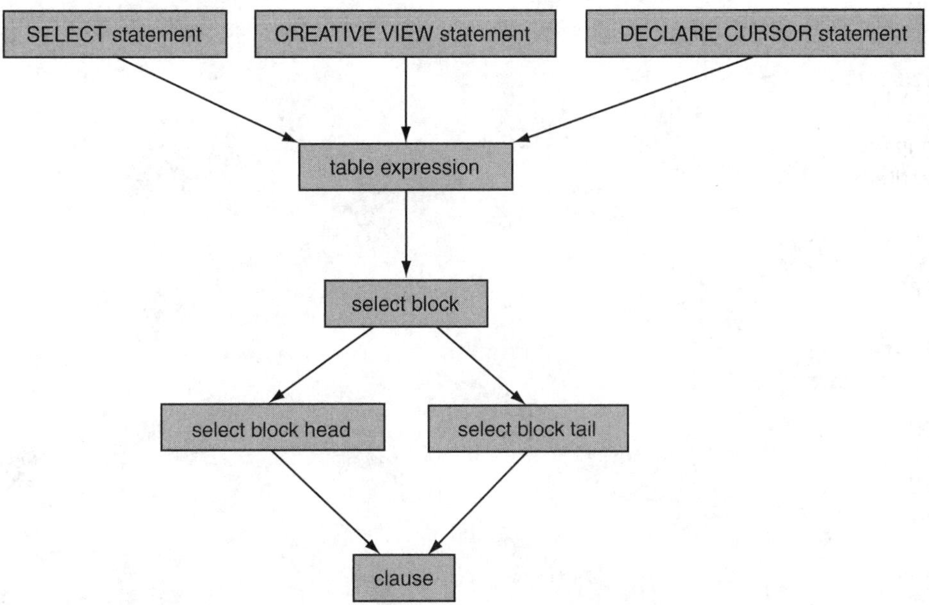

FIGURE 6.2 The relationships between different language constructs

When we use the term *select block* in this book, we mean the combination of a select block head and a select block tail. You will learn about the advantage of naming these two parts individually later in this chapter.

The following rules are important when formulating SELECT statements:

- Each select block (thus, also every table expression and every SELECT statement) consists of at least the SELECT clause. The other clauses, such as WHERE, GROUP BY, and ORDER BY, are optional.
- If a WHERE, GROUP BY, and/or HAVING clause is used, SELECT and FROM clauses are required.
- The order of the clauses within a select block is fixed. For example, a GROUP BY clause may never come in front of a WHERE or FROM clause, and the ORDER BY clause (when used) is always last.
- A HAVING clause can be used within a select block if no GROUP BY clause exists. Most other SQL products do not support this.

Next we give a few examples of correct SELECT statements, table expressions, and select blocks. For the sake of convenience, three dots represent what follows each different clause.

```
SELECT   ...
FROM     ...
ORDER BY ...

SELECT   ...
FROM     ...
GROUP BY ...
HAVING   ...

SELECT   ...
FROM     ...
WHERE    ...

SELECT   ...

SELECT   ...
FROM     ...
WHERE    ...
GROUP BY ...
LIMIT    ...

SELECT   ...
FROM     ...
HAVING   ...
```

Exercise 6.1: Indicate for the following SQL statements whether they are SELECT statements, table expressions, and/or head parts of select blocks. Multiple answers are possible.

1. ```
   SELECT   ...
   FROM     ...
   WHERE    ...
   ORDER BY ...
   ```
2. ```
   SELECT   ...
   FROM     ...
   GROUP BY ...
   ```
3. ```
   CREATE VIEW ...
   SELECT   ...
   FROM     ...
   ```

Exercise 6.2: For the following SQL statement, indicate which part is a table expression and which part is the tail part of a select block.

```
SELECT   ...
FROM     ...
WHERE    ...
ORDER BY ...
```

Exercise 6.3: What is the minimum number of clauses that must be present in a SELECT statement?

Exercise 6.4: Can a SELECT statement have an ORDER BY clause but no WHERE clause?

Exercise 6.5: Can a SELECT statement have a HAVING clause but no GROUP BY clause?

Exercise 6.6: Decide what is incorrect in the following SELECT statements:

1. ```
   SELECT   ...
   WHERE    ...
   ORDER BY ...
   ```
2. ```
   SELECT   ...
   FROM     ...
   HAVING   ...
   GROUP BY ...
   ```
3. ```
   SELECT   ...
   ORDER BY ...
   FROM     ...
   GROUP BY ...
   ```

6.3 Processing the Clauses in a Select Block

Each select block consists of clauses, such as the SELECT, FROM, and ORDER BY clauses. This section explains through examples how the different clauses from a select block are processed. In other words, we show the steps MySQL performs to come to the desired result. Other examples clearly show what the job of each clause is.

In all these examples, the select block forms the entire table expression and the entire SELECT statement.

Later chapters discuss each clause in detail.

Example 6.1: Find the player number for each player who has incurred at least two penalties of more than $25; order the result by player number (smallest number first).

```
SELECT   PLAYERNO
FROM     PENALTIES
WHERE    AMOUNT > 25
GROUP BY PLAYERNO
HAVING   COUNT(*) > 1
ORDER BY PLAYERNO
```

Figure 6.3 shows the order in which MySQL processes the different clauses. You likely noticed immediately that this order differs from the order in which the clauses were entered in the select block (and, therefore, the SELECT statement). Be careful never to confuse these two.

Explanation: Processing each clause results in *one (intermediate result) table* that consists of *zero or more rows* and *one or more columns*. This automatically means that every clause, barring the first, has one table of zero or more rows and one or more columns as its input. The first clause, the FROM clause, retrieves data from the database and has as its input *one or more tables* from the database. Those tables that still have to be processed by a subsequent clause are called *intermediate results*. SQL does not show the user any of the intermediate results; it presents the statement as a single large process. The only table the end user sees is the final result table.

MySQL developers may determine themselves how their product will process the SELECT statements internally. They can switch the order of the clauses or combine the processing of clauses. In fact, they can do whatever they want, as long as the final result of the query is equal to the result they would get if the statement were processed according to the method just described.

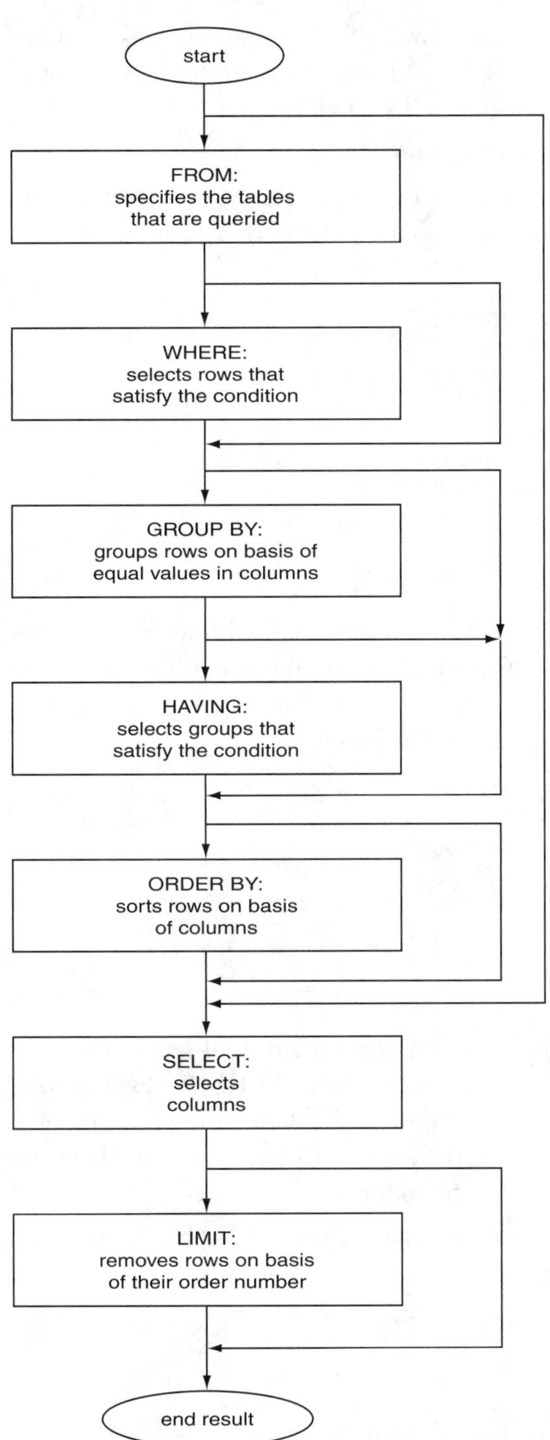

FIGURE 6.3 The clauses of the SELECT statement

Chapter 25, "Using Indexes," examines how MySQL actually processes statements. The method of processing described here is extremely useful if you want to determine the end result of a SELECT statement "by hand."

Let's examine the clauses for the given example one by one.

Only the PENALTIES table is named in the FROM clause. For MySQL, this means that it works with this table. The intermediate result of this clause is an exact copy of the PENALTIES table:

```
PAYMENTNO  PLAYERNO  PAYMENT_DATE  AMOUNT
---------  --------  ------------  ------
        1         6  1980-12-08    100.00
        2        44  1981-05-05     75.00
        3        27  1983-09-10    100.00
        4       104  1984-12-08     50.00
        5        44  1980-12-08     25.00
        6         8  1980-12-08     25.00
        7        44  1982-12-30     30.00
        8        27  1984-11-12     75.00
```

The WHERE clause specifies AMOUNT > 25 as a condition. All rows in which the value in the AMOUNT column is greater than 25 satisfy the condition. Therefore, the rows with payment numbers 5 and 6 are discarded, while the remaining rows form the intermediate result table from the WHERE clause:

```
PAYMENTNO  PLAYERNO  PAYMENT_DATE  AMOUNT
---------  --------  ------------  ------
        1         6  1980-12-08    100.00
        2        44  1981-05-05     75.00
        3        27  1983-09-10    100.00
        4       104  1984-12-08     50.00
        7        44  1982-12-30     30.00
        8        27  1984-11-12     75.00
```

The GROUP BY clause groups the rows in the intermediate result table. The data is divided into groups on the basis of the values in the PLAYERNO column (GROUP BY PLAYERNO). Rows are grouped if they contain equal values in the relevant column. For example, the rows with payment numbers 2 and 7 form one group because the PLAYERNO column has the value of 44 in both rows.

This is the intermediate result (the column name PLAYERNO has been shortened to PNO to conserve some space):

```
PAYMENTNO  PNO  PAYMENT_DATE              AMOUNT
---------  ---  ------------------------  ---------------
{1}          6  {1980-12-08}              {100.00}
{2, 7}      44  {1981-05-05, 1982-12-30}  {75.00, 30.00}
{3, 8}      27  {1983-09-10, 1984-11-12}  {100.00, 75.00}
{4}        104  {1984-12-08}              {50.00}
```

Explanation: Thus, for all but the PLAYERNO column, more than one value can exist in one row. For example, the PAYMENTNO column contains two values in the second and third rows. This is not as strange as it might seem because the data is grouped and each row actually forms a group of rows. A single value for each row of the intermediate table is found only in the PLAYERNO column because this is the column by which the result is grouped. For the sake of clarity, the groups with values have been enclosed by brackets.

In some ways, you can compare this fourth clause, this HAVING clause, with the WHERE clause. The difference is that the WHERE clause acts on the intermediate table from the FROM clause and the HAVING clause acts on the grouped intermediate result table from the GROUP BY clause. The effect is the same; in the HAVING clause, rows are also selected with the help of a condition. In this case, the condition is as follows:

```
COUNT(*) > 1
```

This means that all (grouped) rows made up of more than one row must satisfy the condition. Chapter 10, "SELECT Statement: The GROUP BY Clause," looks at this condition in detail.

The intermediate result is:

```
PAYMENTNO  PNO  PAYMENT_DATE              AMOUNT
---------  ---  ------------------------  ---------------
{2, 7}      44  {1981-05-05, 1982-12-30}  {75.00, 30.00}
{3, 8}      27  {1983-09-10, 1984-11-12}  {100.00, 75.00}
```

The ORDER BY clause has no impact on the contents of the intermediate result, but it sorts the final remaining rows. In this example, the result is sorted on PLAYERNO.

The intermediate result is:

```
PAYMENTNO  PNO  PAYMENT_DATE              AMOUNT
---------  ---  ------------------------  ---------------
{3, 8}      27  {1983-09-10, 1984-11-12}  {100.00, 75.00}
{2, 7}      44  {1981-05-05, 1982-12-30}  {75.00, 30.00}
```

The SELECT clause, which is the last clause in this example, specifies which columns must be present in the final result. In other words, the SELECT clause selects columns.

The end user sees this end result:

```
PLAYERNO
--------
      27
      44
```

Example 6.2: Get the player number and the league number of each player resident in Stratford; order the result by league number.

```
SELECT   PLAYERNO, LEAGUENO
FROM     PLAYERS
WHERE    TOWN = 'Stratford'
ORDER BY LEAGUENO
```

The intermediate result after the FROM clause is:

```
PLAYERNO  NAME       ...  LEAGUENO
--------  ---------  ---  --------
       6  Parmenter  ...  8467
      44  Baker      ...  1124
      83  Hope       ...  1608
       2  Everett    ...  2411
      27  Collins    ...  2513
     104  Moorman    ...  7060
       7  Wise       ...  ?
      57  Brown      ...  6409
      39  Bishop     ...  ?
     112  Bailey     ...  1319
       8  Newcastle  ...  2983
     100  Parmenter  ...  6524
      28  Collins    ...  ?
      95  Miller     ...  ?
```

The intermediate result after the WHERE clause is:

```
PLAYERNO  NAME       ...  LEAGUENO
--------  ---------  ---  --------
       6  Parmenter  ...  8467
      83  Hope       ...  1608
       2  Everett    ...  2411
       7  Wise       ...  ?
      57  Brown      ...  6409
      39  Bishop     ...  ?
     100  Parmenter  ...  6524
```

No GROUP BY clause exists; therefore, the intermediate result remains unchanged. In addition, no HAVING clause exists, so again, the intermediate result remains unchanged.

The intermediate result after the ORDER BY clause is:

```
PLAYERNO  NAME       ...  LEAGUENO
--------  ---------  ---  --------
       7  Wise       ...  ?
      39  Bishop     ...  ?
      83  Hope       ...  1608
       2  Everett    ...  2411
      57  Brown      ...  6409
     100  Parmenter  ...  6524
       6  Parmenter  ...  8467
```

Note that the null values are presented first if the result is sorted. Chapter 12, "SELECT Statement: The ORDER BY Clause," describes this in greater detail.

The SELECT clause asks for the PLAYERNO and LEAGUENO columns. This gives the following final result:

```
PLAYERNO  LEAGUENO
--------  --------
       7  ?
      39  ?
      83  1608
       2  2411
      57  6409
     100  6524
       6  8467
```

The smallest SELECT statement that can be specified consists of one select block with just a SELECT clause.

Example 6.3: How much is 89 × 73?

```
SELECT   89 * 73
```

The result is:

```
89 * 73
-------
   6497
```

The processing of this statement is simple. If no FROM clause is specified, the statement returns a result consisting of one row. This row contains just as many values as there are expressions. In this example, that is also just one.

Exercise 6.7: For the following SELECT statement, determine the intermediate result table after each clause has been processed; give the final result as well.

```
SELECT   PLAYERNO
FROM     PENALTIES
WHERE    PAYMENT_DATE > '1980-12-08'
GROUP BY PLAYERNO
HAVING   COUNT(*) > 1
ORDER BY PLAYERNO
```

6.4 Possible Forms of a Table Expression

We already mentioned that the value of each table expression is a set of rows. We also stated that two forms exist: singular and compound. And we indicated that a singular table expression can consist of a select block. This section introduces new forms of the table expression.

DEFINITION

```
<table expression> ::=
   { <select block head>                |
     ( <table expression> )             |
     <compound table expression> }
   [ <select block tail> ]

<compound table expression> ::=
   <table expression> <set operator> <table expression>

<set operator> ::= UNION
```

This definition shows that a table expression can have three forms. The first form is the familiar form, which uses the head part of a select block. In the second form, the table expression is enclosed in brackets. The third form is the compound table expression, which we have mentioned but not yet clarified. It enables you to specify the tail part of a select block after each form.

As usual, in this book, we illustrate the different forms with examples. We skip the first form because we have already discussed it in great detail. The second form uses brackets.

Example 6.4: Get the contents of the entire TEAMS table.

```
(SELECT   *
 FROM     TEAMS)
```

Explanation: You can specify this statement without brackets; the result is the same. However, you also can formulate the statement as follows:

```
(((((SELECT    *
     FROM      TEAMS)))))
```

Although this is not very useful, it is allowed. Brackets are useful, for example, when multiple select blocks occur within one table expression. We return to this later.

Just as there is a compound version of the scalar expression, a compound version of the table expression exists. A table expression is built from multiple select blocks that are combined with a so-called *set operator*. MySQL supports several set operators. For now, we discuss only one: the *UNION operator*. Chapter 14, "Combining Table Expressions," explains the others in detail.

Example 6.5: Get the numbers of the players who are captains and the numbers of the players who incurred a penalty.

```
SELECT   PLAYERNO
FROM     TEAMS
UNION
SELECT   PLAYERNO
FROM     PENALTIES
```

The result is:

```
PLAYERNO
--------
       6
       8
      27
      44
     104
```

Explanation: This statement consists of two select blocks. The first selects all the captains, and the second selects all the ticketed players. The intermediate result of the first select block is:

```
PLAYERNO
--------
       6
       8
      27
```

The intermediate result of the second select block is:

```
PLAYERNO
--------
       6
       8
      27
      27
      44
      44
      44
     104
```

By linking the select blocks with a `UNION`, MySQL places one intermediate result underneath the other:

```
PLAYERNO
--------
       6
       8
      27
       6
       8
      27
      27
      44
      44
      44
     104
```

In the final step, all the duplicate rows are removed automatically from the result.

In front of and after a `UNION` operator, only the head parts of select blocks appear. This means that a select block tail is allowed only after the last select block. Therefore, the following statement is not allowed:

```
SELECT   PLAYERNO
FROM     TEAMS
ORDER BY PLAYERNO
UNION
SELECT   PLAYERNO
FROM     PENALTIES
```

The tail part of a select block may be used only at the end of the entire table expression, as shown here:

```
SELECT   PLAYERNO
FROM     TEAMS
UNION
SELECT   PLAYERNO
FROM     PENALTIES
ORDER BY PLAYERNO
```

If you want to sort the intermediate result of a select block before it is linked with a UNION operator, you must use brackets. Therefore, the following statement is allowed:

```
(SELECT   PLAYERNO
 FROM     TEAMS
 ORDER BY PLAYERNO)
UNION
(SELECT   PLAYERNO
 FROM     PENALTIES)
ORDER BY PLAYERNO
```

If a set operator is used, the degrees of the select blocks must be equal and the data types of the columns placed below one another should be comparable.

Exercise 6.8: For each committee member, get the player number and the begin and end date. However, the dates should be placed not next to each other, but underneath each other.

Exercise 6.9: Following the previous exercise, now every row must express whether it is a begin or end date.

6.5 What Is a SELECT Statement?

To enable MySQL to process a table expression, the expression must be wrapped in an SQL statement. A table expression can be used in several statements, including the CREATE VIEW and CREATE TABLE statements. However, the SELECT statement is used most often. The first difference between a table expression and a SELECT statement is that query tools such as MySQL Query Browser, Navicat, and WinSQL can process the latter. A table expression, on the other hand, always needs a wrapping statement.

The second difference relates to the clauses. A SELECT statement can contain an additional clause that cannot be specified within a table expression. (See the upcoming definition of the SELECT statement.) Chapter 18, "Loading and Unloading Data," describes this additional clause. Another difference is that FOR UPDATE and LOCK IN SHARE MODE can be specified in a SELECT statement but not in a table expression.

DEFINITION

```
<select statement> ::=
      <table expression>
    [ <into file clause> ]
    [ FOR UPDATE | LOCK IN SHARE MODE ]
```

6.6 What Is a Subquery?

Another table expression can be called from within a table expression. The table expression is called a *subquery*. Alternative names for subquery are *subselect* and *inner select*. The result of the subquery is passed to the calling table expression, which can continue processing.

Grammatically, the difference between a table expression and a subquery is minimal; see the following definition. The difference is mainly in the use.

DEFINITION

```
<subquery> ::= ( <table expression> )
```

Example 6.6: Get the numbers of the players with a number less than 10 and who are male.

```
SELECT   PLAYERNO
FROM    (SELECT   PLAYERNO, SEX
         FROM     PLAYERS
         WHERE    PLAYERNO < 10) AS PLAYERS10
WHERE    SEX = 'M'
```

The result is:

```
PLAYERNO
--------
       2
       6
       7
```

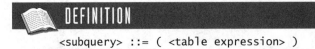

Explanation: This statement is special because it contains a table expression in the FROM clause. As is customary, the FROM clause is processed first and with that the subquery. It is as if the subquery is "called" during the processing of the FROM clause. The table expression in the FROM clause is simple and returns the following intermediate result:

```
PLAYERNO  SEX
--------  ---
       2  M
       6  M
       7  M
       8  F
```

With the specification AS PLAYERS10, this intermediate result receives the name PLAYERS10. This name is called a *pseudonym;* Section 7.5 discusses the pseudonym extensively. These types of pseudonyms are required when using subqueries within the FROM clause.

The intermediate result is passed on to the WHERE clause where the condition SEX = 'M' is used to select the men. Then the SELECT clause is used to select only the PLAYERNO column.

You also can include subqueries within other subqueries. In other words, you can nest subqueries. The following construct is grammatically allowed:

```
SELECT   *
FROM     (SELECT   *
          FROM     (SELECT   *
                    FROM     (SELECT   *
                              FROM     PLAYERS) AS S1) AS S2) AS S3
```

Example 6.7: Get the numbers of the players who have a number greater than 10 and less than 100, for whom the year in which they joined the club is greater than 1980 and who are male.

```
SELECT   PLAYERNO
FROM     (SELECT   PLAYERNO, SEX
          FROM     (SELECT   PLAYERNO, SEX, JOINED
                    FROM     (SELECT   PLAYERNO, SEX, JOINED
                              FROM     PLAYERS
                              WHERE    PLAYERNO > 10) AS GREATER10
                    WHERE    PLAYERNO < 100) AS LESS100
          WHERE    JOINED > 1980) AS JOINED1980
WHERE    SEX = 'M'
```

The result is:

```
PLAYERNO
--------
      57
      83
```

Explanation: This statement has four levels. The inner subquery is used to search for all the players whose player number is greater than 10:

```
PLAYERNO  SEX  JOINED
-------   ----  ------
      27  F      1983
      28  F      1983
      39  M      1980
      44  M      1980
      57  M      1985
      83  M      1982
      95  M      1972
     100  M      1979
     104  F      1984
     112  F      1984
```

The next subquery is used to retrieve from the previous intermediate result all the rows in which the player number is less than 100:

```
PLAYERNO  SEX  JOINED
--------  ---  ------
      27  F      1983
      28  F      1983
      39  M      1980
      44  M      1980
      57  M      1985
      83  M      1982
      95  M      1972
```

The third subquery is used to search the intermediate result for all the rows of which the year of joining the club is greater than 1980. Also the JOINED column is not included in the intermediate result because the table expression on top does not need it. The intermediate result is:

```
PLAYERNO  SEX
--------  ---
      27  F
      28  F
      57  M
      83  M
```

Finally, this intermediate result is searched for the rows in which the SEX column is equal to `M`.

MySQL distinguishes four types of subqueries. The difference among these four is determined by the result of the subquery. The previous subqueries are all *table subqueries* because the result of each subquery is a set of rows. In addition, we have the *row*, the *column*, and the *scalar subquery*. The result of a row subquery is one row with one or more values. The result of a column subquery is a set of rows in which each row consists of just one value. The scalar subquery has only one row, consisting of one value as result. This means that each scalar subquery is, by definition, a row subquery and a column subquery as well, but not vice versa; not every row or column subquery is a scalar subquery. It also holds that each row and each column subquery is a table subquery, but not vice versa.

Column subqueries are not discussed until Chapter 8, "SELECT Statement: The WHERE Clause." For now, we just give a few examples of scalar and row subqueries.

Example 6.8: For each player whose number is less than 60, get the number of years between the year in which that player joined the club and that of player 100.

```
SELECT   PLAYERNO, JOINED -
                   (SELECT   JOINED
                    FROM     PLAYERS
                    WHERE    PLAYERNO = 100)
FROM     PLAYERS
WHERE    PLAYERNO < 60
```

The result is:

```
PLAYERNO  JOINED  - (...
--------  -------------
       2             -4
       6             -2
       7              2
       8              1
      27              4
      28              4
      39              1
      44              1
      57              6
```

Explanation: In this statement, the subquery has been placed inside the SELECT clause. The result of this scalar subquery is 1979. After this result has been determined, the following simple SELECT statement is executed:

```
SELECT   PLAYERNO, JOINED - 1979
FROM     PLAYERS
WHERE    PLAYERNO < 60
```

The scalar subquery has to return zero or one row. If the subquery returns more than one row, MySQL responds with an error message. Therefore, the next statement will not work because the subquery returns too many rows:

```
SELECT    TEAMNO
FROM      TEAMS
WHERE     PLAYERNO =
         (SELECT    PLAYERNO
          FROM      PLAYERS)
```

Almost everywhere a scalar expression can be specified, a scalar subquery can be used.

Example 6.9: Get the numbers of the players who were born in the same year as player 27.

```
SELECT    PLAYERNO
FROM      PLAYERS
WHERE     YEAR(BIRTH_DATE) = (SELECT    YEAR(BIRTH_DATE)
                              FROM      PLAYERS
                              WHERE     PLAYERNO = 27)
```

The result is:

```
PLAYERNO
--------
       6
      27
```

Explanation: The subquery looks for the year of birth of player 27. The result is one row consisting of one value. In other words, this really is a scalar subquery. That one value is `1964`. Next, the following `SELECT` statement is executed:

```
SELECT    PLAYERNO
FROM      PLAYERS
WHERE     YEAR(BIRTH_DATE) = 1964
```

Player 27 appears in the end result as well, of course. If that is not the intention, the `WHERE` clause can be expanded with the condition `AND PLAYERNO <> 27`.

Example 6.10: Get the date of birth of players 27, 44, and 100 as one row (next to each other).

```
SELECT   (SELECT   BIRTH_DATE
          FROM     PLAYERS
          WHERE    PLAYERNO = 27),
         (SELECT   BIRTH_DATE
          FROM     PLAYERS
          WHERE    PLAYERNO = 44),
         (SELECT   BIRTH_DATE
          FROM     PLAYERS
          WHERE    PLAYERNO = 100)
```

The result is:

```
SELECT(... SELECT(... SELECT(...
---------- ---------- ----------
1964-12-28 1963-01-09 1963-02-28
```

Explanation: Using the three scalar subqueries on the position of scalar expressions within a SELECT clause produces the desired result.

Example 6.11: Get the numbers of the players who have the same sex as and live in the same town as player 100.

```
SELECT   PLAYERNO
FROM     PLAYERS
WHERE    (SEX, TOWN) = (SELECT   SEX, TOWN
                        FROM     PLAYERS
                        WHERE    PLAYERNO = 100)
```

The result is:

```
PLAYERNO
--------
       2
       6
       7
      39
      57
      83
     100
```

Explanation: The result of the subquery is one row with two values: ('M', 'Stratford'). This row value is compared to the row expression: (SEX, TOWN). See Sections 5.3 and 5.15 for descriptions of row expressions.

Exercise 6.10: Get the numbers of the committee members who were secretary of the tennis club between January 1, 1990, and December 31, 1994; use subqueries here.

Exercise 6.11: Get the numbers of the teams of which the player with the name Parmenter and initial R is captain; in this example, we assume that no two players have the same name and initials.

Exercise 6.12: Get the name of the player who is captain of the team for which match 6 was played.

Exercise 6.13: Get the numbers of the penalties that are higher than the penalties with payment number 4.

Exercise 6.14: Get the numbers of the players who were born on the same day (for example, Monday or Tuesday) as player 2.

Exercise 6.15: Get the numbers of the committee members who took up a position and who resigned that same position on the same day that player 8 took on and resigned his position as treasurer. Player 8 cannot appear in the end result.

Exercise 6.16: Get the divisions of teams 1 and 2, and place them next to each other.

Exercise 6.17 What is the sum of the penalties with payment numbers 1, 2, and 3?

6.7 Answers

6.1

1. This statement is a SELECT statement and also a table expression. However, it is not a head part of a select block because an ORDER BY clause belongs to the tail part of a select block.
2. This statement is a SELECT statement, a table expression, and the head part of a select block.
3. This statement is not a SELECT statement, but a CREATE VIEW statement. From the word SELECT, it actually is a table expression and also the head part of a select block.

6.2 The statement is a table expression; the ORDER BY clause is the tail part.

6.3 A SELECT statement consists of at least one clause, and that is the SELECT clause.

6.4 Yes.

6.5 Yes, a SELECT statement without GROUP BY clause may have a HAVING clause.

6.6 1. No FROM clause exists.

2. The GROUP BY clause must be specified in front of the HAVING clause.

3. The ORDER BY clause should be the last clause.

6.7 The FROM clause:

```
PAYMENTNO  PLAYERNO  PAYMENT_DATE      AMOUNT
---------  --------  ------------  ----------
        1         6  1980-12-08        100.00
        2        44  1981-05-05         75.00
        3        27  1983-09-10        100.00
        4       104  1984-12-08         50.00
        5        44  1980-12-08         25.00
        6         8  1980-12-08         25.00
        7        44  1982-12-30         30.00
        8        27  1984-11-12         75.00
```

The WHERE clause:

```
PAYMENTNO  PLAYERNO  PAYMENT_DATE      AMOUNT
---------  --------  ------------  ----------
        2        44  1981-05-05         75.00
        3        27  1983-09-10        100.00
        4       104  1984-12-08         50.00
        7        44  1982-12-30         30.00
        8        27  1984-11-12         75.00
```

The GROUP BY clause:

```
PAYMENTNO  PLAYERNO  PAYMENT_DATE              AMOUNT
---------  --------  ------------------------  ---------------
{2, 7}           44  {1981-05-05, 1982-12-30}  {75.00, 30.00}
{3, 8}           27  {1983-09-10, 1984-11-12}  {100.00, 75.00}
{4}             104  {1984-12-08}              {50.00}
```

The HAVING clause:

```
PAYMENTNO  PLAYERNO  PAYMENT_DATE              AMOUNT
---------  --------  ------------------------  ---------------
{2, 7}           44  {1981-05-05, 1982-12-30}  {75.00, 30.00}
{3, 8}           27  {1983-09-10, 1984-11-12}  {100.00, 75.00}
```

The ORDER BY clause:

```
PAYMENTNO  PLAYERNO  PAYMENT_DATE              AMOUNT
---------  --------  ------------------------  ---------------
{3, 8}           27  {1983-09-10, 1984-11-12}  {100.00, 75.00}
{2, 7}           44  {1981-05-05, 1982-12-30}  {75.00, 30.00}
```

```
The SELECT clause:
PLAYERNO
--------
      27
      44
```

6.8
```
SELECT   PLAYERNO, BEGIN_DATE
FROM     COMMITTEE_MEMBERS
UNION
SELECT   PLAYERNO, END_DATE
FROM     COMMITTEE_MEMBERS
RDER BY PLAYERNO
```

6.9
```
SELECT   PLAYERNO, BEGIN_DATE, 'Begin date'
FROM     COMMITTEE_MEMBERS
UNION
SELECT   PLAYERNO, END_DATE, 'End date'
FROM     COMMITTEE_MEMBERS
ORDER BY PLAYERNO
```

6.10
```
SELECT  PLAYERNO
FROM   (SELECT  PLAYERNO
        FROM   (SELECT  PLAYERNO, END_DATE
                FROM   (SELECT  PLAYERNO, BEGIN_DATE,
                                END_DATE
                        FROM    COMMITTEE_MEMBERS
                        WHERE   POSITION = 'Secretary')
                        AS SECRETARIES
                WHERE   BEGIN_DATE >= '1990-01-01')
                AS AFTER1989
        WHERE   END_DATE <= '1994-12-31') AS BEFORE1995
```

6.11
```
SELECT   TEAMNO
FROM     TEAMS
WHERE    PLAYERNO =
        (SELECT   PLAYERNO
         FROM     PLAYERS
         WHERE    NAME = 'Parmenter'
         AND      INITIALS = 'R')
```

6.12
```
SELECT   TEAMNO
FROM     TEAMS
WHERE    PLAYERNO =
        (SELECT   PLAYERNO
         FROM     PLAYERS
         WHERE    NAME =
                 (SELECT   NAME
                  FROM     PLAYERS
                  WHERE    PLAYERNO = 6)
         AND      PLAYERNO <> 6)
```

or

```
SELECT   NAME
FROM     PLAYERS
WHERE    PLAYERNO =
        (SELECT   PLAYERNO
         FROM     TEAMS
         WHERE    TEAMNO =
                 (SELECT   TEAMNO
                  FROM     MATCHES
                  WHERE    MATCHNO = 6))
```

6.13
```
SELECT   PAYMENTNO
FROM     PENALTIES
WHERE    AMOUNT >
        (SELECT   AMOUNT
         FROM     PENALTIES
         WHERE    PAYMENTNO = 4)
```

6.14
```
SELECT   PLAYERNO
FROM     PLAYERS
WHERE    DAYNAME(BIRTH_DATE) =
        (SELECT   DAYNAME(BIRTH_DATE)
         FROM     PLAYERS
         WHERE    PLAYERNO = 2)
```

6.15
```
SELECT   PLAYERNO
FROM     COMMITTEE_MEMBERS
WHERE   (BEGIN_DATE, END_DATE) =
        (SELECT   BEGIN_DATE, END_DATE
         FROM     COMMITTEE_MEMBERS
         WHERE    PLAYERNO = 8
         AND      POSITION = 'Treasurer')
AND      PLAYERNO <> 8
```

6.16
```
SELECT  (SELECT   DIVISION
         FROM     TEAMS
         WHERE    TEAMNO = 1),
        (SELECT   DIVISION
         FROM     TEAMS
         WHERE    TEAMNO = 2)
```

6.17
```
SELECT  (SELECT   AMOUNT
         FROM     PENALTIES
         WHERE    PAYMENTNO = 1) +
        (SELECT   AMOUNT
         FROM     PENALTIES
         WHERE    PAYMENTNO = 2) +
        (SELECT   AMOUNT
         FROM     PENALTIES
         WHERE    PAYMENTNO = 3)
```

CHAPTER 7

SELECT Statement: The FROM Clause

7.1 Introduction

If a table expression contains a FROM clause, the processing starts with this clause. In fact, in this case, it is the starting point of processing a table expression, which is why we discuss this clause in detail first.

This chapter describes the basic features of the FROM clause. In previous chapters, you saw many examples of this clause. The FROM clause is an important clause because each table from which we "use" columns in the other clauses should be specified here. By "using," we mean, for example, that a column appears in a condition or in the SELECT clause. Simply, in the FROM clause, we specify the tables from which the result of a table expression is retrieved.

The FROM clause has many different forms. This chapter starts with the simplest form.

7.2 Table Specifications in the FROM Clause

The FROM clause is used for specifying which tables are to be queried. This is done with *table references*. A table reference consists of a table specification possibly followed by a pseudonym. This section discusses table specifications; later sections cover pseudonyms.

DEFINITION

```
from clause> ::=
   FROM <table reference> [ , <table reference> ]...

<table reference> ::=
   <table specification> [ [ AS ] <pseudonym> ]

<table specification> ::= [ <database name> . ] <table name>

<pseudonym> ::= <name>
```

A table specification normally consists of the name of a table, but you can also specify the name of a view. In both cases, we use the term *table specification.*

Each table is stored in a database. You can refer to a table in two ways. First, you can make a database the current one by using a USE statement. In that case, if a table name is specified in the FROM clause, that table should belong to the current database. Second, you can explicitly extend the table specification with the name of the database to which the table belongs. This feature also enables us to access tables that are part of the current database.

Example 7.1: Create a new database called EXTRA with a new table called CITIES.

```
CREATE DATABASE EXTRA

USE EXTRA

CREATE TABLE CITIES
      (CITYNO      INTEGER NOT NULL PRIMARY KEY,
       CITYNAME    CHAR(20) NOT NULL)

INSERT INTO CITIES VALUES
   (1, 'Stratford')

INSERT INTO CITIES VALUES
   (2, 'Inglewood')
```

Explanation: Do not forget to change the current database into EXTRA with the USE statement after the CREATE DATABASE statement.

Example 7.2: Show the entire contents of the CITIES table; assume that TENNIS is the current database.

```
SELECT   *
FROM     EXTRA.CITIES
```

Explanation: The compound name `EXTRA.CITIES` is the table specification. (Note the full stop between the name of the database and the table name; this full stop is mandatory.) We say that the table name CITIES is *qualified* with the database name EXTRA.

In fact, a table name can always be qualified, even when a table from the current database is queried.

Example 7.3: Show the contents of the TEAMS table.

```
SELECT    *
FROM      TENNIS.TEAMS
```

7.3 Again, the Column Specification

In the previous section, you saw that a table can be qualified with the name of the database. When specifying columns (in the `SELECT` clause, for example), you can also qualify them by specifying the table to which the columns belong. In fact, each column specification consists of three parts; see the definition.

DEFINITION

```
<column specification> ::=
   [ <table specification> . ] <column name>

<table specification> ::=
   [ <database name> . ] <table name>
```

The last part is, of course, the column name itself, such as PLAYERNO or NAME. This is the only mandatory part. The second part is the table name, such as PLAYERS or TEAMS. The first one is the name of the database. You do not have to specify all these parts, but it is not wrong to do so.

Example 7.4: Find the number of each team. Here are three possible solutions; assume that the TEAMS table is stored in the TENNIS database.

```
SELECT    TEAMNO
FROM      TEAMS
```

and

```
SELECT    TEAMS.TEAMNO
FROM      TEAMS
```

and

```
SELECT    TENNIS.TEAMS.TEAMNO
FROM      TENNIS.TEAMS
```

7.4 Multiple Table Specifications in the FROM Clause

Until now, we have used only one table specification in the FROM clause. If you want to present data from different tables in our result table, you must specify multiple tables in the FROM clause.

Example 7.5: Get the team number and the name of the captain of each team.

The TEAMS table holds information about team numbers and the player numbers of each team. However, the names of the captains are stored not in the TEAMS table, but in the PLAYERS table. In other words, we need both tables. Both must be mentioned in the FROM clause.

```
SELECT    TEAMNO, NAME
FROM      TEAMS, PLAYERS
WHERE     TEAMS.PLAYERNO = PLAYERS.PLAYERNO
```

The intermediate result of the FROM clause is:

```
TEAMNO  PLAYERNO  DIVISION  PLAYERNO  NAME         ...
------  --------  --------  --------  ---------    ---
     1         6  first            6  Parmenter    ...
     1         6  first           44  Baker        ...
     1         6  first           83  Hope         ...
     1         6  first            2  Everett      ...
     1         6  first           27  Collins      ...
     1         6  first          104  Moorman      ...
     1         6  first            7  Wise         ...
     1         6  first           57  Brown        ...
     1         6  first           39  Bishop       ...
     1         6  first          112  Bailey       ...
     1         6  first            8  Newcastle    ...
     1         6  first          100  Parmenter    ...
     1         6  first           28  Collins      ...
     1         6  first           95  Miller       ...
     2        27  second           6  Parmenter    ...
     2        27  second          44  Baker        ...
     2        27  second          83  Hope         ...
     2        27  second           2  Everett      ...
     2        27  second          27  Collins      ...
```

```
2       27  second         104  Moorman    ...
2       27  second           7  Wise       ...
2       27  second          57  Brown      ...
2       27  second          39  Bishop     ...
2       27  second         112  Bailey     ...
2       27  second           8  Newcastle  ...
2       27  second         100  Parmenter  ...
2       27  second          28  Collins    ...
2       27  second          95  Miller     ...
```

Explanation: Each row of the PLAYERS table is aligned "beside" each row of the TEAMS table. This results in a table in which the total number of columns equals the number of columns in one table *plus* the number of columns in the other table, and in which the total number of rows equals the number of rows in one table *multiplied* by the number of rows in the other table. We call this result the *Cartesian product* of the tables concerned.

In the `WHERE` clause, each row where the value in the TEAMS.PLAYERNO column equals the one in the PLAYERS.PLAYERNO column is selected:

```
TEAMNO  PLAYERNO  DIVISION  PLAYERNO  NAME       ...
------  --------  --------  --------  ---------  ---
     1         6  first            6  Parmenter  ...
     2        27  second          27  Collins    ...
```

The end result is:

```
TEAMNO  NAME
------  ---------
     1  Parmenter
     2  Collins
```

In this example, it is essential to specify the table name in front of the PLAYERNO column. Without qualifying the column name, it would be impossible for MySQL to determine which column was intended.

Conclusion: If you use a column name that appears in more than one table specified in the `FROM` clause, you *must* include a table specification with the column specification.

Example 7.6: For each penalty, find the payment number, the amount of the penalty, the player number, the name, and the initials of the player who incurred the penalty.

The PENALTIES table contains the payment numbers, the amounts, and the player numbers; the PLAYERS table contains the names and initials. Both tables must be included in the FROM clause:

```
SELECT   PAYMENTNO, PENALTIES.PLAYERNO, AMOUNT,
         NAME, INITIALS
FROM     PENALTIES, PLAYERS
WHERE    PENALTIES.PLAYERNO = PLAYERS.PLAYERNO
```

The intermediate result from the FROM clause is (not all the rows have been included):

```
PAYMENTNO PLAYERNO AMOUNT ... PLAYERNO NAME      INITIALS  ...
--------- -------- ------ --- -------- --------- --------  ---
        1        6 100.00 ...        6 Parmenter R         ...
        1        6 100.00 ...       44 Baker     E         ...
        1        6 100.00 ...       83 Hope      PK        ...
        1        6 100.00 ...        2 Everett   R         ...
        :        :      :            : :         :
        2       44  75.00 ...        6 Parmenter R         ...
        2       44  75.00 ...       44 Baker     E         ...
        2       44  75.00 ...       83 Hope      PK        ...
        2       44  75.00 ...        2 Everett   R         ...
        :        :      :            : :         :
        3       27 100.00 ...        6 Parmenter R         ...
        3       27 100.00 ...       44 Baker     E         ...
        3       27 100.00 ...       83 Hope      PK        ...
        3       27 100.00 ...        2 Everett   R         ...
        :        :      :            : :         :
        :        :      :            : :         :
```

The intermediate result after processing the FROM clause is:

```
PAYMENTNO PLAYERNO AMOUNT ... PLAYERNO NAME      INITIALS  ...
--------- -------- ------ --- -------- --------- --------  ---
        1        6 100.00 ...        6 Parmenter R         ...
        2       44  75.00 ...       44 Baker     E         ...
        3       27 100.00 ...       27 Collins   DD        ...
        4      104  50.00 ...      104 Moorman   D         ...
        5       44  25.00 ...       44 Baker     E         ...
        6        8  25.00 ...        8 Newcastle B         ...
        7       44  30.00 ...       44 Baker     E         ...
        8       27  75.00 ...       27 Collins   DD        ...
```

The end result is:

```
PAYMENTNO  PLAYERNO  AMOUNT  NAME       INITIALS
---------  --------  ------  ---------  --------
        1         6  100.00  Parmenter  R
        2        44   75.00  Baker      E
        3        27  100.00  Collins    DD
        4       104   50.00  Moorman    D
        5        44   25.00  Baker      E
        6         8   25.00  Newcastle  B
        7        44   30.00  Baker      E
        8        27   75.00  Collins    DD
```

To avoid ambiguity, the table name must be specified in front of the PLAYERNO column in the SELECT clause.

The order of the table specifications in a FROM clause does not affect the result of this clause and the end result of the table expression. The SELECT clause is the only clause that determines the order of the columns in the result. The ORDER BY clause determines the order in which rows are presented. Thus, the results of the next two statements are equal:

```
SELECT   PLAYERS.PLAYERNO
FROM     PLAYERS, TEAMS
WHERE    PLAYERS.PLAYERNO = TEAMS.PLAYERNO
```

and

```
SELECT   PLAYERS.PLAYERNO
FROM     TEAMS, PLAYERS
WHERE    PLAYERS.PLAYERNO = TEAMS.PLAYERNO
```

Exercise 7.1: Indicate why these SELECT statements are not correctly formulated:

1. ```
   SELECT   PLAYERNO
   FROM     PLAYERS, TEAMS
   ```
2. ```
   SELECT   PLAYERS.PLAYERNO
   FROM     TEAMS
   ```

Exercise 7.2: For each clause of the following statement, determine the intermediate result and the result. Also give a description of the question that underlies the statement.

```
SELECT   PLAYERS.NAME
FROM     TEAMS, PLAYERS
WHERE    PLAYERS.PLAYERNO = TEAMS.PLAYERNO
```

Exercise 7.3: For each penalty, find the payment number, the amount, and the number and name of the player who incurred it.

Exercise 7.4: For each penalty incurred by a team captain, find the payment number and the captain's name.

7.5 Pseudonyms for Table Names

When multiple table specifications appear in the FROM clause, it is sometimes easier to use so-called *pseudonyms.* Another name for a pseudonym is an *alias.* Pseudonyms are temporary alternative names for table names. In the previous examples, to qualify a column, you specified the full table name. Instead of using table names, you can use pseudonyms.

Example 7.7: For each penalty, get the payment number, the amount of the penalty, the player number, and the name and initials of the player who incurred the penalty. Use pseudonyms.

```
SELECT   PAYMENTNO, PEN.PLAYERNO, AMOUNT,
         NAME, INITIALS
FROM     PENALTIES AS PEN, PLAYERS AS P
WHERE    PEN.PLAYERNO = P.PLAYERNO
```

Explanation: In the FROM clause, the pseudonyms are specified or declared after the table names. In other clauses, you must use these pseudonyms instead of the real table names.

Because pseudonyms have been used, it is *not* possible to mention the original table names in the other clauses anymore. The presence of a pseudonym implies that a table name cannot be used in this SQL statement.

The fact that the pseudonym PEN has been used earlier in the statement (in the SELECT clause) than its declaration (in the FROM clause) does not cause any problems. As you have seen, the FROM clause might not be the first clause specified, but it is the first processed.

The word AS in the definition is optional. So the previous statement has the same result as the following:

```
SELECT    PAYMENTNO, PEN.PLAYERNO, AMOUNT,
          NAME, INITIALS
FROM      PENALTIES PEN, PLAYERS P
WHERE     PEN.PLAYERNO = P.PLAYERNO
```

In both examples, the use of pseudonyms is not vital. However, later this book discusses how to formulate SELECT statements when table names would have to be repeated many times. Adding pseudonyms makes it easier to formulate and read those statements.

A pseudonym must satisfy the naming rules for table names. More about this subject arises in Section 20.8. Additionally, you are not allowed to define two identical pseudonyms in a FROM clause.

Exercise 7.5: For each team, get the number and the last name of the captain.

Exercise 7.6: For each match, get the match number, the last name of the player, and the division of the team.

7.6 Various Examples of Joins

This section looks at some examples to illustrate various aspects of the FROM clause. It also introduces several new terms.

Example 7.8: Get the numbers of the captains who have incurred at least one penalty.

```
SELECT    T.PLAYERNO
FROM      TEAMS AS T, PENALTIES AS PEN
WHERE     T.PLAYERNO = PEN.PLAYERNO
```

Explanation: The TEAMS table includes all the players who are captains. By using the player numbers, we can search the PENALTIES table for those captains who have incurred at least one penalty. For that reason, both tables are included in the FROM clause. The intermediate result from the FROM clause becomes:

```
TEAMNO  PLAYERNO  DIVISION  PAYMENTNO  PLAYERNO  ...
------  --------  --------  ---------  --------  ---
     1         6  first             1         6  ...
     1         6  first             2        44  ...
     1         6  first             3        27  ...
     1         6  first             4       104  ...
     1         6  first             5        44  ...
     1         6  first             6         8  ...
     1         6  first             7        44  ...
     1         6  first             8        27  ...
     2        27  second            1         6  ...
     2        27  second            2        44  ...
     2        27  second            3        27  ...
     2        27  second            4       104  ...
     2        27  second            5        44  ...
     2        27  second            6         8  ...
     2        27  second            7        44  ...
     2        27  second            8        27  ...
```

The intermediate result from the WHERE clause is:

```
TEAMNO  PLAYERNO  DIVISION  PAYMENTNO  PLAYERNO  ...
------  --------  --------  ---------  --------  ---
     1         6  first             1         6  ...
     2        27  second            3        27  ...
     2        27  second            8        27  ...
```

The end result is thus:

```
PLAYERNO
--------
       6
      27
      27
```

When data of different tables is merged into one table, it is called a *join* of tables. The columns on which the join is executed are called the *join columns*. In the previous SELECT statement, these are the columns TEAMS.PLAYERNO and PENALTIES.PLAYERNO. The condition in the WHERE clause, with which we compare the PLAYERNO column of the TEAMS table with the one of the PENALTIES table, is called the *join condition*.

Note that the result of the earlier statement contains duplicate rows. MySQL does not automatically remove duplicate rows from the end result. In our example, player 27 appears twice because she incurred two penalties. When you do not want duplicate rows in your result, you should specify the word DISTINCT directly behind the word SELECT (Chapter 9, "SELECT Statement: SELECT Clause and Aggregation Functions," discusses DISTINCT extensively).

Example 7.9: Get the numbers of the captains who have incurred at least one penalty. Remove the duplicate numbers.

```
SELECT   DISTINCT T.PLAYERNO
FROM     TEAMS AS T, PENALTIES AS PEN
WHERE    T.PLAYERNO = PEN.PLAYERNO
```

The end result then becomes:

```
PLAYERNO
--------
       6
      27
```

Example 7.10: Get the names and initials of the players who have played at least one match. *Note:* A competition player does not have to appear in the MATCHES table (perhaps he or she has been injured for the whole season).

```
SELECT   DISTINCT P.NAME, P.INITIALS
FROM     PLAYERS AS P, MATCHES AS M
WHERE    P.PLAYERNO = M.PLAYERNO
```

The result is:

```
NAME       INITIALS
---------  --------
Parmenter  R
Baker      E
Hope       PK
Everett    R
Collins    DD
Moorman    D
Brown      M
Bailey     IP
Newcastle  B
```

Work out for yourself how this `SELECT` statement could give rise to duplicate values if `DISTINCT` is not used.

A join is not restricted to two tables. A `FROM` clause can contain many tables.

Example 7.11: For each match, get the match number, the player number, the team number, the name of the player, and the division in which the team plays.

```
SELECT   M.MATCHNO, M.PLAYERNO, M.TEAMNO, P.NAME, T.DIVISION
FROM     MATCHES AS M, PLAYERS AS P, TEAMS AS T
WHERE    M.PLAYERNO = P.PLAYERNO
AND      M.TEAMNO = T.TEAMNO
```

The result is:

```
MATCHNO  PLAYERNO  TEAMNO  NAME       DIVISION
-------  --------  ------  ---------  --------
      1         6       1  Parmenter  first
      2         6       1  Parmenter  first
      3         6       1  Parmenter  first
      4        44       1  Baker      first
      5        83       1  Hope       first
      6         2       1  Everett    first
      7        57       1  Brown      first
      8         8       1  Newcastle  first
      9        27       2  Collins    second
     10       104       2  Moorman    second
     11       112       2  Bailey     second
     12       112       2  Bailey     second
     13         8       2  Newcastle  second
```

Example 7.12: Get the payment number, the player number, and the date of each penalty incurred in the year in which the player concerned joined the club.

```
SELECT   PEN.PAYMENTNO, PEN.PLAYERNO, PEN.PAYMENT_DATE
FROM     PENALTIES AS PEN, PLAYERS AS P
WHERE    PEN.PLAYERNO = P.PLAYERNO
AND      YEAR(PEN.PAYMENT_DATE) = P.JOINED
```

The result is:

```
PAYMENTNO  PLAYERNO  PEN.PAYMENT_DATE
---------  --------  ----------------
        3        27  1983-09-10
        4       104  1984-12-08
        5        44  1980-12-08
        6         8  1980-12-08
```

Explanation: Most join conditions compare key columns with each other. However, that is not a requirement. In this example, the date on which the penalty was paid is compared to the year in which the player joined the club.

Exercise 7.7: Get the numbers and names of players who have been chairman.

Exercise 7.8: Get the number of each player who incurred a penalty on the same day that he became a committee member.

7.7 Mandatory Use of Pseudonyms

In some SELECT statements, you have no choice about whether a pseudonym is to be used. This situation arises when the same table is mentioned more than once in the FROM clause. Consider this example.

Example 7.13: Get the numbers of the players who are older than R. Parmenter; in this example, assume that the combination of name and initials is unique.

```
SELECT   P.PLAYERNO
FROM     PLAYERS AS P, PLAYERS AS PAR
WHERE    PAR.NAME = 'Parmenter'
AND      PAR.INITIALS = 'R'
AND      P.BIRTH_DATE < PAR.BIRTH_DATE
```

The intermediate result from the WHERE clause is a multiplication of the PLAYERS table by itself (for simplicity, we have shown only the rows from the PAR.PLAYERS table in which player 6, named R. Parmenter, is found).

```
PLAYERNO  ...  BIRTH_DATE  ...  PLAYERNO  ...  BIRTH_DATE  ...
--------  ---  ----------  ---  --------  ---  ----------  ---
       6  ...  1964-06-25  ...         6  ...  1964-06-25  ...
      44  ...  1963-01-09  ...         6  ...  1964-06-25  ...
      83  ...  1956-11-11  ...         6  ...  1964-06-25  ...
       2  ...  1948-09-01  ...         6  ...  1964-06-25  ...
      27  ...  1964-12-28  ...         6  ...  1964-06-25  ...
     104  ...  1970-05-10  ...         6  ...  1964-06-25  ...
       7  ...  1963-05-11  ...         6  ...  1964-06-25  ...
      57  ...  1971-08-17  ...         6  ...  1964-06-25  ...
      39  ...  1956-10-29  ...         6  ...  1964-06-25  ...
     112  ...  1963-10-01  ...         6  ...  1964-06-25  ...
       8  ...  1962-07-08  ...         6  ...  1964-06-25  ...
     100  ...  1963-02-28  ...         6  ...  1964-06-25  ...
      28  ...  1963-06-22  ...         6  ...  1964-06-25  ...
      95  ...  1963-05-14  ...         6  ...  1964-06-25  ...
       :   :   :            :          :   :   :            :
       :   :   :            :          :   :   :            :
```

The intermediate result of the WHERE clause is:

```
PLAYERNO  ...  BIRTH_DATE  ...  PLAYERNO  ...  BIRTH_DATE  ...
--------  ---  ----------  ---  --------  ---  ----------  ---
      44  ...  1963-01-09  ...         6  ...  1964-06-25  ...
      83  ...  1956-11-11  ...         6  ...  1964-06-25  ...
       2  ...  1948-09-01  ...         6  ...  1964-06-25  ...
       7  ...  1963-05-11  ...         6  ...  1964-06-25  ...
      39  ...  1956-10-29  ...         6  ...  1964-06-25  ...
     112  ...  1963-10-01  ...         6  ...  1964-06-25  ...
       8  ...  1962-07-08  ...         6  ...  1964-06-25  ...
     100  ...  1963-02-28  ...         6  ...  1964-06-25  ...
      28  ...  1963-06-22  ...         6  ...  1964-06-25  ...
      95  ...  1963-05-14  ...         6  ...  1964-06-25  ...
```

The end result is:

```
PLAYERNO
--------
      44
      83
       2
       7
      39
     112
       8
     100
      28
      95
```

In the previous examples, table names were specified in front of column names to identify columns uniquely. That would not help in the previous example because both tables have the same name. In other words, if a FROM clause refers to two tables with the same name, pseudonyms *must* be used.

Note that it would have been sufficient to assign only one of the two tables a pseudonym in the earlier example:

```
SELECT   P.PLAYERNO
FROM     PLAYERS AS P, PLAYERS
WHERE    PLAYERS.NAME = 'Parmenter'
AND      PLAYERS.INITIALS = 'R'
AND      P.BIRTH_DATE < PLAYERS.BIRTH_DATE
```

Exercise 7.9: Get the numbers and names of the players who live in the same town as player 27. Player 27 should not appear in the end result.

Exercise 7.10: Get the number and name of every competition player, as well as the number and name of the captain of each team for which that player has ever competed. The result may *not* contain competition players who are themselves captains of a team. Desired result:

```
PLAYERNO  NAME (PLAYERS)  PLAYERNO  NAME (CAPTAIN)
--------  --------------  --------  --------------
      44  Baker                  6  Parmenter
       8  Newcastle              6  Parmenter
       8  Newcastle             27  Collins
       :  :                      :  :
       :  :                      :  :
```

Exercise 7.11: Get the numbers of the penalties for which the penalty amount is equal to a penalty amount belonging to player 44. The result should not contain the penalties of player 44.

7.8 Tables of Different Databases

In one SELECT statement, tables of different databases may be joined. That makes it necessary to qualify the tables that do not belong to the current database.

Example 7.14: Link the PLAYERS table to the CITIES table from the EXTRA database.

```
SELECT   P.PLAYERNO
FROM     PLAYERS AS P, EXTRA.CITIES AS TOWN
WHERE    P.TOWN = TOWN.CITYNAME
```

The result is:

```
PLAYERNO
--------
       2
       6
       7
       8
      39
      44
      57
      83
     100
```

Explanation: The CITIES table is qualified with the EXTRA database. This statement does not change the current database.

7.9 Explicit Joins in the FROM Clause

So far, we have talked about the concept of joins, but you have not seen the word JOIN in the table expression yet. The reason is that, until now, we have shown only examples in which the join is "hidden" in the SELECT statement. Sometimes this join is referred to as an *implicit join.* In this case, a join is then made up of several specifications from the FROM clause (the table specifications), together with one or more conditions from the WHERE clause.

Explicitly adding the join to the SELECT statement started in the SQL2 standard. This new *explicit join* is entirely specified in the FROM clause, resulting in a considerable increase in features of this clause. The effect is that it is much easier to formulate certain statements. The extended definition of the FROM clause is shown next. Most important in this definition is that a table reference is not restricted to a simple table specification but can form a complete join.

DEFINITION

```
<from clause> ::=
   FROM <table reference> [ , <table reference> ]...

<table reference> ::=
   table specification> [ [ AS ] <pseudonym> ] |
   <join specification>                         |
   ( <join specification> )

<join specification> ::=
   <table reference> <join type> <table reference>
      [ <join condition> ]

<join condition> ::=
    ON <condition> | USING <column list>

<join type> ::=
   [ INNER ] JOIN                               |
   LEFT  [ OUTER ] JOIN                         |
   RIGHT [ OUTER ] JOIN                         |
   NATURAL [ LEFT | RIGHT ] [ OUTER ] JOIN      |
   CROSS JOIN

<column list> ::=
   ( <column name> [ , <column name> ]... )
```

According to this definition, the following FROM clause is correct:

```
FROM     PLAYERS INNER JOIN PENALTIES
         ON (PLAYERS.PLAYERNO = PENALTIES.PLAYERNO)
```

In this example, PLAYERS and PENALTIES are the tables to be joined, and the join condition is placed between brackets after the word ON. The type of join that must be performed is the *inner join*. Consider the meaning of these specifications with an example.

Example 7.15: For each player born after June 1920, find the player number, the name, and the penalty amounts incurred by him or her.

Previous chapters showed that we can answer this question with the following formulation:

```
SELECT   PLAYERS.PLAYERNO, NAME, AMOUNT
FROM     PLAYERS, PENALTIES
WHERE    PLAYERS.PLAYERNO = PENALTIES.PLAYERNO
AND      BIRTH_DATE > '1920-06-30'
```

This has the following result:

```
PLAYERNO  NAME       AMOUNT
--------  ---------  ------
       6  Parmenter  100.00
      44  Baker       75.00
      27  Collins    100.00
     104  Moorman     50.00
      44  Baker       25.00
       8  Newcastle   25.00
      44  Baker       30.00
      27  Collins     75.00
```

This statement also has a "hidden" join. The specifications that together form the join are spread out over the FROM and WHERE clauses. With the new definition of the FROM clause, this join can be presented explicitly; for this, use the FROM clause already given:

```
SELECT   PLAYERS.PLAYERNO, NAME, AMOUNT
FROM     PLAYERS INNER JOIN PENALTIES
         ON (PLAYERS.PLAYERNO = PENALTIES.PLAYERNO)
WHERE    BIRTH_DATE > '1920-06-30'
```

This statement leads to the same result as the previous one; the difference is that now, during the processing of the FROM clause, much more work is done. In the first formulation, the (intermediate) result of the FROM clause is equal to the *Cartesian product* of the two specified tables (see also Section 7.4). For the second formulation, the result is the Cartesian product to which the condition already has been applied. For the processing of the WHERE clause, less work has to be done.

Both statements return the same result, but it is not the desired result. These SELECT statements return only the player number and the name of each player who has incurred at least one penalty; they are missing the players without penalties. That brings us to the specification INNER JOIN. Because MySQL is presenting only data about the players in both the tables PLAYERS and PENALTIES, this join is called an *inner* join. Only those players who appear in the intersection of the sets of the two join columns are included in the end result.

Whether an inner join does or does not give what we want depends entirely, on one hand, on the question and, on the other hand, on the relationship between the join columns. In the previous example, we lose players (from the PLAYERS table) because the sets of the two join columns are not equal; one is a subset of the other. Had the question in the previous example been "For each player who incurred at least one penalty, find the player number…," the formulation of the statement would have been correct.

A certain type of relationship always exists between join columns. "Being a subset of" is just one possibility. Four types of relationships are possible. When a join is specified, it is very important to know what the type of relationship is because it has a serious influence on the result of the SELECT statement in which the join appears.

If C_1 and C_2 are two columns, the four types of relationships between C_1 and C_2 are as follows:

1. The populations of C_1 and C_2 are *equal.*
2. The population of C_1 is a *subset* of the population C_2 (or C_2 is a subset of C_1).
3. The populations of C_1 and C_2 are *conjoint* (they have some values in common).
4. The populations of C_1 and C_2 are *disjoint* (they have no values in common).

Example 7.16: For each team, find the team number and the name of the captain.

With the help of an implicit join:

```
SELECT   TEAMNO, NAME
FROM     TEAMS, PLAYERS
WHERE    TEAMS.PLAYERNO = PLAYERS.PLAYERNO
```

With an explicit join, the previous statement looks as follows:

```
SELECT   TEAMNO, NAME
FROM     TEAMS INNER JOIN PLAYERS
         ON TEAMS.PLAYERNO = PLAYERS.PLAYERNO
```

Explanation: Obviously, the TEAMS and PLAYERS tables are joined with an inner join. The join condition (after the word ON) is used to compare the PLAYERNO columns in the two tables. The results of these two statements are equal. Because the PLAYERNO column in the TEAMS table is a subset of that of the PLAYERS table, the result contains all those players who appear in the TEAMS table (which is in accordance with the question).

The word INNER in the join specification can be omitted. It has been added only to show which type of join is executed. Therefore, the previous statement is equal to the next:

```
SELECT   TEAMNO, NAME
FROM     TEAMS JOIN PLAYERS
         ON TEAMS.PLAYERNO = PLAYERS.PLAYERNO
```

Multiple tables can be joined with one FROM clause. Imagine that T_1, T_2, T_3, and T_4 are tables and C is a join condition to join two tables. Then the following examples are all allowed:

- T_1 INNER JOIN T_2 ON C
- T_1 INNER JOIN T_2 ON C INNER JOIN T_3 ON C
- (T_1 INNER JOIN T_2 ON C) INNER JOIN T_3 ON C
- T_1 INNER JOIN (T_2 INNER JOIN T_3 ON C) ON C
- (T_1 INNER JOIN T_2 ON C) INNER JOIN (T_3 INNER JOIN T_4 ON C) ON C

Exercise 7.12: For each team, find the number and name of the captain. Exercise 7.5 used an implicit join; use an explicit join now.

Exercise 7.13: Find the numbers and names of the players who live in the same town as player 27. Player 27 should be excluded from the end result. Exercise 7.9 used an implicit join; use an explicit join now.

Exercise 7.14: For each match, get the match number, the name of the player, and the division of the team. Exercise 7.6 used an implicit join; use an explicit join now.

7.10 Outer Joins

The only join type discussed so far has been the inner join. However, the additional advantages of this type are limited. It is helpful to be able to indicate more explicitly that the statement performs a join, but this is not a huge improvement. For the other join types, such as *left outer join*, however, statements become considerably clearer, more powerful, and shorter.

This section discusses the left outer and right outer joins.

7.10.1 The Left Outer Join

Let's start with an example.

Example 7.17: For *all* the players, find the player number, name, and penalties incurred by him or her; order the result by player number.

To answer this question, many people would use the following SELECT statement:

```
SELECT   PLAYERS.PLAYERNO, NAME, AMOUNT
FROM     PLAYERS, PENALTIES
WHERE    PLAYERS.PLAYERNO = PENALTIES.PLAYERNO
ORDER BY PLAYERS.PLAYERNO
```

The result is:

```
PLAYERNO  NAME       AMOUNT
--------  ---------  ------
       6  Parmenter  100.00
       8  Newcastle   25.00
      27  Collins    100.00
      27  Collins     70.00
      44  Baker       75.00
      44  Baker       25.00
      44  Baker       30.00
     104  Moorman     50.00
```

However, the result is incomplete because all players who have no penalties are missing.

The intention of this question is to get all the players in the result. To get the missing players in the result as well, a so-called *left outer join* must be specified:

```
SELECT   PLAYERS.PLAYERNO, NAME, AMOUNT
FROM     PLAYERS LEFT OUTER JOIN PENALTIES
         ON PLAYERS.PLAYERNO = PENALTIES.PLAYERNO
ORDER BY PLAYERS.PLAYERNO
```

The result is:

```
PLAYERNO  NAME       AMOUNT
--------  ---------  ------
       2  Everett         ?
       6  Parmenter  100.00
       7  Wise            ?
       8  Newcastle   25.00
      27  Collins    100.00
      27  Collins     75.00
      28  Collins         ?
      39  Bishop          ?
      44  Baker       75.00
      44  Baker       25.00
      44  Baker       30.00
      57  Brown           ?
      83  Hope            ?
      95  Miller          ?
     100  Parmenter       ?
     104  Moorman     50.00
     112  Bailey          ?
```

Explanation: In the FROM clause, the join type is specified between the two tables—in this case, a *left outer join*. In addition, the join condition is specified after the word ON. When the join is specified in this way, MySQL knows that *all* rows from the PLAYERS table *must* appear in the intermediate result of the FROM clause. The columns in the SELECT clause that belong to the PENALTIES table are filled automatically with null values for all those players for whom no penalty was paid.

Note that with all outer joins, the term OUTER can be omitted without any effect on the end result.

Whether outer joins are necessary depends, as mentioned before, on the question and on the relationship between the join columns. Between the populations PLAYERS.PLAYERNO and PENALTIES.PLAYERNO, a subset relationship exists: The population of PENALTIES.PLAYERNO is a subset of the population PLAYERS.PLAYERNO, so a left outer join is useful. The other way would make no sense; see the following example.

Example 7.18: For *each* penalty, get the payment number and the name of the player.

```
SELECT   PAYMENTNO, NAME
FROM     PENALTIES LEFT OUTER JOIN PLAYERS
         ON PENALTIES.PLAYERNO = PLAYERS.PLAYERNO
ORDER BY PAYMENTNO
```

The result is:

```
PAYMENTNO  NAME
---------  ---------
        1  Parmenter
        2  Baker
        3  Collins
        4  Moorman
        5  Baker
        6  Newcastle
        7  Baker
        8  Collins
```

Explanation: In this statement, PENALTIES is the left table. Because there are no penalties that do not belong to a specific player, no penalties are left out. In other words, a left outer join in this example is superfluous. An inner join would have returned the same result.

Example 7.19: For *each* player, find the player number and name, and the numbers and divisions of the teams that he or she captains; order the result by player number.

```
SELECT   P.PLAYERNO, NAME, TEAMNO, DIVISION
FROM     PLAYERS AS P LEFT OUTER JOIN TEAMS AS T
         ON P.PLAYERNO = T.PLAYERNO
ORDER BY P.PLAYERNO
```

The result is:

```
PLAYERNO  NAME       TEAMNO  DIVISION
--------  ---------  ------  --------
       2  Everett         ?  ?
       6  Parmenter       1  first
       7  Wise            ?  ?
       8  Newcastle       ?  ?
      27  Collins         2  second
      28  Collins         ?  ?
      39  Bishop          ?  ?
      44  Baker           ?  ?
      57  Brown           ?  ?
      83  Hope            ?  ?
      95  Miller          ?  ?
     100  Parmenter       ?  ?
     104  Moorman         ?  ?
     112  Bailey          ?  ?
```

Example 7.20: For each player born in Inglewood, find the player number, name, list of penalties, and list of teams for which he or she has played a match.

```
SELECT   PLAYERS.PLAYERNO, NAME, AMOUNT, TEAMNO
FROM     PLAYERS LEFT OUTER JOIN PENALTIES
         ON PLAYERS.PLAYERNO = PENALTIES.PLAYERNO
            LEFT OUTER JOIN MATCHES
            ON PLAYERS.PLAYERNO = MATCHES.PLAYERNO
WHERE    TOWN = 'Inglewood'
```

The result is:

```
PLAYERNO  NAME       AMOUNT  TEAMNO
--------  ---------  ------  ------
       8  Newcastle   25.00       1
       8  Newcastle   25.00       2
      44  Baker       75.00       1
      44  Baker       25.00       1
      44  Baker       30.00       1
```

Explanation: First, the PLAYERS table is joined using a left outer join to the PENALTIES table. The result contains 17 rows consisting of two players from Inglewood: players 8 and 44. Player 8 has incurred only one penalty, and player 44 has three penalties. Then the entire result is joined with the MATCHES table. Because player 8 played for two teams, he appears twice in the result.

Summarizing: A left outer join is useful only if there can exist values in the join column of the left table that do not appear in the join column of the right table.

7.10.2 The Right Outer Join

The right outer join is the mirror image of the left outer join. With the left outer join, all rows from the left table appear in the intermediate result of the FROM clause. With the right outer join, this guarantee is given for the right table.

Example 7.21: For *all* players, get the player number, name, and numbers of the teams for which they are the captain.

```
SELECT   PLAYERS.PLAYERNO, NAME, TEAMNO
FROM     TEAMS RIGHT OUTER JOIN PLAYERS
         ON TEAMS.PLAYERNO = PLAYERS.PLAYERNO
```

The result is:

```
PLAYERNO  NAME       TEAMNO
--------  ---------  ------
       2  Everett         ?
       6  Parmenter       1
       7  Wise            ?
       8  Newcastle       ?
      27  Collins         2
      28  Collins         ?
      39  Bishop          ?
      44  Baker           ?
      57  Brown           ?
      83  Hope            ?
      95  Miller          ?
     100  Parmenter       ?
     104  Moorman         ?
     112  Bailey          ?
```

Explanation: Obviously, players such as 2, 7, and 8 have been included in the result even though they are not captains. If a player was a captain of two teams, he would appear twice in this result.

Exercise 7.15: For all players, get the player number and the list of penalties incurred by them.

Exercise 7.16: For all players, get the player number and a list of the numbers of teams for which they have ever played.

Exercise 7.17: For all players, get the player number, list of penalties they have incurred, and the list of numbers of teams for which they have ever played.

Exercise 7.18: Which of the following FROM clauses would be useful and which would not?

1. ```
   FROM   PENALTIES AS PEN LEFT OUTER JOIN PLAYERS AS P
          ON PEN.PLAYERNO = P.PLAYERNO
   ```
2. ```
   FROM   PENALTIES AS PEN LEFT OUTER JOIN PLAYERS AS P
          ON PEN.PLAYERNO > P.PLAYERNO
   ```
3. ```
   FROM   TEAMS AS T RIGHT OUTER JOIN MATCHES AS M
          ON T.TEAMNO = M.TEAMNO
   ```

Exercise 7.19: Determine the results of the following SELECT statements, given the tables T1, T2, T3, and T4. Each of these tables has only one column.

```
T1  C      T2  C      T3  C      T4  C
-----      -----      -----      -----
    1          2          ?          ?
    2          3          2          2
    3          4                     3
```

1. ```
   SELECT   T1.C, T2.C
   FROM     T1 INNER JOIN T2 ON T1.C = T2.C
   ```
2. ```
   SELECT   T1.C, T2.C
   FROM     T1 LEFT OUTER JOIN T2 ON T1.C = T2.C
   ```
3. ```
   SELECT   T1.C, T2.C
   FROM     T1 RIGHT OUTER JOIN T2 ON T1.C = T2.C
   ```
4. ```
   SELECT   T1.C, T2.C
   FROM     T1 RIGHT OUTER JOIN T2 ON T1.C > T2.C
   ```
5. ```
   SELECT   T1.C, T3.C
   FROM     T1 RIGHT OUTER JOIN T3 ON T1.C = T3.C
   ```

6.
```
SELECT   T1.C, T3.C
FROM     T1 LEFT OUTER JOIN T3 ON T1.C = T3.C
```

7.
```
SELECT   T3.C, T4.C
FROM     T3 LEFT OUTER JOIN T4 ON T3.C = T4.C
```

8.
```
SELECT   T3.C, T4.C
FROM     T3 RIGHT OUTER JOIN T4 ON T3.C = T4.C
```

Exercise 7.20: Which of the following statements are correct? Assume that the column C1 belongs to the table T1, and the column C2 to T2.

1. If C1 is a subset of C2, the result of T1.C1 LEFT OUTER JOIN T2.C2 is equal to an inner join of the same columns.
2. If C2 is a subset of C1, the result of T1.C1 LEFT OUTER JOIN T2.C2 is equal to an inner join of the same columns.
3. The result of T1.C1 LEFT OUTER JOIN T1.C1 is equal to an inner join of the same columns.

7.11 The Natural Join

With the *natural join,* you can shorten the formulation of certain statements somewhat. For many joins, the names of the join columns are equivalent and only one of the join columns in the SELECT clause is retrieved. If this is the case with a join, you can rewrite the join with a natural join.

Example 7.22: For each player who was born after 30 June 1920, and for whom at least one penalty has been incurred, get the number, name, and all penalty amounts.

Without a natural join, this statement looks as follows:

```
SELECT   PLAYERS.PLAYERNO, NAME, AMOUNT
FROM     PLAYERS INNER JOIN PENALTIES
         ON PLAYERS.PLAYERNO = PENALTIES.PLAYERNO
WHERE    BIRTH_DATE > '1920-06-30'
```

The result is:

```
PLAYERNO  NAME       AMOUNT
--------  ---------  ------
       6  Parmenter  100.00
      44  Baker       75.00
      27  Collins    100.00
     104  Moorman     50.00
      44  Baker       25.00
       8  Newcastle   25.00
      44  Baker       30.00
      27  Collins     75.00
```

This statement can be shortened with a natural join and gives the same result:

```
SELECT   PLAYERS.PLAYERNO, NAME, AMOUNT
FROM     PLAYERS NATURAL JOIN PENALTIES
WHERE    BIRTH_DATE > '1920-06-30'
```

Explanation: Now MySQL can add a join condition where the two columns with the same name (PLAYERNO) are compared. In fact, behind the scenes, MySQL transforms the natural join to a normal join.

In a SELECT clause, if we replace all column names with an *, MySQL presents the PLAYERNO column just once. It is assumed that nobody is interested in two columns that are equal.

A natural left outer join also can replace a left outer join this way, and a natural right outer join can replace a right outer join.

7.12 Additional Conditions in the Join Condition

The condition in the FROM clause is primarily meant to be used to join tables. Other conditions that do not really belong to the join are allowed to be included here. However, you should realize that moving a condition from the WHERE clause to the join condition can actually affect the result. The following statement shows that distinction.

Example 7.23: The next SELECT statement contains a left outer join plus an additional condition in the WHERE clause.

```
SELECT   TEAMS.PLAYERNO, TEAMS.TEAMNO, PENALTIES.PAYMENTNO
FROM     TEAMS LEFT OUTER JOIN PENALTIES
         ON TEAMS.PLAYERNO = PENALTIES.PLAYERNO
WHERE    DIVISION = 'second'
```

The result is:

```
PLAYERNO  TEAMNO  PAYMENTNO
--------  ------  ---------
      27       2          3
      27       2          8
```

Explanation: The intermediate result of the FROM clause contains all the rows of the TEAMS table of which the captain appears in the PENALTIES table. If teams disappear from this join, they are brought back again because of the left outer join. In other words, that intermediate result looks as follows (on the left are the columns of the TEAMS table, and on the right are those of the PENALTIES table):

```
TEAMNO PLAYERNO DIVISION PAYNO PLAYERNO PAYMENT_DATE AMOUNT
------ -------- -------- ----- -------- ------------ ------
     1        6 first        1        6 1980-12-08   100.00
     2       27 second       3       27 1983-09-10   100.00
     2       27 second       8       27 1984-11-12    75.00
```

Next, the WHERE clause is processed; only the last two rows are passed on to the SELECT clause.

If we move the condition to the join condition, the following statement arises:

```
SELECT    TEAMS.PLAYERNO, TEAMS.TEAMNO, PENALTIES.PAYMENTNO
FROM      TEAMS LEFT OUTER JOIN PENALTIES
          ON TEAMS.PLAYERNO = PENALTIES.PLAYERNO
          AND DIVISION = 'second'
```

This statement has a result that differs from the previous statement:

```
PLAYERNO  TEAMNO  PAYMENTNO
--------  ------  ---------
       6       1          ?
      27       2          3
      27       2          8
```

Now team 1 does appear in the result, but how did that happen? MySQL processes the explicit join in two steps. During the first step, the join is processed as if no outer join has to be executed, but an inner join does. So first a Cartesian product is created; then all conditions are processed, including the condition on the DIVISION column. This leads to the following result:

```
TEAMNO  PLAYERNO  DIVISION  PAYNO  PLAYERNO  PAYMENT_DATE AMOUNT
------  --------  --------  -----  --------  ------------ ------
     2        27  second        3        27  1983-09-10   100.00
     2        27  second        8        27  1984-11-12    75.00
```

Team 1 does not appear in this intermediate result because it does not play in the second division. During the second step, MySQL checks whether rows from the TEAMS table (because that is the table on the left of the left outer join) have disappeared from this intermediate result. Those rows have to be brought back again. As a result, team 1 is added again:

```
TEAMNO  PLAYERNO  DIVISION  PAYNO  PLAYERNO  PAYMENT_DATE AMOUNT
------  --------  --------  -----  --------  ------------ ------
     2        27  second        3        27  1983-09-10   100.00
     2        27  second        8        27  1984-11-12    75.00
     1         6  first         ?         ?  ?                 ?
```

Because of the absence of a WHERE clause, all these rows are passed on to the SELECT clause, which means that the end result differs from that of the first statement.

Example 7.24: The next SELECT statement contains a full outer join plus an additional condition in the WHERE clause.

```
SELECT   TEAMS.PLAYERNO, TEAMS.TEAMNO, PENALTIES.PAYMENTNO
FROM     TEAMS FULL OUTER JOIN PENALTIES
         ON TEAMS.PLAYERNO = PENALTIES.PLAYERNO
         AND TEAMS.PLAYERNO > 1000
```

The result is:

```
PLAYERNO  TEAMNO  PAYMENTNO
--------  ------  ---------
       ?       ?          3
       ?       ?          8
       ?       ?          1
       ?       ?          6
       ?       ?          2
       ?       ?          5
       ?       ?          7
       ?       ?          4
       6       1          ?
      27       2          ?
```

Explanation: After step 1 of the join has been processed, the intermediate result is empty. The reason is that there are no player numbers greater than 1000. Then during step 2, MySQL checks whether there are rows in the tables TEAMS and PENALTIES that do not appear in the result. That involves all the teams and all the penalties, so they are added again, and a somewhat strange end result occurs.

Conclusion: If an outer join is used, it matters whether certain conditions are placed in the join condition or in the WHERE clause. Therefore, consider carefully where you want to place them. This does not apply to the inner join (work out why for yourself).

7.13 The Cross Join

In MySQL, the *cross join* is nothing more or less than a synonym of the inner join. If you do not include a join condition with the cross join, the result is a Cartesian product.

7.14 Replacing Join Conditions with USING

If the names of the join columns are the same and the condition is that of equality (as it most often is), USING can be used. Therefore, the following two FROM clauses are equal:

```
FROM     TEAMS INNER JOIN PLAYERS
         ON TEAMS.PLAYERNO = PLAYERS.PLAYERNO
```

and

```
FROM     TEAMS INNER JOIN PLAYERS
         USING (PLAYERNO)
```

USING has no influence on the result and does not create any additional possibilities with respect to the other form. It has only two limited advantages. First, the statement is a little shorter and, therefore, easier to read. Second, when a join of two or more columns must be specified, the formulation becomes much more compact.

If USING is used, one of the joined columns automatically is removed from the result.

Example 7.25: Do a left outer join of the PENALTIES table with the TEAMS table.

```
SELECT   *
FROM     PENALTIES LEFT OUTER JOIN TEAMS
         USING (PLAYERNO)
```

The result is:

```
PLAYERNO  PAYMENTNO  PAYMENT_DATE  AMOUNT  TEAMNO  DIVISION
--------  ---------  ------------  ------  ------  --------
       6          1  1980-12-08    100.00       1  first
      44          2  1981-05-05     75.00       ?  ?
      27          3  1983-09-10    100.00       2  second
     104          4  1984-12-08     50.00       ?  ?
      44          5  1980-12-08     25.00       ?  ?
       8          6  1980-12-08     25.00       ?  ?
      44          7  1982-12-30     30.00       ?  ?
      27          8  1984-11-12     75.00       2  second
```

Explanation: From this result, it is clear that the PLAYERNO column is included in the result only once, without having to specify anything.

7.15 The FROM Clause with Table Expressions

Section 6.6 mentioned that the `FROM` clause itself can contain a table expression. The table expression within the `FROM` clause is called a table subquery. This section extends the definition of the `FROM` clause with that table subquery. Next, we present various examples to illustrate the extensive possibilities of table subqueries.

DEFINITION

```
<from clause> ::=
   FROM <table reference> [ , <table reference> ]...

<table reference> ::=
   <table specification> [ [ AS ] <pseudonym> ] |
   <join specification>                          |
   ( <join specification> )                      |
   <table subquery> [ [ AS ] <pseudonym> ]

<table subquery> ::= ( <table expression> )
```

Example 7.26: Get the numbers of the players resident in Stratford.

```
SELECT   PLAYERNO
FROM    (SELECT   *
         FROM     PLAYERS
         WHERE    TOWN = 'Stratford') AS STRATFORDERS
```

Explanation: A table expression in the form of a table subquery is specified in the FROM clause. This subquery returns all the column values of all players from Stratford. The resulting table is named STRATFORDERS and is passed to the other clauses. The other clauses cannot see that the table, which they receive as input, has been generated with a subquery. This statement could have been formulated in the classical way, but we have used this formulation just to start with a simple example.

Example 7.27: Get the number of each player who is a captain of a team playing in the first division.

```
SELECT   SMALL_TEAMS.PLAYERNO
FROM    (SELECT   PLAYERNO, DIVISION
         FROM     TEAMS) AS SMALL_TEAMS
WHERE    SMALL_TEAMS.DIVISION = 'first'
```

The result is:

```
SMALL_TEAMS.PLAYERNO
--------------------
                   6
```

Explanation: With the table expression in the FROM clause, the following intermediate result is created:

```
PLAYERNO  DIVISION
--------  --------
       6  first
      27  second
```

This intermediate table gets the name SMALL_TEAMS. Next, the condition SMALL_TEAMS.DIVISION = 'first' is executed on this table, after which only the PLAYERNO column is retrieved.

Table expressions can be used, for example, to prevent a repeat of complex scalar expressions.

Example 7.28: Get the match number and the difference between the total number of sets won and the total number of sets lost for each match where that difference is greater than 2.

```
SELECT   MATCHNO, DIFFERENCE
FROM    (SELECT   MATCHNO,
                  ABS(WON - LOST) AS DIFFERENCE
         FROM     MATCHES) AS M
WHERE    DIFFERENCE > 2
```

The result is:

```
MATCHNO  DIFFERENCE
-------  ----------
      3           3
      5           3
      7           3
      8           3
     13           3
```

Explanation: The subquery in the FROM clause returns for each match the match number and the difference between the WON and LOST columns. In the main query, a condition is executed on this difference. To refer to that calculation in the main query, a column name has to be introduced in the subquery. For the first time, we have an example in which the specification of a column name is of more use than just to improve the readability of the result.

A special variant of the table expression is the one in which only the SELECT clause is used. This variant can also be used as a table subquery.

Example 7.29: Create a virtual table called TOWNS.

```
SELECT   *
FROM     (SELECT 'Stratford' AS TOWN, 4 AS NUMBER
          UNION
          SELECT 'Plymouth', 6
          UNION
          SELECT 'Inglewood', 1
          UNION
          SELECT 'Douglas', 2) AS TOWNS
ORDER BY TOWN
```

The result is:

```
TOWN       NUMBER
---------  ------
Douglas         2
Inglewood       1
Plymouth        6
Stratford       4
```

Explanation: In this FROM clause, a table is created consisting of two columns (the first an alphanumeric one and the second a numeric one) and four rows. This table is named TOWNS. The first column has the name TOWN and contains the name of a town. The second is named NUMBER and contains a relative indication of the number of residents in that city. Note that an end result is created here without so much as querying one of the existing tables.

The table that is created as a result is a normal table to all the other clauses. For example, a WHERE clause does not know whether the intermediate result from the FROM clause is the contents of a "real" table, a subquery, a view, or a temporarily created table. So we can use all the other operations on this temporarily created table.

Example 7.30: For each player, find the number, the name, the town, and the number of residents living in that town.

```
SELECT   PLAYERNO, NAME, PLAYERS.TOWN, NUMBER * 1000
FROM     PLAYERS,
        (SELECT 'Stratford' AS TOWN, 4 AS NUMBER
         UNION
         SELECT 'Plymouth', 6
         UNION
         SELECT 'Inglewood', 1
         UNION
         SELECT 'Douglas', 2) AS TOWNS
WHERE    PLAYERS.TOWN = TOWNS.TOWN
ORDER BY PLAYERNO
```

The result is:

```
PLAYERNO  NAME       TOWN       NUMBER
--------  ---------  ---------  ------
       2  Everett    Stratford    4000
       6  Parmenter  Stratford    4000
       7  Wise       Stratford    4000
       8  Newcastle  Inglewood    1000
      39  Bishop     Stratford    4000
      44  Baker      Inglewood    1000
      57  Brown      Stratford    4000
      83  Hope       Stratford    4000
      95  Miller     Douglas      2000
     100  Parmenter  Stratford    4000
     112  Bailey     Plymouth     6000
```

Explanation: The PLAYERS table is joined with the TOWNS table. Because an inner join is used, we lose all the players who live in towns that do not appear in the TOWNS table. The next table expression makes sure that we do not lose players from the result:

```
SELECT   PLAYERNO, NAME, PLAYERS.TOWN, NUMBER
FROM     PLAYERS LEFT OUTER JOIN
        (SELECT 'Stratford' AS TOWN, 4 AS NUMBER
         UNION
         SELECT 'Plymouth', 6
         UNION
         SELECT 'Inglewood', 1
         UNION
         SELECT 'Douglas', 2) AS TOWNS
         ON PLAYERS.TOWN = TOWNS.TOWN
ORDER BY PLAYERNO
```

Example 7.31: Find the numbers of the players who live in a town with a population indicator greater than 2.

```
SELECT   PLAYERNO
FROM     PLAYERS LEFT OUTER JOIN
        (SELECT 'Stratford' AS TOWN, 4 AS NUMBER
         UNION
         SELECT 'Plymouth', 6
         UNION
         SELECT 'Inglewood', 1
         UNION
         SELECT 'Douglas', 2) AS TOWNS
         ON PLAYERS.TOWN = TOWNS.TOWN
WHERE    TOWNS.NUMBER > 2
```

The result is:

```
PLAYERNO
--------
       2
       6
       7
      39
      57
      83
     100
     112
```

Example 7.32: Get all possible combinations of the first names `John`, `Mark`, and `Arnold` and the last names `Berg`, `Johnson`, and `Williams`.

```
SELECT   *
FROM     (SELECT 'John' AS FIRST_NAME
          UNION
          SELECT 'Mark'
          UNION
          SELECT 'Arnold') AS FIRST_NAMES,
         (SELECT 'Berg' AS LAST_NAME
          UNION
          SELECT 'Johnson'
          UNION
          SELECT 'Williams') AS LAST_NAMES
```

The result is:

```
FIRST_NAME  LAST_NAME
----------  ---------
John        Berg
Mark        Berg
Arnold      Berg
John        Johnson
Mark        Johnson
Arnold      Johnson
John        Williams
Mark        Williams
Arnold      Williams
```

Example 7.33: For the numbers 10 to 19, find the value to the power of three. However, if the result is greater than 4,000, it should not be included in the result.

```
SELECT   NUMBER, POWER(NUMBER,3)
FROM     (SELECT 10 AS NUMBER UNION SELECT 11 UNION SELECT 12
          UNION
          SELECT 13 UNION SELECT 14 UNION SELECT 15
          UNION
          SELECT 16 UNION SELECT 17 UNION SELECT 18
          UNION
          SELECT 19) AS NUMBERS
WHERE    POWER(NUMBER,3) <= 4000
```

The result is:

```
NUMBER  POWER(NUMBER,3)
------  -------------
    10           1000
    11           1331
    12           1728
    13           2197
    14           2744
    15           3375
```

This statement works well if the numbers are limited. When we want to do the same with 100 or more numbers, the statement is not as simple. In that case, we could try to avoid the problem by generating a long list of numbers in a more creative way.

Example 7.34: Generate the numbers 0 up to and including 999.

```
SELECT   NUMBER
FROM    (SELECT    CAST(CONCAT(DIGIT1.DIGIT,
                   CONCAT(DIGIT2.DIGIT,
                   DIGIT3.DIGIT)) AS UNSIGNED INTEGER)
                   AS NUMBER
         FROM     (SELECT '0' AS DIGIT UNION SELECT '1' UNION
                   SELECT '2' UNION SELECT '3' UNION
                   SELECT '4' UNION SELECT '5' UNION
                   SELECT '6' UNION SELECT '7' UNION
                   SELECT '8' UNION SELECT '9') AS DIGIT1,
                  (SELECT '0' AS DIGIT UNION SELECT '1' UNION
                   SELECT '2' UNION SELECT '3' UNION
                   SELECT '4' UNION SELECT '5' UNION
                   SELECT '6' UNION SELECT '7' UNION
                   SELECT '8' UNION SELECT '9') AS DIGIT2,
                  (SELECT '0' AS DIGIT UNION SELECT '1' UNION
                   SELECT '2' UNION SELECT '3' UNION
                   SELECT '4' UNION SELECT '5' UNION
                   SELECT '6' UNION SELECT '7' UNION
                   SELECT '8' UNION SELECT '9') AS DIGIT3)
                   AS NUMBERS
ORDER BY NUMBER
```

The result is:

```
NUMBER
------
     0
     1
     2
     :
   998
   999
```

Example 7.35: Find the squares of whole numbers between 0 and 999.

```
SELECT   NUMBER AS SQUARE, ROUND(SQRT(NUMBER)) AS BASIS
FROM    (SELECT    CAST(CONCAT(DIGIT1.DIGIT,
                   CONCAT(DIGIT2.DIGIT,
                   DIGIT3.DIGIT)) AS UNSIGNED INTEGER)
                   AS NUMBER
         FROM     (SELECT '0' AS DIGIT UNION SELECT '1' UNION
                   SELECT '2' UNION SELECT '3' UNION
                   SELECT '4' UNION SELECT '5' UNION
                   SELECT '6' UNION SELECT '7' UNION
                   SELECT '8' UNION SELECT '9') AS DIGIT1,
                  (SELECT '0' AS DIGIT UNION SELECT '1' UNION
                   SELECT '2' UNION SELECT '3' UNION
                   SELECT '4' UNION SELECT '5' UNION
                   SELECT '6' UNION SELECT '7' UNION
                   SELECT '8' UNION SELECT '9') AS DIGIT2,
                  (SELECT '0' AS DIGIT UNION SELECT '1' UNION
                   SELECT '2' UNION SELECT '3' UNION
                   SELECT '4' UNION SELECT '5' UNION
                   SELECT '6' UNION SELECT '7' UNION
                   SELECT '8' UNION SELECT '9') AS DIGIT3)
                   AS NUMBERS
WHERE    SQRT(NUMBER) = ROUND(SQRT(NUMBER))
ORDER BY NUMBER
```

The result is:

```
SQUARE  BASIS
------  -----
     0      0
     1      1
     4      2
     :      :
   900     30
   961     31
```

Exercise 7.21: For each player, get the difference between the year they joined the club and the year in which they were born, but return only those players for which that difference is greater than 20.

Exercise 7.22: Get a list of all combinations of three letters that you can make with the letters a, b, c, and d.

Exercise 7.23: Find 10 random integer numbers between 0 and 1,000.

7.16 Answers

7.1 **1.** Both tables have a column called PLAYERNO.

2. The SELECT clause refers to the PLAYERS table even though it is not specified in the FROM clause.

7.2 The question: "Get the name of each player who is captain of a team."

The FROM clause:

```
TEAMNO  PLAYERNO  DIVISION  PLAYERNO  NAME       ...
------  --------  --------  --------  ---------  ---
     1         6  first            6  Parmenter  ...
     1         6  first           44  Baker      ...
     1         6  first           83  Hope       ...
     1         6  first            2  Everett    ...
     1         6  first           27  Collins    ...
     1         6  first          104  Moorman    ...
     1         6  first            7  Wise       ...
     1         6  first           57  Brown      ...
     1         6  first           39  Bishop     ...
     1         6  first          112  Bailey     ...
     1         6  first            8  Newcastle  ...
     1         6  first          100  Parmenter  ...
     1         6  first           28  Collins    ...
     1         6  first           95  Miller     ...
     2        27  second           6  Parmenter  ...
     2        27  second          44  Baker      ...
     2        27  second          83  Hope       ...
     2        27  second           2  Everett    ...
     2        27  second          27  Collins    ...
     2        27  second         104  Moorman    ...
     2        27  second           7  Wise       ...
     2        27  second          57  Brown      ...
     2        27  second          39  Bishop     ...
     2        27  second         112  Bailey     ...
     2        27  second           8  Newcastle  ...
     2        27  second         100  Parmenter  ...
     2        27  second          28  Collins    ...
     2        27  second          95  Miller     ...
```

The WHERE clause:

```
TEAMNO  PLAYERNO  DIVISION  PLAYERNO  NAME       ...
------  --------  --------  --------  ---------  ---
     1         6  first            6  Parmenter  ...
     2        27  second          27  Collins    ...
```

The SELECT clause and also the end result:

```
NAME
---------
Parmenter
Collins
```

7.3
```
SELECT   PAYMENTNO, AMOUNT, PLAYERS.PLAYERNO, NAME
FROM     PENALTIES, PLAYERS
WHERE    PENALTIES.PLAYERNO = PLAYERS.PLAYERNO
```

7.4
```
SELECT   PAYMENTNO, NAME
FROM     PENALTIES, PLAYERS, TEAMS
WHERE    PENALTIES.PLAYERNO = TEAMS.PLAYERNO
AND      TEAMS.PLAYERNO = PLAYERS.PLAYERNO
```

7.5
```
SELECT   T.TEAMNO, P.NAME
FROM     TEAMS AS T, PLAYERS AS P
WHERE    T.PLAYERNO = P.PLAYERNO
```

7.6
```
SELECT   M.MATCHNO, P.NAME, T.DIVISION
FROM     MATCHES AS M, PLAYERS AS P, TEAMS AS T
WHERE    M.PLAYERNO = P.PLAYERNO
AND      M.TEAMNO = T.TEAMNO
```

7.7
```
SELECT   P.PLAYERNO, P.NAME
FROM     PLAYERS AS P, COMMITTEE_MEMBERS AS C
WHERE    P.PLAYERNO = C.PLAYERNO
AND      B.POSITION = 'Chairman'
```

7.8
```
SELECT   DISTINCT CM.PLAYERNO
FROM     COMMITTEE_MEMBERS AS CM, PENALTIES AS PEN
WHERE    CM.PLAYERNO = PEN.PLAYERNO
AND      CM.BEGIN_DATE = PEN.PAYMENT_DATE
```

7.9
```
SELECT   P.PLAYERNO, P.NAME
FROM     PLAYERS AS P, PLAYERS AS P27
WHERE    P.TOWN = P27.TOWN
AND      P27.PLAYERNO = 27
AND      P.PLAYERNO <> 27
```

7.10
```
SELECT   DISTINCT P.PLAYERNO AS PLAYER_PLAYERNO,
         P.NAME AS PLAYER_NAME,
         CAP.PLAYERNO AS CAPTAIN_PLAYERNO,
         CAP.NAME AS CAPTAIN_NAME
FROM     PLAYERS AS P, PLAYERS AS CAP,
         MATCHES AS M, TEAMS AS T
WHERE    M.PLAYERNO = P.PLAYERNO
AND      T.TEAMNO = M.TEAMNO
AND      M.PLAYERNO <> T.PLAYERNO
AND      CAP.PLAYERNO = T.PLAYERNO
```

7.11
```
SELECT   PEN1.PAYMENTNO, PEN1.PLAYERNO
FROM     PENALTIES AS PEN1, PENALTIES AS PEN2
WHERE    PEN1.AMOUNT = PEN2.AMOUNT
AND      PEN2.PLAYERNO = 44
AND      PEN1.PLAYERNO <> 44
```

7.12
```
SELECT   T.TEAMNO, P.NAME
FROM     TEAMS AS T INNER JOIN PLAYERS AS P
         ON T.PLAYERNO = P.PLAYERNO
```

7.13
```
SELECT   P.PLAYERNO, P.NAME
FROM     PLAYERS AS P INNER JOIN PLAYERS AS P27
         ON P.TOWN = P27.TOWN
AND      P27.PLAYERNO = 27
AND      P.PLAYERNO <> 27
```

7.14
```
SELECT   M.MATCHNO, P.NAME, T.DIVISION
FROM    (MATCHES AS M INNER JOIN PLAYERS AS P
         ON M.PLAYERNO = P.PLAYERNO)
         INNER JOIN TEAMS AS T
         ON M.TEAMNO = T.TEAMNO
```

7.15
```
SELECT   PLAYERS.PLAYERNO, PENALTIES.AMOUNT
FROM     PLAYERS LEFT OUTER JOIN PENALTIES
         ON PLAYERS.PLAYERNO = PENALTIES.PLAYERNO
```

7.16
```
SELECT   P.PLAYERNO, M.TEAMNO
FROM     PLAYERS AS P LEFT OUTER JOIN MATCHES AS M
         ON P.PLAYERNO = M.PLAYERNO
```

7.17
```
SELECT   P.PLAYERNO, PEN.AMOUNT, M.TEAMNO
FROM    (PLAYERS AS P LEFT OUTER JOIN MATCHES AS M
         ON P.PLAYERNO = M.PLAYERNO)
         LEFT OUTER JOIN PENALTIES AS PEN
         ON P.PLAYERNO = PEN.PLAYERNO
```

7.18 **1.** The left outer join is used to indicate that all rows that possibly disappear from the left table (the PENALTIES table) still have to be included in the end result. But there are no rows in the PENALTIES table for which the player number does not appear in the PLAYERS table. So the outer join in this `FROM` clause has no use; an inner join would return the same result.

2. The left outer join is used to indicate that all rows that possibly disappear from the left table (the PENALTIES table) still have to be included in the end result. In this example, rows could disappear because a greater-than operator is used in the join condition. Therefore, this `FROM` clause serves a purpose.

3. The right outer join is used to indicate that all rows that possibly disappear from the right table (the MATCHES table) still have to be included in the end result. But there are no rows in the MATCHES table for which the team number does not appear in the TEAMS table. So this `FROM` clause has no use; an inner join would give a similar result.

7.19 **1.**

```
T1.C  T2.C
----  ----
   2     3
   2     3
```

2.

```
T1.C  T2.C
----  ----
   1     ?
   2     2
   3     3
```

3.

```
T1.C  T2.C
----  ----
   2     2
   3     3
   ?     4
```

4.

```
T1.C  T2.C
----  ----
   3     2
   ?     3
   ?     4
```

5.

```
T1.C  T3.C
----  ----
   2     2
   ?     ?
```

6.
```
T1.C  T3.C
----  ----
   1     ?
   2     2
   3     ?
```

7.
```
T3.C  T4.C
----  ----
   ?     ?
   2     2
```

8.
```
T3.C  T4.C
----  ----
   ?     ?
   2     2
   ?     3
```

7.20

1. Correct
2. Incorrect
3. Correct

7.21
```
SELECT   PLAYERNO, DIFFERENCE
FROM    (SELECT   PLAYERNO,
                  JOINED - YEAR(BIRTH_DATE) AS DIFFERENCE
         FROM     PLAYERS) AS DIFFERENCES
WHERE    DIFFERENCE > 20
```

7.22
```
SELECT   LETTER1 || LETTER2 || LETTER3
FROM    (SELECT 'a' AS LETTER1 UNION SELECT 'b'
         UNION SELECT 'c' UNION SELECT 'd') AS LETTERS1,
        (SELECT 'a' AS LETTER2 UNION SELECT 'b'
         UNION SELECT 'c' UNION SELECT 'd') AS LETTERS2,
        (SELECT 'a' AS LETTER3 UNION SELECT 'b'
         UNION SELECT 'c' UNION SELECT 'd') AS LETTERS3
```

7.23
```
SELECT   ROUND(RAND() * 1000)
FROM    (SELECT 0 AS NUMBER UNION SELECT 1 UNION SELECT 2
         UNION
         SELECT 3 UNION SELECT 4 UNION SELECT 5
         UNION
         SELECT 6 UNION SELECT 7 UNION SELECT 8
         UNION
         SELECT 9) AS NUMBERS
```

CHAPTER 8

SELECT Statement: The WHERE Clause

8.1 Introduction

In the WHERE clause, a condition is used to select rows from the intermediate result of the FROM clause. These selected rows form the intermediate result of the WHERE clause. The WHERE clause acts as a kind of filter that removes all the rows for which the condition is not true (but is false or unknown). This chapter describes the different conditions permitted in this clause.

DEFINITION

```
<where clause> ::= WHERE <condition>
```

How is a WHERE clause processed? One by one, each row that appears in the intermediate result table of a FROM clause is evaluated, and the value of the condition is determined. That value can be true, false, or unknown. A row is included in the (intermediate) result of the WHERE clause only if the condition is true. If the condition is false or unknown, the row is kept out of the result. Using a pseudo programming language, this process can be formally described in the following way:

```
WHERE-RESULT := [];
FOR EACH R IN FROM-RESULT DO
   IF CONDITION = TRUE THEN
      WHERE-RESULT :+ R;
ENDFOR;
```

Explanation: The WHERE-RESULT and FROM-RESULT represent two sets in which rows of data can be temporarily stored. R represents a row from a set. The symbol [] represents the empty set. A row is added to the set with the operator :+. This pseudo programming language is used later in the book.

The definition of the term *condition* is shown next. This book considers the terms *condition* and *predicate* as equivalents and uses them interchangeably.

DEFINITION

```
<condition> ::=
   <predicate>                   |
   <predicate> OR <predicate>    |
   <predicate> AND <predicate>   |
   ( <condition> )               |
   NOT <condition>

<predicate> ::=
   <predicate with comparison>     |
   <predicate without comparison>  |
   <predicate with in>             |
   <predicate with between>        |
   <predicate with like>           |
   <predicate with regexp>         |
   <predicate with match>          |
   <predicate with null>           |
   <predicate with exists>         |
   <predicate with any all>
```

Previous chapters gave some examples of possible conditions in the WHERE clause. This chapter describes the following forms:

- The comparison operators
- Conditions coupled with AND, OR, and NOT
- The comparison operators with subquery
- The IN operator with expression list
- The IN operator with subquery
- The BETWEEN operator
- The LIKE operator
- The REGEXP operator
- The MATCH operator

- The NULL operator
- The ANY and ALL operators
- The EXISTS operator

All the conditions described in this chapter consist of one or more expressions. In Chapter 5, "SELECT Statement: Common Elements," you saw that an aggregation function can be a valid expression. However, aggregation functions are not permitted in the condition of a WHERE clause.

8.2 Conditions Using Comparison Operators

The best-known condition is the one in which the values of two expressions are compared. The condition is formed by an expression (for example 83 or 15 * 100), a *comparison operator* or *relation operator* (for example, < or =), and another expression. The value on the left of the operator is compared with the expression on the right. The condition is true, false, or unknown, depending on the operator. MySQL supports the comparison operators shown in Table 8.1.

TABLE 8.1 Overview of Comparison Operators

Comparison Operator	Meaning
=	Equal to
<=>	Equal to also if null
<	Less than
>	Greater than
<=	Less than or equal to
>=	Greater than or equal to
<>	Not equal to
!=	Not equal to

The definition of this condition form is as follows:

DEFINITION

```
<predicate with comparison> ::=
   <scalar expression> <comparison operator>
      <scalar expression> |
   <row expression> <comparison operator> <row expression>

<comparison operator> ::=
   = | <=> | < | > | <= | >= | <> | !=
```

The definition shows that two forms of this predicate exist. The best-known is the one in which the values of scalar expressions are compared. In the other form, row expressions are used. We will start with the first form.

Example 8.1: Get the numbers of the players resident in Stratford.

```
SELECT   PLAYERNO
FROM     PLAYERS
WHERE    TOWN = 'Stratford'
```

The result is:

```
PLAYERNO
--------
       2
       6
       7
      39
      57
      83
     100
```

Explanation: Only for rows in which the value of the TOWN column is equal to `Stratford` is the PLAYERNO printed because then the condition `TOWN = 'Stratford'` is `true`.

If we install MySQL in the default way, capital letters and small letters are considered equal. In other words, the comparisons with the comparison operators are *not case sensitive*). The reason is that `latin1_swedish_ci` is the default *collation.* A collation specifies whether certain letters are seen as equal. If we would work with a different collation, such as `latin1_general_cs`, capitals and small letters are seen as different. Chapter 22, "Character Sets and Collations," discusses collations in detail.

Example 8.2: Get the number, the date of birth, and the year of joining the club for each player who joined 17 years after the year in which he or she was born.

```
SELECT   PLAYERNO, BIRTH_DATE, JOINED
FROM     PLAYERS
WHERE    YEAR(BIRTH_DATE) + 17 = JOINED
```

The result is:

```
PLAYERNO  BIRTH_DATE   JOINED
--------  ----------  -------
      44  1963-01-09     1980
```

The condition in this statement could also be expressed in other ways:

```
WHERE YEAR(BIRTH_DATE) = JOINED - 17
WHERE YEAR(BIRTH_DATE) - JOINED + 17 = 0
```

The first section mentioned that if the condition for a row is `unknown`, it is excluded from the result. Here is an example.

Example 8.3: Get the player numbers for players who have league number 7060.

```
SELECT   PLAYERNO
FROM     PLAYERS
WHERE    LEAGUENO = '7060'
```

The result is:

```
PLAYERNO
--------
     104
```

Explanation: The PLAYERNO is displayed only for rows in which the LEAGUENO is 7060 because only then is the condition `true`. The rows in which the LEAGUENO column has the null value (for players 7, 28, 39, and 95) are not displayed because the value of such a condition is `unknown`.

If one of the scalar expressions in a condition has the null value, regardless of the data type of the expression (numeric, alphanumeric, or date), the condition evaluates to `unknown`. The following table shows what the result of a certain condition can be, depending on whether one or two of the scalar expressions concerned are equal to the null value. Here, the question mark represents any comparison operator (except for <=>):

```
Condition                           Result
-------------------------------     -------------
non-null value ? non-null value     true or false
non-null value ? null value         unknown
null value ? null value             unknown
null value <=> null value           true
```

For some statements, the null value can lead to unexpected results. Here is an example in which the condition at first looks a little peculiar.

Example 8.4: Get the numbers and league numbers of players who actually have a league number.

```
SELECT   PLAYERNO, LEAGUENO
FROM     PLAYERS
WHERE    LEAGUENO = LEAGUENO
```

The result is:

```
PLAYERNO  LEAGUENO
--------  --------
       2  2411
       6  8467
       8  2983
      27  2513
      44  1124
      57  6409
      83  1608
     100  6524
     104  7060
     112  1319
```

Explanation: Each row in which the LEAGUENO column is filled is printed because here LEAGUENO is equal to LEAGUENO. If the LEAGUENO column is not filled, the condition evaluates to `unknown`. Section 8.13 describes a "cleaner" way to formulate the previous query.

For that matter, the condition `LEAGUENO <> LEAGUENO` does not return one single row. If the value of the LEAGUENO column is not equal to null, the condition evaluates to `false`, and if the value equals null, the condition evaluates to `unknown`.

MySQL has a special equal to operator that has the value `true` when the values equal each other or when both are equal to the null value: <=>. The condition is `false` if one of the values is equal to the null value or if both non-null values are unequal. The result of this condition is never `unknown`.

Example 8.5: Get the numbers of the players without league numbers.

```
SELECT   PLAYERNO, LEAGUENO
FROM     PLAYERS
WHERE    LEAGUENO <=> NULL
```

The result is:

```
PLAYERNO
--------
       7
      28
      39
      95
```

Explanation: In the condition LEAGUENO <=> NULL, the special expression NULL is used to check whether the LEAGUENO column is equal to the null value. If the condition LEAGUENO <=> LEAGUENO were used, all rows from the PLAYERS table would have been selected.

The comparison operators <, <=, >, and >= are used to check which value is greater. For numeric values, the answer is always obvious; 1 is less than 2, and 99.99 is greater than 88.3. But how does that work with alphanumeric values, dates, and times? The answer is simple for alphanumeric values: An alphanumeric value is less than another if it comes first in alphabetical order. Consider some examples:

```
Condition             Result
-----------------     ------
'Jim' < 'Pete'        true
'Truth' >= 'Truck'    true
'Jim' = 'JIM'         true
'Jim' > 'JIM'         false
```

But what do we do with special symbols such as the ß and æ? And let us not forget letters with diacritics, such as é, â, and ȩ. Should é come before or after è? And when a rule applies here, does it hold for every language? In other words, what exactly is the order of all kinds of alphanumeric characters? How letters and digits are sorted depends on so-called *character set* and on the previously mentioned *collations*. Again, Chapter 22 discusses these topics in detail.

One date, time, or timestamp is less than another if it comes earlier in time. Some examples follow:

```
Condition                      Result
---------------------------    ------
'1985-12-08' < '1995-12-09'    true
'1980-05-02' > '1979-12-31'    true
'12:00:00'   < '14:00:00'      true
```

Section 5.3 already described row expressions. With comparisons between row expressions, the values with identical positions are compared.

Example 8.6: Find the numbers of the matches in which the number of sets won is equal to 2, and the number of sets lost is equal to 3.

```
SELECT   MATCHNO
FROM     MATCHES
WHERE   (WON, LOST) = (2, 3)
```

The result is:

```
MATCHNO
-------
      2
     11
```

Explanation: MySQL rewrites the condition internally as `(WON = 2) AND (LOST = 3)`.

Instead of using the equal to operator, you can use other comparison operators. However, you must pay attention to how a certain comparison is processed. For example, the condition

```
(2, 4) > (1, 3)
```

is equivalent not to

```
(2 > 1) AND (4 > 3)
```

but to

```
(2 > 1) OR (2 = 1 AND 4 > 3)
```

So first, the first values of both row expressions are compared. If this comparison returns the value `true`, the entire condition is automatically `true`. If this first comparison is not `true`, a check is done to see whether the first two values are equal and whether the second value of the first row expression is greater than the second value of the second row expression. This also means that if the second value of the second row expression is equal to null, the entire condition still can be `true` (if two or more expressions are compared).

For the different comparison operators in the following table, we have indicated how the condition is converted to scalar expressions. The question mark represents one of the operators <, >, <=, or, >=, and E_1, E_2, E_3, E_4, E_5, and E_6 represent random scalar expressions.

Predicate	Converted to scalar expressions
$(E_1, E_2) = (E_3, E_4)$	$(E_1 = E_3)$ AND $(E_2 = E_4)$
$(E_1, E_2) <> (E_3, E_4)$	$(E_1 <> E_3)$ OR $(E_2 <> E_4)$
(E_1, E_2) ? (E_3, E_4)	$(E_1$? $E_3)$ OR $(E_1 = E_3$ AND E_2 ? $E_4)$
(E_1, E_2, E_3) ? (E_4, E_5, E_6)	$(E_1$? $E_4)$ OR $(E_1 = E_4$ AND E_2 ? $E_5)$ OR $(E_1 = E_4$ AND $E_2 = E_5$ AND E_3 ? $E_6)$

The following table contains several examples of comparisons between row expressions and the corresponding results. In particular, pay attention to the examples with null values. If a null value appears in the condition, it does not automatically evaluate to unknown; see the previous example.

```
Predicate               Result
---------------------   -------
(2, 1) > (1, 2)         true
(2, 2) > (1, 1)         true
(1, 2) > (1, 1)         true
(1, 2) > (1, 2)         false
(1, 2) > (1, 3)         false
(2, NULL) > (1, NULL)   true
(NULL, 2) > (1, 1)      unknown
(NULL, 2) > (NULL, 1)   unknown
(2, 1) <> (2, 1)        false
(2, 2) <> (2, 1)        true
(3, 2) <> (2, 1)        true
(3, NULL) <> (2, 1)     true
```

Exercise 8.1: Get the payment number of each penalty greater than $60 (give at least two formulations).

Exercise 8.2: Get the number of each team for which the captain is not player 27.

Exercise 8.3: What is the result of the following SELECT statement?

```
SELECT   PLAYERNO, NAME
FROM     PLAYERS
WHERE    LEAGUENO > LEAGUENO
```

Exercise 8.4: Get the number of each player who won at least one match.

Exercise 8.5: Get the number of each player who played at least one match of five sets.

8.3 Comparison Operators with Subqueries

Chapter 5 mentioned that a scalar expression can also be a subquery. But if it is, it must be a scalar subquery.

Example 8.7: Get the number and name of the player who captains team 1.

```
SELECT    PLAYERNO, NAME
FROM      PLAYERS
WHERE     PLAYERNO =
         (SELECT    PLAYERNO
          FROM      TEAMS
          WHERE     TEAMNO = 1)
```

Explanation: It is obvious in this example that in the condition of the WHERE clause, the value of a "normal" scalar expression, consisting of the column name PLAYERNO, is compared with the value of a subquery. The intermediate result of the subquery is player number 6. This value can now replace the subquery. Next, the following SELECT statement occurs:

```
SELECT    PLAYERNO, NAME
FROM      PLAYERS
WHERE     PLAYERNO = 6
```

The result is:

```
PLAYERNO  NAME
--------  ---------
       6  Parmenter
```

Note that subqueries can be used as expressions only if the subquery returns precisely one value at all times. In other words, it must be a *scalar subquery*. A scalar subquery has one row as result, consisting of one value. Therefore, the following statement is incorrect, and MySQL does not process it:

```
SELECT    *
FROM      PLAYERS
WHERE     BIRTH_DATE <
         (SELECT    BIRTH_DATE
          FROM      PLAYERS)
```

Example 8.8: Find the number and the name and initials of each player who is older than the player with league number 8467.

```
SELECT    PLAYERNO, NAME, INITIALS
FROM      PLAYERS
WHERE     BIRTH_DATE <
         (SELECT    BIRTH_DATE
          FROM      PLAYERS
          WHERE     LEAGUENO = '8467')
```

This subquery always returns at most one value because, as indicated in Section 2.4, the LEAGUENO column cannot contain duplicate values. The intermediate result of that subquery is the date June 25, 1964. The user sees this result:

```
PLAYERNO  NAME       INITIALS
--------  ---------  --------
       2  Everett    R
       7  Wise       GWS
       8  Newcastle  B
      28  Collins    C
      39  Bishop     D
      44  Baker      E
      83  Hope       PK
      95  Miller     P
     100  Parmenter  P
     112  Bailey     IP
```

But what if the subquery does not return a result? In this case, the result of the subquery is equal to the null value. The next, somewhat strange statement returns no rows because no player has league number 9999. The condition in the `WHERE` clause evaluates to `unknown`.

```
SELECT    PLAYERNO, NAME, INITIALS
FROM      PLAYERS
WHERE     BIRTH_DATE <
         (SELECT    BIRTH_DATE
          FROM      PLAYERS
          WHERE     LEAGUENO = '9999')
```

Example 8.9: Get the numbers of the matches played for the team that is captained by player 27.

```
SELECT    MATCHNO
FROM      MATCHES
WHERE     TEAMNO =
         (SELECT    TEAMNO
          FROM      TEAMS
          WHERE     PLAYERNO = 27)
```

The result is:

```
MATCHNO
-------
      9
     10
     11
     12
     13
```

Explanation: The subquery is used to determine the number of the team that is captained by player 27. Next, that result is used in the condition of the main query.

Example 8.10: Get the numbers of the players who have the same league number as player 7. If this player does not have a league number, all players without a league number must be shown.

```
SELECT    PLAYERNO
FROM      PLAYERS
WHERE     LEAGUENO <=>
         (SELECT    LEAGUENO
          FROM      PLAYERS
          WHERE     PLAYERNO = 7)
```

The result is:

```
PLAYERNO
--------
       7
      28
      39
      95
```

Explanation: Of course, this statement returns only one row when that particular player does have a league number.

Example 8.11: Find the number, the town, and the sex of each player living in the same town as player 7 and having the same sex as player 2.

```
SELECT    PLAYERNO, TOWN, SEX
FROM      PLAYERS
WHERE    (TOWN, SEX) =
        ((SELECT    TOWN
          FROM      PLAYERS
          WHERE     PLAYERNO = 7),
         (SELECT    SEX
          FROM      PLAYERS
          WHERE     PLAYERNO = 2))
```

The result is:

```
PLAYERNO  TOWN       SEX
--------  ---------  ---
       2  Stratford  M
       6  Stratford  M
       7  Stratford  M
      39  Stratford  M
      57  Stratford  M
      83  Stratford  M
     100  Stratford  M
```

Explanation: The two scalar subqueries are processed separately. One returns `Stratford` as the answer, and the other returns `M`. After that, the condition `(TOWN, SEX) = ('Stratford', 'M')` is checked for each player separately in the `WHERE` clause. So the two scalar subqueries form one row expression.

If comparisons with row expressions are made, row subqueries can be included.

Example 8.12: Player 6 became secretary of the tennis club on January 1, 1990. Find the numbers of the players who took up a committee position on that same date and also resigned on the same date as player 6.

```
SELECT   DISTINCT PLAYERNO
FROM     COMMITTEE_MEMBERS
WHERE   (BEGIN_DATE, END_DATE) =
        (SELECT    BEGIN_DATE, END_DATE
         FROM      COMMITTEE_MEMBERS
         WHERE     PLAYERNO = 6
         AND       POSITION = 'Secretary'
         AND       BEGIN_DATE = '1990-01-01')
```

The result is:

```
PLAYERNO
--------
       6
       8
      27
```

Explanation: The subquery is a typical row subquery. The result consists of one row with two values at most because each player can hold only one position on a certain date. The combination of PLAYERNO and BEGIN_DATE is the primary key of the COMMITTEE_MEMBERS table. After the subquery has been processed, those two values are compared with the row expression `(BEGIN_DATE, END_DATE)`. Here the same processing rules apply as described in the previous section.

Example 8.13: Get the numbers, names, and initials of all players whose combination of name and initials comes before player 6 in alphabetical order.

```
SELECT   PLAYERNO, NAME, INITIALS
FROM     PLAYERS
WHERE   (NAME, INITIALS) <
        (SELECT    NAME, INITIALS
         FROM      PLAYERS
         WHERE     PLAYERNO = 6)
ORDER BY NAME, INITIALS
```

The result is:

```
PLAYERNO  NAME       INITIALS
--------  ---------  --------
     112  Bailey     IP
      44  Baker      E
      39  Bishop     D
      57  Brown      M
      28  Collins    C
      27  Collins    DD
       2  Everett    R
      83  Hope       PK
      95  Miller     P
     104  Moorman    D
       8  Newcastle  B
     100  Parmenter  P
```

The next example uses the MATCHES_SPECIAL table that was used in Example 5.47.

Example 8.14: Get the numbers of the matches that started after match 1.

```
SELECT   MATCHNO
FROM     MATCHES_SPECIAL
WHERE   (START_DATE, START_TIME) >
        (SELECT   START_DATE, START_TIME
         FROM     MATCHES_SPECIAL
         WHERE    MATCHNO = 1)
```

Explanation: Even though two matches start on the same day, if they start at different times, they can be included in the end result. Without using use row expressions, it would become a complex statement. Try to write this statement without using row expressions.

Exercise 8.6: Find the player number, the name, and the initials of the player who belongs to penalty 4.

Exercise 8.7: Find the player number, the name, and the initials of the player who captains the team belonging to match 2.

Exercise 8.8: Find the player number and name of each player who has the same age as R. Parmenter. R. Parmenter's name and number may not appear in the result.

Exercise 8.9: Find the numbers of all matches played by team 2 in which the number of sets won is equal to the number of sets won in the match with number 6. Exclude match 6 from the result.

Exercise 8.10: Find the number of every match that has the same number of sets won as match 2 and the same number of sets lost as match 8.

Exercise 8.11: Find the numbers, names, and initials of all players whose combination of town, street, and house number comes alphabetically before player 100.

8.4 Comparison Operators with Correlated Subqueries

The previous section contains examples of scalar subqueries, and the previous chapter contains examples of table subqueries. Processing these subqueries is simple for MySQL: Before it processes the main query, it processes the subquery; then it passes this intermediate result to the main query. However, scalar subqueries can also refer to columns of the main query. These are called *correlated subqueries.*

Example 8.15: Get the numbers of the matches played by players living in Inglewood.

```
SELECT   MATCHNO
FROM     MATCHES
WHERE    'Inglewood' =
        (SELECT    TOWN
         FROM      PLAYERS
         WHERE     PLAYERS.PLAYERNO = MATCHES.PLAYERNO)
```

The result is:

```
MATCHNO
-------
      4
      8
     13
```

Explanation: The subquery of this table expression refers to a column belonging to the table specified in the main query: `MATCHES.PLAYERNO`. For this reason, such a subquery is called a *correlated subquery.* By using the qualified column specification, we establish a relationship or correlation between the subquery and the main query.

The effect of a correlated subquery is that MySQL cannot determine the result of the subquery first, but for each row in the main query (every match), the result of the subquery must be determined separately. Because the player belonging to the first match is equal to `6`, the following subquery is executed for this player:

```
SELECT   TOWN
FROM     PLAYERS
WHERE    PLAYERS.PLAYERNO = 6
```

This player does not live in Inglewood, so the first match does not appear in the end result. The next subquery is executed for match 4 with player 44, and he lives in Inglewood. Therefore, match 4 appears in the end result.

```
SELECT   TOWN
FROM     PLAYERS
WHERE    PLAYERS.PLAYERNO = 44
```

The processing of this statement could also be presented as follows with the pseudo programming language:

```
END-RESULT := [];
FOR EACH M IN MATCHES DO
   COUNTER := 0;
   FOR EACH P IN PLAYERS DO
      IF M.PLAYERNO = P.PLAYERNO THEN
         IF 'Inglewood' = P.TOWN THEN
             COUNTER := COUNTER + 1;
         ENDIF;
      ENDIF;
   ENDFOR;
   IF COUNTER > 0 THEN
      END-RESULT :+ W;
   ENDIF;
ENDFOR;
```

Example 8.16: Get the match numbers, the player numbers, and the team numbers of all the matches played by a player who also captains that team.

```
SELECT   MATCHNO, PLAYERNO, TEAMNO
FROM     MATCHES
WHERE    PLAYERNO =
        (SELECT   PLAYERNO
         FROM     TEAMS
         WHERE    TEAMS.PLAYERNO = MATCHES.PLAYERNO)
```

The result is:

```
MATCHNO  PLAYERNO  TEAMNO
-------  --------  ------
      1         6       1
      2         6       1
      3         6       1
      9        27       2
```

Explanation: The correlated subquery is processed for each match separately. For each match, MySQL determines whether there are teams on which the captain is equal to the player who played the match. If so, that match is included in the end result.

Example 8.17: Get the numbers of the matches played by players whose third letter of their name is equal to the third letter of the division in which the team plays.

```
SELECT   MATCHNO
FROM     MATCHES
WHERE    SUBSTR((SELECT   DIVISION
                 FROM     TEAMS
                 WHERE    TEAMS.TEAMNO =
                          MATCHES.TEAMNO),3,1)
         =
         SUBSTR((SELECT   NAME
                 FROM     PLAYERS
                 WHERE    PLAYERS.PLAYERNO =
                          MATCHES.PLAYERNO),3,1)
```

The result is:

```
MATCHNO
-------
      1
      2
      3
```

Exercise 8.12: Get the numbers of the penalties incurred by players who were born after 1965.

Exercise 8.13: Get the payment numbers and the player numbers of all penalties of which the player is also captain of a team.

8.5 Conditions Without a Comparison Operator

The shortest condition is the one in which only one scalar expression is specified. Such a condition is `true` only if the value of that expression is not equal to the number zero. In MySQL, the value `false` is indicated as the number zero; every other value represents the value `true`.

DEFINITION

```
<predicate-without-comparison> ::=
   <scalar expression>
```

Therefore, we can shorten the condition in Example 8.4.

Example 8.18: Get the numbers and league numbers of the players who have a league number.

```
SELECT   PLAYERNO, LEAGUENO
FROM     PLAYERS
WHERE    LEAGUENO
```

The result is similar to the result of Example 8.4.

Example 8.19: Get the numbers of the teams whose number is not equal to 1.

```
SELECT   TEAMNO
FROM     TEAMS
WHERE    TEAMNO - 1
```

The result is:

```
TEAMNO
------
     2
```

Explanation: For the team with team number equal to 1, the expression `TEAMNO - 1` is equal to zero. Conditions with the value zero are not included in the end result because zero is equivalent to `false`.

The following statements are all allowed. Determine their respective results for yourself:

```
SELECT * FROM PLAYERS WHERE 18
SELECT * FROM PLAYERS WHERE NULL
SELECT * FROM PLAYERS WHERE PLAYERNO & 3
SELECT * FROM PLAYERS WHERE YEAR(BIRTH_DATE)
```

8.6 Conditions Coupled with AND, OR, XOR, and NOT

A WHERE clause can contain multiple conditions if the *logical operators* AND, OR, XOR, and NOT are used.

Table 8.2 contains the truth table for two conditions C_1 and C_2, and all possible values for C_1 AND C_2, C_1 OR C_2, C_1 XOR C_2, and NOT C_1.

The operators AND, OR, and NOT do not need much explanation, but XOR probably does. XOR should be read as an exclusive or. A condition with XOR is true if one of the two conditions is equal to true and the other is false; the condition is false if both conditions are true or false. Otherwise, the condition is unknown.

TABLE 8.2 Truth Table for the Logical Operators

C_1	C_2	C_1 AND C_2	C_1 OR C_2	C_1 XOR C_2	NOT C_1
true	true	true	true	false	false
true	false	false	true	true	false
true	unknown	unknown	true	unknown	false
false	true	false	true	true	true
false	false	false	false	false	true
false	unknown	false	unknown	unknown	true
unknown	true	unknown	true	unknown	unknown
unknown	false	false	unknown	unknown	unknown
unknown	unknown	unknown	unknown	unknown	unknown

Example 8.20: Get the number, name, sex, and birth date of each male player born after 1970.

```
SELECT   PLAYERNO, NAME, SEX, BIRTH_DATE
FROM     PLAYERS
WHERE    SEX = 'M'
AND      BIRTH_DATE > '1970-12-31'
```

The result is:

```
PLAYERNO  NAME   SEX  BIRTH_DATE
--------  -----  ---  ----------
      57  Brown  M    1971-08-17
```

Explanation: For every row in the PLAYERS table in which the value in the SEX column equals `M` and the value in the BIRTH_DATE column is greater than `31 December 1970`, four columns are displayed.

Example 8.21: Get the numbers, the names, and the towns of all players who live in Plymouth or Eltham.

```
SELECT   PLAYERNO, NAME, TOWN
FROM     PLAYERS
WHERE    TOWN = 'Plymouth'
OR       TOWN = 'Eltham'
```

The result is:

```
PLAYERNO  NAME     TOWN
--------  -------  --------
      27  Collins  Eltham
     104  Moorman  Eltham
     112  Bailey   Plymouth
```

Note that this `SELECT` statement would produce *no* result if `AND` replaced the logical operator `OR`. Work out for yourself why.

If a `WHERE` clause contains `AND` plus `OR` operators, the `AND` operators are processed first. So in the following `WHERE` clause (assume that C_1, C_2, and C_3 represent conditions)

```
WHERE C1 OR C2 AND C3
```

C_2 AND C_3 is evaluated first. Imagine that the result is A_1, and after this, C_1 OR A_1 is evaluated. This is the final result This process can also be represented as follows:

```
C2 AND C3 --> A1
C1 OR A1  --> result
```

By using brackets, you can influence the order in which the conditions are evaluated. Consider the following `WHERE` clause:

```
WHERE (C1 OR C2) AND C3
```

The processing sequence now becomes this:

```
C1 OR C2  --> A1
A1 AND C3 --> result
```

With any given value for C_1, C_2, and C_3, the result of the first example can differ from the result of the second. Imagine, for example, that C_1 and C_2 are `true` and that

C_3 is `false`. Then the result of the first example without brackets is `true` and that of the second with brackets is `false`.

The `NOT` operator can be specified in front of each condition. The `NOT` operator changes the value of a condition to `false` if it is `true` and `true` if it is `false`; if the condition is `unknown`, it remains `unknown`.

Example 8.22: Get the numbers, names, and towns of players who do *not* live in Stratford.

```
SELECT   PLAYERNO, NAME, TOWN
FROM     PLAYERS
WHERE    TOWN <> 'Stratford'
```

The result is:

```
PLAYERNO  NAME       TOWN
--------  ---------  ---------
       8  Newcastle  Inglewood
      27  Collins    Eltham
      28  Collins    Midhurst
      44  Baker      Inglewood
      95  Miller     Douglas
     104  Moorman    Eltham
     112  Bailey     Plymouth
```

This example can also be formulated as follows:

```
SELECT   PLAYERNO, NAME, TOWN
FROM     PLAYERS
WHERE    NOT (TOWN = 'Stratford')
```

Explanation: Each row in which the condition `TOWN = 'Stratford'` is `true` or `unknown` is not dislayed because the `NOT` operator switches the value `true` to `false`, and `NOT (unknown)` remains `unknown`.

Before Version 5.0.2 of MySQL, using the brackets in this example was important. If no brackets were used in the previous condition, the statement would have returned another result. In that case, the condition `NOT TOWN` would have been executed first. Because every player has a place of residence, the result would have been `true` for each. Next, it would determine whether the value `true` was equal to `Stratford`. Obviously, the result of the statement would have been empty.

Since Version 5.0.2, this does not apply anymore. Now, specifying `NOT TOWN = 'Stratford'` is equivalent to specifying `NOT (TOWN = 'Stratford')`. If you want to have that old behavior back, you must use HIGH_NOT_PRECEDENCE for the SQL_MODE system variable.

Example 8.23: Get the number, the league number, and the phone numbers of all the players who have a league number and a phone number.

```
SELECT   PLAYERNO, LEAGUENO, PHONENO
FROM     PLAYERS
WHERE    LEAGUENO AND PHONENO
```

The result is:

```
PLAYERNO  LEAGUENO  PHONENO
--------  --------  ----------
       2  2411      070-237893
       6  8467      070-476537
       8  2983      070-458458
      27  2513      079-234857
      44  1124      070-368753
      57  6409      070-473458
      83  1608      070-353548
     100  6524      070-494593
     104  7060      079-987571
     112  1319      010-548745
```

Example 8.24: Get the number, town, and date of birth of each player who lives in Stratford or was born in 1963, but do not include those who live in Stratford and were born in 1963.

```
SELECT   PLAYERNO, TOWN, BIRTH_DATE
FROM     PLAYERS
WHERE   (TOWN = 'Stratford' OR  YEAR(BIRTH_DATE) = 1963)
AND NOT (TOWN = 'Stratford' AND YEAR(BIRTH_DATE) = 1963)
```

The result is:

```
PLAYERNO  TOWN       BIRTH_DATE
--------  ---------  ----------
       2  Stratford  1948-09-01
       6  Stratford  1964-06-25
      28  Midhurst   1963-06-22
      39  Stratford  1956-10-29
      44  Inglewood  1963-01-09
      57  Stratford  1971-08-17
      83  Stratford  1956-11-11
      95  Douglas    1963-05-14
     112  Plymouth   1963-10-01
```

The previous statement could have been formulated more elegantly by using the XOR operator:

```
SELECT   PLAYERNO, TOWN, BIRTH_DATE
FROM     PLAYERS
WHERE   (TOWN = 'Stratford') XOR (YEAR(BIRTH_DATE) = 1963)
```

Explanation: This condition is true if one of the two conditions is true and the other is false.

Instead of using the term AND, you may use the symbol &&; instead of using OR, you may use the symbol ||; and you may replace NOT with !. Note however, that this is not according to the SQL standard, which is why we recommend using the words AND, OR, and NOT. Also note that || represents OR only if the SQL_MODE system variable does not have the PIPES_AS_CONCAT; otherwise, it represents a concatenation.

Exercise 8.14: Get the number, name, and town of each female player who is *not* a resident of Stratford.

Exercise 8.15: Find the player numbers of those who joined the club between 1970 and 1980.

Exercise 8.16: Find the numbers, names, and dates of birth of players born in a leap year. Just in case you need a reminder, a leap year is one in which the year figure is divisible by 4, except centuries in which the year figure must be divisible by 400. Therefore, 1900 is not a leap year, but 2000 is.

Exercise 8.17: For each competition player born after 1965 who has won at least one match, get the match number, the name and initials, and the division of the teams in which the player has ever played.

8.7 The IN Operator with Expression List

The condition with the IN *operator* has two forms. This section describes the form in which a series of values is listed. Section 8.8 explains the form in which subqueries are used.

DEFINITION

```
<predicate with in> ::=
   <scalar expression> [ NOT ] IN <scalar expression list> |
   <row expression> [ NOT ] IN <row expression list>

<row expression list> ::=
   ( <scalar expression list>
      [ , <scalar expression list> ]... )

<scalar expression list> ::=
   ( <scalar expression> [ , <scalar expression> ]... )
```

Conditions can become lengthy if you have to check whether a specific value appears within a long list of given values. Consider an example to illustrate this.

Example 8.25: Find the number, name, and town of each player who lives in Inglewood, Plymouth, Midhurst, or Douglas.

```
SELECT   PLAYERNO, NAME, TOWN
FROM     PLAYERS
WHERE    TOWN = 'Inglewood'
OR       TOWN = 'Plymouth'
OR       TOWN = 'Midhurst'
OR       TOWN = 'Douglas'
```

The result is:

```
PLAYERNO  NAME       TOWN
--------  ---------  ---------
       8  Newcastle  Inglewood
      28  Collins    Midhurst
      44  Baker      Inglewood
      95  Miller     Douglas
     112  Bailey     Plymouth
```

The statement and the result are correct, but the statement is rather long. The `IN` operator can simplify the statement:

```
SELECT   PLAYERNO, NAME, TOWN
FROM     PLAYERS
WHERE    TOWN IN ('Inglewood', 'Plymouth', 'Midhurst',
                  'Douglas')
```

This condition is to be read as follows: Each row whose `TOWN` value occurs in the set of four town names satisfies the condition. In this example, the four town names form the *expression list*.

Example 8.26: Get the numbers and years of birth of the players born in 1962, 1963, or 1970.

```
SELECT    PLAYERNO, YEAR(BIRTH_DATE)
FROM      PLAYERS
WHERE     YEAR(BIRTH_DATE) IN (1962, 1963, 1970)
```

The result is:

```
PLAYERNO  YEAR(BIRTH_DATE)
--------  ----------------
       7              1963
       8              1962
      28              1963
      44              1963
      95              1963
     100              1963
     104              1970
     112              1963
```

The previous examples use only literals within the expression list. All forms of scalar expressions can be specified here, including column specifications and scalar subqueries.

Example 8.27: Get the match numbers and the number of sets won and lost for all matches that have two sets won or two sets lost.

```
SELECT    MATCHNO, WON, LOST
FROM      MATCHES
WHERE     2 IN (WON, LOST)
```

The result is:

```
MATCHNO  WON  LOST
-------  ---  ----
      2    2     3
      4    3     2
      9    3     2
     10    3     2
     11    2     3
```

Example 8.28: Find the numbers of the player whose number is equal to `100`, equal to the player number of the penalty with number 1, or equal to the number of the captain of team 2.

```
SELECT    PLAYERNO
FROM      PLAYERS
WHERE     PLAYERNO IN
         (100,
         (SELECT    PLAYERNO
          FROM      PENALTIES
          WHERE     PAYMENTNO = 1),
         (SELECT    PLAYERNO
          FROM      TEAMS
          WHERE     TEAMNO = 2))
```

The result is:

```
PLAYERNO
--------
       6
      27
     100
```

Explanation: The expression list consists of three scalar expressions, of which one is a literal and the other two are scalar subqueries. Make sure that each of the subqueries is really scalar and that they do not return more than one row consisting of one value.

Example 8.29: Get the match numbers and the number of sets won and lost of all matches in which the number of sets won is equal to the match number divided by 2, or equal to the number of sets lost or equal to the number of sets lost belonging to match 1.

```
SELECT    MATCHNO, WON, LOST
FROM      MATCHES
WHERE     WON IN
         (TRUNCATE(MATCHNO / 2,0), LOST,
         (SELECT    LOST
          FROM      MATCHES
          WHERE     MATCHNO = 1))
```

The result is:

```
MATCHNO  WON  LOST
-------  ---  ----
      6    1     3
      7    3     0
     12    1     3
```

Example 8.30: Get the numbers of the matches played by players whose names begin with the capital letters B, C, or E.

```
SELECT   MATCHNO
FROM     MATCHES
WHERE   (SELECT   SUBSTR(NAME,1,1)
         FROM     PLAYERS
         WHERE    PLAYERS.PLAYERNO = MATCHES.PLAYERNO)
         IN ('B','C','E')
```

The result is:

```
MATCHNO
-------
      4
      6
      7
      9
     11
     12
```

The following rules apply to the scalar expressions used with the IN operator: The data types must be comparable, and not every expression form can be used.

How exactly is a condition with IN processed? Imagine that E_1, E_2, E_3, and E_4 are scalar expressions. Then the condition

$$E_1 \text{ IN } (E_2, E_3, E_4)$$

is equivalent to this condition:

$$(E_1 = E_2) \text{ OR } (E_1 = E_3) \text{ OR } (E_1 = E_4)$$

This means that if one of the expressions between brackets is equal to null, the value of the entire condition can still be true. It also means that if E_1 itself is equal to null, the entire condition evaluates to unknown.

Simultaneously, it follows that the condition

$$E_1 \text{ NOT IN } (E_2, E_3, E_4)$$

is equivalent to the condition

$$\text{NOT } (E_1 \text{ IN } (E_2, E_3, E_4))$$

and equivalent to:

$$(E_1 <> E_2) \text{ AND } (E_1 <> E_3) \text{ AND } (E_1 <> E_4)$$

The definition shows that the IN operator can also deal with row expressions.

Example 8.31: Find the match numbers and the number of sets won and lost of all matches that were won 3–1 or 3–2.

```
SELECT   MATCHNO, WON, LOST
FROM     MATCHES
WHERE   (WON, LOST) IN ((3,1),(3,2))
```

The result is:

```
MATCHNO  WON  LOST
-------  ---  ----
      1    3     1
      4    3     2
      9    3     2
     10    3     2
```

Explanation: Because a row expression consisting of two expressions occurs to the left of the `IN` operator, the expression list should also be a list consisting of row expressions.

Example 8.32: Get the numbers, names, and initials of all players whose name and initials are equal to that of players 6 or 27.

```
SELECT   PLAYERNO, NAME, INITIALS
FROM     PLAYERS
WHERE   (NAME, INITIALS) IN
       ((SELECT   NAME, INITIALS
         FROM     PLAYERS
         WHERE    PLAYERNO = 6),
        (SELECT   NAME, INITIALS
         FROM     PLAYERS
         WHERE    PLAYERNO = 27))
```

The result is:

```
PLAYERNO  NAME       INITIALS
--------  ---------  --------
       6  Parmenter  R
      27  Collins    DD
```

Exercise 8.18: Get the payment numbers of every penalty of $50, $75, or $100.

Exercise 8.19: Get the numbers of the players who do not live in Stratford or in Douglas.

Exercise 8.20: Get the numbers of the penalties of which the amount is equal to 100, equal to five times the payment number, or equal to the amount belonging to penalty 2.

Exercise 8.21: Get the numbers of the players who live in the town Stratford and the street Haseltine Lane, or in the town Stratford and the street Edgecombe Way.

8.8 The IN Operator with Subquery

Section 8.7 discussed the first form of the `IN` operator. A row from a table satisfies a condition with the `IN` operator if the value of a particular column occurs in a *fixed* set of expressions. The user has defined the number of elements in the set. The `IN` operator can also take another form in which the set of expressions is not listed, but is *variable*. MySQL determines the set at the point the statement is processed. This section covers this process.

Section 8.7 gave a definition of the condition with the `IN` operator. The definition is extended as follows:

DEFINITION

```
<predicate with in> ::=
  <scalar expression> [ NOT ] IN <scalar expression list> |
  <scalar expression> [ NOT ] IN <column subquery>        |
  <row expression> [ NOT ] IN <row expression list>       |
  <row expression> [ NOT ] IN <table subquery>

<row expression list> ::=
  ( <scalar expression list>
     [ , <scalar expression list> ]... )

<scalar expression list> ::=
  ( <scalar expression> [ , <scalar expression> ]... )

<column subquery> ;
<table subquery>  ::= ( <table expression> )
```

Example 8.33: Get the player number, name, and initials of each player who has played at least one match.

The question in this example actually consists of two parts. First, we need to work out which players have played at least one match. Then we need to look for the numbers, the names, and the initials of these players. The MATCHES table contains the numbers of the players who have played at least one match, so with the following simple SELECT statement, we can determine these numbers:

```
SELECT   PLAYERNO
FROM     MATCHES
```

The result is:

```
PLAYERNO
--------
       6
       6
       6
      44
      83
       2
      57
       8
      27
     104
     112
     112
       8
```

But how do we use those numbers to look up the relevant names and initials of the players from the PLAYERS table? If we use the IN operator, we have to remember the numbers of the previous statement somehow and then type in the following statement:

```
SELECT   PLAYERNO, NAME, INITIALS
FROM     PLAYERS
WHERE    PLAYERNO IN (6, 6, 6, 44, 83, 2, 57, 8, 27,
                      104, 112, 112, 8)
```

The result is:

```
PLAYERNO  NAME       INITIALS
--------  ---------  --------
       2  Everett    R
       6  Parmenter  R
       8  Newcastle  B
      27  Collins    DD
      44  Baker      E
      57  Brown      M
      83  Hope       PK
     104  Moorman    D
     112  Bailey     IP
```

This method works, but it is very clumsy and would be impractical if the MATCHES table contained a large set of different player numbers. Because this type of query is very common, MySQL offers the possibility of specifying column subqueries together with the `IN` operator (note that using subqueries with the previous form of the `IN` operator is allowed, but those are scalar subqueries). The `SELECT` statement for the previous example now looks like this:

```
SELECT    PLAYERNO, NAME, INITIALS
FROM      PLAYERS
WHERE     PLAYERNO IN
         (SELECT    PLAYERNO
          FROM      MATCHES)
```

We have no longer specified an expression list after the `IN` operator as we did in the examples in Section 8.7; we have specified a column subquery. As a result, a column subquery has multiple rows, with each row consisting of one value. In the example, the result would look like the following (remember that this is an intermediate result that the users do not see):

```
(6, 6, 6, 44, 83, 2, 57, 8, 27, 104, 112, 112, 8)
```

When MySQL processes the table expression, it replaces the subquery with the (intermediate) result of the subquery (this is done behind the scenes):

```
SELECT    PLAYERNO, NAME, INITIALS
FROM      PLAYERS
WHERE     PLAYERNO IN (6, 6, 6, 44, 83, 2, 57, 8, 27,
                       104, 112, 112, 8)
```

This is now a familiar statement. The result of this statement is the same as the end result that we have already shown.

The most important difference between the `IN` operator with a set of scalar expressions and a column subquery is that, in the first instance, the set of values is fixed in advance by the user, whereas in the second instance, the values are variable and are determined by MySQL during the processing.

Example 8.34: Get the player number and the name of each player who has played at least one match for the first team.

```
SELECT    PLAYERNO, NAME
FROM      PLAYERS
WHERE     PLAYERNO IN
         (SELECT    PLAYERNO
          FROM      MATCHES
          WHERE     TEAMNO = 1)
```

The intermediate result of the subquery is:

```
(2, 6, 6, 6, 8, 44, 57, 83)
```

The result of the entire statement is:

```
PLAYERNO  NAME
--------  ---------
       2  Everett
       6  Parmenter
       8  Newcastle
      44  Baker
      57  Brown
      83  Hope
```

As you can see, a subquery can also contain conditions; even other subqueries are allowed.

Example 8.35: Get the number and name of each player who has played at least one match for the team that is *not* captained by player 6.

```
SELECT   PLAYERNO, NAME
FROM     PLAYERS
WHERE    PLAYERNO IN
        (SELECT   PLAYERNO
         FROM     MATCHES
         WHERE    TEAMNO NOT IN
                 (SELECT   TEAMNO
                  FROM     TEAMS
                  WHERE    PLAYERNO = 6))
```

The intermediate result of the *sub-subquery* is:

```
(1)
```

The subquery searches all players who do *not* appear in the set of teams captained by player 6. The intermediate result is:

```
(8, 27, 104, 112, 112)
```

The result of the statement is:

```
PLAYERNO  NAME
--------  ---------
       8  Newcastle
      27  Collins
     104  Moorman
     112  Bailey
```

Again, users do not see any of the intermediate results.

When is a condition with an IN operator and a subquery true, when is it false, and when is it unknown? Imagine that C is the name of a column and that v_1, v_2, …, v_n are values from which the intermediate result of subquery S is formed. It follows that

```
C IN (S)
```

is equivalent to:

$$(C = C) \text{ AND } ((C = v_1) \text{ OR } (C = v_2) \text{ OR } \ldots \text{ OR } (C = v_n) \text{ OR false})$$

The following should be noted concerning certain specific situations:

- If C is equal to the null value, the entire condition evaluates to unknown because the condition C = C is equal to unknown; this rule holds independently of the numbers of values in the result of the subquery.
- If C is not equal to the null value and the subquery returns no result, the condition evaluates to false because the last "term" of this "longhand" condition is false.
- If C is not equal to the null value, and if one of the v values is equal to the null value and one of the other v values is not equal to the null value, the condition can be true or unknown.
- If C is not equal to the null value and all v values are equal to the null value, the condition evaluates to unknown.

We can apply the same reasoning to NOT IN. The condition

```
C NOT IN (S)
```

is equivalent to:

$$(C = C) \text{ AND } (C <> v_1) \text{ AND } (C <> v_2) \text{ AND } \ldots \text{ AND } (C <> v_n) \text{ AND true}$$

Note the following concerning certain specific situations:

- If C is equal to the null value, the entire condition evaluates to unknown because the condition C = C is equal to unknown; this rule holds independently of the numbers of values in the result of the subquery.
- If C is not equal to the null value and the subquery returns no result, the condition evaluates to true because the last "term" of this "longhand" condition is true.
- If C is not equal to the null value, and if one of the v values is equal to the null value and one of the other v values is not equal to the null value, the condition can be true or unknown.

- If C is not equal to the null value and all v values are equal to the null value, the condition evaluates to unknown.

Imagine that the year of birth of player 27 is unknown. Will player 27 appear in the end result of the following SELECT statement?

```
SELECT   *
FROM     PLAYERS
WHERE    BIRTH_DATE NOT IN
        (SELECT   BIRTH_DATE
         FROM     PLAYERS
         WHERE    Town = 'London')
```

The answer is no. Only players whose dates of birth are known are included in the end result, so player 27 does not appear.

This IN operator with subquery can be extended with row expressions. In this case, after the IN operator, you have to specify a table expression. The number of expressions in the row expression and the number of expressions in the SELECT clause of the table expressions must be equal. The data types must also be comparable.

Example 8.36: Get all the details of all the rows in the COMMITTEE MEMBERS table that have the same begin and end date as one of those rows for which the position is equal to Secretary.

```
SELECT   *
FROM     COMMITTEE_MEMBERS
WHERE   (BEGIN_DATE, END_DATE) IN
        (SELECT   BEGIN_DATE, END_DATE
         FROM     COMMITTEE_MEMBERS
         WHERE    POSITION = 'Secretary')
```

The result is:

```
PLAYERNO  BEGIN_DATE  END_DATE    POSITION
--------  ----------  ----------  ---------
       6  1990-01-01  1990-12-31  Secretary
       8  1990-01-01  1990-12-31  Treasurer
       8  1991-01-01  1991-12-31  Secretary
      27  1990-01-01  1990-12-31  Member
      27  1991-01-01  1991-12-31  Treasurer
      57  1992-01-01  1992-12-31  Secretary
     112  1992-01-01  1992-12-31  Member
```

Almost all the tables of the standard example in this book have simple primary keys consisting of one column. Imagine that the situation is different and that the primary key of the PLAYERS table is formed by the columns NAME and INITIALS. Foreign keys referring to this primary key will all be compound. In that case, formulating queries is simple if row expressions are used. We illustrate this with a few examples that use slightly adapted versions of the familiar tables PLAYERS and PENALTIES. Assume that the primary key in the PLAYERS_NI table is indeed formed by the combination NAME with INITIALS. In the PENALTIES_NI table, the column PAYMENTNO is still the primary key, but it has been extended with the columns NAME and INITIALS.

Example 8.37: Create the two tables and insert several rows.

```
CREATE TABLE PLAYERS_NI
      (NAME          CHAR(10) NOT NULL,
       INITIALS      CHAR(3) NOT NULL,
       TOWN          VARCHAR(30) NOT NULL,
       PRIMARY KEY (NAME, INITIALS))

INSERT INTO PLAYERS_NI VALUES ('Parmenter', 'R', 'Stratford')

INSERT INTO PLAYERS_NI VALUES ('Parmenter', 'P', 'Stratford')

INSERT INTO PLAYERS_NI VALUES ('Miller', 'P', 'Douglas')

CREATE TABLE PENALTIES_NI
      (PAYMENTNO     INTEGER NOT NULL,
       NAME          CHAR(10) NOT NULL,
       INITIALS      CHAR(3) NOT NULL,
       AMOUNT        DECIMAL(7,2) NOT NULL,
       PRIMARY KEY (PAYMENTNO),
       FOREIGN KEY (NAME, INITIALS)
          REFERENCES PLAYERS_NI (NAME, INITIALS))

INSERT INTO PENALTIES_NI VALUES (1, 'Parmenter', 'R', 100.00)

INSERT INTO PENALTIES_NI VALUES (2, 'Miller', 'P', 200.00)
```

The remaining examples in this section relate to the earlier two tables.

Example 8.38: Get the name, initials, and town of each player who has incurred at least one penalty.

The following SELECT statement, in which no row expressions are used, does not give the correct answer to this question, even though it looks like it will:

```
SELECT   NAME, INITIALS, TOWN
FROM     PLAYERS_NI
WHERE    NAME IN
        (SELECT   NAME
         FROM     PENALTIES_NI)
AND      INITIALS IN
        (SELECT   INITIALS
         FROM     PENALTIES_NI)
```

The result is:

```
NAME       INITIALS  TOWN
---------  --------  ---------
Parmenter  R         Stratford
Parmenter  P         Stratford
Miller     P         Douglas
```

This result is the correct answer with respect to the SELECT statement, but it is *not* the answer to the original question. The fact is, player P. Parmenter has *not* incurred a penalty according to the PENALTIES_NI table. A correct formulation of this question is:

```
SELECT   NAME, INITIALS, TOWN
FROM     PLAYERS_NI
WHERE   (NAME, INITIALS) IN
        (SELECT   NAME, INITIALS
         FROM     PENALTIES_NI)
```

The result is:

```
NAME       INITIALS  TOWN
---------  --------  ---------
Parmenter  R         Stratford
Miller     P         Douglas
```

Another correct solution for this example is given next. This solution does not make use of row expressions, which makes it more difficult to fathom.

```
SELECT   NAME, INITIALS, TOWN
FROM     PLAYERS_NI
WHERE    NAME IN
        (SELECT   NAME
         FROM     PENALTIES_NI
         WHERE    PLAYERS_NI.INITIALS =
                  PENALTIES_NI.INITIALS)
```

Explanation: For every row in the main query (thus, in the PLAYERS_NI table), the subquery looks for rows in the PENALTIES_NI table with identical initials. Next, a verification is carried out to see whether the NAME of the player also appears in those rows (`WHERE NAME IN ...`).

Example 8.39: Get the name, initials, and town of each player who has *not* incurred a penalty.

```
SELECT   NAME, INITIALS, TOWN
FROM     PLAYERS_NI
WHERE   (NAME, INITIALS) NOT IN
        (SELECT   NAME, INITIALS
         FROM     PENALTIES_NI)
```

The result is:

```
NAME       INITIALS  TOWN
---------  --------  ---------
Parmenter  P         Stratford
```

Explanation: The details of a player in the PLAYERS_NI table are included in the result only if there is not one row in the PENALTIES_NI table with the same combination of NAME and INITIALS as the player in the PLAYERS_NI table.

Section 8.16 deals more extensively with the features and limitations of subqueries.

Exercise 8.22: Get the player number and the name of each player who has incurred at least one penalty.

Exercise 8.23: Get the player number and the name of each player who has incurred at least one penalty of more than $50.

Exercise 8.24: Find the team numbers and player numbers of the team captains from the first division who live in Stratford.

Exercise 8.25: Get the player number and the name of each player for whom at least one penalty has been paid and who is not a captain of any team playing in the first division.

Exercise 8.26: What is the result of the following SELECT statement?

```
SELECT   *
FROM     PLAYERS
WHERE    LEAGUENO NOT IN
        (SELECT   LEAGUENO
         FROM     PLAYERS
         WHERE    PLAYERNO IN (28, 95))
```

Exercise 8.27: Get the match number and player number of each match in which the number of sets won and the number of sets lost is equal to at least one of the set scores of a match played by a team from the second division.

Exercise 8.28: Get the numbers and names of those players who live at the same address as at least one other player. "Address" is defined as the combination of town, street, house number, and postcode.

8.9 The BETWEEN Operator

MySQL supports a special operator that enables you to determine whether a value occurs within a given range of values.

DEFINITION

```
<predicate with between> ::=
   <scalar expression> [ NOT ] BETWEEN <scalar expression>
      AND <scalar expression>
```

Example 8.40: Find the number and date of birth of each player born between 1962 and 1964.

```
SELECT    PLAYERNO, BIRTH_DATE
FROM      PLAYERS
WHERE     BIRTH_DATE >= '1962-01-01'
AND       BIRTH_DATE <= '1964-12-31'
```

The result is:

```
PLAYERNO  BIRTH_DATE
--------  ----------
       6  1964-06-25
       7  1963-05-11
       8  1962-07-08
      27  1964-12-28
      28  1963-06-22
      44  1963-01-09
      95  1963-10-01
     100  1963-02-28
     112  1963-10-01
```

This statement can also be written using the `BETWEEN` *operator* (the result remains the same):

```
SELECT    PLAYERNO, BIRTH_DATE
FROM      PLAYERS
WHERE     BIRTH_DATE BETWEEN '1962-01-01' AND '1964-12-31'
```

If E_1, E_2, and E_3 are expressions, the condition

E_1 BETWEEN E_2 AND E_3

is equivalent to this condition:

(E_1 >= E_2) AND (E_1 <= E_3)

From this, we can derive that if one of the three expressions is equal to the null value, the entire condition is unknown or false. Additionally, it follows that

E_1 NOT BETWEEN E_2 AND E_3

is equivalent to

NOT (E_1 BETWEEN E_2 AND E_3)

and equivalent to this:

(E_1 < E_2) OR (E_1 > E_3)

In this case, if E_1 has the null value, the condition evaluates to unknown. The condition is true, for example, if E_1 is not null, E_2 is null, and E_1 is greater than E_3.

Example 8.41: Get the numbers of the matches where the sum of the number of sets won and lost is equal to 2, 3, or 4.

```
SELECT    MATCHNO, WON + LOST
FROM      MATCHES
WHERE     WON + LOST BETWEEN 2 AND 4
```

The result is:

```
MATCHNO  WON + LOST
-------  ----------
      1           4
      3           3
      5           3
      6           4
      7           3
      8           3
     12           4
     13           3
```

Example 8.42: Get the player number, the date of birth, and the name and initials of each player whose birth date is between that of B. Newcastle and P. Miller.

```
SELECT   PLAYERNO, BIRTH_DATE, NAME, INITIALS
FROM     PLAYERS
WHERE    BIRTH_DATE BETWEEN
        (SELECT   BIRTH_DATE
         FROM     PLAYERS
         WHERE    NAME = 'Newcastle'
         AND      INITIALS = 'B')
         AND
        (SELECT   BIRTH_DATE
         FROM     PLAYERS
         WHERE    NAME = 'Miller'
         AND      INITIALS = 'P')
```

The result is:

```
PLAYERNO  BIRTH_DATE  NAME       INITIALS
--------  ----------  ---------  --------
       7  1963-05-11  Wise       GWS
       8  1962-07-08  Newcastle  B
      44  1963-01-09  Baker      E
      95  1963-05-14  Miller     P
     100  1963-02-28  Parmenter  P
```

Exercise 8.29: Get the payment number of each penalty between $50 and $100.

Exercise 8.30: Get the payment number of each penalty that is *not* between $50 and $100.

Exercise 8.31: Get the numbers of the players who joined the club after the age of 16 and before reaching their 40s (we remind you that players can join the club only on January 1 of each year).

8.10 The LIKE Operator

The `LIKE` *operator* selects alphanumeric values with a particular pattern or mask.

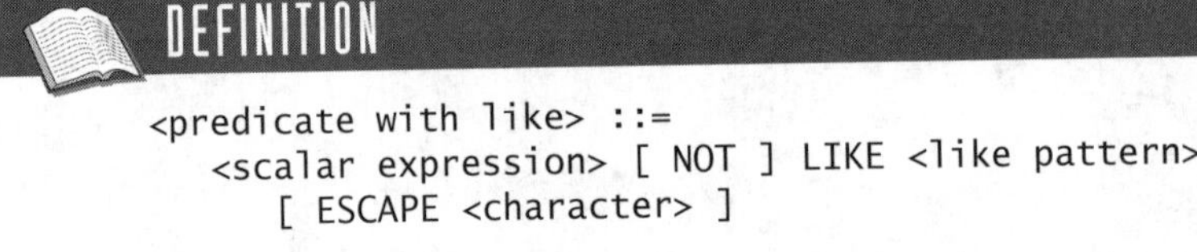

DEFINITION

```
<predicate with like> ::=
   <scalar expression> [ NOT ] LIKE <like pattern>
      [ ESCAPE <character> ]

<like pattern> ::= <scalar alphanumeric expression>
```

Example 8.43: Find the name and number of each player whose name begins with a capital B.

```
SELECT   NAME, PLAYERNO
FROM     PLAYERS
WHERE    NAME LIKE 'B%'
```

The result is:

```
NAME     PLAYERNO
------   --------
Bishop         39
Baker          44
Brown          57
Bailey        112
```

Explanation: After the LIKE operator, you find an alphanumeric literal: 'B%'. Because this literal comes after a LIKE operator and not after a comparison operator, two characters, the percentage sign and the underscore, have a special meaning. Such a literal is called a *pattern* or a *mask*. In a pattern, the percentage sign stands for zero, one, or more characters. The underscore stands for exactly one random character.

The collation is important to the LIKE operator. The previous SELECT statement asked for the players whose names begin with a capital B or with a small b, followed by zero, one, or more characters. If we install MySQL in a default way, we are using the collation latin1_swedish_ci, which considers capital and small letters to be equal. This does not apply to, for example, the collation latin1_general_cs. Chapter 22 discusses collations in detail.

Example 8.44: Get the name and number of each player whose name ends with the small letter r.

```
SELECT   NAME, PLAYERNO
FROM     PLAYERS
WHERE    NAME LIKE '%r'
```

The result is:

```
NAME        PLAYERNO
---------  ---------
Parmenter          6
Baker             44
Miller            95
Parmenter        100
```

Example 8.45: Get the name and number of each player whose name has the letter e as the penultimate letter.

```
SELECT   NAME, PLAYERNO
FROM     PLAYERS
WHERE    NAME LIKE '%e_'
```

The result is:

```
NAME        PLAYERNO
---------   --------
Parmenter          6
Baker             44
Miller            95
Bailey           112
Parmenter        100
```

The pattern does not have to be a simple alphanumeric literal. Each alphanumeric expression is permitted.

Example 8.46: Get the name, town, and number of each player whose name ends with a letter that is equal to the third letter of his or her town.

```
SELECT   NAME, TOWN, PLAYERNO
FROM     PLAYERS
WHERE    NAME LIKE CONCAT('%', SUBSTR(TOWN,3,1))
```

The result is:

```
NAME        TOWN        PLAYERNO
---------   ---------   --------
Parmenter   Stratford          6
Parmenter   Stratford        100
Bailey      Plymouth         112
```

In a pattern, if both the percentage sign and the underscore are absent, the equal to operator can be used. In that case, the condition

```
NAME LIKE 'Baker'
```

is equivalent to this:

```
NAME = 'Baker'
```

Imagine that A is an alphanumeric column and P a pattern; then

```
A NOT LIKE P
```

is equivalent to this:

```
NOT (A LIKE P)
```

If we want to search for one or both of the two special symbols (_ and %), we have to use an *escape symbol.*

Example 8.47: Find the name and number of each player whose name contains an underscore.

```
SELECT   NAME, PLAYERNO
FROM     PLAYERS
WHERE    NAME LIKE '%#_%' ESCAPE '#'
```

Explanation: Because no player satisfies this condition, no result returns. Every character can be specified as an escape symbol. We chose # for this, but symbols such as @, $, and ~ are also allowed. The symbol that follows the escape symbol in a pattern then loses its special meaning. If we had not used the escape symbol in this example, MySQL would have looked for players whose names contain at least one character.

Exercise 8.32: Find the number and name of each player whose name contains the string of letters `is`.

Exercise 8.33: Find the number and name of each player whose name is six characters long.

Exercise 8.34: Find the number and name of each player whose name is at least six characters long.

Exercise 8.35: Find the number and name of each player whose name has an `r` as the third and penultimate letter.

Exercise 8.36: Get the number and name of each player whose town name has the percentage sign in the second and penultimate position.

8.11 The REGEXP Operator

The previous section used the `LIKE` operator to select values with a certain pattern. MySQL supports an additional operator to select rows with the help of patterns: the

REGEXP operator. REGEXP is an abbreviation of *regular expression.* The REGEXP operator has more features but is not part of the SQL standard, as the LIKE operator is. A synonym for the operator REGEXP is RLIKE.

DEFINITION

```
<predicate with rlike> ::=
   <scalar expression> [ NOT ] [ REGEXP | RLIKE ]
      <regexp pattern>

<regexp pattern> ::= <scalar expression>
```

The LIKE operator has two symbols with a special meaning: the percentage sign and the underscore. The REGEXP operator has many more; see Table 8.3.

TABLE 8.3 Special Symbols Belonging to the REGEXP Operator

Special Symbol	Meaning
^	The beginning of the value.
$	The end of the value.
[*abc*]	The rule is satisfied if one of the characters specified between the brackets occurs in the value.
[*a-z*]	The rule is satisfied if one of the characters falling within the range of the characters a and z occurs in the value.
[^*a-z*]	The rule is satisfied if one of the characters falling within the range of the characters a and z does not occur in the value.
.	The rule is satisfied if one random character occurs on the position of the point.
*	The rule is satisfied if what comes in front of the asterisk occurs zero, one, or more times.
()	Brackets can be used to define a set of letters as a group.
+	The rule is satisfied if what comes in front of the plus occurs one or more times.
?	The rule is satisfied if what comes in front of the question mark occurs zero or one time.
{*n*}	The rule is satisfied if what comes in front of the brackets occurs *n* times.
|	This symbol works like an OR operator. The rule is satisfied if what stands left or right of the symbol occurs.
[[.x.]]	X represents a specific symbol. The rule is satisfied if this symbol occurs within the value. The supported symbols are defined in the file regexp/cname.h. Examples of symbols are the backspace, newline, hyphen, plus sign, full stop, and colon.

continues

TABLE 8.3 Continued

Special Symbol	Meaning
[[:<:]] and [[:>:]]	These two symbols represent the beginning and end of a word, respectively.
[[:x:]]	The x indicates a group of characters. The rule is satisfied if one of the characters from the group occurs within the value.

Example 8.48 uses no special symbols.

Example 8.48: Get the name and the number of each player who has the small letter e in his or her name.

```
SELECT   NAME, PLAYERNO
FROM     PLAYERS
WHERE    NAME REGEXP 'e'
```

The result is:

```
NAME       PLAYERNO
---------  --------
Everett           2
Parmenter         6
Wise              7
Newcastle         8
Baker            44
Hope             83
Miller           95
Parmenter       100
Bailey          112
```

Explanation: This statement does not really show the added value of the REGEXP operator because the same result could have been created with the condition NAME LIKE '%e%'.

Obviously, several characters may be used in the pattern, such as NAME REGEXP 'john' and NAME REGEXP 'a_b'.

The collation plays an important role for the LIKE operator. The same applies to the REGEXP operator: For certain collations, capitals and small characters are considered equal. If we had used another collation in the previous example, such as latin1_general_cs, this statement would have had a different result.

Example 8.49: Get the name and number of each player whose name begins with the letter combination ba.

```
SELECT   NAME, PLAYERNO
FROM     PLAYERS
WHERE    NAME REGEXP '^ba'
```

The result is:

```
NAME     PLAYERNO
------   --------
Baker          44
Bailey        112
```

Explanation: Because the symbol ^ is used, MySQL looks for names that begin with the letters ba. Obviously, using ^ makes sense only if it is used at the beginning of the pattern.

Example 8.50: Get the name, the street, and the number of each player whose name ends with the same letter as the first letter of his or her street.

```
SELECT   NAME, STREET, PLAYERNO
FROM     PLAYERS
WHERE    NAME REGEXP CONCAT(SUBSTR(STREET,1,1), '$')
```

The result is:

```
NAME  STREET          PLAYERNO
----  -------------   --------
Wise  Edgecombe Way          7
```

Explanation: The SUBSTR function is used to subtract the first letter of the street, which is the capital letter E in this case. Next, this letter is glued to the dollar sign with the CONCAT function. And because the dollar sign is present, MySQL checks whether any names end with an E. This example shows that complex expressions can be used within a pattern.

Example 8.51: Get the name and number of each player whose name contains the letters a, b, or c.

```
SELECT   NAME, PLAYERNO
FROM     PLAYERS
WHERE    NAME REGEXP '[abc]'
```

The result is:

```
NAME       PLAYERNO
---------  --------
Parmenter         6
Newcastle         8
Collins          27
Collins          28
Bishop           39
Baker            44
Brown            57
Parmenter       100
Moorman         104
Bailey          112
```

The previous pattern could also have been written as `[a-c]`, meaning to look for all the values that contain a letter that falls within the range `a` up to `c`.

Example 8.52: Get the name and the number of each player whose name consists of the pattern `m.n`. The point can be any random character.

```
SELECT   NAME, PLAYERNO
FROM     PLAYERS
WHERE    NAME REGEXP 'm.n'
```

The result is:

```
NAME       PLAYERNO
---------  --------
Parmenter         6
Parmenter       100
Moorman         104
```

Explanation: For the `REGEXP` operator, the point has the same function as the _ for the `LIKE` operator.

Example 8.53: Get the name and number of each player whose name consists of the letters `m`, `e`, or `n`, followed again by `m`, `e`, or `n`.

```
SELECT   NAME, PLAYERNO
FROM     PLAYERS
WHERE    NAME REGEXP '[men][men]'
```

The result is:

```
NAME       PLAYERNO
---------  --------
Parmenter         6
Newcastle         8
Parmenter       100
```

Explanation: This condition is used to check whether the combination mm, me, mn, em, ee, en, nm, ne, or nn occurs somewhere.

Example 8.54: Get the number and the postcode of each player whose postcode has a 3 as third digit.

```
SELECT   PLAYERNO, POSTCODE
FROM     PLAYERS
WHERE    POSTCODE REGEXP '^[0-9][0-9]3'
```

The result is:

```
PLAYERNO  POSTCODE
--------  --------
       6  1234KK
     104  9437AO
```

Example 8.55: Get the street and number of each player whose street name begins with the St and ends with Road.

```
SELECT   STREET, PLAYERNO
FROM     PLAYERS
WHERE    STREET REGEXP '^St.*Road$'
```

The result is:

```
STREET        PLAYERNO
------------  --------
Stoney Road          2
Station Road         8
```

Explanation: The asterisk says something about the character that stands in front of it, which is a point in this pattern. The construct .* indicates that a set of random characters is allowed.

Example 8.56: Find the number and postcode of each player whose postcode consists of one or more digits followed by one or more letters.

```
SELECT   PLAYERNO, POSTCODE
FROM     PLAYERS
WHERE    POSTCODE REGEXP '[0-9][0-9]*[a-z][a-z]*'
```

Explanation: Evidently, the result consists of all the rows from the PLAYERS table.

The asterisk represents zero, one, or more characters. By contrast, the plus sign stands for one or more characters, and the question mark stands for zero or one character. Using the plus, we could simplify the previous condition as follows: `POSTCODE REGEXP '[0-9]+[a-z]+'`.

Example 8.57: Get the name and number of each player whose names does not start with the capital letters A to M.

```
SELECT   NAME, PLAYERNO
FROM     PLAYERS
WHERE    NAME REGEXP '^[^A-M]'
```

The result is:

```
NAME       PLAYERNO
---------  --------
Parmenter         6
Wise              7
Newcastle         8
Parmenter       100
```

Example 8.58: Get the number and name of each player whose name consists of seven or more letters.

```
SELECT   PLAYERNO, NAME
FROM     PLAYERS
WHERE    NAME REGEXP '^[a-z]{7}'
```

The result is:

```
PLAYERNO  NAME
--------  ---------
       2  Everett
       6  Parmenter
       8  Newcastle
      27  Collins
      28  Collins
     100  Parmenter
     104  Moorman
```

Explanation: Names that contain a comma or a blank in the first eight positions do not show up in the result.

Instead of one number, you may specify two. If two numbers are specified, as in {2,5}, the string you are looking for must appear at least twice and at most five times.

Example 8.59: Get the number and name of each player whose name consists of at least six and at most seven letters.

```
SELECT    PLAYERNO, NAME
FROM      PLAYERS
WHERE     NAME REGEXP '^[a-z]{6,7}$'
```

The result is:

```
PLAYERNO  NAME
--------  -------
       2  Everett
      27  Collins
      28  Collins
      39  Bishop
      95  Miller
     104  Moorman
     112  Bailey
```

The symbol * is equivalent to {0,}, + is equivalent to {1,}, and ? is equivalent to {0,1}.

Example 8.60: Get the number and postcode of each player whose postcode contains four 4s in a row.

```
SELECT    PLAYERNO, POSTCODE
FROM      PLAYERS
WHERE     POSTCODE REGEXP '4{4}'
```

The result is:

```
PLAYERNO  POSTCODE
--------  --------
      44  4444LJ
```

Example 8.61: Get the number and street of each player whose street name contains strings Street or Square.

```
SELECT   PLAYERNO, STREET
FROM     PLAYERS
WHERE    STREET REGEXP 'Street|Square'
```

The result is:

```
PLAYERNO  STREET
--------  ------------
      39  Eaton Square
      44  Lewis Street
      95  High Street
     104  Stout Street
```

Example 8.62: Get the number and name of each player whose name contains a space.

```
SELECT   PLAYERNO, NAME
FROM     PLAYERS
WHERE    NAME REGEXP '[[.space.]]'
```

This query does not have a result because no name in the PLAYERS table contains a space.

Example 8.63: Get the number and street of each player whose street name contains the word Street.

```
SELECT   PLAYERNO, STREET
FROM     PLAYERS
WHERE    STREET REGEXP '[[:<:]]Street[[:>:]]'
```

The result is:

```
PLAYERNO  STREET
--------  ------------
      44  Lewis Street
      95  High Street
     104  Stout Street
```

The symbol `[:x:]` enables you to search for specific groups of characters, to so-called character classes. The `x` must be replaced by one of the codes from Table 8.4.

TABLE 8.4 Codes Belonging to the Symbol [[:x:]]

Code	Character Class
alnum	Alphanumeric characters
alpha	Alphabetic characters
blank	Whitespace characters
cntrl	Control characters
digit	Digit characters
graph	Graphic characters
lower	Lowercase alphabetic characters
print	Graphic or space characters
punct	Punctuation characters
space	Space, tab, newline, and carriage return
upper	Uppercase alphabetic characters
xdigit	Hexadecimal digit characters

These special codes appear in these examples of conditions with REGEXP operators. All these conditions return `true` as a result:

```
'AaA' REGEXP '[[:lower:]]+'
'A!!A' REGEXP '[[:punct:]]+'
'A  A' REGEXP '[[:blank:]]+'
```

Exercise 8.37: Get the number and name of each player whose name contains the combination of letters `en`. Use the REGEXP operator.

Exercise 8.38: Get the number and name of each player whose name begins with an `n` and ends with an `e`. Use the REGEXP operator.

Exercise 8.39: Get the number and name of each player whose name is at least nine characters long. Use the REGEXP operator.

8.12 The MATCH Operator

With the LIKE and REGEXP operators, you can look for character strings that appear in a certain column. If you want to store pieces of text in the tables, such as descriptions of products, summaries of books, or complete manuals, the search capabilities of LIKE and REGEXP often do not suffice because you likely want to search for words, not character strings. Specifically, the *MATCH operator* was added to MySQL to search for words in pieces of text.

DEFINITION

```
<predicate with match> ::=
   MATCH ( <column specification>
      [ , <column specification> ]... )
   AGAINST ( <scalar expression> [ <search style> ] )

<column specification> ::=
   [ <table specification> . ] <column name>

<search style> ::=
   IN NATURAL LANGUAGE MODE                          |
   IN NATURAL LANGUAGE MODE WITH QUERY EXPANSION |
   IN BOOLEAN MODE                                   |
   WITH QUERY EXPANSION
```

The different *search styles* are important in this definition. MySQL supports three different search styles: a natural language search, a natural language search with query expansion and a Boolean search. If no search style has been specified, MySQL assumes that the natural language search should be used. MySQL has supported these search styles for some time now. However, only since Version 5.1 has MySQL supported specifying the first two search styles in a MATCH operator.

The sample database does not contain a table with text. To illustrate the MATCH operator and the different search styles, we create a new table.

Example 8.64: Create a table for storing the authors, title, year of publication, and summary of a book.

```
CREATE TABLE BOOKS
      (BOOKNO              INTEGER NOT NULL PRIMARY KEY,
       AUTHORS             TEXT NOT NULL,
       TITLE               TEXT NOT NULL,
       YEAR_PUBLICATION    YEAR NOT NULL,
       SUMMARY             TEXT NOT NULL)
   ENGINE = MyISAM
```

Explanation: The CREATE TABLE statement ends with the specification ENGINE = MyISAM. Section 20.10.1 explains the meaning of this specification. For now, we limit ourselves by stating that we cannot use the MATCH operator without this specification.

Example 8.65: Enter data on five books into the new BOOKS table.

```
SET @@SQL_MODE = 'PIPES_AS_CONCAT'

INSERT INTO BOOKS VALUES (1,
   'Ramez Elmasri and Shamkant B. Navathe',
   'Fundamentals of Database Systems', 2007,
   'This market-leading text serves as a valued resource for '||
   'those who will interact with databases in future courses '||
   'and careers. Renowned for its accessible, comprehensive '||
   'coverage of models and real systems, it provides an '||
   'up-to-date introduction to modern database technologies.')

INSERT INTO BOOKS VALUES (2,
   'George Coulouris, Jean Dollimore and Tim Kindberg',
   'Distributed Systems: Concepts and Design', 2005,
   'This book provides broad and up-to-date coverage of the '||
   'principles and practice in the fast moving area of '||
   'distributed systems. It includes the key issues in the '||
   'debate between components and web services as the way '||
   'forward for industry. The depth of coverage will enable '||
   'students to evaluate existing distributed systems and '||
   'design new ones.')

INSERT INTO BOOKS VALUES (3,
    'Rick van der Lans',
    'Introduction to SQL: Mastering the Relational Database '||
    'Language', 2007,
    'This book provides a technical introduction to the '||
    'features of SQL. Aimed at those new to SQL, but not new '||
    'to programming, it gives the reader the essential skills '||
    'required to start programming with this language. ')

INSERT INTO BOOKS VALUES (4,
    'Chris Date',
    'An Introduction to Database Systems', 2004,
    'Continuing in the eighth edition, this book provides a '||
    'comprehensive introduction to the now very large field of '||
    'database systems by providing a solid grounding in the '||
    'foundations of database technology. This new edition has '||
    'been rewritten and expanded to stay current with database '||
    'system trends.')

INSERT INTO BOOKS VALUES (5,
    'Thomas M. Connolly and Carolyn E. Begg',
    'DataBase Systems: A Practical Approach to Design, '||
    'Implementation and Management',
    2005,
    'A clear introduction to design implementation and management '||
    'issues, as well as an extensive treatment of database '||
    'languages and standards, make this book an indispensable '||
    'complete reference for database students and professionals.')
```

To be able to use the MATCH operator on the TITLE and SUMMARY columns (these are the columns that contain text and words), a special index must be defined on both.

Example 8.66: Create the required indexes.

```
CREATE FULLTEXT INDEX INDEX_TITLE
    ON BOOKS (TITLE)

CREATE FULLTEXT INDEX INDEX_SUMMARY
    ON BOOKS (SUMMARY)
```

Explanation: Special about this statement is the specification FULLTEXT. Section 4.10 briefly explained the concept of an index, and Chapter 25, "Using Indexes," describes it more extensively. For now, we indicate that the term FULLTEXT creates a special kind of index that is required to be able to work with the MATCH operator. If a fulltext index is created, MySQL extracts all the whole words from the individual values. For the title of the book with number 2, that means the words Distributed, Systems, Concepts, and, and Design.

Now we are ready to use the MATCH operator. We begin with an explanation of the natural language search.

Example 8.67: Get the numbers and titles of the books in which the word design occurs.

```
SELECT   BOOKNO, TITLE
FROM     BOOKS
WHERE    MATCH(TITLE) AGAINST ('design')
```

The result is:

```
BOOKNO  TITLE
------  -------------------------------------------------
     2  Distributed Systems: Concepts and Design
     5  DataBase Systems: A Practical Approach to Design,
        Implementation and Management
```

Explanation: The result contains only those rows in which the word design occurs. This example shows that the MATCH operator does not make a distinction between capital and lowercase letters. The operator is not case sensitive.

The previous statement could have been formulated as follows:

```
SELECT   BOOKNO, TITLE
FROM     BOOKS
WHERE    MATCH(TITLE)
         AGAINST ('design' IN NATURAL LANGUAGE MODE)
```

This would have given the same result because the natural language search is the default search style.

A natural language search has three specific characteristics. First, *stopwords* are ignored. Stopwords are words such as *and*, *or*, *the*, and *to*. These words appear so often in texts that searching on them is meaningless. After all, searching for those words would return no result. Second, a natural language search means that if a word appears in more than 50 percent of the rows, it is regarded as a stopword. This means that if you fill the BOOKS table with one row only, any natural language search would return no result. Third, the result of a natural language search is also sorted in such a way that the most relevant rows are presented first.

Example 8.68: Get the numbers and titles of the books in which the word `to` appears.

```
SELECT   BOOKNO, TITLE
FROM     BOOKS
WHERE    MATCH(TITLE) AGAINST ('to')
```

Explanation: This statement returns no result, even though the word `to` appears in four out of five titles. It is a stopword, so it is not indexed.

Example 8.69: Get the numbers and titles of the books in which the word `database` appears.

```
SELECT   BOOKNO, TITLE
FROM     BOOKS
WHERE    MATCH(TITLE) AGAINST ('database')
```

Explanation: This statement with a natural language search returns no result because the word `database` appears in four out of the five books (thus, in more than 50 percent of them): books 1, 3, 4, and 5.

Searching for the word `practical` does give a rather interesting result; see the following example.

Example 8.70: Get the numbers and titles of the books in which the word `practical` appears.

```
SELECT   BOOKNO, TITLE
FROM     BOOKS
WHERE    MATCH(TITLE) AGAINST ('practical')
```

The result is:

```
BOOKNO  TITLE
------  ------------------------------------------------
     5  DataBase Systems: A Practical Approach to Design,
        Implementation and Management
```

Note that if you search for a certain word, the entire word must appear in the title; it cannot be a part of a longer word. If the word `practicality` appeared in the title of a book, it would not satisfy the condition of the previous example.

As mentioned, in a natural language search, the rows are sorted on relevance. The rows in which the searched value appears most are presented first. MySQL can do this by adding a numeric value to the result of a `MATCH` operator, the so-called *relevance value.* If the relevance value is greater than `0`, the row concerned is included in the result. If all rows are found, the result is sorted on those relevance values.

This relevance value can be retrieved.

Example 8.71: Get the numbers and relevance values of the books in which `distributed` appears in the summary.

```
SELECT   BOOKNO, MATCH(SUMMARY) AGAINST ('distributed')
FROM     BOOKS
```

The result is:

```
BOOKNO  MATCH(SUMMARY) AGAINST ('distributed')
------  --------------------------------------
     1                                       0
     2                         1.6928264817988
     3                                       0
     4                                       0
     5                                       0
```

Explanation: The word `distributed` appears twice in the summary of book 2, and that leads to the relevance value `1.6928264817988`.

Another example is the word `principles`. This word appears only once and, because of that, has a lower relevance value, which is `0.99981059964612`.

Example 8.72: Get the numbers and relevance values of the books in which the word `introduction` appears in the title.

```
SELECT   BOOKNO, MATCH(TITLE) AGAINST ('introduction')
FROM     BOOKS
WHERE    MATCH(TITLE) AGAINST ('introduction')
```

The result is:

```
BOOKNO  MATCH(TITLE) AGAINST ('introduction')
------  -------------------------------------
     4                       0.39194306797333
     3                       0.38341854994499
```

Explanation: By adding an `ORDER BY` clause, this sequence can be changed again, of course.

Multiple words may also be specified behind `AGAINST`. In that case, MySQL checks whether one or more of the words appear in the relevant column.

Example 8.73: Get the numbers and titles of the books in which the word `practical` and/or the word `distributed` appears in the title.

```
SELECT   BOOKNO, TITLE
FROM     BOOKS
WHERE    MATCH(TITLE) AGAINST ('practical distributed')
```

The result is:

```
BOOKNO  TITLE
------  --------------------------------------------------
     2  Distributed Systems: Concepts and Design
     5  DataBase Systems: A Practical Approach to Design,
        Implementation and Management
```

It is also possible to search on two or more columns. In that case, a fulltext index must be created on the combination of those columns. If we want to search for words in the TITLE and SUMMARY columns, we must create the following index.

Example 8.74: Create a fulltext index on the combination of TITLE and SUMMARY.

```
CREATE FULLTEXT INDEX INDEX_TITLE_SUMMARY
    ON BOOKS (TITLE, SUMMARY)
```

Now we can search in both columns.

Example 8.75: Get the numbers and titles of the books in which the word `careers` appears in the title and/or the summary.

```
SELECT   BOOKNO, TITLE
FROM     BOOKS
WHERE    MATCH(TITLE, SUMMARY) AGAINST ('careers')
```

The result is:

```
BOOKNO  TITLE
------  --------------------------------
     1  Fundamentals of Database Systems
```

Explanation: The word `careers` appears in the summary of book 1.

The second search style is the *Boolean search.* With this search style, the 50 percent check does not apply; every word counts now.

Example 8.76: Get the numbers and titles of the books in which `database` appears in the title.

```
SELECT   BOOKNO, TITLE
FROM     BOOKS
WHERE    MATCH(TITLE) AGAINST ('database' IN BOOLEAN MODE)
```

The result is:

```
BOOKNO  TITLE
------  ---------------------------------------------------
     1  Fundamentals of Database Systems
     3  Introduction to SQL: Mastering the Relational Database
        Language
     4  An Introduction to Database Systems
     5  DataBase Systems: A Practical Approach to Design,
        Implementation and Management
```

Explanation: Despite the fact that the word `database` appears in more than 50 percent of the rows, it is still included in the result. Compare this result to that of Example 8.69, which uses a natural language search. By adding the specification `IN BOOLEAN MODE`, we force MySQL into a Boolean search: If the value contains the word `database`, it is included in the result; otherwise, it is not.

Example 8.77: Get the numbers and titles of the books in which the word `introduction` appears in the title and/or summary.

```
SELECT   BOOKNO, TITLE
FROM     BOOKS
WHERE    MATCH(TITLE, SUMMARY)
         AGAINST ('introduction' IN BOOLEAN MODE)
```

The result is:

```
BOOKNO  TITLE
------  ----------------------------------------------------
     1  Fundamentals of Database Systems
     3  Introduction to SQL: Mastering the Relational Database
        Language
     4  An Introduction to Database Systems
     5  DataBase Systems: A Practical Approach to Design,
        Implementation and Management
```

Example 8.78: Get the numbers and titles of the books in which the word database and/or the word design appears.

```
SELECT   BOOKNO, TITLE
FROM     BOOKS
WHERE    MATCH(TITLE)
         AGAINST ('database design' IN BOOLEAN MODE)
```

The result is:

```
BOOKNO  TITLE
------  ----------------------------------------------------
     1  Fundamentals of Database Systems
     2  Distributed Systems: Concepts and Design
     3  Introduction to SQL: Mastering the Relational Database
        Language
     4  An Introduction to Database Systems
     5  DataBase Systems: A Practical Approach to Design,
        Implementation and Management
```

In Boolean searches, you may specify several operators before the search words; see Table 8.5. These Boolean search operators affect the end result.

TABLE 8.5 Overview of Boolean Search Operators

+data	Search for the values in which the word data appears.
-data	Search for the values in which the word data does not appear.
>data	Search for the values in which the word data appears, and increase the relevance value 50%.

continues

TABLE 8.5 Continued

BOOLEAN SEARCH OPERATORS	MEANING
<data	Search for the values in which the word data appears and decrease the relevance value 33%.
()	With this, search words can be nested.
~data	Search for the values in which the word data appears, and make the relevance value negative.
data*	Search for the values in which words appear that begin with the term data.
"data data data"	Search for the values in which the phrase data data data appears literally.

Example 8.79: Get the numbers and titles of the books in which the words database and design appear.

```
SELECT   BOOKNO, TITLE
FROM     BOOKS
WHERE    MATCH(TITLE)
         AGAINST ('+database +design' IN BOOLEAN MODE)
```

The result is:

```
BOOKNO  TITLE
------  --------------------------------------------------
     5  DataBase Systems: A Practical Approach to Design,
        Implementation and Management
```

Explanation: The words we are searching need not be right after each other in the text.

Example 8.80: Give the numbers and titles of the books in which the word database appears, but not the word design.

```
SELECT   BOOKNO, TITLE
FROM     BOOKS
WHERE    MATCH(TITLE)
         AGAINST ('+database -design' IN BOOLEAN MODE)
```

The result is:

```
BOOKNO  TITLE
------  ---------------------------------------------------------
     1  Fundamentals of Database Systems
     3  Introduction to SQL: Mastering the Relational Database
        Language
     4  An Introduction to Database Systems
```

If you want to search for a certain phrase, you must place double quotation marks before and after the phrase.

Example 8.81: Get the numbers and titles of the books in which the phrase `design implementation` appears.

```
SELECT   BOOKNO, TITLE
FROM     BOOKS
WHERE    MATCH(TITLE)
         AGAINST ('"design implementation"' IN BOOLEAN MODE)
```

The result is:

```
BOOKNO  TITLE
------  ---------------------------------------------------------
     5  DataBase Systems: A Practical Approach to Design,
        Implementation and Management
```

Explanation: The fact that a comma exists between the two words in the original text is not important.

With the Boolean search, you may also search on parts of words. In that case, we use the asterisk, comparable to using the `LIKE` operator.

Example 8.82: Get the numbers and titles of the books in which words appear that begin with `data`.

```
SELECT   BOOKNO, TITLE
FROM     BOOKS
WHERE    MATCH(TITLE) AGAINST ('data*' IN BOOLEAN MODE)
```

The result is:

```
BOOKNO  TITLE
------  ---------------------------------------------------------
     1  Fundamentals of Database Systems
     2  Distributed Systems: Concepts and Design
     3  Introduction to SQL: Mastering the Relational Database
        Language
     4  An Introduction to Database Systems
     5  DataBase Systems: A Practical Approach to Design,
        Implementation and Management
```

Fulltext indexes are not necessary for the execution of a Boolean search. However, these indexes improve the processing, of course.

The third search style is the *natural language search with query expansion.* In that case, the statement is performed in two steps. Consider an example.

Example 8.83: Get the numbers and titles of the books in which words appear that begin with data.

```
SELECT   BOOKNO, TITLE
FROM     BOOKS
WHERE    MATCH(TITLE) AGAINST ('practical'
         IN NATURAL LANGUAGE MODE WITH QUERY EXPANSION)
```

The following natural language search is processed first:

```
SELECT   BOOKNO, TITLE
FROM     BOOKS
WHERE    MATCH(TITLE) AGAINST ('practical')
```

The intermediate result is:

```
BOOKNO  TITLE
------  -------------------------------------------------
     5  DataBase Systems: A Practical Approach to Design,
        Implementation and Management
```

Next, all words that are found are included in the MATCH operator:

```
SELECT   BOOKNO, TITLE
FROM     BOOKS
WHERE    MATCH(TITLE) AGAINST (' DataBase Systems: A Practical
         Approach to Design, Implementation and Management')
```

The result is:

```
BOOKNO  TITLE
------  -------------------------------------------------
     5  DataBase Systems: A Practical Approach to Design,
        Implementation and Management
     2  Distributed Systems: Concepts and Design
```

Explanation: The term *query expansion* means that the statement is expanded with the words from the first intermediate result. The specification IN NATURAL LANGUAGE MODE may be omitted in the MATCH operator.

Several system variables relate to conditions with the MATCH operator: FT_MAX_WORD_LEN, FT_MIN_WORD_LEN, FT_QUERY_EXPANSION_LIMIT, FT_STOPWORD_FILE, and FT_BOOLEAN_SYNTAX. FT_MAX_WORD_LEN represents the maximum length of words that can be included in a fulltext index. This variable has a standard value of 84. FT_MIN_WORD_LEN represents the minimum length of words that are included. This value is usually equal to 4, which means that it makes no sense to look for words such as SQL.

Example 8.84: Give the numbers and titles of the books in which the word sql appears.

```
SELECT   BOOKNO, TITLE
FROM     BOOKS
WHERE    MATCH(TITLE) AGAINST ('sql')
```

This statement does not have a result because the search word consists of three letters only. You can adjust this variable at MySQL startup. Keep in mind, however, that all relevant indexes have to be rebuilt in this case.

FT_QUERY_EXPANSION_LIMIT indicates the number of top matches executed for queries that include query expansion.

FT_STOPWORD_FILE gives the name of the file containing the stopwords. If the value of this variable is equal to the value built-in, the list is used that is standard included. You will find this list in the manual of MySQL.

FT_BOOLEAN_SYNTAX indicates which operators can be used with Boolean searches.

Exercise 8.40: Get the numbers and summaries of the books in which the word students appears in the summary; use a natural language search.

Exercise 8.41: Get the numbers and summaries of the books in which the word database appears in the summary; use a Boolean search.

Exercise 8.42: Get the numbers and summaries of the books in which the words database and languages appear in the summary; use a natural language search.

Exercise 8.43: Get the numbers and summaries of the books in which the word database but not the word languages appears in the summary; use a Boolean search.

8.13 The IS NULL Operator

The *IS NULL operator* selects rows that have no value in a particular column.

DEFINITION

```
<predicate with null> ::=
   <scalar expression> IS [ NOT ] NULL
```

Example 8.4 showed how to find all players with a league number. This statement can also be formulated in another way that corresponds more to the original question.

Example 8.85: Get the player number and the league number of each player who has a league number.

```
SELECT   PLAYERNO, LEAGUENO
FROM     PLAYERS
WHERE    LEAGUENO IS NOT NULL
```

Explanation: Note that the word IS may *not* be replaced by the equals sign.

This condition could have been simplified by leaving out the specification IS NOT NULL; see Section 8.5. Still, we recommend the previous syntax because it is in accordance with the SQL standard.

If NOT is omitted, you get all the players who have *no* league number.

Example 8.86: Get the name, number, and league number of each player whose league number is *not* equal to 8467.

```
SELECT   NAME, PLAYERNO, LEAGUENO
FROM     PLAYERS
WHERE    LEAGUENO <> '8467'
OR       LEAGUENO IS NULL
```

The result is:

```
NAME       PLAYERNO  LEAGUENO
---------  --------  --------
Everett           2  2411
Wise              7  ?
Newcastle         8  2983
Collins          27  2513
Collins          28  ?
Bishop           39  ?
Baker            44  1124
Brown            57  6409
Hope             83  1608
Miller           95  ?
Parmenter       100  6524
Moorman         104  7060
Bailey          112  1319
```

If the condition LEAGUENO IS NULL were left out, the result would contain only rows in which the LEAGUENO column is not equal to null and not equal to 8467 (see the result table here). This is because the value of the condition LEAGUENO <> '8467' is unknown if the LEAGUENO column has the value null. The result table is:

```
NAME       PLAYERNO  LEAGUENO
---------  --------  --------
Everett           2  2411
Newcastle         8  2983
Collins          27  2513
Baker            44  1124
Brown            57  6409
Hope             83  1608
Parmenter       100  6524
Moorman         104  7060
Bailey          112  1319
```

Imagine that E_1 is an expression; then

```
E1 IS NOT NULL
```

is equivalent to this:

```
NOT (E1 IS NULL)
```

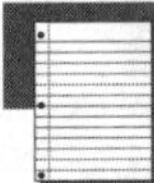

NOTE

A condition with IS NULL or IS NOT NULL can *never* have the value unknown; work this out by yourself.

Exercise 8.44: Get the number of each player who has *no* league number.

Exercise 8.45: Why is the condition in the following SELECT statement not useful?

```
SELECT   *
FROM     PLAYERS
WHERE    NAME IS NULL
```

8.14 The EXISTS Operator

This section discusses another operator with which subqueries can be used in conjunction with main queries: the *EXISTS operator*:

DEFINITION

```
<predicate with exists> ::= EXISTS <table subquery>

<table subquery> ::= ( <table expression> )
```

Example 8.87: Find the names and initials of players for whom at least one penalty has been paid.

The question in this example can be answered using an IN operator:

```
SELECT   NAME, INITIALS
FROM     PLAYERS
WHERE    PLAYERNO IN
        (SELECT   PLAYERNO
         FROM     PENALTIES)
```

The result is:

```
NAME       INITIALS
---------  --------
Parmenter  R
Baker      E
Collins    DD
Moorman    D
Newcastle  B
```

The question can also be answered using the EXISTS operator:

```
SELECT   NAME, INITIALS
FROM     PLAYERS
WHERE    EXISTS
        (SELECT   *
         FROM     PENALTIES
         WHERE    PLAYERNO = PLAYERS.PLAYERNO)
```

But what does this statement mean exactly? For every player in the PLAYERS table, MySQL determines whether the subquery returns a row. In other words, it checks to see whether there is a non-empty result (EXISTS). If the PENALTIES table contains at least one row with a player number that is equal to that of the player concerned, that row satisfies the condition. Consider an example. For the first row in the PLAYERS table, player 6, the following subquery is executed (behind the scenes):

```
SELECT   *
FROM     PENALTIES
WHERE    PLAYERNO = 6
```

The (intermediate) result consists of one row, so in the end result, we see the name and initials of the player whose number is 6.

The previous subquery is executed for the second, third, and subsequent rows of the PLAYERS table. The only thing that changes each time is the value for PLAYERS.PLAYERNO in the condition of the WHERE clause. The subquery can therefore have a different intermediate result for each player in the PLAYERS table.

The difference between how these two different solutions work can best be explained by examples written in the pseudo language introduced in Section 8.1. The formulation with the IN operator is as follows:

```
SUBQUERY-RESULT := [];
FOR EACH PEN IN PENALTIES DO
   SUBQUERY-RESULT :+ PEN;
ENDFOR;
END-RESULT := [];
FOR EACH P IN PLAYERS DO
   IF P.PLAYERNO IN SUBQUERY-RESULT THEN
      END-RESULT :+ P;
   ENDIF;
ENDFOR;
```

The formulation with the EXISTS operator is:

```
END-RESULT := [];
FOR EACH P IN PLAYERS DO
   FOR EACH PEN IN PENALTIES DO
      COUNTER := 0;
      IF P.PLAYERNO = PEN.PLAYERNO THEN
         COUNTER := COUNTER + 1;
      ENDIF;
   ENDFOR;
   IF COUNTER > 0 THEN
      END-RESULT :+ P;
   ENDIF;
ENDFOR;
```

Example 8.88: Get the names and initials of the players who are not team captains.

```
SELECT   NAME, INITIALS
FROM     PLAYERS
WHERE    NOT EXISTS
        (SELECT   *
         FROM     TEAMS
         WHERE    PLAYERNO = PLAYERS.PLAYERNO)
```

The result is:

```
NAME       INITIALS
---------  --------
Everett    R
Wise       GWS
Newcastle  B
Collins    C
Bishop     D
Baker      E
Brown      M
Hope       PK
Miller     P
Parmenter  P
Moorman    D
Bailey     IP
```

A condition that contains only an `EXISTS` operator always has the value `true` or `false` and is never `unknown`. Section 8.16 returns to the `EXISTS` operator and correlated subqueries.

As mentioned before, during the evaluation of a condition with the `EXISTS` operator, MySQL looks to see if the result of the subquery returns rows but does not look at the contents of the rows. This makes what you specify in the `SELECT` clause completely irrelevant. You can even specify a literal. Therefore, the previous statement is equivalent to the following statement:

```
SELECT   NAME, INITIALS
FROM     PLAYERS
WHERE    NOT EXISTS
        (SELECT   'nothing'
         FROM     TEAMS
         WHERE    PLAYERNO = PLAYERS.PLAYERNO)
```

Exercise 8.46: Get the name and initial(s) of each player who is a captain of at least one team.

Exercise 8.47: Get the name and initial(s) of each player who is not a captain of any team in which player 112 has ever played. The player may not be a captain of one of the teams in which player 112 has ever played.

8.15 The ALL and ANY Operators

Another way of using a subquery is with the *`ALL`* and *`ANY` operators*. These operators resemble the `IN` operator with subquery. The *`SOME` operator* has the same meaning as the `ANY` operator; `ANY` and `SOME` are just synonyms.

As the following definition shows, in the ANY and ALL operators, only scalar expressions can be used, not row expressions.

DEFINITION

```
<predicate with any all> ::=
   <scalar expression> <any all operator> <column subquery>

<column subquery> ::= ( <table expression> )

<any all operator> ::=
   <comparison operator> { ALL | ANY | SOME }
```

Example 8.89: Get the player numbers, names, and dates of birth of the oldest players. The oldest players are those whose date of birth is less than or equal to that of every other player.

```
SELECT   PLAYERNO, NAME, BIRTH_DATE
FROM     PLAYERS
WHERE    BIRTH_DATE <= ALL
        (SELECT   BIRTH_DATE
         FROM     PLAYERS)
```

The result is:

```
PLAYERNO  NAME     BIRTH_DATE
--------  -------  ----------
       2  Everett  1948-09-01
```

Explanation: The intermediate result of the subquery consists of the dates of birth of all players. Next, MySQL evaluates each player in the main query and checks whether the date of birth of that player is less than or equal to each date of birth that is in the intermediate result of the subquery.

Example 8.90: Get the player numbers and dates of birth of the players who are older than all the players who have ever played for team 2.

```
SELECT   PLAYERNO, BIRTH_DATE
FROM     PLAYERS
WHERE    BIRTH_DATE < ALL
        (SELECT   BIRTH_DATE
         FROM     PLAYERS AS P INNER JOIN MATCHES AS M
                  ON P.PLAYERNO = M.PLAYERNO
         WHERE    M.TEAMNO = 2)
```

The result is:

```
PLAYERNO  BIRTH_DATE
--------  ----------
       2  1948-09-01
      39  1956-10-29
      83  1956-11-11
```

Explanation: The subquery is used to retrieve the dates of birth of all the players who have ever played a match for team 2. In chronological order, these are 1962-07-08, 1964-12-28, 1970-05-10, 1963-10-01, and 1963-10-01. Next, the main query is used to determine for each player whether his or her date of birth is less than all these five dates. If we had used <= in the condition, player 8 would also have appeared in the result. However, that would not have been right because player 8 has played for team 2, and he is not older than all players because he cannot be older than himself.

Example 8.91: For each team, find the team number and the number of the player with the lowest number of sets won.

```
SELECT   DISTINCT TEAMNO, PLAYERNO
FROM     MATCHES AS M1
WHERE    WON <= ALL
        (SELECT   WON
         FROM     MATCHES AS M2
         WHERE    M1.TEAMNO = M2.TEAMNO)
```

The result is:

```
TEAMNO  PLAYERNO
------  --------
     1        83
     1         8
     2         8
```

Explanation: Again, the SELECT statement contains a correlated subquery. The result is that, for each match (that is found in the main query), a set of matches is retrieved with the subquery. For example, for match 1 (played by team 1), the (intermediate) result of the subquery consists of the matches 1, 2, 3, 4, 5, 6, 7, and 8. These are all matches played with a team number that is equal to the team number belonging to match 1. The final result of the subquery for this first match consists of the won values of those matches—respectively, 3, 2, 3, 3, 0, 1, 3, and 0. Next, MySQL checks whether the won value is smaller than or equal to each of these values. For any match where this is so, the number of the team and player is printed.

For the IN operator, we have shown precisely when such a condition is `true`, `false`, or `unknown`. We can do the same for the `ALL` operator. Imagine that C is the name of the column and that v_1, v_2, …, v_n are values that form the intermediate result of subquery (`S`). It follows that

```
C <= ALL (S)
```

is equivalent to this:

```
(C = C) AND (C <= v1) AND (C = v2) AND ... AND (C = vn) AND true
```

The following should be noted concerning certain specific situations:

- If `C` is equal to the null value, the entire condition evaluates to `unknown` because the condition `C = C` is equal to `unknown`; this rule holds independently of the numbers of values in the result of the subquery.
- If `C` is not equal to the null value and the subquery returns no result, the condition evaluates to `true` because at the end of this "longhand" condition, `true` is specified.
- If `C` is not equal to the null value, and if one of the `v` values is equal to the null value and one of the other `v` values is not equal to the null value, the condition can be `false` or `unknown`.
- If `C` is not equal to the null value and all `v` values are equal to the null value, the condition evaluates to `unknown`.

The following examples illustrate some of these rules.

Example 8.92: Get the highest league number and the corresponding player number.

```
SELECT   LEAGUENO, PLAYERNO
FROM     PLAYERS
WHERE    LEAGUENO >= ALL
        (SELECT   LEAGUENO
         FROM     PLAYERS)
```

Because the LEAGUENO column contains null values, the intermediate result of the subquery will also have null values. Therefore, the following condition is evaluated for each row:

```
(LEAGUENO >= 2411) AND
(LEAGUENO >= 8467) AND
(LEAGUENO >= NULL) AND ... AND true
```

This condition can be true only if all conditions are true, and that does not hold for, among other things, the third condition. So this statement returns an empty result.

We must add a condition to the subquery to eliminate the null value.

```
SELECT    LEAGUENO, PLAYERNO
FROM      PLAYERS
WHERE     LEAGUENO >= ALL
         (SELECT    LEAGUENO
          FROM      PLAYERS
          WHERE     LEAGUENO IS NOT NULL)
```

The result is:

```
LEAGUENO  PLAYERNO
--------  --------
8467             6
```

This result also shows that when a player does not have a league number, he or she will not appear in the final result.

Example 8.93: Find the player number, the town, and the league number for each player who has the lowest league number of all players resident in his or her town.

Many people will execute this statement:

```
SELECT    PLAYERNO, TOWN, LEAGUENO
FROM      PLAYERS AS P1
WHERE     LEAGUENO <= ALL
         (SELECT    P2.LEAGUENO
          FROM      PLAYERS AS P2
          WHERE     P1.TOWN = P2.TOWN)
```

The result is:

```
PLAYERNO  TOWN       LEAGUENO
--------  ---------  --------
      27  Eltham     2513
      44  Inglewood  1124
     112  Plymouth   1319
```

Explanation: This statement returns an unexpected result. Where is Stratford? Where is player 83? Don't forget, he is the one with the lowest league number in Stratford. This statement looks correct, but it is not. We explain the problem step by step. For player 6, who lives in Stratford, for example, the (intermediate) result of the subquery consists of the league numbers 8467, 1608, 2411, 6409, and 6524, and two null values. These are the league numbers of all players living in Stratford. Because the subquery contains a null value, the condition for this player evaluates to unknown. For player 83 with league number 1608, also living in Stratford, the condition evaluates to unknown as well. So both players are not included in the end result.

You can correct this omission by extending the condition in the subquery, as follows:

```
SELECT    PLAYERNO, TOWN, LEAGUENO
FROM      PLAYERS AS P1
WHERE     LEAGUENO <= ALL
         (SELECT   P2.LEAGUENO
          FROM     PLAYERS AS P2
          WHERE    P1.TOWN = P2.TOWN
          AND      LEAGUENO IS NOT NULL)
```

The result is:

```
PLAYERNO  TOWN       LEAGUENO
--------  ---------  --------
      27  Eltham     2513
      44  Inglewood  1124
      83  Stratford  1608
     112  Plymouth   1319
```

Explanation: Player 83 from Stratford has correctly been added to the result.

The ANY operator is the counterpart of ALL. Consider an example.

Example 8.94: Get the player numbers, names, and dates of birth of all players except the oldest.

```
SELECT    PLAYERNO, NAME, BIRTH_DATE
FROM      PLAYERS
WHERE     BIRTH_DATE > ANY
         (SELECT   BIRTH_DATE
          FROM     PLAYERS)
```

The result is:

```
PLAYERNO  NAME       BIRTH_DATE
--------  ---------  ----------
       6  Parmenter  1964-06-25
       7  Wise       1963-05-11
       8  Newcastle  1962-07-08
      27  Collins    1964-12-28
      28  Collins    1963-06-22
```

continues

```
 39  Bishop     1956-10-29
 44  Baker      1963-01-09
 57  Brown      1971-08-17
 83  Hope       1956-11-11
 95  Miller     1963-05-14
100  Parmenter  1963-02-28
104  Moorman    1970-05-10
112  Bailey     1963-10-01
```

Explanation: Again, the intermediate result of the subquery contains all the dates of birth. However, this time we are searching for all the players whose date of birth is greater than at least one date of birth of one other player. When such a date of birth is found, the player is not the oldest. The result of this statement consists of all players except the oldest one, and that is Everett; see the answer in the previous example.

Imagine that C is the name of a column and that v_1, v_2, ..., v_n are values that form the intermediate result of subquery (S). It follows that

```
C > ANY (S)
```

is equivalent to this:

```
(C = C) AND ((C > v1) OR (C > v2) OR ... OR (C > vn) OR false)
```

The following should be noted concerning certain specific situations:

- If C is equal to the null value, the entire condition evaluates to unknown because the condition C = C is equal to unknown; this rule holds independently of the numbers of values in the result of the subquery.
- If C is not equal to the null value and the subquery returns no result, the condition evaluates to false because at the end of this "longhand" condition, false is specified.
- If C is not equal to the null value, and if one of the v values is equal to the null value and one of the other v values is not equal to the null value, the condition can be true or unknown.
- If C is not equal to the null value and all v values are equal to the null value, the condition evaluates to unknown.

Instead of the greater than (>) and the less than or equal to (<=) operators that we used in this section in our two examples, any of the other comparison operators may be used.

Example 8.95: Get the numbers of the players who have incurred at least one penalty that is higher than a penalty paid for player 27; this player may not appear in the result.

```
SELECT   DISTINCT PLAYERNO
FROM     PENALTIES
WHERE    PLAYERNO <> 27
AND      AMOUNT > ANY
        (SELECT   AMOUNT
         FROM     PENALTIES
         WHERE    PLAYERNO = 27)
```

The result is:

```
PLAYERNO
--------
       6
```

Explanation: The main query contains the additional condition `PLAYERNO <> 27` because otherwise this player might also appear in the final result.

Example 8.96: Get the player number, date of birth, and town of each player who is younger than at least one other player from the same town.

```
SELECT   PLAYERNO, BIRTH_DATE, TOWN
FROM     PLAYERS AS P1
WHERE    BIRTH_DATE > ANY
        (SELECT   BIRTH_DATE
         FROM     PLAYERS AS P2
         WHERE    P1.TOWN = P2.TOWN)
```

The result is:

```
PLAYERNO  BIRTH_DATE  TOWN
--------  ----------  ---------
       6  1964-06-25  Stratford
       7  1963-05-11  Stratford
      39  1956-10-29  Stratford
      44  1963-01-09  Inglewood
      57  1971-08-17  Stratford
      83  1956-11-11  Stratford
     100  1963-02-28  Stratford
     104  1970-05-10  Eltham
```

Explanation: Because the subquery is correlated, for each player, the subquery returns another result. The subquery gives the list with dates of birth of all players who live in the same town.

Finally, try to deduce for yourself that the condition `C = ANY (S)` is equivalent to `C IN (S)`. Also try to prove that the condition `C <> ALL (S)` is equivalent to both `C NOT IN (S)` and `NOT (C IN (S))`.

The condition `C = ALL (S)` is, by definition, `false` if the subquery returns multiple, distinct values because the value in a column can never be equal to two or more different values simultaneously. We can illustrate this proposition with a simple example. Imagine that v_1 and v_2 are two different values from the intermediate result of subquery `S`; it follows that `C = ALL (S)` is equal to $(C = v_1)$ AND $(C = v_2)$. By definition, this is `false`.

The opposite applies for the condition `C <> ANY (S)`. If the subquery returns multiple values, the condition is, by definition, `true`. This is because, again, if the intermediate result of subquery `S` consists of the values v_1 and v_2, it follows that `C <> ANY (S)` is equivalent to $(C <> v_1)$ OR $(C <> v_2)$. This, by definition, is `true`.

Exercise 8.48: Find the player number of the oldest players from Stratford.

Exercise 8.49: Find the player number and name of each player who has incurred at least one penalty (do not use the `IN` operator).

Exercise 8.50: Get the payment number, penalty amount, and payment date for each penalty that is the highest of all penalties incurred in the same year.

Exercise 8.51: Get the lowest and highest player numbers in the PLAYER table, and present these two values as one row.

8.16 Scope of Columns in Subqueries

This chapter has shown many SQL statements with subqueries. This section lingers on an important aspect of the subquery: the *scope* of columns. To explain this concept well, we again use *select blocks*. For example, the following table expression is constructed from five select blocks: `S1`, `S2`, `S3`, `S4`, and `S5`.

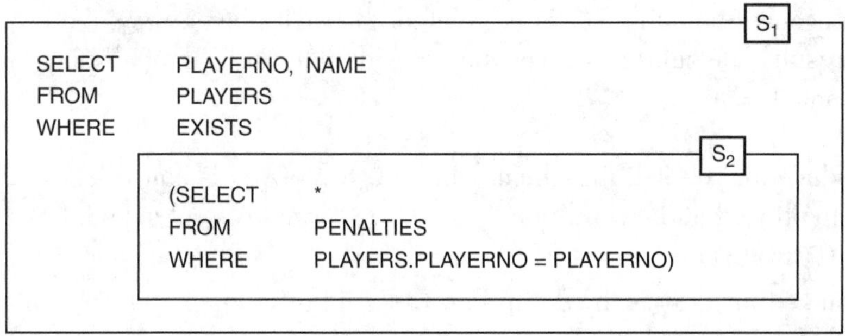

A SELECT clause marks the beginning of a select block. A subquery belongs to the select block formed by the table expression of which it is a subquery. The columns of a table can be used anywhere in the select block in which the table is specified. Therefore, in the example, columns from table A can be used in select blocks S_1, S_3, S_4, and S_5 but not in S_2. We can say, then, that S_1, S_3, S_4, and S_5 together form the scope of the columns from table A. Columns from table B can be used only in select blocks S_3 and S_5, making S_3 and S_5 the scope of the table B columns.

Example 8.97: Get the number and name of each player who has incurred at least one penalty.

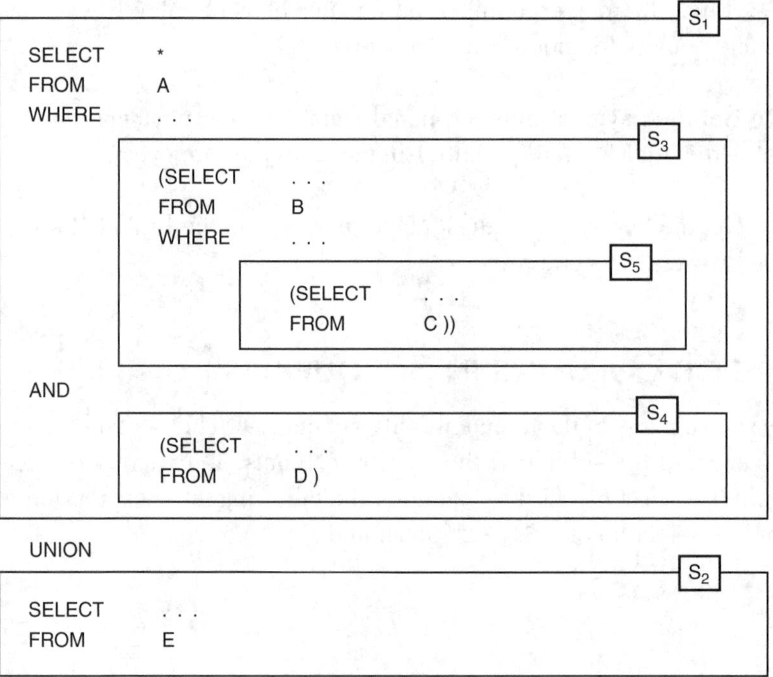

The columns from the PLAYERS table can be used in select blocks S_1 and S_2, but columns from the PENALTIES table can be used only in select block S_2.

In this example, the PLAYERNO column from the PLAYERS table is used in S_2. What would happen if, instead of PLAYERS.PLAYERNO, only PLAYERNO were specified? In that case, MySQL would interpret the column as being PLAYERNO from the PENALTIES table. This would give another result: The NAME of *each* player would be printed because `PLAYERNO = PLAYERNO` is valid for every row in the PENALTIES table.

Select block S_2 is a *correlated subquery* because it contains a column that belongs to a table specified in another select block.

If no table name is specified in front of a column name in a subquery, MySQL first checks whether that column belongs to one of the tables in the `FROM` clause of the subquery. If so, MySQL assumes that the column belongs to that table. If not, MySQL checks whether the column belongs to one of the tables in the `FROM` clause in the select block that the subquery is part of. However, a statement is much easier to read when the table name is explicitly specified in front of the column name.

How does MySQL process the previous statement? Again, we illustrate this by using the intermediate results from the various clauses. The intermediate result of the `FROM` clause in select block S_1 is a copy of the PLAYERS table:

```
PLAYERNO  NAME         ...
--------  ---------    ---
       6  Parmenter    ...
      44  Baker        ...
      83  Hope         ...
       2  Everett      ...
      27  Collins      ...
       :  :             :
       :  :             :
```

When processing the `WHERE` clause, the subquery is executed for each row in the intermediate result. The intermediate result of the subquery for the first row, in which the player number is equal to `6`, looks as follows:

```
PAYMENTNO  PLAYERNO  DATE        AMOUNT
---------  --------  ----------  ------
        1         6  1980-12-08  100.00
```

The PENALTIES table has only one row in which the player number equals the player number from the row in the PLAYERS table. The condition of select block S_1 is `true` because the intermediate result of the select block consists of at least one row.

The intermediate result of the subquery for the second row from select block S_1 consists of three rows:

```
PAYMENTNO  PLAYERNO  DATE        AMOUNT
---------  --------  ----------  ------
        2        44  1981-05-05   75.00
        5        44  1980-12-08   25.00
        7        44  1982-12-30   30.00
```

We see, then, that player 44 appears in the end result. The next player, number 83, is not included in the end result because no row in the PENALTIES table records a player number of 83.

The final result of the statement is:

```
PLAYERNO  NAME
--------  ---------
       6  Parmenter
      44  Baker
      27  Collins
     104  Moorman
       8  Newcastle
```

In processing a correlated subquery, a column from the outer or enveloping select block is considered to be a constant for the subquery.

As already mentioned in Chapter 6, "SELECT Statements, Table Expressions, and Subqueries," in reality, MySQL tries to find a more efficient method. However, regardless of the method, the result is always the same.

The following are a couple alternatives for the previous example.

```
SELECT   PLAYERNO, NAME
FROM     PLAYERS
WHERE    EXISTS
        (SELECT  *
         FROM    PENALTIES
         WHERE   PLAYERS.PLAYERNO = PLAYERS.PLAYERNO)
```

The subquery is executed separately for each player. The `WHERE` clause in the subquery contains a condition that is always `true`, so the subquery always returns rows. The conclusion is, therefore, that this statement returns the names of all players.

The result would be different if the PLAYERNO column in the PLAYERS table did (could) contain null values (work out why for yourself).

This next statement has the same effect as the first example in this section:

```
SELECT   PLAYERNO, NAME
FROM     PLAYERS AS P
WHERE    EXISTS
        (SELECT   *
         FROM     PENALTIES AS PEN
         WHERE    P.PLAYERNO = PEN.PLAYERNO)
```

Note that the pseudonym for the PENALTIES table can be omitted without affecting the result.

Exercise 8.52: For each of the following columns, indicate which select blocks of the SELECT statement they can be used in.

1. $A.C_1$
2. $B.C_1$
3. $C.C_1$
4. $D.C_1$
5. $E.C_1$

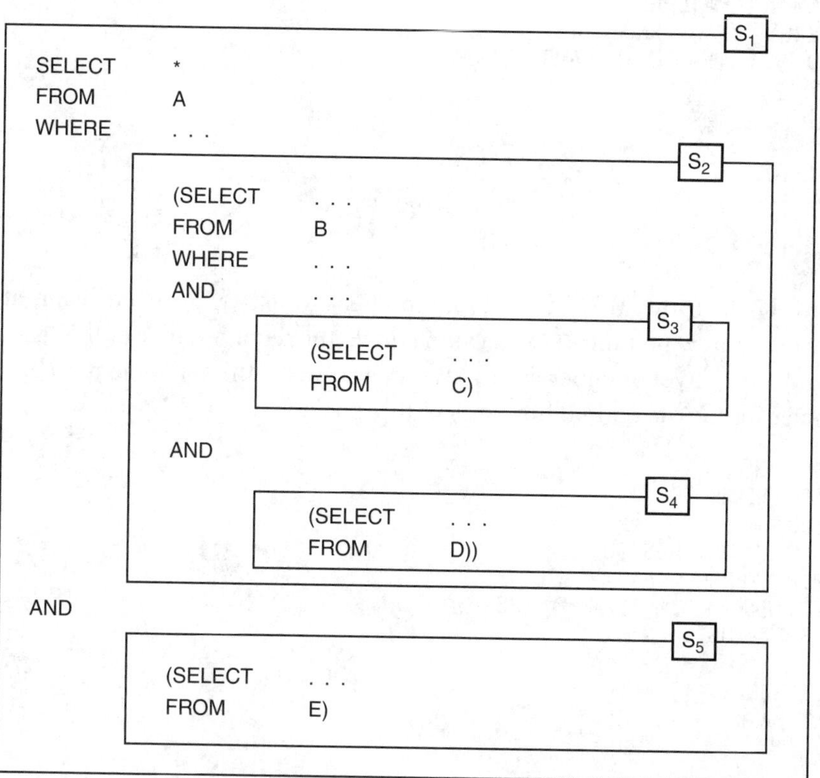

Exercise 8.53: Get the name and initials of each player who has played for a first-division team, who has won at least one match, and who has not incurred a single penalty.

Exercise 8.54: Get the number and name of each player who has played for both the first and second teams.

8.17 More Examples with Correlated Subqueries

A correlated subquery is defined as a subquery in which a column is used that belongs to a table specified in another select block. To make readers more familiar with this type of subquery, we present more examples in this section.

Example 8.98: Get the team number and division of each team in which player 44 has played.

```
SELECT   TEAMNO, DIVISION
FROM     TEAMS
WHERE    EXISTS
        (SELECT   *
         FROM     MATCHES
         WHERE    PLAYERNO = 44
         AND      TEAMNO = TEAMS.TEAMNO)
```

The result is:

```
TEAMNO  DIVISION
------  --------
     1  first
```

Explanation: Look in the MATCHES table to check whether, for each team, at least one row exists in which the TEAMNO value equals the team number of the team concerned and the player number is 44. We now rewrite this statement in the pseudo language already used in other parts of this book.

```
RESULT-MAIN := [];
FOR EACH T IN TEAMS DO
   RESULT-SUB := [];
   FOR EACH M IN MATCHES DO
      IF (M.PLAYERNO = 44)
      AND (T.TEAMNO = M.TEAMNO) THEN
         RESULT-SUB :+ M;
   ENDFOR;
   IF RESULT-SUB <> [] THEN
      RESULT-MAIN :+ T;
ENDFOR;
```

Example 8.99: Get the player number of each player who has incurred more than one penalty.

```
SELECT   DISTINCT PLAYERNO
FROM     PENALTIES AS PEN
WHERE    PLAYERNO IN
        (SELECT   PLAYERNO
         FROM     PENALTIES
         WHERE    PAYMENTNO <> PEN.PAYMENTNO)
```

The result is:

```
PLAYERNO
--------
      27
      44
```

Explanation: For each row in the PENALTIES table, MySQL checks whether there is another row in this table with the same player number but with a different payment number. If so, these players have incurred at least two penalties.

Example 8.100: Get the number and name of each player who has *not* played matches for team 1.

```
SELECT   PLAYERNO, NAME
FROM     PLAYERS
WHERE    1 <> ALL
        (SELECT   TEAMNO
         FROM     MATCHES
         WHERE    PLAYERNO = PLAYERS.PLAYERNO)
```

The result is:

```
PLAYERNO  NAME
--------  ---------
       7  Wise
      27  Collins
      28  Collins
      39  Bishop
      95  Miller
     100  Parmenter
     104  Moorman
     112  Bailey
```

Explanation: The subquery produces a list of team numbers for which a given player has played. The main query presents the names of those players for whom team number 1 does not appear on the list.

Example 8.101: Get the team number of each team in which player 57 has *not* played.

```
SELECT    TEAMNO
FROM      TEAMS
WHERE     NOT EXISTS
         (SELECT   *
          FROM     MATCHES
          WHERE    PLAYERNO = 57
          AND      TEAMNO = TEAMS.TEAMNO)
```

The result is:

```
TEAMNO
------
     2
```

Explanation: Get the numbers of the teams for which, in the MATCHES table, no row appears with the same team number and player number 57.

Example 8.102: Which players have played for all teams named in the TEAMS table?

```
SELECT    PLAYERNO
FROM      PLAYERS AS P
WHERE     NOT EXISTS
         (SELECT   *
          FROM     TEAMS AS T
          WHERE    NOT EXISTS
                  (SELECT   *
                   FROM     MATCHES AS M
                   WHERE    T.TEAMNO = M.TEAMNO
                   AND      P.PLAYERNO = M.PLAYERNO))
```

The result is:

```
PLAYERNO
--------
       8
```

Explanation: We can formulate the original question in another way: Find each player for whom no team exists for which the player concerned has never played. The two subqueries together produce a list of teams for which a specific player has not played. The main query presents those players for whom the result table of the subquery is empty. SQL determines for each player, separately, whether the subquery yields *no* result. Let us consider player 27 as an example. SQL checks whether the following statement has a result for this player:

```
SELECT    *
FROM      TEAMS AS T
WHERE     NOT EXISTS
         (SELECT    *
          FROM      MATCHES AS M
          WHERE     T.TEAMNO = M.TEAMNO
          AND       M.PLAYERNO = 27)
```

This statement has a result if a team exists for which player 27 has never played. Player 27 has not played for team 1, but has for team 2. We conclude that the result of this statement consists of the data from team 1. This means that player 27 does not appear in the end result because the `WHERE` clause specifies players for whom the result of the subquery is empty (`NOT EXISTS`).

We can do the same with player number 8. In this case, the result of the subquery is empty because the player has played for team 1 as well as for team 2. This means that the condition in the main query is `true`, and player 8 is included in the end result.

Example 8.103: Get the player number of each player who has played for at least all the teams for which player 57 has ever played.

```
SELECT    PLAYERNO
FROM      PLAYERS
WHERE     NOT EXISTS
         (SELECT    *
          FROM      MATCHES AS M1
          WHERE     PLAYERNO = 57
          AND       NOT EXISTS
                   (SELECT    *
                    FROM      MATCHES AS M2
                    WHERE     M1.TEAMNO = M2.TEAMNO
                    AND       PLAYERS.PLAYERNO = M2.PLAYERNO))
```

The result is:

```
PLAYERNO
--------
       2
       6
       8
      44
      57
      83
```

Explanation: This statement is very similar to the previous one. However, the question asks not for players who have played for *all* teams, but for teams for which player 57 has also played. This difference is apparent in the first subquery. Here, MySQL does not check all the teams (in contrast to the subquery in the previous example), but only teams for which player 57 has played.

Example 8.104: Get the player number of each player who has played only for the same teams as player 57.

We can formulate this question differently: Get the numbers of the players who, first of all, have played for all the teams for which player 57 has played and, second, have not played for teams for which player 57 has not played. The first part of the question is like the previous one. The second part of the question can be answered with the following SELECT statement. This statement retrieves all players who have competed in teams for which player 57 has not competed:

```
SELECT   PLAYERNO
FROM     MATCHES
WHERE    TEAMNO IN
        (SELECT   TEAMNO
         FROM     TEAMS
         WHERE    TEAMNO NOT IN
                 (SELECT   TEAMNO
                  FROM     MATCHES
                  WHERE    PLAYERNO = 57))
```

Combining this statement with that of the previous question supplies the answer:

```
SELECT   PLAYERNO
FROM     PLAYERS AS P
WHERE    NOT EXISTS
        (SELECT   *
         FROM     MATCHES AS M1
         WHERE    PLAYERNO = 57
         AND      NOT EXISTS
                 (SELECT   *
                  FROM     MATCHES AS M2
                  WHERE    M1.TEAMNO = M2.TEAMNO
                  AND      P.PLAYERNO = M2.PLAYERNO))
AND      PLAYERNO NOT IN
        (SELECT   PLAYERNO
         FROM     MATCHES
         WHERE    TEAMNO IN
                 (SELECT   TEAMNO
                  FROM     TEAMS
                  WHERE    TEAMNO NOT IN
                          (SELECT   TEAMNO
                           FROM     MATCHES
                           WHERE    PLAYERNO = 57)))
```

The result is:

```
PLAYERNO
--------
       2
       6
      44
      57
      83
```

Explanation: Player 57 also appears in the result, of course, but can be removed with a simple condition. Player 8 does not appear in the result because she has played for team 1 as well as for team 2, and player 57 has played only for team 1. Try to fill in a few other player numbers for yourself to check whether the statement is correct.

Exercise 8.55: Find the player number and name of each player who has incurred at least one penalty; use a correlated subquery.

Exercise 8.56: Find the player number and name of each player who has won at least two matches.

Exercise 8.57: Get the name and initials of each player who incurred no penalties between January 1, 1980, and December 31, 1980.

Exercise 8.58: Get the player number of each player who has incurred at least one penalty that is equal to an amount that has occurred at least twice.

8.18 Conditions with Negation

This section discusses an error that programmers often make. This error refers to *conditions with negation.* A condition in which we search for the rows that do not contain a specific value in a column is (informally) called a condition with negation. A negative condition can be made by placing a NOT in front of a positive condition. Two examples demonstrate the problem.

Example 8.105: Get the player numbers of each player who lives in Stratford.

```
SELECT   PLAYERNO
FROM     PLAYERS
WHERE    TOWN = 'Stratford'
```

The result is:

```
PLAYERNO
--------
       2
       6
       7
      39
      57
      83
     100
```

By placing the NOT operator in front of the condition, we get a SELECT statement with a negative condition:

```
SELECT   PLAYERNO
FROM     PLAYERS
WHERE    NOT (TOWN = 'Stratford')
```

The result is:

```
PLAYERNO
--------
       8
      27
      28
      44
      95
     104
     112
```

In this example, we can also specify a negative condition using the comparison operator <> (not equal to):

```
SELECT   PLAYERNO
FROM     PLAYERS
WHERE    TOWN <> 'Stratford'
```

The last example found the players who do *not* live in Stratford by simply adding NOT to the condition. All went well because the SELECT clause contains one of the candidate keys of the PLAYERS table completely, and that is the primary key PLAYERNO. Problems arise, however, if the SELECT clause contains only a part of a candidate key or no candidate key. The next example illustrates this.

Example 8.106: Get the number of each player who has incurred a penalty of $25.

This example and the corresponding SELECT statement appear similar to those of the previous example:

```
SELECT    PLAYERNO
FROM      PENALTIES
WHERE     AMOUNT = 25
```

Now let us find the players who have not incurred a penalty of $25. If we do it in the same way as the last example, the statement looks like this:

```
SELECT    PLAYERNO
FROM      PENALTIES
WHERE     AMOUNT <> 25
```

The result of this is:

```
PLAYERNO
--------
       6
      44
      27
     104
      44
      27
```

If you examine the PENALTIES table, you can see that player 44 incurred a penalty of $25. In other words, the SELECT statement does not return the correct result to the original question. This is because the SELECT clause of this statement contains none of the candidate keys of the PENALTIES table (this table has only one candidate key, PAYMENTNO). The correct answer is obtained by formulating an entirely different statement. We use a subquery coupled with the NOT operator:

```
SELECT    PLAYERNO
FROM      PLAYERS
WHERE     PLAYERNO NOT IN
         (SELECT   PLAYERNO
          FROM     PENALTIES
          WHERE    AMOUNT = 25)
```

The subquery determines which players have incurred a penalty of $25. In the main query, MySQL looks to see which players do *not* appear in the result of the subquery. However, pay attention to the fact that the main query searches not the PENALTIES table, but the PLAYERS table. If the PENALTIES table had been used in the FROM clause in this statement, we would have received a list of all players who had incurred *at least one* penalty that was not equal to $25, and this was not the original question.

Now that we have a negative statement defined using `NOT IN`, it is possible to create the positive `SELECT` statement with a comparable structure:

```
SELECT   PLAYERNO
FROM     PLAYERS
WHERE    PLAYERNO IN
        (SELECT   PLAYERNO
         FROM     PENALTIES
         WHERE    AMOUNT = 25)
```

The result is:

```
PLAYERNO
--------
       8
      44
```

Conclusion: If a `SELECT` clause does not contain a complete candidate key of the table in the `FROM` clause, and if the `WHERE` clause has a negative condition, be very careful!

Exercise 8.59: Get the player number of each player who has not won a single match by winning three sets.

Exercise 8.60: Get the team number and the division of each team for which player 6 has not competed.

Exercise 8.61: Get the player number for each player who has played only in teams for which player 57 has never competed.

8.19 Answers

8.1

```
SELECT   PAYMENTNO
FROM     PENALTIES
WHERE    AMOUNT > 60
```

or

```
SELECT   PAYMENTNO
FROM     PENALTIES
WHERE    60 < AMOUNT
```

or

```
SELECT    PAYMENTNO
FROM      PENALTIES
WHERE     AMOUNT - 60 > 0
```

8.2

```
SELECT    TEAMNO
FROM      TEAMS
WHERE     PLAYERNO <> 27
```

8.3 No row in the PLAYERS table satisfies the condition. No row in which the LEAGUENO column has a value satisfies the condition because the condition is `false`. In addition, each row in which the LEAGUENO column has no value (and thus contains the null value) is not returned.

8.4

```
SELECT    DISTINCT PLAYERNO
FROM      MATCHES
WHERE     WON > LOST
```

8.5

```
SELECT    DISTINCT PLAYERNO
FROM      MATCHES
WHERE     WON + LOST = 5
```

8.6

```
SELECT    PLAYERNO, NAME, INITIALS
FROM      PLAYERS
WHERE     PLAYERNO =
         (SELECT    PLAYERNO
          FROM      PENALTIES
          WHERE     PAYMENTNO = 4)
```

8.7

```
SELECT    PLAYERNO, NAME, INITIALS
FROM      PLAYERS
WHERE     PLAYERNO =
         (SELECT    PLAYERNO
          FROM      TEAMS
          WHERE     TEAMNO =
                   (SELECT    TEAMNO
                    FROM      MATCHES
                    WHERE     MATCHNO = 2))
```

8.8

```
SELECT    PLAYERNO, NAME
FROM      PLAYERS
WHERE     BIRTH_DATE =
         (SELECT    BIRTH_DATE
          FROM      PLAYERS
          WHERE     NAME = 'Parmenter'
          AND       INITIALS = 'R')
AND       NOT (NAME = 'Parmenter'
               AND INITIALS = 'R')
```

8.9
```
SELECT   MATCHNO
FROM     MATCHES
WHERE    WON =
        (SELECT   WON
         FROM     MATCHES
         WHERE    MATCHNO = 6)
AND      MATCHNO <> 6
AND      TEAMNO = 2
```

8.10
```
SELECT   MATCHNO
FROM     MATCHES
WHERE   (WON, LOST) =
       ((SELECT   WON
         FROM     MATCHES
         WHERE    MATCHNO = 2),
        (SELECT   LOST
         FROM     MATCHES
         WHERE    MATCHNO = 8))
```

8.11
```
SELECT   PLAYERNO, TOWN, STREET, HOUSENO
FROM     PLAYERS
WHERE   (TOWN, STREET, HOUSENO) <
        (SELECT   TOWN, STREET, HOUSENO
         FROM     PLAYERS
         WHERE    PLAYERNO = 100)
ORDER BY TOWN, STREET, HOUSENO
```

8.12
```
SELECT   PAYMENTNO
FROM     PENALTIES
WHERE    1965 <
        (SELECT   YEAR(BIRTH_DATE)
         FROM     PLAYERS
         WHERE    PLAYERS.PLAYERNO = PENALTIES.PLAYERNO)
```

8.13
```
SELECT   PAYMENTNO, PLAYERNO
FROM     PENALTIES
WHERE    PLAYERNO =
        (SELECT   PLAYERNO
         FROM     TEAMS
         WHERE    TEAMS.PLAYERNO = PENALTIES.PLAYERNO)
```

8.14
```
SELECT   PLAYERNO, NAME, TOWN
FROM     PLAYERS
WHERE    SEX = 'F'
AND      TOWN <> 'Stratford'
```

or

```
SELECT   PLAYERNO, NAME, TOWN
FROM     PLAYERS
WHERE    SEX = 'F'
AND      NOT (TOWN = 'Stratford')
```

8.15

```
SELECT   PLAYERNO
FROM     PLAYERS
WHERE    JOINED >= 1970
AND      JOINED <= 1980
```

or

```
SELECT   PLAYERNO
FROM     PLAYERS
WHERE    NOT (JOINED < 1970 OR JOINED > 1980)
```

8.16

```
SELECT   PLAYERNO, NAME, BIRTH_DATE
FROM     PLAYERS
WHERE    MOD(YEAR(BIRTH_DATE), 400) = 0
OR      (MOD(YEAR(BIRTH_DATE), 4) = 0
         AND NOT(MOD(YEAR(BIRTH_DATE), 100) = 0))
```

8.17

```
SELECT   MATCHNO, NAME, INITIALS, DIVISION
FROM     MATCHES AS M, PLAYERS AS P, TEAMS AS T
WHERE    M.PLAYERNO = P.PLAYERNO
AND      M.TEAMNO = T.TEAMNO
AND      YEAR(BIRTH_DATE) > 1965
AND      WON > LOST
```

8.18

```
SELECT   PAYMENTNO
FROM     PENALTIES
WHERE    AMOUNT IN (50, 75, 100)
```

8.19

```
SELECT   PLAYERNO
FROM     PLAYERS
WHERE    TOWN NOT IN ('Stratford', 'Douglas')
```

or

```
SELECT   PLAYERNO
FROM     PLAYERS
WHERE    NOT (TOWN IN ('Stratford', 'Douglas'))
```

or

```
SELECT   PLAYERNO
FROM     PLAYERS
WHERE    TOWN <> 'Stratford'
AND      TOWN <> 'Douglas'
```

8.20
```
SELECT    PAYMENTNO
FROM      PENALTIES
WHERE     AMOUNT IN
         (100, PAYMENTNO * 5,
         (SELECT   AMOUNT
          FROM     PENALTIES
          WHERE    PAYMENTNO = 2))
```

8.21
```
SELECT    PLAYERNO, TOWN, STREET
FROM      PLAYERS
WHERE    (TOWN, STREET) IN
        (('Stratford','Haseltine Lane'),
         ('Stratford','Edgecombe Way'))
```

8.22
```
SELECT    PLAYERNO, NAME
FROM      PLAYERS
WHERE     PLAYERNO IN
         (SELECT   PLAYERNO
          FROM     PENALTIES)
```

8.23
```
SELECT    PLAYERNO, NAME
FROM      PLAYERS
WHERE     PLAYERNO IN
         (SELECT   PLAYERNO
          FROM     PENALTIES
          WHERE    AMOUNT > 50)
```

8.24
```
SELECT    TEAMNO, PLAYERNO
FROM      TEAMS
WHERE     DIVISION = 'first'
AND       PLAYERNO IN
         (SELECT   PLAYERNO
          FROM     PLAYERS
          WHERE    TOWN = 'Stratford')
```

8.25
```
SELECT    PLAYERNO, NAME
FROM      PLAYERS
WHERE     PLAYERNO IN
         (SELECT   PLAYERNO
          FROM     PENALTIES)
AND       PLAYERNO NOT IN
         (SELECT   PLAYERNO
          FROM     TEAMS
          WHERE    DIVISION = 'first')
```

or

```
SELECT   PLAYERNO, NAME
FROM     PLAYERS
WHERE    PLAYERNO IN
        (SELECT   PLAYERNO
         FROM     PENALTIES
         WHERE    PLAYERNO NOT IN
                 (SELECT   PLAYERNO
                  FROM     TEAMS
                  WHERE    DIVISION = 'first'))
```

8.26 The result is empty.

8.27

```
SELECT   MATCHNO, PLAYERNO
FROM     MATCHES
WHERE   (WON, LOST) IN
        (SELECT   WON, LOST
         FROM     MATCHES
         WHERE    TEAMNO IN
                 (SELECT   TEAMNO
                  FROM     TEAMS
                  WHERE    DIVISION = 'second'))
```

8.28

```
SELECT   PLAYERNO, NAME
FROM     PLAYERS AS P1
WHERE   (TOWN, STREET, HOUSENO, POSTCODE) IN
        (SELECT   TOWN, STREET, HOUSENO, POSTCODE
         FROM     PLAYERS AS P2
         WHERE    P1.PLAYERNO <> P2.PLAYERNO)
```

8.29

```
SELECT   PAYMENTNO
FROM     PENALTIES
WHERE    AMOUNT BETWEEN 50 AND 100
```

8.30

```
SELECT   PAYMENTNO
FROM     PENALTIES
WHERE    NOT (AMOUNT BETWEEN 50 AND 100)
```

or

```
SELECT   PAYMENTNO
FROM     PENALTIES
WHERE    AMOUNT NOT BETWEEN 50 AND 100
```

or

```
SELECT    PAYMENTNO
FROM      PENALTIES
WHERE     AMOUNT < 50
OR        AMOUNT > 100
```

8.31
```
SELECT    SPELERSNR
FROM      SPELERS
WHERE     JAARTOE BETWEEN
          YEAR(GEB_DATUM + INTERVAL 16 YEAR + INTERVAL 1 DAY)
          AND YEAR(GEB_DATUM + INTERVAL 40 YEAR + INTERVAL -1 DAY)
```

8.32
```
SELECT    PLAYERNO, NAME
FROM      PLAYERS
WHERE     NAME LIKE '%is%'
```

8.33
```
SELECT    PLAYERNO, NAME
FROM      PLAYERS
WHERE     NAME LIKE '______'
```

8.34
```
SELECT    PLAYERNO, NAME
FROM      PLAYERS
WHERE     NAME LIKE '______%'
```

or

```
SELECT    PLAYERNO, NAME
FROM      PLAYERS
WHERE     NAME LIKE '%______'
```

or

```
SELECT    PLAYERNO, NAME
FROM      PLAYERS
WHERE     NAME LIKE '%______%'
```

or

```
SELECT    PLAYERNO, NAME
FROM      PLAYERS
WHERE     LENGTH(RTRIM(NAME)) > 6
```

8.35
```
SELECT    PLAYERNO, NAME
FROM      PLAYERS
WHERE     NAME LIKE '_r%r_'
```

8.36
```
SELECT    PLAYERNO, NAME
FROM      PLAYERS
WHERE     TOWN LIKE '_@%%@%_' ESCAPE '@'
```

8.37
```
SELECT   PLAYERNO, NAME
FROM     PLAYERS
WHERE    NAME REGEXP 'en'
```

8.38
```
SELECT   PLAYERNO, NAME
FROM     PLAYERS
WHERE    NAME REGEXP '^n.*e$'
```

8.39
```
SELECT   PLAYERNO, NAME
FROM     PLAYERS
WHERE    NAME REGEXP ' [a-z]{9}'
```

8.40
```
SELECT   BOOKNO, SUMMARY
FROM     BOOKS
WHERE    MATCH(SUMMARY)
         AGAINST ('students' IN NATURAL LANGUAGE MODE)
```

8.41
```
SELECT   BOOKNO, SUMMARY
FROM     BOOKS
WHERE    MATCH(SUMMARY)
         AGAINST ('database' IN BOOLEAN MODE)
```

8.42
```
SELECT   BOOKNO, SUMMARY
FROM     BOOKS
WHERE    MATCH(SUMMARY)
         AGAINST ('database languages'
         IN NATURAL LANGUAGE MODE)
```

8.43
```
SELECT   BOOKNO, SUMMARY
FROM     BOOKS
WHERE    MATCH(SUMMARY)
         AGAINST ('+database -languages' IN BOOLEAN MODE)
```

8.44
```
SELECT   PLAYERNO
FROM     PLAYERS
WHERE    LEAGUENO IS NULL
```

8.45 The NAME column has been defined as `NOT NULL`. Therefore, the column will never contain a null value, which is why the condition is `false` for each row.

8.46
```
SELECT   NAME, INITIALS
FROM     PLAYERS
WHERE    EXISTS
        (SELECT   *
         FROM     TEAMS
         WHERE    PLAYERNO = PLAYERS.PLAYERNO)
```

8.47
```
SELECT   NAME, INITIALS
FROM     PLAYERS AS P
WHERE    NOT EXISTS
        (SELECT   *
         FROM     TEAMS AS T
         WHERE    T.PLAYERNO = P.PLAYERNO
         AND      EXISTS
                 (SELECT   *
                  FROM     MATCHES AS M
                  WHERE    M.TEAMNO = T.TEAMNO
                  AND      M.PLAYERNO = 112))
```

8.48
```
SELECT   PLAYERNO
FROM     PLAYERS
WHERE    BIRTH_DATE <= ALL
        (SELECT   BIRTH_DATE
         FROM     PLAYERS
         WHERE    TOWN = 'Stratford')
AND      TOWN = 'Stratford'
```

8.49
```
SELECT   PLAYERNO, NAME
FROM     PLAYERS
WHERE    PLAYERNO = ANY
        (SELECT   PLAYERNO
         FROM     PENALTIES)
```

8.50
```
SELECT   PAYMENTNO, AMOUNT, PAYMENT_DATE
FROM     PENALTIES AS PEN1
WHERE    AMOUNT >= ALL
        (SELECT   AMOUNT
         FROM     PENALTIES AS PEN2
         WHERE    YEAR(PEN1.PAYMENT_DATE) =
                  YEAR(PEN2.PAYMENT_DATE))
```

8.51
```
SELECT  (SELECT   PLAYERNO
         FROM     PLAYERS
         WHERE    PLAYERNO <= ALL
                 (SELECT   PLAYERNO
                  FROM     PLAYERS)),
        (SELECT   PLAYERNO
         FROM     PLAYERS
         WHERE    PLAYERNO >= ALL
                 (SELECT   PLAYERNO
                  FROM     PLAYERS))
```

8.52 1. A.C1: S_1, S_2, S_3, S_4, S_5
2. B.C1: S_2, S_3, S_4
3. C.C1: S_3
4. D.C1: S_4
5. E.C1: S_5

8.53
```
SELECT   NAME, INITIALS
FROM     PLAYERS
WHERE    PLAYERNO IN
        (SELECT   PLAYERNO
         FROM     MATCHES
         WHERE    TEAMNO IN
                 (SELECT   TEAMNO
                  FROM     TEAMS
                  WHERE    DIVISION = 'first'))
AND      PLAYERNO IN
        (SELECT   PLAYERNO
         FROM     MATCHES
         WHERE    WON > LOST)
AND      PLAYERNO NOT IN
        (SELECT   PLAYERNO
         FROM     PENALTIES)
```

8.54
```
SELECT   PLAYERNO, NAME
FROM     PLAYERS
WHERE    PLAYERNO IN
        (SELECT   PLAYERNO
         FROM     MATCHES
         WHERE    TEAMNO = 1)
AND      PLAYERNO IN
        (SELECT   PLAYERNO
         FROM     MATCHES
         WHERE    TEAMNO = 2)
```

8.55
```
SELECT   PLAYERNO, NAME
FROM     PLAYERS
WHERE    EXISTS
        (SELECT   *
         FROM     PENALTIES
         WHERE    PLAYERNO = PLAYERS.PLAYERNO)
```

8.56
```
SELECT    PLAYERNO, NAME
FROM      PLAYERS
WHERE     PLAYERNO IN
         (SELECT  PLAYERNO
          FROM    MATCHES AS M1
          WHERE   WON > LOST
          AND     EXISTS
                 (SELECT  *
                  FROM    MATCHES AS M2
                  WHERE   M1.PLAYERNO = M2.PLAYERNO
                  AND     WON > LOST
                  AND     M1.MATCHNO <> M2.MATCHNO))
```

or

```
SELECT    PLAYERNO, NAME
FROM      PLAYERS
WHERE     1 < (SELECT   COUNT(*)
               FROM     MATCHES
               WHERE    WON > LOST
               AND      PLAYERS.PLAYERNO = PLAYERNO)
```

8.57
```
SELECT    NAME, INITIALS
FROM      PLAYERS
WHERE     NOT EXISTS
         (SELECT   *
          FROM     PENALTIES
          WHERE    PLAYERS.PLAYERNO = PLAYERNO
          AND      PAYMENT_DATE BETWEEN '1980-01-01'
                   AND '1980-12-31')
```

8.58
```
SELECT    DISTINCT PLAYERNO
FROM      PENALTIES AS PEN1
WHERE     EXISTS
         (SELECT   *
          FROM     PENALTIES AS PEN2
          WHERE    PEN1.AMOUNT = PEN2.AMOUNT
          AND      PEN1.PAYMENTNO <> PEN2.PAYMENTNO)
```

8.59
```
SELECT    PLAYERNO
FROM      PLAYERS
WHERE     PLAYERNO NOT IN
         (SELECT   PLAYERNO
          FROM     MATCHES WHERE WON = 3)
```

8.60

```
SELECT   TEAMNO, DIVISION
FROM     TEAMS
WHERE    TEAMNO NOT IN
        (SELECT  TEAMNO
         FROM    MATCHES
         WHERE   PLAYERNO = 6)
```

8.61

```
SELECT   DISTINCT PLAYERNO
FROM     MATCHES
WHERE    PLAYERNO NOT IN
        (SELECT  PLAYERNO
         FROM    MATCHES
         WHERE   TEAMNO IN
                (SELECT  TEAMNO
                 FROM    MATCHES
                 WHERE   PLAYERNO = 57))
```

CHAPTER 9

SELECT Statement: SELECT Clause and Aggregation Functions

9.1 Introduction

The WHERE clause, described in the previous chapter, is used to select rows. The intermediate result from this clause forms a *horizontal subset* of a table. In contrast, the SELECT clause selects only columns, not rows; the result forms a *vertical subset* of a table.

The features, limitations, and use of the SELECT clause depend on the presence or absence of a GROUP BY clause. This chapter discusses table expressions *without* a GROUP BY clause. Chapter 10, "SELECT Statement: The GROUP BY Clause," discusses the features of the SELECT clause when the table expression *does* contain a GROUP BY clause.

A large part of this chapter is devoted to so-called *aggregation functions.* Chapter 5, "SELECT Statement: Common Elements," referred to these functions but did not explore them in depth.

DEFINITION

```
<select clause> ::=
   SELECT <select option>... <select element list>

<select option> ::=
   DISTINCT | DISTINCTROW | ALL | HIGH_PRIORITY |
   SQL_BUFFER_RESULT | SQL_CACHE | SQL_NO_CACHE |
   SQL_CALC_FOUND_ROWS | SQL_SMALL_RESULT | SQL BIG_RESULT |
   STRAIGHT_JOIN

<select element list> ::=
   <select element> [ , <select element> ]... |
   *

<select element> ::=
   <scalar expression> [[ AS ] <column name> ] |
   <table specification>.*                     |
   <pseudonym>.*

<column name> ::= <name>
```

9.2 Selecting All Columns (*)

The shortest SELECT clause is the one in which only an asterisk (*) is specified. This asterisk is shorthand notation for all columns in each table mentioned in the FROM clause. Example 9.1 includes two equivalent SELECT statements:

Example 9.1: Get the entire PENALTIES table.

```
SELECT    *
FROM      PENALTIES
```

and

```
SELECT    PAYMENTNO, PLAYERNO, PAYMENT_DATE, AMOUNT
FROM      PENALTIES
```

Explanation: The * symbol, then, does not mean multiplication in this context.

When a FROM clause contains two or more tables, it is sometimes necessary to use a table specification in front of the * symbol to clarify which columns should be presented.

Example 9.2: Get all the information on all the penalties incurred by players who are also captains.

The following three statements are equivalent:

```
SELECT    PENALTIES.*
FROM      PENALTIES INNER JOIN TEAMS
          ON PENALTIES.PLAYERNO = TEAMS.PLAYERNO

SELECT    PENALTIES.PAYMENTNO, PENALTIES.PLAYERNO,
          PENALTIES.PAYMENT_DATE, PENALTIES.AMOUNT
FROM      PENALTIES INNER JOIN TEAMS
          ON PENALTIES.PLAYERNO = TEAMS.PLAYERNO

SELECT    PEN.*
FROM      PENALTIES AS PEN INNER JOIN TEAMS
          ON PEN.PLAYERNO = TEAMS.PLAYERNO
```

The result is:

```
PAYMENTNO  PLAYERNO  PAYMENT_DATE  AMOUNT
---------  --------  ------------  ------
        1         6    1980-12-08  100.00
        3        27    1983-09-10  100.00
        8        27    1984-11-12   75.00
```

9.3 Expressions in the SELECT Clause

In processing the SELECT clause, the intermediate result is evaluated row by row. Each expression gives rise to a value in each result row. Most of the examples of the SELECT clause that we have described so far contain only column names, but an expression can also take the form of a literal, a calculation, or a scalar function.

Example 9.3: For each match, get the match number, the word Tally, the difference between the columns WON and LOST, and the value of the WON column multiplied by 10.

```
SELECT    MATCHNO, 'Tally', WON - LOST,
          WON * 10
FROM      MATCHES
```

The result is:

```
MATCHNO  TALLY  WON - LOST  WON * 10
-------  -----  ----------  --------
      1  Tally           2        30
      2  Tally          -1        20
      3  Tally           3        30
      4  Tally           1        30
      5  Tally          -3         0
      6  Tally          -2        10
      7  Tally           3        30
      8  Tally          -3         0
      9  Tally           1        30
     10  Tally           1        30
     11  Tally          -1        20
     12  Tally          -2        10
     13  Tally          -3         0
```

9.4 Removing Duplicate Rows with DISTINCT

A `SELECT` clause can consist of a number of expressions preceded by the word `DISTINCT` (see the definition at the beginning of this chapter). When `DISTINCT` is specified, MySQL removes duplicate rows from the intermediate result.

Example 9.4: Find all the different town names from the PLAYERS table.

```
SELECT   TOWN
FROM     PLAYERS
```

The result is:

```
TOWN
---------
Stratford
Stratford
Stratford
Inglewood
Eltham
Midhurst
Stratford
Inglewood
Stratford
Stratford
Douglas
Stratford
Eltham
Plymouth
```

In this result table, the towns Stratford, Inglewood, and Eltham appear seven, two, and two times, respectively. If the statement is expanded to include `DISTINCT`

```
SELECT    DISTINCT TOWN
FROM      PLAYERS
```

it produces the following result, in which all duplicate rows are removed:

```
TOWN
---------
Stratford
Midhurst
Inglewood
Plymouth
Douglas
Eltham
```

Example 9.5: Get every existing combination of street and town names.

```
SELECT    STREET, TOWN
FROM      PLAYERS
```

The result is:

```
STREET          TOWN
--------------  ---------
Stoney Road     Stratford
Haseltine Lane  Stratford
Edgecombe Way   Stratford
Station Road    Inglewood
Long Drive      Eltham
Old Main Road   Midhurst
Eaton Square    Stratford
Lewis Street    Inglewood
Edgecombe Way   Stratford
Magdalene Road  Stratford
High Street     Douglas
Haseltine Lane  Stratford
Stout Street    Eltham
Vixen Road      Plymouth
```

This result also contains duplicate rows; for example, Edgecombe Way and Haseltine Lane in Stratford are each mentioned twice. When `DISTINCT` is added:

```
SELECT    DISTINCT STREET, TOWN
FROM      PLAYERS
```

the result is:

```
STREET          TOWN
--------------  ---------
Edgecombe Way   Stratford
Eaton Square    Stratford
Haseltine Lane  Stratford
High Street     Douglas
Lewis Street    Inglewood
Long Drive      Eltham
Magdalena Road  Stratford
Old Main Road   Midhurst
Station Road    Inglewood
Stoney Road     Stratford
Stout Street    Eltham
Vixen Road      Plymouth
```

DISTINCT, then, is concerned with the *whole row,* not only with the expression that directly follows the word DISTINCT in the statement. In these two constructs, the use of DISTINCT is superfluous (but not forbidden):

- When the SELECT clause includes at least one candidate key for each table specified in the FROM clause, DISTINCT is superfluous. The most important property of a candidate key is that the set of columns that forms the candidate key never allows duplicate values, so a table that has a candidate key never has duplicate rows. The inclusion of a candidate key in the SELECT clause offers a guarantee that no duplicate rows will appear in the end result.
- When the table expression results in no rows with values or only one row with values, DISTINCT is superfluous. For equal rows, at least two rows are necessary. For example, if you are looking for players with a certain player number (WHERE PLAYERNO = 45), the statement results in one row if that player number exists; otherwise, no rows result.

The user may specify the word ALL in the same position in the statement where DISTINCT appears. Note that ALL actually has the opposite effect of DISTINCT and does not alter the result of a 'normal' table expression. In other words, the results of the following two statements are equivalent:

```
SELECT   TOWN
FROM     PLAYERS
```

and

```
SELECT   ALL TOWN
FROM     PLAYERS
```

Exercise 9.1: In which of the following statements is DISTINCT superfluous?

1.
```
SELECT   DISTINCT PLAYERNO
FROM     TEAMS
```

2.
```
SELECT   DISTINCT PLAYERNO
FROM     MATCHES
WHERE    TEAMNO = 2
```

3.
```
SELECT   DISTINCT *
FROM     PLAYERS
WHERE    PLAYERNO = 100
```

4.
```
SELECT   DISTINCT M.PLAYERNO
FROM     MATCHES AS M, PENALTIES AS PEN
WHERE    M.PLAYERNO = PEN.PLAYERNO
```

5.
```
SELECT   DISTINCT PEN.PAYMENTNO
FROM     MATCHES AS M, PENALTIES AS PEN
WHERE    M.PLAYERNO = PEN.PLAYERNO
```

6.
```
SELECT   DISTINCT PEN.PAYMENTNO, M.TEAMNO,
         PEN.PLAYERNO
FROM     MATCHES AS M, PENALTIES AS PEN
WHERE    M.PLAYERNO = PEN.PLAYERNO
```

9.5 When Are Two Rows Equal?

When are two rows identical or equal? At first, this seems a trivial question, but are two rows still equal when one of the values is equal to the null value? We answer these two questions somewhat formally.

Imagine that two rows, R_1 and R_2, both consist of n values v_i ($1 <= i <= n$). These two rows R_1 and R_2 are equal under the following conditions:

- The number of values in the rows is equal.
- For each i ($1 <= i <= n$), R_1v_i is equal to R_2v_i, or R_1v_i and R_2v_i are both equal to the null value.

This means, for example, if the value R_1v_3 is equal to the null value and R_2v_3 is not, the rows R_1 and R_2 cannot be equal (regardless of the other values). However, if both R_1v_3 and R_2v_3 are equal to the null value and the other values are all equal, the rows are equal.

Example 9.6: Get all the different league numbers.

```
SELECT   DISTINCT LEAGUENO
FROM     PLAYERS
```

The result is:

```
LEAGUENO
--------
1124
1319
1608
2411
2513
2983
6409
6524
7060
8467
?
```

Explanation: The null value appears only once in the result because rows that consist of only a null value are equal to each other.

This rule does not seem to be in line with the rules in Section 8.2, which stated that two null values are not equal to each other. Also, when comparing row expressions, two null values are not considered to be equal or unequal. For example, the next two conditions both evaluate to *unknown*.

```
NULL = 4
(1, NULL) = (1, NULL)
```

Informally, we could say that MySQL executes a *horizontal comparison* with conditions. The values that must be compared are next to each other, or respectively to the left and right of the comparison operator. That's the difference with DISTINCT. We could state that DISTINCT rows "underneath" each other in the intermediate result are compared instead of rows that are "next to" each other. In other words, with DISTINCT, a *vertical comparison* takes place. In that case, null values are equal to each other. Imagine the intermediate result of a table expression that looks as follows:

```
(1, NULL)
(1, NULL)
```

Two rows are compared vertically when processing DISTINCT. In the end result, only one of the two rows is left.

This rule might look somewhat strange, but it follows the rules of the original relational model.

Example 9.7: Determine which rows DISTINCT will delete.

```
SELECT   DISTINCT *
FROM    (SELECT   1 AS A, 'Hello' AS B, 4 AS C UNION
         SELECT   1, 'Hello', NULL UNION
         SELECT   1, 'Hello', NULL UNION
         SELECT   1, NULL, NULL) AS X
```

The result is:

```
A  B      C
-  -----  -
1  Hello  4
1  Hello  ?
1  ?      ?
```

Exercise 9.2: termine the results of these SELECT statements for the following T table:

```
T:  C1  C2  C3
    --  --  --
    c1  c2  c3
    c2  c2  c3
    c3  c2  ?
    c4  c2  ?
    c5  ?   ?
    c6  ?   ?
```

1. ```
   SELECT   DISTINCT C2
   FROM     T
   ```
2. ```
   SELECT   DISTINCT C2, C3
   FROM     T
   ```

9.6 More Select Options

In addition to DISTINCT and ALL, MySQL supports the following select options: DISTINCTROW, HIGH_PRIORITY, SQL_BUFFER_RESULT, SQL_CACHE, SQL_NO_CACHE, SQL_CALC_FOUND_ROWS, SQL_SMALL_RESULT, SQL BIG_RESULT, and STRAIGHT_JOIN. We describe some here and discuss others later.

DISTINCTROW is a synonym for DISTINCT. We advise using the latter as much as possible because other SQL products do not support DISTINCTROW.

The select option HIGH_PRIORITY deals with locking of data. Chapter 37, "Transactions and Multiuser Usage," discusses this option.

The specification of SQL_BUFFER_RESULT affects the processing speed of SELECT statements. Normally, the rows in the end result of a SELECT statement are locked. At that specific moment, other users cannot update these rows; Chapter 37 describes this extensively. If we specify SQL_BUFFER_RESULT, the end result of the SELECT statement is stored in a temporary table. This makes it possible for other users to update the original data. This requires storage space and additional external memory, but it improves the progress of statements.

The select options SQL_CACHE and SQL_NO_CACHE are relevant when the *query cache* operates in the so-called demand modus. If SQL_CACHE is specified in a SELECT statement, the end result of the statement is stored in this cache, which is not the case with SQL_NO_CACHE. This can considerably affect the processing speed of certain statements. If the result of a certain statement is placed in the query cache and the same statement is executed once again, the result is retrieved directly from the cache. There's no need to access the tables again or to perform joins and sorts, and complex calculations can be left out. This optimization works only if the SELECT statements have been formulated in exactly the same way. When tables from which the end result has been created change, the end result immediately is removed from the cache. This ensures that the results do not show out-of-date data.

With the LIMIT clause, the number of rows in the end result of a SELECT statement can be limited; see Chapter 13, "SELECT Statement: The LIMIT Clause." With the select option SQL_CALC_FOUND_ROWS, you can still query the original number of rows. Chapter 13 revisits this.

The two select options SQL_SMALL_RESULT and SQL_BIG_RESULT give the optimizer of MySQL some information on the size of the end result in advance. This module can use this to its advantage when it must determine the smartest way to process the statement.

With STRAIGHT_JOIN, you indicate that the tables must be joined in the order in which they appear in the FROM clause. Again, this influences the optimizer to improve processing time.

9.7 An Introduction to Aggregation Functions

Expressions in the SELECT clause can contain so-called *aggregation functions* (also called *statistical, group, set*, or *column functions*). If the table expression has *no* GROUP BY clause, an aggregation function in a SELECT clause operates on all rows. If a SELECT clause does contain an aggregation function, the entire table expression yields only one row as an end result (remember, we still assume here that the table expression has *no* GROUP BY clause). In fact, the values of a group of rows are aggregated to one value. For example, all penalty amounts in the PENALTIES table are added up to one value with the SUM function.

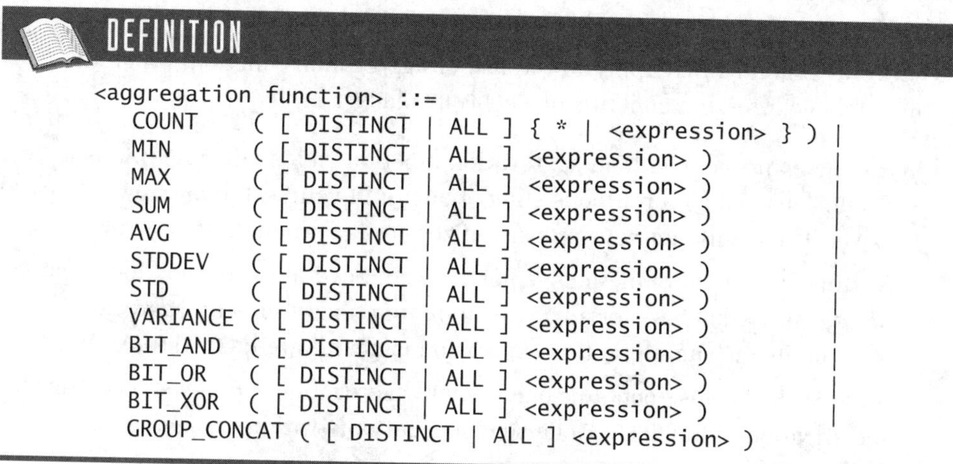

DEFINITION

```
<aggregation function> ::=
   COUNT    ( [ DISTINCT | ALL ] { * | <expression> } ) |
   MIN      ( [ DISTINCT | ALL ] <expression> )           |
   MAX      ( [ DISTINCT | ALL ] <expression> )           |
   SUM      ( [ DISTINCT | ALL ] <expression> )           |
   AVG      ( [ DISTINCT | ALL ] <expression> )           |
   STDDEV   ( [ DISTINCT | ALL ] <expression> )           |
   STD      ( [ DISTINCT | ALL ] <expression> )           |
   VARIANCE ( [ DISTINCT | ALL ] <expression> )           |
   BIT_AND  ( [ DISTINCT | ALL ] <expression> )           |
   BIT_OR   ( [ DISTINCT | ALL ] <expression> )           |
   BIT_XOR  ( [ DISTINCT | ALL ] <expression> )           |
   GROUP_CONCAT ( [ DISTINCT | ALL ] <expression> )
```

Example 9.8: How many players are registered in the PLAYERS table?

```
SELECT   COUNT(*)
FROM     PLAYERS
```

The result is:

```
COUNT(*)
--------
      14
```

Explanation: The function COUNT(*) counts the number of rows that remain after processing the FROM clause. In this case, the number equals the number of rows in the PLAYERS table.

Example 9.9: How many players live in Stratford?

```
SELECT   COUNT(*)
FROM     PLAYERS
WHERE    TOWN = 'Stratford'
```

The result is:

```
COUNT(*)
--------
       7
```

Explanation: Because the SELECT clause is processed *after* the WHERE clause, the number of rows in which the TOWN column has the value Stratford are counted.

The following sections look at various aggregation functions in more detail. We skip only the GROUP_CONCAT function because Chapter 10 discusses this function.

Several general rules apply to the use of aggregation functions when the concerning table expression contains no GROUP BY clause.

- A table expression with an aggregation function yields only one row as a result. This can be a row consisting of only null values, but one row always exists. The result can never consist of zero rows or more than one row.
- Nesting aggregation functions is not allowed. Several expression forms can be used as parameters for an aggregation function but not an aggregation function itself. Therefore, this expression is not allowed: COUNT(MAX(…)).
- If the SELECT clause contains one or more aggregation functions, a column specification in the SELECT clause can occur only within an aggregation function.

The last rule requires some explanation. According to this rule, the following statement is not correct because the SELECT clause contains an aggregation function as an expression, while the column name PLAYERNO occurs outside an aggregation function.

```
SELECT   COUNT(*), PLAYERNO
FROM     PLAYERS
```

The reason for this limitation is that the result of an aggregation function always consists of one value, while the result of a column specification consists of a set of values. MySQL considers this to be incompatible results.

Note, however, that this rule applies only to column specifications and not to, for example, literals and system variables. Therefore, the following statement is correct:

```
SELECT   'The number of players', COUNT(*)
FROM     PLAYERS
```

The result is:

```
'The number of players is'  COUNT(*)
--------------------------  --------
The number of players is          14
```

Chapter 10 extends these rules for the SELECT clause for table expressions that *do* contain a GROUP BY clause.

Exercise 9.3: Is the following SELECT statement correct?

```
SELECT    TEAMNO, COUNT(*)
FROM      MATCHES
```

Exercise 9.4: Find the number of penalties and the highest penalty amount.

9.8 COUNT Function

With the COUNT function, an asterisk (*) or an expression can be specified between brackets. The previous section discussed the first case in which an asterisk is used. This section discusses the other possibilities.

Example 9.10: How many league numbers are there?

```
SELECT    COUNT(LEAGUENO)
FROM      PLAYERS
```

The result is:

```
COUNT(LEAGUENO)
---------------
             10
```

Explanation: The function COUNT(LEAGUENO) is used to count the number of *non-null values* in the LEAGUENO column instead of the number of rows in the intermediate result. So the result is 10, not 14 (the number of non-null values and all values in the column, respectively).

Specifying ALL does not change the result of a query. This applies to all the aggregation functions. Therefore, the previous statement could have been written as follows:

```
SELECT    COUNT(ALL LEAGUENO)
FROM      PLAYERS
```

The COUNT function can also be used to calculate the number of *different* values in a column.

Example 9.11: How many different town names are there in the TOWN column?

```
SELECT    COUNT(DISTINCT TOWN)
FROM      PLAYERS
```

The result is:

```
COUNT(DISTINCT TOWN)
--------------------
                   6
```

Explanation: When DISTINCT is specified in front of the column name, all the duplicate values are removed first; then the addition is carried out.

Example 9.12: Get the number of different characters that start the names of the players.

```
SELECT   COUNT(DISTINCT SUBSTR(NAME, 1, 1))
FROM     PLAYERS
```

The result is:

```
COUNT(DISTINCT SUBSTR(NAME, 1, 1))
----------------------------------
                                 8
```

Explanation: This example shows clearly that all kinds of expression forms can be used within aggregation functions, including scalar functions (see Appendix B, "Scalar Functions," for a description of the SUBSTR function).

Example 9.13: Get the number of different years that appear in the PENALTIES table.

```
SELECT   COUNT(DISTINCT YEAR(PAYMENT_DATE))
FROM     PENALTIES
```

The result is:

```
COUNT(DISTINCT YEAR(PAYMENT_DATE))
----------------------------------
                                 5
```

Example 9.14: Get the number of different town names and the number of sexes represented.

```
SELECT   COUNT(DISTINCT TOWN), COUNT(DISTINCT SEX)
FROM     PLAYERS
```

The result is:

```
COUNT(DISTINCT TOWN)  COUNT(DISTINCT SEX)
--------------------  -------------------
                   6                    2
```

Explanation: More than one aggregation function can be specified in a SELECT clause.

Example 9.15: Get the numbers and names of players who incurred more penalties than they played matches.

```
SELECT   PLAYERNO, NAME
FROM     PLAYERS AS P
WHERE   (SELECT   COUNT(*)
         FROM     PENALTIES AS PEN
         WHERE    P.PLAYERNO = PEN.PLAYERNO)
         >
        (SELECT   COUNT(*)
         FROM     MATCHES AS M
         WHERE    P.PLAYERNO = M.PLAYERNO)
```

The result is:

```
PLAYERNO  NAME
--------  -------
      27  Collins
      44  Baker
```

Explanation: Aggregation functions can appear in the SELECT clause of each table expression, including subqueries.

Example 9.16: For each player, find the player number, the name, and the number of penalties incurred by him or her, but only for players who have at least two penalties.

```
SELECT   PLAYERNO, NAME,
        (SELECT   COUNT(*)
         FROM     PENALTIES
         WHERE    PENALTIES.PLAYERNO = PLAYERS.PLAYERNO)
         AS NUMBER
FROM     PLAYERS
WHERE   (SELECT   COUNT(*)
         FROM     PENALTIES
         WHERE    PENALTIES.PLAYERNO = PLAYERS.PLAYERNO) >= 2
```

The result is:

```
PLAYERNO  NAME     NUMBER
--------  -------  ------
      27  Collins       2
      44  Baker         3
```

Explanation: The correlated subquery in the SELECT clause is used to calculate the number of penalties for each player. That same subquery is used to check whether that number is greater than 1.

This statement can also be formulated in a more compact way by placing the subquery within the FROM clause:

```
SELECT   PLAYERNO, NAME, NUMBER
FROM    (SELECT   PLAYERNO, NAME,
                 (SELECT   COUNT(*)
                  FROM     PENALTIES
                  WHERE    PENALTIES.PLAYERNO =
                           PLAYERS.PLAYERNO)
                  AS NUMBER
         FROM     PLAYERS) AS PN
WHERE    NUMBER >= 2
```

Explanation: The subquery in the FROM clause determines the number, the name, and the number of penalties for each player. Next, this number becomes a column in the intermediate result. After that, a condition can be specified (NUMBER >= 2); finally, the value of that column in the SELECT clause is retrieved.

Example 9.17: Get the total number of penalties followed by the total number of matches.

```
SELECT (SELECT   COUNT(*)
        FROM     PENALTIES),
       (SELECT   COUNT(*)
        FROM     MATCHES)
```

The result is:

```
SELECT ...  SELECT ...
----------  ----------
         8          13
```

Explanation: If the result of a SELECT statement is empty, the COUNT function returns the value 0.

Exercise 9.5: Get the number of different committee positions.

Exercise 9.6: Get the number of league numbers of players resident in Inglewood.

Exercise 9.7: For each team, find the number, division, and number of matches played for that team.

Exercise 9.8: For each player, get the number, name, and number of matches won.

Exercise 9.9: Create a SELECT statement that results in the following table:

```
TABLES             NUMBERS
-----------------  -------
Number of players       14
Number of teams          2
Number of matches       13
```

9.9 MAX AND MIN FUNCTIONS

With the MAX and MIN functions, you can determine the largest and smallest values, respectively, in a column.

Example 9.18: What is the highest penalty?

```
SELECT    MAX(AMOUNT)
FROM      PENALTIES
```

The result is:

```
MAX(AMOUNT)
-----------
     100.00
```

Example 9.19: What is the lowest penalty incurred by a player resident in Stratford?

```
SELECT    MIN(AMOUNT)
FROM      PENALTIES
WHERE     PLAYERNO IN
         (SELECT    PLAYERNO
          FROM      PLAYERS
          WHERE     TOWN = 'Stratford')
```

The result is:

```
MIN(AMOUNT)
-----------
     100.00
```

Example 9.20: How many penalties are equal to the lowest one?

```
SELECT   COUNT(*)
FROM     PENALTIES
WHERE    AMOUNT =
        (SELECT   MIN(AMOUNT)
         FROM     PENALTIES)
```

The result is:

```
COUNT(AMOUNT)
-------------
            2
```

Explanation: The subquery calculates the lowest penalty, which is $25. The SELECT statement calculates the number of penalties equal to the amount of this lowest penalty.

Example 9.21: For each team, find the team number followed by the player number of the player who has won the most matches for that team.

```
SELECT   DISTINCT TEAMNO, PLAYERNO
FROM     MATCHES AS M1
WHERE    WON =
        (SELECT   MAX(WON)
         FROM     MATCHES AS M2
         WHERE    M1.TEAMNO = M2.TEAMNO)
```

The result is:

```
TEAMNO  PLAYERNO
------  --------
     1         6
     1        44
     1        57
     2        27
     2       104
```

Explanation: In the result, more than one player appears for each team because several players won a match in three sets.

Aggregation functions can occur in calculations. Two examples of this follow.

Example 9.22: What is the difference between the highest and lowest penalties in cents?

```
SELECT    (MAX(AMOUNT) - MIN(AMOUNT)) * 100
FROM      PENALTIES
```

The result is:

```
(MAX(AMOUNT) - MIN(AMOUNT)) * 100
---------------------------------
                          7500.00
```

Example 9.23: Of all the players, get the first letter of the last name that is alphabetically sorted last.

```
SELECT    SUBSTR(MAX(NAME), 1, 1)
FROM      PLAYERS
```

The result is:

```
SUBSTR(MAX(NAME), 1, 1)
-----------------------
W
```

Explanation: First, the MAX function finds the last name in alphabetical order; then the scalar function SUBSTR identifies the first letter from this name. See Appendix B for a description of this and other functions.

In principle, DISTINCT can be used with the MAX and MIN functions, but, of course, this does not change the end result (determine why for yourself).

When MAX and MIN functions are processed, two special situations must be taken into consideration:

- If a column in a given row contains only null values, the values of the MIN and MAX functions are also null.
- If the MIN and MAX functions are executed on an empty intermediate result, the value of these functions is also null.

Here is an example of each.

Example 9.24: What is the highest league number of all players from Midhurst?

```
SELECT   MAX(LEAGUENO)
FROM     PLAYERS
WHERE    TOWN = 'Midhurst'
```

The result is:

```
MAX(LEAGUENO)
-------------
?
```

Explanation: The PLAYERS table contains only one player from Midhurst, and she has no league number. That is why the answer to this statement has only one row consisting of the null value.

Example 9.25: What is the lowest league number of all players from Amsterdam? If a player does not exist, print the text `Unknown`.

```
SELECT   CASE WHEN MIN(LEAGUENO) IS NULL
            THEN 'Unknown'
            ELSE MIN(LEAGUENO)
         END
FROM     PLAYERS
WHERE    TOWN = 'Amsterdam'
```

The result is:

```
CASE WHEN ...
-------------
Unknown
```

Example 9.26: For each player who incurred at least one penalty, find the player number, the highest penalty, and the date on which that penalty was paid.

```
SELECT   PLAYERNO, AMOUNT, PAYMENT_DATE
FROM     PENALTIES AS PEN1
WHERE    AMOUNT =
        (SELECT   MAX(AMOUNT)
         FROM     PENALTIES AS PEN2
         WHERE    PEN2.PLAYERNO = PEN1.PLAYERNO)
```

The result is:

```
PLAYERNO  AMOUNT  PAYMENT_DATE
--------  ------  ------------
       6  100.00    1980-12-08
       8   25.00    1980-12-08
      27  100.00    1983-09-10
      44   75.00    1981-05-05
     104   50.00    1984-12-08
```

Example 9.27: For each player, get the player number, the highest penalty amount that was paid for him or her, and the highest number of sets won in a match.

```
SELECT   PLAYERNO,
        (SELECT   MAX(AMOUNT)
         FROM     PENALTIES
         WHERE    PENALTIES.PLAYERNO = PLAYERS.PLAYERNO)
         AS HIGHESTPENALTY,
        (SELECT   MAX(WON)
         FROM     MATCHES
         WHERE    MATCHES.PLAYERNO = PLAYERS.PLAYERNO)
         AS NUMBEROFSETS
FROM     PLAYERS
```

The result is:

```
PLAYERNO  HIGHESTPENALTY  NUMBEROFSETS
--------  --------------  ------------
       2               ?             1
       6          100.00             3
       7               ?             ?
       8           25.00             0
      27          100.00             3
      28               ?             ?
      39               ?             ?
      44           75.00             3
      57               ?             3
      83               ?             0
      95               ?             ?
     100               ?             ?
     104           50.00             3
     112               ?             2
```

Explanation: The two correlated subqueries are processed for each player separately. When no rows are found, the subquery returns a null value.

Example 9.28: Get the number of each player whose lowest penalty amount is equal to his or her highest penalty amount.

```
SELECT    PLAYERNO
FROM      PLAYERS
WHERE    (SELECT   MIN(AMOUNT)
          FROM     PENALTIES
          WHERE    PENALTIES.PLAYERNO = PLAYERS.PLAYERNO) =
         (SELECT   MAX(AMOUNT)
          FROM     PENALTIES
          WHERE    PENALTIES.PLAYERNO = PLAYERS.PLAYERNO)
```

The result is:

```
PLAYERNO
--------
       6
       8
     104
```

Exercise 9.10: Get the lowest number of sets by which a match has been won.

Exercise 9.11: For each player, get the number and the difference between his or her lowest and highest penalty amounts.

Exercise 9.12: Get the number and the date of birth of each player born in the same year as the youngest player who played for the first team.

9.10 The SUM and AVG Function

The SUM function calculates the sum of all values in a particular column. The AVG function calculates the *arithmetic average* of the values in a particular column. Of course, both functions apply only to columns with a numeric data type.

Example 9.29: What is the total amount of penalties incurred by players from Inglewood?

```
SELECT    SUM(AMOUNT)
FROM      PENALTIES
WHERE     PLAYERNO IN
         (SELECT   PLAYERNO
          FROM     PLAYERS
          WHERE    TOWN = 'Inglewood')
```

The result is:

```
SUM(AMOUNT)
-----------
     155.00
```

You can specify the word `ALL` in front of the column name without affecting the result. By adding `ALL`, you explicitly demand that *all* values be considered. In contrast, using `DISTINCT` within the `SUM` function can alter the end result. If you extend the `SUM` function in the previous `SELECT` statement with `DISTINCT`, you get the following result:

```
SELECT   SUM(DISTINCT AMOUNT)
FROM     PENALTIES
WHERE    PLAYERNO IN
        (SELECT   PLAYERNO
         FROM     PLAYERS
         WHERE    TOWN = 'Inglewood')
```

The result is:

```
SUM(AMOUNT)
-----------
     130.00
```

Note that, unlike the `COUNT`, `MIN`, and `MAX` functions, the `SUM` function applies only to columns with a numeric data type. The former three functions can also be applied to columns with alphanumeric and temporal data types.

Example 9.30: Get the average amount of penalties incurred by player 44.

```
SELECT   AVG(AMOUNT)
FROM     PENALTIES
WHERE    PLAYERNO = 44
```

The result is:

```
AVG(AMOUNT)
-----------
      43.33
```

Explanation: The amount $43.33 is the average of the amounts $75, $25, and $30.

Example 9.31: Which players have ever incurred a penalty greater than the average penalty?

```
SELECT   DISTINCT PLAYERNO
FROM     PENALTIES
WHERE    AMOUNT >
        (SELECT   AVG(AMOUNT)
         FROM     PENALTIES)
```

The result is:

```
PLAYERNO
--------
       6
      27
      44
```

Explanation: The average penalty is $60.

Adding the word ALL does not affect the result because it simply reinforces the idea that *all* values are included in the calculation. On the other hand, adding DISTINCT within the AVG function does influence the result.

Example 9.32: What is the *unweighted* arithmetic mean of the penalty amounts? (By "unweighted," we mean that each value is considered only once in the calculation, even when it occurs more than once.)

```
SELECT   AVG(DISTINCT AMOUNT)
FROM     PENALTIES
```

The result is:

```
AVG(DISTINCT AMOUNT)
--------------------
               56.00
```

Explanation: The amount $56 is equal to $100 + $75 + $50 + $30 + $25 divided by 5.

Example 9.33: What is the average length (in number of characters) of the names of the players, and how long is the longest name?

```
SELECT   AVG(LENGTH(RTRIM(NAME))), MAX(LENGTH(RTRIM(NAME)))
FROM     PLAYERS
```

The result is:

```
AVG(LENGTH(RTRIM(NAME)))  MAX(LENGTH(RTRIM(NAME)))
------------------------  ------------------------
                  6.5000                         9
```

Example 9.34: For each penalty, get the payment number, the amount, and the difference between the amount and the average penalty amount.

```
SELECT   PAYMENTNO, AMOUNT,
         ABS(AMOUNT - (SELECT AVG(AMOUNT)
                       FROM   PENALTIES)) AS DIFFERENCE
FROM     PENALTIES AS P
```

The result is:

```
PAYMENTNO  AMOUNT  DIFFERENCE
---------  ------  ----------
        1  100.00       40.00
        2   75.00       15.00
        3  100.00       40.00
        4   50.00       10.00
        5   25.00       35.00
        6   25.00       35.00
        7   30.00       30.00
        8   75.00       15.00
```

Explanation: In this example, the subquery is part of a compound expression. The result of the subquery is subtracted from the AMOUNT column; next, the absolute value of this result is calculated with the scalar function ABS.

For the SUM and AVG functions, the same rules apply as for MIN and MAX:

- If a column in a given row contains only null values, the value of the function is equal to null.
- If some of the values in a column are null, the value of the function is equal to the sum of the average of all *non*-null values divided by the number of *non*-null values (and, therefore, not divided by the total number of values).
- If the intermediate result for which SUM or AVG must be calculated is empty, the result of the function is equal to the null value.

Exercise 9.13: Determine the value of these functions for the following set of values in the NUMBER column: `{ 1, 2, 3, 4, 1, 4, 4, NULL, 5 }`.

1. `COUNT(*)`
2. `COUNT(NUMBER)`
3. `MIN(NUMBER)`
4. `MAX(NUMBER)`
5. `SUM(NUMBER)`
6. `AVG(NUMBER)`
7. `COUNT(DISTINCT NUMBER)`
8. `MIN(DISTINCT NUMBER)`
9. `MAX(DISTINCT NUMBER)`
10. `SUM(DISTINCT NUMBER)`
11. `AVG(DISTINCT NUMBER)`

Exercise 9.14: What is the average penalty for players who have ever competed for team 1?

Exercise 9.15: Get the numbers and names of the players for whom the total amount of penalties is higher than 100.

Exercise 9.16: Get the names and initials of each players who has won for at least one of his matches more sets than player 27 has won in total.

Exercise 9.17: Get the numbers and names of the players for whom the sum of all sets won is equal to 8.

Exercise 9.18: Get the numbers and names of the players for whom the length of their name is greater than the average length.

Exercise 9.19: For each player (also those without penalties), get the player number and the difference between his or her maximum and the average penalty.

Exercise 9.20: For each player, get the average penalty amount in the form of a simple, horizontal histogram. Make use of the scalar function `REPEAT`.

9.11 The VARIANCE and STDDEV Functions

The VARIANCE and STDDEV functions calculate, respectively, the *variance* (sometimes called the *population variance*) and the *standard deviation* (sometimes called the *population standard deviation*) of the values in a particular column. Of course, these functions apply only to columns with a numeric data type.

The VARIANCE function (the VAR function, for short) is used to calculate the variance. Variance is a measurement that indicates how close all values are to the average. In other words, it refers to the *distribution* of all values. The closer each value is to the average, the lower the variance is.

Example 9.35: Get the variance of all penalties incurred by player 44.

```
SELECT   VARIANCE(AMOUNT)
FROM     PENALTIES
WHERE    PLAYERNO = 44
```

The result is:

```
VARIANCE(AMOUNT)
----------------
         505.555
```

Explanation: The variance is calculated on the basis of the following steps:

- Calculate the average of the column concerned.
- For each value in the column, determine how much the value differs from the average.
- Calculate the sum of the squares of the differences.
- Divide the sum by the number of values (in the column).

If you execute these steps for the previous statement, the first step returns the answer: 43.33333, the average of the three values 75, 25, and 30. Next, for each of the three values, the difference with the average is calculated. You can determine this with the following SELECT statement:

```
SELECT   AMOUNT -
        (SELECT   AVG(AMOUNT)
         FROM     PENALTIES
         WHERE    PLAYERNO = 44)
FROM     PENALTIES
WHERE    PLAYERNO = 44
```

This gives the result: 31.666667, -18.33333, and -13.33333. The following SELECT statement calculates the sum of the differences between the squares:

```
SELECT   SUM(P)
FROM    (SELECT    POWER(AMOUNT -
                  (SELECT   AVG(AMOUNT)
                   FROM     PENALTIES
                   WHERE    PLAYERNO = 44),2) AS P
         FROM      PENALTIES
         WHERE     PLAYERNO = 44) AS POWERS
```

The result is 1516.6666666667. In the final step, this amount is divided by the number of values, which gives an end result of 505.5555. To calculate all these steps without the VARIANCE function, you can use the following statement:

```
SELECT   SUM(P) /
        (SELECT COUNT(*) FROM PENALTIES WHERE PLAYERNO = 44)
FROM    (SELECT    POWER(AMOUNT -
                   (SELECT   AVG(AMOUNT)
                   FROM     PENALTIES
                   WHERE    PLAYERNO = 44),2) AS P
         FROM      PENALTIES
         WHERE     PLAYERNO = 44) AS POWERS
```

The STDDEV function calculates the *standard deviation* of a set of values. Standard deviation is another measure of distribution for determining how close the values are to the average. By definition, the standard deviation is equal to the square root of the variance. In other words, the following two expressions are equal: STDDEV(…) and SQRT(VARIANCE(…)).

Example 9.36: Get the standard deviation for all penalties incurred by player 44.

```
SELECT   STDDEV(AMOUNT)
FROM     PENALTIES
WHERE    PLAYERNO = 44
```

The result is:

```
STDDEV(AMOUNT)
--------------
     22.484563
```

The word STDDEV may be abbreviated to STD; this has no effect on the result.

Exercise 9.21: Get the standard deviation of all penalties of player 44 *without* using the STDDEV function.

9.12 The VAR_SAMP and STDDEV_SAMP Functions

The VARIANCE and STDDEV functions operate on all the values in the specified column. For functions, special versions exist that include not all the values in the calculation, but a sample of those values. These are called VAR_SAMP and STDDEV_SAMP, respectively. In the world of statistics, these are called the *sample variance* and the sample *standard deviation*.

Example 9.37: Get the sample variance and the (population) variance of all penalty amounts.

```
SELECT   VAR_SAMP(AMOUNT), VARIANCE(AMOUNT)
FROM     PENALTIES
```

The result is:

```
VAR_SAMP(AMOUNT)  VARIANCE(AMOUNT)
----------------  ----------------
     1062.500000        850.000000
```

Explanation: The formula to calculate the spot check variance is in line with the one of the population variance, but this time, all values are used at random.

Example 9.38: Get the sample standard deviation and the population standard deviation of all penalty amounts.

```
SELECT   STDDEV_SAMP(AMOUNT), STDDEV(AMOUNT)
FROM     PENALTIES
```

The result is:

```
STDDEV_SAMP(AMOUNT)  STDDEV(AMOUNT)
-------------------  --------------
          32.596012       29.154759
```

9.13 The BIT_AND, BIT_OR, and BIT_XOR Functions

Section 5.13.1 describes the binary operators | (or), & (and), and ^ (xor). Equivalent aggregation functions of these operators also exist: BIT_OR, BIT_AND, and BIT_XOR.

For example, the function BIT_OR executes a binary OR on all values that appear in a column.

Example 9.39: Create a new table called BITS, and store three values in it: 001, 011, and 111. (You will need them in the other examples.)

```
CREATE TABLE BITS
      (BIN_VALUE INTEGER NOT NULL PRIMARY KEY)

INSERT INTO BITS
VALUES (CONV(001,2,16)),
       (CONV(011,2,16)),
       (CONV(111,2,16))
```

Example 9.40: Get the result of the BIT_OR function executed on the BIN_VALUE column.

```
SELECT   BIN(BIT_OR(BIN_VALUE))
FROM     BITS
```

The result is:

```
BIN(BIT_OR(BIN_VALUE))
----------------------
111
```

Explanation: Behind the scenes MySQL executes the following expression: (001 | 011) | 111. The result is 111 because on each position of at least one of the three values a 1 occurs.

When you replace BIT_OR by BIT_AND in the previous statement, the result is 001 because on only one position of all the three values a 1 occurs. When you use the BIT_XOR function, the result is 101.

If the BIT_OR and BIT_XOR functions are executed on an empty intermediate result, MySQL returns the number 0 as answer. For BIT_AND, the result is then equal to 18,446,744,073,709,551,615. This is a BIGINTEGER value, of which the binary representation is equal to a long list of 64 ones.

9.14 Answers

9.1 1. Not superfluous
2. Not superfluous
3. Superfluous because a condition appears on the primary key
4. Not superfluous
5. Not superfluous
6. Not superfluous

9.2 1.
```
C2
--
c2
?
```

2.
```
C2  C3
--  --
c2  c3
c2  ?
?   ?
```

9.3 This statement is not correct. An aggregation function is used in the SELECT clause; therefore, all other column names must appear within an aggregation function.

9.4
```
SELECT   COUNT(*), MAX(AMOUNT)
FROM     PENALTIES
```

9.5
```
SELECT   COUNT(DISTINCT POSITION)
FROM     COMMITTEE_MEMBERS
```

9.6
```
SELECT   COUNT(LEAGUENO)
FROM     PLAYERS
WHERE    TOWN = 'Inglewood'
```

9.7
```
SELECT   TEAMNO, DIVISION,
        (SELECT   COUNT(*)
         FROM     MATCHES
         WHERE    TEAMS.TEAMNO = MATCHES.TEAMNO)
FROM     TEAMS
```

9.8
```
SELECT   PLAYERNO, NAME,
        (SELECT   COUNT(*)
         FROM     MATCHES
         WHERE    MATCHES.PLAYERNO = PLAYERS.PLAYERNO
         AND      WON > LOST)
FROM     PLAYERS
```

9.9
```
SELECT 'Number of players' AS TABLES,
        (SELECT COUNT(*) FROM PLAYERS) AS NUMBERS UNION
SELECT 'Number of teams',
        (SELECT COUNT(*) FROM TEAMS) UNION
SELECT 'Number of matches',
        (SELECT COUNT(*) FROM MATCHES)
```

9.10
```
SELECT   MIN(WON)
FROM     MATCHES
WHERE    WON > LOST
```

9.11
```
SELECT   PLAYERNO,
        (SELECT   MAX(AMOUNT)
         FROM     PENALTIES
         WHERE    PENALTIES.PLAYERNO =
                  PLAYERS.PLAYERNO) -
        (SELECT   MIN(AMOUNT)
         FROM     PENALTIES
         WHERE    PENALTIES.PLAYERNO =
                  PLAYERS.PLAYERNO)
FROM     PLAYERS
```

9.12
```
SELECT   PLAYERNO, BIRTH_DATE
FROM     PLAYERS
WHERE    YEAR(BIRTH_DATE) =
        (SELECT   MAX(YEAR(BIRTH_DATE))
         FROM     PLAYERS
         WHERE    PLAYERNO IN
                 (SELECT   PLAYERNO
                  FROM     MATCHES
                  WHERE    TEAMNO = 1))
```

9.13

1. 9
2. 8
3. 1
4. 5
5. 24
6. 3

7. 5
8. 1
9. 5
10. 15
11. 15 / 5 = 3

9.14
```
SELECT   AVG(AMOUNT)
FROM     PENALTIES
WHERE    PLAYERNO IN
        (SELECT   PLAYERNO
         FROM     MATCHES
         WHERE    TEAMNO = 1)
```

9.15
```
SELECT   PLAYERNO, NAME
FROM     PLAYERS
WHERE   (SELECT   SUM(AMOUNT)
         FROM     PENALTIES
         WHERE    PENALTIES.PLAYERNO = PLAYERS.PLAYERNO)
         > 100
```

9.16
```
SELECT   NAME, INITIALS
FROM     PLAYERS
WHERE    PLAYERNO IN
        (SELECT   PLAYERNO
         FROM     MATCHES
         WHERE    WON >
                 (SELECT   SUM(WON)
                  FROM     MATCHES
                  WHERE    PLAYERNO = 27))
```

9.17
```
SELECT   PLAYERNO, NAME
FROM     PLAYERS
WHERE   (SELECT   SUM(WON)
         FROM     MATCHES
         WHERE    MATCHES.PLAYERNO =
                  PLAYERS.PLAYERNO) = 8
```

9.18
```
SELECT   PLAYERNO, NAME
FROM     PLAYERS
WHERE    LENGTH(RTRIM(NAME)) >
        (SELECT   AVG(LENGTH(RTRIM(NAME)))
         FROM     PLAYERS)
```

9.19
```
SELECT    PLAYERNO,
         (SELECT   MAX(AMOUNT)
          FROM     PENALTIES
          WHERE    PENALTIES.PLAYERNO =
                   PLAYERS.PLAYERNO) -
         (SELECT   AVG(AMOUNT)
          FROM     PENALTIES
          WHERE    PENALTIES.PLAYERNO =
                   PLAYERS.PLAYERNO)
FROM      PLAYERS
```

9.20
```
SELECT    PLAYERNO,
          REPEAT('*',
             CAST((SELECT   AVG(AMOUNT)
                   FROM     PENALTIES
                   WHERE    PENALTIES.PLAYERNO =
                            PLAYERS.PLAYERNO)/10
                   AS SIGNED INTEGER))
FROM      PLAYERS
```

9.21
```
SELECT    SQRT(SUM(P) /
         (SELECT COUNT(*) FROM PENALTIES WHERE
                          PLAYERNO = 44))
FROM     (SELECT   POWER(AMOUNT -
                   (SELECT   AVG(AMOUNT)
                   FROM      PENALTIES
                   WHERE     PLAYERNO = 44),2) AS P
          FROM     PENALTIES
          WHERE    PLAYERNO = 44) AS POWERS
```

CHAPTER 10

SELECT Statement: The GROUP BY Clause

10.1 Introduction

The GROUP BY clause groups rows on the basis of similarities among them. For example, we could group all the rows in the PLAYERS table on the basis of the place of residence. The result would be one group of players per town. From there, we could query the number of players in each group. The final result answers the question, how many players live in each town? Other examples are: How many matches has each team played, and how much has each player incurred in penalties? In short, the GROUP BY clause is frequently used to formulate questions based on the word *per*.

By adding aggregation functions, such as COUNT and SUM, to a select block with the use of a GROUP BY clause, data can be *aggregated*. These functions owe their name to this. Aggregation means that we ask for summations, averages, frequencies, and subtotals instead of individual values.

DEFINITION

```
<group by clause> ::=
   GROUP BY <group by specification list> [ WITH ROLLUP ]

<group by specification list> ::=
   <group by specification> [ , <group by specification> ]...

<group by specification> ::=
   <group by expression> [ <sort direction> ]

<group by expression> ::= <scalar expression>

<sort direction> ::= ASC | DESC
```

10.2 Grouping on One Column

The simplest form of the GROUP BY clause is the one in which only one column is grouped. Previous chapters gave several examples of statements with such a GROUP BY clause. For the sake of clarity, we show several other examples in this section.

Example 10.1: Get all the different town names from the PLAYERS table.

```
SELECT   TOWN
FROM     PLAYERS
GROUP BY TOWN
```

The intermediate result from the GROUP BY clause could look similar to this:

```
TOWN       PLAYERNO                    NAME
---------  --------------------------  ----------------------
Stratford  {6, 83, 2, 7, 57, 39, 100}  {Parmenter, Hope, ...}
Midhurst   {28}                        {Collins}
Inglewood  {44, 8}                     {Baker, Newcastle}
Plymouth   {112}                       {Bailey}
Douglas    {95}                        {Miller}
Eltham     {27, 104}                   {Collins, Moorman}
```

Explanation: All rows with the same TOWN form one group. Each row in the intermediate result has one value in the TOWN column, whereas all other columns can contain multiple values. To indicate that these columns are special, the values are placed between brackets. We show those columns in this way for illustrative purposes only; MySQL probably would solve this internally in a different way. Furthermore, these two columns *cannot* be presented like this because a column that is not grouped is completely omitted from the end result. We return to this topic later in the chapter.

The end result of the statement is:

```
TOWN
---------
Stratford
Midhurst
Inglewood
Plymouth
Douglas
Eltham
```

A frequently used term in this particular context is *grouping*. The GROUP BY clause in the previous statement has one grouping, which consists of only one column—the TOWN column. In this chapter, we sometimes represent this as follows: The result is grouped by [TOWN]. Later in this chapter, we give examples of groupings with multiple columns and GROUP BY clauses consisting of multiple groupings.

The earlier question could be solved more easily by leaving out the GROUP BY clause and adding DISTINCT to the SELECT clause instead (work this out by yourself). Using the GROUP BY clause becomes interesting when we extend the SELECT clause with aggregation functions.

Example 10.2: For each town, find the number of players.

```
SELECT   TOWN, COUNT(*)
FROM     PLAYERS
GROUP BY TOWN
```

The result is:

```
TOWN        COUNT(*)
---------   --------
Stratford          7
Midhurst           1
Inglewood          2
Plymouth           1
Douglas            1
Eltham             2
```

Explanation: In this statement, the result is grouped by [TOWN]. The COUNT(*) function is now executed against each grouped row (for each town) instead of against all rows.

In this result, the data is clearly aggregated. The individual data of players cannot be displayed anymore, and the data is aggregated by TOWN. The aggregation level of this result is TOWN.

Example 10.3: For each team, get the team number, the number of matches that has been played for that team, and the total number of sets won.

```
SELECT   TEAMNO, COUNT(*), SUM(WON)
FROM     MATCHES
GROUP BY TEAMNO
```

The result is:

```
TEAMNO  COUNT(*)  SUM(WON)
------  --------  --------
     1         8        15
     2         5         9
```

Explanation: This statement contains one grouping, consisting of the TEAMNO column.

Example 10.4: For each team that is captained by a player resident in Eltham, get the team number and number of matches that has been played for that team.

```
SELECT   TEAMNO, COUNT(*)
FROM     MATCHES
WHERE    TEAMNO IN
        (SELECT   TEAMNO
         FROM     TEAMS INNER JOIN PLAYERS
                  ON TEAMS.PLAYERNO = PLAYERS.PLAYERNO
         WHERE    TOWN = 'Eltham')
GROUP BY TEAMNO
```

The result is:

```
TEAMNO  COUNT(*)
------  --------
     2         5
```

The column on which the result has been grouped might also appear in the SELECT clause as a parameter within an aggregation function. This does not happen often, but it is allowed.

Example 10.5: Get each different penalty amount, followed by the number of times that the amount occurs in the PENALTIES table, and also show the result of that amount multiplied by the number.

```
SELECT   AMOUNT, COUNT(*), SUM(AMOUNT)
FROM     PENALTIES
GROUP BY AMOUNT
```

The PENALTIES table is grouped on the AMOUNT column first. The intermediate result could be presented as follows:

```
PAYMENTNO  PLAYERNO  PAYMENT_DATE              AMOUNT
---------  --------  ------------------------  ------
{5, 6}     {44, 8}   {1980-12-08, 1980-12-08}   25.00
{7}        {44}      {1982-12-30}               30.00
{4}        {104}     {1984-12-08}               50.00
{2, 8}     {44, 27}  {1981-05-05, 1984-11-12}   75.00
{1, 3}     {6, 27}   {1980-12-08, 1983-09-10}  100.00
```

Again, the values of the columns that are not grouped are placed between brackets, and the AMOUNT column shows only one value. However, that is not entirely correct. Behind the scenes, MySQL also creates a group for this column. So the intermediate result should, in fact, be presented as follows:

```
PAYMENTNO  PLAYERNO  PAYMENT_DATE              AMOUNT
---------  --------  ------------------------  ----------------
{5, 6}     {44, 8}   {1980-12-08, 1980-12-08}  {25.00, 25.00}
{7}        {44}      {1982-12-30}              {30.00}
{4}        {104}     {1984-12-08}              {50.00}
{2, 8}     {44, 27}  {1981-05-05, 1984-11-12}  {75.00, 75.00}
{1, 3}     {6, 27}   {1980-12-08, 1983-09-10}  {100.00, 100.00}
```

The values in the AMOUNT column are also represented as a group now. Of course, only equal values appear in each group. And because it is a group, aggregation functions can be used.

The result is:

```
AMOUNT  COUNT(*)  SUM(AMOUNT)
------  --------  -----------
 25.00         2        50.00
 30.00         1        30.00
 50.00         1        50.00
 75.00         2       150.00
100.00         2       200.00
```

However, this book does not present the values of the grouped columns between brackets.

Exercise 10.1: Show the different years in which players joined the club; use the PLAYERS table.

Exercise 10.2: For each year, show the number of players who joined the club.

Exercise 10.3: For each player who has incurred at least one penalty, give the player number, average penalty amount, and number of penalties.

Exercise 10.4: For each team that has played in the first division, give the team number, number of matches, and total number of sets won.

10.3 Grouping on Two or More Columns

A GROUP BY clause can contain two or more columns—or, in other words, a grouping can consist of two or more columns. The next two examples illustrate this topic.

Example 10.6: For the MATCHES table, get all the different combinations of team numbers and player numbers.

```
SELECT   TEAMNO, PLAYERNO
FROM     MATCHES
GROUP BY TEAMNO, PLAYERNO
```

The result is grouped not on one column, but on two. All rows with the same team number and the same player number form a group.

The intermediate result from the GROUP BY clause is:

```
TEAMNO  PLAYERNO  MATCHNO    WON        LOST
------  --------  ---------  ---------  ---------
     1         2  {6}        {1}        {3}
     1         6  {1, 2, 3}  {3, 2, 3}  {1, 3, 0}
     1         8  {8}        {0}        {3}
     1        44  {4}        {3}        {2}
     1        57  {7}        {3}        {0}
     1        83  {5}        {0}        {3}
     2         8  {13}       {0}        {3}
     2        27  {9}        {3}        {2}
     2       104  {10}       {3}        {2}
     2       112  {11, 12}   {2, 1}     {3, 3}
```

The end result is:

```
TEAMNO  PLAYERNO
------  --------
     1         2
     1         6
     1         8
     1        44
     1        57
     1        83
     2         8
     2        27
     2       104
     2       112
```

The sequence of the columns in the GROUP BY clause has no effect on the end result of a statement. The following statement, therefore, is equivalent to the previous one:

```
SELECT   TEAMNO, PLAYERNO
FROM     MATCHES
GROUP BY PLAYERNO, TEAMNO
```

As an example, let us add some aggregation functions to the previous SELECT statement:

```
SELECT   TEAMNO, PLAYERNO, SUM(WON),
         COUNT(*), MIN(LOST)
FROM     MATCHES
GROUP BY TEAMNO, PLAYERNO
```

The result is:

```
TEAMNO  PLAYERNO  SUM(WON)  COUNT(*)  MIN(LOST)
------  --------  --------  --------  ---------
     1         2         1         1          3
     1         6         8         3          0
     1         8         0         1          3
     1        44         3         1          2
     1        57         3         1          0
     1        83         0         1          3
     2         8         0         1          3
     2        27         3         1          2
     2       104         3         1          2
     2       112         3         2          3
```

In this example, the grouping is equal to [TEAMNO, PLAYERNO], and the aggregation level of the result is the combination of team number and player number. This aggregation level is lower than that of a statement in which the grouping is equal to [TEAMNO] or [TOWN].

Example 10.7: For each player who has ever incurred at least one penalty, get the player number, name, and total amount of penalties incurred.

```
SELECT   P.PLAYERNO, NAME, SUM(AMOUNT)
FROM     PLAYERS AS P INNER JOIN PENALTIES AS PEN
         ON P.PLAYERNO = PEN.PLAYERNO
GROUP BY P.PLAYERNO, NAME
```

The result is:

```
P.PLAYERNO  NAME       SUM(AMOUNT)
----------  ---------  -----------
         6  Parmenter       100.00
         8  Newcastle        25.00
        27  Collins         175.00
        44  Baker           130.00
       104  Moorman          50.00
```

Explanation: This example also has a grouping consisting of two columns. The statement would have given the same result if the PEN.PLAYERNO column had also been added to the grouping. Work this out by yourself.

Exercise 10.5: For each combination of won-lost sets in the MATCHES table, get the number of matches won.

Exercise 10.6: Group the matches on town of player and division of team, and get the sum of the number of sets won for each combination of town-division.

Exercise 10.7: For each player who lives in Inglewood, get the name, initials, and number of penalties incurred by him or her.

Exercise 10.8: For each team, get the team number, division, and total number of sets won.

10.4 Grouping on Expressions

Until now, we have shown only examples in which the result was grouped on one or more columns, but what happens when we group on expressions? See the next two examples.

Example 10.8: For each year in the PENALTIES table, get the number of penalties paid.

```
SELECT   YEAR(PAYMENT_DATE), COUNT(*)
FROM     PENALTIES
GROUP BY YEAR(PAYMENT_DATE)
```

The intermediate result from the GROUP BY clause is:

```
YEAR(PAYMENT_DATE)  PAYMENTNO  PLAYERNO    PAYMENT_DATE  AMOUNT
------------------  ---------  ----------  ------------  --------
1980                {1, 5, 6}  {6, 44, 8}  {1980-12-08,  {100.00,
                                             1980-12-08,    25,00,
                                             1980-12-08}    25,00}
1981                {2}        {44}        {1981-05-05}   {75,00}
1982                {7}        {44}        {1982-12-30}   {30,00}
1983                {3}        {27}        {1983-09-10}  {100,00}
1984                {4, 8}     {104, 27}   {1984-12-08,   {50,00,
                                             1984-11-12}    75,00}
```

The result is:

```
YEAR(PAYMENT_DATE)  COUNT(*)
------------------  --------
1980                       3
1981                       1
1982                       1
1983                       1
1984                       2
```

Explanation: The result is now grouped on the values of the scalar expression YEAR(PAYMENT_DATE). Rows for which the value of the expression YEAR(PAYMENT_DATE) is equal form a group.

Example 10.9: Group the players on the basis of their player numbers. Group 1 should contain the players with number 1 up to and including 24. Group 2 should contain the players with numbers 25 up to and including 49, and so on. For each group, get the number of players and the highest player number.

```
SELECT   TRUNCATE(PLAYERNO/25,0), COUNT(*), MAX(PLAYERNO)
FROM     PLAYERS
GROUP BY TRUNCATE(PLAYERNO/25,0)
```

The result is:

```
TRUNCATE(PLAYERNO/25,0)  COUNT(*)  MAX(PLAYERNO)
-----------------------  --------  -------------
                      0         4              8
                      1         4             44
                      2         1             57
                      3         2             95
                      4         3            112
```

The scalar expression on which rows are grouped can be rather complex. This can consist of system variables, user variables, functions, and calculations. Even certain scalar subqueries are allowed.

Exercise 10.9: Group the players on the length of their names and get the number of players for each length.

Exercise 10.10: For each match, determine the difference between the number of sets won and lost, and group the matches on that difference.

Exercise 10.11: For each combination of year-month in the COMMITTEE_MEMBERS table, get the number of committee members who started in that year and that month.

10.5 Grouping of Null Values

If grouping is required on a column that contains null values, all these null values form one group because a GROUP BY clause applies a vertical comparison. This is in accordance with the rules described in Section 9.5.

Example 10.10: Find the different league numbers.

```
SELECT   LEAGUENO
FROM     PLAYERS
GROUP BY LEAGUENO
```

The result is:

```
LEAGUENO
--------
1124
1319
1608
2411
2513
2983
6409
6524
7060
8467
?
```

Explanation: Players 7, 28, 39, and 95 do not have a league number and, therefore, form one group (the last row) in the end result.

10.6 Grouping with Sorting

In many cases, a select block containing a `GROUP BY` clause ends with an `ORDER BY` clause. And many times the columns specified in that `ORDER BY` clause are the same as the ones specified in the `GROUP BY` clause. These statements can be simplified by combining the two clauses.

Example 10.11: For each team, get the number of matches and sort the result in descending order by team number.

The obvious formulation is:

```
SELECT   TEAMNO, COUNT(*)
FROM     MATCHES
GROUP BY TEAMNO
ORDER BY TEAMNO DESC
```

The result is:

```
TEAMNO  COUNT(*)
------  --------
     2         5
     1         8
```

Explanation: The specification DESC is a *sort direction* and indicates that the result must be sorted in a descending order. This statement can be simplified by including the specification DESC in the GROUP BY clause.

```
SELECT   TEAMNO, COUNT(*)
FROM     MATCHES
GROUP BY TEAMNO DESC
```

If the result must have an ascending sort direction, ASC (ascending) must be specified.

10.7 General Rules for the GROUP BY Clause

This section describes a number of important rules for select blocks with a GROUP BY clause.

Rule 1: Section 9.7 gives several rules for the use of aggregation functions in the SELECT clause. For many SQL products, the following rule applies: If a select block has a GROUP BY clause, any column specification in the SELECT clause must exclusively occur as a parameter of an aggregation function, or in the list of columns given in the GROUP BY clause, or in both. Therefore, for most products, the following statement is incorrect because the TOWN column appears in the SELECT clause, yet it is *not* the parameter of an aggregation function and does not occur in the list of columns by which the result is grouped.

```
SELECT   TOWN, COUNT(*)
FROM     PLAYERS
GROUP BY SEX
```

This restriction is because the result of an aggregation function always consists of one value for each group. The result of a column specification on which grouping is performed also always consists of one value per group. These results are compatible. In contrast, the result of a column specification on which *no* grouping is performed consists of a set of values. This would not be compatible with the results of the other expressions in the SELECT clause.

This rule does not apply for MySQL. The previous query will return the following result:

```
TOWN       COUNT(*)
---------  --------
Stratford         9
Inglewood         5
```

The value of the second column is understandable—it is the number of players per sex. But the answer of the first column is unexpected. Why does it show Stratford in the first row and Inglewood in the second? This is strange because, for each sex, there can be multiple towns. The answer is that MySQL itself determines the values to be returned. Those values are selected almost randomly. We can enforce this rule if we add the setting ONLY_FULL_GROUP_BY to the SQL_MODE system variable.

Therefore, we strongly recommend that you do not formulate this type of SQL statement, and instead adhere to this rule that applies to most SQL products.

Rule 2: In most examples, the expressions used to form groups also occur in the SELECT clause. However, that is not necessary. An expression that occurs in the GROUP BY clause *can* appear in the SELECT clause.

Rule 3: An expression that is used to form groups can also occur in the SELECT clause within a compound expression. See the next example.

Example 10.12: Get the list with the different penalty amounts in cents.

```
SELECT   CAST(AMOUNT * 100 AS SIGNED INTEGER)
         AS AMOUNT_IN_CENTS
FROM     PENALTIES
GROUP BY AMOUNT
```

The result is:

```
AMOUNT_IN_CENTS
---------------
           2500
           3000
           5000
           7500
          10000
```

Explanation: A grouping is performed on a simple expression consisting of the column name AMOUNT. In the SELECT clause, that same AMOUNT column occurs within a compound expression. This is allowed.

No matter how complex a compound expression is, if it occurs in a GROUP BY clause, it can be included in its entirety only in the SELECT clause. For example, if the compound expression PLAYERNO * 2 occurs in a GROUP BY clause, the expressions PLAYERNO * 2, (PLAYERNO * 2) - 100 and MOD(PLAYERNO * 2, 3) - 100 can occur in the SELECT clause. On the other hand, the expressions PLAYERNO, 2 * PLAYERNO, PLAYERNO * 100, and 8 * PLAYERNO * 2 are not allowed.

Rule 4: If an expression occurs more than once in a GROUP BY clause, double expressions are simply removed. The GROUP BY clause GROUP BY TOWN, TOWN is converted to GROUP BY TOWN. Also GROUP BY SUBSTR(TOWN,1,1), SEX, SUBSTR(TOWN,1,1) is converted to GROUP BY SUBSTR(TOWN,1,1), SEX.

Rule 5: Section 9.4 described the cases in which the use of DISTINCT in the SELECT clause is superfluous. The rules given in that section apply to SELECT statements without a GROUP BY clause. A different rule exists for SELECT statements with a GROUP BY clause: DISTINCT (if used outside an aggregation function) is superfluous when the SELECT clause includes all the columns specified in the GROUP BY clause. The GROUP BY clause groups the rows in such a way that the column(s) on which they are grouped no longer contain duplicate values.

Exercise 10.12: Describe why the following statements are incorrect:

1.
```
SELECT   PLAYERNO, DIVISION
FROM     TEAMS
GROUP BY PLAYERNO
```
2.
```
SELECT   SUBSTR(TOWN,1,1), NAME
FROM     PLAYERS
GROUP BY TOWN, SUBSTR(NAME,1,1)
```
3.
```
SELECT   PLAYERNO * (AMOUNT + 100)
FROM     PENALTIES
GROUP BY AMOUNT + 100
```

Exercise 10.13: In which of the following statements is DISTINCT superfluous?

1.
```
SELECT   DISTINCT PLAYERNO
FROM     TEAMS
GROUP BY PLAYERNO
```

2.
```
SELECT   DISTINCT COUNT(*)
FROM     MATCHES
GROUP BY TEAMNO
```

3.
```
SELECT   DISTINCT COUNT(*)
FROM     MATCHES
WHERE    TEAMNO = 2
GROUP BY TEAMNO
```

10.8 The GROUP_CONCAT Function

A special aggregation function that MySQL supports is the GROUP_CONCAT function. The value of this function is equal to all values of the specified column belonging to a group. These values are placed behind each other, separated by commas, and are presented as one long alphanumeric value.

Example 10.13: For each team, get the team number and list of players who played matches for that team.

```
SELECT   TEAMNO, GROUP_CONCAT(PLAYERNO)
FROM     MATCHES
GROUP BY TEAMNO
```

The result is:

```
TEAMNO  GROUP_CONCAT(PLAYERNO)
------  ----------------------
     1  6,8,57,2,83,44,6,6
     2  27,104,112,112,8
```

The GROUP_CONCAT function can also be used on the column on which the result is grouped.

Example 10.14: For each team, get the team number and for each player, who played matches for that team, get that same team number.

```
SELECT   TEAMNO, GROUP_CONCAT(TEAMNO)
FROM     MATCHES
GROUP BY TEAMNO
```

The result is:

```
TEAMNO  GROUP_CONCAT(TEAMNO)

------  --------------------
     1  1,1,1,1,1,1,1,1
     2  2,2,2,2,2
```

If a select block contains no GROUP BY clause, the GROUP_CONCAT function is processed on all the values of a column.

Example 10.15: Get all the payment numbers.

```
SELECT   GROUP_CONCAT(PAYMENTNO)
FROM     PENALTIES
```

The result is:

```
GROUP_CONCAT(BETALINGSNR)
-------------------------
1,2,3,4,5,6,7,8
```

The length of the alphanumeric value of a GROUP_CONCAT function is restricted. The system variable GROUP_CONCAT_MAX_LEN indicates the maximum length. This variable has a standard value of 1,024 and can be adjusted with a SET statement.

Example 10.16: Reduce the length of the GROUP_CONCAT function to seven characters and execute the statement of the previous example.

```
SET @@GROUP_CONCAT_MAX_LEN=7

SELECT   TEAMNO, GROUP_CONCAT(TEAMNO)
FROM     MATCHES
GROUP BY TEAMNO
```

The result is:

```
TEAMNO  GROUP_CONCAT(TEAMNO)
------  --------------------
     1  1,1,1,1
     2  2,2,2,2
```

10.9 Complex Examples with GROUP BY

Consider the following examples that illustrate the extensive possibilities of the GROUP BY clause.

Example 10.17: What is the average total amount of penalties for players who live in Stratford and Inglewood?

```
SELECT   AVG(TOTAL)
FROM    (SELECT    PLAYERNO, SUM(AMOUNT) AS TOTAL
         FROM      PENALTIES
         GROUP BY PLAYERNO) AS TOTALS
WHERE    PLAYERNO IN
        (SELECT    PLAYERNO
         FROM      PLAYERS
         WHERE     TOWN = 'Stratford' OR TOWN = 'Inglewood')
```

The result is:

```
AVG(TOTAL)
----------
        85
```

Explanation: The intermediate result of the subquery in the `FROM` clause is a table consisting of two columns, called PLAYERNO and TOTAL, and five rows (players 6, 8, 27, 44, and 104). This table is passed on to the `WHERE` clause, in which a subquery is used to select players from Stratford and Inglewood (players 6, 8, and 44). Finally, the average is calculated in the `SELECT` clause of the column TOTAL.

Example 10.18: For each player (who incurred penalties and is captain), get the player number, name, number of penalties that he or she incurred, and number of teams that he or she captains.

```
SELECT   PLAYERS.PLAYERNO, NAME, NUMBER_OF_PENALTIES,
         NUMBER_OF_TEAMS
FROM     PLAYERS,
        (SELECT    PLAYERNO, COUNT(*) AS NUMBER_OF_PENALTIES
         FROM      PENALTIES
         GROUP BY PLAYERNO) AS NUMBER_PENALTIES,
        (SELECT    PLAYERNO, COUNT(*) AS NUMBER_OF_TEAMS
         FROM      TEAMS
         GROUP BY PLAYERNO) AS NUMBER_TEAMS
WHERE    PLAYERS.PLAYERNO = NUMBER_PENALTIES.PLAYERNO
AND      PLAYERS.PLAYERNO = NUMBER_TEAMS.PLAYERNO
```

The result is:

```
PLAYERNO  NAME       NUMBER_OF_PENALTIES  NUMBER_OF_TEAMS

--------  ---------  -------------------  ---------------
       6  Parmenter                    1                1
      27  Collins                      2                1
```

Explanation: The FROM clause contains two subqueries that both have a GROUP BY clause.

We could more easily formulate the previous statement by including subqueries in the SELECT clause, which eliminates the need for GROUP BY clauses. See the next example, and note that the only difference is that all players appear in the result.

```
SELECT   PLAYERS.PLAYERNO, NAME,
        (SELECT   COUNT(*)
         FROM     PENALTIES
         WHERE    PLAYERS.PLAYERNO =
                  PENALTIES.PLAYERNO) AS NUMBER_OF_PENALTIES,
        (SELECT   COUNT(*)
         FROM     TEAMS
         WHERE    PLAYERS.PLAYERNO =
                  TEAMS.PLAYERNO) AS NUMBER_OF_TEAMS
FROM     PLAYERS
```

Example 10.19: Get the player number and total number of penalties for each player who played a match.

```
SELECT   DISTINCT M.PLAYERNO, NUMBERP
FROM     MATCHES AS M LEFT OUTER JOIN
           (SELECT   PLAYERNO, COUNT(*) AS NUMBERP
            FROM     PENALTIES
            GROUP BY PLAYERNO) AS NP
         ON M.PLAYERNO = NP.PLAYERNO
```

Explanation: In this statement, the subquery creates the following intermediate result (this is the NP table):

```
PLAYERNO  NUMBERP
--------  -------
       6        1
       8        1
      27        2
      44        3
     104        1
```

Next, this table is joined with the MATCHES table. We execute a left outer join, so no players will disappear from this table. The final result is:

```
PLAYERNO  NUMBERP
--------  -------
       2        ?
       6        1
       8        1
      27        2
      44        3
      57        ?
      83        ?
     104        1
     112        ?
```

Example 10.20: Group the penalties on the basis of payment date. Group 1 should contain all penalties between January 1, 1980, and June 30, 1982; group 2 should contain all penalties between July 1, 1981, and December 31, 1982; and group 3 should contain all penalties between January 1, 1983, and December 31, 1984. For each group, get the sum of all penalties.

```
SELECT   GROUPS.PGROUP, SUM(P.AMOUNT)
FROM     PENALTIES AS P,
        (SELECT 1 AS PGROUP, '1980-01-01' AS START,
                '1981-06-30' AS END
         UNION
         SELECT 2, '1981-07-01', '1982-12-31'
         UNION
         SELECT 3, '1983-01-01', '1984-12-31') AS GROUPS
WHERE    P.PAYMENT_DATE BETWEEN START AND END
GROUP BY GROUPS.PGROUP
ORDER BY GROUPS.PGROUP
```

The result is:

```
GROUP  SUM(P.AMOUNT)
-----  -------------
    1         225.00
    2          30.00
    3         225.00
```

Explanation: In the FROM clause, a new (virtual) table is created in which the three groups have been defined. This GROUPS table is joined with the PENALTIES table. A BETWEEN operator is used to join the two tables. Penalties with a payment date that falls outside these groups will not be included in the result.

Example 10.21: For each penalty, get the penalty amount plus the sum of that amount and the amounts of all penalties with a lower payment number (cumulative value).

```
SELECT   P1.PAYMENTNO, P1.AMOUNT, SUM(P2.AMOUNT)
FROM     PENALTIES AS P1, PENALTIES AS P2
WHERE    P1.PAYMENTNO >= P2. PAYMENTNO
GROUP BY P1. PAYMENTNO, P1.AMOUNT
ORDER BY P1. PAYMENTNO
```

For convenience, assume that the PENALTIES table consists of the following three rows only (you can create this, too, by temporarily removing all penalties with a number greater than 3):

```
PAYMENTNO  PLAYERNO  PAYMENT_DATE  AMOUNT
---------  --------  ------------  ------
        1         6  1980-12-08       100
        2        44  1981-05-05        75
        3        27  1983-09-10       100
```

The desired result is:

```
PAYMENTNO  AMOUNT    SUM
---------  ------  -----
        1     100    100
        2      75    175
        3     100    275
```

The intermediate result of the FROM clause (showing only the columns PAYMENTNO and AMOUNT):

```
P1.PAYNO  P1.AMOUNT  P2.PAYNO  P2.AMOUNT
--------  ---------  --------  ---------
       1        100         1        100
       1        100         2         75
       1        100         3        100
       2         75         1        100
       2         75         2         75
       2         75         3        100
       3        100         1        100
       3        100         2         75
       3        100         3        100
```

The intermediate result of the WHERE clause:

```
P1.PAYNO  P1.AMOUNT  P2.PAYNO  P2.AMOUNT
--------  ---------  --------  ---------
       1        100         1        100
       2         75         1        100
       2         75         2         75
       3        100         1        100
       3        100         2         75
       3        100         3        100
```

The intermediate result of the GROUP BY clause:

```
P1.PAYNO  P1.AMOUNT  P2.PAYNO   P2.AMOUNT
--------  ---------  ---------  --------------
       1        100  {1}        {100}
       2         75  {1, 2}     {100, 75}
       3        100  {1, 2, 3}  {100, 75, 100}
```

The intermediate result of the SELECT clause:

```
P1.PAYNO  P1.AMOUNT  SUM(P2.AMOUNT)
--------  ---------  --------------
       1        100             100
       2         75             175
       3        100             275
```

This final result is equal to the desired table.

Most joins in this book (and in the real world) are equi joins. Non-equi joins are rare. However, the previous statement shows an example where non-equi joins can be useful and the powerful statements they can formulate.

Example 10.22: For each penalty, get the payment number, penalty amount, and percentage that the amount forms of the sum of all amounts (use the same PENALTIES table as in the previous example).

```
SELECT   P1.PAYMENTNO, P1.AMOUNT,
         (P1.AMOUNT * 100) / SUM(P2.AMOUNT)
FROM     PENALTIES AS P1, PENALTIES AS P2
GROUP BY P1.PAYMENTNO, P1.AMOUNT
ORDER BY P1.PAYMENTNO
```

The intermediate result of the FROM clause is equal to that of the previous example. However, the intermediate result of the GROUP BY clause differs:

```
P1.PAYNO  P1.AMOUNT  P2.PAYNO   P2.AMOUNT
--------  ---------  ---------  --------------
       1        100  {1, 2, 3}  {100, 75, 100}
       2         75  {1, 2, 3}  {100, 75, 100}
       3        100  {1, 2, 3}  {100, 75, 100}
```

The intermediate result of the SELECT clause is:

```
P1.PAYNO  P1.AMOUNT  (P1.AMOUNT * 100) / SUM(P2.AMOUNT)
--------  ---------  ----------------------------------
       1        100                               36.36
       2         75                               27.27
       3        100                               36.36
```

Determine yourself whether this is the final result.

Exercise 10.14: How many players live in a town, on average?

Exercise 10.15: For each team, get the team number, division, and number of players that played matches for that team.

Exercise 10.16: For each player, get the player number, name, sum of all penalties that he or she incurred, and number of teams from the first division that he or she captains.

Exercise 10.17: For each team captained by a player who lives in Stratford, get the team number and number of players who have won at least one match for that team.

Exercise 10.18: For each player, get the player number, name, and difference between the year in which he or she joined the club and the average year of joining the club.

Exercise 10.19: For each player, get the player number, name, and difference between the year in which he or she joined the club and the average year in which players who live in the same town joined the club.

10.10 Grouping with WITH ROLLUP

The GROUP BY clause has many features to group data and calculate aggregated data, such as the total number of penalties or the sum of all penalties. However, all statements return results in which all data is on the same level of aggregation. But what if we want to see data belonging to different aggregation levels within one statement? Imagine that with one statement we want to see the total penalty amount for each player, followed by the total penalty amount for all players. The forms of the GROUP BY clauses discussed so far do not make this possible. To achieve the desired result, more than two groupings within one GROUP BY clause are required. By adding the specification WITH ROLLUP to the GROUP BY clause, it becomes possible.

Example 10.23: For each player, find the sum of all his or her penalties, plus the sum of all penalties.

Use the UNION operator as a way to combine these two groupings into one statement.

```
SELECT   PLAYERNO, SUM(AMOUNT)
FROM     PENALTIES
GROUP BY PLAYERNO
UNION
SELECT   NULL, SUM(AMOUNT)
FROM     PENALTIES
```

The result is:

```
PLAYERNO  SUM(AMOUNT)
--------  -----------
       6       100.00
       8        25.00
      27       175.00
      44       130.00
     104        50.00
       ?       480.00
```

Explanation: The rows of this intermediate result in which the PLAYERNO column is filled form the result of the first select block. The rows in which PLAYERNO is equal to null make up the result of the second select block. The first five rows contain data on the aggregation level of the player numbers, and the last row contains data on the aggregation level of all rows.

The specification `WITH ROLLUP` has been introduced to simplify this kind of statement. `WITH ROLLUP` can be used to ask for multiple groupings with one `GROUP BY` clause. Using this approach, the previous statement would then be

```
SELECT   PLAYERNO, SUM(AMOUNT)
FROM     PENALTIES
GROUP BY PLAYERNO WITH ROLLUP
```

Explanation: The result of this statement is the same as the previous one. The specification `WITH ROLLUP` indicates that after the result has been grouped on `[PLAYERNO]`, another grouping is needed—in this case, on all rows.

To further define this concept, imagine that the expressions E_1, E_2, E_3, and E_4 are specified in a `GROUP BY` clause. The grouping performed is $[E_1, E_2, E_3, E_4]$. When we add the specification `WITH ROLLUP` to this `GROUP BY` clause, an entire set of groupings is performed: $[E_1, E_2, E_3, E_4]$, $[E_1, E_2, E_3]$, $[E_1, E_2]$, $[E_1]$, and finally `[]`. The specification `[]` means that all rows are grouped into one group. The specified grouping is seen as the highest aggregation level that is asked and also indicates that all higher aggregation levels must be calculated again. To aggregate upward is called rollup. So the result of this statement contains data on five different levels of aggregation.

If an expression occurs in the SELECT clause in which the result of a certain grouping is not grouped, the null value is placed in the result.

Example 10.24: For each combination of sex-town, get the number of players, total number of players per sex, and total number of players in the entire table.

```
SELECT   SEX, TOWN, COUNT(*)
FROM     PLAYERS
GROUP BY SEX, TOWN WITH ROLLUP
```

The result is:

```
SEX  TOWN       COUNT(*)
---  ---------  --------
M    Stratford         7
M    Inglewood         1
M    Douglas           1
M    ?                 9
F    Midhurst          1
F    Inglewood         1
F    Plymouth          1
F    Eltham            2
F    ?                 5
?    ?                14
```

Explanation: This result has three levels of aggregation. Rows 1, 2, 3, 5, 6, 7, and 8 form the lowest level and have been added because of the grouping [SEX, TOWN]; rows 4 and 9 have been added because of the grouping [SEX]; and the last row forms the highest level of aggregation and has been added because of the grouping []. It contains the total number of players.

Exercise 10.20: For each team, get the number of matches played and also the total number of matches.

Exercise 10.21: Group the matches by the name of the player and division of the team, and execute a ROLLUP. Then for each group, get the name of the player, division of the team, and total number of sets won.

10.11 Answers

10.1
```
SELECT   JOINED
FROM     PLAYERS
GROUP BY JOINED
```

10.2
```
SELECT   JOINED, COUNT(*)
FROM     PLAYERS
GROUP BY JOINED
```

10.3
```
SELECT   PLAYERNO, AVG(AMOUNT), COUNT(*)
FROM     PENALTIES
GROUP BY PLAYERNO
```

10.4
```
SELECT   TEAMNO, COUNT(*), SUM(WON)
FROM     MATCHES
WHERE    TEAMNO IN
        (SELECT   TEAMNO
         FROM     TEAMS
         WHERE    DIVISION = 'first')
GROUP BY TEAMNO
```

10.5
```
SELECT   WON, LOST, COUNT(*)
FROM     MATCHES
WHERE    WON > LOST
GROUP BY WON, LOST
ORDER BY WON, LOST
```

10.6
```
SELECT   P.TOWN, T.DIVISION, SUM(WON)
FROM    (MATCHES AS M INNER JOIN PLAYERS AS P
         ON M.PLAYERNO = P.PLAYERNO)
         INNER JOIN TEAMS AS T
         ON M.TEAMNO = T.TEAMNO
GROUP BY P.TOWN, T.DIVISION
ORDER BY P.TOWN
```

10.7
```
SELECT   NAME, INITIALS, COUNT(*)
FROM     PLAYERS AS P INNER JOIN PENALTIES AS PEN
         ON P.PLAYERNO = PEN.PLAYERNO
WHERE    P.TOWN = 'Inglewood'
GROUP BY P.PLAYERNO, NAME, INITIALS
```

10.8
```
SELECT   T.TEAMNO, DIVISION, SUM(WON)
FROM     TEAMS AS T, MATCHES AS M
WHERE    T.TEAMNO = M.TEAMNO
GROUP BY T.TEAMNO, DIVISION
```

10.9
```
SELECT   LENGTH(RTRIM(NAME)), COUNT(*)
FROM     PLAYERS
GROUP BY LENGTH(RTRIM(NAME))
```

10.10
```
SELECT   ABS(WON - LOST), COUNT(*)
FROM     MATCHES
GROUP BY ABS(WON - LOST)
```

10.11
```
SELECT   YEAR(BEGIN_DATE), MONTH(BEGIN_DATE), COUNT(*)
FROM     COMMITTEE_MEMBERS
GROUP BY YEAR(BEGIN_DATE), MONTH(BEGIN_DATE)
ORDER BY YEAR(BEGIN_DATE), MONTH(BEGIN_DATE)
```

10.12

1. Although this column appears in the SELECT clause, the result of the DIVISION column has not been grouped.
2. The NAME column cannot appear like this in the SELECT clause because the result has not been grouped on the full NAME column.
3. The PLAYERNO column appears in the SELECT clause, although the result has not been grouped; furthermore, the column does not appear as a parameter of an aggregation function.

10.13

1. Superfluous
2. Not superfluous
3. Superfluous

10.14
```
SELECT   AVG(NUMBERS)
FROM    (SELECT   COUNT(*) AS NUMBERS
         FROM     PLAYERS
         GROUP BY TOWN) AS TOWNS
```

10.15
```
SELECT   TEAMS.TEAMNO, DIVISION, NUMBER_PLAYERS
FROM     TEAMS LEFT OUTER JOIN
        (SELECT   TEAMNO, COUNT(*) AS NUMBER_PLAYERS
         FROM     MATCHES
         GROUP BY TEAMNO) AS M
         ON (TEAMS.TEAMNO = M.TEAMNO)
```

10.16
```
SELECT    PLAYERS.PLAYERNO, NAME, SUM_AMOUNT,
          NUMBER_TEAMS
FROM     (PLAYERS LEFT OUTER JOIN
         (SELECT   PLAYERNO, SUM(AMOUNT) AS SUM_AMOUNT
          FROM     PENALTIES
          GROUP BY PLAYERNO) AS TOTALS
          ON (PLAYERS.PLAYERNO = TOTALS.PLAYERNO))
             LEFT OUTER JOIN
            (SELECT   PLAYERNO, COUNT(*) AS NUMBER_TEAMS
             FROM     TEAMS
             WHERE    DIVISION = 'first'
             GROUP BY PLAYERNO) AS NUMBERS
             ON (PLAYERS.PLAYERNO = NUMBERS.PLAYERNO)
```

10.17
```
SELECT    TEAMNO, COUNT(DISTINCT PLAYERNO)
FROM      MATCHES
WHERE     TEAMNO IN
         (SELECT   TEAMNO
          FROM     PLAYERS AS P INNER JOIN TEAMS AS T
                   ON P.PLAYERNO = T.PLAYERNO
          AND      TOWN = 'Stratford')
AND       WON > LOST
GROUP BY TEAMNO
```

10.18
```
SELECT    PLAYERNO, NAME, JOINED - AVERAGE
FROM      PLAYERS,
         (SELECT   AVG(JOINED) AS AVERAGE
          FROM     PLAYERS) AS T
```

10.19
```
SELECT    PLAYERNO, NAME, JOINED - AVERAGE
FROM      PLAYERS,
         (SELECT   TOWN, AVG(JOINED) AS AVERAGE
          FROM     PLAYERS
          GROUP BY TOWN) AS TOWNS
WHERE     PLAYERS.TOWN = TOWNS.TOWN
```

10.20
```
SELECT    TEAMNO, COUNT(*)
FROM      MATCHES
GROUP BY TEAMNO WITH ROLLUP
```

10.21
```
SELECT    P.NAME, T.DIVISION, SUM(WON)
FROM     (MATCHES AS M INNER JOIN PLAYERS AS P
          ON M.PLAYERNO = P.PLAYERNO)
          INNER JOIN TEAMS AS T
          ON M.TEAMNO = T.TEAMNO
GROUP BY P.NAME, T.DIVISION WITH ROLLUP
```

CHAPTER 11

SELECT Statement: The HAVING Clause

11.1 Introduction

The purpose of the HAVING clause of a select block is comparable to that of the WHERE clause. The difference is that the WHERE clause is used to select rows after the FROM clause has been processed, whereas the HAVING clause is used to select rows after a GROUP BY clause has been executed. A HAVING clause can be used without a GROUP BY clause.

DEFINITION

```
<having clause> ::=
   HAVING <condition>
```

In the previous chapter, you saw that the GROUP BY clause groups the rows of the result from the FROM clause. The HAVING clause enables you to select groups (with rows) based upon their particular group properties. The condition in the HAVING clause looks a lot like a "normal" condition in the WHERE clause. Nevertheless, one difference exists: Expressions in the condition of a HAVING clause can contain aggregation functions, whereas expressions in the condition of a WHERE clause cannot (unless they appear within a subquery).

Example 11.1: Get the number of each player who has incurred more than one penalty.

```
SELECT    PLAYERNO
FROM      PENALTIES
GROUP BY  PLAYERNO
HAVING    COUNT(*) > 1
```

The intermediate result of the GROUP BY clause looks like this:

```
PAYMENTNO  PLAYERNO  PAYMENT_DATE              AMOUNT
---------  --------  ------------------------  ---------------
{1}               6  {1980-12-08}              {100.00}
{6}               8  {1980-12-08}              {25.00}
{3, 8}           27  {1983-09-10, 1984-11-12}  {100.00, 75.00}
{2, 5, 7}        44  {1981-05-05, 1980-12-08,  {75.00, 25.00,
                      1982-12-30}               30.00}
{4}             104  {1984-12-08}              {50.00}
```

In the HAVING condition, we specified the groups in which the number of rows exceeds 1. This is the intermediate result of the HAVING clause:

```
PAYMENTNO  PLAYERNO  PAYMENT_DATE              AMOUNT
---------  --------  ------------------------  ---------------
{3, 8}           27  {1983-09-10, 1984-11-12}  {100.00, 75.00}
{2, 5, 7}        44  {1981-05-05, 1980-12-08,  {75.00, 25.00,
                      1982-12-30}               30.00}
```

Finally, the end result is this:

```
PLAYERNO
--------
      27
      44
```

Explanation: Just as with the SELECT clause, the value of an aggregation function in a HAVING clause is calculated for each group separately. In the previous example, the number of rows for each group in the intermediate result of the GROUP BY is counted.

11.2 Examples of the HAVING Clause

This section contains examples of applications of aggregation functions in the HAVING clause.

Example 11.2: Get the player number of each player whose last penalty was incurred in 1984.

```
SELECT   PLAYERNO
FROM     PENALTIES
GROUP BY PLAYERNO
HAVING   MAX(YEAR(PAYMENT_DATE)) = 1984
```

The result is:

```
PLAYERNO
--------
      27
     104
```

Explanation: The intermediate result of the GROUP BY clause is equal to the one in Example 11.1. The scalar function YEAR pulls the year figure from each date while processing the HAVING clause. So MySQL searches in the PAYMENT_DATE column for the highest year figures for each row. They are, respectively, 1980-12-08, 1980-12-08, 1984-11-12, 1982-12-30, and 1984-12-08.

Example 11.3: For each player who has incurred more than $150 in total penalties, find the player number and the total amount of penalties.

```
SELECT   PLAYERNO, SUM(AMOUNT)
FROM     PENALTIES
GROUP BY PLAYERNO
HAVING   SUM(AMOUNT) > 150
```

The result is:

```
PLAYERNO  SUM(AMOUNT)
--------  -----------
      27       175.00
```

Example 11.4: For each player who is a captain and who has incurred more than $80 in total penalties, find the player number and the total amount of penalties.

```
SELECT   PLAYERNO, SUM(AMOUNT)
FROM     PENALTIES
WHERE    PLAYERNO IN
        (SELECT   PLAYERNO
         FROM     TEAMS)
GROUP BY PLAYERNO
HAVING   SUM(AMOUNT) > 80
```

The result is:

```
PLAYERNO  SUM(AMOUNT)
--------  -----------
       6       100.00
      27       175.00
```

Example 11.5: Get the player number and the total amount of penalties for the player with the highest penalty total.

```
SELECT   PLAYERNO, SUM(AMOUNT)
FROM     PENALTIES
GROUP BY PLAYERNO
HAVING   SUM(AMOUNT) >= ALL
        (SELECT   SUM(AMOUNT)
         FROM     PENALTIES
         GROUP BY PLAYERNO)
```

The intermediate result of the GROUP BY clause is equal to the one in Example 11.1. The result from the subquery is shown here:

```
AMOUNT
------
100.00
 25.00
175.00
130.00
 50.00
```

For each group (that is, player), MySQL determines whether the result of the function SUM(AMOUNT) is greater than or equal to all values in the result of the subquery. The final result is shown here:

```
PLAYERNO  SUM(AMOUNT)
--------  -----------
      27       175.00
```

11.3 A HAVING Clause but Not a GROUP BY Clause

If a SELECT statement has a HAVING clause but not a GROUP BY clause, all rows of the table are grouped into one row.

Example 11.6: Give the sum of all penalty amounts, but only if that sum is greater than $250.

```
SELECT   SUM(AMOUNT)
FROM     PENALTIES
HAVING   SUM(AMOUNT) >= 250
```

The result is:

```
SUM(AMOUNT)
-----------
     480.00
```

Explanation: Because this statement has a HAVING clause and not a GROUP BY clause, all rows are placed into one group. We refer to this as grouping on [], meaning, we group on zero expressions. This intermediate result could be represented as follows:

```
PAYMENTNO  PLAYERNO      PAYMENT_DATE             AMOUNT
---------  ------------  ------------------------ ---------------
{1, 2, 3,  {6, 44, 27,   {1980-12-08, 1981-05-05,  {100.00, 75.00,
 4, 5, 6,   104, 44, 8,   1983-09-10, 1984-12-08,   100.00, 50.00,
 7, 8}      44, 27}       1980-12-08, 1980-12-08,    25.00, 25.00,
                          1982-12-30, 1984-11-12}    30.00, 75.00}
```

Note that if the grouped row does not satisfy the condition, the result is empty.

Example 11.7: Give the list of the numbers of players who played matches for a team.

```
SELECT    GROUP_CONCAT(PLAYERNO) AS LIST
FROM      MATCHES
HAVING    TRUE
```

The result is:

```
LIST
------------------------------------
2,6,6,6,8,8,27,44,57,83,104,112,112
```

Explanation: Again, we group on []. Because the condition in this HAVING clause is always true, one row appears in the result.

11.4 General Rule for the HAVING Clause

Section 10.7 outlined rules for the use of columns and aggregation functions in the SELECT clause. The HAVING clause requires a similar type of rule, as follows: Each column specification in the HAVING clause must occur within an aggregation function or in the list of columns named in the GROUP BY clause. Therefore, the following statement is incorrect because the BIRTH_DATE column appears in the HAVING clause but does *not* appear within an aggregation function or in the list of columns by which grouping is performed.

```
SELECT   TOWN, COUNT(*)
FROM     PLAYERS
GROUP BY TOWN
HAVING   BIRTH_DATE > '1970-01-01'
```

The reason for this limitation is the same as that for the SELECT clause rule. The result of an aggregation function always consists of one value for each group. In addition, the result of the column specification on which the result is grouped always consists of only one value for each group. However, the result of a column specification, which has *not* been grouped, consists of a set of values. We are then dealing with incompatible results.

Exercise 11.1: In which town do more than four players live?

Exercise 11.2: Get the player number of each player who has incurred more than $150 in penalties.

Exercise 11.3: Get the name, initials, and number of penalties for each player who has incurred more than one penalty.

Exercise 11.4: Get the number of the team for which the most players have played, and give the number of players who have played for this team.

Exercise 11.5: Get the team number and the division of each team for which more than four players have competed.

Exercise 11.6: Get the name and initials of each player who has incurred two or more penalties of more than $40.

Exercise 11.7: Get the name and initials of each player whose total amount of penalties is the highest.

Exercise 11.8: Get the number of each player who has incurred twice as many penalties as player 104. Player 104 should be excluded from the result.

Exercise 11.9: Get the numbers of the players who have incurred as many penalties as player 6. Player 6 should be excluded from the result.

Exercise 11.10: Find the player number and name of each player who has won in total more sets than lost.

11.5 Answers

11.1
```
SELECT   TOWN
FROM     PLAYERS
GROUP BY TOWN
HAVING   COUNT(*) > 4
```

11.2
```
SELECT   PLAYERNO
FROM     PENALTIES
GROUP BY PLAYERNO
HAVING   SUM(AMOUNT) > 150
```

11.3
```
SELECT   NAME, INITIALS, COUNT(*)
FROM     PLAYERS INNER JOIN PENALTIES
         ON PLAYERS.PLAYERNO = PENALTIES.PLAYERNO
GROUP BY PLAYERS.PLAYERNO, NAME, INITIALS
HAVING   COUNT(*) > 1
```

11.4
```
SELECT   TEAMNO, COUNT(*)
FROM     MATCHES
GROUP BY TEAMNO
HAVING   COUNT(*) >= ALL
        (SELECT   COUNT(*)
         FROM     MATCHES
         GROUP BY TEAMNO)
```

11.5
```
SELECT   TEAMNO, DIVISION
FROM     TEAMS
WHERE    TEAMNO IN
        (SELECT   TEAMNO
         FROM     MATCHES
         GROUP BY TEAMNO
         HAVING   COUNT(DISTINCT PLAYERNO) > 4)
```

11.6
```
SELECT   NAME, INITIALS
FROM     PLAYERS
WHERE    PLAYERNO IN
        (SELECT   PLAYERNO
         FROM     PENALTIES
         WHERE    AMOUNT > 40
         GROUP BY PLAYERNO
         HAVING   COUNT(*) >= 2)
```

11.7
```
SELECT   NAME, INITIALS
FROM     PLAYERS
WHERE    PLAYERNO IN
        (SELECT   PLAYERNO
         FROM     PENALTIES
         GROUP BY PLAYERNO
         HAVING   SUM(AMOUNT) >= ALL
                 (SELECT   SUM(AMOUNT)
                  FROM     PENALTIES
                  GROUP BY PLAYERNO))
```

11.8
```
SELECT   PLAYERNO
FROM     PENALTIES
WHERE    PLAYERNO <> 104
GROUP BY PLAYERNO
HAVING   SUM(AMOUNT)  =
        (SELECT   SUM(AMOUNT) * 2
         FROM     PENALTIES
         WHERE    PLAYERNO = 104)
```

11.9
```
SELECT   PLAYERNO
FROM     PENALTIES
WHERE    PLAYERNO <> 6
GROUP BY PLAYERNO
HAVING   COUNT(*) =
        (SELECT   COUNT(*)
         FROM     PENALTIES
         WHERE    PLAYERNO = 6)
```

11.10
```
SELECT   P.PLAYERNO, P.NAME
FROM     PLAYERS AS P, MATCHES AS M1
WHERE    P.PLAYERNO = M1.PLAYERNO
GROUP BY P.PLAYERNO, P.NAME
HAVING   SUM(WON) >
        (SELECT   SUM(LOST)
         FROM     MATCHES AS M2
         WHERE    M2.PLAYERNO = P.PLAYERNO
         GROUP BY M2.PLAYERNO)
```

CHAPTER 12

SELECT Statement: The ORDER BY Clause

12.1 Introduction

In what actual sequence are the rows in the result of a SELECT statement presented? If the SELECT statement has no ORDER BY clause, the sequence is unpredictable. When working through the examples or exercises, you might have found once or twice that the sequence of the rows in your result differs from the one in the book. Adding an ORDER BY clause at the end of a SELECT statement is the only guarantee that the rows in the end result are sorted in a certain way.

DEFINITION

```
<order by clause> ::=
   ORDER BY <sort specification> [ , <sort specification> ]...

<sort specification> ::=
   <column name> [ <sort direction> ]         |
   <scalar expression> [<sort direction> ]    |
   <sequence number> [ <sort direction> ]

<sort direction> ::= ASC | DESC
```

12.2 Sorting on Column Names

Sorting on one column is the simplest method. In this case, the *sorting* consists of one column specification. You may sort on each column specified in the SELECT clause.

Example 12.1: Find the payment number and player number of each penalty incurred; sort the result by player number.

```
SELECT   PAYMENTNO, PLAYERNO
FROM     PENALTIES
ORDER BY PLAYERNO
```

The result is:

```
PAYMENTNO  PLAYERNO
---------  --------
        1         6
        6         8
        3        27
        8        27
        5        44
        2        44
        7        44
        4       104
```

Explanation: The rows are sorted based on the values in the PLAYERNO column, with the lowest value first and the highest value last.

You may sort on more than one column. This could be relevant if the first column consists of duplicate values. For example, the PLAYERNO column in the PENALTIES table contains duplicate values. If we sort on one column only, MySQL is allowed to determine how the rows with duplicate player numbers are sorted. When we add another column for sorting, we explicitly indicate how the duplicate values must be sorted.

Example 12.2: For each penalty, get the player number and the penalty amount; sort the result on both columns.

```
SELECT   PLAYERNO, AMOUNT
FROM     PENALTIES
ORDER BY PLAYERNO, AMOUNT
```

The result is:

```
PLAYERNO  AMOUNT
--------  ------
       6  100.00
       8   25.00
      27   75.00
      27  100.00
      44   25.00
      44   30.00
      44   75.00
     104   50.00
```

Explanation: The result shows that if the player numbers are equal, the penalty amount is used to sort. Two sort keys are needed to get the rows in the desired sequence.

In most cases, sorting is specified on columns and expressions that also appear in the SELECT clause. However, this is not necessary. The ORDER BY clause can contain expressions that do not appear in the SELECT clause.

Example 12.3: Get all penalty amounts, and sort the result on player number and penalty amount.

```
SELECT   AMOUNT
FROM     PENALTIES
ORDER BY PLAYERNO, AMOUNT
```

The result is:

```
AMOUNT
------
100.00
 25.00
 75.00
100.00
 25.00
 30.00
 75.00
 50.00
```

Explanation: When the previous result is compared to the result of Example 12.2, we can see that the rows are indeed sorted on player number, even though this column does not appear in the SELECT clause.

12.3 Sorting on Expressions

Besides sorting on column names, a sorting can consist of scalar expressions.

Example 12.4: For all players, get the last name, initials, and player number; sort the result on the first letter of the last name.

```
SELECT   NAME, INITIALS, PLAYERNO
FROM     PLAYERS
ORDER BY SUBSTR(NAME, 1, 1)
```

The result is:

```
NAME       INITIALS  PLAYERNO
---------  --------  --------
Bishop     D               39
Baker      E               44
Brown      M               57
Bailey     IP             112
Collins    DD              27
Collins    C               28
Everett    R                2
Hope       PK              83
Miller     P               95
Moorman    D              104
Newcastle  B                8
Parmenter  R                6
Parmenter  P              100
Wise       GWS              7
```

Explanation: Because several names begin with the same letter, MySQL can decide the sequence in which the rows with equal letters are presented.

The expressions in the ORDER BY clause can even contain subqueries.

Example 12.5: Get the player number and the amount of all penalties and sort the result on the difference between the amount and the average penalty amount.

```
SELECT   PLAYERNO, AMOUNT
FROM     PENALTIES
ORDER BY ABS(AMOUNT - (SELECT AVG(AMOUNT) FROM PENALTIES))
```

The result is:

```
PLAYERNO  AMOUNT
--------  ------
     104   50.00
      44   75.00
      27   75.00
      44   30.00
      44   25.00
       8   25.00
       6  100.00
      27  100.00
```

Explanation: The value of the subquery is calculated first. Next, the value of the scalar expression is calculated for each row individually; the result is sorted on that.

Subqueries that are used in the ORDER BY clause can even be correlated.

Example 12.6: Get the player number and the amount of all penalties and sort the result on the average penalty amount of each player.

```
SELECT   PLAYERNO, AMOUNT
FROM     PENALTIES AS P1
ORDER BY (SELECT   AVG(AMOUNT)
          FROM     PENALTIES AS P2
          WHERE    P1.PLAYERNO = P2.PLAYERNO)
```

The result is:

```
PLAYERNO  AMOUNT
--------  ------
       8   25.00
      44   75.00
      44   25.00
      44   30.00
     104   50.00
      27  100.00
      27   75.00
       6  100.00
```

Explanation: The average penalty amount of player 8 is 25, so this amount comes first. The penalties of player 44 follow because his average penalty amount is $43.33. The average of player 104 is $50, that of player 27 is $87.50, and, finally, the average penalty amount of player 6 is $100.

12.4 Sorting with Sequence Numbers

In the ORDER BY clause, we can use *sequence numbers* to replace a sorting that consists of column names or expressions. A sequence number assigns a number to the expression in the SELECT clause on which sorting is performed. The next two statements are, therefore, equivalent:

```
SELECT   PAYMENTNO, PLAYERNO
FROM     PENALTIES
ORDER BY PLAYERNO
```

and

```
SELECT   PAYMENTNO, PLAYERNO
FROM     PENALTIES
ORDER BY 2
```

The sequence number 2 stands for the second expression in the SELECT clause. It is not essential to use sequence numbers, but this can simplify the formulation of a statement.

Example 12.7: For each player who has incurred at least one penalty, get the total penalty amount; sort the result on this total.

```
SELECT   PLAYERNO, SUM(AMOUNT)
FROM     PENALTIES
GROUP BY PLAYERNO
ORDER BY 2
```

The result is:

```
PLAYERNO  SUM(AMOUNT)
--------  -----------
       8        25.00
     104        50.00
       6       100.00
      44       130.00
      27       175.00
```

Example 12.8: For each player, get the player number, last name, and sum of his or her penalties; sort the result on this sum.

```
SELECT   PLAYERNO, NAME,
        (SELECT   SUM(AMOUNT)
         FROM     PENALTIES AS PEN
         WHERE    PEN.PLAYERNO=P.PLAYERNO)
FROM     PLAYERS AS P
ORDER BY 3
```

The result is:

```
PLAYERNO  NAME       SELECT SUM
--------  ---------  ----------
       2  Everett             ?
     100  Parmenter           ?
      95  Miller              ?
      83  Hope                ?
      57  Brown               ?
     112  Bailey              ?
      39  Bishop              ?
      28  Collins             ?
       7  Wise                ?
       8  Newcastle       25.00
     104  Moorman         50.00
       6  Parmenter      100.00
      44  Baker          130.00
      27  Collins        175.00
```

Your question might be: Isn't a sequence number a form of an expression as well? The answer is, no. In the ORDER BY clause, the sequence number is not considered to be an expression consisting of one literal. A sequence number is regarded as an exception here.

The previous problem can also be solved by introducing column names in the SELECT clause; see Section 5.4. These column names can also be used to sort rows. The next statement is equivalent, then, to the previous one:

```
SELECT   PLAYERNO, NAME,
        (SELECT   SUM(AMOUNT)
         FROM     PENALTIES AS PEN
         WHERE    PEN.PLAYERNO=P.PLAYERNO) AS TOTAL
FROM     PLAYERS AS P
ORDER BY TOTAL
```

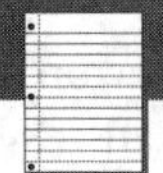

NOTE

Sorting on sequence numbers is allowed, but we discourage the use of this feature. Try to be as explicit as possible when formulating ORDER BY clauses, to avoid any confusion. Use column names when you can.

12.5 Sorting in Ascending and Descending Order

If you do not specify anything after a sorting, MySQL sorts the result in *ascending* order. You can achieve the same result by explicitly specifying ASC (ascending) after the sorting. If you specify DESC (descending), the rows in the result are presented in *descending* order. Sorting values in a descending order always returns the reverse presentation of sorting in an ascending order, regardless of the data type of the values.

Example 12.9: For each penalty, get the player number and penalty amount; sort the result in descending order on player number and in ascending order on penalty amount.

```
SELECT   PLAYERNO, AMOUNT
FROM     PENALTIES
ORDER BY PLAYERNO DESC, AMOUNT ASC
```

The result is:

```
PLAYERNO  AMOUNT
--------  ------
     104   50.00
      44   25.00
      44   30.00
      44   75.00
      27   75.00
      27  100.00
       8   25.00
       6  100.00
```

Sorting numeric values in ascending order is obvious: The lowest value is presented first, and the highest is presented last. Sorting on dates, times, and timestamps is also obvious. In an ascending sort of dates, for example, dates are presented in chronological order.

Sorting alphanumeric values in ascending order is the same as sorting words alphabetically (such as in a dictionary). First come the words beginning with the letter *A*, then those with *B*, and so on. Nevertheless, sorting alphanumeric values is not as simple as it seems. For example, does the lowercase letter *a* come before or after the uppercase *A*? And do digits come before or after letters? And what do we do with letters with diacritics, such as *ë*, *é*, and *è*? And let us not forget special letters, such as *œ*, *ß*, and *Æ*. How letters with diacritics, digits, and special symbols are sorted depends on the *character set* with which you work. In a character set, an internal value is defined for each character. Well-known character sets are American Standard Code for Information Interchange (*ASCII*), Extended Binary Coded Decimal Interchange Code (*EBCDIC*), and *Unicode*. A given operating system usually works with a specific character set. For example, modern versions of Windows use the Unicode character set, while the classic IBM mainframes support the EBCDIC character set. The sequence also depends on the *collations*. Chapter 22, "Character Sets and Collations," discusses character sets and collations in detail.

In this book, we assume that you work with the Unicode character set. Under Windows, it is simple to examine the Unicode character set with the program Character Map, which is one of the accessories of Windows (see Figure 12.1). This figure shows that all uppercase letters come before the lowercase letters and that digits come before uppercase letters.

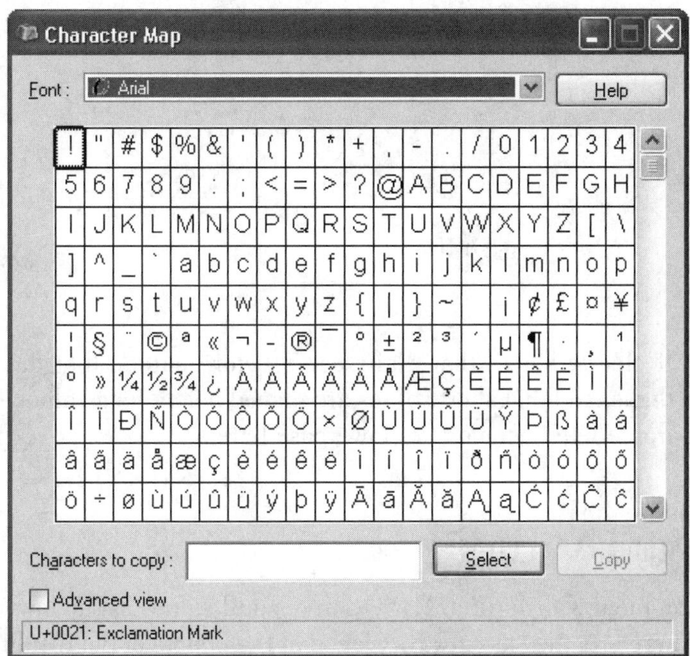

FIGURE 12.1 The program Character Map that shows the Unicode character set

Example 12.10: Create the following CODES table, add the six rows, and see how the different values are sorted.

```
CREATE TABLE CODES
      (CODE   CHAR(4) NOT NULL)

INSERT INTO CODES VALUES ('abc')
INSERT INTO CODES VALUES ('ABC')
INSERT INTO CODES VALUES ('-abc')
INSERT INTO CODES VALUES ('a bc')
INSERT INTO CODES VALUES ('ab')
INSERT INTO CODES VALUES ('9abc')
```

This is the SELECT statement:

```
SELECT   *
FROM     CODES
ORDER BY CODE
```

The result is:

```
CODE
----
-abc
9abc
a bc
ab
abc
ABC
```

Explanation: This result clearly shows that digits come before letters, that the hyphen comes before the digits, and that short values are placed before long values. We can also see that uppercase letters come after lowercase letters.

12.6 Sorting Null Values

Null values introduce a problem with sorting. MySQL treats null values as the lowest values in a column. Therefore, they are always placed at the bottom of the result if the order is descending and at the top if the order is ascending. See the following example and the accompanying result.

Example 12.11: Get the different league numbers and sort the result in descending order.

```
SELECT   DISTINCT LEAGUENO
FROM     PLAYERS
ORDER BY LEAGUENO DESC
```

The result is:

```
LEAGUENO
--------
8467
7060
6524
6409
2983
2513
2411
1608
1319
1124
?
```

Exercise 12.1: Show at least three different ORDER BY clauses that would sort the PLAYERS table in ascending order by player number.

Exercise 12.2: Indicate which of the following SELECT statements are incorrect:

1.
```
SELECT   *
FROM     PLAYERS
ORDER BY 2
```
2.
```
SELECT   *
FROM     PLAYERS
ORDER BY 20 DESC
```
3.
```
SELECT   PLAYERNO, NAME, INITIALS
FROM     PLAYERS
ORDER BY 2, INITIALS DESC, 3 ASC
```
4.
```
SELECT   *
FROM     PLAYERS
ORDER BY 1, PLAYERNO DESC
```

Exercise 12.3: For each match, get the player number, team number, and difference between the number of sets won and the number of sets lost; order the result in ascending order on this difference.

12.7 Answers

12.1

1. ORDER BY 1
2. ORDER BY PLAYERNO
3. ORDER BY 1 ASC
4. ORDER BY PLAYERNO ASC

12.2

1. Correct
2. Incorrect because there is no twentieth column in the PLAYERS table
3. Incorrect because sorting is specified twice on the INITIALS column
4. Incorrect because a column in an ORDER BY clause cannot be specified twice

12.3

```
SELECT   PLAYERNO, TEAMNO, WON - LOST
FROM     MATCHES
ORDER BY 3 ASC
```

CHAPTER 13

SELECT Statement: The LIMIT Clause

13.1 Introduction

Many questions that MySQL will have to process begin with such phrases as "Get the top three..." or "Get the last six..." If we want to know one highest or one lowest value, we can use the MAX and MIN functions, respectively. If we ask for more than one row, it becomes difficult. This is where the *LIMIT clause* is useful. With such a clause, you can extend a select block from which a table expression has been built.

The LIMIT clause is the last clause of a select block with which a subset of the rows can be selected, so the number of rows in the intermediate result can be reduced again. No condition is specified with the LIMIT clause, as with the WHERE and HAVING clauses, but an indication is given of how many of the first and last rows are selected.

DEFINITION

```
<select statement> ::=
   <table expression>

<table expression> ::=
   <select block head> [ <select block tail> ]

<select block head> ::=
   <select clause>
   [ <from clause>
   [ <where clause> ]
   [ <group by clause> ]
   [ <having clause> ] ]

<select block tail> ::=
   <order by clause> |
   <limit clause>    |
   <order by clause> <limit clause>

<limit clause> ::=
   LIMIT [ <fetch offset> , ] <fetch number of rows>       |
   LIMIT <fetch number of rows> [ OFFSET <fetch offset> ]

<fetch number of rows> ;
<fetch offset>             ::= <whole number>
```

Let us begin with a simple example.

Example 13.1: Get the numbers and names of the players with the four highest player numbers.

If only the highest player number should be given, the following SELECT statement would have given the desired result:

```
SELECT   MAX(PLAYERNO)
FROM     PLAYERS
```

The result is:

```
MAX(PLAYERNO)
-------------
          112
```

However, this statement with the MAX function cannot be used to determine the *four* highest player numbers. We can use the following statement for this:

```
SELECT   PLAYERNO, NAME
FROM     PLAYERS AS P1
WHERE    4 >
        (SELECT   COUNT(*)
         FROM     PLAYERS AS P2
         WHERE    P1.PLAYERNO < P2.PLAYERNO)
ORDER BY PLAYERNO DESC
```

The result is:

```
PLAYERNO  NAME
--------  ---------
     112  Bailey
     104  Moorman
     100  Parmenter
      95  Miller
```

However, this is a rather complex statement. The `LIMIT` clause helps simplify this statement:

```
SELECT   PLAYERNO, NAME
FROM     PLAYERS
ORDER BY PLAYERNO DESC
LIMIT    4
```

Explanation: First, the rows are sorted on player number. The `LIMIT` clause states that the first four rows must be retrieved from the intermediate result. MySQL simply removes all rows from the intermediate result that come after the fourth row, regardless of the values in those rows. Because the sequence of the rows in the (intermediate) result has been sorted in a descending order, it is obvious which values remain: those with the highest four player numbers. If this statement had not had an `ORDER BY` clause, the four rows returned would have been unpredictable. This probably would have been the four rows that gave MySQL the least trouble.

If sorting is performed on a column with null values, they are seen as the lowest value.

Example 13.2: Get the five lowest league numbers with the corresponding player numbers and names from the PLAYERS table.

```
SELECT   LEAGUENO, PLAYERNO, NAME
FROM     PLAYERS
ORDER BY LEAGUENO ASC
LIMIT    5
```

The result is:

```
LEAGUENO  PLAYERNO  NAME
--------  --------  -------
       ?         7  Wise
       ?        28  Collins
       ?        39  Bishop
       ?        95  Miller
    1124        44  Baker
```

13.2 Get the Top...

As mentioned, the `LIMIT` clause is used frequently to answer questions about the best, the least, and the lowest. But what exactly is the top three when there are four equal values at the top? We illustrate this problem with several examples.

Example 13.3: Get the numbers of the top three best players. The best player is defined as the person with the highest number of matches won.

```
SELECT   PLAYERNO, COUNT(*) AS NUMBER
FROM     MATCHES
WHERE    WON > LOST
GROUP BY PLAYERNO
ORDER BY NUMBER DESC
LIMIT    3
```

The result is:

```
PLAYERNO  NUMBER
--------  ------
       6       2
      27       1
      44       1
```

Explanation: With the `WHERE` clause, all matches won are selected. The `GROUP BY` clause creates a group for each player. Next, for each group, the player number and the number of matches won are determined. After this, the intermediate result is sorted on the number in descending order; the highest value comes first. When there are equal numbers, a sort must be performed on player numbers. Finally, the first three rows are fetched from that intermediate result.

But why do players 27 and 44 appear in the result? Logically, player 6 appears in the final result because he is the only one who has won two matches. However, four players have won one match: players 27, 44, 57, and 104. This means that, to get the top three players, two must be selected from these four. If no indication is given which two must be selected, MySQL chooses two at random. By adding another sorting, we can explicitly indicate what must happen when equal values exist; see the following example.

Example 13.4: Get the numbers of the best three players. The best player is defined as the person with the highest number of matches won. If players with an equal number exist, only those with the highest player number must be presented.

```
SELECT   PLAYERNO, COUNT(*) AS NUMBER
FROM     MATCHES
WHERE    WON > LOST
GROUP BY PLAYERNO
ORDER BY NUMBER DESC, PLAYERNO DESC
LIMIT    3
```

The result is:

```
PLAYERNO  NUMBER
--------  ------
       6       2
     104       1
      57       1
```

If we want to sort the end result of the previous statement on player number, we need to wrap the entire statement in another statement and add a second `ORDER BY` clause.

Example 13.5: Get the numbers of the best three players and sort the end result on player number; also see Example 13.4.

```
SELECT   *
FROM    (SELECT   PLAYERNO, COUNT(*) AS NUMBER
         FROM     MATCHES
         WHERE    WON > LOST
         GROUP BY PLAYERNO
         ORDER BY NUMBER DESC, PLAYERNO DESC
         LIMIT    3) AS T
ORDER BY 1
```

The result is:

```
PLAYERNO  NUMBER
--------  ------
       6       2
      57       1
     104       1
```

Explanation: By using the `LIMIT` clause to define the select block as a subquery within a `FROM` clause, we can still sort the result in the desired way.

Example 13.6: What is the average of the four lowest penalty amounts?

```
SELECT   AVG(AMOUNT)
FROM    (SELECT    AMOUNT
         FROM      PENALTIES
         ORDER BY  AMOUNT
         LIMIT     4) AS T
```

The result is:

```
AVG(AMOUNT)
-----------
      32.50
```

Explanation: The intermediate result of the subquery consists of the following four rows:

```
AMOUNT
------
 25.00
 25.00
 30.00
 50.00
```

The statistical function `AVG` is applied to these four.

Example 13.7: What is the third highest penalty amount?

```
SELECT   MIN(AMOUNT)
FROM    (SELECT    AMOUNT
         FROM      PENALTIES
         ORDER BY  AMOUNT DESC
         LIMIT     3) AS T
```

The result is:

```
MIN(AMOUNT)
-----------
      75.00
```

Explanation: The intermediate result of the subquery consists of the following four rows:

```
AMOUNT
------
100.00
100.00
 75.00
```

Because the result is sorted in a descending order (ORDER BY AMOUNT DESC), these are the three highest penalty amounts. Next, the MIN function is used to determine the last, or the third highest value. Had we replaced the MIN function with the MAX function and sorted in an ascending order, we would have gotten the third lowest penalty amount.

Example 13.8: Get the three highest penalty amounts and leave out the duplicate amounts.

```
SELECT   DISTINCT AMOUNT
FROM     PENALTIES
ORDER BY AMOUNT DESC
LIMIT    3
```

The result is:

```
AMOUNT
------
100.00
 75.00
 50.00
```

Explanation: The SELECT clause is processed before the LIMIT clause. Because DISTINCT is used here, all duplicate rows are removed first.

Exercise 13.1: Get the payment numbers, penalty amounts, and payment dates of the four highest penalties. If duplicate values exist, the penalties with the most recent payment date are preferred.

Exercise 13.2: Get the match numbers of the matches with the two highest numbers and also the two lowest numbers.

13.3 Subqueries with a LIMIT Clause

The `LIMIT` clause may also be used in select blocks that appear within a subquery. The previous section showed several examples of this; we continue with more in this section.

Example 13.9: Get the numbers of the players with the three lowest player numbers who belong to the group of players with the six highest league numbers.

```
SELECT   PLAYERNO
FROM    (SELECT   PLAYERNO
         FROM     PLAYERS
         WHERE    LEAGUENO IS NOT NULL
         ORDER BY LEAGUENO DESC
         LIMIT    6) AS T
ORDER BY PLAYERNO
LIMIT    3
```

The result is:

```
PLAYERNO
--------
       6
       8
      27
```

Explanation: The subquery (the inner select block) retrieves only the player numbers that belong to the players with the six highest league numbers. The additional condition is necessary to remove the null value. The outer select block looks in this intermediate result for the three lowest player numbers.

Example 13.10: Get the numbers and names of the three players who incurred the highest total amount of penalties.

```
SELECT   PLAYERNO, NAME
FROM     PLAYERS
WHERE    PLAYERNO IN
        (SELECT   PLAYERNO
         FROM    (SELECT   PLAYERNO, SUM(AMOUNT) AS TOTAL
                  FROM     PENALTIES
                  GROUP BY PLAYERNO
                  ORDER BY TOTAL DESC
                  LIMIT    3) AS T)
```

The result is:

```
PLAYERNO  NAME
--------  ---------
       6  Parmenter
      27  Collins
      44  Baker
```

Explanation: The inner subquery has the following intermediate result:

```
PLAYERNO  TOTAL
--------  ------
      27  175.00
      44  130.00
       6  100.00
```

The main query retrieves the number and name of those players for whom the player number appears in the intermediate result of the inner subquery. However, because there are two columns, we cannot link the main query directly to the inner subquery. That is why a subquery comes in between—to retrieve only the player numbers from the intermediate result.

Example 13.11: Get the numbers and names of those players who have incurred at least one penalty that is not equal to one of the two highest nor to one of the two lowest penalties.

```
SELECT   PLAYERNO, NAME
FROM     PLAYERS
WHERE    PLAYERNO IN
        (SELECT   PLAYERNO
         FROM     PENALTIES)
AND      PLAYERNO NOT IN
        (SELECT   PLAYERNO
         FROM     PENALTIES
         ORDER BY AMOUNT DESC
         LIMIT    2)
AND      PLAYERNO NOT IN
        (SELECT   PLAYERNO
         FROM     PENALTIES
         ORDER BY AMOUNT ASC
         LIMIT    2)
```

The result is:

```
PLAYERNO  NAME
--------  -------
     104  Moorman
```

Explanation: The first subquery determines whether a player has incurred a penalty. The second checks whether it is one of the two highest penalties, and the third determines whether it is one of the two lowest.

This statement could have been written as follows:

```
SELECT    PLAYERNO, NAME
FROM      PLAYERS
WHERE     PLAYERNO IN
         (SELECT    PLAYERNO
          FROM      PENALTIES
          WHERE     PLAYERNO NOT IN
                   (SELECT    PLAYERNO
                    FROM      PENALTIES
                    ORDER BY AMOUNT DESC
                    LIMIT     2)
          AND       PLAYERNO NOT IN
                   (SELECT    PLAYERNO
                    FROM      PENALTIES
                    ORDER BY AMOUNT ASC
                    LIMIT     2))
```

Exercise 13.3: Get the numbers and names of players whose number belongs to the lowest ten and whose name alphabetically belongs to the last five from the list of ten.

Exercise 13.4: Get the numbers and names of the two players who have won the most matches. If players have won the same number of matches, give preference to the player with the lower player number.

Exercise 13.5: Get the numbers and names of the two players who have incurred a penalty that belongs to the three highest penalties. If equal penalties exist, give preference to the player whose name comes first alphabetically.

13.4 Limit with an Offset

Normally, the `LIMIT` clause is used to select the head or tail of a list with rows. Adding an *offset* skips several rows.

Example 13.12: Get the numbers and names of the players with the five lowest player numbers, beginning at number 4.

```
SELECT   PLAYERNO, NAME
FROM     PLAYERS
ORDER BY PLAYERNO ASC
LIMIT    5 OFFSET 3
```

The result is:

```
PLAYERNO  NAME
--------  ---------
       8  Newcastle
      27  Collins
      28  Collins
      39  Bishop
      44  Baker
```

Explanation: The players who are dropped from this result are the players with numbers 2, 6, and 7. So an offset equal to 3 means that three rows are skipped.

MySQL has two ways to specify an offset. The last LIMIT clause could have been specified as follows:

```
LIMIT    3, 5
```

However, we recommend using the first formulation, which more explicitly indicates the number of rows that must be presented and the offset.

Exercise 13.6: Get the three highest penalty amounts.

13.5 The Select Option SQL_CALC_FOUND_ROWS

After a SELECT statement has been executed with a LIMIT clause, it sometimes can be useful to ask what the original number of rows in the end result would have been if we had not specified a LIMIT clause. By specifying the select option SQL_CALC_FOUND_ROWS, the total number of rows is determined behind the scenes; see also Section 9.6. After that, you can query this number with a separate SELECT statement.

Example 13.13: Give the first five payment numbers.

```
SELECT   SQL_CALC_FOUND_ROWS PAYMENTNO
FROM     PENALTIES
LIMIT    5
```

The result is:

```
PAYMENTNO
---------
        1
        2
        3
        4
        5
```

With the following statement, we can query the original number of rows now:

```
SELECT   FOUND_ROWS()
```

The result is:

```
FOUND_ROWS()
------------
           8
```

Explanation: FOUND_ROWS is a special scalar function that can be used to query the original number of rows in the end result of the previous SELECT statement.

Note that the select option cannot be specified in the SELECT clause of subqueries.

13.6 Answers

13.1

```
SELECT   PAYMENTNO, AMOUNT, PAYMENT_DATE
FROM     PENALTIES
ORDER BY AMOUNT DESC, PAYMENT_DATE DESC
LIMIT    4
```

13.2

```
(SELECT   MATCHNO
FROM     MATCHES
ORDER BY MATCHNO ASC
LIMIT    2)
UNION
(SELECT   MATCHNO
FROM     MATCHES
ORDER BY MATCHNO DESC
LIMIT    2)
```

13.3
```
SELECT   PLAYERNO, NAME
FROM    (SELECT   PLAYERNO, NAME
         FROM     PLAYERS
         ORDER BY PLAYERNO ASC
         LIMIT    10) AS S10
ORDER BY NAME DESC
LIMIT    5
```

13.4
```
SELECT   PLAYERNO, NAME
FROM     PLAYERS
WHERE    PLAYERNO IN
        (SELECT   PLAYERNO
         FROM    (SELECT   PLAYERNO, COUNT(*) AS NUMBER
                  FROM     MATCHES
                  WHERE    WON > LOST
                  GROUP BY PLAYERNO) AS WINNERS
         ORDER BY NUMBER DESC, PLAYERNO ASC
         LIMIT    2)
```

13.5
```
SELECT   PLAYERNO, NAME
FROM     PLAYERS
WHERE    PLAYERNO IN
        (SELECT   PENALTIES.PLAYERNO
         FROM     PENALTIES INNER JOIN PLAYERS
                  ON PENALTIES.PLAYERNO = PLAYERS.PLAYERNO
         ORDER BY AMOUNT DESC, NAME ASC
         LIMIT    4)
```

13.6
```
SELECT   PAYMENTNO, AMOUNT
FROM     PENALTIES
ORDER BY AMOUNT DESC
LIMIT    1 OFFSET 2
```

CHAPTER 14

Combining Table Expressions

14.1 Introduction

Section 6.4 introduced the term *compound table expression. Set operators* allow us to combine multiple table expressions into one compound table expression. Examples in Section 6.4 and several other chapters used the set operator called `UNION`, which places results of table expressions underneath each other. MySQL supports other set operators besides the `UNION` operator:

- `UNION`
- `UNION DISTINCT`
- `UNION ALL`

Chapter 6, "SELECT Statements, Table Expressions, and Subqueries," defined the table expression and the compound table expression. However, that chapter mentions only the `UNION` operator. Now we extend that definition with the complete set of set operators.

DEFINITION

```
<table expression> ::=
   { <select block head>          |
     ( <table expression> )       |
     <compound table expression> }
   [ <select block tail> ]

<compound table expression> ::=
   <table expression> <set operator> <table expression>

<set operator> ::= UNION | UNION DISTINCT | UNION ALL
```

14.2 Combining with UNION

If two table expressions are combined with the UNION operator, the end result consists of every row that appears in the result of one of the two table expressions or in both. UNION is the equivalent of the operator *union* from set theory.

Example 14.1: Get the player number and town of each player from Inglewood and Plymouth.

```
SELECT    PLAYERNO, TOWN
FROM      PLAYERS
WHERE     TOWN = 'Inglewood'
UNION
SELECT    PLAYERNO, TOWN
FROM      PLAYERS
WHERE     TOWN = 'Plymouth'
```

The result is:

```
PLAYERNO  TOWN
--------  ---------
       8  Inglewood
      44  Inglewood
     112  Plymouth
```

Explanation: Each of the two table expressions returns a table consisting of two columns and zero or more rows. As mentioned, the UNION operator puts the two tables underneath each other. The end result of the entire statement is one table.

Note that the previous statement could, of course, also have been formulated using an OR operator:

```
SELECT    PLAYERNO, TOWN
FROM      PLAYERS
WHERE     TOWN = 'Inglewood'
OR        TOWN = 'Plymouth'
```

However, it is not always possible to replace the UNION operator with an OR operator. Consider an example.

Example 14.2: Get a list of all the dates that appear in the PLAYERS and PENALTIES tables.

```
SELECT    BIRTH_DATE AS DATES
FROM      PLAYERS
UNION
SELECT    PAYMENT_DATE
FROM      PENALTIES
```

The result is:

```
DATES
----------
1948-09-01
1956-10-29
1956-11-11
1962-07-08
1963-01-09
1963-02-28
1963-05-11
1963-05-14
1963-06-22
1963-10-01
1964-06-25
1964-12-28
1970-05-10
1971-08-17
1980-12-08
1981-05-05
1982-12-30
1983-09-10
1984-11-12
1984-12-08
```

This statement cannot be formulated with `OR` because rows from different tables are combined and are not from the same table, as in the previous example.

A special property of the `UNION` operator is that all duplicate (or equal) rows are removed automatically from the end result. Section 9.5 describes the rule concerning the equality of two rows when `DISTINCT` is used in the `SELECT` clause. The same rule also applies, of course, to the `UNION` operator.

Example 14.3: Get the number of each player who has incurred at least one penalty or who is a captain, or for whom both conditions apply.

```
SELECT    PLAYERNO
FROM      PENALTIES
UNION
SELECT    PLAYERNO
FROM      TEAMS
```

The result is:

```
PLAYERNO
--------
       6
       8
      27
      44
     104
```

Explanation: The result obviously shows that all the duplicate rows have been deleted.

You can combine more than two table expressions into one table expression, as in the following example.

Example 14.4: Get the player number of each player who has incurred at least one penalty, who is a captain, who lives in Stratford, or for whom two or three of these conditions apply.

```
SELECT   PLAYERNO
FROM     PENALTIES
UNION
SELECT   PLAYERNO
FROM     TEAMS
UNION
SELECT   PLAYERNO
FROM     PLAYERS
WHERE    TOWN = 'Stratford'
```

The result is:

```
PLAYERNO
--------
       2
       6
       7
       8
      27
      39
      44
      57
      83
     100
     104
```

Exercise 14.1: Get a list of numbers of the players who have ever been committee members, plus the numbers of the players who have incurred at least two penalties.

Exercise 14.2: Determine what the most recent date is: the most recent date of birth or the most recent date on which a penalty has been paid.

14.3 Rules for Using UNION

The following rules for using the UNION operator must be observed:

- The SELECT clauses of all relevant table expressions must have the same number of expressions, and the expressions that are placed under one another must have comparable data types. If this applies, the table expressions are *union compatible.* Note that two data types are comparable if they are the same or if the expressions can be transformed into the same data type by an implicit case.
- An ORDER BY clause can be specified only after the last table expression. The sorting is performed on the entire end result, after all intermediate results have been combined.
- The SELECT clauses should not contain DISTINCT because MySQL automatically removes duplicate rows from the end result when using UNION; thus, an additional DISTINCT is superfluous but allowed.

The following SELECT statements have not been written according to these rules (work through them for yourself):

```
SELECT    *
FROM      PLAYERS
UNION
SELECT    *
FROM      PENALTIES
```

```
SELECT    PLAYERNO
FROM      PLAYERS
WHERE     TOWN = 'Stratford'
ORDER BY 1
UNION
SELECT    PLAYERNO
FROM      TEAMS
ORDER BY 1
```

The UNION operator in combination with the GROUP BY clause offers the possibility of calculating subtotals and totals. Yet the use of WITH ROLLUP results in simpler statements.

Example 14.5: For each combination of team number and player number, get the sum of all sets won and sets lost, and find for each team a subtotal and final total.

```
SELECT   CAST(TEAMNO AS CHAR(4)) AS TEAMNO,
         CAST(PLAYERNO AS CHAR(4)) AS PLAYERNO,
         SUM(WON + LOST) AS TOTAL
FROM     MATCHES
GROUP BY TEAMNO, PLAYERNO
UNION
SELECT   CAST(TEAMNO AS CHAR(4)),
         'subtotal',
         SUM(WON + LOST)
FROM     MATCHES
GROUP BY TEAMNO
UNION
SELECT   'total', 'total', SUM(WON + LOST)
FROM     MATCHES
ORDER BY 1, 2
```

The result is:

```
TEAMNO  PLAYERNO  TOTAL
------  --------  -----
1       2             4
1       44            5
1       57            3
1       6             2
1       8             3
1       83            3
1       subtotal     30
2       104           5
2       112           9
2       27            5
2       8             3
2       subtotal     22
total   total        52
```

Explanation: The statement consists of three table expressions. The first calculates the sum of all sets played for each combination of team number and player number. The second table expression calculates the sum of sets won and lost for each team. In the column PLAYERNO, the word *subtotal* is represented. To make the two table expressions union compatible, the player number in the first table expression of the SELECT clause is converted to an alphanumeric value. The third table expression calculates the total of all sets in the two columns. The ORDER BY clause ensures that the rows in the final result are in the correct sequence.

Instead of using the word UNION, you may specify UNION DISTINCT. This does not change the end result of the statement; it only indicates that duplicate rows are removed.

Exercise 14.3: Indicate which of the following (parts of the) SELECT statements are correct and which are incorrect and state why:

1.
```
SELECT   ...
FROM     ...
GROUP BY ...
HAVING   ...
UNION
SELECT   ...
FROM     ...
ORDER BY ...
```

2.
```
SELECT   PLAYERNO, NAME
FROM     PLAYERS
UNION
SELECT   PLAYERNO, POSTCODE
FROM     PLAYERS
```

3.
```
SELECT   TEAMNO
FROM     TEAMS
UNION
SELECT   PLAYERNO
FROM     PLAYERS
ORDER BY 1
```

4.
```
SELECT   DISTINCT PLAYERNO
FROM     PLAYERS
UNION
SELECT   PLAYERNO
FROM     PENALTIES
ORDER BY 1
```

5.
```
SELECT   ...
FROM     ...
GROUP BY ...
ORDER BY ...
UNION
SELECT   ...
FROM     ...
```

Exercise 14.4: If we assume the original contents of the sample tables, how many rows appear in the end result of each of the following statements?

1. ```
   SELECT    TOWN
   FROM      PLAYERS
   UNION
   SELECT    TOWN
   FROM      PLAYERS
   ```
2. ```
   SELECT    PLAYERNO
   FROM      PENALTIES
   UNION
   SELECT    PLAYERNO
   FROM      PLAYERS
   ```
3. ```
   SELECT    YEAR(BIRTH_DATE)
   FROM      PLAYERS
   UNION
   SELECT    YEAR(PAYMENT_DATE)
   FROM      PENALTIES
   ```

14.4 Keeping Duplicate Rows

All previous examples made it clear that duplicate rows are automatically removed from the end result if the set operator UNION is used. You can suppress duplicate row removal by using the ALL version of this operator.

If two table expressions are combined with the UNION ALL operator, the end result consists of the resulting rows from both of the table expressions. The only difference between UNION and UNION ALL is that when you use UNION, the duplicate rows are automatically removed, whereas when you use UNION ALL, they are retained.

The result of the following statement shows that duplicate rows are not removed.

Example 14.6: Combine the set of player numbers from the PENALTIES table with the one from the TEAMS table. Do not remove duplicate rows.

```
SELECT   PLAYERNO
FROM     PENALTIES
UNION ALL
SELECT   PLAYERNO
FROM     TEAMS
```
```

The result is:

```
PLAYERNO
--------
       6
      44
      27
     104
      44
       8
      44
      27
       6
      27
```

Exercise 14.5: Get the numbers of players and add the number of teams.

Exercise 14.6: Get the squares for the numbers 0 up to and including 9, and carry the numbers to the third power. Do not remove duplicate numbers.

14.5 Set Operators and the Null Value

MySQL automatically removes duplicate rows from the result if the UNION operator is specified. That is why the following (somewhat peculiar) SELECT statement produces only one row, even if both individual table expressions have one row as their intermediate result:

```
SELECT   PLAYERNO, LEAGUENO
FROM     PLAYERS
WHERE    PLAYERNO = 27
UNION
SELECT   PLAYERNO, LEAGUENO
FROM     PLAYERS
WHERE    PLAYERNO = 27
```

But what happens to null values? What is the result of the previous statement if we substitute player number 7 for 27? Player 7 has no league number. Maybe you think that the statement will produce two rows now because the two null values are not considered equivalent. However, this is not true. MySQL produces only one row in this situation. MySQL considers null values to be equivalent when set operators are processed. In other words, the rule used here to determine whether two rows are equal is the same as the one for DISTINCT; see Section 9.5. This is in accordance with the theory of the original relational model defined by E. F. Codd (see [CODD90]).

14.6 Answers

14.1
```
SELECT   PLAYERNO
FROM     COMMITTEE_MEMBERS
UNION
SELECT   PLAYERNO
FROM     PENALTIES
GROUP BY PLAYERNO
HAVING   COUNT(*) >= 2
```

14.2
```
SELECT   MAX(ADATE)
FROM    (SELECT   MAX(BIRTH_DATE) AS ADATE
         FROM     PLAYERS
         UNION
         SELECT   MAX(PAYMENT_DATE) AS ADATE
         FROM     PENALTIES) AS TWODATES
```

14.3
1. Correct
2. Correct, even though the lengths of the columns NAME and POSTCODE are not equal
3. Correct
4. Correct, even though, in a `SELECT` clause, `DISTINCT` is superfluous with a `UNION` operator
5. Incorrect because when a `UNION` operator is used, only the last `SELECT` statement can include an `ORDER BY` clause

14.4
1. 6
2. 14
3. 412

14.5
```
SELECT   SUM(NUMBER)
FROM    (SELECT   COUNT(*) AS NUMBER
         FROM     PLAYERS
         UNION ALL
         SELECT   COUNT(*) AS NUMBER
         FROM     TEAMS) AS NUMBERS
```

14.6
```
SELECT   POWER(DIGIT,2)
FROM    (SELECT 0 AS DIGIT UNION SELECT 1 UNION
         SELECT 2 UNION SELECT 3 UNION
         SELECT 4 UNION SELECT 5 UNION
         SELECT 6 UNION SELECT 7 UNION
         SELECT 8 UNION SELECT 9) AS DIGITS1
UNION ALL
SELECT   POWER(DIGIT,3)
FROM    (SELECT 0 AS DIGIT UNION SELECT 1 UNION
         SELECT 2 UNION SELECT 3 UNION
         SELECT 4 UNION SELECT 5 UNION
         SELECT 6 UNION SELECT 7 UNION
         SELECT 8 UNION SELECT 9) AS DIGITS2
ORDER BY 1
```

CHAPTER 15

The User Variable and the SET Statement

15.1 Introduction

In MySQL, we can define variables—the *user variables* or *user-defined variables.* We can assign values to user variables and use them in the same place where scalar expressions normally are used. As a result, the statement becomes partly variable. By changing the value of the user variable, the statement changes.

Before you introduce a user variable, you must define it. You do this with the special *SET statement* or with a SELECT statement.

After defining a variable, you must assign a value; otherwise, the variable has the null value. Again, with SET and SELECT statements, a value can be assigned explicitly to a user variable.

Section 5.6 briefly described the user variable; this chapter contains a more complete description and also explains the DO statement.

15.2 Defining Variables with the SET Statement

The definition of the SET statement follows:

DEFINITION

```
<set statement> ::=
   SET <user variable definition>
       [ , <user variable definition> ]...

<user variable definition> ::=
   <user variable> { = | := } <scalar expression>
```

Example 15.1: Define the user variable `PI` and initialize this with the value `3.141592654`.

```
SET @PI = 3.141592654
```

Explanation: The `@` symbol must always appear in front of a user variable, to distinguish user variables from column names. The new value stands behind the equal to operator. It may be any random, compound scalar expression, as long as no column specifications appear in it.

The data type of the user variable is derived from the value of the scalar expression. So in the previous example, it is a decimal. The data type of the variable can change later if a new value with another data type is assigned.

A simple `SELECT` statement can retrieve the value of a user variable. The result is a table with one row.

Example 15.2: Get the value of the user variable `PI`.

```
SELECT   @PI
```

The result is:

```
@PI
-----------
3.141592654
```

A defined user variable, such as `PI`, may be used in other SQL statements after it has been created.

Example 15.3: Get the last name, place of residence, and postcode of all players with a number less than the value of the user variable `PI` that was just created.

```
SELECT   NAME, TOWN, POSTCODE
FROM     PLAYERS
WHERE    PLAYERNO < @PI
```

The result is:

```
NAME     TOWN        POSTCODE
-------  ---------   --------
Everett  Stratford   3575NH
```

One `SET` statement can define multiple variables simultaneously.

Example 15.4: Define three new user variables.

```
SET @ABC = 5, @DEF = 'Inglewood',
    @GHI = DATE('2004-01-01')
```

The scalar expression that is used to assign a value to a variable may be compound. Calculations, functions, system variables, and other user variables are allowed, along with subqueries.

Example 15.5: Define the user variable `PI` with the help of a formula.

```
SET @PI = CAST(22 AS BINARY)/7
```

Example 15.6: Define a user variable that has the player number of the captain of team 1 as a value.

```
SET @ANR = (SELECT   PLAYERNO
            FROM     TEAMS
            WHERE    TEAMNO = 1)
```

In an expression that is used to assign a value to a user variable, other user variables may be specified as well. The statement `SET @A = @B + 1` is allowed. However, be careful with the following construct: `SET @A = 5, @B = @A`. After this statement, the variable `B` does *not* have the value `5`. `B` gets the old value of `A`. MySQL determines the values of all expressions first and only then assigns the values to the variables. Therefore, this `SET` statement does not have the same result as the following two `SET` statements: `SET @A = 5 and SET @B = @A`.

You also may use the `:=` symbol instead of the equal to symbol `=`. This has no effect on the result.

15.3 Defining Variables with the SELECT Statement

Instead of using the SET statement, you may use the SELECT statement to define a user variable. Note that, because it is a SELECT statement, there will be a result in the form of a table. Compare that to a SET statement that does not return a table as a result. Consider an example.

Example 15.7: Create the user variable PLAYERNO and initialize it with the value 5.

```
SELECT    @PLAYERNO := 7
```

The result is:

```
@PLAYERNO := 7
--------------
             7
```

Explanation: With the SET statement, the symbols = and := may be used to assign a value; with the SELECT statement, only the symbol := is allowed. This is because the expression @PLAYERNO = 7 is seen as a condition that has the value 0 or 1 as a result. Also in the SELECT statement, any random scalar expression may be used to assign a value to a user variable—even a column specification is allowed here.

Multiple variables also may be defined with a SELECT statement.

Example 15.8: Define the user variables NAME, TOWN, and POSTCODE, and assign values.

```
SELECT    @NAME := 'Johnson', @TOWN := 'Inglewood',
          @POSTCODE := '1234AB'
```

You could have achieved the same result by retrieving the values from the PLAYERS table.

Example 15.9: Define the user variables NAME, TOWN, and POSTCODE, and give them the values that belong to player 2.

```
SELECT    @NAME := NAME, @TOWN := TOWN,
          @POSTCODE := POSTCODE
FROM      PLAYERS
WHERE     PLAYERNO = 2
```

The result is:

```
@NAME := NAME  @TOWN := TOWN  @POSTCODE := POSTCODE
-------------  -------------  ---------------------
Everett        Stratford      3575NH
```

Example 15.10: Define the user variables `PENALTIESTOTAL` and `NUMBERPENALTIES`, and give them the values that belong to player 2.

```
SELECT    @PENALTIESTOTAL := SUM(AMOUNT),
          @NUMBERPENALTIES := COUNT(*)
FROM      PENALTIES
```

The result is:

```
@PENALTIESTOTAL := SUM(AMOUNT)  @NUMBERPENALTIES := COUNT(*)
------------------------------  ----------------------------
                        480.00                             8
```

If the `SELECT` statement used returns more than one row, the values of the last row are assigned to the variables.

Example 15.11: Define the user variable `PLAYERNO` and assign the value of the highest player number from the PLAYERS table.

```
SELECT    @PLAYERNO := PLAYERNO
FROM      PLAYERS
ORDER BY PLAYERNO DESC

SELECT    @PLAYERNO
```

The result is:

```
@PLAYERNO
---------
        2
```

As mentioned, user variables may be used anywhere scalar expressions are allowed—for example, also in the `WHERE` clause. Note that when they are used in a `WHERE` or `HAVING` clause, they must be defined first with another statement. Remember that the `WHERE` clause is executed before the `SELECT` clause. Therefore, the following statement does *not* return the players whose numbers are less than 7.

```
SELECT    @PNR7 := 7
FROM      PLAYERS
WHERE     PLAYERNO < @PNR7
```

15.4 Application Areas for User Variables

User variables have several application areas. For example, the result of one `SELECT` statement can be passed to another.

Example 15.12: Get the name of the captain of team 1.

```
SET @CNO = (SELECT    PLAYERNO
            FROM      TEAMS
            WHERE     TEAMNO = 1)

SELECT    NAME
FROM      PLAYERS
WHERE     PLAYERNO = @CNO
```

Explanation: The SET statement finds the player number of the captain of team 1. Next, the SELECT statement looks for the name of that player. The variable CNO acts as an intermediary between these two statements.

Another area of application is to prevent repeated execution of the same expression. It is better to define the expression once and use it many times. Especially if it concerns a complex value, this could be useful and even improve the processing speed.

Example 15.13: Give all data of the penalties of which the payment number is smaller than the result of the expression (((3/7)*100)/124)+3 and the player number is greater than that same expression.

```
SET @VAR = (((3/7)*100)/124)+3

SELECT    *
FROM      PENALTIES
WHERE     PAYMENTNO < @VAR
AND       PLAYERNO > @VAR
```

The result is:

```
PAYMENTNO  PLAYERNO  PAYMENT_DATE  AMOUNT
---------  --------  ------------  ------
        1         6  1980-12-08    100.00
        2        44  1981-05-05     75.00
        3        27  1983-09-10    100.00
```

15.5 Life Span of User Variables

User variables exist as long as your session has not finished. So when you log off and on again, you lose all user variables, including their values. If you want to save the values for a future session, you must register them in a special table with an INSERT statement. You must create that table yourself.

Example 15.14: Create two user variables that you can use again in future sessions.

First, you must create a table in which these variables can be stored.

```
CREATE TABLE VARIABLES
      (VARNAME   CHAR(30) NOT NULL PRIMARY KEY,
       VARVALUE  CHAR(30) NOT NULL)
```

Next, define and initialize the two variables and store them in the new table:

```
SET @VAR1 = 100, @VAR2 = 'John'

INSERT INTO VARIABLES VALUES ('VAR1', @VAR1)

INSERT INTO VARIABLES VALUES ('VAR2', @VAR2)
```

After this, log off. This finishes the actual session. Then log on again to start a new session. Then retrieve the values of the variables with two SELECT statements:

```
SELECT   @VAR1 := VARVALUE
FROM     VARIABLES
WHERE    VARNAME = 'VAR1'

SELECT   @VAR2 := VARVALUE
FROM     VARIABLES
WHERE    VARNAME = 'VAR2'

SELECT   @VAR1, @VAR2
```

The result is:

```
@VAR1  @VAR2
-----  -----
  100  John
```

Exercise 15.1: Define the user variable TODAY and assign the date of today by using a SET and a SELECT statement.

Exercise 15.2: Get the penalties that were incurred more than five years ago, and use the variable defined in the previous example.

Exercise 15.3: Rewrite the following SET statement to a SELECT statement:

```
SET @VAR = (SELECT SUM(AMOUNT) FROM PENALTIES)
```

15.6 The DO Statement

A special and simple SQL statement is the *DO statement*. In a DO statement, one or more scalar expressions are formulated, which MySQL processes one by one. However, the results of these expressions are not shown, as with a SELECT statement. This can be useful, for example, for calling a function that executes something into the background for which we do not need to see a result.

DEFINITION

```
<do statement> ::=
   DO <scalar expression>
      [ , <scalar expression> ]...
```

Example 15.15: Add two years to today.

```
DO CURRENT_DATE + INTERVAL 2 YEAR
```

Section 37.13 gives some examples that clearly show the use of this DO statement.

15.7 Answers

15.1 SET @TODAY = CURRENT_DATE

and

SELECT @TODAY := CURRENT_DATE

15.2

```
SELECT    *
FROM      PENALTIES
WHERE     PENALTIES_DATE < @TODAY - INTERVAL 5 YEAR
```

15.3

```
SELECT    @VAR := SUM(AMOUNT)
FROM      PENALTIES
```

CHAPTER 16

The HANDLER Statement

16.1 Introduction

So far, we have discussed only the SELECT statement for querying table data. Typical of this statement is that it always returns a set of rows. The statement is representative of the declarative character of the SQL language.

MySQL supports an additional statement to retrieve data: the *HANDLER statement.* This statement enables us to browse the data of a table row by row. For some applications, this statement is more suitable than the SELECT statement, such as for applications in which the data of a table is always processed row by row.

However, the HANDLER statement does not have all the features of the SELECT statement. In addition, the HANDLER statement has not been included in the SQL standard; it is specific to MySQL.

16.2 A Simple Example of the HANDLER Statement

We start with a simple example to explain the way the HANDLER statement works.

Example 16.1: Browse the PENALTIES table row by row; each time, show the data of the row concerned.

```
HANDLER PENALTIES OPEN
```

This statement does not have a result. The effect is that we indicate which table we would like to browse. In fact, we declare a *handler* here called PENALTIES. After that, we can retrieve the first row:

```
HANDLER PENALTIES READ FIRST
```

The result is:

```
PAYMENTNO  PLAYERNO  PAYMENT_DATE  AMOUNT
---------  --------  ------------  ------
        1         6  1980-12-08    100.00
```

This presents the first row. Next, we can retrieve the following row:

```
HANDLER PENALTIES READ NEXT
```

The result is:

```
PAYMENTNO  PLAYERNO  PAYMENT_DATE  AMOUNT
---------  --------  ------------  ------
        2        44  1981-05-05     75.00
```

We can keep retrieving rows until they are all presented. The HANDLER statement returns an empty result if we execute NEXT again after the last row has been retrieved. When we are finished, we must close the handler:

```
HANDLER PENALTIES CLOSE
```

As mentioned, this was a simple example. The difference with the SELECT statement is obvious: the SELECT statement returns all relevant rows at once, whereas the HANDLER statement returns only one row at a time. The next sections discuss in detail the features for opening a handler, browsing the rows, and closing a handler.

16.3 Opening a Handler

Note the following definition of the *HANDLER OPEN statement*. A table specification indicates which table will be queried. If no explicit handler name is specified, the name of the opened handler is the same as that of the table.

DEFINITION

```
<handler open statement> ::=
   HANDLER <table specification> OPEN [ AS <handler name> ]

<table specification> ::= [ <database name> . ] <table name>
```

MySQL registers a handler internally; it does not store it in the catalog. For the handler, MySQL lists, among other things, the table to be browsed, the index to use, and the current row. A handler one user creates is invisible to another user. Handlers can be opened more than once, but they must be closed again every time.

16.4 Browsing the Rows of a Handler

With the *HANDLER READ statement,* we can browse the rows of an opened handler. This statement offer many features; see the following definition.

DEFINITION

```
<handler read statement> ::=
   HANDLER <handler name> READ <read specification>
      [ <where clause> ]
      [ <limit clause> ]

<read specification> ::=
   FIRST                                            |
   NEXT                                             |
   { <index name> { FIRST | NEXT | PREV | LAST } } |
   { <index name> { = | > | >= | <= | < }
      <scalar expression list> }

<scalar expression list> ::=
   ( <scalar expression> [ , <scalar expression> ]... )
```

Section 16.2 gave examples in which the read specification consists of `FIRST` and `NEXT`. Evidently, `FIRST` refers to the first row, and `NEXT` refers to the next row. But what exactly is the first row? Because there are no additional specifications, MySQL decides the order in which the rows are presented. We can enforce a certain order by specifying an index. MySQL shows the rows in the order determined by the specified index. By way of illustration, we create an additional index on the PENALTIES table in the following example.

Example 16.2: Create an index on the AMOUNT column of the PENALTIES table.

```
CREATE INDEX PENALTIES_AMOUNT ON PENALTIES (AMOUNT)
```

Example 16.3: From the PENALTIES table, get all rows sorted by penalty amount (the smallest value first).

```
HANDLER PENALTIES OPEN AS P

HANDLER P READ PENALTIES_AMOUNT FIRST
```

The result is:

```
PAYMENTNO  PLAYERNO  PAYMENT_DATE  AMOUNT
---------  --------  ------------  ------
        5        44  1980-12-08     25.00
```

Explanation: The penalty with payment number 1 is not the first row now (as in the example of Section 16.2); payment number 5 is the first. The amount for that penalty is equal to 25, which is the lowest amount in the table.

Get the following row:

```
HANDLER P READ PENALTIES_AMOUNT NEXT
```

The result is:

```
PAYMENTNO  PLAYERNO  PAYMENT_DATE  AMOUNT
---------  --------  ------------  ------
        6         8  1980-12-08     25.00
```

We are not restricted to retrieving the next row only. With LAST, we can jump to the last row at once, and we can use PREV to retrieve the previous row.

We can add a WHERE clause if we do not want to browse all the rows of a table. Here, the WHERE clause has the same function as the SELECT statement: It works as a filter.

Example 16.4: From the PENALTIES table, get only those rows for which the player number is greater than 100; sort the rows on penalty amount.

```
HANDLER PENALTIES OPEN AS P

HANDLER P READ PENALTIES_AMOUNT FIRST WHERE PLAYERNO > 100
```

The result is:

```
PAYMENTNO  PLAYERNO  PAYMENT_DATE  AMOUNT
---------  --------  ------------  ------
        4       104  1984-12-08     50.00
```

Explanation: Clearly, the first row differs from the one in the previous example.

Note, however, that with NEXT, the WHERE clause must be repeated:

```
HANDLER P READ PENALTIES_AMOUNT NEXT WHERE PLAYERNO > 100
```

Not all conditions that can be used in the WHERE clause of a SELECT statement are allowed in the HANDLER READ statement. For example, subqueries are not permitted. On the other hand, scalar functions; the BETWEEN, LIKE, and IN operators; and logical operators can be used.

We can also retrieve multiple rows with a HANDLER READ statement. For this, we add a LIMIT clause.

Example 16.5: Get all the rows from the PENALTIES table, sort them on penalty amount, and get three rows at a time.

```
HANDLER PENALTIES OPEN AS P

HANDLER P READ PENALTIES_AMOUNT FIRST LIMIT 3
```

The result is:

```
PAYMENTNO  PLAYERNO  PAYMENT_DATE  AMOUNT
---------  --------  ------------  ------
        5        44  1980-12-08     25.00
        6         8  1980-12-08     25.00
        7        44  1982-12-30     30.00
```

Here, the function of the LIMIT clause is not equal to that of the SELECT statement. Adding a LIMIT clause to a SELECT statement restricts the total number of rows in the end result. With the HANDLER statement, this clause determines the number of rows retrieved with one HANDLER READ statement.

We can also specify which row to begin with. This is done by specifying a value for the indexed column.

Example 16.6: Get all the rows from the PENALTIES table, sort them on penalty amount, and start with a penalty of which the amount is equal to $30.

```
HANDLER PENALTIES OPEN AS P

HANDLER P READ PENALTIES_AMOUNT = (30.00)
```

The result is:

```
PAYMENTNO  PLAYERNO  PAYMENT_DATE  AMOUNT
---------  --------  ------------  ------
        7        44  1982-12-30     30.00
```

Behind the scenes, MySQL browses all the rows until one satisfies the condition AMOUNT = (30.00). With NEXT, we go on browsing:

```
HANDLER P READ PENALTIES_AMOUNT NEXT
```

The result is:

```
PAYMENTNO  PLAYERNO  PAYMENT_DATE  AMOUNT
---------  --------  ------------  ------
        4       104  1984-12-08     50.00
```

Instead of using the equal-to operator, other comparison operators can be used.

MySQL assigns indexes the name PRIMARY to indexes that are created because of a primary key. If you use this name within a HANDLER statement, note that it must be placed between quotation marks because it is a reserved word; see Section 20.8.

If the relevant index has been defined on two or more columns, we can specify multiple values between brackets. To illustrate this, we create an additional index.

Example 16.7: Create an index on the AMOUNT and PLAYERNO columns of the PENALTIES table.

```
CREATE INDEX AMOUNT_PLAYERNO ON PENALTIES (AMOUNT, PLAYERNO)
```

Example 16.8: Get all the rows from the PENALTIES table, sort them on penalty amount, and begin with a penalty of which the amount is equal to $30 and the player number is equal to 44.

```
HANDLER PENALTIES OPEN AS P

HANDLER P READ AMOUNT_PLAYERNO > (30.00, 44) LIMIT 100
```

The result is:

```
PAYMENTNO  PLAYERNO  PAYMENT_DATE  AMOUNT
---------  --------  ------------  ------
        4       104  1984-12-08     50.00
        8        27  1984-11-12     75.00
        2        44  1981-05-05     75.00
        1         6  1980-12-08    100.00
        3        27  1983-09-10    100.00
```

The number of values that is specified between brackets must be equal to or less than the number of columns of the index. We specified `LIMIT 100` to give us more than one row, and we assume that no more than 100 rows will be returned.

16.5 Closing a Handler

In the end, the `HANDLER CLOSE` statement must close each handler.

DEFINITION

```
<handler close statement> ::=
   HANDLER <handler name> CLOSE
```

If an application is stopped, all the handlers that are still open are automatically closed.

Exercise 16.1: Show all `HANDLER` statements that are needed to show all rows from the MATCHES table. The order of the rows is not important.

Exercise 16.2: Show all `HANDLER` statements that are needed to show all rows from the MATCHES table, sorted on match number.

Exercise 16.3: Show all `HANDLER` statements that are needed to show all rows from the MATCHES table in descending order sorted on match number, but only the rows of players 6, 104, and 112.

16.6 Answers

16.1

```
HANDLER MATCHES OPEN AS M1

HANDLER M1 READ FIRST

HANDLER M1 READ NEXT
```

The previous statement must be executed several times.

```
HANDLER M1 CLOSE
```

16.2
```
HANDLER MATCHES OPEN AS M2

HANDLER M2 READ 'PRIMARY' FIRST

HANDLER M2 READ 'PRIMARY' NEXT
```
The previous statement must be executed several times.
```
HANDLER M2 CLOSE
```

16.3
```
HANDLER MATCHES OPEN AS M3

HANDLER M3 READ 'PRIMARY' LAST
   WHERE PLAYERNO IN (6, 104, 112)

HANDLER M3 READ 'PRIMARY' PREV
   WHERE PLAYERNO IN (6, 104, 112)
```
The previous statement must be executed several times.
```
HANDLER M3 CLOSE
```

CHAPTER 17

Updating Tables

17.1 Introduction

MySQL offers various statements for updating the contents (the column values in the rows) of tables. Statements exist for inserting new rows, changing column values, and deleting rows. This chapter describes the extensive features of these statements.

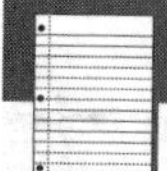

NOTE

In most examples of this book, we assume that the tables contain their original contents. If you execute the statements discussed in this chapter, you will change the contents of the tables. Consequently, the results of your statements in the next examples can differ from those in the book. On the web site of the book, www.r20.nl, you can read how to restore the original contents of the tables after an update.

17.2 Inserting New Rows

In MySQL, you can use the `INSERT` *statement* to add rows to an existing table. With this statement, you can add new rows and populate a table with rows taken from another table.

DEFINITION

```
<insert statement> ::=
   INSERT [ IGNORE ] [ INTO ] <table specification>
   <insert specification> [ <on duplicate key specification> ]

<insert specification> ::=
   [ <column list> ] <values clause>                        |
   [ <column list> ] <table expression>                     |
   SET <column assignment> [ , <column assignment> ]...

<column list> ::=
   ( <column name> [ , <column name> ]... )

<values clause> ::=
   VALUES <row expression> [ , <row expression> ]...

<row expression> ::=
   <scalar row expression>

<on duplicate key specification> ::=
   ON DUPLICATE KEY UPDATE <column assignment>
      [ , <column assignment> ]...

<column assignment> ::=
   <column name> = <scalar expression>
```

Section 4.7, among others, contains several examples of INSERT statements. This section shows other simple examples to illustrate the possibilities of the INSERT statement.

Example 17.1: The tennis club has a new team. This third team is captained by player 100 and will compete in the third division.

```
INSERT INTO TEAMS (TEAMNO, PLAYERNO, DIVISION)
VALUES (3, 100, 'third')
```

Explanation: Behind the term INSERT INTO, the name of the table is specified for which rows must be added. Following that are the names of the columns of that table; finally, a VALUES clause specifies the values of the new row. The structure of a VALUES clause is simple and consists of one or more row expressions, with each row expression consisting of one or more scalar expressions.

You can omit the word INTO with MySQL, but all other SQL products require it; therefore, we recommend always including the word.

You do not have to specify column names if a value is specified for all columns of the table concerned. The TEAMS table contains three columns, and three values have been specified; thus, we could have omitted the column names:

```
INSERT INTO TEAMS
VALUES (3, 100, 'third')
```

If column names are omitted, MySQL assumes that the order in which the values are entered is the same as the default sequence of the columns (see COLUMN_NO in the COLUMNS table).

You are not required to specify columns in the default sequence. Therefore, the next statement is equivalent to the previous two:

```
INSERT INTO TEAMS (PLAYERNO, DIVISION, TEAMNO)
VALUES (100, 'third', 3)
```

If the column names had *not* been specified in this statement, the result would have been entirely different. MySQL would have considered the value 100 to be a TEAMNO, the value 'third' a PLAYERNO, and the value 3 a DIVISION. Of course, the insert would not have been performed at all because the value 'third' is an alphanumeric literal, and the PLAYERNO column has a numeric data type.

For all columns in the CREATE TABLE statement that have been defined as NOT NULL, a value *must* be specified (work out for yourself why). The following statement is therefore not correct because the PLAYERNO column has been defined as NOT NULL and does not have a value in the INSERT statement:

```
INSERT INTO TEAMS
       (TEAMNO, DIVISION)
VALUES (3, 'third')
```

However, the next example is correct.

Example 17.2: Add a new player.

```
INSERT INTO PLAYERS
       (PLAYERNO, NAME, INITIALS, SEX,
        JOINED, STREET, TOWN)
VALUES (611, 'Jones', 'GG', 'M', 1977, 'Green Way', 'Stratford')
```

In all columns that have not been specified in the INSERT statement, null values are entered.

Instead of using a literal, you can specify a null value. Then the concerning row is filled with the null value. In the following statement, the LEAGUENO column, among other things, is filled with the null value:

```
INSERT INTO PLAYERS
       (PLAYERNO, NAME, INITIALS, BIRTH_DATE,
        SEX, JOINED, STREET, HOUSENO, POSTCODE,
        TOWN, PHONENO, LEAGUENO)
VALUES (611, 'Jones', 'GG', NULL, 'M', 1977,
        'Green Way', NULL, NULL, 'Stratford', NULL, NULL)
```

Because it is possible to specify more than one row expression in a VALUES clause, one INSERT statement can add multiple new rows.

Example 17.3: Add four new teams.

```
INSERT INTO TEAMS (TEAMNO, PLAYERNO, DIVISION)
VALUES (6, 100, 'third'),
       (7,  27, 'fourth'),
       (8,  39, 'fourth'),
       (9, 112, 'sixth')
```

Explanation: The new rows are separated by apostrophes within the VALUES clause.

Instead of using literals, you may also include expressions within the VALUES clause, and these expressions can be compound. Therefore, calculations, scalar functions, and even scalar subqueries are allowed.

Example 17.4: Create a new table in which the number of players and the sum of all penalties is stored.

```
CREATE TABLE TOTALS
       (NUMBERPLAYERS   INTEGER NOT NULL,
        SUMPENALTIES    DECIMAL(9,2) NOT NULL)

INSERT INTO TOTALS (NUMBERPLAYERS, SUMPENALTIES)
VALUES ((SELECT COUNT(*) FROM PLAYERS),
        (SELECT SUM(AMOUNT) FROM PENALTIES))
```

Explanation: Remember that each subquery must always be placed between brackets in this construct.

MySQL has an alternative formulation for adding a new row to a table. Example 17.1 contains the following INSERT statement:

```
INSERT INTO TEAMS (TEAMNO, PLAYERNO, DIVISION)
VALUES (3, 100, 'third')
```

This statement can also be rewritten as follows:

```
INSERT INTO TEAMS SET
   TEAMNO = 3, PLAYERNO = 100, DIVISION = 'third'
```

This formulation is somewhat old. Here we can enter only one row per statement.

MySQL checks whether the new data that has been entered with an INSERT statement satisfies all the integrity constraints. For example, by adding a new row, it is possible to create duplicate rows in a primary key. With a normal INSERT statement, MySQL gives an error message and interrupts the processing of the statement. Adding IGNORE prevents the error message from appearing. However, the entire INSERT statement is still stopped.

Example 17.5: Add team 1 to the TEAMS table again.

```
INSERT IGNORE INTO TEAMS VALUES (1, 39, 'second')
```

Explanation: Usually, this statement results in an error message because the TEAMS table already contains a team number 1. However, now that the term IGNORE has been added, an error message will not be presented. The new row is not entered. If there is no team with the number 1, the INSERT statement will actually be processed.

You can add an ON DUPLICATE KEY *specification* to each INSERT statement. This specification becomes active if the row that is added causes trouble with the primary key or one of the alternate keys. When a new row conflicts with an existing row, we can indicate that the values in the existing row must be adjusted.

Example 17.6: Add team 1 to the TEAMS table again. If team 1 already exists, enter 39 as the player number and 'second' as the division.

```
INSERT INTO TEAMS VALUES (1, 39, 'second')
ON DUPLICATE KEY UPDATE PLAYERNO = 39, DIVISION='second'
```

Explanation: In fact, the following statements are executed behind the scenes:

```
INSERT INTO TEAMS VALUES (1, 39, 'second')

IF TEAMNO 1 IS NOT UNIQUE
   BEGIN
      UPDATE   TEAMS
      SET      PLAYERNO = 39,
               DIVISION='second'
      WHERE    TEAMNO = 1
   END
```

The changes behind the word UPDATE should satisfy the same requirements and display the same behavior as that of the UPDATE statement; see Section 17.4.

17.3 Populating a Table with Rows from Another Table

In the previous section, we showed only examples of INSERT statements in which new rows are added. With the INSERT statement, we can fill a table with rows from another table (or other tables). You could say that data is *copied* from one table to another. Instead of using the VALUES clause, we use a table expression in the INSERT statement.

Example 17.7: Create a separate table in which the number, name, town, and telephone number of each noncompetition player are recorded.

We start by creating a new table:

```
CREATE TABLE RECR_PLAYERS
      (PLAYERNO    SMALLINT NOT NULL,
       NAME        CHAR(15) NOT NULL,
       TOWN        CHAR(10) NOT NULL,
       PHONENO     CHAR(13),
       PRIMARY KEY (PLAYERNO))
```

The following INSERT statement populates the RECR_PLAYERS table with data about recreational players registered in the PLAYERS table:

```
INSERT   INTO RECR_PLAYERS
        (PLAYERNO, NAME, TOWN, PHONENO)
SELECT   PLAYERNO, NAME, TOWN, PHONENO
FROM     PLAYERS
WHERE    LEAGUENO IS NULL
```

After this INSERT statement, the contents of the new table look like this:

```
PLAYERNO  NAME     TOWN       PHONENO
--------  -------  ---------  ----------
       7  Wise     Stratford  070-347689
      28  Collins  Midhurst   071-659599
      39  Bishop   Stratford  070-393435
      95  Miller   Douglas    070-867564
```

Explanation: The first part of the INSERT statement is a normal INSERT statement. The second part is based not on a VALUES clause, but on a table expression. The result of a table expression is a number of rows with values. However, these rows are not displayed on the screen, but are stored directly in the RECR_PLAYERS table.

The rules that apply to the first form of the INSERT statement also apply here. The next two statements, then, have an equivalent result to the previous INSERT statement:

```
INSERT   INTO RECR_PLAYERS
SELECT   PLAYERNO, NAME, TOWN, PHONENO
FROM     PLAYERS
WHERE    LEAGUENO IS NULL

INSERT   INTO RECR_PLAYERS
        (TOWN, PHONENO, NAME, PLAYERNO)
SELECT   TOWN, PHONENO, NAME, PLAYERNO
FROM     PLAYERS
WHERE    LEAGUENO IS NULL
```

Several other rules apply:

- The table to which rows are added can be the same as the one from which they are copied. In this case, the result of the SELECT statement is determined first to avoid a continuous loop; see the next example.
- The table expression is a fully fledged table expression and, therefore, can include subqueries, joins, set operators, GROUP BY and ORDER BY clauses, functions, and so on.
- The number of columns in the INSERT INTO clause must be equal to the number of expressions in the SELECT clause of the table expression.
- The data types of the columns in the INSERT INTO clause must conform to the data types of the expressions in the SELECT clause.

We use two examples to illustrate the first rule.

Example 17.8: Duplicate the number of rows in the RECR_PLAYERS table.

```
INSERT   INTO RECR_PLAYERS
        (PLAYERNO, NAME, TOWN, PHONENO)
SELECT   PLAYERNO + 1000, NAME, TOWN, PHONENO
FROM     RECR_PLAYERS
```

Explanation: One thousand is added to the value of the PLAYERNO column to make sure no problems arise with the primary key.

Example 17.9: Add all penalties to the PENALTIES table for which the amount is greater than the average amount.

```
INSERT   INTO PENALTIES
SELECT   PAYMENTNO + 100, PLAYERNO, PAYMENT_DATE, AMOUNT
FROM     PENALTIES
WHERE    AMOUNT >
        (SELECT   AVG(AMOUNT)
         FROM     PENALTIES)
```

Exercise 17.1: Add a new row to the PENALTIES table; the payment number is 15, this concerns player 27, the payment date was 1985-11-08, and the penalty amount is $75.

Exercise 17.2: Add all the penalties to the PENALTIES table for which the amount is smaller than the average amount, plus all penalties of player 27. Make sure that the penalty numbers remain unique.

17.4 Updating Values in Rows

You can change values in a table with the `UPDATE` statement. A table reference indicates which table needs to be updated. The `WHERE` clause of an `UPDATE` statement specifies which rows must be changed; the `SET` clause is used to assign new values to one or more columns.

DEFINITION

```
<update statement> ::=
   UPDATE [ IGNORE ] <table reference>
   SET <column assignment> [ , <column assignment> ]...
   [ <where clause> ]
   [ <order by clause> ]
   [ <limit clause> ]

<table reference> ::=
   <table specification> [ [ AS ] <pseudonym> ]

<pseudonym> ::= <name>

<column assignment> ::=
   <column name> = <scalar expression>
```

Example 17.10: Update the league number for player 95 to 2,000.

```
UPDATE   PLAYERS
SET      LEAGUENO = '2000'
WHERE    PLAYERNO = 95
```

Explanation: For *every* row in the PLAYERS table (`UPDATE PLAYERS`) in which the player number equals 95 (`WHERE PLAYERNO = 95`), you must change the LEAGUENO to 2,000 (`SET LEAGUENO = '2000'`). The last specification is called a column assignment.

In most examples, it is not necessary, but you can specify a pseudonym behind a table name, just as in a `SELECT` statement. The earlier `UPDATE` statement has the same result as the following:

```
UPDATE   PLAYERS AS P
SET      P.LEAGUENO = '2000'
WHERE    P.PLAYERNO = 95
```

A literal is specified in the column assignment of this first example. Because of this, the LEAGUENO column gets a new value that replaces the existing value. A column assignment can also contain complex expressions that can even refer to the column that is updated.

Example 17.11: Increase all penalties by 5 percent.

```
UPDATE   PENALTIES
SET      AMOUNT = AMOUNT * 1.05
```

Explanation: Because the WHERE clause has been omitted, as in the previous example, the update is performed on all rows in the table concerned. In this example, the amount in each row of the PENALTIES table increases by 5 percent.

Example 17.12: Set the number of sets won to 0 for all competitors resident in Stratford.

```
UPDATE   MATCHES
SET      WON = 0
WHERE    PLAYERNO IN
        (SELECT   PLAYERNO
         FROM     PLAYERS
         WHERE    TOWN = 'Stratford')
```

The earlier examples show SET clauses with only one column assignment. You are allowed to update multiple columns with one statement simultaneously.

Example 17.13: The Parmenter family has moved to 83 Palmer Street in Inglewood, the postcode has become 1234UU, and the telephone number is unknown.

```
UPDATE   PLAYERS
SET      STREET   = 'Palmer Street',
         HOUSENO  = '83',
         TOWN     = 'Inglewood',
         POSTCODE = '1234UU',
         PHONENO  = NULL
WHERE    NAME     = 'Parmenter'
```

Explanation: In this case, the PHONENO column has been filled with the null value. Remember the comma between two items. With this statement, both players named Parmenter are moved to the same address.

Be careful when the column that is updated is used in the expressions of column assignments.

The following statement could give the impression that the values of the STREET and TOWN columns for player 44 are exchanged:

```
UPDATE   PLAYERS
SET      STREET   = TOWN,
         TOWN     = STREET
WHERE    PLAYERNO = 44
```

Explanation: These are the original contents of the PLAYERS table:

```
PLAYERNO  STREET        TOWN
--------  ------------  ---------
44        Lewis Street  Inglewood
```

The result of the UPDATE statement is:

```
PLAYERNO  STREET     TOWN
--------  ---------  ------------
44        Inglewood  Lewis Street
```

So the values of the columns have not been switched, but now the question is, why not? This is caused by the processing method of the UPDATE statement. For each row, MySQL checks whether the condition in the WHERE clause is true. If so, the value of the expression of the first column assignment is determined first, and this value is assigned to the column concerned. The value of the second expression is determined next, and that value also is assigned to the column concerned. In this example, first the value of the TOWN column is assigned to the STREET column. After that, the value of the STREET column in the second column assignment is calculated, which already is the TOWN column. It looks as if MySQL processed the following statements in succession:

```
UPDATE   PLAYERS
SET      STREET   = TOWN
WHERE    PLAYERNO = 44

UPDATE   PLAYERS
SET      TOWN     = STREET
WHERE    PLAYERNO = 44
```

When exchanging values, the values of one of the columns must be entered in a temporary table.

Expressions consisting of scalar subqueries can also be used in the SET clause.

Example 17.14: Create a new table to store for each player the player number, the number of matches he or she played, and the sum of all penalties incurred by him or her.

```
CREATE TABLE PLAYERS_DATA
      (PLAYERNO         INTEGER NOT NULL PRIMARY KEY,
       NUMBER_MAT       INTEGER,
       SUM_PENALTIES    DECIMAL(7,2))

INSERT INTO PLAYERS_DATA (PLAYERNO)
SELECT PLAYERNO FROM PLAYERS

UPDATE   PLAYERS_DATA AS PD
SET      NUMBER_MAT =    (SELECT   COUNT(*)
                          FROM     MATCHES AS M
                          WHERE    M.PLAYERNO = PD.PLAYERNO),
         SUM_PENALTIES = (SELECT   SUM(AMOUNT)
                          FROM     PENALTIES AS PEN
                          WHERE    PEN.PLAYERNO = PD.PLAYERNO)
```

Explanation: In the UPDATE clause of the UPDATE statement, a pseudonym (PD) is used to reference this table in the subqueries. Note that this example does not require the use of the pseudonym.

In a subquery used in a SET clause, it is *not* allowed to specify the table that is updated.

Example 17.15: Subtract the average penalty amount from each penalty amount.

The following solution is therefore not allowed:

```
UPDATE   PENALTIES
SET      AMOUNT = AMOUNT - (SELECT   AVG(AMOUNT)
                            FROM     PENALTIES)
```

To create a comparable result, this statement must be divided into two parts:

```
SET @AVERAGE_AMOUNT = (SELECT AVG(AMOUNT) FROM PENALTIES)

UPDATE   PENALTIES
SET      AMOUNT = AMOUNT - @AVERAGE_AMOUNT
```

When an ORDER BY clause is added to an UPDATE statement, the sequence in which the rows must be updated is specified.

Example 17.16: Increase all penalties by 5 percent and begin with the highest amount.

```
UPDATE   PENALTIES
SET      AMOUNT = AMOUNT * 1.05
ORDER BY AMOUNT DESC
```

This can be useful and even necessary for certain changes on multiple rows. Imagine that we want to increase the payment number of all penalties by 1. If MySQL started processing with the penalty holding payment number 1, this new value 2 would conflict with the existing payment number 2. To make sure no conflicts arise, we can force MySQL to begin with the last penalty by adding an ORDER BY clause—see the following example.

Example 17.17: Increase all payment numbers by 1.

```
UPDATE   PENALTIES
SET      PAYMENTNO = PAYMENTNO + 1
ORDER BY PAYMENTNO DESC
```

Including an ORDER BY clause can also be useful when a LIMIT clause is added as well.

Example 17.18: Increase the four highest penalties by 5 percent.

```
UPDATE   PENALTIES
SET      AMOUNT = AMOUNT * 1.05
ORDER BY AMOUNT DESC, PLAYERNO ASC
LIMIT    4
```

Explanation: An additional sorting on the PLAYERNO column has been added to the ORDER BY clause to indicate clearly which rows must be updated if equal penalty amounts exist.

MySQL checks whether the new rows that have been entered with an UPDATE statement, satisfy all integrity constraints. For example, a certain update could create duplicate values in a primary key. With a normal UPDATE statement, MySQL gives an error message and interrupts the processing of the statement. As with the INSERT statement, you can add IGNORE to have this error message ignored. In this situation, the entire update is stopped.

Example 17.19: For the match with number 4, increase the number by 1 and make the number of sets won 2 and the number of sets lost 3.

```
UPDATE   IGNORE MATCHES
SET      MATCHNO = MATCHNO + 1,
         WON = 2,
         LOST = 3
WHERE    MATCHNO = 4
```

Explanation: Because you added the term IGNORE, no error messages arise when the increase of the match number causes conflicts. If match number 5 does not exist, the UPDATE statement is processed correctly.

Exercise 17.3: Change the value F in the SEX column of the PLAYERS table to W (woman).

Exercise 17.4: Update the SEX column in the PLAYERS table as follows: Where M is recorded, change it to F, and where F exists, change it to M.

Exercise 17.5: Increase all penalties that are higher than the average penalty by 20 percent.

17.5 Updating Values in Multiple Tables

MySQL enables you to change data in two or more tables with only one UPDATE statement. For this, the definition of the UPDATE statement has been adjusted somewhat; you may specify more than one table in the UPDATE clause.

DEFINITION

```
<update statement> ::=
   UPDATE [ IGNORE ] <table reference>
      [ , <table reference> ]...
   SET <update> [ , <update> ]...
   [ <where clause> ]
   [ <order by clause> ]
   [ <limit clause> ]

<table reference> ::=
   <table specification> [ [ AS ] <pseudonym> ]

<pseudonym> ::= <name>

<update> ::=
   <column name> = <scalar expression>
```

Before we give an example of an update on two tables, we give an example in which two tables are mentioned in the UPDATE clause but only one table is updated.

Example 17.20: Set the number of sets won to 0 for all matches that have been played for a team in the first division.

```
UPDATE   MATCHES AS M, TEAMS AS T
SET      WON = 0
WHERE    T.TEAMNO = M.TEAMNO
AND      T.DIVISION = 'first'
```

Explanation: Two tables are mentioned in the UPDATE clause, but the SET clause contains only columns of one table. When processing this statement, MySQL first executes the following SELECT statement:

```
SELECT   ...
FROM     MATCHES AS M, TEAMS AS T
WHERE    T.TEAMNO = M.TEAMNO
AND      T.DIVISION = 'first'
```

This statement is derived from the UPDATE statement. The SELECT clause of this statement is insignificant. After MySQL processes the FROM and WHERE clauses, several rows are selected in both tables. These rows satisfy the join condition and the condition T.DIVISION = 'first'. The actual update is performed on those selected rows. Because the SET clause contains only columns of the MATCHES table, only the selected rows in that table are updated.

This statement could also have been solved with a subquery in the WHERE clause:

```
UPDATE   MATCHES
SET      WON = 0
WHERE    TEAMNO IN
        (SELECT   TEAMNO
         FROM     TEAMS
         WHERE    DIVISION = 'first')
```

Example 17.21: Set the number of sets won to 0 for all matches that have been played for a team in the first division and set the number of the captain to 112 for those first-division teams.

```
UPDATE   MATCHES AS M, TEAMS AS T
SET      M.WON = 0,
         T.PLAYERNO = 112
WHERE    T.TEAMNO = M.TEAMNO
AND      T.DIVISION = 'first'
```

Explanation: This statement actually updates data in two tables. The SET clause clearly shows that the WON column from the MATCHES table and the PLAYERNO column from the TEAMS table have been updated. The update concerns all rows from both tables for which the conditions in the WHERE clause are true.

The advantage of updating multiple tables with one statement is that either the entire statement is executed or none of it is. If we had split the statement into two UPDATE statements and a problem arose after the first was processed but before the processing of the second, the first update could be performed, but the second could not. With one statement, this is impossible.

Example 17.22: If the player with number 2 appears in all five tables of the sample database, that number must be changed to 1 in all five tables.

```
UPDATE    PLAYERS AS P,
          TEAMS AS T,
          MATCHES AS M,
          PENALTIES AS PEN,
          COMMITTEE_MEMBERS AS C
SET       P.PLAYERNO   = 1,
          T.PLAYERNO   = 1,
          M.PLAYERNO   = 1,
          PEN.PLAYERNO = 1,
          C.PLAYERNO   = 1
WHERE     P.PLAYERNO   = T.PLAYERNO
AND       T.PLAYERNO   = M.PLAYERNO
AND       M.PLAYERNO   = PEN.PLAYERNO
AND       PEN.PLAYERNO = C.PLAYERNO
AND       C.PLAYERNO   = 2
```

Explanation: If player 2 appears in all tables, all join conditions are `true`, and in all tables the player number is changed to 1.

Exercise 17.6: Change the division in `'third'` for all teams that are captained by a player living in Stratford.

Exercise 17.7: Use one statement to change the amounts of all penalties in $50 and the divisions of all teams in `'fourth'`.

17.6 Substituting Existing Rows

With the INSERT statement, new rows are added to a table. The *REPLACE statement* can also add new rows, but there is a difference. When a new row is added, the assigned primary key or one of the alternate keys conflicts with that of an existing row. In that case, the INSERT statement rejects the addition, but the old row is overwritten by the new row in the REPLACE statement. The new row essentially replaces the old row. In fact, REPLACE changes into a kind of UPDATE statement. The structure of this statement looks very much like that of the INSERT statement.

DEFINITION

```
<replace statement> ::=
   REPLACE [ IGNORE ] [ INTO ] <table specification>
   <insert specification>

<insert specification> ::=
   [ <column list> ] <values clause>                      |
   [ <column list> ] <table expression>                   |
   SET <column assignment> [ , <column assignment> ]...

<column list> ::=
   ( <column name> [ , <column name> ]... )

<values clause> ::=
   VALUES <row expression> [ , <row expression> ]...

<row expression> ::=
   <scalar row expression>

<column assignment> ::=
   <column name> = <scalar expression>
```

By way of illustration, we convert several INSERT statements from the previous sections into REPLACE statements.

Example 17.23: Add a new player; if the primary keys already exist, the old values must be overwritten (based upon Example 17.2).

```
REPLACE INTO PLAYERS
       (PLAYERNO, NAME, INITIALS, SEX,
        JOINED, STREET, TOWN)
VALUES (611, 'Jones', 'GG', 'M', 1977, 'Green Way', 'Stratford')
```

Explanation: If player 611 already exists, the values in the REPLACE statement overwrite the existing values.

Example 17.24: Add four new teams; if the primary keys already exist, the old values must be overwritten (based upon Example 17.3).

```
REPLACE INTO TEAMS (TEAMNO, PLAYERNO, DIVISION)
VALUES (6, 100, 'third'),
       (7,  27, 'fourth'),
       (8,  39, 'fourth'),
       (9, 112, 'sixth')
```

Example 17.25: Double the number of rows in the RECR_PLAYERS table; if the primary keys already exist, the old values must be overwritten (based upon Example 17.8).

```
REPLACE INTO RECR_PLAYERS
       (PLAYERNO, NAME, TOWN, PHONENO)
SELECT  PLAYERNO + 1000, NAME, TOWN, PHONENO
FROM    RECR_PLAYERS
```

Of course, it is not allowed to add an `ON DUPLICATE KEY` specification to the `REPLACE` statement. The `IGNORE` option works as it does with the `INSERT` and `UPDATE` statements.

17.7 Deleting Rows from a Table

The `DELETE` statement removes rows from a table. The definition of the `DELETE` statement reads as follows:

DEFINITION

```
<delete statement> ::=
   DELETE [ IGNORE ]
   FROM    <table reference>
   [ <where clause> ]
   [ <order by clause> ]
   [ <limit clause> ]

<table reference> ::=
   <table specification> [ [ AS ] <pseudonym> ]

<pseudonym> ::= <name>
```

Example 17.26: Delete all penalties incurred by player 44.

```
DELETE
FROM    PENALTIES
WHERE   PLAYERNO = 44
```

or:

```
DELETE
FROM    PENALTIES AS PEN
WHERE   PEN.PLAYERNO = 44
```

If the WHERE clause is omitted, all the rows of the specified table are deleted. This is not the same as dropping a table with the DROP statement. DELETE removes only the contents, whereas the DROP statement also deletes the definition of the table from the catalog. After the DELETE statement, the table remains intact.

Example 17.27: Delete all players for whom the year in which they joined the club is greater than the average year that all players from Stratford joined the club.

```
DELETE
FROM     PLAYERS
WHERE    JOINED >
        (SELECT   AVG(JOINED)
         FROM     PLAYERS
         WHERE    TOWN = 'Stratford')
```

Explanation: As with the UPDATE statement, some SQL products do not allow subqueries in the WHERE clause of a DELETE statement to refer to the table from which rows are deleted. Again, this restriction does not apply to MySQL.

As with the UPDATE statement, an ORDER BY clause and a LIMIT clause may be specified in a DELETE statement. The effect and method of processing are comparable.

Example 17.28: Delete the four highest penalties.

```
DELETE
FROM     PENALTIES
ORDER BY AMOUNT DESC, PLAYERNO ASC
LIMIT    4
```

Example 17.29: Remove all players and do not return an error message if something goes wrong during the processing.

```
DELETE   IGNORE
FROM     PLAYERS
```

Explanation: You may specify an IGNORE option in the DELETE statement as well.

Exercise 17.8: Delete all penalties incurred by player 44 in 1980.

Exercise 17.9: Delete all penalties incurred by players who have ever played for a team in the second division.

Exercise 17.10: Delete all players who live in the same town as player 44 but keep the data about player 44.

17.8 Deleting Rows from Multiple Tables

MySQL enables you to delete data from two or more tables with one DELETE statement. You can formulate these DELETE statements in two ways. The possibilities of these two are the same.

DEFINITION

```
<delete statement> ::=
   { DELETE [ IGNORE ]
     <table reference> [ , <table reference> ]...
     FROM <table reference> [ , <table reference> ]...
     [ <where clause> ] } |
   { DELETE [ IGNORE ]
     FROM <table reference> [ , <table reference> ]...
     USING <table reference> [ , <table reference> ]...
     [ <where clause> ] }

<table reference> ::=
   <table specification> [ [ AS ] <pseudonym> ]

<pseudonym> ::= <name>
```

As with the UPDATE statement, we first give an example that mentions multiple tables but removes rows from only one table.

Example 17.30: Delete all matches of all players living in Inglewood.

```
DELETE   MATCHES
FROM     MATCHES, PLAYERS
WHERE    MATCHES.PLAYERNO = PLAYERS.PLAYERNO
AND      PLAYERS.TOWN = 'Inglewood'
```

Explanation: As with the UPDATE statement, the following SELECT statement is executed first:

```
SELECT   ...
FROM     MATCHES, PLAYERS
WHERE    MATCHES.PLAYERNO = PLAYERS.PLAYERNO
AND      PLAYERS.TOWN = 'Inglewood'
```

With this, rows in both tables are selected. Because only the MATCHES table is mentioned in the `DELETE` clause of the `DELETE` statement, only the selected rows from this table are removed.

In the `DELETE` clause, only table references may be specified that also appear in the `FROM` clause. Therefore, the following statement is incorrect because the MATCHES table gets the pseudonym `M`. The statement would have been correct if, in the `DELETE` clause, the name `MATCHES` also was replaced by `M`.

```
DELETE    MATCHES
FROM      MATCHES AS M, PLAYERS
WHERE     M.PLAYERNO = PLAYERS.PLAYERNO
AND       PLAYERS.TOWN = 'Inglewood'
```

Example 17.31: Delete all data about team 1 from the TEAMS and MATCHES tables.

```
DELETE    TEAMS, MATCHES
FROM      TEAMS, MATCHES
WHERE     TEAMS.TEAMNO = MATCHES.TEAMNO
AND       TEAMS.TEAMNO = 1
```

Explanation: All rows that satisfy the join and the condition `TEAMS.TEAMNO = 1` are deleted now, including those from the TEAMS table as well as from the MATCHES table.

The second formulation for this statement looks as follows:

```
DELETE
FROM      TEAMS, MATCHES
USING     TEAMS, MATCHES
WHERE     TEAMS.TEAMNO = MATCHES.TEAMNO
AND       TEAMS.TEAMNO = 1
```

The table references in the first formulation in the `DELETE` clause are now in the `FROM` clause, and those in the `FROM` clause are in the `USING` clause. In brief, everything is descended one line.

Exercise 17.11: Delete all penalties and matches of player 27, but only if player 27 appears in both tables.

Exercise 17.12: Delete all penalties and matches of player 27, regardless of whether the player appears in both tables.

17.9 The TRUNCATE Statement

If all rows from a large table must be removed, it could take a lot of time. For this special case, MySQL has the *TRUNCATE statement.* With this statement, all rows are deleted at once. In most cases, the rows are removed faster than when a DELETE statement is used.

DEFINITION

```
<truncate statement> ::=
   TRUNCATE TABLE <table specification>
```

Example 17.32: Delete all committee members.

```
TRUNCATE TABLE COMMITTEE_MEMBERS
```

17.10 Answers

17.1
```
INSERT INTO PENALTIES
VALUES (15, 27, '1985-11-08', 75)
```

17.2
```
INSERT   INTO PENALTIES
SELECT   PAYMENTNO + 1000, PLAYERNO, PAYMENT_DATE, AMOUNT
FROM     PENALTIES
WHERE    AMOUNT >
        (SELECT   AVG(AMOUNT)
         FROM     PENALTIES)
UNION
SELECT   PAYMENTNO + 2000, PLAYERNO, PAYMENT_DATE, AMOUNT
FROM     PENALTIES
WHERE    PLAYERNO = 27
```

17.3
```
UPDATE   PLAYERS
SET      SEX = 'W'
WHERE    SEX = 'F'
```

17.4
```
UPDATE    PLAYERS
SET       SEX = 'X'
WHERE     SEX = 'F'

UPDATE    PLAYERS
SET       SEX = 'F'
WHERE     SEX = 'M'

UPDATE    PLAYERS
SET       SEX = 'M'
WHERE     SEX = 'X'
```

or

```
UPDATE    PLAYERS
SET       SEX = CASE SEX
                   WHEN 'F' THEN 'M'
                   ELSE 'F'
                END
```

17.5
```
UPDATE    PENALTIES
SET       AMOUNT = AMOUNT * 1.2
WHERE     AMOUNT >
         (SELECT   AVG(AMOUNT)
          FROM     PENALTIES)
```

17.6
```
UPDATE    TEAMS AS T, PLAYERS AS P
SET       DIVISION = 'third'
WHERE     T.PLAYERNO = P.PLAYERNO
AND       P.TOWN = 'Stratford'
```

17.7
```
UPDATE    PENALTIES, TEAMS
SET       AMOUNT = 50,
          DIVISION = 'fourth'
```

17.8
```
DELETE
FROM      PENALTIES
WHERE     PLAYERNO = 44
AND       YEAR(PAYMENT_DATE) = 1980
```

17.9
```
DELETE
FROM      PENALTIES
WHERE     PLAYERNO IN
         (SELECT   PLAYERNO
          FROM     MATCHES
          WHERE    TEAMNO IN
                  (SELECT   TEAMNO
                   FROM     TEAMS
                   WHERE    DIVISION = 'second'))
```

17.10
```
DELETE
FROM     PLAYERS
WHERE    TOWN =
        (SELECT   TOWN
         FROM     PLAYERS
         WHERE PLAYERNO = 44)
AND      PLAYERNO <> 44
```

17.11
```
DELETE   PEN, M
FROM     PENALTIES AS PEN, MATCHES AS M
WHERE    PEN.PLAYERNO = M.PLAYERNO
AND      PEN.PLAYERNO = 27
```

17.12
```
DELETE   PEN, M
FROM     PENALTIES AS PEN, MATCHES AS M
WHERE    PEN.PLAYERNO = 27
AND      M.PLAYERNO = 27
```

CHAPTER 18

Loading and Unloading Data

18.1 Introduction

All SQL statements use data that is stored in tables of a database. However, sometimes we want to take the data out of the database and store it in an *output file*. Other programs that do not support SQL then can process this file. This process is called *unloading data*.

The opposite of loading data is, obviously, *loading data*. Here, data stored in files is added to the database. These files are created by another program or supplied by a company, for example. Usually, this file is called the *input file*.

Loading and unloading data can also transfer data from one MySQL database to another. For example, this can be useful if we want to build a second version of the database somewhere else.

When unloading data, MySQL uses the SELECT statement; it uses the special LOAD statement when loading data. The next two sections discuss the features of these two statements.

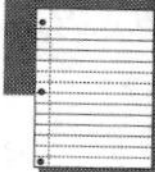

NOTE

Section 20.11 discusses the CSV storage engine. This subject is also related to loading and unloading data.

18.2 Unloading Data

The result of every SELECT statement can be written to a file. For this, an additional clause has been added to the SELECT statement, the *INTO FILE clause*.

DEFINITION

```
<select statement> ::=
   <table expression>
   [ <into file clause> ]
   [ FOR UPDATE | LOCK IN SHARE MODE ]

<into file clause> ::=
   INTO OUTFILE '<file name>' <export option>... |
   INTO DUMPFILE '<file name>'                   |
   INTO <user variable> [ , <user variable> ]...

<export option> ::=
   FIELDS [ TERMINATED BY <alphanumeric literal> ]
          [ [ OPTIONALLY ] ENCLOSED BY <alphanumeric literal> ]
          [ ESCAPED BY <alphanumeric literal> ] |
    LINES TERMINATED BY <alphanumeric literal>
```

Example 18.1: Unload all the data of the TEAMS table.

```
SELECT    *
FROM      TEAMS
INTO      OUTFILE 'C:/TEAMS.TXT'
```

The contents of the output file look as follows:

```
1    6    first
2    27    second
```

Explanation: The output file is called TEAMS.TXT. The file may not exist in the specified directory. Additionally, the specified directory must exist. Tab symbols separate the values in the rows, and each row starts on a new line.

Example 18.2: Unload all the data of the TEAMS table, place commas between the values, and terminate every row with a question mark.

```
SELECT    *
FROM      TEAMS
INTO      OUTFILE 'C:/TEAMS.TXT'
          FIELDS TERMINATED BY ','
          LINES TERMINATED BY '?'
```

The file TEAMS.TXT looks as follows:

```
1,6,first?2,27,second?
```

Explanation: The data is written to the output file called TEAMS.TXT. Commas are placed between the different column values, and a question mark is placed after each row. Because of this, a row no longer starts on a new line. The alphanumeric literal used may consist of more than one letter or symbol.

In this and the following examples, we use very simple SELECT statements, but note that every SELECT statement is allowed.

If necessary, we also can place values in the output file between quotation marks or other symbols. We can do this by extending the FIELDS TERMINATED specification.

Example 18.3: Unload all the data of the TEAMS table, place commas between the values, terminate every row with a question mark, and place the alphanumeric values between double quotation marks.

```
SELECT   *
FROM     TEAMS
INTO     OUTFILE 'C:/TEAMS.TXT'
         FIELDS TERMINATED BY ','
            OPTIONALLY ENCLOSED BY '"'
         LINES TERMINATED BY '?'
```

The file TEAMS.TXT looks as follows:

```
1,6,"first"?2,27,"second"?
```

Explanation: Only the alphanumeric values are placed between double quotation marks now. If we want to place all the values between quotation marks, we must omit the word OPTIONALLY; see the following example.

Example 18.4: Unload all the data of the TEAMS table.

```
SELECT   *
FROM     TEAMS
INTO     OUTFILE 'C:/TEAMS.TXT'
         FIELDS TERMINATED BY ','
            ENCLOSED BY '"'
         LINES TERMINATED BY '?'
```

The file TEAMS.TXT looks as follows:

```
"1","6","first"?"2","27","second"?
```

If a column contains null values, they are represented in the output file with the code \N.

Example 18.5: Unload all the data of the TEAMS table.

```
SELECT    *, NULL
FROM      TEAMS
INTO      OUTFILE 'C:/TEAMS.TXT'
          FIELDS TERMINATED BY ','
             ENCLOSED BY '"'
          LINES TERMINATED BY '?'
```

The file TEAMS.TXT looks as follows:

```
"1","6","first",\N?"2","27","second",\N?
```

Instead of a backslash in front of the capital letter N, you may use another symbol.

Example 18.6: Unload all the data of the TEAMS table and present the null values with the code *N.

```
SELECT    *, NULL
FROM      TEAMS
INTO      OUTFILE 'C:/TEAMS.TXT'
          FIELDS TERMINATED BY ','
             ENCLOSED BY '"'
             ESCAPED BY '*'
          LINES TERMINATED BY '?'
```

The file TEAMS.TXT looks as follows:

```
"1","6","first",*N?"2","27","second",*N?
```

Table 5.1 contained several special symbols that may be included within an alphanumeric literal. These special symbols may also be used as symbols within an INTO FILE clause.

Example 18.7: Unload all the data of the TEAMS table, place commas between the values, terminate every row with a carriage return, and place the alphanumeric values between double quotation marks.

```
SELECT    *
FROM      TEAMS
INTO      OUTFILE 'C:/TEAMS.TXT'
          FIELDS TERMINATED BY ','
             OPTIONALLY ENCLOSED BY '"'
          LINES TERMINATED BY '\n'
```

The file TEAMS.TXT looks as follows:

```
1,6,"first"
2,27,"second"
```

The first example of this section did not include a FIELDS or LINES specification. MySQL interprets this as the following specification:

```
FIELDS TERMINATED BY '\t' ENCLOSED BY '' ESCAPE BY '\\'
LINES TERMINATED BY '\n'
```

Instead of using OUTFILE, you may also use DUMPFILE. All the rows are placed right after each other without any markings between the values and the rows; it becomes one long value.

Example 18.8: Unload all the data of the TEAMS table in a dumpfile.

```
SELECT    *
FROM      TEAMS
INTO      DUMPFILE 'C:/TEAMS.DUMP'
```

In a special form of the INTO FILE clause, the result is not written to a file, but is assigned to user variables. This works only if the SELECT statement returns just one row.

Example 18.9: Assign the data of team 1 to the user variables V1, V2, and V3. Next, show the values of these variables.

```
SELECT    *
FROM      TEAMS
WHERE     TEAMNO = 1
INTO      @V1, @V2, @V3

SELECT    @V1, @V2, @V3
```

The result is:

```
@V1  @V2  @V3
---  ---  -----
  1    6  first
```

18.3 Loading Data

The *LOAD statement* is the opposite of the SELECT statement with an INTO FILE clause.

DEFINITION

```
<load statement> ::=
   LOAD DATA [ LOW_PRIORITY ] [ CONCURRENT ] [ LOCAL ]
      INFILE '<file name>'
      [ REPLACE | IGNORE ]
      INTO TABLE <table specification>
      [ <fields specification> ]
      [ <lines specification> ]
      [ IGNORE <whole number> LINES ]
      [ { <column name> | <user variable> }
         [ , { <column name> | <user variable> } ]... ]
      [ <set statement> ]

<fields specification> ::=
   FIELDS [ TERMINATED BY <alphanumeric literal> ]
          [ [ OPTIONALLY ] ENCLOSED BY <alphanumeric literal> ]
          [ ESCAPED BY <alphanumeric literal> ]

<lines specification> ::=
   LINES [ TERMINATED BY <alphanumeric literal> ]
         [ STARTING BY <alphanumeric literal> ]
```

In all examples in this section, we assume that the TEAMS table is empty.

Example 18.10: Load the data of the file TEAMS.TXT, created in Example 18.2, in the TEAMS table.

```
LOAD DATA INFILE 'C:/TEAMS.TXT'
REPLACE
INTO TABLE TEAMS
FIELDS TERMINATED BY ','
LINES TERMINATED BY '?'
```

Explanation: After this statement, the TEAMS table is filled with the original data again.

In this example, a file is loaded that has been created with a SELECT statement. That is not a necessity; input files can also be created by hand or with other programs.

If the term REPLACE is specified and if there are rows in the table of which the value of the primary key or that of an unique index equals that of a row in the input file, the new data overwrites the existing data. When IGNORE is specified, the new data is ignored, and no error message is given. If neither term is specified and a value already appears, an error message is returned and loading is stopped.

If we include the specification IGNORE followed by a number, MySQL skips the first rows of the input file.

Example 18.11: Load the data from the file TEAMS.TXT, created in Example 18.2, in the TEAMS table, but skip the first row.

```
LOAD DATA INFILE 'C:/TEAMS.TXT'
REPLACE
INTO TABLE TEAMS
FIELDS TERMINATED BY ','
LINES TERMINATED BY '?'
IGNORE 1 LINES
```

By including column names, we can determine which value in the file must go to which column.

Example 18.12: Load the data from the file TEAMS.TXT, as created in Example 18.2, in the TEAMS table, but switch the columns PLAYERNO and TEAMNO. Next, show the contents of the TEAMS table.

```
LOAD DATA INFILE 'C:/TEAMS.TXT'
REPLACE
INTO TABLE TEAMS
FIELDS TERMINATED BY ','
LINES TERMINATED BY '?'
(PLAYERNO,TEAMNO,DIVISION)

SELECT * FROM TEAMS
```

The result is:

```
TEAMNO  PLAYERNO  DIVISION
------  --------  --------
     6         1  first
    27         2  second
```

Example 18.13: Load the data from the file TEAMS.TXT, created in Example 18.2, in the TEAMS table, and assign the value xxx to the DIVISION column. Next, show the contents of the TEAMS table.

```
LOAD DATA INFILE 'C:/TEAMS.TXT'
REPLACE
INTO TABLE TEAMS
FIELDS TERMINATED BY ','
LINES TERMINATED BY '?'
SET DIVISION='xxx'

SELECT * FROM TEAMS
```

The result is:

```
TEAMNO  PLAYERNO  DIVISION
------  --------  --------
     1         6  xxx
     2        27  xxx
```

Instead of using a literal, more complex expressions can be used in this special SET statement. Scalar functions, system variables, and calculations are all allowed. We can even use the value of a column.

Example 18.14: Load the data from the file TEAMS.TXT, created in Example 18.2, in the TEAMS table, and use the user variable DIV to fill the DIVISION. Next, show the contents of the TEAMS table.

```
LOAD DATA INFILE 'C:/TEAMS.TXT'
REPLACE
INTO TABLE TEAMS
FIELDS TERMINATED BY ','
LINES TERMINATED BY '?'
(TEAMNO,PLAYERNO,@DIV)
SET DIVISION=SUBSTRING(@DIV,1,1)

SELECT * FROM TEAMS
```

The result is:

```
TEAMNO  PLAYERNO  DIVISION
------  --------  --------
     1         6  f
     2        27  s
```

Explanation: This statement is processed as follows. Space is reserved in internal memory to keep one row with data. Because rows are added to the TEAMS table, MySQL knows that this row consists of three values and that the column names of that row are equal to TEAMNO, PLAYERNO, and DIVISION, successively. MySQL retrieves this data from the catalog, including the data types of the columns. If this space is reserved, the first row of the file is read. The first value of this row is assigned to the column TEAMNO of the temporary row, the second to the column PLAYERNO, and the third value to the user variable DIV, not to the DIVISION column. Next, the SET statement is processed. This means that the first symbol of the user variable DIV is determined, and that result is assigned to the DIVISION column of the temporary row. Only now is this temporary row stored in the TEAMS table, so we can continue with the next row.

By way of illustration, the following more complex specification is allowed:

```
(@A,PLAYERNO,@B)
SET TEAMNO=@A*@B, PLAYERNO=PLAYERNO,
    DIVISION=SUBSTRING(CURRENT_USER(),1,1)
```

As with UPDATE and DELETE statements, LOW_PRIORITY may be specified. Loading then is executed only if no other SQL users are reading the data with SELECT statements. Chapter 37, "Transactions and Multiuser Usage," returns to this topic.

If CONCURRENT is specified during the loading of a MyISAM table, the loading can happen concurrently with the processing of SELECT statements.

The specification LOCAL refers to the location of the input file. Does the file reside on the server on which the database server runs as well, or does it reside on the machine on which the program runs, the client? If LOCAL is specified, the input file should be on the client and is sent to the server. If LOCAL is not specified, MySQL assumes that the file is on the server in the designated directory.

Example 18.15: Load the data from the input file TEAMS2.TXT. This file has the following contents:

```
This is the beginning
/*/1,6,first
/*/2,27,second
This is the end
```

Next, show the contents of the TEAMS table.

```
LOAD DATA INFILE 'C:/TEAMS2.TXT'
REPLACE
INTO TABLE TEAMS
FIELDS TERMINATED BY ','
LINES TERMINATED BY '\r'
      STARTING BY '/*/'

SELECT * FROM TEAMS
```

The result is:

```
TEAMNO  PLAYERNO  DIVISION
------  --------  --------
     6         1  first
    27         2  second
```

Explanation: With the STARTING BY specification, we indicate which lines in the input file to include. In this example, all lines that begin with the code /*/ are included.

CHAPTER 19

Working with XML Documents

19.1 XML IN A NUTSHELL

Extensible Markup Language (XML) is the most popular language for exchanging data electronically. For example, if a company wants to send an electronic invoice to a customer, it can put the invoice data in an XML document and send it through the Internet. The web site of a travel agency also might communicate with that of an airline to reserve seats, which can be done using XML documents. Some ATM machines even communicate with computers in the main office using XML documents.

XML is not a programming language, such as Java, PHP, or C#. Nor is it a database language, such as SQL. It is a language in which data such as addresses, invoices, articles, and bills of materials can be recorded. The power of XML is that an XML document contains not only the data itself, but also the metadata. In a document, we record the value Inglewood and also describe that Inglewood is the name of a town.

The best way to explain what this language looks like is to show an example. Following is a simple example of an XML document that includes some data of the player with number 6:

```
<player>
   <number>6</number>
   <name>
      <lastname>Parmenter</lastname>
      <initials>R</initials>
   </name>
   <address>
      <street>Haseltine Lane</street>
      <houseno>80</houseno>
      <postcode>1234KK</postcode>
      <town>Stratford</town>
   </address>
</player>
```

This example clearly shows that data and metadata go hand in hand. For example, the number 6 is enclosed by the *tags* `<number>` and `</number>`. The tag `<number>` indicates the beginning, and `</number>` indicates the end. A start tag and end tag together form an *element,* so `<number>` and `</number>` together from the element number. This example clearly shows that XML is not a programming or database language.

An XML document has a hierarchic structure. In the previous example, the element `player` forms the top. The elements `number`, `name`, and `address` form the next level. The `name` element itself consists of two subelements: `lastname` and `initials`.

Each element may contain *attributes.* The previous example can also be structured as follows. Here the element number has been replaced by the attribute number:

```
<player number=6>
   <name>
      <lastname>Parmenter</lastname>
      <initials>R</initials>
   </name>
   <address>
      <street>Haseltine Lane</street>
      <houseno>80</houseno>
      <postcode>1234KK</postcode>
      <town>Stratford</town>
   </address>
</player>
```

Like SQL, XML is standardized. The World Wide Web Consortium (W3C) manages the XML standard. The first version of this standard appeared in 1998. Version 3, the most recent version, was published in 2004. Without a doubt, new versions will appear.

Storing XML documents in a MySQL database has always been possible. Each XML document can be seen as a long alphanumeric value and can be stored in a column with an alphanumeric data type, such as TEXT or LONGTEXT. Since

Version 5.1.5, MySQL also supports special scalar functions to query and update these stored XML documents in a smart way. These functions form the topic of this chapter.

For more information on XML, refer to the website of the W3C (www.w3c.org) and to [HARO04] and [BENZ03].

19.2 Storing XML Documents

As mentioned, storing XML documents has always been possible. Here we create a special version of the MATCHES table to register several XML documents. Figure 19.1 shows the three documents to store in this table.

Example 19.1: Create the XML_MATCHES table.

```
CREATE TABLE XML_MATCHES
      (MATCHNO       INTEGER NOT NULL PRIMARY KEY,
       MATCH_INFO    TEXT)
```

Explanation: The last column can be used to store XML documents.

Example 19.2: Add three rows to the new XML_MATCHES table.

```
INSERT INTO XML_MATCHES VALUES (1,
'<match number=1>Match info of 1
    <team>Team info of 1
       <number>1</number>
       <division>first</division>
    </team>
    <player>Player info of 6
       <number>6</number>
       <name>The name of 6
          <lastname>Parmenter</lastname>
          <initials>R</initials>
       </name>
       <address>The address of 6
          <street>Haseltine Lane</street>
          <houseno>80</houseno>
          <postcode>1234KK</postcode>
          <town>Stratford</town>
       </address>
    </player>
    <sets>Info about sets of 1
       <won>3</won>
       <lost>1</lost>
    </sets>
</match>')
```

```
INSERT INTO XML_MATCHES VALUES (9,
'<match number=9>Match info of 9
    <team>Team info of 2
       <number>2</number>
       <division>second</division>
    </team>
    <player>Player info of 27
       <number>27</number>
       <name>The name of 27
          <lastname>Collins</lastname>
          <initials>DD</initials>
       </name>
       <address>The address of 27
          <street>Long Drive</street>
          <houseno>804</houseno>
          <postcode>8457DK</postcode>
          <town>Eltham</town>
       </address>
       <phones>Phone numbers of 27
          <number>1234567</number>
          <number>3468346</number>
          <number>6236984</number>
          <number>6587437</number>
       </phones>
    </player>
    <sets>Info about sets of 9
       <won>3</won>
       <lost>2</lost>
    </sets>
 </match>')

INSERT INTO XML_MATCHES VALUES (12,
'<match number=12>Match info of 12
    <team>Team info of 2
       <number>2</number>
       <division>second</division>
    </team>
    <player>Player info of 8
       <number>8</number>
       <name>The name of 8
          <lastname>Newcastle</lastname>
          <initials>B</initials>
       </name>
```

```
      <address>The first address van 8
         <street>Station Road</street>
         <houseno>4</houseno>
         <postcode>6584RO</postcode>
         <town>Inglewood</town>
      </address>
      <address>The second address of 8
         <street>Trolley Lane</street>
         <houseno>14</houseno>
         <postcode>2728YG</postcode>
         <town>Douglas</town>
      </address>
   </player>
   <sets>Info about sets of 12
      <won>1</won>
      <lost>3</lost>
   </sets>
</match>')
```

Explanation: This data deviates somewhat from the data in the original database.

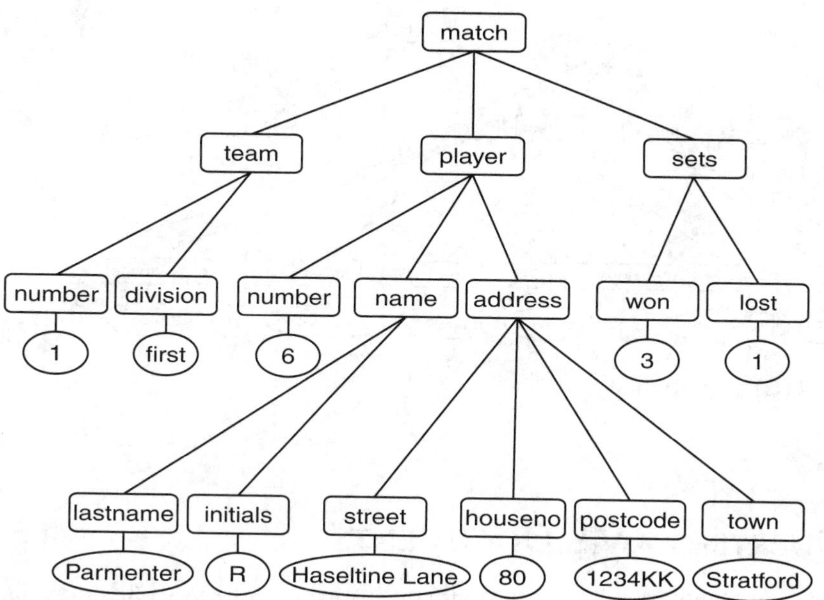

FIGURE 19.1(A) Graphic representation of the three XML documents

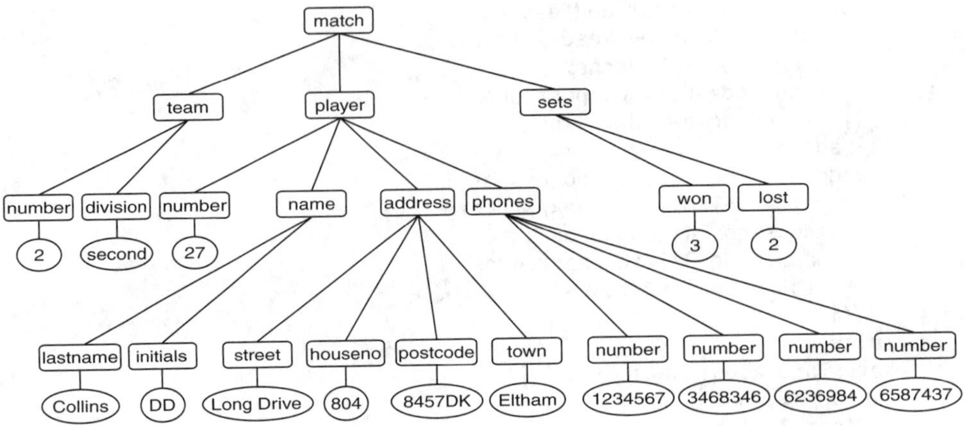

FIGURE 19.1(B) continued

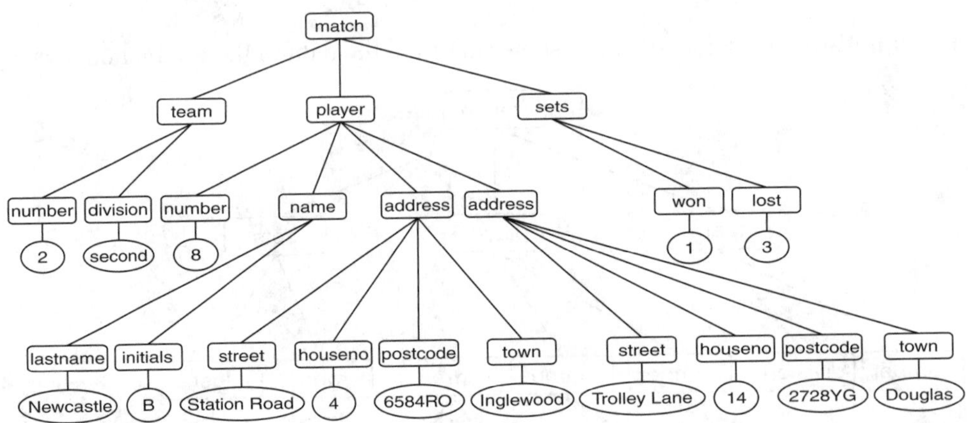

FIGURE 19.1(C) continued

19.3 Querying XML Documents

Several additional standards have been defined for working with XML documents. One of these standards is called *XPath* (XML Path Language). XPath is a language specially developed for selecting element values from a certain XML document, like a miniature query language. MySQL uses this language to query XML documents stored in tables.

We can use the EXTRACTVALUE function to extract values from an XML document. The first parameter of this function refers to a column or expression that has an XML document as a value. The second parameter contains the query and, thus, an XPath expression.

This chapter uses examples to give you an idea of what is possible with this scalar function and XPath. If we described all the features, this chapter would turn into a complete book by itself. Hopefully, this chapter will help get you started. See [KAY04] for an extensive description of XPath.

Example 19.3: Get the match number and division of the team for each match.

```
SELECT   MATCHNO,
         EXTRACTVALUE(MATCH_INFO, '/match/team/division')
                            AS DIVISION
FROM     XML_MATCHES
```

The result is:

```
MATCHNO  DIVISION
-------  --------
      1  first
      9  second
     12  second
```

Explanation: The specification `/match/team/division` is an XPath expression. This should be read as follows: Get the value of the `division` element that belongs hierarchically to the `team` element, which belongs hierarchically to the `match` element. Note that the `match` element must be the top element of the XML document. The expression `/team` would mean: Get the value of the top element `/team`. Because `team` is not a top element, nothing would be found.

Example 19.4: For each match of which the number of sets won is equal to 3, get the match number and the last name of the player concerned.

```
SELECT   MATCHNO,
         EXTRACTVALUE(MATCH_INFO,
         '/match/player/name/lastname')
         AS PLAYER
FROM     XML_MATCHES
WHERE    EXTRACTVALUE(MATCH_INFO,
         '/match/sets/won') = 3
```

The result is:

```
MATCHNO  PLAYER
-------  ---------
      1  Parmenter
      9  Collins
```

Explanation: As with every scalar function, we may use EXTRACTVALUE in other clauses than the SELECT clause. The XPath expression /match/player/name/lastname returns the value of the lastname element that belongs to the name element, which belongs to the player element, which belongs hierarchically to the match element.

If the element that an XPath expression returns has no value, that expression returns an alphanumeric value without characters (or an empty string) as result.

Example 19.5: From the following XML document, get the value of the team element.

```
SELECT    EXTRACTVALUE('
             <team>
                <number>2</number>
                <division>second</division>
             </team>'
          ,'/team') = '' AS TEAM
```

The result is:

```
TEAM
----
   0
```

Explanation: The result of the expression in the SELECT clause is 0. This means that the value of the EXTRACTVALUE function is indeed an empty string. Because all the elements in the XML_MATCHES table have a value, we do not use XML_MATCHES in this example. This example also shows that the first parameter of the EXTRACTVALUE function does not have to be a column. It may be any alphanumeric value, as long as its value is a XML document.

If the result of an XPath expression consists of multiple values, they are glued together and separated by spaces.

Example 19.6: Get all the phone numbers of player 27 who belongs to match 9.

```
SELECT    MATCHNO, EXTRACTVALUE(MATCH_INFO,
          '/match/player/phones/number')
          AS PHONES
FROM      XML_MATCHES
WHERE     MATCHNO = 9
```

The result is:

```
MATCHNO  PHONES
-------  ------------------------------
      9  1234567 3468346 6236984 6587437
```

All the previous examples retrieved only values of elements that did not contain any subelements. You may use EXTRACTVALUE to use the value of one of the higher elements.

Example 19.7: Get the values of the player elements.

```
SELECT   MATCHNO, EXTRACTVALUE(MATCH_INFO,
         '/match/player')
         AS PLAYERS
FROM     XML_MATCHES
```

The result is:

```
MATCHNO  PLAYERS
-------  ----------------
      1  Player info of 6




      9  Player info of 27




     12  Player info of 8



```

Explanation: This result demands an explanation—because why are all those empty lines included? MySQL generates many spaces. They become more visible when they are replaced by another symbol:

```
SELECT   REPLACE(EXTRACTVALUE(MATCH_INFO,
         '/match/player'), ' ', '#')
         AS PLAYER_INFO
FROM     XML_MATCHES
```

The result is:

```
PLAYER INFO
-----------------
Player info of 6
########
########
########
####
Player info of 27
########
########
########
########
####
Player info of 8
########
########
########
########
####
```

The value of an element player is the combination of a piece of text (`Player info of ...`) and a number of subelements. The first match has three subelements (`number`, `name`, and `address`), the second match has four elements (`number`, `name`, `address`, and `phones`), and the third match has four elements (`number`, `name`, and two `addresses`). For each match, the text is displayed, followed by an empty line for each subelement, followed by an additional empty line.

XPath enables you to formulate powerful queries. For example, the asterisk can specify a random element. The XPath expression in Example 19.4 can also be written as follows: `/*/*/*/lastname`.

Example 19.8: Get the match number, the team number, and the player number of each match.

```
SELECT    MATCHNO, EXTRACTVALUE(MATCH_INFO,
          '/match/*/number')
          AS NUMBERS
FROM      XML_MATCHES
```

The result is:

```
MATCHNO  NUMBERS
-------  -------
      1  1 6
      9  2 27
     12  2 8
```

Explanation: The XPath expression `/match/*/number` returns the value of each `number` element that belongs to any element that subsequently belongs to the `match` element. It does not matter to XPath whether they are different kinds of numbers. In fact, XPath treats everything as alphanumeric values.

This expression `/match/*/*/number` would have returned all the phone numbers. The reason is that XPath returns the value of each `number` element that belongs to any element that subsequently belongs to any element and that belongs to the `match` element.

If we place two slashes (//) right behind each other, it means that it does not matter how many elements are in between hierarchically. Thus, the expression `/match//number` is equivalent to the expressions `/match/*/number`, plus `/match/*/*/number`, plus `/match/*/*/*/number`, etc.

Example 19.9: Get the match number, team number, player number, and phone numbers for each match.

```
SELECT    MATCHNO, EXTRACTVALUE(MATCH_INFO,
          '/match//number')
          AS NUMBERS
FROM      XML_MATCHES
```

The result is:

```
MATCHNO  NUMBERS
-------  -----------------------------------
      1  1 6
      9  2 27 1234567 3468346 6236984 6587437
     12  2 8
```

This statement can still be simplified because we know that all stored documents have `match` as the top element.

```
SELECT    MATCHNO,
          EXTRACTVALUE(MATCH_INFO, '//number')
          AS NUMBERS
FROM      XML_MATCHES
```

Example 19.10: For match 1, get all the data from the XML document.

```
SELECT    EXTRACTVALUE(MATCH_INFO, '/match//*')
          AS EVERYTHING
FROM      XML_MATCHES
WHERE     MATCHNO = 1
```

The result is:

```
EVERYTHING
------------------------
Team info of 1
   1
   first
Player info of 6
   6
   The name of 6
      Parmenter
      R
   The address of 6
      Haseltine Lane
      80
      1234KK
      Stratford
Info about sets of 1
   3
   1
```

Explanation: The specification //* actually refers to the values of all elements that belong directly or indirectly to the match element. The expression /match/player//* would return all the information on players.

You can retrieve the values of multiple elements with the | symbol.

Example 19.11: For each match, get the match number, followed by the town of the player concerned and the number of sets won.

```
SELECT   MATCHNO, EXTRACTVALUE(MATCH_INFO,
         '//town|//won')
         AS TOWN_WON
FROM     XML_MATCHES
```

The result is:

```
MATCHNO  TOWN_WON
-------  -------------------
      1  Stratford 3
      9  Eltham 3
     12  Inglewood Douglas 1
```

Explanation: We could have obtained the same result with a concatenation of two EXTRACTVALUE functions (such as the following), but the previous formulation is more efficient.

```
SELECT   MATCHNO,
         CONCAT(EXTRACTVALUE(MATCH_INFO, '//town'),
                ' ',
                EXTRACTVALUE(MATCH_INFO, '//won'))
         AS TOWN_WON
FROM     XML_MATCHES
```

You also can retrieve the value of an attribute. In the XML_MATCHES table, the `match` element has an attribute.

Example 19.12: For each match, get the match number and the number that occurs in the XML document concerned.

```
SELECT   MATCHNO, EXTRACTVALUE(MATCH_INFO,
         '/match/@number')
         AS XML_MATCHNO
FROM     XML_MATCHES
```

The result is:

```
MATCHNO  XML_MATCHNO
-------  -----------
      1            1
      9            9
     12           12
```

Explanation: By specifying the `@` symbol in front of the attribute number, we tell XPath that we are looking for an attribute.

In an XPath expression, you may include simple calculations as well.

Example 19.13: For each match, get the match number, followed by the number of sets won plus 10.

```
SELECT   MATCHNO, EXTRACTVALUE(MATCH_INFO,
         '/match/sets/won+10')
         AS WON_PLUS_10
FROM     XML_MATCHES
```

The result is:

```
MATCHNO  WON_PLUS_10
-------  -----------
      1           13
      9           13
     12           11
```

19.4 Querying Using Positions

On a level in a hierarchy, multiple instances of an element can occur. For example, player 8 belonging to match 12 has two addresses, and player 27 has four phone numbers at match 9. If we are interested in only one, we can specify a sequence number between square brackets in an XPath expression.

Example 19.14: For each match, get the match number and the town of the first address of the player who played the match.

```
SELECT   MATCHNO, EXTRACTVALUE(MATCH_INFO,
         '/match/player/address[1]/town')
         AS TOWN
FROM     XML_MATCHES
```

The result is:

```
MATCHNO  TOWN
-------  ---------
      1  Stratford
      9  Eltham
     12  Inglewood
```

Explanation: Because we specified `address[1]`, only the first address is returned. If we had specified `address[2]`, the result would have been as follows:

```
MATCHNO  TOWN
-------  ----------
      1
      9
     12  Douglas
```

The asterisk and the square brackets may also be combined.

Example 19.15: For each match, get the match number and the value of the first element.

```
SELECT   MATCHNO, EXTRACTVALUE(MATCH_INFO,
         '/match/player/*[1]')
         AS A_VALUE
FROM     XML_MATCHES
```

The result is:

```
MATCHNO  A_VALUE
-------  -------
      1        6
      9       27
     12        8
```

Explanation: The `player` element has four subelements: `number`, `name`, `address`, and `phones`. In all three XML documents, the `number` element is specified first every time. If this had not been the case, this statement could have given values of different elements.

For example, the expression `/match/player/address/*[3]` gives the third element (the postcode) of the address of the player of a match. The expression `/match/player/*[2]/*[2]` returns the second element (the initials) of the second element (the name) of the player of a match.

With the special XPath function `last()`, we can retrieve the last subelement.

Example 19.16: For each match, get the last phone number of the relevant player.

```
SELECT   MATCHNO, EXTRACTVALUE(MATCH_INFO,
         '/match/player/phones/number[last()]')
         AS LAST
FROM     XML_MATCHES
```

The result is:

```
MATCHNO  LAST
-------  -------
      1
      9  6587437
     12
```

Explanation: The players belonging to matches 1 and 12 do not have a phone number. The number `6587437` is indeed the last number of the player belonging to match 9. The expression `/match/player/phones/number[last()-1]` returns the penultimate phone number.

19.5 The Extended Notation of XPath

The examples in the previous sections used the so-called shortened notation form (abbreviated syntax) of XPath. An extended notation (expanded syntax) also exists. For example, the expression `/match/team/number` is equivalent to `/child::match/child::team/child::number`. And the expression `/match//number` is equivalent to `/child::match/descendant-or-self::node()/child::number`. With this extended notation, we can easily browse an XML document. From an element, we can step up, down, or aside in the hierarchy to another element. Here are a few examples of this notation.

Example 19.17: For each match, get the match number and team number of the corresponding team.

```
SELECT    MATCHNO, EXTRACTVALUE(MATCH_INFO,
          '/child::match/child::team/child::number ')
          AS NUMBERS
FROM      XML_MATCHES
```

The result is:

```
MATCHNO  NUMBERS
-------  -------
      1        1
      9        2
     12        2
```

Example 19.18: For each match, get all address information for the corresponding player.

```
SELECT    EXTRACTVALUE(MATCH_INFO,
          '/match/player/address/descendant::* ')
          AS ADDRESS_INFO
FROM      XML_MATCHES
```

The result is:

```
ADDRESS INFO
-------------------------------------------------------------

Haseltine Lane 80 1234KK Stratford
Long Drive 804 8457DK Eltham
Station Road 4 6584RO Inglewood Trolley Lane 14 2728YG Douglas
```

Explanation: `descendant` returns not only the subelements, but also the sub-subelements and the sub-sub-subelements, and so on.

In the previous example, all subelements of address had only a piece of text as the value. In that case, all words of a value are shown. If the subelements contain subelements themselves, the EXTRACTVALUE function returns the entire hierarchy.

Example 19.19: For each match, get all the data of the player concerned.

```
SELECT   EXTRACTVALUE(MATCH_INFO,
         '/match/player/descendant::* ')
         AS PLAYER_INFO
FROM     XML_MATCHES
```

The result is:

```
PLAYER INFO
-------------------------------------
6 The name of 6
           Parmenter
           R
        The address of 6
           Haseltine Lane
           80
           1234KK
           Stratford

27 The name of 27
           Collins
           DD
        The address of 27
           Long Drive
           804
           8457DK
           Eltham
        Phone numbers of 27
           1234567
           3468346
           6236984
           6587437

8 The name of 8
           Newcastle
           B
        The first address of 8
           Station Road
           4
           6584RO
           Inglewood
        The second address of 8
           Trolley Lane
           14
           2728YG
           Douglas
```

We can also retrieve the value of the parent and the ancestor of a certain element. The former gives the value of the element that is above, and the latter gives the top of the hierarchy.

Example 19.20: For each match, get all the data of the player concerned.

```
SELECT    EXTRACTVALUE(MATCH_INFO,
          '/match/player/descendant::* ')
          AS PLAYER_INFO
FROM      XML_MATCHES
```

19.6 XPath Expressions with Conditions

Conditions can be added to an XPath expression.

Example 19.21: For each match, get the player number, but only if that number is equal to 8.

```
SELECT    MATCHNO, EXTRACTVALUE(MATCH_INFO,
          '/match/player[number=8]')
          AS PLAYER8
FROM      XML_MATCHES
```

The result is:

```
MATCHNO  PLAYER8
-------  ----------------
      1
      9
     12  Player info of 8
```

Explanation: If a row does not satisfy the condition, the result is an empty string. The row itself will appear in the result because the condition is not in the WHERE clause, but in the SELECT clause. If we move the condition to the WHERE clause, we can use the EXTRACTVALUE function to select rows.

Example 19.22: Get only those matches for which the player number is equal to 8.

```
SELECT    MATCHNO, EXTRACTVALUE(MATCH_INFO,
          '/match/player')
          AS PLAYER8
FROM      XML_MATCHES
WHERE     EXTRACTVALUE(MATCH_INFO,
          '/match/player[number=8]') <> ''
```

The result is:

```
MATCHNO  PLAYER8
-------  ----------------
     12  Player info of 8
```

In conditions, only the comparison operators = and != (unequal to) can be used, plus the logical operators and and or.

Example 19.23: Get only those matches in which the number of sets won is equal to 3 and the number of sets lost is equal to 1.

```
SELECT   MATCHNO, EXTRACTVALUE(MATCH_INFO,
         '/match/sets')
         AS THREE_AND_ONE
FROM     XML_MATCHES
WHERE    EXTRACTVALUE(MATCH_INFO,
         '/match/sets[won=3 and lost=1]') <>''
```

The result is:

```
MATCHNO  THREE_AND_ONE
-------  --------------------
      1  Info about sets of 1
```

19.7 CHANGING XML DOCUMENTS

To replace an entire XML document by another, use a normal UPDATE statement. The new XML document is included in the SET clause. However, if we want to change a part of an XML document, such as the value of one element, we have to use the special function UPDATEXML.

UPDATEXML has three parameters. The first parameter identifies the document that must be changed. The second parameter contains an XPath expression with which we indicate which elements need to be changed. The third parameter is the new piece of the XML document that must be inserted.

Example 19.24: For match 1, change the number of sets lost to 2. Show the result next.

```
UPDATE   XML_MATCHES
SET      MATCH_INFO =
         UPDATEXML(MATCH_INFO,
         '/match/sets/lost',
         '<lost>2</lost>')
WHERE    MATCHNO = 1

SELECT   EXTRACTVALUE(MATCH_INFO,
         '/match/sets/lost') AS LOST
FROM     XML_MATCHES
WHERE    MATCHNO = 1
```

The result is:

```
LOST
----
   2
```

Example 19.25: For match 3, change the address to Jolly Lane 30, Douglas, 5383GH. Show the result next.

```
UPDATE   XML_MATCHES
SET      MATCH_INFO =
         UPDATEXML(MATCH_INFO,
         '/match/player/address',
         '<address>The new address of 8
             <street>Jolly Lane</street>
             <houseno>30</houseno>
             <postcode>5383GH</postcode>
             <town>Douglas</town>
          </address>')
WHERE    MATCHNO = 1

SELECT   EXTRACTVALUE(MATCH_INFO,
         '/match/player/address/*') AS NEW_ADDRESS
FROM     XML_MATCHES
WHERE    MATCHNO = 1
```

The result is:

```
NEW_ADDRESS
----------------------------
Jolly Lane 30 5383GH Douglas
```

Part III

Creating Database Objects

This third part describes how *database objects* are created. *Database object* is the generic term for, among other things, tables, keys, views, and indexes. These are the objects that we must create and that together form a database.

Chapter 20, "Creating Tables," describes all the statements for creating tables and details the properties of the different data types.

When tables are created, it is possible to specify integrity constraints. Chapter 21, "Specifying Integrity Constraints," explains these constraints and also reviews primary keys, alternate keys, foreign keys, and check integrity constraints, along with some other topics.

Chapter 22, "Character Sets and Collations," explains the terms *character set* and *collation,* and illustrates how MySQL supports them.

This book has not yet addressed the special data types ENUM and SET. By using these data types, it becomes possible to store multiple values in a column of a row. Chapter 23, "The ENUM and SET Types," focuses completely on creating and changing columns with these data types.

Chapter 24, "Changing and Dropping Tables," concentrates entirely on the SQL statements and the features for changing and deleting existing tables. Changes might include adding new columns, updating data types, and deleting columns.

Chapter 25, "Using Indexes," describes how to use indexes to reduce the required processing time of certain SQL statements. This chapter gives an overview of how indexes work internally and gives guidelines on which columns to index.

Chapter 26, "Views," deals with views, or virtual tables. With views, we define a "layer" on top of the tables so that the users can see the tables in a form that is most suitable for them.

Chapter 27, "Creating Databases," discusses creating, updating, and deleting entire databases.

Chapter 28, "Users and Data Security," handles data security. We explain which SQL statements to use to create new users (with passwords) and discuss how to authorize these users to perform certain statements against certain data.

CHAPTER 20

Creating Tables

20.1 Introduction

This chapter describes the statements for creating, updating, and deleting tables. We take the view that the user knows what data must be stored and what the structure of the data is—that is, what tables are to be created and what the appropriate columns are. In other words, the user has a ready-to-use database design at his or her disposal.

20.2 Creating New Tables

You can use the *CREATE TABLE statement* to construct new tables to store rows of data. The definition of this statement is complex and extensive. For that reason, we explain the statement's features step by step and build up the definition slowly. The following sections and chapters explain the concepts of column definition, table integrity constraint, column integrity constraint, data type, and index definition. First, we focus on the core of the CREATE TABLE statement.

DEFINITION

```
<create table statement> ::=
   CREATE [ TEMPORARY ] TABLE [ IF NOT EXISTS ]
      <table specification> <table structure>

<table specification> ::= [ <database name> . ] <table name>

<table structure> ::= <table schema>

<table schema> ::=
   ( <table element> [ , <table element> ]... )

<table element> ::=
   <column definition>           |
   <table integrity constraint>  |
   <index definition>

<column definition> ::=
   <column name> <data type> [ <null specification> ]
      [ <column integrity constraint> ]

<null specification> ::= [ NOT ] NULL

<column integrity constraint> ::=
   PRIMARY KEY                  |
   UNIQUE [ KEY ]               |
   <check integrity constraint>

<table integrity constraint> ::=
   <primary key>                |
   <alternate key>              |
   <foreign key>                |
   <check integrity constraint>
```

We begin with a simple example.

Example 20.1: Show the statement to create the PLAYERS table in the tennis club database.

```
CREATE   TABLE PLAYERS
        (PLAYERNO      INTEGER NOT NULL PRIMARY KEY,
         NAME          CHAR(15) NOT NULL,
         INITIALS      CHAR(3) NOT NULL,
         BIRTH_DATE    DATE NULL,
         SEX           CHAR(1) NOT NULL,
         JOINED        SMALLINT NOT NULL,
         STREET        VARCHAR(30) NOT NULL,
         HOUSENO       CHAR(4) NULL,
         POSTCODE      CHAR(6) NULL,
         TOWN          VARCHAR(30) NOT NULL,
         PHONENO       CHAR(13) NULL,
         LEAGUENO      CHAR(4) UNIQUE)
```

We explain this statement step by step. The name of this table is PLAYERS. The table is created in the current database. Two tables belonging to the same database cannot have the same name.

The *table schema* of a table consists of one or more *table elements*. These elements determine how the table looks and what data we can store in it. Table elements include, for example, column definitions and integrity constraints, such as primary and foreign keys. Chapter 21, "Specifying Integrity Constraints," discusses these concepts. In this chapter, we concentrate primarily on column definitions and primary keys.

A *column definition* contains a column name, a data type, possibly a null specification, and a column integrity constraint. It is not allowed to have duplicate column names in one table. However, two different tables may have similar column names, such as the columns with the name PLAYERNO that appear in all tables.

You must specify a data type for a column to indicate what kind of values can be entered in a column. In other words, the data type of a column restricts the type of values that can be entered. Therefore, it is important to choose a suitable data type. Section 5.2 describes the data types of literals in detail. The next section discusses all data types and their respective qualities as they appear in a `CREATE TABLE` statement.

For every column, you can include a *null specification* (see Section 1.3.2). Again, we emphasize that MySQL supports the *null value* as a possible value for a column in a row. The null value can be compared to "value unknown" or "value not present" and should not be confused with the number zero or a set of spaces. In a `CREATE TABLE` statement, you can specify `NOT NULL` after the data type of a column. This indicates which columns *cannot* contain null values. In other words, every `NOT NULL` column must contain a value in every row. If only `NULL` is specified, null values are allowed. Not including a null specification is equal to specifying `NULL`.

A column definition may end with a column integrity constraint. This could be a primary key, for example. Specifying the term `PRIMARY KEY` after a column makes this column the primary key of the table. In the previous example, PLAYERNO is the primary key. This specification can appear only within one column definition of a table. After this, MySQL guarantees that the column concerned does not contain duplicate values. If `PRIMARY KEY` is specified, the column can no longer contain null values; it is as if the null specification `NOT NULL` has been included implicitly.

Another column integrity constraint is `UNIQUE`. After this specification, MySQL enforces that this column must not contain duplicate values. We can specify `UNIQUE` for multiple column definitions belonging to the same table. A difference with `PRIMARY KEY` is that `UNIQUE` columns can contain null values; that is why we can define the LEAGUENO column as `UNIQUE`.

Section 21.6 discusses the check integrity constraint.

Imagine that a new table is built in the current database. If we want to create a table in another database, we must specify a database name in front of the table name.

Example 20.2: Create the PENALTIES table in the database called TEST.

```
CREATE   TABLE TEST.PENALTIES
        (PAYMENTNO        INTEGER NOT NULL PRIMARY KEY,
         PLAYERNO         INTEGER NOT NULL,
         PAYMENT_DATE     DATE NOT NULL,
         AMOUNT           DECIMAL(7,2) NOT NULL)
```

Explanation: However, the TEST database should exist (see Section 4.4 on creating databases). After this statement, the TEST database is not automatically the current database; the current database remains unchanged.

Exercise 20.1: Do you have to specify a data type for each column?

Exercise 20.2: What should be defined first in a column definition, the null specification or the data type?

20.3 Data Types of Columns

Chapter 5, "SELECT Statement: Common Elements," extensively discusses the concept of data type. In that chapter, we showed how literals and expressions can have different data types. In this section, we explain how these data types within CREATE TABLE statements must be defined. We also discuss the properties and limitations of each data type. The definition of *data type* follows:

DEFINITION

```
<data type> ::=
   <numeric data type> [ <numeric data type option>... ]         |
   <alphanumeric data type> [ <alphanumeric data type option>.. ] |
   <temporal data type>                                           |
   <blob data type>                                               |
   <geometric data type>                                          |
   <complex data type>
```

continues

```
<numeric data type> ::=
   <integer data type> |
   <decimal data type> |
   <float data type>   |
   <bit data type>

<integer data type> ::=
   TINYINT   [ ( <presentation width> ) ] |
   INT1      [ ( <presentation width> ) ] |
   BOOLEAN                                |
   SMALLINT  [ ( <presentation width> ) ] |
   INT2      [ ( <presentation width> ) ] |
   MEDIUMINT [ ( <presentation width> ) ] |
   INT3      [ ( <presentation width> ) ] |
   MIDDLEINT [ ( <presentation width> ) ] |
   INT       [ ( <presentation width> ) ] |
   INTEGER   [ ( <presentation width> ) ] |
   INT4      [ ( <presentation width> ) ] |
   BIGINT    [ ( <presentation width> ) ] |
   INT8      [ ( <presentation width> ) ]

<decimal data type> ::=
   DEC     [ ( <precision> [ , <scale> ] ) ] |
   DECIMAL [ ( <precision> [ , <scale> ] ) ] |
   NUMERIC [ ( <precision> [ , <scale> ] ) ] |
   FIXED   [ ( <precision> [ , <scale> ] ) ]

<float data type> ::=
   FLOAT [ ( <length> ) | ( <presentation width> , <scale> ) ] |
   FLOAT4 [ ( <presentation width> , <scale>) ]                |
   REAL [ ( <presentation width> , <scale>) ]                  |
   DOUBLE [ PRECISION ] [ ( <presentation width> , <scale>) ]

<bit data type> ::=
   BIT [ ( <length> ) ]

<alphanumeric data type> ::=
   [ NATIONAL ] CHAR [ ( <length> ) ]                 |
   [ NATIONAL ] CHARACTER [ ( <length> ) ]            |
   NCHAR [ ( <length> ) ]                             |
   [ NATIONAL ] VARCHAR ( <length> )                  |
   [ NATIONAL ] CHAR VARYING ( <length> )             |
   [ NATIONAL ] CHARACTER VARYING ( <length> )        |
   NCHAR VARYING ( <length> )                         |
   TINYTEXT                                           |
   TEXT ( <length> )                                  |
   MEDIUM TEXT                                        |
   LONG VARCHAR                                       |
   LONGTEXT
```

continues

```
<temporal data type> ::=
   DATE                          |
   DATETIME                      |
   TIME                          |
   TIMESTAMP                     |
   YEAR [ ( 2 ) | ( 4 ) ]

<blob data type> ::=
   BINARY    [ ( <length> ) ] |
   VARBINARY ( <length> )     |
   TINYBLOB                   |
   BLOB ( <length> )          |
   MEDIUMBLOB                 |
   LONG VARBINARY             |
   LONGBLOB

<geometric data type> ::=
   GEOMETRY           |
   GEOMETRYCOLLECTION |
   LINESTRING         |
   MULTILIMESTRING    |
   MULTIPOINT         |
   MULTIPOLYGON       |
   POINT              |
   POLYGON

<complex data type> ::=
   ENUM ( <alphanumeric expression list> ) |
   SET ( <alphanumeric expression list> )

<numeric data type option> ::=
   UNSIGNED              |
   ZEROFILL              |
   AUTO_INCREMENT        |
   SERIAL DEFAULT VALUE

<alphanumeric data type option> ::=
   CHARACTER SET <name> |
   COLLATE <name>

<presentation width>      ;
<precision>               ;
<scale>                   ;
<length>                  ::= <whole number>
```

20.3.1 The Integer Data Types

Columns with an integer data type can store whole numbers or integers. For example, all primary keys in the tables of the sample database are integers and, for that reason, have an integer data type.

MySQL supports various integer data types. The differences between the data types stem from their different sizes. Table 20.1 shows which integer data types are supported and their respective ranges. For example, columns with the data type `INTEGER` can store values that are less than or equal to `2.147.483.647`. After that, the column is "full."

TABLE 20.1 Ranges of Different Integer Data Types

Integer Literal	Range
TINYINT	-2^7 up to and including $+2^7-1$, or –128 up to and including 127
SMALLINT	-2^{15} up to and including $+2^{15}-1$, or –32,768 up to and including 32,767
MEDIUMINT	-2^{23} up to and including $+2^{23}-1$, or –8,388,608 up to and including 8,388,607
INTEGER	-2^{31} up to and including $+2^{31}-1$ or –2,147,483,648 up to and including 2,147,483,647
BIGINT	-2^{63} up to and including $+2^{63}-1$, or –9,223,372,036,854,775,808 up to and including 9,223,372,036,854,775,807

Every data type also has a synonym; see Table 20.2. We recommend that you use the names from Table 20.1 because most other SQL products support them.

TABLE 20.2 Synonyms for the Names of Integer Data Types

Original Data Type	Synonyms
TINYINT	INT1
SMALLINT	INT2
MEDIUMINT	INT3, MIDDLEINT
INTEGER	INT, INT4
BIGINT	INT8

For each integer data type, you may specify a display width. However, the width does not indicate how big or wide the values that are stored can be. Instead, applications and tools can use the width to display the values in a certain way. Imagine that the PLAYERS column has a width of four positions. Applications can then decide to always reserve at least four positions for each value.

Example 20.3: Create a table with one integer data type and add a row.

```
CREATE TABLE WIDTH (C4 INTEGER(4))

INSERT INTO WIDTH VALUES (1)
```

Next, when we retrieve the contents of this table with the statement `SELECT * FROM WIDTH`, we can see that the value `1` has been moved to the right and that room has been made for four digits:

```
C4
----
   1
```

If the value is too large for the width—for example, if we store the number `10,000` in the WIDTH table—most applications will reserve more positions. The specified width is seen as only the minimal width. So the width has to do with the display of integers, not with storage.

The data type `BOOLEAN` is equal to `TINYINT(1)`. Up to Version 5.0.2, the same applied to the `BIT` data type. From Version 5.0.3 onward, `BIT` is no longer a numeric data type, but a separate data type.

20.3.2 The Decimal Data Types

For the storage of nonwhole numbers, MySQL has several decimal data types. This data type can be used to store amounts and measurement data, for example. For this data type you can specify how many digits you can have in front of and after the decimal point. For example, in `DECIMAL(12,4)`, the first number (`12`) represents the *precision* and the second number (`4`) represents the *scale*. This means that columns with this data type can have a maximum of eight digits in front of the decimal point (scale minus precision) and four after it (the precision), or the range of this data type is –99,999,999.9999 up to and including 99,999,999.9999. The scale of a decimal data type must always be equal to or smaller than the precision.

If the precision is specified and the scale is not, the scale is equal to `0`. If neither is specified, the precision is equal to `10`, and the scale is equal to `0`. The precision is at least equal to `1` but never more than `30`. Note that when the specified precision is equal to `0`, MySQL thinks that no precision has been specified; therefore, it becomes equal to `10`.

The name `DECIMAL` may be abbreviated to `DEC`. The names `NUMERIC` and `FIXED` can be used as synonyms for `DECIMAL`.

20.3.3 The Float Data Types

The float data type is used to store very big or very small numbers. This could be numbers consisting of, for example, 30, 100, or even more digits in front of the decimal point, or it could be numbers with many digits after the decimal point. Consider numbers in which the number of digits after the decimal point is infinite, such as the well-known number pi and the fraction [1/3]. However, because a restricted amount of storage space is available for a float value, the real numbers are not stored. If a number is very big or very small, an approximation of that number is stored. This is why they are sometimes called *estimated* values.

In columns with a decimal data type, the decimal point has the same position in every value. This does not apply to the float data type; in every value, the decimal point can be somewhere else. In other words, the decimal point "floats around." This is why we call it a floating decimal point.

MySQL has two float data types: *single precision* and *double precision*. They differ in the amount of storage space that is reserved for a value. Because of this, they differ in range. The range of the single-precision float data type is between –3.402823466E38 and –1.175494351E-38, and between 1.175494351E-38 and 3.402823466E38. The range of the double precision is bigger: from –1.7976931348623157E308 to –2.2250738585072014E-308, and from 2.2250738585072014E-308 to 1.7976931348623157E308.

The length that can be specified in a float data type determines the type of the float data type. It is single precision if the length is between 0 and 24, and double precision if the length is between 25 and 53.

Example 20.4: Create a new table consisting of two columns; one has a single-precision data type. Store several float values in it and show the contents of this table next.

```
CREATE TABLE MEASUREMENTS
      (NR INTEGER, MEASUREMENT_VALUE FLOAT(1))

INSERT INTO MEASUREMENTS VALUES
   (1, 99.99),
   (2, 99999.99),
   (3, 99999999.99),
   (4, 99999999999.99),
   (5, 99999999999999.99),
   (6, 0.999999),
   (7, 0.9999999),
   (8, 99999999.9999),
   (9, (1.0/3))

SELECT * FROM MEASUREMENTS
```

The result is:

```
NO  MEASUREMENT_VALUE
--  -----------------
 1              99.99
 2             100000
 3             1e+008
 4             1e+011
 5             1e+014
 6           0.999999
 7                  1
 8             1e+008
 9           0.333333
```

Explanation: In the first row, the actual value can be stored; therefore, an estimate is not necessary. However, that is not the case in rows 2, 3, 4, and 5. The number of digits in front of the decimal point is too big. For that reason, the value is rounded in these four rows, and MySQL can just store the simple value `1.0E+xx`. Row 6 is stored accurately. The number of digits after the decimal point is high, but not in front of the decimal point. In row 7, the number of digits after the decimal point is indeed too big, and the value is rounded to `1`. For the value in row 8, an estimate is stored as well. The result of the division `1.0 / 3` is rounded after six digits after the decimal point.

If we create the previous table again, but this time with `FLOAT(30)` as the data type instead of `FLOAT(1)`, the following result arises:

```
NO  MEASUREMENT_VALUE
--  -----------------
 1              99.99
 2           99999.99
 3        99999999.99
 4     99999999999.99
 5    100000000000000
 6           0.999999
 7          0.9999999
 8      99999999.9999
 9        0.333333333
```

Explanation: More storage space is available, so the need to store an estimate is reduced. Rows 1, 2, 3, 4, 6, 7, and 8 all contain actual numbers, not estimates. Row 5 stores an estimate, and in row 9, the number was rounded after nine digits after the decimal point.

With the float data type, you may specify two parameters instead of one. If only one parameter is specified (the length), it determines whether it is a single- or double-precision float data type. If two parameters exist, MySQL interprets the first one differently. In this case, the two parameters are seen as the width and the scale and are used to present the float values. If the width and scale are specified, this is automatically a single-precision float data type.

Example 20.5: Create a new version of the MEASUREMENTS table (see Example 20.4) in which the column with the float data type has a width of ten positions and a scale of 3. Store the same float values in it, and show the contents of this table next.

```
CREATE TABLE MEASUREMENTS
      (NR INTEGER, MEASUREMENT_VALUE FLOAT(10,3))

INSERT INTO MEASUREMENTS VALUES
   (1, 99.99),
   (2, 99999.99),
   (3, 99999999.99),
   (4, 99999999999.99),
   (5, 99999999999999.99),
   (6, 0.999999),
   (7, 0.9999999),
   (8, 99999999.9999),
   (9, (1.0/3))

SELECT * FROM MEASUREMENTS
```

The result is:

```
NO  MEASUREMENT_VALUE
--  -----------------
1              99.990
2           99999.992
3        10000000.000
4        10000000.000
5        10000000.000
6               1.000
7               1.000
8        10000000.000
9               0.333
```

Explanation: Now a floating decimal point is no longer used. All values have three digits after the decimal point (the scale) and a maximum of six positions in front of the decimal point (width minus 1 for the point minus the scale). In that respect, the width of the float data type looks much like the width of an integer data type. The behavior starts to look somewhat like that of a decimal data type. The difference is that, with the float data type, if necessary, estimates of values are still stored, and that never happens with decimal values.

The width of the float data type must be between `1` and `255`, and the scale must be between `0` and `30`.

Synonyms for `FLOAT` with a width and scale are `REAL` and `FLOAT4`. Behind both data types, only a width and a scale are specified, not a length. `DOUBLE` and `DOUBLE PRECISION` are also synonyms for `FLOAT` but always have a double-precision character. In other words, specifying `DOUBLE` is equivalent to specifying `FLOAT(30)`; only a width and a scale may be specified behind these data types as well.

20.3.4 The Bit Data Type

The bit data type is used to store bit-based values. If no length is specified, the maximum length is `1`. The maximum length that can be specified is `64`.

20.3.5 The Alphanumeric Data Types

MySQL supports the following alphanumeric data types (*string data types*) for storing alphanumeric values: `CHAR`, `VARCHAR`, `LONG VARCHAR`, and `LONGTEXT`. Each alphanumeric data type is suitable for storing words, names, text, and codes.

Each column with an alphanumeric data type has an assigned character set and collation; see Chapter 22, "Character Sets and Collations." MySQL must make sure that if we store common letters, letters with diacritics (such as é, á, and ç), and special symbols (such as ?, %, and >) in the database and retrieve them later, they still look the same. This could mean that MySQL has to perform several translations. Imagine that the data is stored in a database that has been installed on a UNIX machine. However, the data is displayed on a Windows machine. The different machines could present a certain letter or symbol internally in a different way. By using an alphanumeric data type, we indicate that all internal translations must be done automatically and transparently. MySQL is responsible for this.

An alphanumeric column has a *maximum length*. This length indicates how many characters, at most, can be stored in the column concerned. However, do not confuse the number of characters with the number of bytes that those values will occupy on disk; that depends on the chosen character set. With the ASCII character set, each character uses 1 byte; in other character sets, this could go up to 4 bytes per character (which means that an alphanumeric value of, for example, ten characters could occupy 40 bytes on disk). Again, see Chapter 22.

The alphanumeric data types can be divided into two groups: those with a fixed length (`CHAR`) and those with a variable length (`VARCHAR`, `LONG VARCHAR`, and `LONGTEXT`). Fixed or variable has to do with the way in which the values are stored on the hard disk. For example, if `CHARACTER(20)` is used in a `CREATE TABLE` statement, we have to assume that each value that we store in that column indeed occupies 20 characters on disk. If we store a value consisting of only 4 characters, then 16 spaces are added to fill the 20 characters. The other three data types store only relevant characters. This is where the data types `VARCHAR` and `LONG VARCHAR` get their names: `VARCHAR` stands for `VARYING CHARACTER`, which refers to an alphanumeric value with variable length. In many SQL statements, the difference between CHAR and `VARCHAR` has no effect; it mainly has to do with performance and storage space.

Table 20.3 shows the maximum length for the different alphanumeric data types.

TABLE 20.3 Maximum Length of Alphanumeric Data Types

Alphanumeric Data Type	Maximum Length
CHAR	255 (2^8–1) characters
VARCHAR	255 (2^8–1) characters and from version 5.03 65,535 (2^{16}–1) characters
LONG VARCHAR	16,777,215 (2^{24}–1) characters
LONGTEXT	4,294,967,295 (2^{32}–1) characters

For the CHAR data type, a value between 0 and 255 *may* be specified; for VARCHAR, a value between 0 and 255 *must* be specified. If the length is equal to 0, only the null value or an empty numeric value ('') can be stored.

Many of these data types also have synonyms. Synonyms for the CHAR data type are CHARACTER, NCHAR, NATIONAL CHAR, and NATIONAL CHARACTER. Synonyms for VARCHAR are CHAR VARYING, CHARACTER VARYING, NATIONAL VARCHAR, NATIONAL CHAR VARYING, NATIONAL CHARACTER VARYING, and TEXT. The data type TINYTEXT is equivalent to VARCHAR with a maximum length of 255. The data type MEDIUMTEXT is a synonym for LONG VARCHAR. We recommend that you use the names in Table 20.8 as much as possible, to simplify a possible switch to other SQL products.

20.3.6 The Temporal Data Types

MySQL supports five temporal data types: DATE, TIME, DATETIME, TIMESTAMP, and YEAR. The DATE data type is used to record dates in a column. The TIME data type represents a time of the day. The DATETIME and TIMESTAMP data types are both combinations of a date and a time. YEAR is used to record year values. YEAR can have a parameter, whose value has to be 2 or 4. The value 2 means that only the last two digits of a year can be stored; the value 4 means all four, so the millenniums as well. Chapter 5 extensively describes these data types and their features.

The required storage space for columns with the DATE and TIME data types is 3 bytes, for DATETIME 8 bytes, for TIMESTAMP 4 bytes, and, finally, for columns with the YEAR data type only 1 byte.

20.3.7 The Blob Data Types

Section 20.3.5 showed that when alphanumeric columns are used, MySQL must make sure that an a remains an a and a b a b. Sometimes we want to store strings of bytes that MySQL does not use. These bytes must be stored and retrieved again without any form of translation This is necessary for the storage of, for example, digital photographs, video, and scanned documents. MySQL supports the *blob data type* for storing this data. *Blob* stands for binary large object—in other words, it is an object that consists of many bytes.

Blob data types have several features in common with the alphanumeric data types. First, both have two versions: those with a fixed length and those with a variable length. Second, blob data types have a maximum length.

MySQL supports the following blob data types: BINARY, VARBINARY, and LONG VARBINARY.

TABLE 20.4 Maximum Length of Blob Data Types

BINARY	255 (28–1) CHARACTERS
BINARY	255 (2^8–1) characters
VARBINARY	255 (2^8–1) characters and, from Version 5.03, 65,535 (2^{16}–1) characters
BLOB	65,535 (2^{16}–1) characters
LONG VARBINARY	16,777,215 (2^{24}–1) characters
LONGBLOB	4,294,967,295 (2^{32}–1) characters

A synonym for `BINARY` is `TINYBLOB`, and a synonym for `LONG VARBINARY` is `MEDIUMBLOB`.

20.3.8 The Geometric Data Types

For the storage data on geometric figures, such as dots, lines, planes, and polygons, MySQL supports several special geometric data types. For the processing of values belonging to these data types, several scalar functions have been added. Because the processing of geometric data is relevant for only a small group of applications, we skip these data types in this book.

Exercise 20.3: Describe in your own words the differences among the numeric data types integer, decimal, and float.

Exercise 20.4: When would you prefer an alphanumeric data type with a variable length to one with a fixed length?

Exercise 20.5: Determine acceptable data types for the following columns:

- Phone number at which a player can be reached
- Age of a player in whole months
- Name of the company where the player works
- Number of children a player has
- Date of a player's first match for the club

Exercise 20.6: Write a `CREATE TABLE` statement for a table with the name DEPARTMENT and with these columns: DEPNO (unique code consisting of always five characters), BUDGET (maximum amount of 999,999), and LOCATION (name of maximum 30 characters). The DEPNO column always has a value.

20.4 Adding Data Type Options

After some alphanumeric data types and all numeric data types, you may specify so-called *data type options.* A data type option changes the properties and features of the data type and, thus, the column. MySQL supports two data type options for the alphanumeric data types: `CHARACTER SET` and `COLLATE`. Chapter 22 discusses this extensively. This section is completely devoted to the data type options of the numeric columns.

For every numeric data type except `BIT`, one or more of the following data type options may be added: `UNSIGNED`, `ZEROFILL`, `AUTO_INCREMENT`, and `SERIAL DEFAULT VALUE`.

For the sake of clarity, data type options are specified behind the data type in a column definition and in front of the null specification and integrity constraints.

20.4.1 The Data Type Option UNSIGNED

When you specify the data type option `UNSIGNED`, values smaller than zero are no longer allowed, only positive numbers. The primary keys of all tables from the sample database contain no negative values, so they could all be defined as `UNSIGNED`.

`UNSIGNED` can be used at every numeric data type. By adding `UNSIGNED` to a column with an integer data type, the range changes; see Table 20.5. In fact, the maximum value allowed increases with two.

TABLE 20.5 Range of Unsigned Integer Data Types

Integer Literal	Range
TINYINT UNSIGNED	0 up to and including $+2^8-1$, or 255
SMALLINT UNSIGNED	0 up to and including $+2^{16}-1$, or 65.535
MEDIUMINT UNSIGNED	0 up to and including $+2^{24}-1$, or 16.777.215
INTEGER UNSIGNED	0 up to and including $+2^{32}-1$, or 4.294.967.295
BIGINT UNSIGNED	0 up to and including $+2^{64}-1$, or 18.446.744.073.709.551.615

Example 20.6: Create a new variant of the PENALTIES table in which all key columns are defined as `INTEGER UNSIGNED`.

```
CREATE TABLE PENALTIESDEF
      (PAYMENTNO     INTEGER UNSIGNED NOT NULL PRIMARY KEY,
       PLAYERNO      INTEGER UNSIGNED NOT NULL,
       PAYMENT_DATE  DATE NOT NULL,
       AMOUNT        DECIMAL(7,2) NOT NULL)
```

The range does not change when UNSIGNED is added to a decimal data type. However, the additional byte reserved for the storage of the minus symbol can be left out, thus saving storage space. If a column may not contain values smaller than 0, UNSIGNED also works as an integrity constraint, which is an additional advantage.

UNSIGNED may be used in combination with a float data type.

20.4.2 The Data Type Option ZEROFILL

Adding ZEROFILL affects the way in which numeric values are presented. If the width of a numeric value is smaller than that of the maximum width allowed, the value is filled in the front with zeroes.

Example 20.7: Create the WIDTH table from Example 20.3 again, but add ZEROFILL to the column this time.

```
CREATE TABLE WIDTH (C4 INTEGER(4) ZEROFILL)

INSERT INTO WIDTH VALUES (1)

INSERT INTO WIDTH VALUES (200)
```

If we retrieve the contents of the C4 columns, we see that every integer value has been moved to the right and that, respectively, three zeroes and one zero in the front have been added:

```
C4
----
0001
0200
```

If ZEROFILL is specified, the column automatically is set UNSIGNED.

The effect of ZEROFILL at decimal data types is equivalent to that at the integer data types.

Example 20.8: Create a new version of the PENALTIES table in which the AMOUNT column (with a decimal data type) is extended with ZEROFILL. Show the contents of this column.

```
CREATE   TABLE PENALTIES
        (PAYMENTNO      INTEGER NOT NULL PRIMARY KEY,
         PLAYERNO       INTEGER NOT NULL,
         PAYMENT_DATE   DATE NOT NULL,
         AMOUNT         DECIMAL(7,2) ZEROFILL NOT NULL)

SELECT AMOUNT FROM PENALTIES
```

The result is:

```
AMOUNT
--------
00100.00
00075.00
00100.00
00050.00
00025.00
00025.00
00030.00
00075.00
```

Example 20.9: Create a new version of the MEASUREMENTS table (see Example 20.4) in which the column with the float data type has a precision of 19 and a scale of 3. Store several float values in it. Show the contents of this table next.

```
CREATE TABLE MEASUREMENTS (NO INTEGER,
   MEASUREMENT_VALUE FLOAT(19,3) ZEROFILL)

INSERT INTO MEASUREMENTS VALUES
   (1, 99.99),
   (2, 99999.99),
   (3, 99999999.99),
   (4, 99999999999.99),
   (5, 99999999999999.99),
   (6, 0.999999),
   (7, 0.9999999),
   (8, 99999999.9999),
   (9, (1.0/3))

SELECT * FROM MEASUREMENTS
```

The result is:

```
NO  MEASUREMENT_VALUE
--  -------------------
 1  000000000000099.990
 2  000000000099999.992
 3  000000100000000.000
 4  000099999997952.000
 5  100000000376832.000
 6  000000000000001.000
 7  000000000000001.000
 8  000000100000000.000
 9  000000000000000.333
```

Explanation: The width of the float data type is large enough now for all values in the column. However, it is also obvious that for all rows except Row 1, an estimated value is presented.

20.4.3 The Data Type Option AUTO_INCREMENT

All the primary keys of the tables in the sample database contain simple sequence numbers. Every time a new row is added, a new number must be assigned. This new number can be calculated by determining the highest number issued and adding 1 to it. This is the application's responsibility. This could be done more easily by having MySQL generate the numbers itself. For this, the option AUTO_INCREMENT must be added to the data type of the column. However, this is allowed only for integer data types.

NOTE

Not all storage engines support the AUTO_INCREMENT option, but InnoDB and MyISAM do.

Example 20.10: Create a new table called CITY_NAMES with an AUTO_INCREMENT column.

```
CREATE TABLE CITY_NAMES
      (SEQNO    INTEGER UNSIGNED AUTO_INCREMENT
                NOT NULL PRIMARY KEY,
       NAME     VARCHAR(30) NOT NULL)
```

Explanation: MySQL sets each column with the AUTO_INCREMENT option automatically on NOT NULL. The AUTO_INCREMENT option can be used for only one column per table. The option UNSIGNED is used so that the numbering will continue up to 4,294,967,295 and doesn't stop at 2,147,483,647.

If a null value is specified for the AUTO_INCREMENT column in the INSERT statement, or if no value is specified, MySQL determines what the next sequence number should be.

Example 20.11: Add three new rows to the CITY_NAMES table and show the contents next.

```
INSERT INTO CITY_NAMES VALUES (NULL, 'London')

INSERT INTO CITY_NAMES VALUES (NULL, 'New York')

INSERT INTO CITY_NAMES (NAME) VALUES ('Paris')

SELECT * FROM CITY_NAMES
```

The result is:

```
SEQNO  NAME
-----  --------
    1  London
    2  New York
    3  Paris
```

Explanation: The first two rows specify null values, and these are replaced by the sequence numbers 1 and 2. In the third row, no value is specified, so MySQL fills the row with sequence number 3. Make sure that the first sequence number given is 1, not 0.

MySQL remembers what the last given sequence number is. When assigning a new sequence number, the last sequence number is located and the highest value in the column is determined. The next sequence number is the highest of the two plus (possibly) 1. This means that if we specify a normal value with an INSERT statement, we could get gaps in the set of sequence numbers. MySQL does not guarantee the absence of holes in the numbering; it only guarantees that the generated numbers will be unique.

Example 20.12: Add two new rows to the CITY_NAMES table, in which the first row has the sequence number 8; show the new contents again next.

```
INSERT INTO CITY_NAMES VALUES (8, 'Bonn')

INSERT INTO CITY_NAMES VALUES (NULL, 'Amsterdam')

SELECT * FROM CITY_NAMES
```

The result is:

```
SEQNO  NAME
-----  ---------
    1  London
    2  New York
    3  Paris
    8  Bonn
    9  Amsterdam
```

Example 20.13: Remove all rows from the CITY_NAMES table and then add two again. Show the new contents next.

```
DELETE FROM CITY_NAMES

INSERT INTO CITY_NAMES VALUES (NULL, 'Phoenix')

INSERT INTO CITY_NAMES VALUES (NULL, 'Rome')
```

The result is:

```
SEQNO  NAME
-----  -------
   10  Phoenix
   11  Rome
```

Explanation: Clearly, even though all rows have been removed, the numbering continues from where it was. If we want to start again at 1, we must delete the entire table and re-create it.

By default, a sequence number starts at 1 and is subsequently incremented by 1. You can change the starting value with the system variable AUTO_INCREMENT_OFFSET. The system variable AUTO_INCREMENT_INCREMENT indicates the value by which the generated numbers are incremented. By default, this variable is equal to 1, but you can change it with the SET statement.

Example 20.14: Start the sequence numbers at 10 and increase them every time by 10. Next, create a new table.

```
SET @@AUTO_INCREMENT_OFFSET = 10,
    @@AUTO_INCREMENT_INCREMENT = 10

CREATE TABLE T10
      (SEQNO  INTEGER AUTO_INCREMENT NOT NULL PRIMARY KEY)

INSERT INTO T10 VALUES (NULL),(NULL)

SELECT * FROM T10
```

The result is:

```
SEQNO
-----
   10
   20
```

20.4.4 The Data Type Option SERIAL DEFAULT VALUE

Finally, the data type option SERIAL DEFAULT VALUE is shorthand for and equivalent to the specification of AUTO_INCREMENT NOT NULL UNIQUE.

20.5 Creating Temporary Tables

In most cases, the tables that we create are granted a long life. Applications will use them for months or even years. The tables created with a CREATE TABLE statement are, therefore, sometimes called *permanent tables*. Usually, multiple SQL users and several applications use permanent tables.

However, sometimes *temporary tables* are needed. Unlike permanent tables, temporary tables have a short lifespan and are visible only for the SQL users who created them; essentially, one SQL user owns a temporary table for a limited time span. Temporary tables are useful, for example, for temporarily storing the results of complex SELECT statements. Afterward, other statements can repeatedly access those tables.

MySQL supports temporary tables. After they have been created, they act as permanent tables. Every SELECT, UPDATE, INSERT, and DELETE statement can be executed on these tables. A DROP TABLE statement can remove a temporary table, but if that does not happen, MySQL removes them automatically when the session ends.

You can use the CREATE TABLE statement to create a temporary table; you simply have to add the word TEMPORARY.

Example 20.15: Create the temporary table SUMPENALTIES and store in it the sum of all penalties.

```
CREATE TEMPORARY TABLE SUMPENALTIES
      (TOTAL DECIMAL(10,2))

INSERT INTO SUMPENALTIES
SELECT SUM(AMOUNT)
FROM   PENALTIES
```

Explanation: From now on, only the SQL user who started the application in which this table was created can access it.

The name of a temporary table can be equal to the name of an existing permanent table. In that case, the permanent table is not removed, but the temporary table of the current SQL user hides the permanent one. See the following example.

Example 20.16: Create a permanent table and a temporary table with similar names.

```
CREATE TABLE TESTTABLE (C1 INTEGER)

INSERT INTO TESTTABLE VALUES (1)

CREATE TEMPORARY TABLE TESTTABLE (C1 INTEGER, C2 INTEGER)

INSERT INTO TESTTABLE VALUES (2, 3)

SELECT * FROM TESTTABLE
```

The result is:

```
C1  C2
--  --
 2   3
```

Explanation: The result of the SELECT statement clearly shows that the contents of the temporary table are presented instead of those of the permanent table. This example also shows that, in this situation, the two tables involved need not have the same table schema.

If a DROP TABLE statement is executed on the TESTTABLE after the SELECT statement and, subsequently, a SELECT statement is executed again, the original permanent table appears again and the following result is presented:

```
C1
--
 1
```

20.6 What If the Table Already Exists?

If we process a CREATE TABLE statement with a table name that already exists, MySQL returns an error message. Adding IF NOT EXISTS represses this error message.

Example 20.17: Create the TEAMS table and do not give an error message if a table exists with a similar name.

```
CREATE   TABLE IF NOT EXISTS TEAMS
        (TEAMNO       INTEGER NOT NULL PRIMARY KEY,
         PLAYERNO     INTEGER NOT NULL,
         DIVISION     CHAR(6) NOT NULL)
```

Explanation: If the TEAMS table already exists, MySQL does not return an error message. Of course, the statement also will not be processed, even though that seems to be the case.

The specification `IF NOT EXISTS` can also be used with temporary tables. In that case, this specification suppresses an error message only when you create a temporary table with the same name as that of an existing temporary table .

20.7 Copying Tables

All `CREATE TABLE` statements shown in this chapter and the previous chapters assume that the table is created from scratch. However, it is also possible to create a new table that is based on an existing table. The specifications and/or the contents of the existing tables are used to create the new table and possibly fill it as well.

DEFINITION

```
<create table statement> ::=
   CREATE [ TEMPORARY ] TABLE [ IF NOT EXISTS ]
      <table specification> <table structure>

<table structure> ::=
   LIKE <table specification>                  |
   ( LIKE <table specification> )              |
   <table contents>                            |
   <table schema> [ <table contents> ]

<table contents> ::=
   [ IGNORE | REPLACE ] [ AS ] <table expression>

<table schema> ::=
   ( <table element> [ , <table element> ]... )
```

Example 20.18: Create a copy of the TEAMS table called TEAMS_COPY1.

```
CREATE TABLE TEAMS_COPY1 LIKE TEAMS
```

Explanation: A new table was created with the same structure as the TEAMS table. Column names, data types, null specifications, and indexes were all copied, but not the contents of the table. Therefore, this table is still empty after this statement. The foreign keys and the specialized privileges that might be present have not been copied, either.

The specification LIKE TEAMS also can be placed between brackets, but this does not affect the result.

In another way of copying that includes copying the data, a table expression is used.

Example 20.19: Create a copy of the TEAMS table called TEAM_COPY2 and copy the contents as well.

```
CREATE TABLE TEAMS_COPY2 AS
(SELECT    *
 FROM      TEAMS)
```

Explanation: During the processing of the statement, MySQL first determines the structure of the result of the SELECT statement. This involves determining how many columns the result contains (three, in this example) and what the data types of these columns are (INTEGER for TEAMNO, INTEGER for PLAYERNO, and CHAR(6) for DIVISION, respectively). MySQL also determines what the null specification is: It checks each column to see whether null values are allowed. Next, a CREATE TABLE statement is executed behind the scenes. The table that is created has the same structure as the original TEAMS table. Finally, the result of the SELECT statement is added to the new table. In fact, the entire TEAMS table is copied in this example.

For MySQL, the word AS and the brackets around the table expression can be omitted. However, we recommend using them as much as possible because many other SQL products require them.

When you create a copy like this, indexes and integrity constraints are not copied. MySQL cannot derive from a SELECT statement what the indexes and integrity constraints should be.

This example used a simple table expression. However, any table expression can be used, including the complex forms. The table expression can contain subqueries, set operators, and GROUP BY clauses.

If we want the column names of the new table to differ from those in the original table, we have to specify those new names in the table expression.

Example 20.20: Create a copy of the TEAMS table and assign the columns TEAMNO and PLAYERNO different names—respectively, TNO and PNO. Show the contents of this new table next.

```
CREATE TABLE TEAMS_COPY3 AS
(SELECT    TEAMNO AS TNO, PLAYERNO AS PNO, DIVISION
 FROM      TEAMS)

SELECT    *
FROM      TEAMS_COPY3
```

The result is:

```
TNO  PNO  DIVISION
---  ---  --------
  1    6  first
  2   27  second
```

Example 20.21: Create a copy of the TEAMS table but without the DIVISION column and only with the teams of player 27.

```
CREATE TABLE TEAMS_COPY4 AS
(SELECT   TEAMNO, PLAYERNO
 FROM     TEAMS
 WHERE    PLAYERNO = 27)
```

Example 20.22: Create a *temporary* copy of the TEAMS table and assign this table the same name.

```
CREATE TEMPORARY TABLE TEAMS AS
 (SELECT   *
  FROM     TEAMS
```

Explanation: Chapter 17, "Updating Tables," contains several INSERT, UPDATE, and DELETE statements that change the contents of the permanent TEAMS table. If you want to return to the original contents of the tables, you must remove the available rows and add the common rows again. You can simplify this process by using temporary tables. After the earlier CREATE TABLE statement has been processed, you can process transactions on the TEAMS table to your heart's content. If the application is stopped or started again, or after the temporary table has been removed, the original TEAMS table, including the original contents, reappears.

If you want to change certain properties of a column, such as the data type or the null specification, during the copying, you must add a table schema to the CREATE TABLE statement.

Example 20.23: Create a copy of the TEAMS table in which null values are allowed in the PLAYERNO column and in which the data type of the DIVISION column is extended from six to ten characters.

```
CREATE TABLE TEAMS_COPY5
      (TEAMNO     INTEGER NOT NULL PRIMARY KEY,
       PLAYERNO   INTEGER NULL,
       DIVISION   CHAR(10) NOT NULL) AS
(SELECT   *
 FROM     TEAMS)
```

Explanation: Columns in which the properties do not change can be omitted from the table schema. The following statement would give the same result:

```
CREATE TABLE TEAMS_COPY5
      (PLAYERNO   INTEGER NULL,
       DIVISION   CHAR(10) NOT NULL) AS
(SELECT   *
 FROM     TEAMS)
```

Make sure that all column names that appear in the table schema are equal to the names of the original columns. MySQL considers columns with unfamiliar names as new columns.

Example 20.24: Create a copy of the TEAMS table, but the PLAYERNO column should now allow null values. In addition, a new column called COMMENT must be added. Show the contents of this table next.

```
CREATE TABLE TEAMS_COPY6
      (PLAYERNO    INTEGER NULL,
       COMMENT     VARCHAR(100)) AS
(SELECT   *
 FROM     TEAMS)

SELECT * FROM TEAMS_COPY6
```

The result is:

```
COMMENT  TEAMNO  PLAYERNO  DIVISION
-------  ------  --------  --------
?             1         6  first
?             2        27  second
```

Explanation: The result shows that the TEAMS_COPY6 table has an additional column compared to the TEAMS table. This new column is filled with null values, of course. You can add columns to existing tables in another way, but Chapter 24, "Changing and Dropping Tables," explains that.

The table expression can give a result with column values that conflict with the present primary or alternate keys. Specifying the concept `IGNORE` instructs MySQL to ignore these rows; they then are not added to the new table, and no error message is returned. If `REPLACE` is specified, the existing rows are overwritten.

Example 20.25: Create a copy of the TEAMS table in which an additional row is added.

```
CREATE   TABLE TEAMS_COPY7
        (TEAMNO INTEGER NOT NULL PRIMARY KEY)
REPLACE AS
(SELECT   * FROM TEAMS
 UNION ALL
 SELECT   2, 27, 'third'
 ORDER BY 1, 3 DESC)

SELECT * FROM TEAMS_COPY7
```

The result is:

```
TEAMNO  PLAYERNO  DIVISION
------  --------  --------
     1         6  first
     2        27  third
```

Explanation: The result of the table expression consists of the following three rows:

```
TEAMNO  PLAYERNO  DIVISION
------  --------  --------
     1         6  first
     2        27  second
     2        27  third
```

Team 2 appears twice in this list. Because we specified `REPLACE`, the last of the two rows overwrites the first. An `ORDER BY` clause has been added to make sure that the row in which the DIVISION column is equal to `'third'` is processed last. If `IGNORE` had been specified, the first row of team 2 would have stayed in the result.

Exercise 20.7: Create a table called P_COPY with the same table schema as the PLAYERS table.

Exercise 20.8: Create a table called P2_COPY with the same table schema and contents as the PLAYERS table.

Exercise 20.9: Create a table called NUMBERS that contains only the player numbers of players resident in Stratford.

20.8 Naming Tables and Columns

Users may select names for columns and tables. MySQL has only the following restrictions:

- Two tables belonging to the same database may not have the same name.
- Two columns in a table may not have the same name.
- The length of a table or column name is restricted to 64 characters.
- A name may consist of only letters, digits, and the special symbols _ and $.
- Each name must begin with a letter or digit.
- Table and column names may not be reserved words; Appendix A, "Syntax of SQL," includes a list of all reserved words.

You can avoid the restrictions imposed by the last two rules by placing a grave accent (or back tick) in front of and after the table name. The table names `SELECT` and `FAMOUS PLAYERS` are incorrect, but `'SELECT'` and `'FAMOUS PLAYERS'` are correct. However, this means that everywhere these table names are used, grave accents must be included. Instead of the grave accents, we could use the double quotation marks; however, the `SQL_MODE` variable must be set to `ANSI_QUOTES` then:

```
SET @@SQL_MODE='ANSI_QUOTES'
```

Defining sensible names for tables and columns is extremely important. Column and table names are used in almost every statement. Awkward names, especially during interactive use of SQL, can lead to irritating mistakes, so observe the following naming conventions:

- Keep the table and column names short but not cryptic (so PLAYERS instead of PLYRS).
- Use the plural form for table names (so PLAYERS instead of PLAYER), so that statements "flow" better.
- Do not use *information-bearing names* (so PLAYERS instead of PLAYERS_2, where the digit 2 represents the number of indexes on the table); if this information changed, it would be necessary to change the table name together with all the statements that use the table.
- Be consistent (PLAYERNO and TEAMNO instead of PLAYERNO and TEAMNUM).
- Avoid names that are too long (so STREET instead of STREETNAME).

- As much as possible, give columns with comparable populations the same name (so PLAYERNO in PLAYERS, PLAYERNO in TEAMS, and PLAYERNO in PENALTIES).

To prevent potential problems, avoid words that have a special meaning within the operating system, such as CON and LPT.

20.9 Column Options: Default and Comment

A table schema consists of column definitions, among other things. Section 20.2 mentioned that a column definition consists of a column name, a data type, possibly a null specification, and some column integrity constraints. Several column options can be added to each column definition as well. This section covers column options.

DEFINITION

```
<column definition> ::=
   <column name> <data type> [ <null specification> ]
      [ <column integrity constraint> ] [ <column option>... ]

<column option> ::=
   DEFAULT <literal>                    |
   COMMENT <alphanumeric literal>
```

The first column option is the *default value*, which is used when a new row is added to a table and no value has been specified for that column.

Example 20.26: Create the PENALTIES table in which the default value of the AMOUNT column is equal to 50 and the default value for the PAYMENT_DATE is 1 January 1990.

```
CREATE TABLE PENALTIES
      (PAYMENTNO     INTEGER NOT NULL PRIMARY KEY,
       PLAYERNO      INTEGER NOT NULL,
       PAYMENT_DATE  DATE NOT NULL DEFAULT '1990-01-01',
       AMOUNT        DECIMAL(7,2) NOT NULL DEFAULT 50.00)
```

Next, we add a new row with an INSERT statement in which we do not specify a value for the columns PAYMENT_DATE and AMOUNT.

```
INSERT   INTO PENALTIES
         (PAYMENTNO, PLAYERNO)
VALUES   (15, 27)
```

After this statement, the new PENALTIES table contains the following contents:

```
PAYMENTNO  PLAYERNO  PAYMENT_DATE  AMOUNT
---------  --------  ------------  ------
       15        27  1990-01-01     50.00
```

Instead of specifying no value in the INSERT statement, we can include the specification DEFAULT. The previous INSERT statement then looks as follows:

```
INSERT   INTO PENALTIES
         (PAYMENTNO, PLAYERNO, PAYMENT_DATE, AMOUNT)
VALUES   (15, 27, DEFAULT, DEFAULT)
```

In the UPDATE statement, DEFAULT also can replace an existing value by the default value of the column.

Example 20.27: Replace the amount of all penalties by the default value.

```
UPDATE   PENALTIES
SET      AMOUNT = DEFAULT
```

Note that DEFAULT is not a system variable and, therefore, cannot appear within compound expressions. The scalar function DEFAULT can be used to retrieve the default value of a column. Of course, this function can be included within expressions.

Example 20.28: Replace the amount of all penalties by the year of the default value of the PAYMENT_DATE column and multiply this by 10.

```
UPDATE   PENALTIES
SET      AMOUNT = YEAR(DEFAULT(PAYMENT_DATE))*10
```

Default values cannot be specified for columns with the data types BLOB or TEXT or one of the geometric data types.

The second column option is COMMENT, which you can use to add a comment to each column. This documentation about the columns is stored in the catalog and is available to every SQL user. The comment can be 255 characters long at most.

Example 20.29: Create the PENALTIES table and add a comment to each column. Show the comment as it is stored in the catalog tables next.

```
CREATE TABLE PENALTIES
      (PAYMENTNO   INTEGER  NOT NULL PRIMARY KEY
          COMMENT    'Primary key of the table',
       PLAYERNO      INTEGER  NOT NULL
          COMMENT    'Player who has incurred the penalty',
       PAYMENT_DATE  DATE     NOT NULL
          COMMENT    'Date on which the penalty has been paid',
       AMOUNT        DECIMAL(7,2) NOT NULL
          COMMENT   'Amount of the penalty in dollars')

SELECT   COLUMN_NAME, COLUMN_COMMENT
FROM     INFORMATION_SCHEMA.COLUMNS
WHERE    TABLE_NAME = 'PENALTIES'
```

The result is:

```
COLUMN_NAME   COLUMN_COMMENT
------------  ---------------------------------------
PAYMENTNO     Primary key of the table
PLAYERNO      Player who has incurred the penalty
PAYMENT_DATE  Date on which the penalty has been paid
AMOUNT        Amount of the penalty in dollars
```

20.10 Table Options

In a CREATE TABLE statement, several *table options* can be specified behind the table structure. Most table options involve how and where table data is stored. This section explains a few of these options. Chapter 22 extensively discusses the table options CHARACTER SET and COLLATE.

DEFINITION

```
<create table statement> ::=
   CREATE [ TEMPORARY ] TABLE [ IF NOT EXISTS ]
      <table specification> <table structure> [ <table option>... ]

<table option> ::=
   ENGINE = <engine name>                                          |
   TYPE = <engine name>                                            |
   UNION = ( <table name> [ , <table name> ]... )                  |
   INSERT_METHOD = { NO | FIRST | LAST }                           |
   AUTO_INCREMENT = <whole number>                                 |
   COMMENT = <alphanumeric literal>                                |
   AVG_ROW_LENGTH = <whole number>                                 |
   MAX_ROWS = <whole number>                                       |
   MIN_ROWS = <whole number>                                       |
   [ DEFAULT ] CHARACTER SET { <name> | DEFAULT }                  |
   [ DEFAULT ] COLLATE { <name> | DEFAULT }                        |
   DATA DIRECTORY = <directory>                                    |
   INDEX DIRECTORY = <directory>                                   |
   CHECK_SUM = { 0 | 1 }                                           |
   DELAY_KEY_WRITE = { 0 | 1 }                                     |
   PACK_KEYS = { 0 | 1 | DEFAULT }                                 |
   PASSWORD = <alphanumeric literal>                               |
   RAID_TYPE = { 1 | STRIPED | RAIDO }                             |
   RAID_CHUNKS = <whole number>                                    |
   RAID_CHUNKSIZE = <whole number>                                 |
   ROW_FORMAT = { DEFAULT | DYNAMIC | FIXED | COMPRESSED }
```

20.10.1 The ENGINE Table Option

Probably the most important table option is `ENGINE`, which indicates the *storage engine* of the table. A storage engine determines how data is stored and how it can be accessed, as well as how transactions are processed. The cleverness and power of a storage engine strongly influences the required storage space and the speed with which SQL statements are processed; different storage engines have different qualities. Some storage engines are very well suited when many complex `SELECT` statements must be processed, while others are more focused on quickly implementing updates. Other engines are optimized to keep temporary tables efficiently in internal memory.

MySQL allows another storage engine to be defined for each table. If a storage engine has not been defined in a `CREATE TABLE` statement, MySQL selects the default storage engine; this depends on the version of MySQL. For quite a long time now, a storage engine called MyISAM has been the default engine; at the beginning of MySQL, it was one called ISAM. If you want to create a table but you don't want to use the default storage engine, and if you don't want to be dependent on what the default is, you can specify the desired storage engine in the `CREATE TABLE` statement.

MySQL includes a number of storage engines, and this list has grown over the years. You can see which engines are included and installed with a `SHOW` statement.

Example 20.30: Show all registered storage engines.

```
SHOW ENGINES
```

The result is (created with Version 5.0):

```
ENGINE      SUPPORT  COMMENT
----------  -------  ------------------------------------------------
MyISAM      YES      Default engine as of MySQL 3.23 with great
                     performance
MEMORY      YES      Hash based, stored in memory, useful for temporary
                     tables
HEAP        YES      Alias for MEMORY
MERGE       YES      Collection of identical MyISAM tables
MRG_MYISAM  YES      Alias for MERGE
ISAM        NO       Obsolete storage engine, now replaced by MyISAM
MRG_ISAM    NO       Obsolete storage engine, now replaced by MERGE
InnoDB      DEFAULT  Supports transactions, row-level locking, and
                     foreign keys
INNOBASE    YES      Alias for INNODB
BDB         NO       Supports transactions and page-level locking
BERKELEYDB  NO       Alias for BDB
NDBCLUSTER  NO       Clustered, fault-tolerant, memory-based tables
NDB         NO       Alias for NDBCLUSTER
EXAMPLE     NO       Example storage engine
ARCHIVE     NO       Archive storage engine
CSV         NO       CSV storage engine
FEDERATED   NO       Federated MySQL storage engine
BLACKHOLE   NO       /dev/null storage engine (anything you write to
                     it disappears)
```

A number of these storage engines exist but are not available for the database on which this `SHOW` statement has been executed, so, they are not a standard accessory. These are the ones for which `NO` is specified in the SUPPORT column.

You can see that InnoDB is the default storage engine (the SUPPORT column includes DEFAULT) for Version 5.0. This is an ideal storage engine for "normal" use. InnoDB supports transactions, the definition of foreign keys, and locking on row level—in short, it is a classic and mature storage engine for applications that must process many SELECT statements or update much data. The engine is strong enough to handle many applications concurrently. For most applications, this default engine is the right one.

As indicated, in Version 5.1 of MySQL, MyISAM is the default storage engine. This storage engine once replaced the ISAM storage engine. However, MyISAM was more powerful. MyISAM and InnoDB are highly competitive engines; choosing will be difficult.

Example 20.31: Create a new table named SEXES and store it with the MyISAM storage engine.

```
CREATE TABLE SEXES
   (SEX CHAR(1) NOT NULL PRIMARY KEY)
   ENGINE = MYISAM
```

A synonym for the table option ENGINE is TYPE. However, the use of ENGINE is recommended.

Example 20.32: Get the names of the storage engines used by the tables PLAYERS, PENALTIES, and the new table SEXES; see Example 20.3.1.

```
SELECT   TABLE_NAME, ENGINE
FROM     INFORMATION_SCHEMA.TABLES
WHERE    TABLE_NAME IN ('PLAYERS', 'PENALTIES', 'SEXES')
```

The result is:

```
TABLE_NAME  ENGINE
----------  ------
penalties   InnoDB
sexes       MyISAM
players     InnoDB
```

The storage engine called MEMORY (formerly called HEAP) makes sure that data is not stored on hard disk, but remains in memory. By doing so, adding, updating, and querying in these tables is processed very fast. Notice, however, that when the database server is stopped, the contents of those tables are deleted because the data is not stored on disk. When the database server is started again, those tables will be empty. So these do look like temporary tables, but temporary tables disappear completely when the application stops. Anyone can access the tables that use MEMORY, just like all the other permanent tables.

We recommend using the MEMORY storage engine when temporary tables are created; see the next example.

Example 20.33: As in Example 20.15, create the temporary table SUMPENALTIES and make use of the MEMORY storage engine.

```
CREATE TEMPORARY TABLE SUMPENALTIES
   (TOTAL DECIMAL(10,2))
   ENGINE = MEMORY
```

The storage engine MERGE enables us to treat multiple tables as if they are one. Imagine that the PENALTIES table contains so many rows that we decide to create a separate PENALTIES table for each year. In other words, we create three tables: PENALTIES_1990, PENALTIES_1991, and PENALTIES_1992. These three tables have the same table schema and, therefore, the same columns. However, the disadvantage of dividing this table is that when a SELECT statement must access the three tables simultaneously, we must use the UNION operator. This can be prevented by using the MERGE storage engine.

Example 20.34: Create the three tables PENALTIES_1990, PENALTIES_1991, and PENALTIES_1992, as just described, and make use of the MERGE storage engine.

```
CREATE TABLE PENALTIES_1990
   (PAYMENTNO INTEGER NOT NULL PRIMARY KEY)
   ENGINE=MYISAM

INSERT INTO PENALTIES_1990 VALUES (1),(2),(3)

CREATE TABLE PENALTIES_1991
   (PAYMENTNO INTEGER NOT NULL PRIMARY KEY)
   ENGINE=MYISAM

INSERT INTO PENALTIES_1991 VALUES (4),(5),(6)

CREATE TABLE PENALTIES_1992
   (PAYMENTNO INTEGER NOT NULL PRIMARY KEY)
   ENGINE=MYISAM

INSERT INTO PENALTIES_1992 VALUES (7),(8),(9);

CREATE TABLE PENALTIES_ALL
   (PAYMENTNO INTEGER NOT NULL PRIMARY KEY)
   ENGINE = MERGE
   UNION  = (PENALTIES_1990,PENALTIES_1991,PENALTIES_1992)
   INSERT_METHOD = NO

SELECT * FROM PENALTIES_ALL
```

The result is:

```
PAYMENTNO
---------
        1
        2
        3
        4
        5
        6
        7
        8
        9
```

Explanation: MERGE works only if the underlying tables have MyISAM as its storage engine. This is why all three have an ENGINE table option. In the CREATE TABLE statement of the PENALTIES_ALL table, we use three table options: ENGINE, UNION, and INSERT_METHOD. The first table option gets the value MERGE. The second option, UNION, indicates which tables should be merged. The third table option, INSERT_METHOD, indicates whether INSERT statements can be executed on the PENALTIES_ALL table. NO means that it is not allowed, of course. If FIRST is specified, the rows are added to the table mentioned first (PENALTIES_1990); with LAST, the rows are added to the table mentioned last.

You can achieve the same with a view; see Section 4.11.

Example 20.35: Create a view that merges the contents of the three tables from Example 20.34.

```
CREATE VIEW PENALTIES_ALL AS
SELECT * FROM PENALTIES_1990
UNION
SELECT * FROM PENALTIES_1991
UNION
SELECT * FROM PENALTIES_1992
```

The use of views gives more possibilities than the MERGE storage engine for merging tables into one table. The only disadvantage is that a view is based on the UNION operator and cannot process INSERT statements. Chapter 26, "Views," covers views in greater depth and discusses their possibilities and limitations.

You can determine the default storage engine with the system variable STORAGE_ENGINE. You can use the SET statement to change the value of this variable.

For a more detailed description of the storage engines, refer to the MySQL manuals.

Many of the other table options are relevant only for the MyISAM storage engine: CHECKSUM, DATA and INDEX DIRECTORY, DELAY_KEY_WRITE, INSERT_METHOD, PACK_KEYS, RAID_TYPE, RAID_CHUNKS, RAID_CHUNKSIZE, and ROW_FORMAT.

Because the default storage engine changes regularly, it is important to specify the desired engine when creating tables. Only then can you be certain which engine is used.

20.10.2 The AUTO_INCREMENT Table Option

Section 20.4.3 discussed the AUTO_INCREMENT data type option. If a table is still empty, 1 is the first sequence number assigned. By including the table option AUTO_INCREMENT, we can deviate from that.

Example 20.36: Create a new table called CITY_NAMES with an AUTO_INCREMENT column, and start the numbering at 10.

```
CREATE TABLE CITY_NAMES
      (SEQNO   INTEGER AUTO_INCREMENT NOT NULL PRIMARY KEY,
       NAME    VARCHAR(30) NOT NULL)
   AUTO_INCREMENT = 10

INSERT INTO CITY_NAMES VALUES (NULL, 'London')

INSERT INTO CITY_NAMES VALUES (NULL, 'New York')

INSERT INTO CITY_NAMES VALUES (NULL, 'Paris')

SELECT * FROM CITY_NAMES
```

The result is:

```
SEQNO  NAME
-----  --------
   10  London
   11  New York
   12  Paris
```

20.10.3 The COMMENT Table Option

The column option COMMENT enables you to store some documentation about columns in the catalog. The table option COMMENT also makes this possible for tables.

Example 20.37: Create the PENALTIES table, and add comment to the columns and to the table. Next, show the comment about the table as it is stored in the catalog tables.

```
CREATE TABLE PENALTIES
      (PAYMENTNO      INTEGER  NOT NULL PRIMARY KEY
          COMMENT     'Primary key of the table',
       PLAYERNO       INTEGER  NOT NULL
          COMMENT     'Player who has incurred the penalty',
       PAYMENT_DATE   DATE     NOT NULL
          COMMENT    'Date on which the penalty has been paid',
       AMOUNT         DECIMAL(7,2) NOT NULL
          COMMENT    'Sum of the penalty in Euro''s')
   COMMENT = 'Penalties that have been paid by the tennis club'

SELECT   TABLE_NAME, TABLE_COMMENT
FROM     INFORMATION_SCHEMA.TABLES
WHERE    TABLE_NAME = 'PENALTIES'
```

The result is:

```
TABLE_NAME  TABLE_COMMENT
----------  ------------------------------------
PENALTIES   Penalties that have been paid by the
            tennis club;InnoDB free: 3072 kB
```

Explanation: Behind the stored comment, you see some more comments that the InnoDB storage engine added.

20.10.4 The AVG_ROW_LENGTH, MAX_ROWS, and MIN_ROWS Table Options

The table option AVG_ROW_LENGTH returns an estimate of the average length in bytes that is occupied by the rows of a table. MAX_ROWS and MIN_ROWS estimate the maximum number and minimum number of rows of a table, respectively. Storage engines can use these values when they build the tables concerned. Especially when a table becomes bigger and the MyISAM storage engine is used, it is better to specify these table options. This could prevent MySQL from suddenly indicating that a table is full.

Example 20.38: Create the MATCHES table again and indicate that the number of rows is between one million and two million.

```
CREATE TABLE MATCHES
   (MATCHNO     INTEGER NOT NULL PRIMARY KEY,
    TEAMNO      INTEGER NOT NULL,
    PLAYERNO    INTEGER NOT NULL,
    WON         SMALLINT NOT NULL,
    LOST        SMALLINT NOT NULL)
   AVG_ROW_LENGTH = 15
   MAX_ROWS = 2000000
   MIN_ROWS = 1000000
```

20.11 The CSV Storage Engine

Chapter 18, "Loading and Unloading Data," discussed loading and unloading of data. Data stored in tables can be written to external files using a SELECT statement. A LOAD statement can copy data from external files to tables. You can access external data in another way through the CSV storage engine. This special storage engine was developed to access data stored not in the database, but in external files. These files must have a certain structure: The values in the rows must be separated by commas (*CSV* stands for *comma-separated value*). This implies that a file created with a SELECT INTO statement can be accessed through a CSV table.

Example 20.39: Create a new version of the TEAMS table and use the CSV storage engine. Next, add two rows.

```
CREATE   TABLE TEAMS_CSV
        (TEAMNO       INTEGER NOT NULL,
         PLAYERNO     INTEGER NOT NULL,
         DIVISION     CHAR(6) NOT NULL)
   ENGINE = CSV

INSERT INTO TEAMS_CSV VALUES (1, 6, 'first')

INSERT INTO TEAMS_CSV VALUES (2, 27, 'second')
```

As a result of this statement, a file named TEAMS_CSV.CSV is created. This file is stored in the directory of the current database and has the following contents:

```
"1","6","first"
"2","27","second"
```

Files that were created outside the MySQL environment can also be accessed in this way with MySQL. Suppose that we created a file with a SELECT INTO statement and that we want to access it. The following example illustrates how to do that.

Example 20.40: Copy all data of the MATCHES table to a file, put commas between the values, begin each row on a new line, and place all values between double quotes.

```
SELECT   *
FROM     MATCHES
INTO     OUTFILE 'C:/MATCHES_EXTERN.TXT'
         FIELDS TERMINATED BY ',' ENCLOSED BY '"'
```

This new file looks as follows:

```
"1","1","6","3","1"
"2","1","6","2","3"
"3","1","6","3","0"
"4","1","44","3","2"
"5","1","83","0","3"
"6","1","2","1","3"
"7","1","57","3","0"
"8","1","8","0","3"
"9","2","27","3","2"
"10","2","104","3","2"
"11","2","112","2","3"
"12","2","112","1","3"
"13","2","8","0","3"
```

Of course, we can load this file with a LOAD statement. However, we could also create a CSV table. For this, we begin with creating the following empty table (make sure that the structure of the table corresponds to that of the file):

```
CREATE   TABLE MATCHES_CSV
        (MATCHNO     INTEGER NOT NULL,
         TEAMNO      INTEGER NOT NULL,
         PLAYERNO    INTEGER NOT NULL,
         WON         SMALLINT NOT NULL,
         LOST        SMALLINT NOT NULL)
   ENGINE = CSV
```

A FLUSH TABLE *statement* guarantees that MySQL "releases" the table:

```
FLUSH TABLE MATCHES_CSV
```

Next, we change the name of the MATCHES_EXTERNAL.TXT file to MATCHES_CSV.CSV. Finally, we can execute SELECT statements on this table:

```
SELECT   *
FROM     MATCHES_CSV
WHERE    MATCHNO <= 4
```

The result is:

```
MATCHNO  TEAMNO  PLAYERNO  WON  LOST
-------  ------  --------  ---  ----
      1       1         6    3     1
      2       1         6    2     3
      3       1         6    3     0
      4       1        44    3     2
```

20.12 Tables and the Catalog

Section 4.16 mentioned that the catalog stores descriptions of tables. Two of these catalog tables are used to record tables and columns: TABLES and COLUMNS. We give the descriptions of these tables next. Other chapters explain some of the columns.

The TABLE_CREATOR and TABLE_NAME columns form the primary key of the table.

TABLE 20.6 Description of the TABLE catalog table

Column Name	Data Type	Description
TABLE_CREATOR	CHAR	Name of the database (not the owner) in which the table was created. MySQL does not recognize an owner of a table, as other SQL products do, which is why the database name was chosen.
TABLE_NAME	CHAR	Name of the table.
CREATE_TIMESTAMP	TIMESTAMP	Date and time the table was created.
COMMENT	CHAR	Comments that were entered using the `COMMENT` statement.

The three columns TABLE_CREATOR, TABLE_NAME, and COLUMN_NAME form the primary key of the COLUMNS table.

TABLE 20.7 Description of the COLUMNS Catalog Table

Column Name	Data Type	Description
TABLE_CREATOR	CHAR	Name of the database in which the table was created; see the TABLES table.
TABLE_NAME	CHAR	Name of the table of which the column is a part.
COLUMN_NAME	CHAR	Name of the column.
COLUMN_NO	NUMERIC	Sequence number of the column within the table. This sequence reflects the order in which columns appear in the `CREATE TABLE` statement.
DATA_TYPE	CHAR	Data type of the column.
CHAR_LENGTH	NUMERIC	If the `DATA_TYPE` is equal to alphanumeric, the length is indicated here.
PRECISION	NUMERIC	If the value of `DATA_TYPE` is equal to `N`(umeric), the number of digits in front of the decimal point is indicated. For all other data types, the value is equal to `0`.
SCALE	NUMERIC	If the value of `DATA_TYPE` is equal to `N`(umeric), the number of digits after the decimal point is indicated. For all other data types, the value is equal to `0`.
NULLABLE	CHAR	If the column has been defined as `NOT NULL`, the value is equal to `NO`; otherwise, it is equal to `YES`.
COMMENT	CHAR	Comments that have been entered using the `COMMENT` statement.

Example 20.41: For each column in the PLAYERS table (which was created in the TENNIS database), get the name, the data type, and the length and indicate whether it is a `NULL` column.

```
SELECT   COLUMN_NAME, DATA_TYPE, CHAR_LENGTH, NULLABLE
FROM     COLUMNS
WHERE    TABLE_NAME = 'PLAYERS'
AND      TABLE_CREATOR = 'TENNIS'
ORDER BY COLUMN_NO
```

The result is:

```
COLUMN_NAME  DATA_TYPE  CHAR_LENGTH  NULLABLE
-----------  ---------  -----------  --------
PLAYERNO     INT                  ?  NO
NAME         CHAR                15  NO
INITIALS     CHAR                 3  NO
BIRTH_DATE   DATE                 ?  YES
SEX          CHAR                 1  NO
JOINED       SMALLINT             ?  NO
STREET       VARCHAR             30  NO
HOUSENO      CHAR                 4  YES
POSTCODE     CHAR                 6  YES
TOWN         VARCHAR             30  NO
PHONENO      CHAR                13  YES
LEAGUENO     CHAR                 4  YES
```

Example 20.42: For each of the tables of the tennis club, get the number of rows and the number of columns.

```
SELECT   'PLAYERS' AS TABLE_NAME, COUNT(*) AS NUMBER_ROWS,
        (SELECT   COUNT(*)
         FROM     COLUMNS
         WHERE    TABLE_NAME = 'PLAYERS'
         AND      TABLE_CREATOR = 'TENNIS') AS P
FROM     PLAYERS
UNION
SELECT   'TEAMS', COUNT(*),
        (SELECT   COUNT(*)
         FROM     COLUMNS
         WHERE    TABLE_NAME = 'TEAMS'
         AND      TABLE_CREATOR = 'TENNIS') AS T
FROM     TEAMS
UNION
SELECT   'PENALTIES', COUNT(*),
        (SELECT   COUNT(*)
         FROM     COLUMNS
         WHERE    TABLE_NAME = 'PENALTIES'
         AND      TABLE_CREATOR = 'TENNIS') AS PEN
FROM     PENALTIES
UNION
SELECT   'MATCHES', COUNT(*),
        (SELECT   COUNT(*)
         FROM     COLUMNS
         WHERE    TABLE_NAME = 'MATCHES'
         AND      TABLE_CREATOR = 'TENNIS') AS M
FROM     MATCHES
```

continues

```
UNION
SELECT    'COMMITTEE_MEMBERS', COUNT(*),
         (SELECT    COUNT(*)
          FROM      COLUMNS
          WHERE     TABLE_NAME = 'COMMITTEE_MEMBERS'
          AND       TABLE_CREATOR = 'TENNIS') AS CM
FROM      COMMITTEE_MEMBERS
ORDER BY 1
```

The result is:

```
TABLE_NAME         NUMBER_ROWS  NUMBER_COLUMNS
-----------------  -----------  --------------
COMMITTEE_MEMBERS           17               4
PENALTIES                    8               4
PLAYERS                     14              13
TEAMS                        2               3
MATCHES                     13               5
```

In the catalog called INFORMATION_SCHEMA, table and column data is stored in the tables TABLES and COLUMNS, respectively.

Exercise 20.10: Show how the TABLES and COLUMNS tables are filled after the execution of the `CREATE TABLE` statement in Exercise 20.6.

20.13 Answers

20.1 Yes, a data type is mandatory.

20.2 First the data type.

20.3 Own words.

20.4 Variable length is useful when the difference between the longest value possible for a column and the average length is considerable. If both are equal, a fixed length for a column is preferable.

20.5 `CHARACTER(13)`. No phone number in the world is longer than 13 digits.
`SMALLINT or DECIMAL(3,0).`
`VARCHAR(50). Company names can be very long.`
`SMALLINT.`
`DATE.`

20.6
```
CREATE TABLE DEPARTMENT
     ( DEPNO     CHAR(5) NOT NULL PRIMARY KEY,
       BUDGET    DECIMAL(8,2),
       LOCATION  VARCHAR(30))
```

20.7
```
CREATE TABLE P_COPY LIKE PLAYERS
```

20.8
```
CREATE TABLE P2_COPY AS (SELECT * FROM PLAYERS)
```

20.9
```
CREATE TABLE NUMBERS AS
(SELECT   PLAYERNO
 FROM     PLAYERS
 WHERE    TOWN = 'Stratford')
```

20.10 The TABLES table:

```
CREATOR TABLE_NAME CREATE_TIMESTAMP    COMMENT
------- ---------- ------------------- --------------------
TENNIS  DEPARTMENT 2005-08-29 11:43:48 InnoDB free: 10240 kB
```

The COLUMNS table:

```
TABLE_CREATOR TABLE_NAME COLUMN_NAME COLUMN_NO
------------- ---------- ----------- ---------
TENNIS        DEPARTMENT DEPNO               1
TENNIS        DEPARTMENT BUDGET              2
TENNIS        DEPARTMENT LOCATION            3

DATA_TYPE CHAR_LENGTH PRECISION SCALE NULLABLE COMMENT
--------- ----------- --------- ----- -------- -------
CHAR                5         ?     ? NO       ?
DECIMAL             ?         8     2 YES      ?
VARCHAR            30         ?     ? YES      ?
```

CHAPTER 21

Specifying Integrity Constraints

21.1 Introduction

Chapter 1, "Introduction to MySQL," discussed the fact that enforcement of *data integrity* in the database is one of the most important responsibilities of a database server. By data integrity, we mean *consistency* and *correctness* of the data. Data is consistent if individual items do not contradict one another. Data is correct if it satisfies all relevant rules, which can be company rules but also be tax rules, laws of nature, and so on. For example, if in the example database the total number of sets in a match is greater than five, this data item is incorrect.

MySQL can take care of data integrity if *integrity constraints* (or constraints) are defined. After each update, MySQL tests whether the new database contents still comply with the relevant integrity constraints. In other words, it checks whether the state of the database is still *valid*. A valid update transforms the valid state of a database to a new valid state. Therefore, the specification of integrity constraints places restrictions on the possible values of a table.

Integrity constraints are the rules with which the contents of a database must comply at all times; they describe which updates to the database are permitted.

Several integrity constraints can be defined within a `CREATE TABLE` statement. For each column, `NOT NULL` can be specified, for example. This means that the null value is not permitted—in other words, the column must be populated. Section 20.2 discussed this integrity constraint. This chapter covers all other kinds of integrity constraints. Primary and foreign keys are other examples of integrity constraints.

DEFINITION

```
<create table statement> ::=
   CREATE [ TEMPORARY ] TABLE [ IF NOT EXISTS ]
      <table specification> <table structure>

           <table structure> ::= <table schema>

           <table schema> ::= ( <table element> [ , <table element> ]... )

           <table element> ::=
              <column definition>           |
              <table integrity constraint> |
              <index definition>

           <column definition> ::=
              <column name> <data type> [ <null specification> ]
                 [ <column integrity constraint> ]

           <null specification> ::= [ NOT ] NULL

           <column integrity constraint> ::=
              PRIMARY KEY                   |
              UNIQUE [ KEY ]                |
              <check integrity constraint>

           <table integrity constraint> ::=
              [ CONSTRAINT [ <constraint name> ] ]
              { <primary key>                 |
                <alternate key>               |
                <foreign key>                 |
                <check integrity constraint> }

           <primary key> ::=
              PRIMARY KEY [ <index name> ]
              [ { USING | TYPE } <index type> ] <column list>

           <alternate key> ::=
              UNIQUE [ INDEX | KEY ] [ <index name> ]
              [ { USING | TYPE } <index type> ] <column list>

           <foreign key> ::=
              FOREIGN KEY [ <index name> ]
                 <column list> <referencing specification>

           <referencing specification> ::=
              REFERENCES <table specification> <column list>
                 [ <referencing action>... ]
```

continues

```
<referencing action> ::=
   ON { UPDATE | DELETE }
      { CASCADE | RESTRICT | SET NULL | NO ACTION | SET DEFAULT } |
   [ MATCH FULL | MATCH PARTIAL | MATCH SIMPLE ]

 <column list> ::=
   ( <column name> [ , <column name> ]... )

<check integrity constraint> ::= CHECK ( <condition> )

<column list> ::=
   <column name> [ , <column name> ]...

<table name>      ;
<constraint name> ;
   <index name>      ::= <name>
```

21.2 Primary Keys

A *primary key* is (informally) known as a column or group of columns of a table of which the values are always unique. Null values are not permitted in columns that form part of a primary key. In the example in Section 20.2, the column PLAYERNO is defined as the primary key of the PLAYERS table.

Primary keys can be defined in two ways: as column or table integrity constraints. In the first case, the term `PRIMARY KEY` is simply added to the column definition.

Example 21.1: Create the PLAYERS table, including the primary key.

```
CREATE TABLE PLAYERS (
       PLAYERNO      INTEGER NOT NULL PRIMARY KEY,
       :             :
       LEAGUENO      CHAR(4))
```

Explanation: The primary key is defined after the null specification. The null specification may also be specified behind the primary key.

In this example, we can also define the primary key as a table integrity constraint:

```
CREATE TABLE PLAYERS (
       PLAYERNO      INTEGER NOT NULL,
       :             :
       LEAGUENO      CHAR(4),
       PRIMARY KEY   (PLAYERNO))
```

You can define primary keys over multiple columns in a table. These are called *composite* primary keys. The COMMITTEE_MEMBERS table contains such a composite primary key. A composite primary key can be defined as only a table integrity constraint. All relevant columns are placed between brackets.

Example 21.2: Create a DIPLOMAS table to record, among other things, which course members followed on which date; the STUDENT, COURSE, and DDATE columns form a composite primary key.

```
CREATE   TABLE DIPLOMAS
        (STUDENT      INTEGER NOT NULL,
         COURSE       INTEGER NOT NULL,
         DDATE        DATE NOT NULL,
         SUCCESSFUL   CHAR(1),
         LOCATION     VARCHAR(50),
         PRIMARY KEY (STUDENT, COURSE, DDATE))
```

Explanation: By defining the primary key on the three columns, you can ensure that a student can obtain only one diploma for each course on a specific date.

If a column that is part of a primary key has not been defined as `NOT NULL`, MySQL defines the column as `NOT NULL`. In fact, you could omit the specification `NOT NULL` in the PLAYERNO column in the previous examples; however, we do not recommend that. For the sake of clarity, it is better to include this null specification.

In principle, any column or group of columns can function as a primary key. Nevertheless, primary key columns must follow a number of rules. Some of these rules stem from the theory of the relational model; MySQL enforces others. We advise you to follow these rules when you define primary keys:

- Only one primary key can be defined for each table. This rule comes from the relational model and applies to MySQL as well.
- The theory (the relational model) requires that one primary key be defined for each table. However, MySQL does not enforce this; you can create tables without a primary key. Still, we strongly recommend that you specify a primary key for each base table. The main reason is that, without a primary key, it is possible (accidentally or deliberately) to store two identical rows in a table; as a result, the two rows no longer would be distinguishable from one another. In query processes, they would satisfy the same conditions, and in updating, they would always be updated together, so a high probability exists that eventually the database would become corrupted.

- Two different rows in a table may never have the same value for the primary key. In the literature, this is called the *uniqueness rule.* As an example, the TOWN column in the PLAYERS table should not be specified as a primary key because many players live in the same town.
- A primary key is not correct if it is possible to delete a column from the primary key and have this "smaller" primary key still satisfy the uniqueness rule. This rule is called the *minimality rule.* In short, this means that a primary key should not consist of an unnecessarily high number of columns. Imagine that we defined PLAYERNO with NAME as the primary key for the PLAYERS table. We already know that player numbers are unique, so in this case, the primary key contains more columns than necessary and, therefore, does not satisfy the minimality rule.
- A column name may occur only once in the column list of a primary key.
- The populations of the columns belonging to a primary key may not contain null values. This rule is known as either the *first integrity constraint* or the *entity integrity constraint.* What would happen if we allowed null values in a primary key? It would be possible to insert two rows with null values as the primary key values and other columns with identical data. These two rows would not be uniquely identifiable and would always satisfy the same conditions for selection or updating. In fact, you cannot break this rule because MySQL requires that the columns concerned be defined as NOT NULL.

MySQL automatically creates an index for each primary key. Usually the name of that index is equal to PRIMARY. However, you may come up with your own name for this index.

Example 21.3: Create the same DIPLOMAS table as in Example 21.2 but now name the index created for the primary key as INDEX_PRIM.

```
CREATE   TABLE DIPLOMAS
        (STUDENT      INTEGER NOT NULL,
         COURSE       INTEGER NOT NULL,
         DDATE        DATE NOT NULL,
         SUCCESSFUL   CHAR(1),
         LOCATION     VARCHAR(50),
            PRIMARY KEY INDEX_PRIM (STUDENT, COURSE, DDATE))
```

Chapter 25, "Using Indexes," returns to the topic of defining indexes.

Exercise 21.1: Do you have to specify a NOT NULL integrity constraint for a column defined as the primary key?

Exercise 21.2: What is the minimum and maximum number of primary keys that can be defined for each table?

Exercise 21.3: Define the primary key for the MATCHES table.

21.3 Alternate Keys

In the relational model, an alternate key is, like a primary key, a column or group of columns of a table of which the values are unique at all times. Chapter 1 indicated that an alternate key is a candidate key that is not chosen to be the primary key. A table may have many alternate keys but may have only one primary key.

Example 21.4: Define the PLAYERNO column in the TEAMS table as if it is an alternate key (we assume in this example that a player may captain only one team).

```
CREATE   TABLE TEAMS
        (TEAMNO      INTEGER NOT NULL,
         PLAYERNO    INTEGER NOT NULL UNIQUE,
         DIVISION    CHAR(6) NOT NULL,
         PRIMARY KEY (TEAMNO))
```

Explanation: The word `UNIQUE` indicates that PLAYERNO is an alternate key and that the values must remain unique.

The previous statement could also have been defined as follows. The alternate key is defined as a table integrity constraint.

```
CREATE   TABLE TEAMS
        (TEAMNO      INTEGER NOT NULL,
         PLAYERNO    INTEGER NOT NULL,
         DIVISION    CHAR(6) NOT NULL,
         PRIMARY KEY (TEAMNO),
         UNIQUE (PLAYERNO))
```

According to the relational model, an alternate key may not contain null values. MySQL deviates from this. In MySQL, alternate keys are allowed to have null values. Separately, we must use the `NULL` or `NOT NULL` specification to indicate whether null values are allowed. For example, we can see the LEAGUENO column in the PLAYERS table as an alternate key that allows null values; see the next example.

Example 21.5: Define the PLAYERNO column in the PLAYERS table as an alternate key.

```
CREATE   TABLE PLAYERS
        (PLAYERNO      INTEGER NOT NULL,
         NAME          CHAR(15) NOT NULL,
         INITIALS      CHAR(3) NOT NULL,
         BIRTH_DATE    DATE,
         SEX           CHAR(1) NOT NULL,
         JOINED        SMALLINT NOT NULL,
         STREET        VARCHAR(30) NOT NULL,
         HOUSENO       CHAR(4),
         POSTCODE      CHAR(6),
         TOWN          VARCHAR(30) NOT NULL,
         PHONENO       CHAR(13),
         LEAGUENO      CHAR(4) UNIQUE,
         PRIMARY KEY   (PLAYERNO))
```

Explanation: The LEAGUENO column can now have multiple null values.

Each table can have several alternate keys, and they may even overlap. We can define one alternate key on the columns C_1 and C_2 and another on C_2 with C_3. There is overlap on the C_2 column, then, which MySQL allows. Alternative keys may also overlap with the primary key. However, it makes no sense to define a set of columns as an alternate key when that set is a superset of the columns of another key. If a primary key has been defined on the column C_1, for example, the definition of an alternate key on the columns C_1 and C_2 is unnecessary. The primary key already guarantees the uniqueness of the combination C_1, C_2. However, MySQL allows this construct, so be careful that you do not make mistakes.

Exercise 21.4: Indicate what is incorrect in the following CREATE TABLE statements:

1.
```
CREATE TABLE T1
        (C1  INTEGER NOT NULL,
         C2  INTEGER NOT NULL UNIQUE,
         C3  INTEGER NOT NULL,
         PRIMARY KEY (C1, C4))
```

2.
```
CREATE TABLE T1
        (C1  INTEGER NOT NULL PRIMARY KEY,
         C2  INTEGER NOT NULL,
         C3  INTEGER UNIQUE,
         PRIMARY KEY (C1, C2, C1))
```

3.
```
CREATE TABLE T1
        (C1  INTEGER NOT NULL PRIMARY KEY,
         C2  INTEGER NOT NULL,
         C3  INTEGER UNIQUE,
         UNIQUE (C2, C3))
```

21.4 Foreign Keys

In the sample database, a number of rules are associated with the relationships between the tables; see Chapter 2, "The Tennis Club Sample Database." For example, all player numbers stored in the TEAMS table must exist in the PLAYERNO column of the PLAYERS table. Also all team numbers in the MATCHES table must appear in the TEAMNO column of the TEAMS table. This type of relationship is called a *referential integrity constraint.* Referential integrity constraints are a special type of integrity constraint that can be implemented as a foreign key with the CREATE TABLE statements. We give a number of examples here.

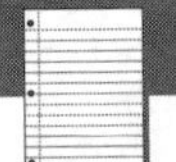

NOTE

Foreign keys can be used only for tables that are created with the storage engine InnoDB; the others do not support foreign keys (see Section 20.10.1). This is one of the reasons to prefer InnoDB. Because of this, we assume in this chapter that InnoDB is the default storage engine. If that is not the case, you can achieve this with the following SET statement:

```
SET @@STORAGE_ENGINE = 'InnoDB'
```

Example 21.6: Create the TEAMS table so that all player numbers (captains) must appear in the PLAYERS table. We assume that the PLAYERS table has already been created with the PLAYERNO column as the primary key.

```
CREATE   TABLE TEAMS
        (TEAMNO        INTEGER NOT NULL,
         PLAYERNO      INTEGER NOT NULL,
         DIVISION      CHAR(6) NOT NULL,
         PRIMARY KEY (TEAMNO),
         FOREIGN KEY (PLAYERNO)
            REFERENCES PLAYERS (PLAYERNO))
```

Explanation: The foreign key specification has been added to the CREATE TABLE statement. Each foreign key specification consists of three parts. The first part indicates which column (or combination of columns) is the foreign key. This is the specification FOREIGN KEY (PLAYERNO). In the second part, we indicate the table and column(s) the foreign key refers to (REFERENCES PLAYERS (PLAYERNO)). The third part is the referencing action (this does not appear in this example but is discussed in the next section).

Foreign keys can refer to only primary and alternate keys. A foreign key cannot refer to a random group of columns; it must be a combination of columns for which the combined value is guaranteed unique.

Before we give a detailed explanation of this example, we introduce two new terms. The table in which a foreign key is defined is called a *referencing table*. A table to which a foreign key points is called a *referenced table*. Thus, in the previous example, TEAMS is the referencing table, and PLAYERS is the referenced table.

What is the actual effect of defining a foreign key? After the statement has been executed, MySQL guarantees that each non-null value inserted in the foreign key already occurs in the primary key of the referenced table. In the previous example, this means that for each new player number in the TEAMS table, a check is carried out on whether that number already occurs in the PLAYERNO column (primary key) of the PLAYERS table. If this is not the case, the user or application receives an error message, and the update is rejected. This also applies to updating the PLAYERNO column in the TEAMS table with the UPDATE statement. We could also say that MySQL guarantees that the population of the PLAYERNO column in the TEAMS table is always a subset of the PLAYERNO column in the PLAYERS table. This means, for example, that the following SELECT statement never returns any rows:

```
SELECT   *
FROM     TEAMS
WHERE    PLAYERNO NOT IN
        (SELECT   PLAYERNO
         FROM     PLAYERS)
```

Naturally, the definition of a foreign key has a huge influence on the updating of the tables involved. We illustrate this with a number of examples. We assume here that the PLAYERS and TEAM tables have the same data as the tables described in Chapter 2.

1. Deleting a player from the PLAYERS table is now permitted only if that player is not a captain.
2. Updating a player number of a player in the PLAYERS table is possible only if that player is not a captain.
3. When inserting new players into the PLAYERS table, the foreign key enforces no restrictions.
4. When deleting existing teams from the TEAMS table, the foreign key enforces no restrictions.

5. Updating a player number of a captain in the TEAMS table is permitted only if the new player number already occurs in the PLAYERS table.
6. Inserting new teams into the TEAMS table is permitted only if the player number of the captain already occurs in the PLAYERS table.

Where clarity on terminology is concerned, we refer to the PLAYERNO column in the TEAMS table as the foreign key; the referential integrity constraint is the check stating that each player number added to the TEAMS table must occur in the PLAYERS table.

The following rules apply when a foreign key is specified:

- The referenced table must already have been created by a `CREATE TABLE` statement or must be the table that is currently being created. In the latter case, the referencing table is the same as the referenced table.
- A primary key *must* be defined for the referenced table.
- A column name (or combination of column names) must be specified behind the referenced table name. This column (or combination) must be the primary key of this table.
- A null value is permitted in a foreign key, although a primary key can never contain null values. This means that the contents of a foreign key are correct if each non-null value occurs in a specific primary key.
- The number of columns in the foreign key must be the same as the number of columns in the primary key of the referenced table
- The data types of the columns in the foreign key must match those of the corresponding columns in the primary key of the referenced table.

Next we give the definitions of three tables from the sample database, including all primary and foreign keys.

Example 21.7: Create the TEAMS table, including all relevant primary and foreign keys.

```
CREATE   TABLE TEAMS
        (TEAMNO     INTEGER NOT NULL,
         PLAYERNO   INTEGER NOT NULL,
         DIVISION   CHAR(6) NOT NULL,
         PRIMARY KEY (TEAMNO),
         FOREIGN KEY (PLAYERNO) REFERENCES PLAYERS (PLAYERNO))
```

Explanation: Team captains must be players who occur in the PLAYERS table. Players who are captains cannot be deleted.

Example 21.8: Create the MATCHES table, including all relevant primary and foreign keys.

```
CREATE   TABLE MATCHES
        (MATCHNO      INTEGER NOT NULL,
         TEAMNO       INTEGER NOT NULL,
         PLAYERNO     INTEGER NOT NULL,
         WON          INTEGER NOT NULL,
         LOST         INTEGER NOT NULL,
         PRIMARY KEY (MATCHNO),
         FOREIGN KEY (TEAMNO) REFERENCES TEAMS (TEAMNO),
         FOREIGN KEY (PLAYERNO) REFERENCES PLAYERS (PLAYERNO))
```

Explanation: A match may be played only by someone who appears in the PLAYERS table and only for a team that appears in the TEAMS table. Players and teams may be deleted only if their numbers do not occur in the MATCHES table.

Example 21.9: Create the PENALTIES table, including all relevant primary and foreign keys.

```
CREATE   TABLE PENALTIES
        (PAYMENTNO      INTEGER NOT NULL,
         PLAYERNO       INTEGER NOT NULL,
         PAYMENT_DATE   DATE NOT NULL,
         AMOUNT         DECIMAL(7,2) NOT NULL,
         PRIMARY KEY (PAYMENTNO),
         FOREIGN KEY (PLAYERNO) REFERENCES PLAYERS (PLAYERNO))
```

Explanation: A penalty can be inserted only for a player who appears in the PLAYERS table. A player can be deleted from the PLAYERS table only if he or she has no penalties.

For the sake of clarity, we note that the following constructs *are* permitted:

- A foreign key may consist of one or more columns. This means that if a foreign key consists of two columns, for example, the primary key of the referenced table must also consist of two columns.
- A column may be part of several different foreign keys.
- A subset of columns in a primary key, or the entire set of columns in a primary key, may form a foreign key.

The referenced and referencing table associated with a foreign key may be the same. Such a table is called a *self-referencing table*, and the construct is called *self-referential integrity*. Consider an example:

```
CREATE   TABLE EMPLOYEES
        (EMPLOYEE_NO  CHAR(10) NOT NULL,
         MANAGER_NO   CHAR(10),
         PRIMARY KEY  (EMPLOYEE_NO),
         FOREIGN KEY  (MANAGER_NO)
            REFERENCES EMPLOYEES (EMPLOYEE_NO))
```

Exercise 21.5: Describe the reason for defining foreign keys.

Exercise 21.6: Indicate which updates are no longer allowed after the following definition:

```
CREATE   TABLE MATCHES
        (MATCHNO      INTEGER NOT NULL,
         TEAMNO       INTEGER NOT NULL,
         PLAYERNO     INTEGER NOT NULL,
         WON          INTEGER NOT NULL,
         LOST         INTEGER NOT NULL,
         PRIMARY KEY  (MATCHNO),
         FOREIGN KEY  (TEAMNO)
            REFERENCES TEAMS (TEAMNO),
         FOREIGN KEY  (PLAYERNO)
            REFERENCES PLAYERS (PLAYERNO))
```

Exercise 21.7: Describe the concept of self-referential integrity.

Exercise 21.8: Can a self-referencing table be created with one CREATE TABLE statement?

21.5 The Referencing Action

The previous section deferred the discussion of one part of the foreign key: the *referencing action.* In that section, we assumed that a player can be deleted only if he or she had not played a match. By defining a referencing action, we can change this behavior.

Referencing actions can be defined for each foreign key. A referencing action consists of two parts: In the first part, we indicate the statement to which the referencing action applies. Two statements are relevant here: the UPDATE and DELETE statements. In the second part, we specify which action is taken. Five possible actions exist: CASCADE, RESTRICT, SET NULL, NO ACTION, and SET DEFAULT. We explain what these different actions mean next.

If you do not specify referencing actions, by default, the following two referencing actions are used:

```
ON UPDATE RESTRICT
ON DELETE RESTRICT
```

Example 21.10: Create the PENALTIES table with two referencing actions.

```
CREATE   TABLE PENALTIES
        (PAYMENTNO      INTEGER NOT NULL,
         PLAYERNO       INTEGER NOT NULL,
         PAYMENT_DATE   DATE NOT NULL,
         AMOUNT         DECIMAL(7,2) NOT NULL,
         PRIMARY KEY   (PAYMENTNO),
         FOREIGN KEY   (PLAYERNO) REFERENCES PLAYERS (PLAYERNO)
            ON UPDATE   RESTRICT
            ON DELETE   RESTRICT)
```

Explanation: The first referencing action specifies explicitly that if the number of a players in the PLAYERS table for whom penalties occur in the PENALTIES table is updated (UPDATE), that update must be rejected (RESTRICT). The same applies to the second referencing action: If a player for whom penalties occur in the PENALTIES table is removed (DELETE) from the PLAYERS table, the delete must be rejected (RESTRICT).

When CASCADE is used instead of RESTRICT, the behavior changes.

Example 21.11: Create the PENALTIES table with a CASCADE referencing action for the DELETE statement.

```
CREATE   TABLE PENALTIES
        (PAYMENTNO      INTEGER NOT NULL,
         PLAYERNO       INTEGER NOT NULL,
         PAYMENT_DATE   DATE NOT NULL,
         AMOUNT         DECIMAL(7,2) NOT NULL,
         PRIMARY KEY (PAYMENTNO),
         FOREIGN KEY (PLAYERNO) REFERENCES PLAYERS (PLAYERNO)
            ON DELETE CASCADE)
```

Explanation: If a player is deleted, all his or her penalties are automatically removed as well. Imagine that the following DELETE statement is executed:

```
DELETE
FROM      PLAYERS
WHERE     PLAYERNO = 127
```

MySQL automatically executes the following DELETE statement (behind the scenes):

```
DELETE
FROM      PENALTIES
WHERE     PLAYERNO = 127
```

If we had specified ON UPDATE CASCADE, the same would have applied to changing the player numbers. If a player number in the PLAYERS table is updated, all player numbers in the PENALTIES table are updated accordingly.

If we replace the word CASCADE with SET NULL, which is the third possibility, we have another result:

Example 21.12: Create the PENALTIES table with a SET NULL referencing action for the DELETE statement.

```
CREATE   TABLE PENALTIES
        (PAYMENTNO     INTEGER NOT NULL,
         PLAYERNO      INTEGER NOT NULL,
         PAYMENT_DATE  DATE NOT NULL,
         AMOUNT        DECIMAL(7,2) NOT NULL,
         PRIMARY KEY  (PAYMENTNO),
         FOREIGN KEY  (PLAYERNO) REFERENCES PLAYERS (PLAYERNO)
            ON DELETE SET NULL)
```

If you delete a player, the player number is replaced by the null value in all rows of the PENALTIES table in which that player number appears.

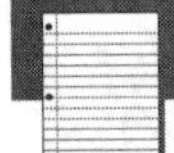

NOTE

The previous statement is actually a little strange because the PLAYERNO column in the PENALTIES table has been defined as NOT NULL. This means that no null values can be entered. Still, MySQL will accept the previous CREATE TABLE statement.

An alternative to SET NULL is SET DEFAULT. Instead of the null value, the default value is specified, but only if a default value has been specified for the column.

The three MATCH specifications have been added, but MySQL will not yet process them. Other SQL products support these options, which is why they have been added.

The referencing action NO ACTION is equal to RESTRICT.

A foreign key may use different actions for the two statements. For example, you can define a foreign key with the referencing actions ON UPDATE RESTRICT and ON DELETE CASCADE.

You may include a MATCH specification in the definition of a referencing action, but MySQL ignores it. This specification relates to whether a foreign key allows null values.

Exercise 21.9: Not specifying referencing actions is equal to specifying which referencing actions?

Exercise 21.10: Which update restrictions does the following definition impose?

```
CREATE   TABLE MATCHES
        (MATCHNO       SMALLINT NOT NULL,
         TEAMNO        SMALLINT NOT NULL,
         PLAYERNO      SMALLINT NOT NULL,
         WON           SMALLINT NOT NULL,
         LOST          SMALLINT NOT NULL,
         PRIMARY KEY  (MATCHNO),
         FOREIGN KEY  (TEAMNO)
            REFERENCES TEAMS
            ON UPDATE CASCADE
            ON DELETE RESTRICT,
         FOREIGN KEY  (PLAYERNO)
            REFERENCES PLAYERS
            ON UPDATE RESTRICT
            ON DELETE CASCADE)
```

21.6 Check Integrity Constraints

Primary, alternate, and foreign keys are examples of common integrity constraints. In addition, each database has a number of special integrity constraints. For example, the SEX column in the PLAYERS table can contain only two types of values: M or F. Likewise, the value of the AMOUNT column must be greater than 0. We can specify such rules with *check integrity constraints.*

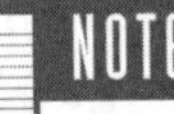

NOTE

In MySQL, check integrity constraints can be included in the CREATE TABLE statements; unfortunately, they are not enforced yet. This will change in a future version.

Example 21.13: Create a special version of the PLAYERS table with only the columns PLAYERNO and SEX and take into account that the SEX column may contain only the values M or F.

```
CREATE   TABLE PLAYERS_X
        (PLAYERNO  INTEGER NOT NULL,
         SEX       CHAR(1) NOT NULL
                   CHECK(SEX IN ('M', 'F')))
```

Explanation: The check integrity constraint specifies which values are permitted. Because CHECK is included within the definition of the column itself, only the column SEX may occur in the condition. This is why this form is called a *column integrity constraint.*

Example 21.14: Create another version of the PLAYERS table containing only the columns PLAYERNO and BIRTH_DATE and take into account that all values in the BIRTH_DATE column must be greater than 1 January 1920.

```
CREATE   TABLE PLAYERS_Y
        (PLAYERNO    INTEGER NOT NULL,
         BIRTH_DATE  DATE NOT NULL
                     CHECK(BIRTH_DATE > '1920-01-01'))
```

If an integrity constraint is specified in which two or more columns of a table are compared to each other, the column integrity constraint must be defined as a *table integrity constraint.*

Example 21.15: Create another version of the PLAYERS table that contains only the columns PLAYERNO, BIRTH_DATE, and JOINED and take into account that all the values in the BIRTH_DATE column must be smaller than the values in the JOINED column. In other words, a player can join the tennis club only after he or she has been born.

```
CREATE   TABLE PLAYERS_Z
        (PLAYERNO     SMALLINT NOT NULL,
         BIRTH_DATE   DATE,
         JOINED       SMALLINT NOT NULL,
         CHECK(YEAR(BIRTH_DATE) < JOINED))
```

The specification `NOT NULL` is a special variant of the check integrity constraint. Instead of `NOT NULL`, we can specify the following column integrity constraint for all columns concerned: `CHECK(COLUMN IS NOT NULL)`. However, we advise you to use the null specification because MySQL checks this in a more efficient way.

Be sure that a combination of check integrity constraints does not mean that a table (or column) can no longer be filled. MySQL does not check this. For example, after the following statement, it is no longer possible to enter rows in the PLAYERS_W table:

```
CREATE   TABLE PLAYERS_W
        (PLAYERNO     SMALLINT,
         BIRTH_DATE   DATE     NOT NULL,
         JOINED       SMALLINT NOT NULL,
         CHECK(YEAR(BIRTH_DATE) < JOINED),
         CHECK(BIRTH_DATE > '1920-01-01'),
         CHECK(JOINED  < 1880))
```

The scalar expressions we used in the check integrity constraints in the earlier examples are all simple. However, MySQL allows more complex expressions.

Example 21.16: Create another version of the PLAYERS table containing only the columns PLAYERNO and SEX and make sure that all values in the SEX column appear in the SEX column of the original PLAYERS table.

```
CREATE   TABLE PLAYERS_V
        (PLAYERNO   SMALLINT NOT NULL,
         SEX        CHAR(1) NOT NULL
                    CHECK(SEX IN
                       (SELECT SEX FROM PLAYERS)))
```

Exercise 21.11: Define a check integrity constraint that guarantees that each penalty amount in the PENALTIES table is greater than zero.

Exercise 21.12: Define a check integrity constraint that guarantees that, in the MATCHES table, the total number of sets won is always greater than the number of sets lost, and make sure that the total is less than 6.

Exercise 21.13: Define a check integrity constraint that guarantees that, in the COMMITTEE_MEMBERS table, the begin date is always less than the end date and that the begin date must be after 31 December 1989.

21.7 Naming Integrity Constraints

If an INSERT, UPDATE, or DELETE statement violates an integrity constraint, MySQL returns an error message and rejects the update. One update can result in the violation of more than one integrity constraint. In that case, the application receives several error messages. To indicate exactly which integrity constrains were violated, a name can be assigned to each integrity constraint; the error message then includes the name, to make the message more meaningful to the application.

If no names have been specified, MySQL comes up with a name itself. You can see that in the catalog tables; see Section 21.9.

Example 21.17: Create the same DIPLOMAS table as in Example 21.2; however, the primary key should have a name this time.

```
CREATE   TABLE DIPLOMAS
        (STUDENT      INTEGER NOT NULL,
         COURSE       INTEGER NOT NULL,
         DDATE        DATE NOT NULL,
         SUCCESSFUL   CHAR(1),
         LOCATION     VARCHAR(50),
         CONSTRAINT   PRIMARY_KEY_DIPLOMAS
            PRIMARY KEY (STUDENT, COURSE, DDATE))
```

Assigning the name is done by specifying the name behind the word CONSTRAINT in front of the integrity constraint (in this case, the primary key).

Example 21.18: Create the PLAYERS table and assign names to the primary key and to the various check integrity constraints.

```
CREATE   TABLE PLAYERS
        (PLAYERNO      INTEGER NOT NULL,
         NAME          CHAR(15) NOT NULL,
         INITIALS      CHAR(3) NOT NULL,
         BIRTH_DATE    DATE,
         SEX           CHAR(1) NOT NULL,
         JOINED        SMALLINT NOT NULL,
         STREET        VARCHAR(30)  NOT NULL,
         HOUSENO       CHAR(4),
         POSTCODE      CHAR(6),
         TOWN          VARCHAR(30) NOT NULL,
         PHONE         CHAR(13),
         LEAGUENO      CHAR(4),
         CONSTRAINT PRIMARY_KEY_PLAYERS
            PRIMARY KEY(PLAYERNO),
         CONSTRAINT JOINED
            CHECK(JOINED > 1969),
         CONSTRAINT POSTCODE_SIX_CHARACTERS_LONG
            CHECK(POSTCODE LIKE '______'),
         CONSTRAINT ALLOWED_VALUES_SEX
            CHECK(SEX IN ('M', 'F')))
```

We recommend assigning names as often as possible when defining integrity constraints, to more easily refer to them when deleting integrity constraints, for example. This implies that we prefer the table integrity constraint to the column integrity constraint because it is not possible to assign a name to the latter.

21.8 Deleting Integrity Constraints

If a table is deleted with a DROP TABLE statement, all integrity constraints are automatically deleted. All foreign keys for which the table is the referenced table are also deleted. With the ALTER TABLE statement, integrity constraints can be dropped independently without dropping the table itself. Chapter 24, "Changing and Dropping Tables," describes this feature in detail.

21.9 Integrity Constraints and the Catalog

INFORMATION_SCHEMA contains several tables in which we can find data on integrity constraints. The TABLE_CONSTRAINTS table records which integrity constraints have been defined on a table. The KEY_COLUMN_USAGE table indicates the columns for which an integrity constraint has been defined. The REFERENTIAL_CONSTRAINTS table stores foreign keys.

21.10 Answers

21.1 A primary key cannot contain null values. MySQL does not require that `NOT NULL` be defined for each column belonging to a primary key. MySQL will define the column as `NOT NULL` itself.

21.2 For each table, only one primary key can be defined, but it is not mandatory.

21.3
```
CREATE   TABLE MATCHES
        (MATCHNO      INTEGER NOT NULL,
         TEAMNO       INTEGER NOT NULL,
         PLAYERNO     INTEGER NOT NULL,
         WON          INTEGER NOT NULL,
         LOST         INTEGER NOT NULL,
         PRIMARY KEY  (MATCHNO))
```

or

```
CREATE   TABLE MATCHES
        (MATCHNO      INTEGER NOT NULL PRIMARY KEY,
         TEAMNO       INTEGER NOT NULL,
         PLAYERNO     INTEGER NOT NULL,
         WON          INTEGER NOT NULL,
         LOST         INTEGER NOT NULL)
```

21.4 Column C4 in the definition of the primary key does not exist.

Column C1 is defined as the primary key twice; this is not permitted.

The first alternate key on the column C3 is a subset of the second on the columns C2 and C3.

21.5 Foreign keys are defined to force MySQL to check that no incorrect data can be entered in the tables.

21.6 The following updates are no longer permitted:

- Deleting a player from the PLAYERS table is now permitted only if that player has played no matches.
- Updating a player number in the PLAYERS table is possible only if that player has played no matches.
- Deleting a team from the TEAMS table is now permitted only if no matches have been played for that team.
- Updating a team number in the TEAMS table is possible only if no matches have been played for that team.

- The foreign keys have not imposed any restrictions on inserting new players into the PLAYERS table.
- The foreign keys have not imposed any restrictions on inserting new teams into the TEAMS table.
- The foreign keys have not imposed any restrictions on deleting matches from the MATCHES table.
- Updating a player number in the MATCHES table is permitted only if the new player number already occurs in the PLAYERS table.
- Updating a team number in the MATCHES table is permitted only if the new team number already occurs in the TEAMS table.
- Inserting new matches in the MATCHES table is permitted only if the new player number already occurs in the PLAYERS table and the new team number already occurs in the TEAMS table.

21.7 If the referencing table and the referenced table are the same for the same foreign key, we call this self-referential integrity.

21.8 Yes.

21.9 This is the same as the specification of `ON UPDATE RESTRICT` and `ON DELETE RESTRICT`.

21.10 The following updates are no longer permitted:

- Updating a player from the PLAYERS table is now permitted only if that player has played no matches: `ON UPDATE RESTRICT`.
- Deleting a player number in the PLAYERS table is allowed: `ON DELETE CASCADE`.
- Deleting a team from the TEAMS table is not permitted: `ON DELETE RESTRICT`.
- Updating a team number in the TEAMS table is allowed: `ON UPDATE CASCADE`.
- The foreign keys have not imposed any restrictions on inserting new players into the PLAYERS table.
- The foreign keys have not imposed any restrictions on inserting new teams into the TEAMS table
- The foreign keys have not imposed any restrictions on deleting matches from the MATCHES table.

- Updating a player number in the MATCHES table is permitted only if the new player number already occurs in the PLAYERS table.
- Updating a team number in the MATCHES table is permitted only if the new team number already occurs in the TEAMS table.
- Inserting new matches in the MATCHES table is permitted only if the new player number already occurs in the PLAYERS table and the new team number already occurs in the TEAMS table.

21.11
```
CHECK(AMOUNT > 0)
```

21.12
```
CHECK(WON > LOST AND WON + LOST < 6)
```

21.13
```
CHECK(BEGIN_DATE BETWEEN '1990-01-01' AND
      COALESCE(END_DATE, '9999-01-01'))
```

CHAPTER 22

Character Sets and Collations

22.1 Introduction

This book has described the concepts *character sets* and *collation* a few times. What exactly do these concepts mean, and how does MySQL handle them? This chapter addresses these topics.

Alphanumeric values consist of letters, digits, and special symbols. Before these values can be stored, the letters, digits, and symbols must be converted into numeric codes. Something like a translation table must be built that contains a unique numeric code for each relevant character. Therefore, each character gets a position in that translation table. Such a translation table is called a character set in the SQL world. The literature sometimes uses the terms *code character set* and *character encoding*.

For a character set, an *encoding scheme* must exist. The character set indicates only that, for example, the uppercase letter A has the position 41 and that the lowercase letter h has the position 68. But how will we store that in bytes? For each translation table, several encoding schemes can be invented; the more creative you are, the more schemes you can come up with. At first, you always think of a fixed number of bits and bytes for each character. So for the storage of a character set consisting of a maximum of 256 characters, we can decide to reserve 8 bits for each character. But we could also decide to use flexible storage. For characters that occur frequently, for example, we reserve 4 bits; for the others, we reserve 8 or 12.

Morse code also uses flexible lengths. In Morse, dots and dashes represent letters. However, not every letter has the same number of dots or dashes. The letter e, for example, is only one dash, whereas the c is built up from a dash, a dot, a dash, and finally a dot—four symbols for one letter. Such a solution can also serve as an encoding scheme for a character set.

So the encoding scheme contains information about how positions such as 1, 100, and 1,000 are stored on hard disk or in internal memory.

In MySQL, the concepts of character set and encoding scheme are seen as synonyms. A character set is a combination of a translation table with an encoding scheme.

Through the years, many character sets have been invented. The first standardized character set was the American Standard Code for Information Interchange (ASCII), and the American National Standards Institute (ANSI) defined its first version in 1960. Another well-known character set is Extended Binary Coded Decimal Interchange Code (EBCDIC), invented by IBM for its System 360 operating system. It has been the standard on the IBM mainframes since 1964.

With ASCII, the number of characters was limited to a maximum of 256 (2^8) characters. That used to be enough, but nowadays applications and their users require much more. Applications must be capable of handling special letters such as ß, Ð, Œ, and æ, as well as letters with all sorts of diacritics, such as ş, ũ, and ĕ. And that is not to mention the languages in which other letters are used. Think about languages from the Middle East and the Far East. In short, 256 positions are no longer sufficient; character sets must be able to code thousands of different characters. *Unicode* (short for Universal Code) is one of the most used new character sets, but others also can hold large sets of characters.

Different encoding schemes exist for Unicode, including *UTF-8*, *UTF-16*, and *UTF-32*. UTF stands for Unicode Transformation Format. These encoding schemes vary in the minimum of number bytes they reserve for one character.

The concept of *collation* deals with the sort order or the grouping of the characters. If numeric values are sorted or compared, it is always obvious how that must be done. The number `10` is smaller than the number `100`, so `10` comes before `100` when sorted. Sorting and comparing alphanumeric values is not always that simple. If we have to place the words `Monkey` and `monkey` in alphabetical order, which one comes first, the spelling with the uppercase letter or the one with the lowercase letter? If we sort on the positions of the characters, the spelling with the uppercase letters comes first with character sets such as ASCII and Unicode. But is that what you want? If so, does that mean that a user living in Georgia wants that as well? It becomes even more difficult when we want to sort the Dutch words `scène`, `schaaf`, and `scepter`. These words begin to differ only on the third letter. When we look at the ASCII codes for these three letters, `scepter` comes first, then `schaaf`, and finally `scène`. However, most users would like to see `scepter` and `scène` behind each other. But then the question is, which of these two comes first?

To shed some light on this, the collation was added. If a character set is assigned to a column, a collation can be specified; for one character set, several collations can be relevant. A collation always belongs to only one character set.

22.2 Available Character Sets and Collations

During MySQL installation, a number of character sets is introduced. You can retrieve this list by using a special SHOW statement or by querying a catalog table.

Example 22.1: Show the available character sets.

```
SHOW CHARACTER SET
```

or

```
SELECT   CHARACTER_SET_NAME, DESCRIPTION,
         DEFAULT_COLLATE_NAME, MAXLEN
FROM     INFORMATION_SCHEMA.CHARACTER_SETS
```

The results of both statements are the same, except for the column names:

```
CHARSET  DESCRIPTION                  DEFAULT COLLATION   MAXLEN
-------  ---------------------------  -----------------   ------
big5     Big5 Traditional Chinese     big5_chinese_ci          2
dec8     DEC West European            dec8_swedish_ci          1
cp850    DOS West European            cp850_general_ci         1
hp8      HP West European             hp8_english_ci           1
koi8r    KOI8-R Relcom Russian        koi8r_general_ci         1
latin1   ISO 8859-1 West European     latin1_swedish_ci        1
latin2   ISO 8859-2 Central European  latin2_general_ci        1
swe7     7bit Swedish                 swe7_swedish_ci          1
ascii    US ASCII                     ascii_general_ci         1
:
utf8     UTF-8 Unicode                utf8_general_ci          3
ucs2     UCS-2 Unicode                ucs2_general_ci          2
:
cp932    SJIS for Windows Japanese    cp932_japanese_ci        2
eucjpms  UJIS for Windows Japanese    eucjpms_japanese_ci      3
```

Explanation: The column on the left contains the name of the character set. We use this name in SQL statements to indicate which character set must be applied. The second column contains a short description of each character set. The third column contains the default collation of each character set. And on the complete right side, you can find the maximum number of bytes reserved for a character. For example, this is 3 bytes for the last one.

In the SELECT statement, the column names, not a *, have been specified to make sure that the SELECT statement presents the columns in the same order as the SHOW statement.

All available collations can be retrieved as well.

Example 22.2: Show the available collations for the character set `utf8`.

```
SHOW COLLATION LIKE 'utf8%'
```

or

```
SELECT   *
FROM     INFORMATION_SCHEMA.COLLATIONS
WHERE    COLLATION_NAME LIKE 'utf8%'
```

The results of both statements are the same, except for the column names:

```
COLLATION            CHARSET  ID  DEFAULT  COMPILED  SORTLEN
------------------   -------  --- -------  --------  -------
utf8_general_ci      utf8      33 Yes      Yes             1
utf8_bin             utf8      83          Yes             1
utf8_unicode_ci      utf8     192          Yes             8
utf8_icelandic_ci    utf8     193          Yes             8
utf8_latvian_ci      utf8     194          Yes             8
utf8_romanian_ci     utf8     195          Yes             8
utf8_slovenian_ci    utf8     196          Yes             8
utf8_polish_ci       utf8     197          Yes             8
utf8_estonian_ci     utf8     198          Yes             8
utf8_spanish_ci      utf8     199          Yes             8
utf8_swedish_ci      utf8     200          Yes             8
utf8_turkish_ci      utf8     201          Yes             8
utf8_czech_ci        utf8     202          Yes             8
utf8_danish_ci       utf8     203          Yes             8
utf8_lithuanian_ci   utf8     204          Yes             8
utf8_slovak_ci       utf8     205          Yes             8
utf8_spanish2_ci     utf8     206          Yes             8
utf8_roman_ci        utf8     207          Yes             8
utf8_persian_ci      utf8     208          Yes             8
```

Explanation: The column on the left contains the names of the collations that we can use in SQL statements. The second column contains the name of the character set to which the collation belongs. ID contains a unique number of the sequence. The DEFAULT column indicates whether the collation is the default for this character set. The last two columns we ignore.

22.3 Assigning Character Sets to Columns

Each alphanumeric column has a character set. When a table is created, a character set can explicitly be assigned to each column. For this, a data type option is used.

Example 22.3: Create a new table with two alphanumeric columns and assign the character set ucs2 to both.

```
CREATE TABLE TABUCS2
      (C1  CHAR(10)      CHARACTER SET ucs2
                         NOT NULL PRIMARY KEY,
       C2  VARCHAR(10)   CHARACTER SET ucs2)
```

Explanation: The character set is included as data type option and, therefore, is placed after the data type and in front of the null specification and primary key. You may enter the name of the character set in uppercase or lowercase letters. You may also specify the name as an alphanumeric literal. CHARACTER SET may be abbreviated to CHAR SET or CHARSET.

Columns belonging to the same table can have different character sets. This can be useful for registering a company name in different languages, for example.

If a character set has not explicitly been defined for a column, the default character set is used.

Example 22.4: Create a new table with two alphanumeric columns, do not assign a character set, and look in the catalog tables next to see what the default character set is.

```
CREATE TABLE TABDEFKARSET
      (C1   CHAR(10) NOT NULL,
       C2   VARCHAR(10))

SELECT   COLUMN_NAME, CHARACTER_SET_NAME
FROM     INFORMATION_SCHEMA.COLUMNS
WHERE    TABLE_NAME = 'TABDEFKARSET'
```

The result is:

```
COLUMN_NAME  CHARACTER_SET_NAME
-----------  ------------------
C1           latin1
C2           latin1
```

The default character set is latin1 for both columns. But where exactly has that default been defined? A default character set can be defined on three levels, on the table, database, or database server level. Section 20.10 describes the table options, one of which is the character set. The CHARACTER SET table option specifies the default character set.

Example 22.5: Create a new table with two alphanumeric columns and define `utf8` as the default character set.

```
CREATE TABLE TABUTF8
      (C1   CHAR(10) NOT NULL,
       C2   VARCHAR(10))
   DEFAULT CHARACTER SET utf8

SELECT   COLUMN_NAME, CHARACTER_SET_NAME
FROM     INFORMATION_SCHEMA.COLUMNS
WHERE    TABLE_NAME = 'TABUTF8'
```

The result is:

```
COLUMN_NAME  CHARACTER_SET_NAME
-----------  ------------------
C1           utf8
C2           utf8
```

If no default character set has been defined for a table, MySQL checks whether one has been defined on the database level.

Each created database has a default character set, which is `latin1` if nothing has been specified. Chapter 27, "Creating Databases," shows how you can specify and change this default character set.

Every time the MySQL database server is started, a file is read. On Windows, this file is called `my.ini`; on Linux, it is `my.cnf`. This file contains the values for some parameters, one of which is the default character set. So this is the third level on which a character set can be defined. If a default character set is missing on the table or database level, this character set is used.

Character sets that have been assigned once explicitly do not change if we change the default of the table, database, or database server later.

Exercise 22.1: Are the internal byte codes of two characters belonging to the same character set but with different collations equal?

Exercise 22.2: Show the `SELECT` statement with which the number of collations for each character set can be determined.

22.4 Assigning Collations to Columns

Each column should also have a collation. If this has not been specified, MySQL uses the default collation that belongs to the character set. The next example shows how such a default collation of a character set can be retrieved.

Example 22.6: Get the collations of the columns of the tables created in Examples 22.3 and 22.4.

```
SELECT    TABLE_NAME, COLUMN_NAME, COLLATION_NAME
FROM      INFORMATION_SCHEMA.COLUMNS
WHERE     TABLE_NAME IN ('TABUCS2', 'TABDEFKARSET')
```

The result is:

```
TABLE_NAME    COLUMN_NAME  COLLATION_NAME
------------  -----------  -----------------
tabdefkarset  C1           latin1_swedish_ci
tabdefkarset  C2           latin1_swedish_ci
tabucs2       C1           ucs2_general_ci
tabucs2       C2           ucs2_general_ci
```

Of course, it is possible to explicitly specify a collation with the data type option COLLATE.

Example 22.7: Create a new table with two alphanumeric columns, define utf8 as the character set, and use two different collations.

```
CREATE TABLE TABCOLLATE
      (C1   CHAR(10)
            CHARACTER SET utf8
            COLLATE utf8_romanian_ci NOT NULL,
       C2   VARCHAR(10)
            CHARACTER SET utf8
            COLLATE utf8_spanish_ci)

SELECT    COLUMN_NAME, CHARACTER_SET_NAME, COLLATION_NAME
FROM      INFORMATION_SCHEMA.COLUMNS
WHERE     TABLE_NAME = 'TABCOLLATE'
```

The result is:

```
COLUMN_NAME  CHARACTER_SET_NAME  COLLATION_NAME
-----------  ------------------  ----------------
C1           utf8                utf8_romanian_ci
C2           utf8                utf8_spanish_ci
```

Explanation: The name of the collation may also be written in uppercase letters and may be placed between brackets. If a character set and a collation are specified, the character set should go first.

If all alphanumeric columns of a table need to have the same collation, a default collation can be defined for the entire table. Even though the character sets have their own collations, that of the table still takes priority.

Example 22.8: Create a new table with two alphanumeric columns and define utf8 as character set and utf8_romanian_ci as the collation.

```
CREATE TABLE TABDEFCOL
      (C1   CHAR(10) NOT NULL,
       C2   VARCHAR(10))
   CHARACTER SET utf8
   COLLATE utf8_romanian_ci

SELECT   COLUMN_NAME, CHARACTER_SET_NAME, COLLATION_NAME
FROM     INFORMATION_SCHEMA.COLUMNS
WHERE    TABLE_NAME = 'TABDEFCOL'
```

The result is:

```
COLUMN_NAME  CHARACTER_SET_NAME  COLLATION_NAME
-----------  ------------------  ----------------
C1           utf8                utf8_romanian_ci
C2           utf8                utf8_romanian_ci
```

It is also possible to specify a default collation on the database level; see Chapter 27.

22.5 Expressions with Character Sets and Collations

The character set and the collation play a big part in the processing of alphanumeric expressions. Especially when making comparisons and sorting data, MySQL must include the character sets and collation of the expressions concerned. You may not compare two alphanumeric values belonging to two different collations. We can conclude that two expressions with two different character sets cannot be compared either because, by definition, they have different collations.

Example 22.9: Create a new table with two columns based upon different character sets.

```
CREATE TABLE TWOCHARSETS
      (C1   CHAR(10) CHARACTER SET 'latin1' NOT NULL,
       C2   VARCHAR(10) CHARACTER SET 'hp8')

INSERT INTO TWOCHARSETS VALUES ('A', 'A')

SELECT   *
FROM     TWOCHARSETS
WHERE    C1 = C2
```

MySQL returns an error message when processing this SELECT.

Example 22.10: Create a new table with two columns based upon the same character set, but with different collations.

```
CREATE TABLE TWOCOLL
      (C1   CHAR(10) COLLATE  'latin1_general_ci' NOT NULL,
       C2   VARCHAR(10) COLLATE 'latin1_danish_ci')

INSERT INTO TWOCOLL VALUES ('A', 'A')

SELECT   *
FROM     TWOCOLL
WHERE    C1 = C2
```

Explanation: Both the columns C1 and C2 have the character set latin1 (the default of the database), but their collations differ; as a result, comparisons, such as in the earlier SELECT statement, will lead to error messages.

To be able to compare two values with different collations, we could change the collation of one. We would then specify the term COLLATE behind the column concerned, followed by the name of the sequence:

```
SELECT   *
FROM     TWOCOLL
WHERE    C1 COLLATE latin1_danish_ci = C2
```

Because of this, the definition of the alphanumeric expression is extended somewhat:

DEFINITION

```
<alphanumeric expression> ::=
   <alphanumeric scalar expression> |
   <alphanumeric row expression>    |
   <alphanumeric table expression>

<alphanumeric scalar expression> ::=
   <singular alphanumeric scalar expression>
      COLLATE <collation name>                 |
   <compound alphanumeric scalar expression>

<alphanumeric singular scalar expression> ::=
   _<character set name> <alphanumeric literal> |
   <alphanumeric column specification>          |
   <alphanumeric user variable>                 |
   <alphanumeric system variable>               |
   <alphanumeric cast expression>               |
   <alphanumeric case expression>               |
   NULL                                         |
   ( <alphanumeric scalar expression> )         |
   <alphanumeric scalar function>               |
   <alphanumeric aggregation function>          |
   <alphanumeric scalar subquery>
```

Clearly, we can specify only a collation that belongs to the character set of the column or expression. The following statement also returns an error message because utf8_general_ci is not a collation that belongs to latin1:

```
SELECT   *
FROM     TWOCOLL
WHERE    C1 COLLATE utf8_general_ci = C2
```

What exactly is the character set of an alphanumeric literal? If nothing is specified, that is the default character set of the database. If we want to assign a literal another character set, we should place the name of the character set in front of the literal. And in front of that name, the underscore symbol must be placed.

Example 22.11: Present the word database in the utf8 character set.

```
SELECT   _utf8'database'
```

To retrieve the collation of a certain expression, we added the COLLATE function.

Example 22.12: Get the collation of the expressions _utf8'database' and _utf8'database' COLLATE utf8_bin and of the NAME column of the PLAYERS table.

```
SELECT   COLLATION(_utf8'database'),
         COLLATION(_utf8'database' COLLATE utf8_bin),
         COLLATION((SELECT MAX(NAME) FROM PLAYERS))
```

The result is:

```
COLLATION(_utf8'database')  COLLATION(...)  COLLATION(...)
--------------------------  --------------  -----------------
utf8_general_ci             utf8_bin        latin1_swedish_ci
```

With the CHARSET function, we retrieve the character set.

Example 22.13: Get the character sets of the expression _utf8'database' and of the NAME column of the PLAYERS table.

```
SELECT   CHARSET(_utf8'database'),
         CHARSET((SELECT MAX(NAME) FROM PLAYERS))
```

The result is:

```
CHARSET(_utf8'database')  CHARSET((...))
------------------------  --------------
utf8                      latin1
```

Exercise 22.3: How does a comparison look in which two alphanumeric expressions with the same character set but with different collations are compared on the basis of a third collation?

22.6 Sorting and Grouping with Collations

COLLATE may also be used in ORDER BY clauses to specify a sorting on another collation.

Example 22.14: Sort the two names Muller and Müller with two different collations: latin1_swedish_ci and latin1_german2_ci.

```
SELECT _latin1'Muller' AS NAME
UNION
SELECT CONCAT('M', _latin1 x'FC', 'ller')
ORDER BY NAME COLLATE latin1_swedish_ci
```

The result is:

```
NAME
------
Muller
Müller
```

Explanation: The first select block returns the name `Muller` with the character set `latin1`; the second select block returns the name `Müller`. When we change the collation to `latin1_german2_ci` in this statement, the two rows are flipped in sequence, as the following result shows:

```
NAME
------
Müller
Muller
```

For the grouping of data, a check is done to see whether values in a column are equal. If that is the case, they are joined in one group. If the column contains alphanumeric values, the collation plays a big part. In one collation, two different characters might be seen as equal; in another sequence, they might be considered unequal.

Example 22.15: Create a table in which the characters *e*, *é*, and *ë* are stored.

```
CREATE TABLE LETTERS
   (SEQNO    INTEGER NOT NULL PRIMARY KEY,
    LETTER   CHAR(1) CHARACTER SET UTF8 NOT NULL)

INSERT INTO LETTERS VALUES (1, 'e'), (2, 'é'),(3, 'ë')

SELECT   LETTER, COUNT(*)
FROM    (SELECT   LETTER COLLATE latin2_czech_cs AS LETTER
         FROM     LETTERS) AS LATIN2_CZECH_LETTERS
GROUP BY LETTER
```

The result is:

```
LETTER  COUNT(*)
------  --------
e              1
é              1
ë              1
```

Explanation: In the subquery, all letters are converted into the `latin2_czech_cs` collation. The result shows that all letters are considered to be nonequal. If we change the collation, we get another result:

```
SELECT   LETTER, COUNT(*)
FROM    (SELECT   LETTER COLLATE latin2_croatian_ci AS LETTER
         FROM     LETTERS) AS LATIN2_CROATIAN_LETTERS
GROUP BY LETTER
```

The result is:

```
LETTER  COUNT(*)
------  --------
e              3
```

Now all three characters form one group and are grouped together. So be careful when you group and sort alphanumeric values when collations are involved.

Exercise 22.4: Determine the character set and collation of the TOWN column in the PLAYERS table.

Exercise 22.5: Sort the players on the basis of the TOWN column but use a collation other than the one in the previous exercise.

22.7 The Coercibility of Expressions

For many expressions and statements, MySQL can decide which collation must be used. For example, if we sort the values of a column or we compare a column with itself, the collation of the relevant column is used; see the following example.

Example 22.16: Use the LETTERS table from Example 22.15, and sort this table on the LETTER column.

```
SELECT   LETTER
FROM     LETTERS
ORDER BY LETTER
```

Which collation is used if we compare values that are of the same character set but that have different collations? MySQL solves this problem by means of the *coercibility*. Each expression has a coercibility value between `0` and `5`. If two expressions are compared with different coercibility values, the collation of the expression with the lowest coercibility value is selected. These are the rules for coercibility:

- If an explicit collation is assigned to an expression, the coercibility is equal to 0.
- The concatenation of two alphanumeric expressions with different collations gives a coercibility equal to 1.
- The coercibility of a column specification is 2.
- The value of functions such as USER() and VERSION() has a coercibility of 3.
- The coercibility of an alphanumeric literal is 4.
- The null value of an expression that has a null value as a result, has 5 as coercibility.

For the comparison COLUMN1 = 'e', the column specification COLUMN1 has a coercibility of 2, and the literal has a coercibility of 4. This implies that MySQL will use the collation of the column specification.

You can retrieve the coercibility of an expression with the COERCIBILITY *function.*

Example 22.17: Get the coercibility value of several expressions.

```
SELECT   COERCIBILITY('Rick' COLLATE latin1_general_ci) AS C0,
         COERCIBILITY(TEAMNO) AS C2,
         COERCIBILITY(USER()) AS C3,
         COERCIBILITY('Rick') AS C4,
         COERCIBILITY(NULL) AS C5
FROM     TEAMS
WHERE    TEAMNO = 1
```

The result is:

```
C0  C2  C3  C4  C5
--  --  --  --  --
 0   2   3   4   5
```

22.8 Related System Variables

Various system variables have a relationship with character sets and collations. Table 22.1 contains their names and the corresponding explanations.

TABLE 22.1 System Variables for Character Sets and Collations

System Variable	Explanation
CHARACTER_SET_CLIENT	The character set of the statements sent from the client to the server.
CHARACTER_SET_CONNECTION	The character set of the client/server connection.
CHARACTER_SET_DATABASE	The default character set of the current database. The value of this variable can change every time the USE statement is used to "jump" to another database. If there is no current database, this variable has the value of the CHARACTER_SET_SERVER variable.
CHARACTER_SET_RESULTS	The character set of the end results of SELECT statements that are sent from the server to the client.
CHARACTER_SET_SERVER	The default character set of the server.
CHARACTER_SET_SYSTEM	The character set of the system. This character set is used for the names of database objects, such as tables and columns, but also for the names of functions that are stored in the catalog tables. The value of this variable is always equal to utf8.
CHARACTER_SET_DIR	The name of the directory in which the files with all the character sets are registered.
COLLATION_CONNECTION	The character set of the current connection.
COLLATION_DATABASE	The default collation of the current database. The value of this variable can change every time the USE statement is used to "jump" to another database. If there is no current database, this variable has the value of the COLLATION_SERVER variable.
COLLATION_SERVER	The default collation of the server.

Besides CHARACTER_SET_DIR, the value of each of these system variables can be retrieved with the help of @ symbols within SQL statements.

Example 22.18: Give the value of the default collation of the current database.

```
SELECT @@COLLATION_DATABASE
```

The result is:

```
@@COLLATION_DATABASE
--------------------
latin1_swedish_ci
```

Example 22.19: Give the values of the system variables whose names begin with CHARACTER_SET.

```
SHOW VARIABLES LIKE 'CHARACTER_SET%'
```

The result is:

```
VARIABLE_NAME              VALUE
------------------------   ------------------------------------
character_set_client       latin1
character_set_connection   latin1
character_set_database     latin1
character_set_results      latin1
character_set_server       latin1
character_set_system       utf8
character_sets_dir         C:\Program Files\MySQL\MySQL Server
                           5.0\share\charsets/
```

22.9 Character Sets and the Catalog

In the catalog called INFORMATION_SCHEMA, we can find information on character sets in the CHARACTER_SETS table and on collations in the COLLATIONS tables. The COLLATION_CHARACTER_SET_APPLICABILITY table indicates which character set belongs to which collation.

22.10 Answers

22.1 The internal byte codes are not equal then.

22.2
```
SELECT   CHARACTER_SET_NAME, COUNT(*)
FROM     INFORMATION_SCHEMA.COLLATIONS
GROUP BY CHARACTER_SET_NAME
```

22.3
```
EXPRESSION1 COLLATE utf8 = EXPRESSION2 COLLATE utf8
```

22.4
```
SELECT CHARSET((SELECT MAX(TOWN) FROM PLAYERS)),
       COLLATION((SELECT MAX(TOWN) FROM PLAYERS))
```

22.5
```
SELECT   TOWN
FROM     PLAYERS
ORDER BY TOWN COLLATE latin1_danish_ci
```

CHAPTER 23

The ENUM and SET Types

23.1 Introduction

Two special data types have not been discussed at all in this book: *ENUM* (enumeration) and *SET*. Both data types can be used if the number of values that a column may contain is restricted. For example, in the SEX column of the PLAYERS table, only two values may be entered: M or F. And in the POSITION column of the COMMITTEE_MEMBERS table, only the values Member, Secretary, Treasurer, or Chairman may appear. For both columns, the number of permitted values is restricted. This differs from columns such as PLAYERNO and AMOUNT, which must fulfill certain conditions but ultimately may contain all kinds of values.

The way the PLAYERS and COMMITTEE_MEMBERS tables have been defined now makes it possible to store all kinds of values also in the columns mentioned. Nothing keeps us from entering the sex X or the function Warehouseman. We could let MySQL check whether the value entered is correct with the help of the data types ENUM and SET. For columns with these two data types, the set of permitted values has been defined. The difference between the two is that with ENUM, only one value can be chosen; with SET (the word already indicates it), this can be more than one.

DEFINITION

```
<data type> ::=
   <numeric data type> [ <numeric data type option>... ]         |
   <alphanumeric data type> [ <alphanumeric data type option> ] |
   <temporal data type>                                          |
   <blob data type>                                              |
   <geometric data type>                                         |
   <complex data type>

<complex data type> ::=
   ENUM ( <alphanumeric expression list> ) |
   SET ( <alphanumeric expression list> )

<alphanumeric expression list> ::=
   <alphanumeric scalar expression>
         [ , <alphanumeric scalar expression> ]...
```

23.2 The ENUM Data Type

When defining a column with an ENUM data type, the list of permitted values is given.

Example 23.1: Create a special variant of the PLAYERS table in which only the columns PLAYERNO, NAME, INITIALS, BIRTH_DATE, and SEX are included. The SEX column may contain only two values: M and F.

```
CREATE TABLE PLAYERS_SMALL
      (PLAYERNO     INTEGER NOT NULL PRIMARY KEY,
       NAME         CHAR(15) NOT NULL,
       INITIALS     CHAR(3) NOT NULL,
       BIRTH_DATE   DATE,
       SEX          ENUM ('M','F'))
```

Explanation: Behind the term ENUM, all legal values are specified between brackets. A maximum of 65,536 can be entered. This example uses alphanumeric literals, but more complex expressions are also allowed. Note that all expressions must have an alphanumeric data type.

You cannot adjust the set of permitted values later; you must remove the existing table with a DROP TABLE statement and build it again afterward, or you must remove the column and then it add again.

Example 23.2: Add several rows to the PLAYERS_SMALL table (see Example 23.1) and show the contents of the table next.

```
INSERT INTO PLAYERS_SMALL
VALUES (24, 'Jones', 'P', '1985-04-22', 'M')

INSERT INTO PLAYERS_SMALL
VALUES (25, 'Marx', 'L', '1981-07-01', 'F')

INSERT INTO PLAYERS_SMALL
VALUES (111, 'Cruise', 'T', '1982-11-11', 'm')

INSERT INTO PLAYERS_SMALL
VALUES (199, 'Schroder', 'L', '1970-02-12', 'X')

INSERT INTO PLAYERS_SMALL
VALUES (201, 'Lie', 'T', '1972-02-12', NULL)

SELECT * FROM PLAYERS_SMALL
```

The result is:

```
PLAYERNO  NAME      INITIALS  BIRTH_DATE  SEX
--------  --------  --------  ----------  ---
      24  Jones     P         1985-04-22  M
      25  Marx      L         1981-07-01  F
     111  Cruise    T         1982-11-11  M
     199  Schroder  L         1970-02-12
     201  Lie       T         1972-02-12  ?
```

Explanation: The table stores the first two rows introduced with `INSERT` statements without a problem. In the third row, the value of the SEX column is not an uppercase letter. MySQL converts the letter into a capital itself, so the value is presented in an uppercase letter. Value `X` in row four is not allowed. MySQL adds the row nevertheless and returns no error message, but it stores a special value, called the *error value*. In the result, it looks like a blank. The fifth row has been added to show that null values can be entered explicitly (provided that the column has not been defined as `NOT NULL`).

MySQL does *not* store the values `M` and `F` internally. It assigns a sequence number to each value from the list of permitted values. The first value (`M`, in our example) gets sequence number `1`, the second `2`, and so on. We can see these internal values if we include the column with the `ENUM` data type in a numeric expression.

Example 23.3: For each row from the PLAYERS_SMALL table, get the player number, SEX column, and internal value of that column.

```
SELECT   PLAYERNO, SEX, SEX * 1
FROM     PLAYERS_SMALL
```

The result is:

```
PLAYERNO  SEX  SEX * 1
--------  ---  -------
      24   M         1
      25   F         2
     111   M         1
     199             0
     201   ?         ?
```

Explanation: Because the SEX column occurs in a numeric expression, MySQL assumes that the internal value is used for a calculation. The first three rows contain the internal values of, respectively, `M`, `F`, and again `M`. The error value remains equal to zero, which you can see clearly now. In the last row, the null value just remains the null value.

When `ENUM` values are compared and sorted, MySQL works with the internal values. Sometimes this leads to unexpected results. The internal value of `M` equals `1`, and that of `F` is `2`. Sorting would put the males at the beginning of the list, and that is probably not what you want.

Example 23.4: For each row from the PLAYERS_SMALL table, get the player number and sex; sort the result on sex.

```
SELECT   PLAYERNO, SEX
FROM     PLAYERS_SMALL
ORDER BY SEX
```

The result is:

```
PLAYERNO  SEX
--------  ---
     201  ?
     199
      25  F
      24  M
     111  M
```

Explanation: In this result, the females are placed before the males. However, this is not because the F comes before the M in alphabetical order; it is the result of sorting on those internal values. Therefore, it is important that the values in the list be specified in the correct order.

Chapter 21, "Specifying Integrity Constraints," describes the check integrity constraints. As mentioned, this category of integrity constraints can already be entered, but MySQL is not capable of checking them yet. A future version of MySQL will remedy that; we recommend that you avoid using the ENUM data type to prepare for this. Instead, use a normal alphanumeric data type and add a check integrity constraint. The first reason for this is that when values are sorted and compared, the behavior of MySQL will probably be more like you would expect. The second reason is that no other SQL products support the ENUM data type, whereas many support the check integrity constraint.

Another way to limit the set of permitted values of a column is to create a separate table consisting of one column in which all those permitted values are stored. Additionally, the original ENUM column must be defined as a foreign key pointing to this new table; see the following example.

Example 23.5: Create a separate table for the registration of the permitted values of the SEX column.

```
CREATE TABLE SEXES
      (SEX          CHAR(1) NOT NULL PRIMARY KEY)

INSERT INTO SEXES VALUES ('M'),('F')

CREATE TABLE PLAYERS_SMALL2
      (PLAYERNO       INTEGER NOT NULL PRIMARY KEY,
       NAME           CHAR(15) NOT NULL,
       INITIALS       CHAR(3) NOT NULL,
       BIRTH_DATE     DATE,
       SEX            CHAR(1),
       FOREIGN KEY (SEX) REFERENCES SEXES (SEX))
```

This approach has a dual advantage. First, standard SQL is used now. Second, it is easier to extend the list of permitted values without having to delete a table temporarily.

Exercise 23.1: Create the MATCHES table again and make sure that the columns WON and LOST can contain only the values 0, 1, 2, and 3.

Exercise 23.2: Determine the result of the following INSERT statement:

1. `INSERT INTO MATCHES VALUES (1,1,27,'1','2')`
2. `INSERT INTO MATCHES VALUES (2,1,27,'4','2')`
3. `INSERT INTO MATCHES VALUES (3,1,27,'','2')`
4. `INSERT INTO MATCHES VALUES (4,1,27,NULL,'2')`

23.3 The SET Data Type

The SET data type looks like the ENUM data type. A list of permitted values is specified here as well. However, the difference is that a column with the SET data type can contain more than one value from the list. Normally, we store in a specific row only one value per column. For example, a player has only one name, one town, and one year of birth. The SET data type makes it possible to record in a row multiple values in one column. That way, we can store, for example, several phone numbers of a player without having to create a separate table. The SET data type can also be used when a team can play in several divisions. However, this data type can be used only if the number of permitted values is not too large because a column with a SET data type can contain a maximum of 64 values only.

Example 23.6: Imagine that teams can play in more than one division; four divisions exist called first, second, third, and fourth.

```
CREATE TABLE TEAMS_NEW
      (TEAMNO     INTEGER NOT NULL PRIMARY KEY,
       PLAYERNO   INTEGER NOT NULL,
       DIVISION   SET ('first','second','third','fourth'))
```

Explanation: Behind the word SET, the permitted values have been specified between brackets. These must always be alphanumeric expressions, so even if the permitted values are a series of numbers, they must be written as alphanumeric literals.

The permitted values are sometimes called the *elements.* Here, the list of permitted values in the DIVISION column consists of four elements.

When rows are added to a table, special rules govern the formulation of the elements of a SET data type. These elements must be specified as one alphanumeric value and must be separated by quotation marks.

Example 23.7: Add several rows to the TEAMS_NEW table and show the contents of the table next.

```
INSERT INTO TEAMS_NEW VALUES (1, 27, 'first')

INSERT INTO TEAMS_NEW VALUES (2, 27, 'first,third')

INSERT INTO TEAMS_NEW VALUES (3, 27, 'first,third,sixth')

INSERT INTO TEAMS_NEW VALUES (4, 27, 'first,fifth')

INSERT INTO TEAMS_NEW VALUES (5, 27, NULL)

INSERT INTO TEAMS_NEW VALUES (6, 27, 7)

INSERT INTO TEAMS_NEW VALUES (7, 27, CONV(1001,2,10))

SELECT * FROM TEAMS_NEW
```

The result is:

```
TEAMNO  PLAYERNO  DIVISION
------  --------  ------------------
     1        27  first
     2        27  first,third
     3        27  first,third
     4        27  first
     5        27  ?
     6        27  first,second,third
     7        27  first,fourth
```

Explanation: In the first row, a team is added that plays in only one division: the first league. The team in the second row plays in two divisions. Notice that the two values have been specified not as two separate literals, but as one—therefore, as `'first,third'` and not as `'first', 'third'`. The third row contains the incorrect value `sixth`. This value is simply ignored. In the fifth row, the null value has been entered; as a result, that team does not play for a single division. The last two rows need some explanation. As with the `ENUM` data type, the actual values are not stored but exist as a string of 64 bits. In this string, the first bit (counted from the right side) is `1` if the first value occurs in this column; otherwise, it is `0`. The second bit to the right is `1` if the second value occurs in the set, and so on. The bit pattern for the division of team 1 is, therefore `1`; the bit pattern for team 2 is `101` (first and third); and the bit pattern for team 7 is `1001` (first and fourth). So by adding the number `7` in row 6, we add the bit pattern `111`, and that means the divisions first, second, and third. In row 7, we add the bit pattern `1001`, and that means the second and fifth values, or the first and fourth divisions.

Example 23.8: Show the internal values of the DIVISION column in the TEAMS_NEW table.

```
SELECT    TEAMNO, DIVISION * 1, BIN(DIVISION * 1)
FROM      TEAMS_NEW
```

The result is:

```
TEAMNO  DIVISION * 1  BIN(DIVISION * 1)
------  ------------  -----------------
     1             1                  1
     2             5                101
     3             5                101
     4             1                  1
     5             ?                  ?
     6             7                111
     7             9               1001
```

Explanation: By multiplying the DIVISION column by 1, we show the numeric internal value of this column. With the `BIN` function, we can convert a decimal value into the binary equivalent and can see the bit pattern that MySQL uses.

Note that this bit pattern can be very long.

Example 23.9: Create a table with one column that can store only the numbers `1` up to and including `40`.

```
CREATE TABLE SERIES_NUMBERS
      (NUMBERS SET
          ('1','2','3','4','5','6','7','8','9','10',
           '11','12','13','14','15','16','17','18','19','20',
           '21','22','23','24','25','26','27','28','29','30',
           '31','32','33','34','35','36','37','38','39','40'))

INSERT INTO SERIES_NUMBERS VALUES ('1'),('20'),('40')

SELECT    NUMBERS, BIN(NUMBERS * 1)
FROM      SERIES_NUMBERS
```

The result is:

```
NUMBERS  BIN(NUMBERS * 1)
-------  ----------------------------------------
      1                                         1
     20                      10000000000000000000
     40  1000000000000000000000000000000000000000
```

Example 23.10: Add two new rows to the TEAMS_NEW table and show the contents of the table next.

```
INSERT INTO TEAMS_NEW VALUES (8, 27, 'eighth')

INSERT INTO TEAMS_NEW VALUES (9, 27, '')

SELECT    TEAMNO, DIVISION, DIVISION * 1, BIN(DIVISION * 1)
FROM      TEAMS_NEW
WHERE     TEAMNO IN (8, 9)
```

The result is:

```
TEAMNO  DIVISION  DIVISION * 1  BIN(DIVISION * 1)
------  --------  ------------  -----------------
     8                       0                  0
     9                       0                  0
```

Explanation: Both rows contain values that do not belong to the list of permitted values. Furthermore, both rows do not contain correct values; `'eighth'` and the empty alphanumeric literal are not valid values. When not one correct value has been entered, the value `0` is stored. This means that there are no correct values for that team.

If in an `INSERT` statement duplicate values have been specified, MySQL will automatically delete them.

When retrieving information about teams on the basis of specific divisions, you must formulate the conditions very carefully.

Example 23.11: Get the numbers of the teams that play in the first division.

```
SELECT    TEAMNO
FROM      TEAMS_NEW
WHERE     DIVISION = 'first'
```

The result is:

```
TEAMNO
------
     1
     4
```

Explanation: MySQL returns only those teams that play in the first division. For example, team 3 plays in the first division, but it is not included in the end result because this team also plays in the third division. With the condition `DIVISION = 'first,third'`, we find all the teams that play in the first and in the third divisions, but not in any other.

For many queries, we have to use so-called bit operators; see Section 5.13.1.

Example 23.12: Get the numbers and divisions of all teams that play in at least the third division.

```
SELECT   TEAMNO, DIVISION
FROM     TEAMS_NEW
WHERE    DIVISION & POWER(2,3-1) = POWER(2,3-1)
```

The result is:

```
TEAMNO  DIVISION
------  --------------------
     2  first,third
     3  first,third
     6  first,second,third
```

Explanation: With the `POWER` function, we can determine the decimal value of the third division. The third division is the third element. This gives the decimal value `4`, and that equals the bit pattern `100`. Next, the `&` operator (or the `AND` operator) checks whether the value of the DIVISION column on the third position to the right contains a `1`.

For a better reading of the statement, we have used the `POWER` function here; it stands out more clearly now that we are looking for the row where position 3 has been filled. The same result can be achieved with the condition `DIVISION & CONV(100,2,10) = CONV(100,2,10)`. Here `100` is the binary value of `4`. However, the statement is processed faster if these functions are replaced by the literal `4`.

Example 23.13: Get the numbers and divisions of all teams playing in the first and fourth divisions.

```
SELECT   TEAMNO, DIVISION
FROM     TEAMS_NEW
WHERE    DIVISION & 9 = 9
```

The result is:

```
TEAMNO  DIVISION
------  ------------
     7  first,fourth
```

Explanation: The code 9 is used here because the first division has the bit pattern 1 and the fourth division has the bit pattern 1000 (or 8). The sum of these two numbers is 9.

Example 23.14: For each team, get the team number and number of elements in the DIVISION column.

```
SELECT   TEAMNO,
         LENGTH(REPLACE(CONV((DIVISION * 1),10,2),'0',''))
         AS NUMBER
FROM     TEAMS_NEW
```

The result is:

```
TEAMNO  NUMBER
------  ------
     1       1
     2       2
     3       2
     4       1
     5       ?
     6       3
     7       2
     8       0
     9       0
```

Explanation: You can use the REPLACE function to delete all zeroes from the bit pattern, and you can add the remaining ones with the LENGTH function. The number of ones represents the number of divisions.

Example 23.15: Create a report that displays the teams on a vertical axis and the divisions in which they play on a horizontal axis.

```
SELECT   TEAMNO,
         CASE WHEN (DIVISION & POWER(2,1-1) = POWER(2,1-1)) = 1
            THEN 'YES' ELSE 'NO' END AS FIRST,
         CASE WHEN (DIVISION & POWER(2,2-1) = POWER(2,2-1)) = 1
            THEN 'YES' ELSE 'NO' END AS SECOND,
         CASE WHEN (DIVISION & POWER(2,3-1) = POWER(2,3-1)) = 1
            THEN 'YES' ELSE 'NO' END AS THIRD,
         CASE WHEN (DIVISION & POWER(2,4-1) = POWER(2,4-1)) = 1
            THEN 'YES' ELSE 'NO' END AS FOURTH
FROM     TEAMS_NEW
```

The result is:

```
TEAMNO  FIRST  SECOND  THIRD  FOURTH
------  -----  ------  -----  ------
     1  YES    NO      NO     NO
     2  YES    NO      YES    NO
     3  YES    NO      YES    NO
     4  YES    NO      NO     NO
     5  NO     NO      NO     NO
     6  YES    YES     YES    NO
     7  YES    NO      NO     YES
     8  NO     NO      NO     NO
     9  NO     NO      NO     NO
```

Example 23.16: For each combination of divisions available, get the number of teams that belong to it.

```
SELECT   DIVISION, COUNT(*)
FROM     TEAMS_NEW
WHERE    DIVISION > 0
OR       DIVISION IS NULL
GROUP BY DIVISION
```

The result is:

```
DIVISION                  COUNT(*)
------------------        --------
?                                1
first                            2
first,third                      2
first,second,third               1
first,fourth                     1
```

Explanation: The first condition has been added to leave out the rows that contain only error values. The second condition has been added to include the rows with null values in the result.

No special SQL statement exists for adding new elements to the list of a certain row. However, we can use an UPDATE statement to add a value as a third or fourth division, but that must be done with the OR operator.

Example 23.17: Insert the fact that team 1 also plays in the third division.

```
UPDATE   TEAMS_NEW
SET      DIVISION = DIVISION | POWER(2,3-1)
WHERE    TEAMNO = 1
```

Explanation: By executing the `OR` operator on the DIVISION column and on the value of the `POWER` function, a new bit pattern is created in which the bit for the third division is always active, regardless of what the value was. The expression `POWER(2,3-1)` can be replaced again by `CONV(100,2,10)`.

Example 23.18: Delete the third division for all teams.

```
UPDATE   TEAMS_NEW
SET      DIVISION = DIVISION & CONV(1011,2,10)
```

Explanation: In the bit pattern, the third position to the right is a zero because the value of the third division is in the third position.

Example 23.19: For each team, delete all divisions.

```
UPDATE   TEAMS_NEW
SET      DIVISION = 0
```

Explanation: Only four ones have been used because the list contains only four elements.

Finally, as with the `ENUM` data type, `SET` has not been implemented in many SQL products. Therefore, use it to a limited degree.

23.4 Answers

23.1
```
CREATE TABLE MATCHES
       (MATCHNO      INTEGER NOT NULL PRIMARY KEY,
        TEAMNO       INTEGER NOT NULL,
        PLAYERNO     INTEGER NOT NULL,
        WON          ENUM('0','1','2','3') NOT NULL,
        LOST         ENUM('0','1','2','3') NOT NULL)
```

23.2
1. This statement is accepted.
2. The value `4` cannot be entered in the WON column; MySQL will enter an error value.
3. This statement is accepted.
4. This statement is not accepted because the WON column cannot contain null values. The entire statement will not be processed.

CHAPTER 24

Changing and Dropping Tables

24.1 Introduction

The UPDATE, INSERT, and DELETE statements are used to update the contents of a table. In MySQL, we can also change the *structure* of a table, even when that table contains millions of rows. We can add columns, change the data type of an existing column, add integrity constraints, and even delete entire tables. This chapter describes all the features for dropping tables (with the DROP TABLE statement), renaming them (with the RENAME statement), and changing them (with the ALTER TABLE statement).

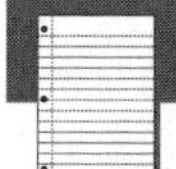

NOTE

Most examples in this book assume that each table contains its original contents. If you execute the statements in this chapter with MySQL, you change the structure and the contents, of course. Because of this, the results of your statements in the following examples could differ from those in the book. On the website of the book, www.r20.nl, you find information on how to restore the tables to their original structure.

24.2 Deleting Entire Tables

The *DROP TABLE statement* is used to delete a table. MySQL also removes the descriptions of the table from all relevant catalog tables, along with all integrity constraints, indexes, and privileges that are "linked" to that table. In fact, MySQL removes each database object that has no right to exist after the table has been deleted.

```
<drop table statement> ::=
   DROP [ TEMPORARY ] { TABLE | TABLES } [ IF EXISTS ]
   <table specification> [ , <table specification> ]...
   [ CASCADE | RESTRICT ]
```

Example 24.1: Delete the PLAYERS table.

```
DROP TABLE PLAYERS
```

Explanation: After this statement has been processed, the table no longer exists. Furthermore, all linked database objects, such as indexes, views, and privileges, are removed as well.

A table can be removed only if no foreign keys point to the table—in other words, the table cannot be a referenced table. In that case, either the relevant foreign key or the entire referencing table must be removed first.

When the word TEMPORARY is added, a temporary table is removed (unless a temporary table exists with the specified name). IF EXISTS can be added to repress an error message if the table mentioned does not exist.

Example 24.2: Delete the table TAB1 that belongs to the database DB8.

```
DROP TABLE DB8.TAB1
```

Explanation: By qualifying the table name with a database name, you can remove tables from other databases.

It is possible to remove multiple tables simultaneously with one DROP TABLE statement.

Example 24.3: Delete all five tables of the tennis club.

```
DROP TABLES COMMITTEE_MEMBERS, MATCHES, TEAMS,
     PENALTIES, PLAYERS
```

The options RESTRICT and CASCADE may be added but do not have any effect yet. If they are activated in a future version of MySQL, the specification of CASCADE will mean that all tables that are "linked" to the specified table via foreign keys are removed. With the statement DROP TABLE PLAYERS CASCADE, we would remove the entire database at once. The specification of RESTRICT means that a table can be removed only if no foreign keys point to the relevant table. The statement DROP TABLE PLAYERS RESTRICT would fail because of the various foreign keys, but it would be possible to execute DROP TABLE COMMITTEE_MEMBERS RESTRICT.

24.3 Renaming Tables

The *RENAME TABLE statement* gives an existing table a new name.

DEFINITION

```
<rename table statement> ::=
   RENAME { TABLE | TABLES } <table name change>
      [ , <table name change> ]...

<table name change> ::= <table name> TO <table name>
```

Example 24.4: Change the name of the PLAYERS table to TENNIS_PLAYERS.

```
RENAME TABLE PLAYERS TO TENNIS_PLAYERS
```

All other database objects that refer to this table are changed accordingly. Assigned privileges do not disappear, foreign keys remain, and views that use this renamed table keep working.

One RENAME TABLE statement can change the names of multiple tables at once.

Example 24.5: Change the name of the PLAYERS table to TENNIS_PLAYERS and that of COMMITTEE_MEMBERS to MEMBERS.

```
RENAME TABLES PLAYERS TO TENNIS_PLAYERS,
       COMMITTEE_MEMBERS TO MEMBERS
```

24.4 Changing the Table Structure

MySQL supports the ALTER TABLE statement for this for changing many aspects of the table structure. Because this statement offers so many possibilities, we describe its features in several sections. This section describes the possibilities for altering the table itself. The following section discusses the ways to change the specifications of columns. Section 24.6 covers the possibilities of changing integrity constraints. Section 25.5 describes how to change existing indexes (after we explain how indexes are created).

 DEFINITION

```
<alter table statement> ::=
   ALTER [ IGNORE ] TABLE <table specification>
   <table structure change>

<table structure change> ::=
   <table change>                  |
   <column change>                 |
   <integrity constraint change> |
   <index change>

<table change> ::=
   RENAME [ TO | AS ] <table name>                                      |
   <table options>...                                                   |
   CONVERT TO CHARACTER SET { <character set name> | DEFAULT }
      [ COLLATE <collation name> ]                                      |
   ORDER BY <sort specification>
      [ , <sort specification> ]...                                     |
   { ENABLE | DISABLE } KEYS

<sort specification> ::= <column name> [ <sort direction> ]

<sort direction> ::= { ASC | DESC }

<table name>         ;
<column name>        ;
<character set name> ;
<collation name>     ::= <name>
```

Example 24.6: Change the name of the PLAYERS table to TENNIS_PLAYERS.

```
ALTER TABLE PLAYERS RENAME TO TENNIS_PLAYERS
```

Explanation: The result of this statement is, of course, equal to that of the RENAME TABLE statement; see Section 24.3. The word `TO` can be replaced by `AS`, and it can be omitted.

Each table option described in Section 20.10 may be changed.

Example 24.7: Set the numbering of the CITY_NAMES table to `10,000`, and change the comment.

```
ALTER TABLE CITY_NAMES
   AUTO_INCREMENT = 10000
   COMMENT = 'New comment'
```

An ALTER TABLE statement also can change the default character set and collation. Obviously, this no longer has any effect on the existing columns of a table; those properties have already been assigned to those columns. However, for the columns that are added with another ALTER TABLE statement later, it is still relevant.

If we want to change the character set of existing columns, we use the CONVERT feature of the ALTER TABLE statement.

Example 24.8: For all alphanumeric columns in the PLAYERS table, change the character set to utf8 and set the collation to utf8_general_ci.

```
ALTER TABLE PLAYERS
   CONVERT TO CHARACTER SET utf8 COLLATE utf8_general_ci
```

You may add IGNORE to each ALTER TABLE statement. The same rule applies here: If the processing of the statement would result in error messages, they are repressed.

The features ENABLE and DISABLE KEYS apply only to tables that work with the MyISAM storage engine. If updates are executed on a table, MySQL updates the indexes automatically. The automatic update of the indexes can be switched off with ALTER TABLE ... DISABLE KEYS and can be switched on again with ENABLE KEYS.

To increase the processing time of SELECT statements with sort specifications, the rows of a table can be sorted explicitly on a specific column or combination of columns; see also Section 25.3.

Example 24.9: Sort all players in the PLAYERS table on league number in descending order.

```
ALTER TABLE PLAYERS ORDER BY LEAGUENO DESC
```

Exercise 24.1: Change the storage engine of the TEAMS table to MyISAM.

Exercise 24.2: Sort the COMMITTEE_MEMBERS table on player number in ascending order and next sort on function in descending order.

24.5 Changing Columns

The ALTER TABLE statement can change many properties of columns.

DEFINITION

```
<alter table statement> ::=
   ALTER [ IGNORE ] TABLE <table specification>
   <table structure change>

<table structure change> ::=
   <table change>                  |
   <column change                  |
   <integrity constraint change>   |
   <index change>

<column change> ::=
   ADD [ COLUMN ] <column definition>
      [ FIRST | AFTER <column name> ]                              |
   ADD [ COLUMN ] <table schema>                                   |
   DROP [ COLUMN ] <column name> [ RESTRICT | CASCADE ]            |
   CHANGE [ COLUMN ] <column name> <column definition>
      [ FIRST | AFTER <column name> ]                              |
   MODIFY [ COLUMN ] <column definition>
      [ FIRST | AFTER <column name> ]                              |
   ALTER [ COLUMN ] { SET DEFAULT <expression> | DROP DEFAULT }

<column definition> ::=
   <column name> <data type> [ <null specification> ]
      [ <column integrity constraint> ] [ <column option>... ]

<table name>          ;
<column name>         ;
<index name>          ;
<constraint name>     ;
<character set name>  ;
<collation name>      ::= <name>
```

Example 24.10: Add a new column called TYPE to the TEAMS table. This column shows whether it is a ladies' or a men's team.

```
ALTER   TABLE TEAMS
ADD     TYPE CHAR(1)
```

The TEAMS table now looks like this:

```
TEAMNO  PLAYERNO  DIVISION  TYPE
------  --------  --------  ----
     1         6  first     ?
     2        27  second    ?
```

Explanation: In all rows, the TYPE column is filled with the null value. This is the only possible value that MySQL can use to fill the column (how would MySQL know, for example, whether team 1 is a men's team?). The new column automatically becomes the last column unless the "position" is specified.

Because you may specify a full column definition, you may also enter a null specification, integrity constraints, and column options.

The word COLUMN may be added but does not change the result.

Example 24.11: Add a new column called TYPE to the TEAMS table. This column shows whether it is a ladies' or a men's team. The column must be placed right behind the TEAMNO column.

```
ALTER   TABLE TEAMS
ADD     TYPE CHAR(1) AFTER TEAMNO
```

This TEAMS table now looks like this:

```
TEAMNO  TYPE  PLAYERNO  DIVISION
------  ----  --------  --------
     1     ?         6  first
     2     ?        27  second
```

Explanation: By replacing AFTER TEAMNO by FIRST, the new column is positioned at the beginning.

With a somewhat different formulation, two or more new columns can be added at once.

Example 24.12: Add two new columns to the TEAMS table.

```
ALTER   TABLE TEAMS
ADD    (CATEGORY  VARCHAR(20) NOT NULL,
        IMAGO     INTEGER DEFAULT 10)
```

Explanation: The CATEGORY column has been defined as NOT NULL. This means that MySQL cannot assign a null value to each row for this column. Depending on the data type, MySQL fills in an actual value: the value 0 for numeric columns, the empty string for alphanumeric columns, the date 0000-00-00 for date data types, and the time 00:00:00 for time data types.

Example 24.13: Delete the TYPE column from the TEAMS table.

```
ALTER   TABLE TEAMS
DROP    TYPE
```

Explanation: All other database objects that depend on this column, such as privileges, indexes, and views, will also be deleted.

Example 24.14: In the TEAMS table, change the column name BIRTH_DATE to DATE_OF_BIRTH.

```
ALTER   TABLE PLAYERS
CHANGE  BIRTH_DATE DATE_OF_BIRTH DATE
```

Explanation: Behind the column name, a new column definition is specified. Because we want to change only the column name, we leave the other specifications unchanged so they remain equal to those of the original column. But we are allowed to change those as well.

Example 24.15: Increase the length of the TOWN column from 30 to 40.

```
ALTER   TABLE PLAYERS
CHANGE  TOWN TOWN VARCHAR(40) NOT NULL
```

The length of a data type may be increased or decreased. In the case of the latter, the existing values are shortened.

Example 24.16: Shorten the length of the TOWN column to five characters.

```
ALTER   TABLE PLAYERS
CHANGE  TOWN TOWN VARCHAR(5) NOT NULL
```

Example 24.17: Change the data type of the PLAYERNO column in the PLAYERS table from `INTEGER` to `SMALLINT`.

```
ALTER   TABLE PLAYERS
CHANGE  PLAYERNO PLAYERNO SMALLINT
```

When data types are changed, the usual rule is that it must be possible to transform the values in the column into the new data type. So the previous example is executed correctly because the current player numbers fit into the `SMALLINT` data type.

Example 24.18: Move the TOWN column to the second position.

```
ALTER   TABLE PLAYERS
CHANGE  TOWN TOWN VARCHAR(5) NOT NULL AFTER PLAYERNO
```

Specifications that are not mentioned, such as the comment and the character set, remain unchanged.

ALTER TABLE MODIFY can also change properties of columns; you do not have to specify the new column names first. That also means that, when using MODIFY, you cannot change the column name itself.

Example 24.19: Rewrite Example 24.18 with MODIFY.

```
ALTER   TABLE PLAYERS
MODIFY  TOWN VARCHAR(5) NOT NULL AFTER PLAYERNO
```

Example 24.20: Assign the default value Member to the POSITION column of the COMMITTEE_MEMBERS table.

```
ALTER   TABLE COMMITTEE_MEMBERS
ALTER   POSITION SET DEFAULT 'Member'
```

or

```
ALTER   TABLE COMMITTEE_MEMBERS
MODIFY  POSITION CHAR(20) DEFAULT 'Member'
```

Example 24.21: Delete the default value of the POSITION column in the COMMITTEE_MEMBERS table.

```
ALTER   TABLE COMMITTEE_MEMBERS
ALTER   POSITION DROP DEFAULT
```

Exercise 24.3: Change the column name POSITION in the COMMITTEE_MEMBERS table to COMMITTEE_POSITION.

Exercise 24.4: Next, increase the length of the COMMITTEE_POSITION column from 20 to 30.

Exercise 24.5: Assign the default value Stratford to the TOWN column in the PLAYERS table.

24.6 Changing Integrity Constraints

Chapter 21, "Specifying Integrity Constraints," we extensively discussed the different kinds of integrity constraints that you can add to a table. With the ALTER TABLE statement, you can add or delete constraints afterward.

DEFINITION

```
<alter table statement> ::=
   ALTER [ IGNORE ] TABLE <table specification>
   <table structure change>

<table structure change> ::=
   <table change>                     |
   <column change>                    |
   <integrity constraint change> |
   <index change>

<integrity constraint change> ::=
   ADD <primary key>                      |
   DROP PRIMARY KEY                       |
   ADD <alternate key>                    |
   DROP FOREIGN KEY <index name>          |
   ADD <foreign key>                      |
   ADD <check integrity constraint>   |
   DROP CONSTRAINT <constraint name>

<primary key> ::=
   [ CONSTRAINT [ <constraint name> ] ]
   PRIMARY KEY [ <index name> ]
   [ { USING | TYPE } <index type> ] <column list>

<alternate key> ::=
   [ CONSTRAINT [ <constraint name> ] ]
   UNIQUE [ INDEX | KEY ] [ <index name> ]
   [ { USING | TYPE } <index type> ] <column list>

<foreign key> ::=
   [ CONSTRAINT [ <constraint name> ] ]
   FOREIGN KEY [ <index name> ] <column list>
   <referencing specification>

<check integrity constraint> ::=
   [ CONSTRAINT [ <constraint name> ] ] CHECK ( <condition> )

<column list> ::= ( <column name> [ , <column name> ]... )

<table name>       ;
<database name>    ;
<column name>      ;
<index name>       ;
<constraint name> ::= <name>
```

The syntax for adding integrity constraints with an ALTER TABLE statement is identical to the syntax for table integrity constraints in the CREATE TABLE statement. We refer to Chapter 21 for this.

Consider this special situation: Imagine that two tables, T_1 and T_2, both have a foreign key referring to the other table. This is called *cross-referential integrity*. Cross-referential integrity can cause problems. If T_1 is defined and T_2 does not yet exist, the foreign key cannot be defined. You can solve this problem by adding one of the two foreign keys later with an `ALTER TABLE` statement.

Example 24.22: Create the two tables T_1 and T_2.

```
CREATE TABLE T1
      (A INTEGER NOT NULL PRIMARY KEY,
       B INTEGER NOT NULL)

CREATE TABLE T2
      (A INTEGER NOT NULL PRIMARY KEY,
       B INTEGER NOT NULL,
       CONSTRAINT C1 CHECK (B > 0),
       CONSTRAINT FK1 FOREIGN KEY (A) REFERENCES T1 (A))

ALTER TABLE T1
   ADD CONSTRAINT FK2 FOREIGN KEY (A) REFERENCES T2 (A)
```

Explanation: After these three statements, the cross-referential integrity is defined.

To remove integrity constraints, you can use the `DROP` version of the `ALTER TABLE` statement. Consider some examples:

Example 24.23: Delete the primary key from the PLAYERS table.

```
ALTER TABLE PLAYERS DROP PRIMARY KEY
```

Example 24.24: Delete the foreign key called `FK2` that refers from the T_1 to the T_2 table; see the previous example.

```
ALTER TABLE T1 DROP CONSTRAINT FK2
```

With `DROP CONSTRAINT`, all kinds of integrity constraints can be removed, including primary and alternate keys, and check integrity constraints.

Example 24.25: Delete the check integrity constraint C_1 that is defined on the B column of the T_2 table.

```
ALTER TABLE T2 DROP CONSTRAINT C1
```

It is easier to delete an integrity constraint later if a name has explicitly been specified because then it is not necessary to determine which name MySQL has assigned to it.

24.7 Answers

24.1
```
ALTER TABLE TEAMS
    ENGINE = MYISAM
```

24.2
```
ALTER TABLE COMMITTEE_MEMBERS
    ORDER BY PLAYERNO ASC, POSITION DESC
```

24.3
```
ALTER TABLE COMMITTEE_MEMBERS
    CHANGE POSITION COMMITTEE_POSITION CHAR(20)
```

24.4
```
ALTER TABLE COMMITTEE_MEMBERS
    MODIFY COMMITTEE_POSITION CHAR(30)
```

24.5
```
ALTER TABLE PLAYERS
    ALTER TOWN SET DEFAULT 'Stratford'
```

CHAPTER 25

Using Indexes

25.1 Introduction

Some SQL statements, such as the CREATE TABLE and GRANT statements, have a reasonably constant execution time. It does not matter under which circumstances such statements are executed; they always need a certain execution time, and it cannot be reduced. However, this is not the case for all statements. The time required to process SELECT, UPDATE, and DELETE statements varies. One SELECT statement might be processed in two seconds, and another could take minutes. You can influence the required execution time for this type of statement.

Many techniques exist for reducing the execution time of SELECT, UPDATE, and DELETE statements, ranging from reformulating statements to purchasing faster computers. This chapter describes one technique—using indexes to strongly influence execution times.

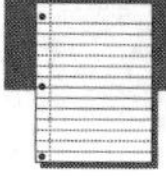

NOTE

The next few sections provide useful background information on how MySQL uses indexes rather than explain SQL statements.

25.2 Rows, Tables, and Files

This book assumes that if we add rows, they are stored in tables. However, a table is a concept that MySQL understands but the operating system does not. This section explains how rows are actually stored on hard disk. This information is important to understand before we concentrate on the workings of an index.

Rows are stored in *files*. Depending on the storage engine of the table, rows of different tables are stored in the same or different files. `MyISAM` creates a separate file for each table. On the other hand, `InnoDB` places tables into one file, unless explicitly specified not to do so.

Each file is divided into *data pages*, or *pages*, for short. Figure 25.1 shows a file that contains the data of the PLAYERS table. The file consists of five pages (the horizontal gray strips form the boundaries between the pages). In other words, the data of the PLAYERS table is spread over five pages of this file.

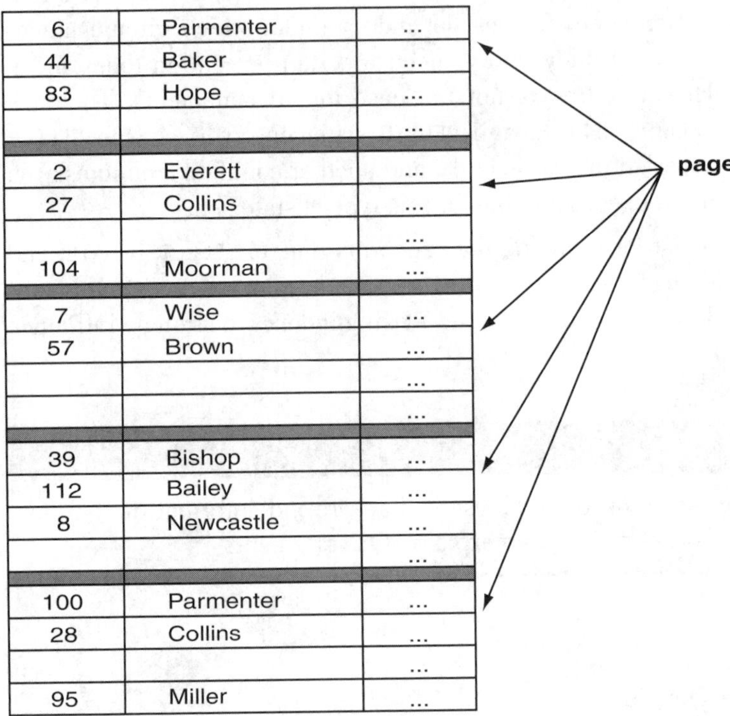

FIGURE 25.1 The rows of a table are stored in pages.

In this example, each page clearly has enough space for four rows and is not completely filled. How do these "gaps" arise? When new rows are added, MySQL automatically stores them after the last row of the final page. If that page is full, an empty page is added to the file. So a gap is created not during the process of adding rows, but when rows are deleted. MySQL does not fill the gaps automatically. If it did, MySQL would need to find an empty space when a row is added; for large tables, this would take too much time. Imagine that the table contains one million rows and that all pages are full except for the penultimate page. If a new row had to be stored in a gap, first all other rows would need to be accessed to locate a gap. Again, this would delay processing and explains why rows are inserted at the end.

In this example, we have also assumed that a page consists of a maximum of four rows. Two factors determine how many rows really fit in a page: the size of the page and the length of the rows. The size of a page depends on the operating system and the storage engine. Sizes such as 2K, 4K, 8K, and 32K are very common. The length of a row from the PLAYERS table is about 90 bytes. This means that approximately 45 rows would fit into a 4K page.

It is important to realize that pages always form the unit of I/O. If an operating system retrieves data from a hard disk, it occurs page by page. Systems such as UNIX or Windows do not retrieve 2 bytes from disk. Instead, they collect the page in which these 2 bytes are stored. Therefore, a database server can ask an operating system to retrieve one page from the file, but not just one row.

Two steps are required to retrieve a row from a table. First, the page in which the row is recorded is collected from disk. Second, we need to find the row in the page. This step takes place entirely within internal memory. Each row has a unique identification. This *row identification* consists of two parts: a page identification and a specification that indicates which row is involved. This row-identification process looks different for each storage engine.

25.3 How Does an Index Work?

MySQL has several methods of accessing rows in a table. The two best-known methods are the *sequential access method* (also called *scanning* or *browsing*) and the *indexed access method.*

The sequential access method is best described as browsing a table row by row. Each row in a table is read. If only one row needs to be found in a table with many rows, this method is very time-consuming and inefficient, comparable to going through a telephone book page by page. If you are looking for the number of someone whose name begins with an *L*, you certainly do not want to start looking under the letter *A*.

When MySQL uses the indexed access method, it reads only the rows that exhibit the required characteristics. However, an *index* is necessary. An index is a type of alternative access to a table and can be compared to the index in a book.

An index in MySQL is built like a *tree* consisting of a number of *nodes*. Figure 25.2 shows an index on the PLAYERNO column. Notice that this is a simplified version of an actual index tree. Nevertheless, the example is detailed enough to show how MySQL handles indexes. At the top of the figure (in the light gray area) is the index itself, and at the bottom are two columns of the PLAYERS table: PLAYERNO and NAME. The long rectangles represent the nodes of the index. The node at the top forms the starting point of the index and is known as the *root*. Each node contains up to three values from the PLAYERNO column. Each value in a node points to another node or to a row in the PLAYERS table, and each row in the table is referenced through one node. A node that points to a row is called a *leaf page*. The values in a node have been ordered. For each node except the root, the values in that node are always less than or equal to the value that points to that node. Leaf pages are themselves linked to one another. A leaf page has a pointer to the leaf page with the next set of values. Figure 25.2 represents these pointers with open arrows.

What does a pointer from a leaf page to a row in the PLAYERS table really look like? A pointer is nothing more than arow identification. We introduced this concept in the previous section. Because arow identification consists of two parts, the same also applies to an index pointer. The two parts are the page in which the row occurs, and the entity of the list that indicates the location of the row within the page.

Broadly speaking, MySQL supports three algorithms for using indexes. The first algorithm is for searching rows in which a particular value occurs. The second algorithm is for browsing through an entire table or a part of a table via an ordered column. The third algorithm is used if several values of a column must be retrieved. We illustrate these algorithms with three examples. The first example is how MySQL uses the index to select particular rows.

Example 25.1: Imagine that all rows with player number 44 must be found.

Step 1. Look for the root of the index. This root becomes the active node.

Step 2. Is the active node a leaf page? If so, continue with step 4. If not, continue with step 3.

Step 3. Does the active node contain the value 44? If so, the node to which this value points becomes the active node; go back to step 2. If not, choose the lowest value that is greater than 44 in the active node. The node to which this value points becomes the active node; go back to step 2.

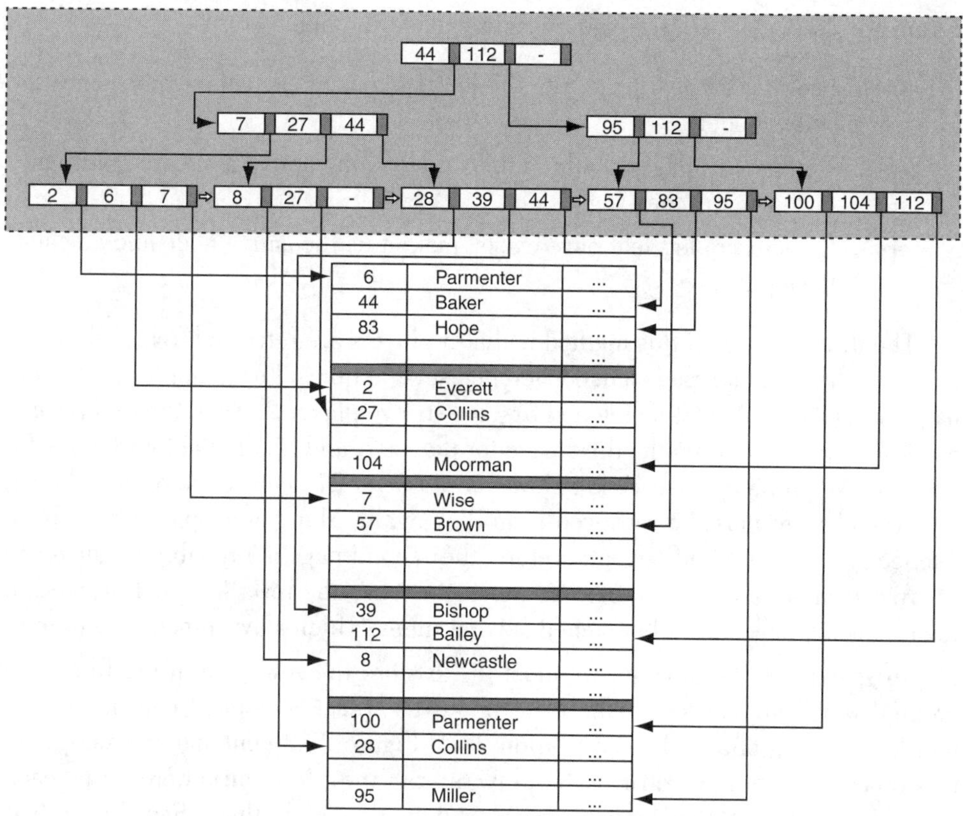

FIGURE 25.2 Example of an index tree

Step 4. Look for the value 44 in the active node. Now this value points to all pages in which rows of the PLAYERS table appear, and the value of the PLAYERNO column is 44. Retrieve all these pages from the database for further processing.

Step 5. For each page, find the row where the value of the PLAYERNO column is equal to 44.

Without browsing all the rows, MySQL has found the desired row(s). In most cases, the time spent answering this type of question can be reduced considerably if MySQL uses an index.

In the next example, MySQL uses the index to retrieve ordered rows from a table.

Example 25.2: Get all players ordered by player number.

Step 1. Look for the leaf page with the lowest value. This leaf page becomes the active node.

Step 2. Retrieve all pages to which the values in the active node are pointing, for further processing.

Step 3. If a subsequent leaf page exists, make this the active node and go back to step 2.

The disadvantage of this method is that if players are retrieved from disk, there is a good chance that a page must be fetched several times. For example, the second page in Figure 25.2 must be fetched first to retrieve player 2. Next, the first page is needed for player 6, then the third page for player 7, and finally the fourth page for player 8. No problem exists so far. However, if player 27 needs to be retrieved next, the second page must be retrieved from disk again. Many other pages have been fetched since the second page; therefore, the second page is probably no longer in internal memory and cannot be read again. Because the rows were not ordered in the file, many pages must be fetched several times, which slows processing time.

To speed up this process, we must try to store the rows within the file in an ordered way. The `ORDER BY` clause in the `ALTER TABLE` statement can be used to reorder the rows of a table; see Section 24.4. Figure 25.3 contains an example of this process. If we now retrieve the players from the file in an ordered way, each page is probably fetched only once. MySQL understands that when player 6 is retrieved, the correct page is already in the internal memory from when player 2 was retrieved. The same applies to player 7.

The third algorithm is a combination of the first two.

Example 25.3: Get all players numbers 39 through 95.

Step 1. Look for the root of the index. This root becomes the active node.

Step 2. Is the active node a leaf page? If so, continue with step 4. If not, continue with step 3.

Step 3. Does the active node contain the value `39`? If so, the node to which this value points becomes the active node; go back to step 2. If not, choose the lowest value that is greater than `39` in the active node. The node to which this value points becomes the active node; go back to step 2.

Step 4. Look for the value `39` in the active node.

Step 5. In the active node, retrieve all rows that belong to the values between `39` and `95`. If `95` appears in this node, you are ready. Otherwise, continue with step 6.

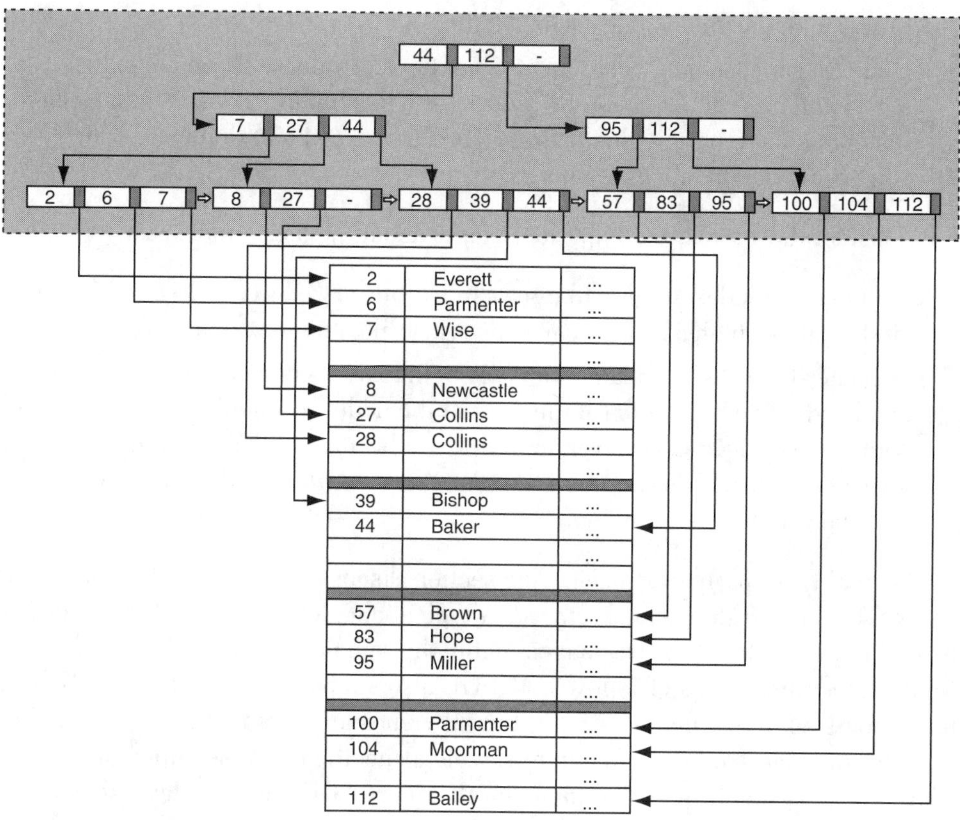

FIGURE 25.3 Example of a clustered index

Step 6. If a subsequent leaf page exists, make this the active node and go back to step 5.

This algorithm can be useful when a `SELECT` statement contains conditions with a `BETWEEN`, a greater than operator, or certain `LIKE` operators.

See the following remarks about indexes:

- If values in a table are updated or rows are added or deleted, MySQL automatically updates the index, so the index tree is always consistent with the contents of the table.
- In the previous table, an index was defined on the PLAYERNO column of the PLAYERS table. This is the primary key of this table and contains no duplicate values. An index can also be defined on a nonunique column, such as the NAME column. As a result, one value in a leaf page points to multiple rows—one pointer for each row in which the value occurs.

- You can define many indexes on a table.
- Indexes can also be defined on combinations of values. Those are called *compound indexes* or *composite indexes.* Each value in a node is then a concatenation of the individual values. The leaf pages point to rows in which that combination of values appears.

Consider these two other important points about the use of indexes:

- Nodes of an index are just like rows in a table, stored in files. Therefore, an index takes up physical storage space (just like an index in a book).
- Updates to tables can lead to updates to indexes. When an index must be updated, MySQL tries to fill the gaps in the nodes to complete the process as quickly as possible; however, an index can become so "full" that new nodes must be added. This can require a total *reorganization* of the index, which can be very time-consuming.

Several types of indexes exist. This section discussed what is called the *B-tree* index. The letter *B* stands for *balanced.* A typical characteristic of a B-tree index is that all the branches of the tree have roughly the same length. Later in this chapter, we describe other types of indexes. MySQL also supports the *hash index.* With a hash index, no tree structure is built, but all values are kept in a list that points to the relevant pages and rows. When retrieving a specific row based upon one value, a hash index is very fast. For example, for the query, "Give me the player with number 27," a hash index would be perfect. However, hash indexes are not useful for sorting rows or fetching a row based on subvalues, such as, "Give the players whose names begin with a capital *P*." The hash index can be combined with tables that are kept in internal memory. These are the tables that have been built with the `MEMORY` storage engine; see Section 20.10.1.

As we already mentioned, this section presents a very simplified picture of how an index works. In reality, a node in an index tree can accommodate not just three, but many values, for example. For a more detailed description of indexes, see [ELMA06].

25.4 Processing a SELECT Statement: The Steps

Chapter 6, "SELECT Statements, Table Expressions, and Subqueries," described which clauses are executed successively during the processing of a `SELECT` statement. These clauses form a *basic strategy* for processing a statement. In a basic strategy, we assume sequential access to the data. This section discusses how using an index can change the basic strategy to an *optimized strategy.*

MySQL tries to choose the most efficient strategy for processing each statement. This analysis is performed by a module within MySQL called the *optimizer.* (The analysis of statements is also referred to as *query optimization.*) The optimizer defines a number of alternative strategies for each statement. It estimates which strategy is likely to be the most efficient, based upon factors such as the expected execution time, the number of rows, and the presence of indexes (in the absence of indexes, this can be the basic strategy). MySQL then executes the statement according to its chosen strategy.

See the next examples of optimized processing strategies.

Example 25.4: Get all information about player 44; we assume that there is an index defined on the PLAYERNO column.

```
SELECT    *
FROM      PLAYERS
WHERE     PLAYERNO = 44
```

The FROM clause: Usually, all rows would be retrieved from the PLAYERS table. Speeding up the processing by using an index means that only the rows in which the value in the PLAYERNO column is 44 are fetched.

The intermediate result is:

```
PLAYERNO  NAME   ...
--------  -----  ---
      44  Baker  ...
```

The WHERE clause: In this example, this clause was processed simultaneously with the FROM clause.

The SELECT clause: All columns are presented.

The difference between the basic strategy and this "optimized" strategy can be represented in another way.

The basic strategy is:

```
RESULT := [];
FOR EACH P IN PLAYERS DO
   IF P.PLAYERNO = 44 THEN
      RESULT :+ P;
ENDFOR;
```

The optimized strategy is:

```
RESULT := [];
FOR EACH P IN PLAYERS WHERE PLAYERNO = 44 DO
   RESULT :+ P;
ENDFOR;
```

With the first strategy, the FOR EACH statement fetches all rows. The second strategy works much more selectively. When an index is used, only those rows in which the player number is 44 are retrieved.

Example 25.5: Get the player number and town of each player whose player number is less than 10 and who lives in Stratford; order the result by player number.

```
SELECT   PLAYERNO, TOWN
FROM     PLAYERS
WHERE    PLAYERNO < 10
AND      TOWN = 'Stratford'
ORDER BY PLAYERNO
```

The FROM clause: Fetch all rows in which the player number is less than 10. Again, use the index on the PLAYERNO column. Fetch the rows in ascending order using the ORDER BY clause. This is simple because the values in an index are always ordered.

The intermediate result is:

```
PLAYERNO  ...  TOWN       ...
--------  ---  ---------  ---
       2  ...  Stratford  ...
       6  ...  Stratford  ...
       7  ...  Stratford  ...
       8  ...  Inglewood  ...
```

The WHERE clause: The WHERE clause specifies two conditions. Each row in the intermediate result satisfies the first condition, which has already been evaluated in the FROM clause. Now only the second condition must be evaluated.

The intermediate result is:

```
PLAYERNO  ...  TOWN       ...
--------  ---  ---------  ---
       2  ...  Stratford  ...
       6  ...  Stratford  ...
       7  ...  Stratford  ...
```

The ORDER BY clause: Because we used an index while processing the FROM clause, no extra sorting needs to be done.

The SELECT clause: Two columns are selected. The end result is:

```
PLAYERNO  TOWN
--------  ---------
       2  Stratford
       6  Stratford
       7  Stratford
```

Next we show the basic strategy and the optimized strategy for this example.

The basic strategy is:

```
RESULT := [];
FOR EACH P IN PLAYERS DO
   IF (P.PLAYERNO < 10)
   AND (P.TOWN = 'Stratford') THEN
      RESULT :+ P;
ENDFOR;
```

The optimized strategy is:

```
RESULT := [];
FOR EACH P IN PLAYERS WHERE PLAYERNO < 10 DO
   IF P.TOWN = 'Stratford' THEN
      RESULT :+ P;
ENDFOR;
```

Example 25.6: Get the name and initials of each player who lives in the same town as player 44.

```
SELECT   NAME, INITIALS
FROM     PLAYERS
WHERE    TOWN =
        (SELECT   TOWN
         FROM     PLAYERS
         WHERE    PLAYERNO = 44)
```

We again show both strategies for this example.

The basic strategy is:

```
RESULT := [];
FOR EACH P IN PLAYERS DO
   HELP := FALSE;
   FOR EACH P44 IN PLAYERS DO
      IF (P44.TOWN = P.TOWN)
      AND (P44.PLAYERNO = 44) THEN
         HELP := TRUE;
   ENDFOR;
   IF HELP = TRUE THEN
      RESULT :+ P;
ENDFOR;
```

The optimized strategy is:

```
RESULT := [];
FIND P44 IN PLAYERS WHERE PLAYERNO = 44;
FOR EACH P IN PLAYERS WHERE TOWN = P44.TOWN DO
   RESULT :+ P;
ENDFOR;
```

These were three relatively simple examples. As the statements become more complex, it also becomes more difficult for MySQL to determine the optimal strategy, which adds to the processing time. The quality of the optimizer is an important factor here.

If you want to know more about the optimization of SELECT statements, see [KIM85]. However, you do not actually need this knowledge to understand SQL statements, which is why we have given only a summary of the topic.

Exercise 25.1: For the following two statements, write the basic strategy and an optimized strategy; assume that an index has been defined on each column.

1.
```
SELECT   *
FROM     TEAMS
WHERE    TEAMNO > 1
AND      DIVISION = 'second'
```

2.
```
SELECT   P.PLAYERNO
FROM     PLAYERS AS P, MATCHES AS M
WHERE    P.PLAYERNO = M.PLAYERNO
AND      BIRTH_DATE > '1963-01-01'
```

25.5 Creating Indexes

The definition of the *CREATE INDEX statement* follows:

DEFINITION

```
<create index statement> ::=
   CREATE [ <index type> ] INDEX <index name>
   [ USING { BTREE | HASH } ]
   ON <table specification>
   ( <column in index> [ , <column in index> ]... )

<index type> ::= UNIQUE | FULLTEXT | SPATIAL

<column in index> ::= <column name> [ ASC | DESC ]
```

Example 25.7: Create an index on the POSTCODE column of the PLAYERS table.

```
CREATE   INDEX PLAY_PC
ON       PLAYERS (POSTCODE ASC)
```

Explanation: In this example, a nonunique index is created (correctly). The inclusion of ASC or DESC indicates whether the index should be built in ascending (ASC) or descending (DESC) order. If neither is specified, MySQL uses ASC as its default. If a certain column in a SELECT statement is sorted in descending order, processing is quicker if a descending-order index is defined on that column.

If we do not assign the USING specification, MySQL normally creates a B-tree. So the previous statement could have been formulated as follows:

```
CREATE    INDEX PLAY_PC USING BTREE
ON        PLAYERS (POSTCODE ASC)
```

However, if the relevant table has been built with the MEMORY storage engine, MySQL uses the hash index.

Example 25.8: Create a hash index on the TOWN column of the PLAYERS table.

```
CREATE    INDEX PLAY_TOWN USING HASH
ON        PLAYERS (TOWN)
```

Example 25.9: Create a compound index on the WON and LOST columns of the MATCHES table.

```
CREATE    INDEX MAT_WL
ON        MATCHES (WON, LOST)
```

Explanation: Multiple columns may be included in the definition of an index as long as they all belong to the same table.

Example 25.10: Create a unique index on the NAME and INITIALS columns of the PLAYERS table.

```
CREATE    UNIQUE INDEX NAMEINIT
ON        PLAYERS (NAME, INITIALS)
```

Explanation: After this statement has been entered, MySQL prevents two equal combinations of name and initials from being inserted into the PLAYERS table. The same could have been achieved by defining the column combination as an alternate key.

You can create indexes at any time; you do not need to create all the indexes for a table right after the CREATE TABLE statement. You can also create indexes on tables that already have data in them. Obviously, creating a unique index on a table in which the column concerned already contains duplicate values is not possible. MySQL identifies this and does not create the index. The user needs to remove the duplicate values first. The following SELECT statement helps locate the duplicate C values (C is the column on which the index must be defined):

```
SELECT   C
FROM     T
GROUP BY C
HAVING   COUNT(*) > 1
```

Besides UNIQUE, MySQL has two other special index types: *FULLTEXT* and *SPATIAL*. FULLTEXT indexes can be used in combination only with tables that are defined with the MyISAM storage engine. After they have been created, the special full-text queries containing the MATCH operator can be used; see Section 8.12. This is useful for alphanumeric columns in which names and text are stored.

The SPATIAL index can be used to index columns with geometric data types. We do not discuss the SPATIAL index or geometric data types in this book.

Indexes can also be entered with an ALTER TABLE statement; see the following definition.

DEFINITION

```
<alter table statement> ::=
   ALTER TABLE <table specification> <table structure change>

<table structure change> ::=
   <table change>                |
   <column change>               |
   <integrity constraint change> |
   <index change>

<index change> ::=
   ADD [ <index type> ] INDEX <index name>
   [ USING { BTREE | HASH } ]
   ( <column in index> [ , <column in index> ]... )

<index type> ::= UNIQUE | FULLTEXT | SPATIAL

<column in index> ::= <column name> [ ASC | DESC ]
```

Example 25.11: Create a nonunique index on the DIVISION column of the TEAMS table.

```
ALTER TABLE TEAMS
ADD   INDEX TEAMS_DIVISION USING BTREE (DIVISION)
```

Example 25.12: Create a unique hash index to the PLAYERS table on the combination of the columns TOWN, STREET, and BIRTH_DATE.

```
ALTER TABLE PLAYERS
ADD   UNIQUE INDEX TEAMS_DIVISION
      USING HASH (TOWN, STREET, BIRTH_DATE)
```

25.6 Defining Indexes Together with the Tables

The previous section showed how indexes can be created with a CREATE INDEX or an ALTER TABLE statement. In both cases, the indexes are created after the tables have been created and perhaps filled with rows. Indexes can also be created with the table. We can include the index definition within the CREATE TABLE statement.

DEFINITION

```
<create table statement> ::=
   CREATE [ TEMPORARY ] TABLE [ IF NOT EXISTS ]
      <table specification> <table structure>

<table structure> ::=
   <table schema>

<table schema> ::=
   ( <table element> [ , <table element> ]... )

<table element> ::=
   <column definition>          |
   <table integrity constraint> |
   <index definition>

<index definition> ::=
   <index type> { INDEX | KEY } [ <index name> ]
   [ USING { BTREE | HASH } ]
   ( <column in index> [ , <column in index> ]... )

<index type> ::= UNIQUE | FULLTEXT | SPATIAL

<column in index> ::= <column name> [ ASC | DESC ]

<table name>       ;
<index name>       ::= <name>
```

Example 25.13: Create the MATCHES table with a compound index on the WON and LOST columns; see also Example 25.9.

```
CREATE TABLE MATCHES
      (MATCHNO      INTEGER NOT NULL PRIMARY KEY,
       TEAMNO       INTEGER NOT NULL,
       PLAYERNO     INTEGER NOT NULL,
       WON          SMALLINT NOT NULL,
       LOST         SMALLINT NOT NULL,
       INDEX MAT_WL (WON, LOST))
```

Explanation: The syntax for the index as a table element looks much like that of the CREATE INDEX statement. The result is also the same.

Index types such as UNIQUE, FULLTEXT, and SPATIAL may also be added.

Example 25.14: Create the PLAYERS table with a unique hash index on the NAME and INITIALS columns; see also Example 25.10.

```
CREATE   TABLE PLAYERS
        (PLAYERNO      INTEGER NOT NULL PRIMARY KEY,
         NAME          CHAR(15) NOT NULL,
         INITIALS      CHAR(3) NOT NULL,
         BIRTH_DATE    DATE,
         SEX           CHAR(1) NOT NULL,
         JOINED        SMALLINT NOT NULL,
         STREET        VARCHAR(30) NOT NULL,
         HOUSENO       CHAR(4),
         POSTCODE      CHAR(6),
         TOWN          VARCHAR(30) NOT NULL,
         PHONENO       CHAR(13),
         LEAGUENO      CHAR(4),
         UNIQUE INDEX NAMEINIT USING HASH (NAME, INITIALS))
```

25.7 Dropping Indexes

The DROP INDEX statement is used to remove indexes.

DEFINITION

```
<drop index statement> ::=
   DROP INDEX <index name> ON <table specification>
```

Example 25.15: Remove the three indexes that were defined in the previous examples.

```
DROP INDEX PLAY_PC ON PLAYERS

DROP INDEX MATD_WL ON MATCHES

DROP INDEX NAMEINIT ON PLAYERS
```

Explanation: When you drop an index, the index type is not mentioned. In other words, you do not need to specify the words UNIQUE, FULLTEXT, and SPATIAL. Neither is it necessary to indicate whether it is a B-tree of hash index.

Instead of using the DROP INDEX statement, you can use the ALTER TABLE statement to remove an index.

DEFINITION

```
<alter table statement> ::=
   ALTER [ IGNORE ] TABLE <table specification>
      <table structure change>

<table structure change> ::=
   <table change>                |
   <column change>               |
   <integrity constraint change> |
   <index change>

<index change> ::=
   DROP { INDEX | KEY } <index name>
```

25.8 Indexes and Primary Keys

MySQL creates a unique index automatically if a primary or alternate key is defined within a CREATE TABLE statement or with an ALTER TABLE statement. MySQL determines the name of the index based on a set of rules. The index for a primary key is called PRIMARY. For an alternate key, the name of the first column of the key is used. If more than one alternate key exists for which the name begins with a certain column name, a sequence number is placed behind the column name.

Example 25.16: Create the T1 table with one primary key and three alternate keys.

```
CREATE TABLE T1
      (COL1   INTEGER NOT NULL,
       COL2   DATE NOT NULL UNIQUE,
       COL3   INTEGER NOT NULL,
       COL4   INTEGER NOT NULL,
       PRIMARY KEY (COL1, COL4),
       UNIQUE (COL3, COL4),
       UNIQUE (COL3, COL1))
```

After the table has been created, MySQL executes the following `CREATE INDEX` statements behind the scenes:

```
CREATE UNIQUE INDEX "PRIMARY" USING BTREE
ON     T1 (COL1, COL4)

CREATE UNIQUE INDEX COL2 USING BTREE
ON     T1 (COL2)

CREATE UNIQUE INDEX COL3 USING BTREE
ON     T1 (COL3, COL4)

CREATE UNIQUE INDEX COL3_2 USING BTREE
ON     T1 (COL3, COL1)
```

Be sure that the name `PRIMARY` is placed between double quotes because it is a reserved word; see Section 20.8.

25.9 The Big PLAYERS_XXL Table

In the next sections, as well as in other chapters, we use a special version of the PLAYERS table. This new table contains the same columns as the original PLAYERS table. However, the new table might hold thousands of rows, not just 14. This is why we called the table PLAYERS_XXL.

The original PLAYERS table contains normal values, such as `Inglewood` and `Parmenter`. The PLAYERS_XXL table contains artificially created data. The POSTCODE column, for example, contains values such as `p4` and `p25`, and the STREET column contains values such as `street164` and `street83`. The following sections show how this big table can be created and filled.

Example 25.17: Create the PLAYERS_XXL table.

```
CREATE TABLE PLAYERS_XXL
      (PLAYERNO      INTEGER NOT NULL PRIMARY KEY,
       NAME          CHAR(15) NOT NULL,
       INITIALS      CHAR(3) NOT NULL,
       BIRTH_DATE    DATE,
       SEX           CHAR(1) NOT NULL,
       JOINED        SMALLINT NOT NULL,
       STREET        VARCHAR(30) NOT NULL,
       HOUSENO       CHAR(4),
       POSTCODE      CHAR(6),
       TOWN          VARCHAR(30) NOT NULL,
       PHONENO       CHAR(13),
       LEAGUENO      CHAR(8))
```

Example 25.18: Then create the stored procedure FILL_PLAYERS_XXL.

```
CREATE PROCEDURE FILL_PLAYERS_XXL
   (IN NUMBER_PLAYERS INTEGER)
BEGIN
   DECLARE COUNTER INTEGER;
   TRUNCATE TABLE PLAYERS_XXL;
   COMMIT WORK;
   SET COUNTER = 1;
   WHILE COUNTER <= NUMBER_PLAYERS DO
    INSERT INTO PLAYERS_XXL VALUES(
     COUNTER,
     CONCAT('name',CAST(COUNTER AS CHAR(10))),
     CASE MOD(COUNTER,2) WHEN 0 THEN 'vl1' ELSE 'vl2' END,
     DATE('1960-01-01') + INTERVAL (MOD(COUNTER,300)) MONTH,
     CASE MOD(COUNTER,20) WHEN 0 THEN 'F' ELSE 'M' END,
     1980 + MOD(COUNTER,20),
     CONCAT('street',CAST(COUNTER /10 AS UNSIGNED INTEGER)),
     CAST(CAST(COUNTER /10 AS UNSIGNED INTEGER)+1 AS CHAR(4)),
     CONCAT('p',MOD(COUNTER,50)),
     CONCAT('town',MOD(COUNTER,10)),
     '070-6868689',
     CASE MOD(COUNTER,3) WHEN 0
        THEN NULL ELSE cast(COUNTER AS CHAR(8)) END);
    IF MOD(COUNTER,1000) = 0 THEN
     COMMIT WORK;
    END IF;
    SET COUNTER = COUNTER + 1;
   END WHILE;
   COMMIT WORK;
END
```

Explanation: This stored procedure has been created, but the table is not yet filled.

Example 25.19: Fill the PLAYERS_XXL table.

```
CALL FILL_PLAYERS_XXL(100000)
```

Explanation: With this statement, the PLAYERS_XXL table is filled with 100,000 rows. The stored procedure begins by emptying the table using a TRUNCATE statement. Next, the number of rows specified in the CALL statement are added. See Chapter 37, "Transactions and Multiuser Usage," for a description of the COMMIT statement.

Example 25.20: Create the following indexes on the PLAYERS_XXL table.

```
CREATE INDEX PLAYERS_XXL_INITIALS
   ON PLAYERS_XXL(INITIALS)

CREATE INDEX PLAYERS_XXL_POSTCODE
   ON PLAYERS_XXL(POSTCODE)

CREATE INDEX PLAYERS_XXL_STREET
   ON PLAYERS_XXL(STREET)
```

25.10 Choosing Columns for Indexes

To be absolutely sure that inefficient processing of SELECT statements is not due to the absence of an index, you could create an index on every column and combination of columns. If you intend to enter only SELECT statements against the data, this could be a good approach. However, such a solution raises a number of problems, such as the cost of index storage space. Another important disadvantage is that each update (INSERT, UPDATE, or DELETE statement) requires a corresponding index update and reduces the processing speed. So you need to make a choice. We discuss some guidelines next.

25.10.1 A Unique Index on Candidate Keys

In CREATE TABLE statements, we can specify primary and alternate keys. The result is that the relevant column(s) will never contain duplicate values. It is recommended that an index be defined on each candidate key so that the uniqueness of new values can be checked quickly. As mentioned in Section 25.8, MySQL automatically creates a unique index for each candidate key.

25.10.2 An Index on Foreign Keys

Joins can take a long time to execute if no indexes are defined on the join columns. For a large percentage of joins, the join columns are also keys of the tables concerned. They can be primary and alternate keys, but they may also be foreign keys. According to the first rule of thumb, you should define an index on the primary and alternate key columns. Indexes on foreign keys remain.

25.10.3 An Index on Columns Included in Selection Criteria

In some cases, SELECT, UPDATE, and DELETE statements can be executed faster if an index has been defined on the columns named in the WHERE clause.

See this example:

```
SELECT   *
FROM     PLAYERS
WHERE    TOWN = 'Stratford'
```

Rows are selected on the basis of the value in the TOWN column, and processing this statement could be more efficient if an index were created on this column. Earlier sections of this chapter discussed this extensively.

An index is worthwhile not just when the = operator is used, but also for <, <=, >, and >=. (Note that the <> operator does not appear in this list.) However, this saves time only when the number of rows selected is a small percentage of the total number of rows in the table.

This section started with "In some cases." So when is it necessary to define an index? This depends on several factors, of which the most important are the number of rows in the table (or the cardinality of the table), the number of different values in the column concerned (or the cardinality of the column), and the distribution of values within the column. We explain these rules and illustrate them with some figures created from a test performed with MySQL.

This test uses the PLAYERS_XXL table; see the previous section. The results of the tests are represented in three diagrams; see Figure 25.4. Diagrams A, B, and C contain the processing times of the following SELECT statements, respectively:

```
SELECT    COUNT(*)
FROM      PLAYERS_XXL
WHERE     INITIALS = 'in1'

SELECT    COUNT(*)
FROM      PLAYERS_XXL
WHERE     POSTCODE = 'p25'

SELECT    COUNT(*)
FROM      PLAYERS_XXL
WHERE     STREET = 'street164'
```

Each SELECT statement has been executed on the PLAYERS_XXL table with three different sizes: small (100,000 rows), medium (500,000 rows), and large (1,000,000 rows). Each statement has also been executed with (light gray bars) and without (dark gray bars) an index. Each of the three statements was run in six different environments. To give reliable figures, each statement was run several times in each environment, and the average processing speed is shown in seconds in the diagrams.

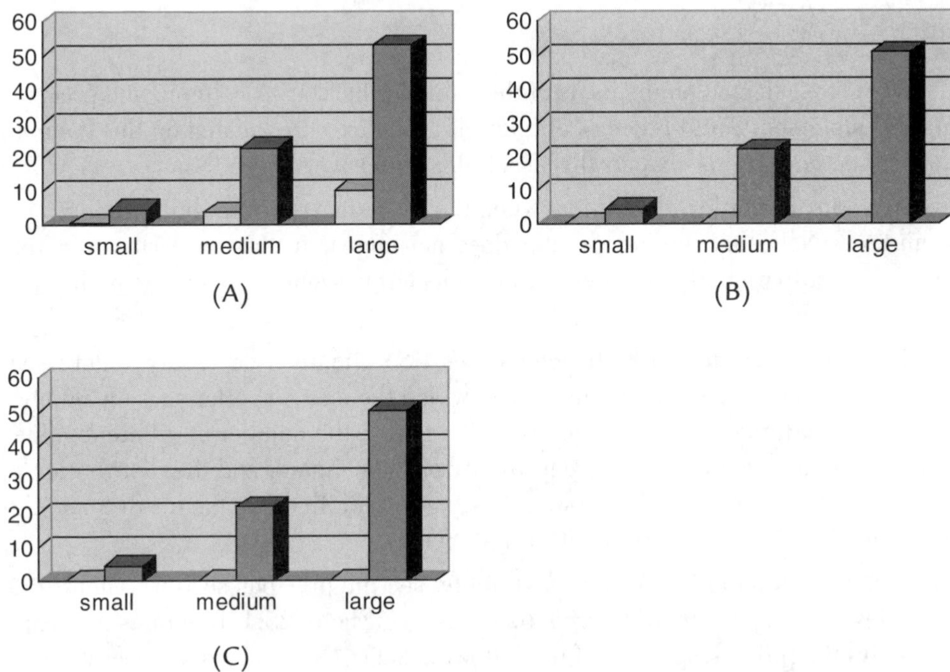

FIGURE 25.4 The impact of the cardinality of a column on the processing speed

It is important to know that the INITIALS column contains only two different values, `in1` and `in2`; the POSTCODE column contains 50 different values; and, in the STREET column, every value occurs ten times at most. This means that the first `SELECT` statement contains a condition on a column with a low cardinality, the third statement has a condition on a column with a high cardinality, and the second statement has a condition on a column with an average cardinality.

The following rules can be derived from the results. First, all three diagrams show that the larger the table is, the bigger the impact of the index is. Of course, we can define an index on a table consisting of 20 rows, but the effect is minimal. Whether a table is large enough for it to be worth defining an index depends entirely on the system on which the application runs. You need to try for yourself.

Second, the diagrams show that the effect of an index on a column with a low cardinality (so few different values) is minimal; see diagram A in Figure 25.4. As the table becomes larger, the processing speed starts to improve somewhat, but it remains minimal. For the third statement with a condition on the STREET column, the opposite applies. Here the presence of an index has a major impact on the processing speed. Moreover, as the database gets larger, that difference becomes more apparent. Diagram B in Figure 25.4 confirms the results for a table with an average cardinality.

The third significant factor in deciding whether you will define an index is the distribution of the values within a column. In the previous statements, each column has an equal distribution of values. (Each value occurs the same number of times within the column.) What if that is not the case? Figure 25.5 shows the results of the following two statements:

```
SELECT   COUNT(*)
FROM     PLAYERS_XXL
WHERE    SEX = 'M'

SELECT   COUNT(*)
FROM     PLAYERS_XXL
WHERE    SEX = 'F'
```

For these tests, the division of the values in the SEX column is as follows: The `M` value is present in 95 percent of the rows, and the `F` value is present in 5 percent of the rows. This is an extreme example of an unequal distribution and indicates the difference clearly. In diagram A in Figure 25.5, we can see that the impact of the index is minimal; however, the impact in diagram B in that figure is large. If an index is defined, counting all women in the large PLAYERS table is carried out approximately 180 times faster.

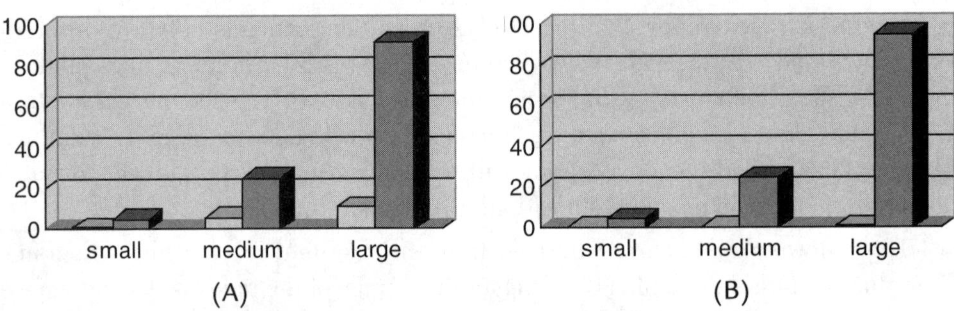

FIGURE 25.5 The impact on the processing speed of the distribution of values within a column

25.10.4 An Index on a Combination of Columns

If a WHERE clause contains an AND operator, an index is usually defined on the combination of columns to ensure more efficient processing. See the following example:

```
SELECT    *
FROM      PLAYERS
WHERE     NAME = 'Collins'
AND       INITIALS = 'DD'
```

The associated index is:

```
CREATE    INDEX NAMEINIT
ON        PLAYERS (NAME, INITIALS)
```

In some cases, when you are executing such a SELECT statement, it can suffice to have an index on only one of the columns. Imagine that duplicate names seldom occur in the NAME column and that this is the only column with an index. MySQL usually finds all the rows that satisfy the condition NAME = 'Collins' by using this index. Only infrequently does it retrieve a few too many rows. In this case, an index on the combination of columns takes up more storage space than necessary and will not significantly improve the processing speed of the SELECT statement.

Indexes defined on combinations of columns are also used for selections in which only the first column (or columns) of the index is specified. Therefore,

MySQL uses the previous NAMEINIT index to process the condition `NAME = 'Collins'`, but not for `INITIALS = 'DD'` because the INITIALS column is not the first one in the NAMEINIT index.

25.10.5 An Index on Columns Used for Sorting

If MySQL needs to sort the result of a `SELECT` statement by a column that has no index, a separate (time-consuming) sort process must be performed. You can avoid this extra sorting if you define a clustered index on the relevant column. When the rows are fetched from the database (with the `FROM` clause), this index can be used. The intermediate result from the `FROM` clause is already ordered by the correct column, so no extra sorting is necessary. This rule is valid only if the column concerned does not contain many null values (because null values are not stored in an index) and if the `SELECT` statement does not have a `WHERE` clause with a condition that can be optimized.

When exactly does MySQL perform a sort? If you add an `ORDER BY` clause to a `SELECT` statement, there is a good chance that SQL performs a sort. In addition, when columns are to be grouped (with the `GROUP BY` clause), all the rows must be sorted first. MySQL can process a `GROUP BY` clause more quickly when the rows are already ordered. If you use `DISTINCT` in the `SELECT` clause, all rows must be ordered (behind the scenes) to determine whether they are equal. Therefore, the order rule again applies: MySQL can process `DISTINCT` more quickly when the rows are already ordered.

Finally, note that it makes little sense to define two indexes on the same column or combination of columns. Therefore, consult the COLUMNS_IN_INDEX table for whether an index has already been defined on a column or on a combination of columns.

25.11 Indexes and the Catalog

As with tables and columns, indexes are recorded in catalog tables—the INDEXES table and the COLUMNS_IN_INDEX table. The descriptions of these table columns are given here. The columns INDEX_CREATOR and INDEX_NAME are the primary key of the INDEXES table.

TABLE 25.1 Description of the INDEXES Catalog Table

Column Name	Data Type	Description
INDEX_CREATOR	CHAR	Name of the database in which the index is created
INDEX_NAME	CHAR	Name of the index
CREATE_TIMESTAMP	DATETIME	Date and time the index was created
TABLE_CREATOR	NUMERIC	Name of the database in which the table was created
TABLE_NAME	CHAR	Name of the table on which the index is defined
UNIQUE_ID	CHAR	Whether the index is unique (YES) or not (NO)
INDEX_TYPE	CHAR	Form of the index: BTREE or HASH

The columns on which an index is defined are recorded in a separate table—the COLUMNS_IN_INDEX table. The columns INDEX_CREATOR, INDEX_NAME, and COLUMN_NAME form the primary key of this table.

TABLE 25.2 Description of the COLUMNS_IN_INDEX Catalog Table

Column Name	Data Type	Description
INDEX_CREATOR	CHAR	Name of the database in which the index was created
INDEX_NAME	CHAR	Name of the index
TABLE_CREATOR	NUMERIC	Name of the database in which the table was created
TABLE_NAME	CHAR	Name of the table on which the index is defined
COLUMN_NAME	CHAR	Name of the column on which the index is defined
COLUMN_SEQ	NUMERIC	Sequence number of the column in the index
ORDERING	CHAR	Has the value ASC if the index has been built in ascending order; otherwise, has the value DESC

The sample indexes from this section are recorded in the INDEXES and COLUMNS_IN_INDEX tables, as follows (we assume that all the tables and indexes are created in the TENNIS database):

```
INDEX_CREATOR  INDEX_NAME  TABLE_NAME  UNIQUE_ID  INDEX_TYPE
-------------  ----------  ----------  ---------  ----------
TENNIS         PLAY_PC     PLAYERS     NO         BTREE
TENNIS         MAT_WL      MATCHES     NO         BTREE
TENNIS         NAMEINIT    PLAYERS     YES        BTREE

INDEX_NAME  TABLE_NAME  COLUMN_NAME  COLUMN_SEQ  ORDERING
----------  ----------  -----------  ----------  --------
PLAY_PC     PLAYERS     POSTCODE     1           ASC
MAT_WL      MATCHES     WON          1           ASC
MAT_WL      MATCHES     LOST         2           ASC
NAMEINIT    PLAYERS     NAME         1           ASC
NAMEINIT    PLAYERS     INITIALS     2           ASC
```

Example 25.21: Determine which base table has more than one index.

```
SELECT   TABLE_CREATOR, TABLE_NAME, COUNT(*)
FROM     INDEXES
GROUP BY TABLE_CREATOR, TABLE_NAME
HAVING   COUNT(*) > 1
```

Explanation: If a particular base table appears more than once in the INDEXES table, it is based upon more than one index.

Example 25.22: Determine which base table does not have any unique index.

```
SELECT   TABLE_CREATOR, TABLE_NAME
FROM     TABLES AS TAB
WHERE    NOT EXISTS
        (SELECT   *
         FROM     INDEXES AS IDX
         WHERE    TAB.TABLE_CREATOR = IDX.TABLE_CREATOR
         AND      TAB.TABLE_NAME = TAB.TABLE_NAME
         AND      IDX.UNIQUE_ID = 'YES')
```

In the INFORMATION_SCHEMA catalog, we can find data on indexes in the STATISTICS table.

We also can retrieve information about indexes with a `SHOW` statement. If we use this statement, more information in the indexes is presented.

DEFINITION

```
<show index statement> ::=
   SHOW { INDEX | KEY } { FROM | IN }
   <table specification> [ { FROM | IN } <database name> ]
```

Example 25.23: Get information about the indexes of the PLAYERS table.

```
SHOW INDEX FROM PLAYERS
```

25.12 Answers

25.1 1. Basic strategy:

```
RESULT := [];
FOR EACH T IN TEAMS DO
   IF (T.TEAMNO > 1)
   AND (T.DIVISION = 'second') THEN
      RESULT :+ T;
ENDFOR;
```

Optimized strategy:

```
RESULT := [];
FOR EACH T IN TEAMS
WHERE DIVISION = 'second' DO
   IF T.TEAMNO > 1 THEN
      RESULT :+ T;
ENDFOR;
```

2. Basic strategy:

```
RESULT := [];
FOR EACH P IN PLAYERS DO
   FOR EACH M IN MATCHES DO
      IF P.PLAYERNO = M.PLAYERNO AND
         P.BIRTH_DATE > '1963-01-01' THEN
         RESULT :+ P;
   ENDFOR;
ENDFOR;
```

Optimized strategy:

```
RESULT := [];
FOR EACH P IN PLAYERS
HERE P.BIRTH_DATE > '1963-01-01' DO
  FOR EACH M IN MATCHES DO
      IF M.PLAYERNO = P.PLAYERNO THEN
         RESULT :+ P;
  ENDFOR;
ENDFOR;
```

CHAPTER 26

Views

26.1 INTRODUCTION

MySQL supports two types of tables: real tables, generally known as base tables, and derived tables, also called *views*. Base tables are created with CREATE TABLE statements and are the only ones in which data can be stored. Examples are the PLAYERS and TEAMS tables from the tennis club database.

A derived table, or view, stores *no* rows itself. Instead, it serves as a prescription or formula for combining certain data from base tables to make a "virtual" table. The word *virtual* is used because the contents of a view exist only when it is used in a statement. At that moment, MySQL retrieves the prescription that makes up the *view formula*, executes it, and presents the user with what seems to be a real table.

This chapter describes how views are created and how they can be used. Some useful applications include simplifying routine statements and reorganizing tables. Two sections cover restrictions on querying and updating views.

26.2 CREATING VIEWS

Views are created with the CREATE VIEW statement.

DEFINITION

```
<create view statement> ::=
   CREATE [ OR REPLACE ] VIEW <view name> [ <column list> ]
      AS <table expression>
      [ WITH [ CASCADED | LOCAL ] CHECK OPTION ]
```

Example 26.1: Create a view that holds all town names from the PLAYERS table and show the virtual contents of this new view.

```
CREATE   VIEW TOWNS AS
SELECT   DISTINCT TOWN
FROM     PLAYERS

SELECT   *
FROM     TOWNS
```

The result is:

```
TOWN
---------
Stratford
Inglewood
Eltham
Midhurst
Douglas
Plymouth
```

Example 26.2: Create a view that holds the player numbers and league numbers of all players who have a league number and show the virtual contents of this view.

```
CREATE   VIEW CPLAYERS AS
SELECT   PLAYERNO, LEAGUENO
FROM     PLAYERS
WHERE    LEAGUENO IS NOT NULL

SELECT   *
FROM     CPLAYERS
```

The result is:

```
PLAYERNO  LEAGUENO
--------  --------
      44  1124
     112  1319
      83  1608
       2  2411
      27  2513
       8  2983
      57  6409
     100  6524
     104  7060
       6  8467
```

These two `CREATE VIEW` statements create two views: TOWNS and CPLAYERS. A table expression defines the contents of each view and forms the view formula.

These two views can be queried just like base tables, and the CPLAYERS view can even be updated (see Section 26.8).

Example 26.3: Get the player and league numbers for competition players whose numbers are between 6 and 44.

```
SELECT   *
FROM     CPLAYERS
WHERE    PLAYERNO BETWEEN 6 AND 44
```

The result is:

```
PLAYERNO  LEAGUENO
--------  --------
       6  8467
      44  1124
      27  2513
       8  2983
```

If we did not use the CPLAYERS view for the same question but instead accessed the PLAYERS table directly, we would need a more complex SELECT statement to retrieve the same information:

```
SELECT   PLAYERNO, LEAGUENO
FROM     PLAYERS
WHERE    LEAGUENO IS NOT NULL
AND      PLAYERNO BETWEEN 6 AND 44
```

Example 26.4: Remove the competition player whose league number is 7060.

```
DELETE
FROM     CPLAYERS
WHERE    LEAGUENO = '7060'
```

When this statement is executed, it deletes the row in the base (PLAYERS) table in which the LEAGUENO column equals 7060.

The contents of a view are not stored, but are instead derived when the view is referenced. This means that the contents, by definition, are always in line with the contents of the base tables. Every update made to the data in a base table is immediately visible in a view. Users don't need to be concerned about the integrity of the contents of the view, as long as the integrity of the base tables is maintained. We return to the subject of updating views in Section 26.8.

Another view may be specified in a view formula. In other words, we may nest views.

Example 26.5: Create a view that holds all competition players whose player numbers are between 6 and 27, and show the virtual contents of this view.

```
CREATE   VIEW SEVERAL AS
SELECT   *
FROM     CPLAYERS
WHERE    PLAYERNO BETWEEN 6 AND 27

SELECT   *
FROM     SEVERAL
```

The result is:

```
PLAYERNO  LEAGUENO
--------  --------
       6  8467
       8  2983
      27  2513
```

In most cases, table expressions retrieve data from base tables or views; however, table expressions can give a result without accessing a table (see Example 7.34). Therefore, views do not have to be defined on base tables. See this example:

Example 26.6: Create a view in which the digits 0 through 9 appear, and show its contents.

```
CREATE VIEW DIGITS AS
SELECT 0 DIGIT UNION SELECT 1 UNION
SELECT 2 UNION SELECT 3 UNION
SELECT 4 UNION SELECT 5 UNION
SELECT 6 UNION SELECT 7 UNION
SELECT 8 UNION SELECT 9

SELECT * FROM DIGITS
```

The result is:

```
DIGIT
-----
    0
    1
    2
    3
    4
    5
    6
    7
    8
    9
```

Behind the word CREATE, we can specify OR REPLACE. If the name of the view already exists, the new view formula overwrites the old one.

26.3 The Column Names of Views

The column names in a view default to the column names in the SELECT clause. For example, the two columns in the SEVERAL view are called PLAYERNO and LEAGUENO. A view, therefore, inherits the column names. You can also explicitly define the column names of views.

Example 26.7: Create a view that holds the player number, name, initials, and date of birth of each player who lives in Stratford.

```
CREATE   VIEW STRATFORDERS (PLAYERNO, NAME, INIT, BORN) AS
SELECT   PLAYERNO, NAME, INITIALS, BIRTH_DATE
FROM     PLAYERS
WHERE    TOWN = 'Stratford'

SELECT   *
FROM     STRATFORDERS
WHERE    PLAYERNO > 90
```

Note the column names in the result:

```
PLAYERNO  NAME       INITIALS  BORN
--------  ---------  --------  ----------
     100  Parmenter  P         1963-02-08
```

These new column names are permanent. You can no longer refer to the columns PLAYERNO or BIRTH_DATE in the STRATFORDERS view.

MySQL allows an expression in the SELECT clause of a view formula to be a function or calculation instead of a column specification. The name of the column is equal to the expression.

Example 26.8: For each town, create a view that holds the place name and number of players who live in that town and then show the contents of the view.

```
CREATE   VIEW RESIDENTS AS
SELECT   TOWN, COUNT(*)
FROM     PLAYERS
GROUP BY TOWN

SELECT   TOWN, "COUNT(*)"
FROM     RESIDENTS
```

The result is:

```
TOWN       COUNT(*)
---------  --------
Douglas           1
Eltham            2
Inglewood         2
Midhurst          1
Plymouth          1
Stratford         7
```

Explanation: This view has two column names: TOWN and COUNT(*). Note that the name COUNT(*) must be enclosed by double quotes.

Exercise 26.1: Create a view called NUMBERPLS that contains all the team numbers and total number of players who have played for that team. (Assume that at least one player has competed for each team.)

Exercise 26.2: Create a view called WINNERS that contains the number and name of each player who, for at least one team, has won one match.

Exercise 26.3: Create a view called TOTALS that records the total amount of penalties for each player who has incurred at least one penalty.

26.4 Updating Views: WITH CHECK OPTION

We have already seen a number of examples where underlying tables are being updated through views. Careful with updating views, it can have unexpected results. The following example illustrates this situation.

Example 26.9: Create a view that holds all players born earlier than 1960.

```
CREATE   VIEW VETERANS AS
SELECT   *
FROM     PLAYERS
WHERE    BIRTH_DATE < '1960-01-01'
```

Now we would like to change the date of birth of the veteran whose player number is 2 from 1 September 1948 to 1 September 1970. The update statement reads:

```
UPDATE   VETERANS
SET      BIRTH_DATE = '1970-09-01'
WHERE    PLAYERNO = 2
```

This update is correct. The date of birth of player number 2 in the PLAYERS table is changed. However, the unexpected effect of this update is that player number 2 no longer appears if we look at the *view* using a SELECT statement. This is because the player ceased to satisfy the condition specified in the view formula after the update occurred.

If you extend the view definition using the so-called WITH CHECK OPTION, MySQL ensures that such an unexpected effect does not arise.

The view definition then becomes this:

```
CREATE   VIEW VETERANS AS
SELECT   *
FROM     PLAYERS
WHERE    BIRTH_DATE < '1960-01-01'
WITH     CHECK OPTION
```

If a view includes the WITH CHECK OPTION clause, all changes on the view with UPDATE, INSERT, and DELETE statements are checked for validity:

- An UPDATE statement is correct if the updated rows still belong to the (virtual) contents of the view.
- An INSERT statement is correct if the new rows belong to the (virtual) contents of the view.
- A DELETE statement is correct if the deleted rows belong to the (virtual) contents of the view.

As mentioned earlier, views can be nested, or in other words, a view can be stacked on top of another view. You might wonder to what extent the check of the WITH CHECK OPTION can be carried out. If we specify WITH CASCADED CHECK OPTION, all views are checked. When WITH LOCAL CHECK OPTION is used, checks that relate to conditions in the view being updated are the only ones checked. CASCADED is the default option.

Example 26.10: Create a view of all players born earlier than 1960 and who live in Inglewood.

```
CREATE   VIEW INGLEWOOD_VETERANS AS
SELECT   *
FROM     VETERANS
WHERE    TOWN = 'Inglewood'
WITH     CASCADED CHECK OPTION
```

Explanation: If we use an INSERT statement to add a player to this view, he or she must live in Inglewood and must have been born earlier than January 1, 1960. When we leave out CASCADED, every player who we add to the INGLEWOOD_VETERANS table must live in Inglewood. MySQL no longer carries out the check.

The WITH CHECK OPTION can be used only in conjunction with views that can be updated according to the rules mentioned in Section 26.8.

26.5 Options of Views

You can define special options such as privileges and method of processing for each view.

DEFINITION

```
<create view statement> ::=
   CREATE [ OR REPLACE ]
      [ DEFINER = { <user name> | CURRENT_USER } ]
      [ SQL SECURITY { DEFINER | INVOKER } ]
      [ ALGORITHM = { MERGE | TEMPTABLE | UNDEFINED } ]
      VIEW <viewnaam> [ <column list> ] AS <table expression>
      [ WITH [ CASCADED | LOCAL ] CHECK OPTION ]
```

With the *definer option,* we can indicate who the creator, or the *definer,* of the view is. If this option is not specified, the user who creates the view is the definer. We can change this by creating a view for another SQL user.

Example 26.11: Create a view with user JACO as the definer.

```
CREATE   DEFINER = 'JACO'@'%' VIEW JACO_VIEW AS
SELECT   *
FROM     PLAYERS
WHERE    PLAYERNO > 100
```

Specifying the term CURRENT_USER as the definer has the same result as omitting the definer option.

A user might have the privilege to query a view, but what happens if that view queries tables for which that same user has no SELECT privilege? The SQL SECURITY option determines the outcome. If SQL SECURITY has not been specified, the rule is that the user who creates the view must have SELECT privileges on the queries tables. For example, if the view V_1 queries the table T_1, the definer of the view must have SELECT privilege for T_1. Other users of V_1 do not need those privileges. Not specifying an SQL SECURITY option is equal to specifying SQL SECURITY DEFINER. If we specify SQL SECURITY INVOKER, the users of the view must explicitly be granted the required privileges for the tables accessed. Therefore, every user who queries V_1 should be granted the SELECT privilege for the T_1 table.

The ALGORITHM option indicates how the view must be processed internally. Two methods can process a statement on a view. In the first method, called MERGE, the SELECT statement with which the view is queried is combined with the view formula. As a result, one (combined) SELECT statement is processed. With the method called TEMPTABLE, a SELECT statement on a view is processed in two steps. During step 1, the intermediate result of the view formula is determined and stored in a temporary table. In step 2, the SELECT statement is executed on this intermediate result. If the ALGORITHM option has not been specified or if it is set to UNDEFINED, MySQL determines which method it will apply.

Example 26.12: Create a view processed using the MERGE method for which the user should have the right privileges.

```
CREATE   SQL SECURITY INVOKER
         ALGORITHM = MERGE
         VIEW SIMPLE_VIEW AS
SELECT   PLAYERNO
FROM     PLAYERS
WHERE    PLAYERNO > 100
```

All options, including the creator and even the view formula, can be changed later with an ALTER USER *statement.*

DEFINITION

```
<alter view statement> ::=
   ALTER
      [ DEFINER = { <user name> | CURRENT_USER } ]
      [ SQL SECURITY { DEFINER | INVOKER } ]
      [ ALGORITHM = { MERGE | TEMPTABLE | UNDEFINED } ]
      VIEW <view name> [ <column list> ] AS <table expression>
      [ WITH [ CASCADED | LOCAL ] CHECK OPTION ]
```

26.6 Deleting Views

The DROP VIEW *statement* is used to delete a view. By using this statement, every other view that references the dropped view is also dropped automatically. When a base table is dropped, all views that have been defined directly or indirectly on that table are also dropped.

DEFINITION

```
<drop view statement> ::=
   DROP VIEW [ IF EXISTS ] <table specification>
      [ , <table specification> ]...
      [ RESTRICT | CASCADE ]
```

Example 26.13: Drop the CPLAYERS view.

```
DROP VIEW CPLAYERS
```

When `IF EXISTS` is specified, no error messages appear if the view that must be dropped does not exist. `RESTRICT` and `CASCADE` can be specified, but they have no effect.

26.7 Views and the Catalog

Information about views is recorded in various tables. In the VIEWS table, a row is stored for each view. The column VIEW_ID forms the primary key of this catalog table. The columns VIEW_NAME and CREATOR form an alternate key.

TABLE 26.1 Description of the VIEWS Catalog Table

Column Name	Data Type	Description
VIEW_CREATOR	CHAR	Name of the database to which the view belongs
VIEW_NAME	CHAR	Name of the view
CREATE_TIMESTAMP	TIMESTAMP	Date on which the view was created; however, this column is not filled by MySQL
WITHCHECKOPT	CHAR	Value is `YES` if the view is defined with `WITH CHECK, CASCADED`, or `LOCAL OPTION`); otherwise, it has the value `NO`
IS_UPDATABLE	CHAR	Value is `YES` if the view can be updated; otherwise, it has the value `NO`
COMMENT	CHAR	Comment that is entered with the `COMMENT` statement
VIEWFORMULA	CHAR	The view formula (table expression)

The columns of the view inherit the data type of the column expressions from the `SELECT` clause of the view formula.

Example 26.14: Can a table called STOCK be created in the TENNIS DATABASE, or does that name already exist?

```
SELECT   TABLE_NAME
FROM     TABLES
WHERE    TABLE_NAME = 'STOCK'
AND      TABLE_CREATOR = 'TENNIS'
UNION
SELECT   VIEW_NAME
FROM     VIEWS
WHERE    VIEW_NAME = 'STOCK'
AND      VIEW_CREATOR = 'TENNIS'
```

Explanation: The `SELECT` statement checks whether a table or view was created with the name STOCK in the TENNIS database. If the statement has a result, this table name cannot be used again.

The VIEWS table in the INFORMATION_SCHEMA catalog contains data on views.

26.8 Restrictions on Updating Views

`INSERT`, `UPDATE`, and `DELETE` statements may be executed on views. However, MySQL has several restrictions. For example, rows of some views may not be deleted or updated. This section covers the restrictions that apply to updating views.

A view can be updated only if a one-to-one correspondence exists between the rows of the view and the rows of the underlying table. Additionally, the view formula should satisfy the following conditions. The first seven conditions apply to all update statements.

1. The `SELECT` clause may *not* contain `DISTINCT`.
2. The `SELECT` clause may *not* contain aggregation functions.
3. The `FROM` clause may *not* contain more than *one* table.
4. The `WHERE` clause may *not* contain a correlated subquery.
5. The `SELECT` statement may *not* contain a `GROUP BY` clause (or a `HAVING` clause).
6. The `SELECT` statement may *not* contain an `ORDER BY` clause.
7. The `SELECT` statement may *not* contain set operators.

In addition, the following restriction holds for the UPDATE statement:

8. A virtual column may *not* be updated.

   The BEGIN_AGE column in the following view may not be updated (though the PLAYERNO column may be updated):

```
CREATE   VIEW AGES (PLAYERNO, BEGIN_AGE) AS
SELECT   PLAYERNO, JOINED - YEAR(BIRTH_DATE)
FROM     PLAYERS
```

   In addition, the following restriction holds for the INSERT statement:

9. The SELECT clause must contain, from the table that is specified in the FROM clause, all columns in which the null value is not allowed or for which no default value is specified.

This is why INSERT statements may not be performed against the following view—it does not contain all NOT NULL columns, such as SEX and TOWN:

```
CREATE   VIEW PLAYERS_NAMES AS
SELECT   PLAYERNO, NAME, INITIALS
FROM     PLAYERS
```

Exercise 26.4: This chapter has shown many examples of views. For each of the following views, indicate whether an UPDATE, INSERT, or DELETE statement may be performed:

1. TOWNS
2. CPLAYERS
3. SEVERAL
4. DIGITS
5. STRATFORDERS
6. RESIDENTS
7. VETERANS
8. TOTALS
9. AGES

26.9 Processing View Statements

How will statements that access views be processed? The processing steps (see Chapter 6, "SELECT Statements, Table Expressions, and Subqueries") cannot be executed one by one, as happens for base tables. MySQL reaches the FROM clause and attempts to fetch rows from the database; it encounters a problem because a view contains no stored rows. So which rows must be retrieved from the database when a statement refers to a view? MySQL knows that it is working with a view (thanks to a routine look in the catalog). To process the steps, MySQL can choose between two methods called *substitution* and *materialization.*

With the first method, the view formula is merged into the SELECT statement. This method is called substitution because the view name in the SELECT statement is replaced (substituted) by the view formula. Next, the obtained SELECT statement is processed. The following example illustrates this method.

Example 26.15: Create a view of all data of the players who incurred a penalty. Next, give the number of each player from the COST_RAISERS view who has incurred at least one penalty and lives in Stratford.

```
CREATE   VIEW COST_RAISERS AS
SELECT   *
FROM     PLAYERS
WHERE    PLAYERNO IN
        (SELECT   PLAYERNO
         FROM     PENALTIES)

SELECT   PLAYERNO
FROM     COST_RAISERS
WHERE    TOWN = 'Stratford'
```

The first processing step comprises the merging of the view formula into the SELECT statement and produces the following statement:

```
SELECT   PLAYERNO
FROM    (SELECT   *
         FROM     PLAYERS
         WHERE    PLAYERNO IN
                 (SELECT   PLAYERNO
                  FROM     PENALTIES)) AS VIEWFORMULA
WHERE    TOWN = 'Stratford'
```

Now this statement can be processed by moving through the remaining steps.

The final result is:

```
PLAYERNO
--------
       6
```

See the next example that uses the STRATFORDERS view from Section 26.3.

Example 26.16: Delete all Stratford people born later than 1965.

```
DELETE
FROM     STRATFORDERS
WHERE    BORN > '1965-12-31'
```

After the name has been substituted by the view formula, the statement reads:

```
DELETE
FROM     PLAYERS
WHERE    BIRTH_DATE > '1965-12-31'
AND      TOWN = 'Stratford'
```

Another method of processing is called materialization. In this method, the table expression of the view formula processes first, which gives an intermediate result. Next, the actual SELECT statement is executed on that intermediate result. If we would process Example 26.15 through materialization, the following statement would be executed first:

```
SELECT   *
FROM     PLAYERS
WHERE    PLAYERNO IN
        (SELECT   PLAYERNO
         FROM     PENALTIES)
```

This gives the following intermediate result (for simplicity, only the columns PLAYERNO and TOWN have been displayed):

```
PLAYERNO  TOWN
--------  ---------
       6  Stratford
       8  Inglewood
      27  Eltham
      44  Inglewood
     104  Eltham
```

MySQL keeps this intermediate result in internal memory. After that, the following statement is executed:

```
SELECT   PLAYERNO
FROM     <intermediate result>
WHERE    TOWN = 'Stratford'
```

Both methods have their advantages and disadvantages. MySQL itself determines which method should be used in each situation; however, the user can choose the processing method by specifying it in the view definition.

Example 26.17: Create a view of all data of the players who incurred a penalty and make sure that MySQL uses the materialization method during the processing.

```
CREATE   VIEW EXPENSIVE_PLAYERS AS
         ALORITHM = TEMPTABLE
SELECT   *
FROM     PLAYERS
WHERE    PLAYERNO IN
        (SELECT   PLAYERNO
         FROM     PENALTIES)
```

Explanation: With the word TEMPTABLE, we indicate that a temporary table must be created during the processing of SELECT statements on this view—that a materialization must be carried out. If MERGE is specified as algorithm, the substitution method is used. With UNDEFINED, MySQL makes the decision itself.

Exercise 26.5: How will the following statements appear after the view formula has been included through the substitution method?

1.
```
SELECT   YEAR(BORN) - 1900 AS DIFFERENCE, COUNT(*)
FROM     STRATFORDERS
GROUP BY DIFFERENCE
```
2.
```
SELECT   COST_RAISERS.PLAYERNO
FROM     COST_RAISERS, STRATFORDERS
WHERE    COST_RAISERS.PLAYERNO = STRATFORDERS.PLAYERNO
```
3.
```
UPDATE   STRATFORDERS
SET      BORN = '1950-04-04'
WHERE    PLAYERNO = 7
```

26.10 Application Areas for Views

Views can be used in a variety of applications. This section covers some of them. There is no significance to the order in which they are discussed.

26.10.1 Simplification of Routine Statements

Statements that are used frequently or are structurally similar can be simplified through the use of views.

Example 26.18: Imagine that these two statements are frequently entered.

```
SELECT   *
FROM     PLAYERS
WHERE    PLAYERNO IN
        (SELECT   PLAYERNO
         FROM     PENALTIES)
AND      TOWN = 'Stratford'
```

and

```
SELECT    TOWN, COUNT(*)
FROM      PLAYERS
WHERE     PLAYERNO IN
         (SELECT   PLAYERNO
          FROM     PENALTIES)
GROUP BY TOWN
```

Both statements are concerned with the players who have incurred at least one penalty, so this subset of players can be defined by a view:

```
CREATE    VIEW PPLAYERS AS
SELECT    *
FROM      PLAYERS
WHERE     PLAYERNO IN
         (SELECT   PLAYERNO
          FROM     PENALTIES)
```

Now the two previous SELECT statements can be greatly simplified by using the PPLAYERS view:

```
SELECT    *
FROM      PPLAYERS
WHERE     TOWN = 'Stratford'
```

and

```
SELECT    TOWN, COUNT(*)
FROM      PPLAYERS
GROUP BY TOWN
```

Example 26.19: Imagine that the PLAYERS table is often joined with the MATCHES table.

```
SELECT    ...
FROM      PLAYERS, MATCHES
WHERE     PLAYERS.PLAYERNO = MATCHES.PLAYERNO
AND       ...
```

In this case, the SELECT statement becomes simpler if the join is defined as a view:

```
CREATE    VIEW PLAY_MAT AS
SELECT    ...
FROM      PLAYERS, MATCHES
WHERE     PLAYERS.PLAYERNO = MATCHES.PLAYERNO
```

The join now takes this simplified form:

```
SELECT   ...
FROM     PLAY_MAT
WHERE    ...
```

26.10.2 Reorganizing Tables

Tables are designed and implemented on the basis of a particular situation. The situation can sometimes change, which means that the structure also changes. For example, a new column might be added to a table, or two tables might be joined to make a single table. In most cases, the reorganization of a table structure requires altering already developed and operational statements. Such changes can be time-consuming and expensive. Appropriate use of views can keep this time and cost to a minimum. Let us see how.

Example 26.20: For each competition player, get the name, initials, and divisions in which he or she has ever played.

```
SELECT   DISTINCT NAME, INITIALS, DIVISION
FROM     PLAYERS AS P, MATCHES AS M, TEAMS AS T
WHERE    P.PLAYERNO = M.PLAYERNO
AND      M.TEAMNO = T.TEAMNO
```

The result is:

```
NAME       INITIALS  DIVISION
---------  --------  --------
Parmenter  R         first
Baker      E         first
Hope       PK        first
Everett    R         first
Collins    DD        second
Moorman    D         second
Brown      M         first
Bailey     IP        second
Newcastle  B         first
Newcastle  B         second
```

For unknown reasons, the TEAMS and MATCHES tables need to be reorganized; they are combined to form one table, the RESULT table, shown here:

```
MATCH_NO  TEAMNO  PLAYERNO  WON  LOST  CAPTAIN  DIVISION
--------  ------  --------  ---  ----  -------  --------
       1       1         6    3     1        6  first
       2       1         6    2     3        6  first
       3       1         6    3     0        6  first
       4       1        44    3     2        6  first
       5       1        83    0     3        6  first
       6       1         2    1     3        6  first
       7       1        57    3     0        6  first
       8       1         8    0     3        6  first
       9       2        27    3     2       27  second
      10       2       104    3     2       27  second
      11       2       112    2     3       27  second
      12       2       112    1     3       27  second
      13       2         8    0     3       27  second
```

The CAPTAIN column in the RESULT table is the former PLAYERNO column from the TEAMS table. This column has been given another name; otherwise, there would have been two columns called PLAYERNO. All statements that refer to the two tables, including the previous SELECT statement, now need to be rewritten. To prevent the need for a total rewrite, a better solution is to define two views that represent the former TEAMS and MATCHES tables, respectively:

```
CREATE   VIEW TEAMS (TEAMNO, PLAYERNO, DIVISION) AS
SELECT   DISTINCT TEAMNO, CAPTAIN, DIVISION
FROM     RESULT

CREATE   VIEW MATCHES AS
SELECT   MATCHNO, TEAMNO, PLAYERNO,
         WON, LOST
FROM     RESULT
```

The virtual contents of each of these two views are the same as the contents of the two original tables. No statements need to be rewritten, including the SELECT statement from the beginning of this section.

Of course, you cannot manage every reorganization of a table with views. It might be decided, for example, to store data about male and female players in separate tables. Both tables contain the same columns as the PLAYERS table but omit the SEX column. It is possible to reconstruct the original PLAYERS table with a view using the UNION operator; however, inserts on this view are not allowed.

26.10.3 Stepwise Development of SELECT Statements

Imagine that you need to answer the following question: For each player from Stratford who has incurred a penalty that is greater than the average penalty for players from the second team and who played for at least one first-division team, get the name and initials. You could write a huge SELECT statement to answer this, but you could also develop a query in a stepwise fashion.

First, we create a view of all the players who have incurred at least one penalty that is greater than the average penalty for players from the second team:

```
CREATE   VIEW GREATER AS
SELECT   DISTINCT PLAYERNO
FROM     PENALTIES
WHERE    AMOUNT >
        (SELECT   AVG(AMOUNT)
         FROM     PENALTIES
         WHERE    PLAYERNO IN
                 (SELECT   PLAYERNO
                  FROM     MATCHES
                  WHERE    TEAMNO = 2))
```

Then we create a view of all players who have competed for a team in the first division:

```
CREATE   VIEW FIRST AS
SELECT   DISTINCT PLAYERNO
FROM     MATCHES
WHERE    TEAMNO IN
        (SELECT   TEAMNO
         FROM     TEAMS
         WHERE    DIVISION = 'first')
```

Using these two views, we can answer the original question:

```
SELECT   NAME, INITIALS
FROM     PLAYERS
WHERE    TOWN = 'Stratford'
AND      PLAYERNO IN
        (SELECT   PLAYERNO
         FROM     GREATER)
AND      PLAYERNO IN
        (SELECT   PLAYERNO
         FROM     FIRST)
```

We can split the problem into “mini-problems” and execute it in steps, creating one long SELECT statement.

26.10.4 Specifying Integrity Constraints

Use the WITH CHECK OPTION clause to implement rules that restrict the possible set of values that may be entered into columns.

Example 26.21: The SEX column in the PLAYERS table may contain either the value `'M'` or the value `'F'`. Using the `WITH CHECK OPTION` clause provides an automatic control for this. The following view should be defined:

```
CREATE   VIEW PLAYERSS AS
SELECT   *
FROM     PLAYERS
WHERE    SEX IN ('M', 'F')
WITH     CHECK OPTION
```

We don't give anyone the privilege of accessing the PLAYERS table directly; instead, others need to use the PLAYERSS view. The `WITH CHECK OPTION` clause tests every `UPDATE` and `INSERT` statement to determine whether the value in the SEX column falls into the permitted range.

Note: If the desired check can be defined with a check integrity constraint, we recommend that you use it in this application.

26.10.5 Data Security

Views can also be used to protect parts of tables. Chapter 28, "Users and Data Security," covers this topic in detail.

Exercise 26.6: Decide whether the following reorganizations of the database structure are possible through the use of views.

1. The NAME column is added to the PENALTIES table but also remains in the PLAYERS table.
2. The TOWN column is removed from the PLAYERS table and placed together with the PLAYERNO column in a separate table.

26.11 Answers

26.1
```
CREATE   VIEW NUMBERPLS (TEAMNO, NUMBER) AS
SELECT   TEAMNO, COUNT(*)
FROM     MATCHES
GROUP BY TEAMNO
```

26.2
```
CREATE   VIEW WINNERS AS
SELECT   PLAYERNO, NAME
FROM     PLAYERS
WHERE    PLAYERNO IN
        (SELECT   PLAYERNO
         FROM     MATCHES
         WHERE    WON > LOST)
```

26.3

```
CREATE   VIEW TOTALS (PLAYERNO, SUM_PENALTIES) AS
SELECT   PLAYERNO, SUM(AMOUNT)
FROM     PENALTIES
GROUP BY PLAYERNO
```

26.4

VIEW	UPDATE	INSERT	DELETE
TOWNS	No	No	No
CPLAYERS	Yes	No	Yes
SEVERAL	Yes	No	Yes
DIGITS	No	No	No
STRATFORDERS	Yes	No	Yes
RESIDENTS	No	No	No
VETERANS	Yes	Yes	Yes
TOTALS	No	No	No
AGES	Yes	No	Yes

26.5

1.

```
SELECT   YEAR(BORN) - 1900 AS DIFFERENCE, COUNT(*)
FROM    (SELECT   PLAYERNO, NAME,
                  INITIALS, BIRTH_DATE AS BORN
         FROM     PLAYERS
         WHERE    TOWN = 'Stratford') AS STRATFORDERS
GROUP BY DIFFERENCE
```

2.

```
SELECT   EXPENSIVE.PLAYERNO
FROM    (SELECT   *
         FROM     PLAYERS
         WHERE    PLAYERNO IN
                 (SELECT   PLAYERNO
                  FROM     PENALTIES)) AS EXPENSIVE,
        (SELECT   PLAYERNO, NAME,
                  INITIALS, BIRTH_DATE AS BORN
         FROM     PLAYERS
         WHERE    TOWN = 'Stratford') AS STRATFORDERS
WHERE    EXPENSIVE.PLAYERNO = STRATFORDERS.PLAYERNO
```

3.

```
UPDATE   PLAYERS
SET      BIRTH_DATE = '1950-04-04'
WHERE    PLAYERNO = 7
```

26.6

1. Yes
2. Yes, but the view can be queried only, not updated, because the view formula contains a join.

CHAPTER 27

Creating Databases

27.1 Introduction

Each table that is created is stored in a database. During MySQL installation, two databases are created automatically and used to store the catalog tables. We do not recommend adding your own tables to these databases. It is better to create new databases for this by using the *CREATE DATABASE statement*. Section 4.4 contains an example of this statement. In this relatively short chapter, we deal with this statement at great length.

27.2 Databases and the Catalog

MySQL stores information on databases in the catalog table called INFORMATION_SCHEMA.

Example 27.1: Show the names of all databases.

```
SELECT   SCHEMA_NAME
FROM     INFORMATION_SCHEMA.SCHEMATA
```

The result is:

```
SCHEMA_NAME
------------------
information_schema
mysql
tennis
test
```

Explanation: No catalog table called DATABASES exists. Instead, this table is called SCHEMATA. This is somewhat confusing. MySQL is one of the few products that use the terms database and schema interchangeably.

The previous result contains four databases. MySQL created the first two, INFORMATION_SCHEMA and MYSQL, during installation. If you remove these databases, MySQL can no longer function. The last two databases were created separately.

The tables of a database can be retrieved by querying the catalog table TABLES and specifying the database name or schema name in the condition.

Example 27.2: Show the names of the tables belonging to the TENNIS database.

```
SELECT   TABLE_NAME
FROM     INFORMATION_SCHEMA.TABLES
WHERE    TABLE_SCHEMA = 'TENNIS'
ORDER BY TABLE_NAME
```

The result is:

```
TABLE_NAME
-----------------
COMMITTEE_MEMBERS
PENALTIES
PLAYERS
TEAMS
MATCHES
```

27.3 Creating Databases

With the CREATE DATABASE statement, you can create new databases. During this process, you can specify a default character set and a default collation.

DEFINITION

```
<create database statement> ::=
   CREATE DATABASE [ IF NOT EXISTS ] <database name>
      [ <database option>... ]

<database option> ::=
   [ DEFAULT ] CHARACTER SET <character set name> |
   [ DEFAULT ] COLLATE <collation name>

<database name>       ;
<character set name> ;
<collation name>      ::= <name>
```

Example 27.3: Create a new database called TENNIS2.

```
CREATE DATABASE TENNIS2
   DEFAULT CHARACTER SET utf8
   DEFAULT COLLATE utf8_general_ci
```

Explanation: This creates a new database without tables. If you want to use this database, do not forget to make it the current database using the USE statement.

Example 27.4: For each database, get the name and default character set and collation.

```
SELECT   SCHEMA_NAME, DEFAULT_CHARACTER_SET_NAME,
         DEFAULT_COLLATION_NAME
FROM     INFORMATION_SCHEMA.SCHEMATA
```

The result is:

```
SCHEMA_NAME         DEFAULT_CHARACTER_SET_NAME  DEFAULT_COLLATION_NAME
------------------  --------------------------  ----------------------
information_schema  utf8                        utf8_general_ci
mysql               latin1                      latin1_swedish_ci
tennis              latin1                      latin1_swedish_ci
tennis2             utf8                        utf8_general_ci
test                latin1                      latin1_swedish_ci
```

27.4 Changing Databases

You can change the existing default character set and collation with an *ALTER DATABASE statement*. These new defaults apply only to the tables and columns that are created after the update.

DEFINITION

```
<alter database statement> ::=
   ALTER DATABASE [ <database name> ]
      [ <database option>... ]

<database option> ::=
   [ DEFAULT ] CHARACTER SET <character set name> |
   [ DEFAULT ] COLLATE <collation name>

<database name>       ;
<character set name> ;
<collation name>      ::= <name>
```

Example 27.5: Change the character set and collation of the TENNIS2 database.

```
ALTER DATABASE TENNIS2
   DEFAULT CHARACTER SET sjis
   DEFAULT COLLATE sjis_japanese_ci
```

Explanation: The TENNIS2 database does not have to be current for this statement.

Example 27.6: Define hp8 as the default character set for the TENNIS database and then create a new table with two alphanumeric columns. Do not assign a character set. Look in the catalog tables to see what the default collation is.

```
ALTER DATABASE TENNIS CHARACTER SET hp8

CREATE TABLE CHARSETHP8
      (C1  CHAR(10) NOT NULL,
       C2  VARCHAR(10))

SELECT   COLUMN_NAME, CHARACTER_SET_NAME, COLLATION_NAME
FROM     INFORMATION_SCHEMA.COLUMNS
WHERE    TABLE_NAME = 'CHARSETHP8'
```

The result is:

```
COLUMN_NAME  CHARACTER_SET_NAME  COLLATION_NAME
-----------  ------------------  --------------
K1           hp8                 hp8_english_ci
K2           hp8                 hp8_english_ci
```

The default of the database is, of course, the default collation (latin1_swedish_ci) of the default character set (latin1). With ALTER DATABASE, you can change this default.

Example 27.7: Change the default collation of the TENNIS database to hp8_bin.

```
ALTER DATABASE TENNIS COLLATE hp8_bin
```

27.5 Dropping Databases

One of the most drastic SQL statements is the *DROP DATABASE statement*. This statement removes the entire database at once. All tables of that database will disappear permanently, so be very careful.

```
<drop database statement> ::=
   DROP DATABASE [ IF NOT EXISTS ] <database name>

<database name> ::= <name>
```

Example 27.8: Drop the TENNIS2 database.

```
DROP DATABASE TENNIS2
```

If you add `IF NOT EXISTS`, no error messages are presented when the database mentioned does not exist.

CHAPTER 28

Users and Data Security

28.1 Introduction

This chapter describes the features that MySQL offers for protecting data in the tables against deliberate or accidental unauthorized use: SQL users, passwords, and privileges.

SQL users must be known to MySQL before they can access the database data. Chapter 3, "Installing the Software," showed you how one user is created automatically during the installation of MySQL, and Chapter 4, "SQL in a Nutshell," showed how a new SQL user called BOOKSQL was introduced. Logging on to MySQL without an existing user name is just not possible.

A password can also be assigned to each SQL user. When a password is required, accessing the database data becomes even more difficult because the name of an SQL user is no longer sufficient. After following the procedure described in this book for installing the sample database, the user BOOKSQL has the password BOOKSQLPW. You have probably entered this password many times and perhaps already have discovered what happens if you make a typing error—no access.

New SQL users are not allowed to access tables belonging to other SQL users, not even with the SELECT statement. Nor can they immediately create their own tables. New SQL users must explicitly be granted privileges. We can indicate, for example, that an SQL user is allowed to query a certain table or change specific columns of a table. Another SQL user might be allowed to create tables, and another user might be allowed to create and remove complete databases.

The privileges that can be granted are divided into four groups:

- *Column privileges* relate to one specific column of a table, such as the privilege to update the values in the AMOUNT column of the PENALTIES table with UPDATE statements.
- *Table privileges* relate to all data of one specific table, such as the privilege to query all the data of the PLAYERS table with SELECT statements.
- *Database privileges* relate to all tables of one specific database, such as the privilege to create new tables in the existing TENNIS database.
- *User privileges* relate to all databases that are known to MySQL, such as the privilege to remove existing databases or to create new ones.

This chapter explains how new SQL users can be entered and how privileges can be assigned with the *GRANT statement*. The catalog stores all privileges. We also describe how privileges can be recalled with the *REVOKE statement* and how SQL users can be removed from the catalog.

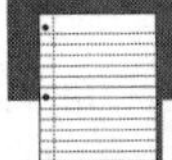

NOTE

For convenience, this chapter uses the term *user* instead of the somewhat longer *SQL user*. See Section 4.3 to understand the difference between the two terms.

28.2 Adding and Removing Users

We can add other users in addition to BOOKSQL. Section 4.3 showed an example of how to add a new user. This section explains the process in more detail.

To add new users in the catalog, MySQL uses the simple *CREATE USER statement*.

DEFINITION

```
<create user statement> ::=
   CREATE USER <user specification>
      [ , <user specification> ]...

<user specification> ::=
   <user name> [ IDENTIFIED BY [ PASSWORD ] <password> ]

<user name> ::=
   <name> | '<name>' | '<name>'@'<host name>'

<password> ::= <alphanumeric literal>
```

In a CREATE USER statement, a *user name* and a *password* are entered. In most SQL products, the user name and password are just names consisting of letters and numbers.

Example 28.1: Introduce two new users: CHRIS with the password CHRISSEC and PAUL with the password LUAP.

```
CREATE USER
   'CHRIS'@'localhost' IDENTIFIED BY 'CHRISSEC',
   'PAUL'@'localhost' IDENTIFIED BY 'LUAP'
```

Explanation: Behind the user name, the term `localhost` is specified. This term specifies the *host* from which the user creates a connection with MySQL. We return to this topic later. If the name of a user or host contains special characters, quotation marks must be placed before and after it—for example `'CHRIS'@'localhost'` or `'CHRIS'@'xxx.r20.com'`. Quotation marks *must* always be placed before and after the password.

This example specified a certain host; however, the percent sign may be used to indicate a group of hosts.

Example 28.2: Add three new users and then show the contents of the USERS catalog view.

```
CREATE USER
   'CHRIS1'@'sql.r20.com' IDENTIFIED BY 'CHRISSEC1',
   'CHRIS2'@'%' IDENTIFIED BY 'CHRISSEC2',
   'CHRIS3'@'%.r20.com' IDENTIFIED BY 'CHRISSEC3'

SELECT   *
FROM     USERS
WHERE    USER_NAME LIKE '''CHRIS%'
ORDER    BY 1
```

The result is:

```
USER_NAME
----------------------
'CHRIS1'@'SQL.R20.COM'
'CHRIS2'@'%'
'CHRIS3'@'%.R20.COM'
```

Explanation: Now the user named CHRIS1 is allowed to log on to MySQL from the host called `sql.r20.com`. CHRIS2 may log on from every host, and CHRIS3 may log on from all hosts whose names end with `r20.com`. *Not* specifying a host is equal to specifying the host `'%'`.

If two users have the same user name but different hosts, MySQL regards them as different users, allowing us to assign different sets of privileges to the two users.

If no password is entered, the relevant user is allowed to log on without a password. However, this is not a good idea from a security standpoint.

Users who have just been introduced do not have many privileges yet. They can log on to MySQL, but they cannot use the `USE` statement to make any database current that has been created by users; therefore, they cannot access the tables of those databases. They are allowed to perform only operations for which no privileges are required, such as querying the list of all storage engines and character sets with a `SHOW` statement. However, they are allowed to work with the INFORMATION_SCHEMA databases and execute statements such as `SELECT TABLE_NAME FROM TABLES`. They can see only the tables of the catalog itself.

We can use the *DROP USER statement* to remove users from the system, and all their privileges are also removed automatically.

DEFINITION

```
<drop user statement> ::=
   DROP USER <user name> [ , <user name> ]...

<user name> ::=
   <name> | '<name>' | '<name>'@'<host name>'
```

Example 28.3: Drop the user JIM.

```
DROP USER JIM
```

If the removed user has created tables, indexes, or other database objects, they remain because MySQL does not register who created the objects.

Exercise 28.1: Create a user with the name RONALDO and password NIKE.

Exercise 28.2: Remove user RONALDO.

28.3 Changing the Names of Users

The name of an existing SQL user can be later changed with the *RENAME USER statement.*

DEFINITION

```
<rename user statement> ::=
   RENAME USER <user name> TO <user name>
      [ , <user name> TO <user name> ]...

<user name> ::=
   <name> | '<name>' | '<name>'@'<host name>'
```

Example 28.4: Change the names of the users CHRIS1 and CHRIS2 to COMBO1 and COMBO2, respectively, and then show the contents of the USERS catalog view.

```
RENAME USER
   'CHRIS1'@'sql.r20.com' TO 'COMBO1'@'sql.r20.com',
   'CHRIS2'@'%' TO 'COMBO2'@'sql.r20.com'

SELECT   *
FROM     USERS
WHERE    USER_NAME LIKE '''COMBO%'
ORDER    BY 1
```

The result is:

```
USER_NAME
----------------------
'COMBO1'@'SQL.R20.COM'
'COMBO2'@'SQL.R20.COM'
```

This statement cannot be used to change the password of a user. A separate SQL statement is available for this; see the following section.

28.4 Changing Passwords

Each user has the right to change his or her own password, or that of someone else, by using the SET PASSWORD statement.

DEFINITION

```
<set password statement> ::=
   SET PASSWORD [ FOR <user name> ]
      = PASSWORD( <password> )

<password> ::= <alphanumeric literal>
```

Example 28.5: Change the password of JOHN to JOHN1.

```
SET PASSWORD FOR 'JOHN'= PASSWORD('JOHN1')
```

Explanation: In this statement, we assume that JOHN enters this statement himself.

If JOHN wants to change the password of another user, he needs to specify the name of that user.

Example 28.6: Change the password of ROB to ROBSEC.

```
SET PASSWORD FOR ROB = PASSWORD('ROBSEC')
```

28.5 Granting Table and Column Privileges

MySQL supports the following table privileges.

- SELECT—This privilege gives a user the right to access the specified table with the SELECT statement. He or she can also include the table in a view formula. However, a user must have the SELECT privilege for every table (or view) specified in a view formula.
- INSERT—This privilege gives a user the right to add rows to the specified table with the INSERT statement.
- DELETE—This privilege gives a user the right to remove rows from the specified table with the DELETE statement.
- UPDATE—This privilege gives a user the right to change values in the specified table with the UPDATE statement.
- REFERENCES—This privilege gives a user the right to create foreign keys that refer to the specified table.
- CREATE—This privilege gives a user the right to create a table with the specified name.
- ALTER—This privilege gives a user the right to change the table with the ALTER TABLE statement.
- INDEX—This privilege gives a user the right to define indexes on the table.
- DROP—This privilege gives a user the right to remove the table.
- ALL or ALL PRIVILEGES—This privilege is a shortened form for all the privileges named.

A table privilege may be granted only by users who own enough privileges.

DEFINITION

```
<grant statement> ::=
   <grant table privilege statement>

<grant table privilege statement> ::=
   GRANT <table privileges>
   ON    <table specification>
   TO    <grantees>
   [ WITH <grant option>... ]

<table privileges> ::=
   ALL [ PRIVILEGES ] |
   <table privilege> [ , <table privileges> ]...

<table privileges> ::=
   SELECT                          |
   INSERT                          |
   DELETE [ <column list> ]        |
   UPDATE [ <column list> ]        |
   REFERENCES [ <column list> ]    |
   CREATE                          |
   ALTER                           |
   INDEX [ <column list> ]         |
   DROP

<grantees> ::=
   <user specification> [ , <user specification> ]...

<user specification> ::=
   <user name> [ IDENTIFIED BY [ PASSWORD ] <password> ]

<user name> ::=
   <name> | '<name>' | '<name>'@'<host name>'

<grant option> ::=
   GRANT OPTION                                |
   MAX_CONNECTIONS_PER_HOUR <whole number>     |
   MAX_QUERIES_PER_HOUR <whole number>         |
   MAX_UPDATES_PER_HOUR <whole number>         |
   MAX_USER_CONNECTIONS <whole number>

<column list> ::=
   ( <column name> [ , <column name> ]... )
```

See these examples of how table privileges must be granted. We assume, unless otherwise mentioned, that the user called BOOKSQL enters the statements.

Example 28.7: Give JAMIE the SELECT privilege on the PLAYERS table.

```
GRANT    SELECT
ON       PLAYERS
TO       JAMIE
```

Explanation: After this GRANT statement has been processed, JAMIE may use a USE statement to log on to the TENNIS database. After that, she may use any SELECT statement to query the PLAYERS table, regardless of who has created the table.

If privileges are granted to a user who does not exist yet, MySQL creates this user by automatically executing a CREATE USER statement. The statement does not specify a host, which means that the new user is granted '%' as host. No password has been specified, either, so JAMIE is allowed to log on without entering a password. For security purposes, it would be better to specify a user name and password for this user.

Example 28.8: Give the new user BOB the SELECT privilege on the PLAYERS table.

```
GRANT    SELECT
ON       PLAYERS
TO       'BOB'@'localhost' IDENTIFIED BY 'BOBPASS'
```

Multiple table privileges can be granted to multiple users simultaneously.

Example 28.9: Give JAMIE and PETE the INSERT and UPDATE privileges for all columns of the TEAMS table.

```
GRANT    INSERT, UPDATE
ON       TEAMS
TO       JAMIE, PETE
```

Granting one table privilege does not automatically lead to another. If we grant an INSERT privilege to a user, he or she does not automatically receive the SELECT privilege. It needs to be granted separately.

With several privileges, including UPDATE and REFERENCES, you can indicate the columns to which the privilege applies. In that case, we call it *column privileges.* When you do not specify a column, as in the previous examples, the privilege applies to *all* columns of the table.

Example 28.10: Give PETE the UPDATE privilege for the columns PLAYERNO and DIVISION of the TEAMS table.

```
GRANT   UPDATE (PLAYERNO, DIVISION)
ON      TEAMS
TO      PETE
```

Exercise 28.3: Give RONALDO the SELECT and INSERT privileges on the PLAYERS table.

Exercise 28.4: Give RONALDO the UPDATE privilege for the columns STREET, HOUSENO, POSTCODE, and TOWN of the PLAYERS table.

28.6 Granting Database Privileges

Table privileges apply to a specific table. MySQL also supports privileges for an entire database, such as the privilege to create tables or views in a specific database.

MySQL supports the following database privileges:

- SELECT—This privilege gives the user the right to access all tables and views of the specified database with the SELECT statement.
- INSERT—This privilege gives the user the right to add rows to all tables of the specified database with the INSERT statement.
- DELETE—This privilege gives the user the right to remove rows from all tables of the specified database with the DELETE statement.
- UPDATE—This privilege gives the user the right to update values in all tables of the specified database with the UPDATE statement.
- REFERENCES—This privilege gives the user the right to create foreign keys that point to tables of the specified database.
- CREATE—This privilege gives the user the right to create new tables in the specified database with the CREATE TABLE statement.
- ALTER—This privilege gives the user the right to alter all tables of the specified database with the ALTER TABLE statement.
- DROP—This privilege gives the user the right to remove all tables and views of the specified database.
- INDEX—This privilege gives the user the right to define and remove indexes on all tables of the specified database.

- CREATE TEMPORARY TABLES—This privilege gives the user the right to create temporary tables in the specified database.
- CREATE VIEW—This privilege gives the user the right to create new views in the specified database with the CREATE VIEW statement.
- SHOW VIEW—This privilege gives the user the right to look at the view definitions of existing views in the specified database with the SHOW VIEW statement.
- CREATE ROUTINE—This privilege gives the user the right to create new stored procedures and stored functions for the specified database; see Chapters 31, "Stored Procedures," and 32, "Stored Functions."
- ALTER ROUTINE—This privilege gives the user the right to update and remove existing stored procedures and stored functions of the specified database.
- EXECUTE ROUTINE—This privilege gives the user the right to invoke existing stored procedures and stored functions of the specified database.
- LOCK TABLES—This privilege gives the user the right to block existing tables of the specified database; see Section 37.9.
- ALL or ALL PRIVILEGES—This privilege is a shortened form for all the privileges named.

The definition of the following GRANT statement resembles the one for granting table privileges. However, two important differences exist: The list with privileges is longer, and the ON clause looks different.

DEFINITION

```
<grant statement> ::=
   <grant database privilege statement>

<grant database privilege statement> ::=
   GRANT <database privileges>
   ON    [ <database name> . ] *
   TO    <grantees>
   [ WITH <grant option>... ]

<database privileges> ::=
   ALL [ PRIVILEGES ] |
   <database privilege> [ , <database privilege> ]...
```

continues

```
<database privilege> ::=
   SELECT                  |
   INSERT                  |
   DELETE                  |
   UPDATE                  |
   REFERENCES              |
   CREATE                  |
   ALTER                   |
   DROP                    |
   INDEX                   |
   CREATE TEMPORARY TABLES |
   CREATE VIEW             |
   SHOW VIEW               |
   CREATE ROUTINE          |
   ALTER ROUTINE           |
   EXECUTE ROUTINE         |
   LOCK TABLES

<grantees> ::=
   <user specification> [ , <user specification> ]...

<user specification> ::=
   <user name> [ IDENTIFIED BY [ PASSWORD ] <password> ]

<user name> ::=
   <name> | '<name>' | '<name>'@'<host name>'
```

Example 28.11: Give PETE the SELECT privilege for all tables in the TENNIS database.

```
GRANT   SELECT
ON      TENNIS.*
TO      PETE
```

Explanation: This privilege applies to all existing tables and also any tables that are added to the TENNIS database later.

Example 28.12: Give JIM the privilege to create, update, and remove new tables and views in the TENNIS database.

```
GRANT   CREATE, ALTER, DROP, CREATE VIEW
ON      TENNIS.*
TO      JIM
```

Similar to table privileges, granting one database privilege does not imply another. JIM is now allowed to create new tables and views, but he may not access them yet. For that to occur, he needs to be granted a separate SELECT privilege or more privileges.

Example 28.13: Give PETE the SELECT privilege to query all catalog tables in the INFORMATION_SCHEMA database.

```
GRANT    SELECT
ON       INFORMATION_SCHEMA.*
TO       PETE
```

Example 28.14: Give ALYSSA the SELECT and INSERT privileges for all tables in the current database.

```
GRANT    SELECT, INSERT
ON       *
TO       ALYSSA
```

Explanation: The asterisk represents the current database here.

Exercise 28.5: Give JACO and DIANE the INSERT privilege on all tables of the TENNIS database.

28.7 Granting User Privileges

The most effective privileges are the user privileges. For all statements for which database privileges need to be granted, user privileges can be defined as well. For example, by granting someone the privilege CREATE on the user level, this user can create new databases as well as tables in all databases (instead of in one specific database). MySQL also supports the following user privileges:

- CREATE USER—This privilege gives a user the right to create and remove new users.
- SHOW DATABASE—This privilege gives a user the right to look at the definitions of all databases with the SHOW DATABASE statement.

We list other user privileges, but we don't explain them in this book because they are primarily used in managing the database server instead of programming with SQL.

DEFINITION

```
<grant statement> ::=
   <grant user privilege statement>

<grant user privilege statement> ::=
   GRANT <user privileges>
   ON    *.*
   TO    <grantees>
   [ WITH <grant option>... ]

<user privileges> ::=
   ALL [ PRIVILEGES ] |
   <user privilege> [ , <user privilege> ]...

<user privilege> ::=
   SELECT                  |
   INSERT                  |
   DELETE                  |
   UPDATE                  |
   REFERENCES              |
   CREATE                  |
   ALTER                   |
   DROP                    |
   INDEX                   |
   CREATE TEMPORARY TABLES |
   CREATE VIEW             |
   SHOW VIEW               |
   CREATE ROUTINE          |
   ALTER ROUTINE           |
   EXECUTE ROUTINE         |
   LOCK TABLES             |
   CREATE USER             |
   SHOW DATABASES          |
   FILE                    |
   PROCESS                 |
   RELOAD                  |
   REPLICATION CLIENT      |
   REPLICATION SLAVE       |
   SHUTDOWN                |
   SUPER                   |
   USAGE

<grantees> ::=
   <user specification> [ , <user specification> ]...

<user specification> ::=
   <user name> [ IDENTIFIED BY [ PASSWORD ] <password> ]

<user name> ::=
   <name> | '<name>' | '<name>'@'<host name>'
```

Example 28.15: Give MAX the CREATE, ALTER, and DROP privileges for all tables of all databases.

```
GRANT   CREATE, ALTER, DROP
ON      *.*
TO      MAX
```

Explanation: User MAX now has the privileges to create, drop, and alter all existing and future databases.

Example 28.16: Give ALYSSA the privilege to create new users.

```
GRANT   CREATE USER
ON      *.*
TO      ALYSSA
```

The user called *root* gets the following privilege during the installation of MySQL:

```
GRANT   ALL PRIVILEGES
ON      *.*
TO      ROOT
```

To summarize privileges, Table 28.1 lists the levels at which certain SQL statement privileges can be granted.

TABLE 28.1 Overview of Privileges

Statement	User Privilege	Database Privilege	Table Privilege	Column Privilege
SELECT	yes	yes	yes	no
INSERT	yes	yes	yes	no
DELETE	yes	yes	yes	yes
UPDATE	yes	yes	yes	yes
REFERENCES	yes	yes	yes	yes
CREATE	yes	yes	yes	no
ALTER	yes	yes	yes	no
DROP	yes	yes	yes	no
INDEX	yes	yes	yes	yes
CREATE TEMPORARY TABLES	yes	yes	no	no
CREATE VIEW	yes	yes	no	no
SHOW VIEW	yes	yes	no	no
CREATE ROUTINE	yes	yes	no	no
ALTER ROUTINE	yes	yes	no	no

continues

TABLE 28.1 Continued

Statement	User Privilege	Database Privilege	Table Privilege	Column Privilege
EXECUTE ROUTINE	yes	yes	no	no
LOCK TABLES	yes	yes	no	no
CREATE USER	yes	no	no	no
SHOW DATABASES	yes	no	no	no
FILE	yes	no	no	no
PROCESS	yes	no	no	no
RELOAD	yes	no	no	no
REPLICATION CLIENT	yes	no	no	no
REPLICATION SLAVE	yes	no	no	no
SHUTDOWN	yes	no	no	no
SUPER	yes	no	no	no
USAGE	yes	no	no	no

28.8 Passing on Privileges: WITH GRANT OPTION

A GRANT statement can be concluded with the WITH GRANT OPTION. By using this statement, all users specified in the TO clause can *themselves* pass on the privilege (or part of the privilege) to other users, even if they are not the owner of it.

Example 28.17: Give JIM the REFERENCES privilege on the TEAMS table and allow him to pass it on to other users.

```
GRANT    REFERENCES
ON       TEAMS
TO       JIM
WITH     GRANT OPTION
```

Because of the WITH GRANT OPTION clause, JIM can pass on this privilege to PETE, for example:

```
GRANT    REFERENCES
ON       TEAMS
TO       PETE
```

JIM can himself extend the statement by using WITH GRANT OPTION so that PETE, in turn, can pass on the privilege.

So if a user has been granted the WITH GRANT OPTION on a specific table, it applies to all the privileges that the user has on that table. The next example illustrates this.

Example 28.18: Give MARC the INSERT and SELECT privileges for the COMMITTEE_MEMBERS table. He may pass both privileges to other users.

```
GRANT    INSERT
ON       COMMITTEE_MEMBERS
TO       MARC

GRANT    SELECT
ON       COMMITTEE_MEMBERS
TO       MARC
WITH     GRANT OPTION
```

Explanation: With these two statements, it might look as if MARC has the privilege to pass on only SELECT, but that is not the case. WITH GRANT OPTION applies to all relevant table privileges.

Example 28.19: Give SAM the SELECT privilege for all tables in all databases, which he can pass on to other users.

```
GRANT    SELECT
ON       *.*
TO       SAM
WITH     GRANT OPTION
```

Explanation: This example shows that WITH GRANT OPTION can be added to every kind of privilege, including database and user privileges.

28.9 Restricting Privileges

It is also possible to grant usage restrictions to a user, such as how many times someone may query the database per hour.

Example 28.20: Give JIM the right to process only one SELECT statement per hour.

```
GRANT    SELECT
ON       *
TO       JIM
WITH     MAX_QUERIES_PER_HOUR 1
```

In addition to MAX_QUERIES_PER_HOUR, you are allowed to specify MAX_CONNECTIONS_PER_HOUR, MAX_UPDATES_PER_HOUR, and MAX_USER_CONNECTIONS. For the first three specifications, the rule applies that if the value is equal to 0, no restrictions are in effect.

28.10 Recording Privileges in the Catalog

Several catalog tables are used to record users, roles, and privileges:

- The USERS table records users.
- The ROLES table stores roles.
- The USER_ROLES table records which user has which role.
- The COLUMN_AUTHS table contains information about the privileges granted on specific columns.
- The TABLE_AUTHS table contains information about privileges on specific tables.

The USERS table contains only one column, the name of the user. This column also forms the primary key of this table.

TABLE 28.2 Description of the USERS Catalog Table

Column Name	Data Type	Description
USER_NAME	CHAR	Name of the user followed by the name of the host

The column privileges are recorded in a separate catalog table, the COLUMN_AUTHS table. The primary key of this table is formed by the columns GRANTOR, TABLE_NAME, GRANTEE, and COLUMN_NAME. The table has the following structure:

TABLE 28.3 Description of the COLUMN_AUTHS Catalog Table

Column Name	Data Type	Description
GRANTOR	CHAR	User who granted the privilege.
GRANTEE	CHAR	User who received the privilege.
TABLE_CREATOR	CHAR	Name of the database of the table on which the privilege is granted.
TABLE_NAME	CHAR	Table or view on which the privilege is granted.
COLUMN_NAME	CHAR	Column name on which the privilege is granted.
PRIVILEGE	CHAR	Type of privilege.
WITHGRANTOPT	LOGICAL	If this column is filled with the value YES, the user can pass on the privilege to other users; otherwise, the value of this column is equal to NO.

The TABLE_AUTHS table has the following structure. The columns GRANTOR, GRANTEE, TABLE_CREATOR, TABLE_NAME, and PRIVILEGE form the primary key of this table. You can see that the column privileges are *not* recorded in this table.

TABLE 28.4 Description of the TABLE_AUTHS catalog table

Column Name	Data Type	Description
GRANTOR	CHAR	User who granted the privilege.
GRANTEE	CHAR	User who received the privilege.
TABLE_CREATOR	CHAR	Name of the database of the table on which the privilege is granted.
TABLE_NAME	CHAR	Table or view on which the privilege is granted.
PRIVILEGE	CHAR	Type of privilege.
WITHGRANTOPT	CHAR	If this column is filled with the value YES, the user can pass on the privilege to other users; otherwise, the value of this column is equal to NO.

The DATABASE_AUTHS table has the following structure. The primary key of this table is formed by the columns GRANTOR, GRANTEE, DATABASE_NAME, and PRIVILEGE.

TABLE 28.5 Description of the DATABASE_AUTHS Catalog Table

Column Name	Data Type	Description
GRANTOR	CHAR	User who granted the privilege.
GRANTEE	CHAR	User who received the privilege.
DATABASE_NAME	CHAR	Database on which the privilege is granted.
PRIVILEGE	CHAR	Type of privilege.
WITHGRANTOPT	CHAR	If this column is filled with the value YES, the user can pass on the privilege to other users; otherwise, the value of this column is equal to NO.

The USER_AUTHS table has the following structure. The primary key of this table is formed by the columns GRANTOR, GRANTEE, and PRIVILEGE.

TABLE 28.6 Description of the USER_AUTHS Catalog Table

Column Name	Data Type	Description
GRANTOR	CHAR	User who granted the privilege.
GRANTEE	CHAR	User who received the privilege.
PRIVILEGE	CHAR	Type of privilege; if this column is filled with the value USAGE, this user does not have any user privilege.
WITHGRANTOPT	CHAR	If this column is filled with the value YES, the user can pass the privilege on to other users; otherwise, the value of this column is equal to NO.

Example 28.21: Which users are allowed to query the PLAYERS table in the TENNIS database?

```
SELECT   GRANTEE
FROM     USER_AUTHS
WHERE    PRIVILEGE = 'SELECT'
UNION
SELECT   GRANTEE
FROM     DATABASE_AUTHS
WHERE    DATABASE_NAME = 'TENNIS'
AND      PRIVILEGE = 'SELECT'
UNION
SELECT   GRANTEE
FROM     TABLE_AUTHS
WHERE    TABLE_CREATOR = 'TENNIS'
AND      PRIVILEGE = 'SELECT'
AND      TABLE_NAME = 'PLAYERS'
```

Explanation: This example requires a search in three tables because SELECT privileges can be defined on three levels.

The tables USER_PRIVILEGES, SCHEMA_PRIVILEGES, TABLE_PRIVILEGES, and COLUMN_PRIVILEGES, all belonging to the catalog called INFORMATION_SCHEMA, contain information on privileges.

28.11 Revoking Privileges

To withdraw privileges from a user without deleting that user from the USERS table, use the *REVOKE statement.* This statement has the opposite effect of the GRANT statement.

DEFINITION

```
<revoke statement> ::=
   <revoke table privilege statement>    |
   <revoke database privilege statement |
   <revoke user privilege>

<revoke table privilege statement> ::=
   REVOKE  [ <table privileges> ] [ GRANT OPTION ]
   ON      <table specification>
   FROM    <user name> [ , <user name> ]...

<table privileges> ::=
   ALL [ PRIVILEGES ] |
   <table privilege> [ , <table privilege> ]...

<table privilege> ::=
   SELECT                          |
   INSERT                          |
   DELETE [ <column list> ]        |
   UPDATE [ <column list> ]        |
   REFERENCES [ <column list> ]    |
   CREATE                          |
   ALTER                           |
   INDEX [ <column list> ]         |
   DROP

<revoke database privilege statement> ::=
   REVOKE  [ <database privileges> ] [ GRANT OPTION ]
   ON      [ <database name> . ] *
   FROM    <user name> [ , <user name> ]...

<database privileges> ::=
   ALL [ PRIVILEGES ] |
   <database privilege> [ , <database privilege> ]...

<database privilege> ::=
   SELECT                   |
   INSERT                   |
   DELETE                   |
   UPDATE                   |
   REFERENCES               |
   CREATE                   |
   ALTER                    |
   DROP                     |
   INDEX                    |
   CREATE TEMPORARY TABLES  |
   CREATE VIEW              |
   SHOW VIEW                |
   CREATE ROUTINE           |
   ALTER ROUTINE            |
   EXECUTE ROUTINE          |
   LOCK TABLES
```

continues

```
<revoke user privilege statement> ::=
   REVOKE  [ <user privileges> ] [ GRANT OPTION ]
   ON      *.*
   FROM    <user name> [ , <user name> ]...

<user privileges> ::=
   ALL [ PRIVILEGES ] |
   <user privilege> [ , <user privilege> ]...

<user privilege> ::=
   SELECT                  |
   INSERT                  |
   DELETE                  |
   UPDATE                  |
   REFERENCES              |
   CREATE                  |
   ALTER                   |
   DROP                    |
   INDEX                   |
   CREATE TEMPORARY TABLES |
   CREATE VIEW             |
   SHOW VIEW               |
   CREATE ROUTINE          |
   ALTER ROUTINE           |
   EXECUTE ROUTINE         |
   LOCK TABLES             |
   CREATE USER             |
   SHOW DATABASES          |
   FILE                    |
   PROCESS                 |
   RELOAD                  |
   REPLICATION CLIENT      |
   REPLICATION SLAVE       |
   SHUTDOWN                |
   SUPER                   |
   USAGE

<user name> ::=
   <name> | '<name>' | '<name>'@'<host name>'
```

Example 28.22: Withdraw JIM's SELECT privilege on the PLAYERS table (assume that the situation is as it was at the end of Section 28.10).

```
REVOKE   SELECT
ON       PLAYERS
FROM     JIM
```

The relevant privilege is now deleted from the catalog.

Example 28.23: Withdraw JIM's REFERENCES privilege on the TEAMS table.

```
REVOKE   REFERENCES
ON       TEAMS
FROM     JIM
```

This privilege is withdrawn, in addition to all the privileges that are directly or indirectly dependent on it. In the example, PETE also loses his REFERENCES privilege on the TEAMS table.

If a privilege has been granted with a WITH GRANT OPTION, it is not withdrawn when a table privilege is removed. The next example is based upon the privileges that were granted in Example 28.18.

Example 28.24: Withdraw MARC's INSERT and SELECT privileges on the COMMITTEE_MEMBERS table.

```
REVOKE  INSERT, SELECT
ON      COMMITTEE_MEMBERS
FROM    MARC
```

The WITH GRANT OPTION remains after this statement, so if we want to grant MARC a new table privilege on the same table again, he can immediately pass it on to other users. An additional REVOKE statement is required to withdraw MARC's WITH GRANT privilege.

```
REVOKE  GRANT OPTION
ON      COMMITTEE_MEMBERS
FROM    MARC
```

A user can be granted overlapping privileges. For example, he could receive the table privilege UPDATE on the PLAYERS table and also the user privilege UPDATE for all tables in all databases. If one of the two is withdrawn, the other privilege remains.

28.12 Security of and Through Views

A GRANT statement can refer not only to tables, but also to views (see the definition of the GRANT statement in Section 28.5). Let us look at this more closely.

Because privileges can also be granted for views, it is possible to provide users with access to only a part of a table or only to information derived or summarized from tables. See the following examples of both features.

Example 28.25: Give DIANE the privilege to read only the names and addresses of noncompetitive players.

First, DIANE must be entered with a CREATE USER statement.

```
CREATE USER 'DIANE'@'localhost' IDENTIFIED BY 'SECRET'
```

Second, a view is created specifying which data she may see.

```
CREATE   VIEW NAME_ADDRESS AS
SELECT   NAME, INITIALS, STREET, HOUSENO,
         TOWN
FROM     PLAYERS
WHERE    LEAGUENO IS NULL
```

The last step is to grant DIANE the SELECT privilege on the NAME_ADDRESS view:

```
GRANT   SELECT
ON      NAME_ADDRESS
TO      DIANE
```

With this statement, DIANE has access to only that part of the PLAYERS table defined in the view formula of NAME_ADDRESS.

Example 28.26: Restrict user GERARD to view only the number of players in each town. First, we introduce GERARD.

```
CREATE USER 'GERARD'@'localhost' IDENTIFIED BY 'XYZ1234'
```

The view that we use looks like this:

```
CREATE   VIEW RESIDENTS (TOWN, NUMBER_OF) AS
SELECT   TOWN, COUNT(*)
FROM     PLAYERS
GROUP BY TOWN
```

Now we give GERARD the privilege for the previous view:

```
GRANT   SELECT
ON      RESIDENTS
TO      GERARD
```

All types of table privileges can be granted on views.

28.13 Answers

28.1
```
CREATE  USER RONALDO IDENTIFIED BY 'NIKE'
```

28.2
```
DROP    USER RONALDO
```

28.3
```
GRANT   SELECT, INSERT
ON      PLAYERS
TO      RONALDO
```

28.4
```
GRANT   UPDATE(STREET, HOUSENO, POSTCODE, TOWN)
ON      PLAYERS
TO      RONALDO
```

28.5
```
GRANT   INSERT
ON      TENNIS.*
TO      JACO, DIANE
```

CHAPTER 29

Statements for Table Maintenance

29.1 Introduction

MySQL supports several SQL statements that relate to the maintenance and management of databases. For example, with one we can repair a damaged table, and with another one we can check whether a table with indexes is still correct. Generally, database managers, not developers, use these statements. Still, we discuss them here to be complete.

This chapter discusses the following statements:

- ANALYZE TABLE
- CHECKSUM TABLE
- OPTIMIZE TABLE
- CHECK TABLE
- REPAIR TABLE
- BACKUP TABLE
- RESTORE TABLE

These statements belong to the group called *table maintenance statements.*

Note that MySQL also supports special utilities with which comparable actions can be performed. Because this book focuses on the SQL dialect of MySQL, we leave those utilities aside.

29.2 The ANALYZE TABLE Statement

If the optimizer determines the processing strategy for an SQL statement, it starts by gathering some information. An important piece of required information is the *cardinality* of the data in an indexed column—that is, how many different values are there in a column on which an index has been defined? The catalog stores this cardinality, and we can retrieve it with a *SHOW INDEX statement*, for example.

Example 29.1: Show the cardinalities of the indexes belonging to the PLAYERS table.

```
SHOW INDEX FROM PLAYERS
```

The result follows (only a few columns have been shown, for the sake of clarity):

```
TABLE    KEY_NAME  COLUMN_NAME  CARDINALITY
-------  --------  -----------  -----------
PLAYERS  PRIMARY   PLAYERNO              14
```

The cardinality of an indexed column is not automatically updated. If a new player is added, we cannot assume that the cardinality increases by 1. Also, when we create a new index, the cardinality is not calculated immediately; that would take too much time.

Example 29.2: Create an index on the TOWN column of the PLAYERS table; next, show the cardinality of that new index.

```
CREATE INDEX PLAYERS_TOWN
    ON PLAYERS (TOWN)

SHOW INDEX FROM PLAYERS
```

The result follows (only a few columns have been shown, for the sake of clarity):

```
TABLE    KEY_NAME         COLUMN_NAME  CARDINALITY
-------  ---------------  -----------  -----------
SPELERS  PRIMARY          PLAYERNO              14
SPELERS  PLAYERS_TOWN     TOWN                   ?
```

Explanation: Clearly, the cardinality of the PLAYERS_TOWN index has not been updated.

The special *ANALYZE TABLE statement* can update the cardinalities of indexed columns.

DEFINITION

```
<analyze table statement> ::=
   ANALYZE [ <analyze option> ]
      TABLE <table specification> [ , <table specification> ]...

<table specification> ::= [ <database nam > . ] <table name>

<analyze option> ::= NO_WRITE_TO_BINLOG | LOCAL
```

Example 29.3: Update the cardinalities of the indexes belonging to the PLAYERS table and show those cardinalities next.

```
ANALYZE TABLE PLAYERS

SHOW INDEX FROM PLAYERS
```

The result follows (only a few columns have been shown):

```
TABLE    KEY_NAME       COLUMN_NAME  CARDINALITY
-------  ------------   -----------  -----------
PLAYERS  PRIMARY        PLAYERNO              14
PLAYERS  PLAYERS_TOWN   TOWN                   7
```

All updates executed on a MySQL database are also written to a binary log file. It falls outside the context of this book to explain this. However, developers should realize that data is written not only to the database, but to this log file as well. Data resulting from processing the ANALYZE TABLE statement is also written to this log file. You can switch off this function by specifying the option NO_WRITE_TO_BINLOG. The term LOCAL is a synonym for NO_WRITE_TO_BINLOG. If this is switched off, the ANALYZE TABLE statement finishes more quickly.

29.3 The CHECKSUM TABLE Statement

For each table, a *checksum* can be retrieved. Sometimes, when data is transferred, some data gets lost or changed by mistake. To detect such a problem, a checksum can be calculated in advance and afterward. After the data has been transferred, a check tells us whether the two checksums are still the same. If so, the data was transferred correctly. For example, the formula used to calculate a checksum can be compared to the check digit used for Universal Product Codes and International Standard Book Numbers.

For each table created with the MyISAM storage engine, the checksum is stored in the table. This is called a *live checksum.* If rows are added or values are changed, the live checksum is updated immediately.

The *CHECKSUM TABLE statement* retrieves the checksum of a table.

DEFINITION

```
<checksum table statement> ::=
   CHECKSUM TABLE <table specification> [ , <table specification> ]...
     [ <checksum option> ]

<table specification> ::= [ <database name> . ] <table name>

      <checksum option> ::= QUICK | EXTENDED
```

Example 29.4: Determine the value of the checksum of the PLAYERS table.

```
CHECKSUM TABLE PLAYERS
```

The result is:

```
TABLE            CHECKSUM
--------------   ----------
TENNIS.PLAYERS   3394683388
```

You can specify `QUICK` or `EXTENDED` behind a `CHECKSUM TABLE` statement. If the latter is used, the original table is analyzed and the checksum is calculated. Even if the table has been built with MyISAM, the live checksum is not used, but the checksum is calculated. If `QUICK` is used, MySQL returns the value of the live checksum if it concerns a MyISAM table (and this is done very quickly). Otherwise, MySQL returns the value `null`.

Not specifying `QUICK` and `EXTENDED` is equal to specifying the latter.

29.4 The OPTIMIZE TABLE Statement

If you continuously create and remove files on your own computer, you know that your hard disk splits into fragments. In other words, your hard disk becomes a real mess, which reduces the speed of the machine.

The same applies to tables. If we continuously update a table with `INSERT`, `DELETE`, and `UPDATE` statements, the internal structure of the table becomes fragmented, which reduces the speed of SQL statements on this table. In this case, it is time to organize the data in the table properly. You can do this with the *OPTIMIZE TABLE statement*.

This statement also works with tables created with the MyISAM or the InnoDB storage engine.

DEFINITION

```
<optimize table statement> ::=
   OPTIMIZE [ <optimize option> ]
      TABLE <table specification> [ , <table specification> ]...

<table specification> ::= [ <database name> . ] <table name>

<optimize option> ::= NO_WRITE_TO_BINLOG | LOCAL
```

Example 29.5: Optimize the PLAYERS table.

```
OPTIMIZE TABLE PLAYERS
```

The result is:

```
TABLE           OP        MSG_TYPE  MSG_TEXT
--------------  --------  --------  --------
TENNIS.PLAYERS  optimize  status    OK
```

In fact, you should periodically execute an `OPTIMIZE TABLE` statement on tables that are updated frequently.

As with the `ANALYZE TABLE` statement, you can turn off the writing to the log file by specifying `NO_WRITE_TO_BINLOG` or `LOCAL`.

29.5 The CHECK TABLE Statement

Sometimes things go wrong with a database. When new data is written to the hard disk at a time an error occurs, the question is whether the table is still correct. Or has the table been updated correctly, but the indexes of the table haven't? Another problem could be that the computer on which MySQL runs is turned off suddenly, with no chance for MySQL to close the database properly. In all circumstances, the state of the data is not clear. Odds are, a table or an index has been damaged. Maybe the pointers between the table and an index are no longer correct.

You might notice, for example, that a table is damaged when MySQL displays the following error message after querying a table:

```
Incorrect key file for table: '    '. Try to repair it.
```

If you question the condition of the data, use the *`CHECK TABLE` statement* to check whether everything is still correct. This statement checks one or more tables with their corresponding indexes.

DEFINITION

```
<check table statement> ::=
   CHECK TABLE <table specification> [ , <table specification> ]...
      [ <check option> ]...

<table specification> ::= [ <database name> . ] <table name>

<check option> ::=
   FOR UPGRADE | QUICK | FAST | MEDIUM | EXTENDED | CHANGED
```

Example 29.6: Check whether the PLAYERS table is still correct.

```
CHECK TABLE PLAYERS
```

The result is:

```
TABLE           OP     MSG_TYPE  MSG_TEXT
--------------  -----  --------  --------
TENNIS.PLAYERS  check  status    OK
```

Explanation: The result shows whether the table is still correct. In this case, the table proves to be okay. Another message could be: `Table is already up to date`. In all other cases, a problem exists with the table. In that case, the table must be repaired; see the following section.

MySQL keeps track in the catalog of when a table was checked last. Each time the CHECK TABLE is executed for a table, it stores this information.

Example 29.7: Show when the PLAYERS table was checked last.

```
SELECT   TABLE_NAME, CHECK_TIME
FROM     INFORMATION_SCHEMA.TABLES
WHERE    TABLE_NAME = 'PLAYERS'
AND      TABLE_SCHEMA = 'TENNIS'
```

The result is:

```
TABLE_NAME  CHECK_TIME
----------  -------------------
PLAYERS     2006-08-21 16:44:25
```

A CHECK TABLE statement can include different options. If we specify FOR UPGRADE, MySQL determines whether the table, which might have been created with an older version of MySQL, is compatible with the version of MySQL that is currently being used. This could happen, for example, when we decide to record values with a certain data type differently.

The other options apply only to tables created with the MyISAM storage engine.

- `QUICK`—This is the fastest option. The rows in the table you are working with are not checked for incorrect links. This option is recommended if you do not really expect any problems.
- `FAST`—This option checks only whether the tables have been closed correctly. This option is recommended if you do not expect serious problems or right after a power failure that probably did not cause any problems.
- `CHANGED`—This is comparable to the `FAST` option, but it checks only tables that changed after the previous `CHECK` statement.
- `MEDIUM`—This option checks whether the links between the index data and the table data are correct. In addition, the checksum of all keys are compared to the checksum of all the rows. This is the default option.
- `EXTENDED`—This is the most extensive and, therefore, slowest option. All the checks performed by the other options are now checked in detail.

29.6 The REPAIR TABLE Statement

The `CHECK TABLE` statement can detect a problem in a table. If a table or index appears to be damaged, we can try to repair it with the `REPAIR TABLE` *statement*. If that does not work, we can deploy utilities such as myisamchk.

Note that the REPAIR TABLE statement works only for tables created with the MyISAM and the ARCHIVE storage engines.

DEFINITION

```
<repair table statement> ::=
   REPAIR [ <repair option> ]
      TABLE <table specification> [ , <table specification> ]...
      [ QUICK ] [ EXTENDED ] [ USE_FRM ]

<table specification> ::= [ <database name> . ] <table name>

<repair option> ::= NO_WRITE_TO_BINLOG | LOCAL
```

Example 29.8: Suppose that the PLAYERS table is damaged. Make sure that it is repaired.

```
REPAIR TABLE PLAYERS
```

The result is:

```
TABLE           OP      MSG_TYPE  MSG_TEXT
--------------  ------  --------  --------
TENNIS.PLAYERS  repair  status    OK
```

We can also include options with the REPAIR TABLE statement to indicate how thorough the repair must be.

- QUICK—This is the fastest option. Here, MySQL tries to repair only the index tree.
- EXTENDED—With this option, the index is rebuilt row by row instead of creating the entire index at once.
- USE_FRM—This option must be used if the MYI file is missing completely or if the header is damaged. The entire index is then set up once again.

As with the ANALYZE TABLE statement, you can turn off writing to the log file by specifying NO_WRITE_TO_BINLOG or LOCAL.

29.7 The BACKUP TABLE Statement

With the *BACKUP TABLE statement,* we can make a backup (as the name implies) of one or more tables. Make sure they are MyISAM tables.

Note that the BACKUP TABLE and RESTORE TABLE statements are referred to as *deprecated.* That means that these statements will slowly disappear. In the end, more powerful alternatives will appear. Therefore, we limit ourselves to a short overview.

```
<backup table statement> ::=
   BACKUP TABLE <table specification>
      [ , <table specification> ]...
      TO <directory>

<table specification> ::= [ <database name> . ] <table name>
```

Example 29.9: Create a backup of the PLAYERS table and store it in the directory called C:/WORKING_AREA.

```
BACKUP TABLE PLAYERS TO 'C:/WORKING_AREA'
```

The result is:

```
TABLE           OP      MSG_TYPE  MSG_TEXT
--------------  ------  --------  --------
TENNIS.PLAYERS  backup  status    OK
```

Explanation: The specified directory should already exist. After this statement, this directory contains a few files: one for the table (FRM file) and one for each index (MYD file).

29.8 The RESTORE TABLE Statement

With the RESTORE TABLE statement, we can retrieve a backup of one or more tables created with the BACKUP TABLE statement. The data in the backup files is read into a table again.

DEFINITION

```
<restore table statement> ::=
   RESTORE TABLE <table specification> [ , <table specification> ]...
      FROM <directory>

<table specification> ::= [ <database name> . ] <table name>
```

Example 29.10: Restore the PLAYERS table with data from the backup created in the previous section.

```
RESTORE TABLE PLAYERS FROM 'C:/WORKING_AREA'
```

The result is:

```
TABLE           OP      MSG_TYPE  MSG_TEXT
--------------  ------  --------  --------
TENNIS.PLAYERS  backup  status    OK
```

Explanation: The specified table should not exist yet.

CHAPTER 30

The SHOW, DESCRIBE, and HELP Statements

30.1 Introduction

Everywhere in this book you can see examples of the *SHOW statement*. With these statements, you can show information stored in the catalog tables. Consider a SHOW statement as a predefined SELECT statement on the catalog. The result of this statement is a table, just as with a SELECT statement. This chapter lists all the SHOW statements with their corresponding definitions and discusses the DESCRIBE and the HELP statements. These three statements belong to the group called the *informative statements*.

Note that all the SHOW and DESCRIBE statements access the tables in the MYSQL and INFORMATION_SCHEMA databases, not our catalog views.

30.2 Overview of SHOW Statements

SHOW CHARACTER SET: Shows the list of several or all of the character sets that MySQL supports.

DEFINITION

```
<show character set statement> ::=
   SHOW CHARACTER SET [ LIKE <alphanumeric literal> ]
```

SHOW COLLATION: Shows the list of several or all the collations that MySQL supports.

DEFINITION

```
<show collation statement> ::=
   SHOW COLLATION [ LIKE <alphanumeric literal> ]
```

SHOW COLUMN TYPES: Shows information about all data types.

DEFINITION

```
<show column types statement> ::=
   SHOW COLUMN TYPES
```

SHOW COLUMNS: Shows information about all columns of one or more tables.

DEFINITION

```
<show columns statement> ::=
   SHOW [ FULL ] COLUMNS { FROM | IN } <table specification>
      [ { FROM | IN } <database name> ]
      [ LIKE <alphanumeric literal> ]
```

SHOW CREATE DATABASE: Shows the CREATE DATABASE statement for a certain database.

DEFINITION

```
<show create database statement> ::=
   SHOW CREATE DATABASE [ IF NOT EXISTS ] <database name>
```

SHOW CREATE EVENT: Shows the CREATE EVENT statement for a certain event.

DEFINITION

```
<show create event statement> ::=
   SHOW CREATE EVENT [ <database name> . ] <event name>
```

SHOW CREATE FUNCTION: Shows the CREATE FUNCTION statement for a certain stored function.

DEFINITION

```
<show create function statement> ::=
   SHOW CREATE FUNCTION
      [ <database name> . ] <stored function name>
```

SHOW CREATE PROCEDURE: Shows the CREATE PROCEDURE statement for a certain stored procedure.

DEFINITION

```
<show create procedure statement> ::=
   SHOW CREATE PROCEDURE
      [ <database name> . ] <stored procedure name>
```

SHOW CREATE TABLE: Shows the CREATE TABLE statement for a certain table.

DEFINITION

```
<show create table statement> ::=
   SHOW CREATE TABLE <table specification>
```

SHOW CREATE VIEW: Shows the CREATE VIEW statement for a certain view.

DEFINITION

```
<show create view statement> ::=
   SHOW CREATE VIEW <table specification>
```

SHOW DATABASES: Shows a list of several or all created databases.

DEFINITION

```
<show databases statement> ::=
   SHOW DATABASES [ LIKE <alphanumeric literal> ]
```

All users are allowed to execute the SHOW DATABASES statement. If you want only users who were granted the privilege for the SHOW DATABASES statement to execute this statement, you must switch the value of the system variable SKIP_SHOW_DATABASE to ON.

SHOW ENGINE: Shows the status of a certain storage engine.

DEFINITION

```
<show engine statements::=
   SHOW ENGINE <engine name> { LOGS | STATUS }
```

SHOW ENGINES: Shows the list of all storage engines that MySQL supports.

DEFINITION

```
<show engines statement> ::=
   SHOW [ STORAGE ] ENGINES
```

SHOW EVENTS: Shows the list of all events.

DEFINITION

```
<show events statement> ::=
   SHOW EVENTS [ FROM <database name> ]
      [ LIKE <alphanumeric literal> ]
```

SHOW FUNCTION STATUS: Shows the status of a certain stored function.

DEFINITION

```
<show function status statement> ::=
   SHOW FUNCTION STATUS [ LIKE <alphanumeric literal> ]
```

SHOW GRANTS: Shows information about the privileges of certain users.

DEFINITION

```
<show grants statement> ::=
   SHOW ACCOUNTS [ FOR <user name> ]
```

SHOW INDEX: Shows information about the indexes of several tables.

```
<show index statement> ::=
   SHOW { INDEX | KEY } { FROM | IN }
      <table specification> [ { FROM | IN } <database name> ]
```

SHOW PRIVILEGES: Shows the list of all privileges that MySQL recognizes.

DEFINITION

```
<show privileges statement> ::=
   SHOW PRIVILEGES
```

SHOW PROCEDURE STATUS: Shows the status of a certain stored procedure.

DEFINITION

```
<show procedure status statement> ::=
   SHOW PROCEDURE STATUS [ LIKE <alphanumeric literal> ]
```

SHOW TABLE TYPES: This statement is an outdated alternative for `SHOW ENGINES`. Use the latter as much as possible.

DEFINITION

```
<show table types statement> ::=
   SHOW TABLE TYPES
```

SHOW TABLES: Shows information about several tables.

DEFINITION

```
<show tables statement> ::=
   SHOW [ FULL ] TABLES [ { FROM | IN } <database name> ]
      [ LIKE <alphanumeric literal> ]
```

SHOW TRIGGERS: Shows information about several triggers.

DEFINITION

```
<show triggers statement> ::=
   SHOW TRIGGERS [ FROM <database name> ]
      [ LIKE <alphanumeric literal> ]
```

SHOW VARIABLES: Shows the values of several or all system and user variables.

DEFINITION

```
<show variables statement> ::=
   SHOW [ GLOBAL | SESSION ] VARIABLES
      [ LIKE <alphanumeric literal> ]
```

30.3 Additional SHOW Statements

Besides the SHOW statements described in the previous section, MySQL offers several others that we can use to study the status of the database server itself:

- SHOW BINLOG EVENTS
- SHOW ERRORS
- SHOW INNODB STATUS
- SHOW LOGS
- SHOW MASTER LOGS
- SHOW MASTER STATUS
- SHOW OPEN TABLES
- SHOW PROCESSLIST
- SHOW SLAVE HOSTS
- SHOW SLAVE STATUS
- SHOW STATUS
- SHOW TABLE STATUS
- SHOW WARNINGS

However, these SHOW statements do not show any catalog information, which is why we do not discuss them.

30.4 The DESCRIBE Statement

The result of the `DESCRIBE` *statement* is equal to that of the `SHOW COLUMNS` statement. The statement gives information about the columns of a table. The statement has been added because many other SQL products also support this statement.

DEFINITION

```
<describe statement> ::=
   { DESCRIBE | DESC } <table specification>
      [ <column name> | <alphanumeric literal> ]
```

Examples of the `DESCRIBE` statement are shown here:

```
DESCRIBE PLAYERS

DESCRIBE PLAYERS TOWN

DESCRIBE PLAYERS 'G%'
```

The special symbols `%` en `_` may be used within the alphanumeric literals; they have the same function as when used with the `LIKE` operator.

30.5 The HELP Statement

With the `HELP` *statement*, we can retrieve information from the MySQL reference manual.

DEFINITION

```
<help statement> ::=
   HELP <alphanumeric literal>
```

Examples of the `HELP` statement are shown here:

```
HELP 'CREATE TABLE'
HELP 'date'
```

The following `HELP` statement returns all the topics you can retrieve information on.

```
HELP 'contents'
```

The result is:

```
SOURCE_CATEGORY_NAME  NAME
--------------------  --------------------------  ---
Contents              Account Management
Contents              Administration
Contents              Data Definition
Contents              Data Manipulation
Contents              Data Types
Contents              Functions
Contents              Functions and Modifiers for Use
                      with GROUP BY
Contents              Geographic Features
Contents              Language Structure
:                     :
```

After that, you can use the different categories in a HELP statement again—for example, HELP 'data types'.

Part IV

Procedural Database Objects

In Section 1.4, we mentioned that, for a long time SQL, was a purely declarative language, but this changed in 1986–1987 when SQL products on the market began to support so-called *stored procedures.* That changed the character of SQL. A stored procedure can informally be described as a piece of code that can be called from applications, among other things. This piece of code consists of well-known SQL statements, such as `INSERT` and `SELECT`, but also procedural statements, such as `IF-THEN-ELSE` and `WHILE DO`. Because stored procedures offered many practical advantages, other vendors started to implement them. This meant the end of the pure declarative character of SQL. Since their inclusion in the SQL2 standard, stored procedures have formed a real part of the language.

Later, other nondeclarative database objects were added, such as stored functions and triggers. These are all database objects that we create with `CREATE` statements and store in the catalog. They differ, however, because they are based on procedural code. That is why we call them *procedural database objects.*

Since version 5.0, MySQL has supported stored procedures, stored functions, triggers, and events. This part discusses these four procedural database objects.

CHAPTER 31

Stored Procedures

31.1 Introduction

This chapter covers the procedural database object called the *stored procedure* or database procedure. We start by giving its definition:

> A **stored procedure** is a certain piece of code (the procedure) consisting of declarative and procedural SQL statements stored in the catalog of a database that can be activated by calling it from a program, a trigger, or another stored procedure.

Thus, a stored procedure is a piece of code. This code can consist of declarative SQL statements, such as `CREATE`, `UPDATE`, and `SELECT`, possibly complemented with procedural statements, such as `IF-THEN-ELSE` and `WHILE-DO`. The code from which a stored procedure is built is, therefore, not a part of a program, but is stored in the catalog.

Calling a stored procedure is comparable to calling a "normal" procedure (otherwise called a function or routine) in procedural languages. For calling stored procedures, a new SQL statement has been introduced. When calling stored procedures, you can also specify input and output parameters. As the definition indicates, stored procedures can be called from other stored procedures, just as functions in C can call other functions. The definition states that triggers also can activate stored procedures; Chapter 33, "Triggers," returns to this subject.

We can best illustrate a stored procedure and shows its possibilities with a number of examples. Therefore, this chapter includes several examples of increasing complexity.

31.2 An Example of a Stored Procedure

We start with a simple example.

Example 31.1: Create a stored procedure that removes all matches played by a specific player.

```
CREATE PROCEDURE DELETE_MATCHES
   (IN P_PLAYERNO INTEGER)
BEGIN
   DELETE
   FROM   MATCHES
   WHERE  PLAYERNO = P_PLAYERNO;
END
```

Explanation: The *CREATE PROCEDURE statement* is one SQL statement, just as CREATE TABLE and SELECT are. The statement consists of several other SQL statements. We return to this subject and discuss it extensively later in this chapter. Each stored procedure consists of at least three parts: a list of parameters, a body, and a name.

The previous procedure has only one parameter: P_PLAYERNO (the player number). The word IN indicates that this parameter is an input parameter. The value of this parameter can be used within the procedure, but after the execution of the procedure, the variable used at the call remains unchanged.

Between the keywords BEGIN and END, the *procedure body* is specified. In this example, the body is very simple because it consists of only a single DELETE statement. New in this statement is the use of the parameter P_PLAYERNO. This is the rule: Everywhere a scalar expression is allowed, a parameter may be used.

The names of the procedures within a database must be unique, just like the names of tables.

The result of the previous CREATE PROCEDURE statement is not the execution of the DELETE statement; the syntax of the statement is merely verified and, if it is correct, is stored in the catalog. This is comparable to creating views.

To activate a stored procedure, a separate SQL statement must be used: the *CALL statement*.

Example 31.2: Remove all matches of player 8 by using the DELETE_MATCHES procedure.

```
CALL DELETE_MATCHES (8)
```

Explanation: This statement is straightforward. The value of the player number assigned to the parameter P_PLAYERNO is included between the brackets. If we compare this with classic programming languages, the CREATE PROCEDURE statement is comparable to the declaration of a procedure; with CALL, the procedure is invoked.

Figure 31.1 shows how a stored procedure is processed. The left block represents the program from which the procedure is called, the middle block represents the database server, and the right side represents the database and its catalog. The process begins when the procedure is called from the program (step 1). The database server receives this call and finds the matching procedure in the catalog (step 2). Next, the procedure is executed (step 3). This can result in inserting new rows or, in the situation of the DELETE_MATCHES procedure, removing rows. When the procedure is finished, the result of the procedure is returned (step 4). No communication takes place between the database server and the program during the execution of the procedure.

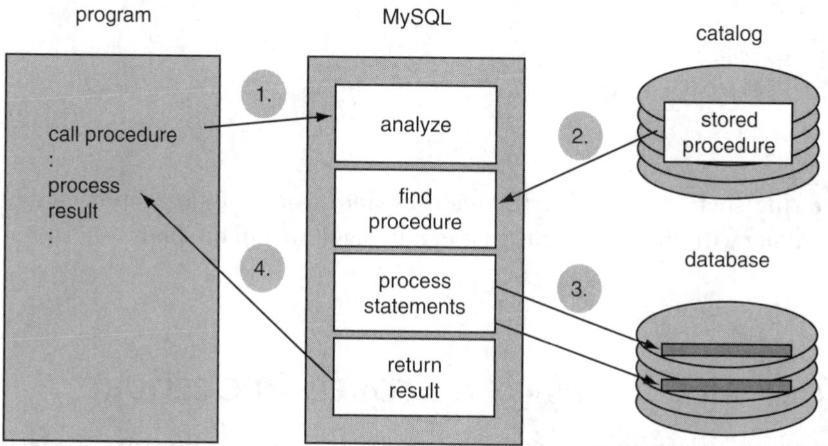

FIGURE 31.1 The processing steps of a stored procedure

How the database server really calls and processes the stored procedure is not important to the programmer or the program. The processing of a stored procedure can be seen as an extension of the processing of the program itself. Imagine that a program calling the stored procedure DELETE_MATCHES looks as follows:

```
Answer := 'Y';
WHILE answer = 'Y' DO
   PRINT 'Do you want to remove all matches of another player (Y/N)? '
   READ answer
   IF answer = 'Y' THEN
      PRINT 'Enter a player number: ';
      READ pno;
      CALL DELETE_MATCHES(pno);
   ENDIF;
ENDWHILE;
```

The final result of this program is the same as if we replaced the stored procedure call with the body of the procedure itself:

```
Answer := 'Y';
WHILE answer = 'Y' DO
   PRINT 'Do you want to remove all matches of another player (Y/N)? '
   READ answer
   IF answer = 'Y' THEN
      PRINT 'Enter a player number: ';
      READ pno;
      DELETE
      FROM   MATCHES
      WHERE  PLAYERNO = :pno;
   ENDIF;
ENDWHILE;
```

The following sections describe the features and syntax of stored procedures step by step, along with the statements that can be used within the body of a stored procedure.

31.3 The Parameters of a Stored Procedure

A stored procedure has zero, one, or multiple parameters. Through these parameters, the procedure is capable of communicating with the outside world. Three types of parameters are supported. With input parameters, data can be passed to a stored procedure. For example, the procedure in Example 31.1 contained one input parameter: The player number of the matches that must be removed. The stored procedure uses output parameters when an answer or result must be returned. For example, we could create a stored procedure that finds the name of a player. That name is the output parameter then. The third type is the input/output parameter. As the name suggests, this parameter can act as an input as well as an output parameter.

DEFINITION

```
<create procedure statement> ::=
   CREATE PROCEDURE <procedure name> ( [ <parameter list> ] )
      <routine body>

<parameter list> ::=
   <parameter specification> [ , <parameter specification> ]...

<parameter specification> ::=
   [ IN | OUT | INOUT ] <parameter> <data type>
```

A stored procedure does not need parameters, but opening and closing brackets are still required.

Make sure that the names of parameters are not equal to the names of columns. If we want to change P_PLAYERNO in the previous example to PLAYERNO, MySQL will not return an error message; the DELETE statement will consider the second PLAYERNO as the name of the column, not of the parameter. As a result, with every call, the stored procedure will remove all the players.

31.4 The Body of a Stored Procedure

The *body* of a stored procedure contains all the statements that must be executed when the procedure is called. The body always begins with BEGIN and ends with END. In between, all statement types can be specified. These can be the well-known SQL statements from the previous chapters (thus, all DDL, DCL, and DML statements), but procedural statements are allowed as well. These are other versions of statements that we see in all procedural programming languages, such as IF-THEN-ELSE and WHILE-DO. Additionally, special statements can fetch the results of SELECT statement into a stored procedure, local variables can be declared, and you can assign values to them.

DEFINITION

```
<create procedure statement> ::=
   CREATE PROCEDURE <procedure name> ( [ <parameter list> ] )
      <routine body>

<routine body> ::= <begin-end block>

<begin-end block> ::=
   [ <label> : ] BEGIN <statement list> END [ <label> ]

<statement list> ::= { <body statement> ; }...

<statement in body> ::=
   <declarative statement> |
   <procedural statement>

<declarative statement> ::=
   <ddl statement> |
   <dml statement> |
   <dcl statement>

<procedural statement> ::=
   <begin-end block>                   |
   <call statement>                    |
   <close statement>                   |
   <declare condition statement>       |
   <declare cursor statement>          |
   <declare handler statement>         |
   <declare variable statement>        |
   <fetch cursor statement>            |
   <flow control statement>            |
   <open cursor statement>             |
   <set statement>
```

With a begin-end block, statements can be grouped into one statement. Sometimes such a block is called a *compound statement*. In fact, the body of a stored procedure is a begin-end block. Blocks may be nested. In other words, you can define subblocks within begin-end blocks, so this is a legal body of a stored procedure:

```
BEGIN
   BEGIN
      BEGIN
      END;
   END;
END
```

Note that each statement, including each begin-end block, must end with a semicolon. However, this is not required for the begin-end block that indicates the end of the procedure body.

You may assign a *label* to a begin-end block. In fact, the block is named with it:

```
BLOCK1 : BEGIN
   BLOCK2 : BEGIN
      BLOCK3 : BEGIN
      END BLOCK1;
   END BLOCK2;
END BLOCK3
```

Labeling blocks has two advantages. First, labeling makes it easier to determine which BEGIN belongs to which END, especially when many blocks exist within a stored procedure. Second, certain SQL statements, such as LEAVE and ITERATE, need these names. Section 31.7 returns to this topic.

A closing label behind END is not necessary. However, if it is used, it must refer to a label that stands in front of a BEGIN. The following code is not allowed, for example:

```
BLOCK1 : BEGIN
   SET VAR1 = 1;
END BLOCK2
```

The following statement is not correct, either. The name of the closing label BLOCK2 does exist, but it belongs to the wrong BEGIN.

```
BLOCK1 : BEGIN
   BLOCK2 : BEGIN
      SET VAR1 = 1;
   END
END BLOCK2
```

31.5 Local Variables

Within a stored procedure, *local variables* can be declared. They can be used to store temporary intermediate results. If we need a local variable within a stored procedure, we must introduce it first with a DECLARE VARIABLE statement. MySQL thus differs from similar languages such as PHP, in which a variable is declared implicitly if it is used.

With a declaration, the data type of the variable is determined, and an initial value can be specified. The supported data types are those that may be used in CREATE TABLE statements; see Section 20.3.

DEFINITION

```
<declare variable statement> ::=
   DECLARE <local variable list> <data type>
      [ DEFAULT <scalar expression> ]

<local variable list> ::=
   <local variable> [ , <local variable> ]...
```

Example 31.3: Declare a numeric and an alphanumeric variable.

```
DECLARE NUM1 DECIMAL(7,2);
DECLARE ALPHA1 VARCHAR(20);
```

Multiple variables carrying the same data type can be declared with one DECLARE VARIABLE statement.

Example 31.4: Declare two integer variables.

```
DECLARE NUMBER1, NUMBER2 INTEGER;
```

Adding a default expression gives variables an initial value.

Example 31.5: Create a stored procedure in which an initial value is assigned to a local variable. Next, call this stored procedure.

```
CREATE PROCEDURE TEST
   (OUT NUMBER1 INTEGER)
BEGIN
   DECLARE NUMBER2 INTEGER DEFAULT 100;
   SET NUMBER1 = NUMBER2;
END

CALL TEST (@NUMBER)

SELECT @NUMBER
```

The result is:

```
@NUMBER
-------
    100
```

Explanation: If DECLARE VARIABLE statements are used, they must be included as the first statements of a begin-end block.

The expression for the default value is not limited to literals, but may consist of compound expressions, including scalar subqueries.

Example 31.6: Create a stored procedure in which a local variable is initiated with the number of players in the PLAYERS table.

```
CREATE PROCEDURE TEST
   (OUT NUMBER1 INTEGER)
BEGIN
   DECLARE NUMBER2 INTEGER
      DEFAULT (SELECT COUNT(*) FROM PLAYERS);
   SET NUMBER1 = NUMBER2;
END
```

Local variables can be declared within each begin-end block. After the declaration, the variables can be used in the relevant block, including all subblocks of that block. Those variables are unknown in the other blocks. In the following construct, the variable V1 may be used in all blocks. V2, on the other hand, can be used only in the first subblock, called B2. In the second subblock B3, this variable is unknown, so the SET statement will not be accepted. The last SET statement will also not be accepted.

```
B1 : BEGIN
   DECLARE V1 INTEGER;
   B2 : BEGIN
      DECLARE V2 INTEGER;
      SET V2 = 1;
      SET V1 = V2;
   END B2;
   B3 : BEGIN
      SET V1 = V2;
   END B3;
   SET V2 = 100;
END B1
```

Do not confuse local variables with user variables; see Chapter 15, "The User Variable and the SET Statement." The first difference is that no @ symbol is used in front of local variables. Another difference is that user variables exist during the entire session. Local variables disappear immediately after the processing of the begin-end block in which they have been declared is finished. User variables can be used within and outside a stored procedure, whereas local variables have no meaning outside a procedure.

Also note that MySQL does not support arrays as local variables.

31.6 The SET Statement

The SET statement is part of SQL itself. Section 15.2 describes how a value can be assigned to user variables with the SET statement. The same statement can assign a value to a local variable. You can use any random expression here as well.

DEFINITION

```
<set statement> ::=
   SET <local variable definition>
      [ , <local variable definition> ]...

<local variable definition> ::=
   <local variable> { = | := } <scalar expression>
```

The previous sections showed several examples of the SET statement. The following examples are also correct:

```
SET VAR1 = 1;
SET VAR1 := 1;
SET VAR1 = 1, VAR2 = VAR1;
```

In the last example, a value is assigned to VAR1 first, and that value is next assigned to VAR2 via VAR1.

31.7 Flow-Control Statements

The well-known procedural statements can be used within the body of a stored procedure. Consider their definitions:

DEFINITION

```
<flow control statement> ::=
   <if statement>          |
   <case statement>        |
   <while statement>       |
   <repeat statement>      |
   <loop statement>        |
   <leave statement>       |
   <iterate statement>

<if statement> ::=
   IF <condition> THEN <statement list>
      [ ELSEIF <condition> THEN <statement list> ]...
      [ ELSE <statement list> ]
   END IF

<case statement> ::=
   { CASE <scalar expression>
        WHEN <scalar expression> THEN <statement list>
        [ WHEN <scalar expression> THEN <statement list> ]...
        [ ELSE <statement list> ]
     END CASE } |
   { CASE
        WHEN <condition> THEN <statement list>
        [ WHEN <condition> THEN <statement list> ]...
        [ ELSE <statement list>
     END CASE }

<while statement> ::=
   [ <label> : WHILE <condition> DO <statement list>
   END WHILE [ <label> ]

<repeat statement> ::=
   [ <label> : ] REPEAT <statement list>
   UNTIL <condition>
   END REPEAT <label>

<loop statement> ::=
   [ <label> : ] LOOP <statement list>
   END LOOP [ <label> ]

<leave statement> ::= LEAVE <label>

<iterate statement> ::= ITERATE <label>

<statement list> ::= { <statement in body> ; }...

<begin-end block> ::=
   [ <label> : ] BEGIN <statement list> END [ <label> ]

<label> ::= <name>
```

We begin with examples of the `IF` statement.

Example 31.7: Create a stored procedure that determines which of the two input parameters is highest.

```
CREATE PROCEDURE DIFFERENCE
   (IN P1 INTEGER,
    IN P2 INTEGER,
    OUT P3 INTEGER)
BEGIN
   IF P1 > P2 THEN
      SET P3 = 1;
   ELSEIF P1 = P2 THEN
      SET P3 = 2;
   ELSE
      SET P3 = 3;
   END IF;
END
```

Explanation: The `ELSE` clause is not mandatory, and you may specify many `ELSEIF` clauses.

Example 31.8: Create a stored procedure that generates numbers according to the Fibonacci algorithm.

A Fibonacci algorithm generates numbers as follows. You start with two numbers, such as 16 and 27. The first generated number is the sum of those two, which is 43. Then the second generated number is the sum of the number that was generated last (43), plus the number in front of that: 27, result 70. The third number is 70 plus 43, giving 113. The fourth number is 113 plus 70, and so on. If the sum exceeds a specific maximum, that maximum is subtracted. In the following examples, we assume that the maximum equals 10,000. If this problem is to be solved with stored procedures, the calling program must remember the two previous numbers because a stored procedure does not have a memory. For every call, these two numbers must be included. The procedure itself looks as follows:

```
CREATE PROCEDURE FIBONACCI
   (INOUT NUMBER1 INTEGER,
    INOUT NUMBER2 INTEGER,
    INOUT NUMBER3 INTEGER)
BEGIN
   SET NUMBER3 = NUMBER1 + NUMBER2;
   IF NUMBER3 > 10000 THEN
      SET NUMBER3 = NUMBER3 - 10000;
   END IF;
   SET NUMBER1 = NUMBER2;
   SET NUMBER2 = NUMBER3;
END
```

Call this stored procedure three times, beginning with the values 16 and 27:

```
SET @A=16, @B=27

CALL FIBONACCI(@A,@B,@C)

SELECT @C

CALL FIBONACCI(@A,@B,@C)

SELECT @C

CALL FIBONACCI(@A,@B,@C)

SELECT @C
```

The results of the three SELECT statements are, respectively, 43, 70, and 113. Here we indicate how this procedure can be called from a program (our pseudo language is used with this):

```
number1 := 16;
number2 := 27;

counter := 1;
while counter <= 10 do
   CALL FIBONACCI (:number1, :number2, :number3);
   print 'The number is ', number3;
   counter := counter + 1;
endwhile;
```

Example 31.9: Create a stored procedure that indicates which table, PLAYERS or PENALTIES, has the largest number of rows.

```
CREATE PROCEDURE LARGEST
   (OUT T CHAR(10))
BEGIN
   IF (SELECT COUNT(*) FROM PLAYERS) >
      (SELECT COUNT(*) FROM PENALTIES) THEN
      SET T = 'PLAYERS';
   ELSEIF (SELECT COUNT(*) FROM PLAYERS) =
          (SELECT COUNT(*) FROM PENALTIES) THEN
      SET T = 'EQUAL';
   ELSE
      SET T = 'PENALTIES';
   END IF;
END
```

Explanation: As this example shows, conditions are allowed to contain scalar subqueries. However, this stored procedure would be more efficient if the results of the subqueries were assigned to local variables first and, subsequently, if the values of the variables were compared in the condition. In the previous example, the subqueries are sometimes executed twice.

The CASE statement makes it possible to specify complex IF-THEN-ELSE constructs. The IF statement in Example 31.7, for example, can be rewritten as follows:

```
CASE
   WHEN P1 > P2 THEN SET P3 = 1;
   WHEN P1 = P2 THEN SET P3 = 2;
   ELSE SET P3 = 3;
END CASE;
```

MySQL supports three statements for creating loops: the WHILE, REPEAT, and LOOP statements.

Example 31.10: Create a stored procedure that calculates the number of years, months, and days between two dates.

```
CREATE PROCEDURE AGE
   (IN  START_DATE  DATE,
    IN  END_DATE    DATE,
    OUT YEARS       INTEGER,
    OUT MONTHS      INTEGER,
    OUT DAYS        INTEGER)
BEGIN
   DECLARE NEXT_DATE, PREVIOUS_DATE DATE;

   SET YEARS = 0;
   SET PREVIOUS_DATE = START_DATE;
   SET NEXT_DATE = START_DATE + INTERVAL 1 YEAR;
   WHILE NEXT_DATE < END_DATE DO
      SET YEARS = YEARS + 1;
      SET PREVIOUS_DATE = NEXT_DATE;
      SET NEXT_DATE = NEXT_DATE + INTERVAL 1 YEAR;
   END WHILE;

   SET MONTHS = 0;
   SET NEXT_DATE = PREVIOUS_DATE + INTERVAL 1 MONTH;
   WHILE NEXT_DATE < END_DATE DO
      SET MONTHS = MONTHS + 1;
      SET PREVIOUS_DATE = NEXT_DATE;
      SET NEXT_DATE = NEXT_DATE + INTERVAL 1 MONTH;
   END WHILE;

   SET DAYS = 0;
   SET NEXT_DATE = PREVIOUS_DATE + INTERVAL 1 DAY;
   WHILE NEXT_DATE <= END_DATE DO
      SET DAYS = DAYS + 1;
      SET PREVIOUS_DATE = NEXT_DATE;
      SET NEXT_DATE = NEXT_DATE + INTERVAL 1 DAY;
   END WHILE;
END
```

This stored procedure works as follows:

```
SET @START = '1991-01-12'

SET @END = '1999-07-09'

CALL AGE (@START, @END, @YEAR, @MONTH, @DAY)

SELECT @START, @END, @YEAR, @MONTH, @DAY
```

Explanation: The first loop determines the number of intervening years, the second indicates the number of months, and the last indicates the number of days. Of course, scalar functions can achieve the same in a more simple way; we used this method only to illustrate the WHILE statement.

With a WHILE statement, a check is done first to see whether the specified condition is true; only then the statement is executed. With the REPEAT statement, the statements are executed first; then a check is done to see whether the condition is true. The first WHILE statement from Example 31.10 can be rewritten as follows:

```
SET YEARS = -1;
SET NEXT_DATE = START_DATE;
REPEAT
   SET PREVIOUS_DATE = NEXT_DATE;
   SET NEXT_DATE = PREVIOUS_DATE + INTERVAL 1 YEAR;
   SET YEARS = YEARS + 1;
UNTIL NEXT_DATE > END_DATE END REPEAT;
```

Before we explain the LOOP statement, we describe the LEAVE statement, which can stop the processing of a begin-end block early. However, the relevant block must have a label.

Example 31.11: Create a stored procedure in which a block is ended prematurely.

```
CREATE PROCEDURE SMALL_EXIT
   (OUT P1 INTEGER, OUT P2 INTEGER)
BEGIN
   SET P1 = 1;
   SET P2 = 1;
   BLOCK1 : BEGIN
      LEAVE BLOCK1;
      SET P2 = 3;
   END;
   SET P1 = 4;
END
```

If we call this stored procedure, the value of the second parameter is equal to 1, and the value of P1 is equal to 4. The SET statement that comes immediately after the LEAVE statement is not executed, contrary to the SET statement specified after BLOCK1 that is actually executed.

With the LOOP statement, we do not use a condition; we use a LEAVE statement to end the loop.

The first WHILE statement from Example 31.10 can be rewritten as follows:

```
SET YEARS = 0;
SET PREVIOUS_DATE = START_DATE;
SET NEXT_DATE = START_DATE + INTERVAL 1 YEAR;
YEARS_LOOP: LOOP
   IF NEXT_DATE > END_DATE THEN
      LEAVE YEARS_LOOP;
   END IF;
   SET YEARS = YEARS + 1;
   SET PREVIOUS_DATE = NEXT_DATE;
   SET NEXT_DATE = NEXT_DATE + INTERVAL 1 YEAR;
END LOOP YEARS_LOOP;
```

Example 31.12: Create a stored procedure that does not respond for a certain number of seconds.

```
CREATE PROCEDURE WAIT
   (IN WAIT_SECONDS INTEGER)
BEGIN
   DECLARE END_TIME INTEGER
      DEFAULT NOW() + INTERVAL WAIT_SECONDS SECOND;
   WAIT_LOOP: LOOP
      IF NOW() > END_TIME THEN
         LEAVE WAIT_LOOP;
      END IF;
   END LOOP WAIT_LOOP;
END
```

Explanation: If we call this stored procedure with CALL(5), MySQL checks whether the 5 seconds have passed. If so, we leave the loop with the LEAVE statement.

The ITERATE statement is the counterpart of the LEAVE statement. The difference between the two is that, with the LEAVE statement, we leave a loop early, whereas we restart the loop with ITERATE.

Example 31.13: Create a stored procedure with an `ITERATE` statement.

```
CREATE PROCEDURE AGAIN
   (OUT RESULT INTEGER)
BEGIN
   DECLARE COUNTER INTEGER DEFAULT 1;
   SET RESULT = 0;
   LOOP1: WHILE COUNTER <= 1000 DO
      SET COUNTER = COUNTER + 1;
      IF COUNTER > 100 THEN
         LEAVE LOOP1;
      ELSE
         ITERATE LOOP1;
      END IF;
      SET RESULT = COUNTER * 10;
   END WHILE LOOP1;
END
```

Explanation: The value of the parameter `RESULT` is always equal to 0. The stored procedure will never come at the statement `SET RESULT = COUNTER * 10`. The reason is that the `IF` statement leads to the processing of the `LEAVE` statement (and then we leave the loop) or to the processing of the `ITERATE` statement. In that case, the processing jumps again to the loop with the name `LOOP1`.

31.8 Calling Stored Procedures

A procedure can be called from a program, from interactive SQL, and from stored procedures. In all three cases, the `CALL` statement is used.

DEFINITION

```
<call statement> ::=
   CALL [ <database name> . ] <stored procedure name>
      ( [ <scalar expression> [ , <scalar expression> ]... ] )
```

In spite of the fact that the statement is not complex, certain rules apply. The number of expressions in the expression list must always equal the number of parameters of the stored procedure. The name of a database may be specified in front of the procedure name. MySQL automatically places that same database name in the DML statements in front of each table name. This does not apply when a database name is explicitly specified in front of a table name, of course.

Any scalar expression may be used as an input parameter of a stored procedure. MySQL calculates the value of that expression before the value is passed on to the procedure.

Example 31.14: Call the stored procedure called `WAIT` from Example 31.12 and wait just as many seconds as there are rows in the PENALTIES table.

```
CALL WAIT ((SELECT COUNT(*) FROM PENALTIES))
```

Stored procedures can call themselves *recursively*. This is illustrated next with an example that uses a special version of the PLAYERS table, called the PLAYERS_WITH_PARENTS table. Most columns from the original PLAYERS table have been removed, and two columns have been added instead: FATHER_PLAYERNO and MOTHER_PLAYERNO. These two columns contain player numbers and are filled if the father and/or mother of the player concerned also plays at the tennis club. See Figure 31.2 for an overview of the family relationships among several players.

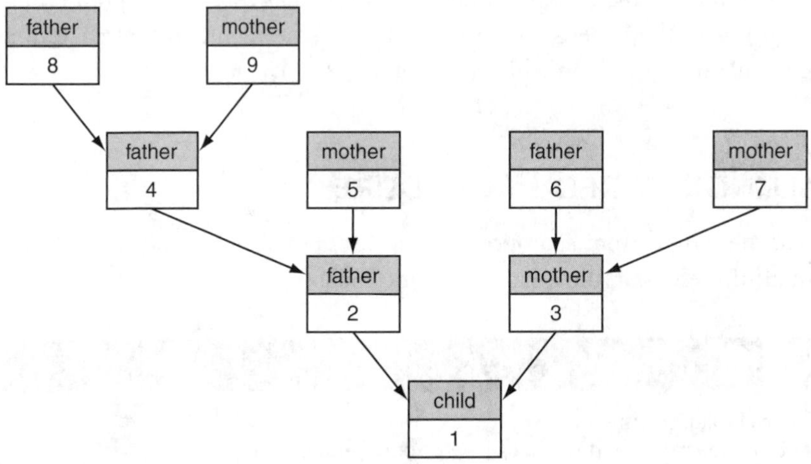

FIGURE 31.2 The family relationships among several players

```
CREATE TABLE PLAYERS_WITH_PARENTS
      (PLAYERNO          INTEGER NOT NULL PRIMARY KEY,
       FATHER_PLAYERNO   INTEGER,
       MOTHER_PLAYERNO   INTEGER)

ALTER TABLE PLAYERS_WITH_PARENTS ADD
   FOREIGN KEY (FATHER_PLAYERNO)
      REFERENCES PLAYERS_WITH_PARENTS (PLAYERNO)
```

```
ALTER TABLE PLAYERS_WITH_PARENTS ADD
   FOREIGN KEY (MOTHER_PLAYERNO)
      REFERENCES PLAYERS_WITH_PARENTS (PLAYERNO)

INSERT INTO PLAYERS_WITH_PARENTS VALUES
   (9,NULL,NULL), (8,NULL,NULL), (7,NULL,NULL), (6,NULL,NULL),
   (5,NULL,NULL), (4,8,9), (3,6,7), (2,4,5), (1,2,3)
```

Example 31.15: Develop a stored procedure that calculates for a specific player the number of parents, grandparents, great-grandparents, and so on, who also play for the club. After that, call the stored procedure for the players.

```
CREATE PROCEDURE TOTAL_NUMBER_OF_PARENTS
   (IN P_PLAYERNO INTEGER,
    INOUT NUMBER INTEGER)
BEGIN
   DECLARE V_FATHER, V_MOTHER INTEGER;
   SET V_FATHER =
      (SELECT   FATHER_PLAYERNO
       FROM     PLAYERS_WITH_PARENTS
       WHERE    PLAYERNO = P_PLAYERNO);
   SET V_MOTHER =
      (SELECT   MOTHER_PLAYERNO
       FROM     PLAYERS_WITH_PARENTS
       WHERE    PLAYERNO = P_PLAYERNO);

   IF V_FATHER IS NOT NULL THEN
      CALL TOTAL_NUMBER_OF_PARENTS (V_FATHER, NUMBER);
      SET NUMBER = NUMBER + 1;
   END IF;

   IF V_MOTHER IS NOT NULL THEN
      CALL TOTAL_NUMBER_OF_PARENTS (V_MOTHER, NUMBER);
      SET NUMBER = NUMBER + 1;
   END IF;
END

SET @NUMBER = 0

CALL TOTAL_NUMBER_OF_PARENTS (1, @NUMBER)

SELECT @NUMBER
```

Explanation: The result of the last SELECT statement is 8. Apart from the way this procedure works, you can clearly see the recursive style of calling procedures. But how does it work, precisely? We assume that the procedure is called with the number of a player—for example, 27—as the first parameter and a variable in which the number of ancestors is recorded as the second parameter. However, this variable first must be initialized and set to 0; otherwise, the procedure will not work correctly. The first SELECT statement determines the player numbers of the father and mother. If the father is indeed a member of the club, the procedure TOTAL_NUMBER_OF_PARENTS is again called (recursively), this time with the player number of the father as the input parameter. When this procedure has finished, the number of ancestors of the father is shown. Next, we add 1 because the father himself must also be counted as the ancestor of the child. Thus, it is possible that, for the father, TOTAL_NUMBER_OF_PARENTS is activated for the third time because he, in turn, has a father or mother who is still a member of the club. After the number of ancestors has been determined for the father, the same is done for the mother.

In practice, the need to walk through a hierarchy from top to bottom, or vice versa, and perform calculations occurs often. For example, a production company records which products are a part of other products. A car consists of, among other things, a chassis and an engine. The engine itself contains spark plugs, a battery, and other parts, and this hierarchy goes on and on. Another example involves departments in large companies. Departments consist of smaller departments, which, in turn, consist of even smaller departments. No doubt you can think of many more examples.

31.9 Querying Data with SELECT INTO

Quite often we want to retrieve data from the tables into the stored procedure. We can fetch data in two ways. First, if only one row with data must be fetched, we can easily do this with a special version of the SELECT statement: the *SELECT INTO statement.* Second, to fetch multiple rows, the concept of a cursor has been added. This section describes the SELECT INTO statement; Section 31.11 explains the cursor.

DEFINITION

```
<select into statement> ::=
      <select clause>
      <into clause>
   [ <from clause>
   [ <where clause> ]
   [ <group by clause> ]
   [ <having clause> ]
   [ <select block tail> ] ]

<select block tail> ::=
   <order by clause> |
   <limit clause>    |
   <order by clause> <limit clause>

<into clause> ::=
   INTO <local variable> [ , <local variable> ]...
```

Special to the SELECT INTO statement is the new clause, called INTO. Here, we specify the names of variables. For each expression in the SELECT clause, a variable must be specified. After processing the SELECT INTO statement, the values of that expression are assigned to the variables.

Example 31.16: Create a stored procedure that calculates the total amount of all the penalties of a certain player. After that, call the procedure for player 27.

```
CREATE PROCEDURE TOTAL_PENALTIES_PLAYER
   (IN P_PLAYERNO INTEGER,
    OUT TOTAL_PENALTIES DECIMAL(8,2))
BEGIN
   SELECT SUM(AMOUNT)
   INTO   TOTAL_PENALTIES
   FROM   PENALTIES
   WHERE  PLAYERNO = P_PLAYERNO;
END

CALL TOTAL_PENALTIES_PLAYER (27, @TOTAL)

SELECT @TOTAL
```

Explanation: The result of the SELECT INTO statement is assigned to the output parameter TOTAL_PENALTIES.

Example 31.15 shows another example in which the SELECT INTO statement can be used. One SELECT INTO statement can replace the first two SET statements with subqueries (to improve the processing speed):

```
SELECT   FATHER_PLAYERNO, MOTHER_PLAYERNO
INTO     V_FATHER, V_MOTHER
FROM     PLAYERS_WITH_PARENTS
WHERE    PLAYERNO = P_PLAYERNO
```

Example 31.17: Create a stored procedure that retrieves the address of a player.

```
CREATE PROCEDURE GIVE_ADDRESS
   (IN  P_PLAYERNO SMALLINT,
    OUT P_STREET   VARCHAR(30),
    OUT P_HOUSENO  CHAR(4),
    OUT P_TOWN     VARCHAR(30),
    OUT P_POSTCODE CHAR(6))
BEGIN
   SELECT TOWN, STREET, HOUSENO, POSTCODE
   INTO   P_TOWN, P_STREET, P_HOUSENO, P_POSTCODE
   FROM   PLAYERS
   WHERE  PLAYERNO = P_PLAYERNO;
END
```

Example 31.18: Example 31.8 shows how the next value of a Fibonacci series can be calculated with a stored procedure. The disadvantage of this solution is that the stored procedure has three parameters, of which only one is relevant to the calling program: the third parameter. It would be better if we could remember the two first parameters within the stored procedure, but then the stored procedure would need a memory, which is kept between two calls. No such memory exists, but we can simulate it by storing the values of these variables in a table. For this, we can use the following table:

```
CREATE TABLE FIBON
      (NUMBER1   INTEGER NOT NULL PRIMARY KEY,
       NUMBER2   INTEGER NOT NULL)
```

We need a stored procedure to assign an initial value to the two columns; see the next example. The DELETE statement is used to empty the table in case it contains remnants of a previous exercise. Next, we use an INSERT statement to give the columns an initial value:

```
CREATE PROCEDURE FIBONACCI_START()
BEGIN
   DELETE FROM FIBON;
   INSERT INTO FIBON (NUMBER, NUMBER2) VALUES (16, 27);
END
```

The original procedure, called FIBONACCI, now looks as follows:

```
CREATE PROCEDURE FIBONACCI_GIVE
   (INOUT NUMBER INTEGER)
BEGIN
   DECLARE N1, N2 INTEGER;
   SELECT NUMBER1, NUMBER2
   INTO   N1, N2
   FROM   FIBON;
   SET NUMBER = N1 + N2;
   IF NUMBER > 10000 THEN
      SET NUMBER = NUMBER - 10000;
   END IF;
   SET N1 = N2;
   SET N2 = NUMBER;
   UPDATE FIBON
   SET    NUMBER1 = N1,
          NUMBER2 = N2;
END
```

A SELECT INTO statement retrieves the last two values. The procedure is probably obvious. The part of a program in which the procedures are called might look like this:

```
CALL FIBONACCI_START()

CALL FIBONACCI_GIVE(@C)

SELECT @C

CALL FIBONACCI_GIVE(@C)

SELECT @C

CALL FIBONACCI_GIVE(@C)

SELECT @C
```

The first advantage of the previous solution is that when a procedure is called, only one parameter must be passed. The second advantage has to do with the way the Fibonacci algorithm works: In the second solution, the internal workings are more hidden from the calling program.

Example 31.19: Create a stored procedure that removes a player. Imagine that the following rule applies: A player can be removed only if he or she has incurred no penalty and only if he or she is not a captain of a team. We also assume that no foreign keys have been defined.

```
CREATE PROCEDURE DELETE_PLAYER
   (IN P_PLAYERNO INTEGER)
BEGIN
   DECLARE NUMBER_OF_ PENALTIES INTEGER;
   DECLARE NUMBER_OF_TEAMS  INTEGER;
   SELECT COUNT(*)
   INTO   NUMBER_OF_PENALTIES
   FROM   PENALTIES
   WHERE  PLAYERNO = P_PLAYERNO;

   SELECT COUNT(*)
   INTO   NUMBER_OF_TEAMS
   FROM   TEAMS
   WHERE  PLAYERNO = P_PLAYERNO_;

   IF NUMBER_OF_PENALTIES = 0 AND NUMBER_OF_TEAMS = 0 THEN
      CALL DELETE_MATCHES (P_PLAYERNO);
      DELETE FROM PLAYERS
      WHERE  PLAYERNO = P_PLAYERNO;
   END IF;
END
```

This stored procedure can be optimized by checking, after the first SELECT statement, whether the number of penalties is not equal to zero. If this is the case, the procedure can be interrupted because the second SELECT statement is no longer necessary.

31.10 Error Messages, Handlers, and Conditions

All the error messages MySQL supports have a unique code, called the *MySQL error code,* a piece of describing text, and a code called SQLSTATE. SQLSTATE has been added to comply with the SQL standard. The SQLSTATE codes are not unique; several error codes can have the same SQLSTATE. For example, SQLSTATE 23000 belongs to, among other things, the following error codes:

Error 1022, "Can't write; duplicate key in table"

Error 1048, "Column cannot be null"

Error 1052, "Column is ambiguous"

Error 1062, "Duplicate entry for key"

The manuals of MySQL list all the error messages and their respective codes.

Processing SQL statements in stored procedures can lead to error messages. For example, when a new row is added but the value in the primary key already exists, or when an index is removed that does not exist, MySQL stops the processing of the stored procedure. We illustrate this with an example.

Example 31.20: Create a stored procedure with which an existing team number is entered.

```
CREATE PROCEDURE DUPLICATE
   (OUT P_PROCESSED SMALLINT)
BEGIN
   SET P_PROCESSED = 1;
   INSERT INTO TEAMS VALUES (2,27,'third');
   SET P_PROCESSED = 2;
END

CALL DUPLICATE(PROCESSED)
```

Explanation: Because team 2 already exists, the INSERT statement results in an error message. MySQL immediately stops the processing of the stored procedure. The last SET statement is no longer processed, and the parameter PROCESSED is not set to 2.

With a special version of the DECLARE statement, the *DECLARE HANDLER statement,* we can prevent MySQL from stopping the processing:

DEFINITION

```
<declare handler statement> ::=
   DECLARE <handler type> HANDLER FOR <condition value list>
      <procedural statement>

<handler type> ::=
   CONTINUE |
   EXIT     |
   UNDO

<condition value list> ::=
   <condition value> [ , <condition value> ]...

<condition value> ::=
   SQLSTATE [ VALUE ] <sqlstate value> |
   <mysql error code>                  |
   SQLWARNING                          |
   NOT FOUND                           |
   SQLEXCEPTION                        |
   <condition name>
```

The DECLARE HANDLER statement defines a so-called *handler.* that indicates what should happen if the processing of an SQL statement leads to a certain error message. The definition of a handler consists of three parts: the type of handler, the condition, and the action.

Three types of handlers exist: CONTINUE, EXIT, and UNDO. When we specify a CONTINUE handler, MySQL does not interrupt the processing of the stored procedure, whereas an EXIT handler does stop the processing.

Example 31.21: Create a stored procedure with which a team number is entered. If that number already exists, the processing of the procedure should continue. When the processing finishes, the output parameter then contains the SQLSTATE code of the possible error message.

```
CREATE PROCEDURE SMALL_MISTAKE1
   (OUT ERROR CHAR(5))
BEGIN
   DECLARE CONTINUE HANDLER FOR SQLSTATE '23000'
      SET ERROR = '23000';
   SET ERROR = '00000';
   INSERT INTO TEAMS VALUES (2,27,'third');
END
```

Explanation: After the call of this stored procedure, the ERROR parameter has the value 23000. But how does it work? Obviously, the INSERT statement leads to an error message of which the SQLSTATE code is 23000. When an error occurs, MySQL checks whether a handler has been defined for this code, which happens to be the case in this example. Next, MySQL executes the additional statement belonging to the DECLARE statement (SET ERROR = '23000'). After that, MySQL checks what kind of handler it is; in this case, it is a *CONTINUE handler*. Because of this, the processing of the stored procedure continues. If the INSERT statement could have been executed without mistakes, the ERROR parameter would have had the value 00000.

You may define several handlers within a stored procedure, as long as they apply to different error messages.

Example 31.22: Create a special version of the previous example.

```
CREATE PROCEDURE SMALL_MISTAKE2
   (OUT ERROR CHAR(5))
BEGIN
   DECLARE CONTINUE HANDLER FOR SQLSTATE '23000'
      SET ERROR = '23000';
   DECLARE CONTINUE HANDLER FOR SQLSTATE '21S01'
      SET ERROR = '21S01';
   SET ERROR = '00000';
   INSERT INTO TEAMS VALUES (2,27,'third',5);
END
```

Explanation: The error message with SQLSTATE code 21S01 returns if the number of values in the INSERT statement does not comply with the number of columns in the table. In this example, the output parameter will have the value 21S01 when the procedure is processed.

Instead of using an SQLSTATE code, you can define an error code. The handlers in the previous example could have been defined as follows:

```
DECLARE CONTINUE HANDLER FOR 1062 SET ERROR = '23000';
DECLARE CONTINUE HANDLER FOR 1136 SET ERROR = '21S01';
```

The *SQLWARNING handler* is activated for all SQLSTATE codes beginning with 01, the *NOT FOUND handler* for all codes beginning with 02, and the *SQLEXCEPTION handler* for all codes that do not begin with 01 or 02. The three handlers can be used when you do not want to define a separate handler for every error message possible.

Example 31.23: Create a stored procedure with which a team number can be entered. If something goes wrong with the processing of the INSERT statement, the procedure has to continue.

```
CREATE PROCEDURE SMALL_MISTAKE3
   (OUT ERROR CHAR(5))
BEGIN
   DECLARE CONTINUE HANDLER FOR SQLWARNING, NOT FOUND,
      SQLEXCEPTION SET ERROR = 'XXXXX';
   SET ERROR = '00000';
   INSERT INTO TEAMS VALUES (2,27,'third');
END
```

To improve the readability, we can give certain SQLSTATE and error codes a name and use this name later with the declaration of a handler. A *DECLARE CONDITION statement* can define a condition.

DEFINITION

```
<declare condition statement> ::=
   DECLARE <condition name> CONDITION FOR
   { SQLSTATE [ VALUE ] <sqlstate value> } | <mysql error code>
```

Example 31.24: Change the stored procedure SMALL_MISTAKE1 and use conditions instead of handlers.

```
CREATE PROCEDURE SMALL_MISTAKE4
   (OUT ERROR CHAR(5))
BEGIN
   DECLARE NON_UNIQUE CONDITION FOR SQLSTATE '23000';
   DECLARE CONTINUE HANDLER FOR NON_UNIQUE
      SET ERROR = '23000';
   SET ERROR = '00000';
   INSERT INTO TEAMS VALUES (2,27,'third');
END
```

Explanation: The condition NON_UNIQUE can be used instead of the SQLSTATE code.

Handlers and conditions can be defined within each begin-end block. A handler is relevant for all SQL statements that belong to the same block, plus all its subblocks.

Example 31.25: Develop a stored procedure called SMALL_MISTAKE5.

```
CREATE PROCEDURE SMALL_MISTAKE5
   (OUT ERROR CHAR(5))
BEGIN
   DECLARE NON_UNIQUE CONDITION FOR SQLSTATE '23000';
   DECLARE CONTINUE HANDLER FOR NON_UNIQUE
      SET ERROR = '23000';
   BEGIN
      DECLARE CONTINUE HANDLER FOR NON_UNIQUE
         SET ERROR = '23000';
   END;
   BEGIN
      DECLARE CONTINUE HANDLER FOR NON_UNIQUE
         SET ERROR = '00000';
      INSERT INTO TEAMS VALUES (2,27,'third');
   END;
END
```

Explanation: In this procedure, the parameter ERROR will have the value 00000 when something goes wrong with the INSERT statement.

In fact, the rules for the range of handlers are equivalent to those of declared variables.

Two or more handlers cannot be defined for the same error message and within the same begin-end block. For example, the following two statements in the same stored procedure are not allowed:

```
DECLARE CONTINUE HANDLER FOR SQLSTATE '23000'
   SET ERROR = '23000';
DECLARE EXIT HANDLER FOR SQLSTATE '23000'
   SET ERROR = '24000';
```

However, the same handler can be defined in a subblock; see the following example:

```
CREATE PROCEDURE SMALL_MISTAKE6 ()
BEGIN
   DECLARE CONTINUE HANDLER FOR SQLSTATE '23000'
      SET @PROCESSED = 100;
   BEGIN
      DECLARE CONTINUE HANDLER FOR SQLSTATE '23000'
         SET @PROCESSED = 200;
      INSERT INTO TEAMS VALUES (2,27,'third');
   END;
END
```

If the processing of the INSERT statement goes wrong, MySQL checks whether a relevant DECLARE HANDLER statement appears within that same begin-end block. If so, it is activated; otherwise, MySQL tries to find a relevant handler in the surrounding begin-end block.

31.11 Retrieving Data with a Cursor

SELECT INTO statements return one row with values only. Because of this, they can easily be fetched into a stored procedure. Normal SELECT statements, which *can* return more than one row, are more complex to deal with. A special concept, called the *cursor*, has been added to handle this. Four special SQL statements are required to work with a cursor: DECLARE CURSOR, OPEN CURSOR, FETCH CURSOR, and CLOSE CURSOR.

If we declare a cursor with the DECLARE CURSOR statement, we link it to a table expression. With the special OPEN CURSOR statement, we can instruct MySQL to process the table expression of the cursor. Next, we can use FETCH CURSOR statements to retrieve the created result row by row into the stored procedure. At a certain moment, only one row from the result is visible: the current row. It is as if an arrow points to one row from the result—hence the name cursor. With the FETCH CURSOR statement, we move this cursor to the next row. When all rows have been processed, we can remove the result with a CLOSE CURSOR statement.

DEFINITION

```
<declare cursor statement> ::=
   DECLARE <cursor name> CURSOR FOR <table expression>

<open statement> ::=
   OPEN <cursor name>

<fetch statement> ::=
   FETCH <cursor name>
      INTO <local variable> [ , <local variable> ]...

<close statement> ::=
   CLOSE <cursor name>
```

We begin with a simple example and explain the cursor in detail.

Example 31.26: Create a stored procedure that counts the number of rows in the PLAYERS table.

```
CREATE PROCEDURE NUMBER_OF_PLAYERS
   (OUT NUMBER INTEGER)
BEGIN
   DECLARE A_PLAYERNO INTEGER;
   DECLARE FOUND BOOLEAN DEFAULT TRUE;
   DECLARE C_PLAYERS CURSOR FOR
      SELECT PLAYERNO FROM PLAYERS;
   DECLARE CONTINUE HANDLER FOR NOT FOUND
      SET FOUND = FALSE;
   SET NUMBER = 0;
   OPEN C_PLAYERS;
   FETCH C_PLAYERS INTO A_PLAYERNO;
   WHILE FOUND DO
      SET NUMBER = NUMBER + 1;
      FETCH C_PLAYERS INTO A_PLAYERNO;
   END WHILE;
   CLOSE C_PLAYERS;
END
```

Explanation: Obviously, we could have solved this problem with a COUNT function, but we used this solution to illustrate how a cursor works. A cursor is declared with the *DECLARE CURSOR statement*. This can be compared somewhat to the declaration of local variables. Informally, the table expression SELECT PLAYERNO FROM PLAYERS receives the name C_PLAYERS in this example. Through the name of the cursor, we can refer to the table expression in other statements. Note, however, that at the declaration of the cursor, the table expression is not processed yet.

The name of the cursor must satisfy the same rules that apply to table names; see Chapter 20, "Creating Tables." Two different cursors within one stored procedure may have the same name.

A DECLARE CURSOR statement does nothing itself; it is a typical declaration. Only by using an *OPEN CURSOR statement* does a cursor become active and are the result of the table expression determined. In the previous example, the cursor with the name C_PLAYERS is opened. The result of the table expression is available after the OPEN CURSOR statement has been processed. Where MySQL stores the result is not important to us. Within a program, a cursor may be opened several times. Each time, the result might contain other rows because other users or the program itself has updated the tables.

After the OPEN CURSOR statement, the result of the table expression is determined, but it is still unknown to the stored procedure. With the *FETCH CURSOR statement,* we can look at the rows in the result of the table expression by browsing them one by one and, if necessary, update them. In other words, the FETCH CURSOR statement fetches the result into the stored procedure. The first FETCH CURSOR statement that is executed fetches the first row, the second FETCH CURSOR statement the second row, and so on. The values of the fetched row are assigned to the variables. In this example, only one variable exists, called A_PLAYERNO. Note, however, that a FETCH CURSOR statement can be used only after the cursor has been opened (with an OPEN CURSOR statement).

In the stored procedure, we browse all the rows of the result with a WHILE statement. If the FETCH statement fetches the last row, the variable FOUND becomes equal to true, and the WHILE statement stops.

The FETCH CURSOR statement has an INTO clause that has the same meaning as the INTO clause in the SELECT-INTO clause. The number of variables in the INTO clause in the FETCH CURSOR statement also must be equal to the number of expressions in the SELECT clause of the DECLARE CURSOR statement. A table expression in a DECLARE CURSOR statement may *not* contain an INTO clause. The FETCH CURSOR statement takes over this function. Figure 31.3 indicates the position of the cursor after certain SQL statements.

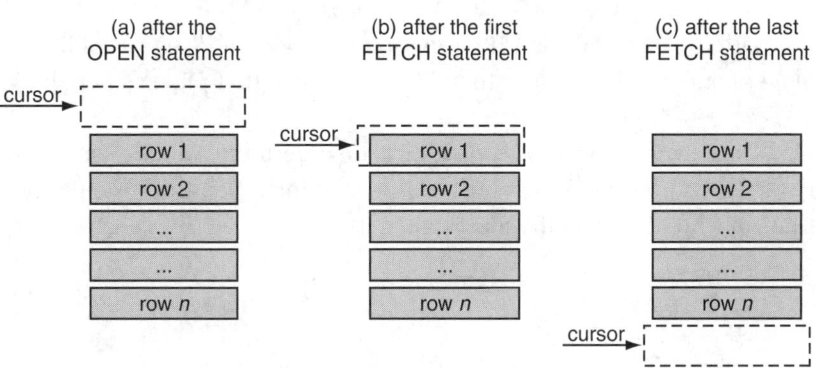

FIGURE 31.3 The position of the cursor after specific SQL statements

The CLOSE CURSOR *statement* closes a cursor so that the result of the table expression is no longer available. It is not necessary to fetch rows until the last row before closing the cursor; you should close a cursor as soon as possible because keeping the result of the cursor costs computer resources. We recommend that you close a cursor before it is opened again and before a stored procedure is completed.

Example 31.27: Create a stored procedure that removes all the penalties of the players who are older than 30 years.

```
CREATE PROCEDURE DELETE_OLDER_THAN_30()
BEGIN
   DECLARE V_AGE, V_PLAYERNO,V_YEARS,
      V_MONTHS, V_DAYS INTEGER;
   DECLARE V_BIRTH_DATE DATE;
   DECLARE FOUND BOOLEAN DEFAULT TRUE;
   DECLARE C_PLAYERS CURSOR FOR
      SELECT PLAYERNO, BIRTH_DATE
      FROM   PLAYERS;
   DECLARE CONTINUE HANDLER FOR NOT FOUND
      SET FOUND = FALSE;
   OPEN C_PLAYERS;
   FETCH C_PLAYERS INTO V_PLAYERNO, V_BIRTH_DATE;
   WHILE FOUND DO
      CALL AGE (V_BIRTH_DATE, NOW(), V_YEARS,
         V_MONTHS, V_DAYS);
      IF V_YEARS > 30 THEN
         DELETE FROM PENALTIES WHERE PLAYERNO = V_PLAYERNO;
      END IF;
      FETCH C_PLAYERS INTO V_PLAYERNO, V_BIRTH_DATE;
   END WHILE;
   CLOSE C_PLAYERS;
END
```

Explanation: With the cursor C_PLAYERS, we walk through the PLAYERS table. If the age of a player concerned is greater than 30, we remove that player's penalties.

Example 31.28: Develop a stored procedure to determine whether a player belongs to the top three players of the club. In this example, "top three" is defined as the three players who have won the most total sets.

```
CREATE PROCEDURE TOP_THREE
   (IN P_PLAYERNO INTEGER,
    OUT OK BOOLEAN)
BEGIN
   DECLARE A_PLAYERNO, BALANCE, SEQNO INTEGER;
   DECLARE FOUND BOOLEAN;
   DECLARE BALANCE_PLAYERS CURSOR FOR
      SELECT   PLAYERNO, SUM(WON) - SUM(LOST)
      FROM     MATCHES
      GROUP BY PLAYERNO
      ORDER BY 2;
   DECLARE CONTINUE HANDLER FOR NOT FOUND
      SET FOUND = FALSE;
   SET SEQNO = 0;
   SET FOUND = TRUE;
```

```
    SET OK = FALSE;
    OPEN BALANCE_PLAYERS;
    FETCH BALANCE_PLAYERS INTO A_PLAYERNO, BALANCE;
    WHILE FOUND AND SEQNO < 3 AND OK = FALSE DO
       SET SEQNO = SEQNO + 1;
       IF A_PLAYERNO = P_PLAYERNO THEN
          SET OK = TRUE;
       END IF;
       FETCH BALANCE_PLAYERS INTO A_PLAYERNO, BALANCE;
    END WHILE;
    CLOSE BALANCE_PLAYERS;
END
```

Explanation: The stored procedure uses a cursor to determine for each player the difference between the total number of sets won and the total number of sets lost (the balance). These players are ordered by balance: the player with the largest difference first and the one with the smallest last. With the `WHILE` statement, we browse the first three rows of this result. The parameter `OK` has the value `true` if the entered player number is equal to one of the first three players.

`SELECT INTO` statements and cursors may contain variables. By changing the value of a variable before opening a cursor, we can get different results.

Example 31.29: Create a stored procedure that counts the number of penalties of a certain player in the PENALTIES table.

```
CREATE PROCEDURE NUMBER_PENALTIES
   (IN  V_PLAYERNO INTEGER,
    OUT NUMBER INTEGER)
BEGIN
   DECLARE A_PLAYERNO INTEGER;
   DECLARE FOUND BOOLEAN DEFAULT TRUE;
   DECLARE C_PLAYERS CURSOR FOR
      SELECT PLAYERNO
      FROM   PENALTIES
      WHERE  PLAYERNO = V_PLAYERNO;
   DECLARE CONTINUE HANDLER FOR NOT FOUND
      SET FOUND = FALSE;
   SET NUMBER = 0;
   OPEN C_PLAYERS;
   FETCH C_PLAYERS INTO A_PLAYERNO;
   WHILE FOUND DO
      SET NUMBER = NUMBER + 1;
      FETCH C_PLAYERS INTO A_PLAYERNO;
   END WHILE;
   CLOSE C_PLAYERS;
END
```

Explanation: This stored procedure could have been formulated more simply, of course, but it shows the use of variables (in this case, V_PLAYERNO) in the table expressions of cursors. If we change the value of the variable after the OPEN CURSOR statement, it has no effect on the cursor. The value of the variable is queried only when the cursor is opened again.

31.12 Including SELECT Statements Without Cursors

You may include SELECT statements that return more than one row within a stored procedure without using cursors. The result of the SELECT statement is sent directly to the calling program; the stored procedure itself cannot do anything with this result.

Example 31.30: Create a stored procedure that shows all the rows from the TEAMS table.

```
CREATE PROCEDURE ALL_TEAMS()
BEGIN
   SELECT * FROM TEAMS;
END
```

Next, call this stored procedure with a CALL statement:

```
CALL ALL_TEAMS()
```

The result is:

```
TEAMNO  PLAYERNO  DIVISION
------  --------  --------
     1         6  first
     2        27  second
```

It looks as if the CALL statement was a SELECT statement.

When you work this way, it is important that the calling program be capable of picking up the results of the SELECT statement. Programs such as Navicat, WinSQL, and mysql can do this and simply show the table.

A stored procedure may contain multiple SELECT statements.

Example 31.31: Create a stored procedure that shows the number of rows from the TEAMS table and the number of rows from the PENALTIES table.

```
CREATE PROCEDURE NUMBERS_OF_ROWS()
BEGIN
   SELECT COUNT(*) FROM TEAMS;
   SELECT COUNT(*) FROM PENALTIES;
END

CALL NUMBER_OF_ROWS()
```

The result is:

```
COUNT(*)
--------
       2

COUNT(*)
--------
       8
```

31.13 Stored Procedures and User Variables

Section 5.6 described user variables. In stored procedures, it is possible to refer to this group of variables. User variables always have a global character. Even though they are created within a stored procedure, they remain after the stored procedure has stopped. User variables that were created outside the stored procedure still maintain their value within the stored procedure.

Example 31.32: Develop a stored procedure that sets the value of the user variable VAR1 to 1.

```
CREATE PROCEDURE USER_VARIABLE ()
BEGIN
   SET @VAR1 = 1;
END

CALL USER_VARIABLE ()

SELECT @VAR1
```

Explanation: After calling the procedure, VAR1 will have the value 1.

31.14 Characteristics of Stored Procedures

We can specify characteristics of a stored procedure between the parameters and the body of a stored procedure. Most characteristics tell MySQL something about the nature of the procedure. If we specify NO SQL, for example, we indicate that the procedure does not contain SQL statements and, therefore, will not access the database.

DEFINITION

```
<create procedure statement> ::=
   CREATE [ <definer option> ]
      PROCEDURE <procedure name> ( [ <parameter list> ] )
      [ <routine characteristic>... ]
      <routine body>

<definer option> ::=
   DEFINER = { <user name> | CURRENT_USER }

<routine characteristic> ::=
   LANGUAGE SQL                                   |
   [ NOT ] DETERMINISTIC                          |
   { CONTAINS SQL | NO SQL | READS SQL DATA |
     MODIFIES SQL DATA } |
   SQL SECURITY { DEFINER | INVOKE }              |
   COMMENT <alphanumeric literal>
```

The *definer* of the procedure is the user who defined the procedure and has prompted the processing of a CREATE PROCEDURE. Behind the word CREATE, we can specify another user name with a definer option. This means that this user is seen as the definer of the procedure.

Example 31.33: Develop a stored procedure that returns pi^2. User CHRIS3 should be the definer.

```
CREATE DEFINER = 'CHRIS3'@'%' PROCEDURE PIPOWER
   (OUT VAR1 DECIMAL(10,5))
BEGIN
   SET VAR1 = POWER(PI(),2);
END
```

Instead using of a specific user name, you may specify CURRENT_USER. This is the same as when the definer option has not been specified.

With LANGUAGE SQL, we indicate that the body of the procedure consists of statements described in this book. The body is not formulated in Java or PHP. In the future, we will be able to write the stored procedures in other languages in addition to using SQL.

The characteristic DETERMINISTIC indicates that the result of the procedure for specific values for the input parameters is always equal. For example, the procedure from Example 31.28 is not deterministic because when the contents of the queried tables change, the result of the procedure changes, too. If nothing is specified, MySQL assumes that the procedure is not deterministic.

Example 31.34: Develop a deterministic stored procedure that calculates the square of the square of a number.

```
CREATE PROCEDURE POWERPOWER
   (IN P1 INTEGER, OUT P2 INTEGER)
   DETERMINISTIC
BEGIN
   SET P2 = POWER(POWER(P1,2),2);
END
```

MySQL can use this characteristic to optimize the processing of a procedure. Imagine that a procedure is called twice in the same transaction with the same parameters. If we had indicated that the procedure is deterministic, this procedure would have to be called just once.

The third characteristic says something about the SQL statements used within the stored procedure. `CONTAINS SQL` does not need further explanation. `NO SQL` implies that the procedure contains only procedural statements. `READS SQL DATA` indicates that the procedure only queries data, and `MODIFIES SQL DATA` indicates that the procedure also adds, changes, and removes data. MySQL does not check on this characteristic; it just accepts the following procedure.

Example 31.35: Develop a stored procedure that has `NO SQL` as a characteristic but that does contain SQL statements.

```
CREATE PROCEDURE CLEANUP ()
    NO SQL
BEGIN
   DELETE FROM PENALTIES;
END
```

As its name implies, the characteristic `SQL SECURITY` relates to security. A stored procedure can contain all kinds of SQL statements with which data can be queried and changed. Suppose that the stored procedure `P1` adds a row to the PLAYERS table. If `P1` is accessed, should the user responsible for the call have the privilege to add rows to the PLAYERS table? If `SQL SECURITY` has not been specified, the caller does not need that specific of privileges. However, the user who creates the stored procedure must have the right privileges. When a stored procedure is called and `SQL SECURITY INVOKER` has been specified, a check is done to see whether the caller (the invoker) has sufficient privileges himself. Specifying `SQL SECURITY DEFINER` is equivalent to not specifying the `SQL SECURITY` characteristic.

The last characteristic is COMMENT. As with tables, we can store comments in the catalog.

An *ALTER PROCEDURE statement* can adjust the characteristics later.

DEFINITION

```
<alter procedure statement> ::=
   ALTER PROCEDURE [ <database name> . ] <procedure name>
      [ <routine characteristic>... ]

<routine characteristic> ::=
   LANGUAGE SQL                                      |
   [ NOT ] DETERMINISTIC                             |
   { CONTAINS SQL | NO SQL | READS SQL DATA |
     MODIFIES SQL DATA } |
   SQL SECURITY { DEFINER | INVOKE }                 |
   COMMENT <alphanumeric literal>
```

31.15 Stored Procedures and the Catalog

We have not defined a catalog view for stored procedures; you must access the catalog of MySQL directly. This catalog table is called ROUTINES.

Example 31.36: Get the columns of the ROUTINES table.

```
SELECT   COLUMN_NAME
FROM     INFORMATION_SCHEMA.COLUMNS
WHERE    TABLE_SCHEMA = 'INFORMATION_SCHEMA'
AND      TABLE_NAME = 'ROUTINES'
ORDER BY ORDINAL_POSITION
```

The result is:

```
COLUMN_NAME
------------------
SPECIFIC_NAME
ROUTINE_CATALOG
ROUTINE_SCHEMA
ROUTINE_NAME
ROUTINE_TYPE
DTD_IDENTIFIER
ROUTINE_BODY
ROUTINE_DEFINITION
EXTERNAL_NAME
EXTERNAL_LANGUAGE
```

```
PARAMETER_STYLE
IS_DETERMINISTIC
SQL_DATA_ACCESS
SQL_PATH
SECURITY_TYPE
CREATED
LAST_ALTERED
SQL_MODE
ROUTINE_COMMENT
DEFINER
```

A `SHOW` statement also exists for retrieving information on stored procedures from the catalog.

Example 31.37: Get the characteristics of the procedure called `FIBONACCI`.

```
SHOW PROCEDURE STATUS LIKE 'FIBONACCI'
```

Example 31.38: Get the `CREATE PROCEDURE` statement for the procedure called `FIBONACCI`.

```
SHOW CREATE PROCEDURE FIBONACCI
```

The result is:

```
PROCEDURE  SQL_MODE  CREATE PROCEDURE
---------  --------  ------------------------------------
FIBONACCI            CREATE PROCEDURE 'tennis'.'FIBONACCI'
                        (INOUT NUMBER1 INTEGER,
                         INOUT NUMBER2 INTEGER,
                         INOUT NUMBER3 INTEGER)
                     BEGIN
                        SET NUMBER3 = NUMBER1 + NUMBER2;
                        IF NUMBER3 > 10000 THEN
                           SET NUMBER3 = NUMBER3 - 10000;
                        END IF;
                        SET NUMBER1 = NUMBER2;
                        SET NUMBER2 = NUMBER3;
                     END
```

31.16 Removing Stored Procedures

As with tables, views, and indexes, you can remove stored procedures from the catalog. For this, MySQL supports the *DROP PROCEDURE statement.*

DEFINITION

```
<drop procedure statement> ::=
   DROP PROCEDURE [ IF EXISTS ]
      [ <database name> . ] <procedure name>
```

Example 31.39: Remove the DELETE_PLAYER procedure.

```
DROP PROCEDURE DELETE_PLAYER
```

31.17 Security with Stored Procedures

Not every SQL user may call a stored procedure; to access tables and views, privileges must be granted with the GRANT statement. A special privilege, called EXECUTE, handles this. The definition of this form of the GRANT statement looks as follows:

DEFINITION

```
<grant statement> ::=
   <grant execute privilege statement>

<grant execute privilege statement> ::=
   GRANT EXECUTE
   ON    PROCEDURE <stored procedure name>
   TO    <grantees>
   [ WITH <grant option>... ]

<grantees> ::=
   <user specification> [ , <user specification> ]...

<user specification> ::=
   <user name> [ IDENTIFIED BY [ PASSWORD ] <password> ]

<user name> ::=
   <name> | '<name>' | '<name>'@'<host name>'

<grant option> ::=
   GRANT OPTION                              |
   MAX_CONNECTIONS_PER_HOUR <whole number>   |
   MAX_QUERIES_PER_HOUR <whole number>       |
   MAX_UPDATES_PER_HOUR <whole number>       |
   MAX_USER_CONNECTIONS <whole number>
```

Example 31.40: Give John the privilege to call the DELETE_MATCHES procedure.

```
GRANT EXECUTE
ON    PROCEDURE DELETE_MATCHES
TO    JOHN
```

However, John does *not* need to have a privilege for the SQL statements executed within the procedure. With respect to the DELETE_MATCHES procedure, John does not need an explicit DELETE privilege for the MATCHES table.

The developer who created the procedure does need this privilege. In other words, if a user creates a stored procedure, he or she must have privileges for all SQL statements executed within the procedure.

For most products, it also holds that a procedure will not be executed if the owner of a stored procedure loses several privileges after the procedure has been created correctly. SQL sends an error message when the procedure is called.

31.18 Advantages of Stored Procedures

Several examples have shown the features of stored procedures. This section covers the advantages of stored procedures, including maintenance, performance, security, and centralization.

The first advantage, maintenance, has to do with the way applications can be set up with stored procedures. If a specific set of updates on the database logically forms a unit, and if this set of updates is used in multiple applications, it is better to put them in one procedure. Examples include removing all player data (at least five statements) and calculating the number of ancestors of a player. For this, you simply activate the procedure in the programs. This improves the productivity, of course, and prevents a programmer from implementing the set of updates incorrectly in his or her program.

The second advantage of stored procedures relates to performance. If an application activates a procedure and waits for completion, the amount of communication between the application and the database server is minimal. This contrasts with the application sending each SQL statement separately to the database server. Especially now that more applications access the database server through a network, it is important to minimize the amount of communication and reduce the possibility that the network will get overloaded. Briefly, stored procedures can minimize network traffic.

Stored procedures do not depend on a particular host language; they can be called from different host languages. This means that if multiple languages are used for development, certain common code does not have to be duplicated (for each language). For example, a specific stored procedure can be called from an online Java application, from a batch application written in C, or from a PHP program operating in an Internet environment.

CHAPTER 32

Stored Functions

32.1 Introduction

Stored functions show a strong resemblance to stored procedures: They are pieces of code consisting of SQL and procedural statements that are stored in the catalog and can be called from applications and SQL statements. However, a few differences exist:

- A stored function can have input parameters but does not have output parameters. The stored function itself is the output parameter. The next sections illustrate this with examples.
- After stored functions have been created, all kinds of expressions can invoke them in the same way they invoke the familiar scalar functions. Therefore, we do not call stored functions using a `CALL` statement.
- Stored functions must contain a `RETURN` statement. This special SQL statement is not allowed in stored procedures.

The definition of the `CREATE FUNCTION` procedure looks very much like that of the stored procedure. The definition also starts with a name followed by parameters, and it ends with a body, but a few small differences exist. Because a stored function can have only input parameters, you cannot specify `IN`, `OUT`, and `INOUT`. The `RETURNS` *specification* follows the parameters and indicates the data type of the value that the stored function returns.

DEFINITION

```
<create function statement> ::=
   CREATE FUNCTION <function name>
      ( [ <parameter list> ] )
      RETURNS <data type>
      <routine body>

<parameter list> ::=
   <parameter specification>
      [ , <parameter specification> ]...

<parameter specification> ::= <parameter> <data type>

<routine body> ::= <begin-end block>

<begin-end block> ::=
   [ <label> : ] BEGIN <statement list> END [ <label> ]

<statement list> ::= { <statement in body> ; }...

<statement in body> ::=
   <declarative statement> |
   <procedural statement>

<procedural statement> ::=
   <begin-end block>                |
   <call statement>                 |
   <close statement>                |
   <declare condition statement>    |
   <declare cursor statement>       |
   <declare handler statement>      |
   <declare variable statement>     |
   <fetch cursor statement>         |
   <flow control statement>         |
   <open cursor statement>          |
   <set statement>                  |
   <return statement>

<return statement> ::= RETURN <scalar expression>
```

32.2 Examples of Stored Functions

We begin with several examples.

Example 32.1: Create a stored function that returns the American dollar value of the penalty amounts. After that, for each penalty with a number less than 4, get the payment number and euro and dollar value of each penalty amount.

```
CREATE FUNCTION DOLLARS(AMOUNT DECIMAL(7,2))
   RETURNS DECIMAL(7,2)
BEGIN
   RETURN AMOUNT * (1 / 0.8);
END

SELECT   PAYMENTNO, AMOUNT, DOLLARS(AMOUNT)
FROM     PENALTIES
WHERE    PAYMENTNO <= 3
```

The result is:

```
PAYMENTNO  AMOUNT  DOLLARS(AMOUNT)
---------  ------  ---------------
        1  100.00           125.00
        2   75.00            93.75
        3  100.00           125.00
```

Explanation: The fact that the result of the stored function has a decimal data type is specified after RETURNS. With the special RETURN statement, we give the stored function a value. Each stored function must contain at least one RETURN statement.

You can see that this new stored function can be called as if it is a scalar function supplied by MySQL. No visible difference exists between calling a scalar function, such as SUBSTR and COS, and calling a stored function.

Example 32.2: Create a stored function that returns the number of players in the PLAYERS table as a result. After that, call this stored function.

```
CREATE FUNCTION NUMBER_OF_PLAYERS()
   RETURNS INTEGER
BEGIN
   RETURN (SELECT COUNT(*) FROM PLAYERS);
END

SELECT NUMBER_OF_PLAYERS()
```

Explanation: This example shows first that SQL statements are allowed within stored functions and, second, that the RETURN statement may contain complex compound expressions.

Example 32.3: Create two stored functions that determine, respectively, the number of penalties and the number of matches of a certain player. After that, get the numbers, names, and initials of those players whose number of penalties is greater than the number of matches.

```
CREATE FUNCTION NUMBER_OF_PENALTIES
   (P_PLAYERNO INTEGER)
   RETURNS INTEGER
BEGIN
   RETURN (SELECT   COUNT(*)
           FROM     PENALTIES
           WHERE    PLAYERNO = P_PLAYERNO);
END

CREATE FUNCTION NUMBER_OF_MATCHES
   (P_PLAYERNO INTEGER)
   RETURNS INTEGER
BEGIN
   RETURN (SELECT   COUNT(*)
           FROM     MATCHES
           WHERE    PLAYERNO = P_PLAYERNO);
END

SELECT   PLAYERNO, NAME, INITIALS
FROM     PLAYERS
WHERE    NUMBER_OF_PENALTIES(PLAYERNO) >
         NUMBER_OF_MATCHES(PLAYERNO)
```

The result is:

```
PLAYERNO  NAME     INITIALS
--------  -------  --------
      27  Collins        DD
      44  Baker           E
```

Example 32.4: Create a stored function that makes the SELECT statement in Example 23.12 easier to read. The statement is:

```
SELECT   TEAMNO, DIVISION
FROM     TEAMS_NEW
WHERE    DIVISION & POWER(2,3-1) = POWER(2,3-1)
```

We create the following stored function:

```
CREATE FUNCTION POSITION_IN_SET
   (P_COLUMN BIGINT, POSITION SMALLINT)
   RETURNS BOOLEAN
BEGIN
   RETURN (P_COLUMN & POWER(2, POSITION-1) =
           POWER(2,POSITION-1));
END
```

The SELECT statement then looks as follows:

```
SELECT   TEAMNO, DIVISION
FROM     TEAMS_NEW
WHERE    POSITION_IN_SET(DIVISION, 3)
```

Example 32.5: Create a stored function that calculates the number of days between two dates, using the same arithmetic method as in Example 31.10.

```
CREATE FUNCTION NUMBER_OF_DAYS
   (START_DATE DATE,
    END_DATE DATE)
    RETURNS INTEGER
BEGIN
   DECLARE DAYS INTEGER;
   DECLARE NEXT_DATE, PREVIOUS_DATE DATE;
   SET DAYS = 0;
   SET NEXT_DATE = START_DATE + INTERVAL 1 DAY;
   WHILE NEXT_DATE <= END_DATE DO
      SET DAYS = DAYS + 1;
      SET PREVIOUS_DATE = NEXT_DATE;
      SET NEXT_DATE = NEXT_DATE + INTERVAL 1 DAY;
   END WHILE;
   RETURN DAYS;
END
```

Explanation: All statements, such as DECLARE, SET, and WHILE, may be used.

Example 32.6: Create a stored function for removing a player, with the same functionality as the stored procedure in Example 31.19. Imagine that the rule applies that a player can be removed only if he or she has not incurred a penalty and if he or she is not a captain. We also assume that no foreign keys have been defined.

```
CREATE FUNCTION DELETE_PLAYER
   (P_PLAYERNO INTEGER)
   RETURNS BOOLEAN
BEGIN
   DECLARE NUMBER_OF_PENALTIES INTEGER;
   DECLARE NUMBER_OF_TEAMS  INTEGER;
   DECLARE EXIT HANDLER FOR SQLWARNING RETURN FALSE;
   DECLARE EXIT HANDLER FOR SQLEXCEPTION RETURN FALSE;

   SELECT COUNT(*)
   INTO   NUMBER_OF_PENALTIES
   FROM   PENALTIES
   WHERE  PLAYERNO = P_PLAYERNO;

   SELECT COUNT(*)
   INTO   NUMBER_OF_TEAMS
   FROM   TEAMS
   WHERE  PLAYERNO = P_PLAYERNO;

   IF NUMBER_OF_PENALTIES = 0 AND NUMBER_OF_TEAMS = 0 THEN
      DELETE FROM MATCHES
      WHERE  PLAYERNO = P_PLAYERNO;
      DELETE FROM PLAYERS
      WHERE  PLAYERNO = P_PLAYERNO;
   END IF;
   RETURN TRUE;
END
```

Explanation: If the stored function is processed correctly, this function returns 0 as result; otherwise, the value is 1.

Example 32.7: Create a stored function that does not do anything but call the stored procedure NUMBER_OF_PLAYERS that we created in Example 31.26.

```
CREATE FUNCTION GET_NUMBER_OF_PLAYERS()
   RETURNS INTEGER
BEGIN
   DECLARE NUMBER INTEGER;
   CALL NUMBER_OF_PLAYERS(NUMBER);
   RETURN NUMBER;
END
```

Explanation: Stored functions and stored procedures cannot have identical names. Therefore, the name of the function has been changed somewhat. The example proofs that stored procedures can be called from stored functions.

Example 32.8: Create a stored function that determines whether two periods overlap in time.

```
CREATE FUNCTION OVERLAP_BETWEEN_PERIODS
   (PERIOD1_START DATETIME,
    PERIOD1_END DATETIME,
    PERIOD2_START DATETIME,
    PERIOD2_END DATETIME)
    RETURNS BOOLEAN
BEGIN
   DECLARE TEMPORARY_DATE DATETIME;
   IF PERIOD1_START > PERIOD1_END THEN
      SET TEMPORARY_DATE = PERIOD1_START;
      SET PERIOD1_START = PERIOD1_END;
      SET PERIOD1_END = TEMPORARY_DATE;
   END IF;
   IF PERIOD2_START > PERIOD2_END THEN
      SET TEMPORARY_DATE = PERIOD2_START;
      SET PERIOD2_START = PERIOD2_END;
      SET PERIOD2_END = TEMPORARY_DATE;
   END IF;
   RETURN NOT(PERIOD1_END < PERIOD2_START OR
              PERIOD2_END < PERIOD1_START);
END
```

Explanation: The stored function has four parameters. The first two represent the begin date and end date of the first period, and the next two represent the begin date and end date of the second parameter. The value of this stored function is `true` (1) or `false` (0). The first `IF` statement determines whether the start date of the first period is older than the begin date. If not, the values of these two variables are switched. With the second `IF` statement, we do the same thing for the start and end dates of the second period. Next, we determine whether the two functions overlap. They do *not* overlap when the first period ends before the second period begins or when the second period ends before the first begins.

You can use this stored function to formulate certain queries more elegantly; see following the example.

Example 32.9: Get the data of those players who were committee members in the period of June 30, 1991, until June 30, 1992.

```
SELECT   *
FROM     COMMITTEE_MEMBERS
WHERE    OVERLAP_BETWEEN_PERIODS(BEGIN_DATE,END_DATE,
         '1991-06-30','1992-06-30')
ORDER BY 1, 2
```

The result is:

```
PLAYERNO  BEGIN_DATE  END_DATE    FUNCTION
--------  ----------  ----------  ---------
       2  1990-01-01  1992-12-31  Chairman
       6  1991-01-01  1992-12-31  Member
       6  1992-01-01  1993-12-31  Treasurer
       8  1991-01-01  1991-12-31  Secretary
      27  1991-01-01  1991-12-31  Treasurer
      57  1992-01-01  1992-12-31  Secretary
     112  1992-01-01  1992-12-31  Member
```

32.3 More on Stored Functions

As mentioned, stored functions and stored procedures have much in common. The stored functions are also stored in the ROUTINES catalog table. You can retrieve information about them with SELECT and SHOW statements.

For a stored function, you can specify a definer and the same set of characteristics as for a stored procedure. Refer to Section 31.14 for a detailed description of the definer option and the characteristics. The ALTER FUNCTION statement can change those characteristics.

DEFINITION

```
<create function statement> ::=
   CREATE [ <definer option> ]
      FUNCTION [ <database name> . ] <function name>
      ( [ <parameter list> ] )
      RETURNS <data type>
      [ <routine characteristic>... ]
      <routine body>

<definer option> ::=
   DEFINER = { <user name> | CURRENT_USER }

<alter function statement> ::=
   ALTER FUNCTION [ <database name> . ] <function name>
      [ <routine characteristic>... ]

<routine characteristic> ::=
   LANGUAGE SQL                                  |
   [ NOT ] DETERMINISTIC                         |
   { CONTAINS SQL | NO SQL | READS SQL DATA |
     MODIFIES SQL DATA } |
   SQL SECURITY { DEFINER | INVOKE }             |
   COMMENT <alphanumeric literal>
```

To be able to call stored functions, you must assign privileges with GRANT statements.

DEFINITION

```
<grant statement> ::=
   <grant execute privilege statement>

<grant execute privilege statement> ::=
   GRANT EXECUTE
   ON    FUNCTION <stored procedure name>
   TO    <grantees>
   [ WITH <grant option>... ]

<grantees> ::=
   <user specification> [ , <user specification> ]...

<user specification> ::=
   <user name> [ IDENTIFIED BY [ PASSWORD ] <password> ]

<user name> ::=
   <name> | '<name>' | '<name>'@'<host name>'

<grant option> ::=
   GRANT OPTION                            |
   MAX_CONNECTIONS_PER_HOUR <whole number> |
   MAX_QUERIES_PER_HOUR <whole number>     |
   MAX_UPDATES_PER_HOUR <whole number>     |
   MAX_USER_CONNECTIONS <whole number>
```

32.4 Removing Stored Functions

A DROP statement also exists for the stored function.

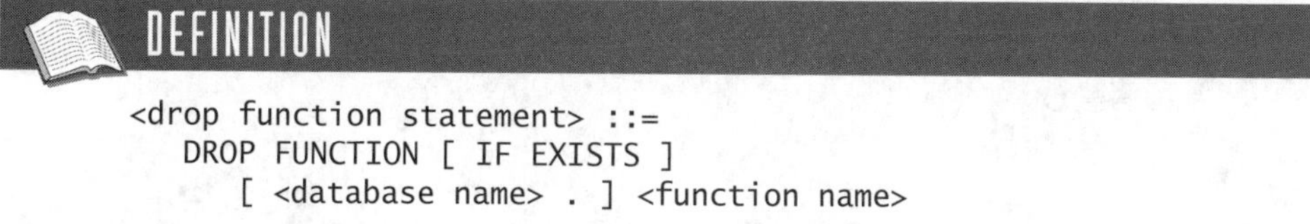

DEFINITION

```
<drop function statement> ::=
   DROP FUNCTION [ IF EXISTS ]
      [ <database name> . ] <function name>
```

Example 32.10: Remove the PLACE_IN_SET stored function.

```
DROP FUNCTION PLACE_IN_SET
```

CHAPTER 33

Triggers

33.1 Introduction

A database server is passive by nature. It performs an action only if we explicitly ask for it with, for example, an SQL statement. This chapter describes the database concept that turns a passive database server into an active one. This concept is called a *trigger*. As with stored procedures, we start by giving a definition:

> A **trigger** is a piece of code consisting of procedural and declarative statements stored in the catalog and activated by the database server if a specific operation is executed on the database—and only then when a certain condition holds.

A trigger shows many similarities to a stored procedure. First, the trigger is also a procedural database object stored in the catalog. Second, the code itself consists of declarative and procedural SQL statements. Therefore, `UPDATE`, `SELECT`, `CREATE`, `IF-THEN-ELSE`, and `WHILE-DO` statements can occur within a trigger.

However, one important difference exists between the two concepts. The way in which triggers are called deviates from that of stored procedures. Triggers *cannot* be called explicitly either from a program or from a stored procedure. No `CALL` or `EXECUTE TRIGGER` statement or similar statement is available. MySQL itself calls triggers transparently, without the programs or users being aware of it.

But how and when are triggers called? MySQL calls a trigger when a program, interactive user, or stored procedure executes a specific database operation, such as adding a new row to a table or removing all rows. So MySQL executes triggers automatically, and it is impossible to either activate triggers or switch them off from a program.

Note that this book describes Version 5.0.7 of MySQL. Triggers were already supported, but still in a limited way. Therefore, some of the statements in this book will not work yet. During the writing of the book, we found that the possibilities of triggers in Version 5.0.10 had already improved. This will surely continue to improve in later versions.

33.2 An Example of a Trigger

Most examples in this section and the next section use a new table in the database of the tennis club: the CHANGES table. Imagine that this table records which users have updated the PLAYERS table and at what moment.

Example 33.1: Create the CHANGES table.

```
CREATE TABLE CHANGES
       (USER              CHAR(30) NOT NULL,
        CHA_TIME          TIMESTAMP NOT NULL,
        CHA_PLAYERNO      SMALLINT NOT NULL,
        CHA_TYPE          CHAR(1) NOT NULL,
        CHA_PLAYERNO_NEW  INTEGER,
        PRIMARY KEY       (USER, CHA_TIME,
                          CHA_PLAYERNO, CHA_TYPE))
```

Explanation: The meaning of the first two columns is obvious. The third column, CHA_PLAYERNO, records the player number of the player who was added or removed, or whose column value was changed. If the player number of a player is changed, the new player number is recorded in the CHA_PLAYERNO_NEW column. Therefore, this column is used only when the player number is updated; otherwise, a null value is stored. The CHA_TYPE column stores the type of change: `I`(nsert), `U`(pdate), or `D`(elete). The columns USER, CHA_TIME, CHA_PLAYERNO, and CHA_TYPE form the primary key of this table. In other words, if a user executes two changes of the same type on the same player at the same moment, this needs to be recorded only once.

The definition of the *`CREATE TRIGGER` statement* follows. Triggers consist of three main elements: the *trigger moment,* the *trigger event,* and the *trigger action.* These elements appear clearly in the definition. For a description of the concept of statement, refer to Section 31.4.

DEFINITION

```
<create trigger statement> ::=
   CREATE [ <definer option> ]
      TRIGGER <trigger name>
      <trigger moment>
      <trigger event>
      <trigger action>

<definer option> ::=
   DEFINER = { <user name> | CURRENT_USER }

<trigger moment> ::= BEFORE | AFTER

<trigger event> ::=
   { INSERT | DELETE | UPDATE }
   ON <table specification> FOR EACH ROW

<trigger action> ::= <statement>
```

We begin with a simple example that uses a minimal set of specifications.

Example 33.2: Create the trigger that updates the CHANGES table automatically as new rows are added to the PLAYERS table.

```
CREATE TRIGGER INSERT_PLAYERS
   AFTER
   INSERT ON PLAYERS FOR EACH ROW
   BEGIN
      INSERT INTO CHANGES
         (USER, CHA_TIME, CHA_PLAYERNO,
          CHA_TYPE, CHA_PLAYERNO_NEW)
      VALUES (USER, CURDATE(), NEW.PLAYERNO, 'I', NULL);
   END
```

Explanation: As with every SQL statement for creating a database object, the statement begins by assigning a name to the trigger: INSERT_PLAYER. All the other specifications follow.

The second line contains the trigger moment (AFTER). This element specifies when the trigger must be started. In this case it happens *after* the INSERT statement on the PLAYERS table has been processed.

The third line contains the trigger event. This element specifies the operations for which the trigger must be activated—in this case, at an INSERT statement on the

PLAYERS table. Sometimes this is called the *triggering statement*, and the PLAYERS table is called the *triggering table*. If the triggering statement has occurred, the body of the trigger, or the *trigger action*, must be executed. The trigger action usually consists of a number of statements that are executed. We focus on the trigger action in more detail shortly.

The word AFTER as a trigger moment is important. If we use a SELECT statement in the trigger action to query the number of rows of the PLAYERS table, the row added is actually counted. This is because the trigger action starts after the triggering statement has been processed. If we had specified BEFORE, the row would not have been included because the trigger action would have been executed first. AFTER is usually used if we want to execute several more changes after the triggering statement and BEFORE if we want to verify whether the new data satisfies the constraints applied.

The trigger event contains the specification FOR EACH ROW. This is used to specify that, for each individual row inserted into the PLAYERS table, the trigger action must be activated. So if we add a set of rows to the PLAYERS table with one INSERT SELECT statement in one operation, the trigger still is executed for each row (see Section 17.3 for a description of this statement). The counterpart of FOR EACH ROW is FOR EACH STATEMENT. However, MySQL does not support this option yet. If we had been able to specify this, the trigger would have been activated only once for each triggering statement. This means that if we inserted a thousand rows with one INSERT SELECT statement, the trigger would still be executed only once. Alternatively, if we remove a million rows with one DELETE statement, and if the triggering statement is a DELETE, the trigger is still executed only once if FOR EACH STATEMENT is specified.

A trigger action can be as simple or as complex as the body of a stored procedure. The trigger action in our example is very simple because it consists of only one INSERT statement. This additional INSERT statement inserts one row into the CHANGES table that consists of four values: the value of the system variable USER, the system date and time, the player number of the new player, and the literal 'I' to indicate that it is an INSERT.

NEW is specified in front of the column name PLAYERNO. This is an important specification. If a row is inserted, it looks as if there is a table called NEW. The column names of this NEW table are equal to those of the triggering table (those in which the new row appears). As a result of specifying NEW in front of PLAYERNO, the player number that is added to the PLAYERS table is used. Its use will be obvious when we change rows in the PLAYERS table.

Triggers may also call stored procedures. Therefore, we can divide the previous CREATE TRIGGER statement into two parts. First, we create a stored procedure:

```
CREATE PROCEDURE INSERT_CHANGE
   (IN CPNO         INTEGER,
    IN CTYPE        CHAR(1),
    IN CPNO_NEW     INTEGER)
BEGIN
   INSERT INTO CHANGES (USER, CHA_TIME, CHA_PLAYERNO,
                        CHA_TYPE, CHA_PLAYERNO_NEW)
   VALUES (USER, CURDATE(), CPNO, CTYPE, CPNO_NEW);
END
```

Next, we create the trigger:

```
CREATE TRIGGER INSERT_PLAYER
   AFTER INSERT ON PLAYERS FOR EACH ROW
   BEGIN
      CALL INSERT_CHANGE(NEW.PLAYERNO, 'I', NULL);
   END
```

Two triggers cannot have the same trigger moment and the same trigger event for one table. We cannot define two `BEFORE DELETE` or two `AFTER INSERT` triggers on a table. Thus, if we want to invoke two pieces of code for a specific table, we must combine those pieces of code into one trigger.

For each trigger, a definer option can be defined, as for a stored procedure. If a user name is specified, this user becomes the owner of the trigger.

33.3 More Complex Examples

The previous section contained one example of a trigger. This section gives some other examples.

Example 33.3: Create the trigger that updates the CHANGES table automatically when rows from the PLAYERS table are removed.

```
CREATE TRIGGER DELETE_PLAYER
   AFTER DELETE ON PLAYERS FOR EACH ROW
   BEGIN
      CALL INSERT_CHANGE (OLD.PLAYERNO, 'D', NULL);
   END
```

Explanation: This trigger is almost the same as the one in Example 33.2. However, two differences exist. In the first place, the triggering statement is, of course, a `DELETE`. Second—and this is an important difference—the keyword `OLD` is now specified instead of `NEW`. After we remove a row, a table called `OLD` exists with column names that are equal to those of the triggering table, in which the removed row occurs.

When you update rows, the NEW and the OLD tables both exist. The row with the old values appears in the OLD table, and the new row appears in the NEW table.

Example 33.4: Create the trigger that updates the CHANGES table automatically when rows in the PLAYERS table change.

```
CREATE TRIGGER UPDATE_PLAYER
   AFTER UPDATE ON PLAYERS FOR EACH ROW
   BEGIN
      CALL INSERT_CHANGES
         (NEW.PLAYERNO, 'U', OLD.PLAYERNO);
   END
```

After the UPDATE specification, you can specify which update of which columns the trigger must be activated for.

These examples demonstrate one of the advantages of stored procedures: Code that has already been developed can be reused. This is an advantage in terms of both productivity and maintenance.

Triggers can also be used efficiently to record redundant data.

For the following example, we use a new table called PLAYERS_MAT that stores the player number and the number of matches for each player.

Example 33.5: Create the PLAYERS_MAT table and fill it with relevant data from the PLAYERS and MATCHES tables.

```
CREATE TABLE PLAYERS_MAT
      (PLAYERNO INTEGER NOT NULL PRIMARY KEY,
       NUMBER_OF_MATCHES INTEGER NOT NULL)

INSERT INTO PLAYERS_MAT (PLAYERNO, NUMBER_OF_MATCHES)
SELECT    PLAYERNO,
         (SELECT   COUNT(*)
          FROM     MATCHES AS M
          WHERE    P.PLAYERNO = M.PLAYERNO)
FROM      PLAYERS AS P
```

Example 33.6: Create a trigger on the PLAYERS table that ensures that if a new player is added, he or she is also added to the PLAYERS_MAT table.

```
CREATE TRIGGER INSERT_PLAYERS
   AFTER INSERT ON PLAYERS FOR EACH ROW
   BEGIN
      INSERT INTO PLAYERS_MAT
      VALUES(NEW.PLAYERNO, 0);
   END
```

Explanation: A new player cannot have matches yet, which is why the number is set to 0.

Example 33.7: Create a trigger on the PLAYERS table that ensures that if a new player is removed, he or she is also removed from the PLAYERS_MAT table.

```
CREATE TRIGGER DELETE_PLAYERS
   AFTER DELETE ON PLAYERS FOR EACH ROW
   BEGIN
      DELETE FROM PLAYERS_MAT
      WHERE PLAYERNO = OLD.PLAYERNO;
   END
```

Explanation: This can also be done with a foreign key.

Example 33.8: Create a trigger on the MATCHES table that ensures that if a new match is added for a player, this information is also passed on to the PLAYERS_MAT table.

```
CREATE TRIGGER INSERT_MATCHES
   AFTER INSERT ON MATCHES FOR EACH ROW
   BEGIN
      UPDATE PLAYERS_MAT
      SET    NUMBER_OF_MATCHES = NUMBER_OF_MATCHES + 1
      WHERE  PLAYERNO = NEW.PLAYERNO;
   END
```

Example 33.9: Create a trigger on the MATCHES table that ensures that if an existing match for a player is removed, this information is also passed on to the PLAYERS_MAT table.

```
CREATE TRIGGER DELETE_MATCHES
   AFTER DELETE ON MATCHES FOR EACH ROW
   BEGIN
      UPDATE PLAYERS_MAT
      SET    NUMBER_OF_MATCHES = NUMBER_OF_MATCHES - 1
      WHERE  PLAYERNO = OLD.PLAYERNO;
   END
```

Several other triggers are needed, but these examples give an idea of what is required. The main advantage of all these triggers is that no program has to worry about updating the PLAYERS_MAT table. As long as the triggers exist, the contents of this table are equal to the contents of the PLAYERS and MATCHES tables.

Example 33.10: Imagine that the PLAYERS table contains a column called SUM_PENALTIES. This column contains, for each player, the sum of his or her penalties. Now we want to create triggers that automatically record the values in this column. For this, we must create two triggers.

```
CREATE TRIGGER SUM_PENALTIES_INSERT
   AFTER INSERT ON PENALTIES FOR EACH ROW
   BEGIN
      DECLARE TOTAL DECIMAL(8,2);

      SELECT   SUM(AMOUNT)
      INTO     TOTAL
      FROM     PENALTIES
      WHERE    PLAYERNO = NEW.PLAYERNO;

      UPDATE   PLAYERS
      SET      SUM_PENALTIES = TOTAL
      WHERE    PLAYERNO = NEW.PLAYERNO
   END

CREATE TRIGGER SUM_PENALTIES_DELETE
   AFTER DELETE, UPDATE ON PENALTIES FOR EACH ROW
   BEGIN
      DECLARE TOTAL DECIMAL(8,2);

      SELECT   SUM(AMOUNT)
      INTO     TOTAL
      FROM     PENALTIES
      WHERE    PLAYERNO = OLD.PLAYERNO;

      UPDATE   PLAYERS
      SET      SUM_PENALTIES = TOTAL
      WHERE    PLAYERNO = OLD.PLAYERNO
   END
```

Explanation: The first trigger is activated when a new penalty is added; the second is activated when a penalty is deleted or when a penalty amount changes. If a player is added, the new sum of the penalty amounts of that new player (NEW.PLAYERNO) is determined. Next, an UPDATE statement updates the PLAYERS table. We use the local variable TOTAL.

Of course, we also can combine the UPDATE and SELECT statements. Then the trigger action consists of only one statement:

```
UPDATE   PLAYERS
SET      SUM_PENALTIES = (SELECT   SUM(AMOUNT)
                          FROM     PENALTIES
                          WHERE    PLAYERNO = NEW.PLAYERNO)
WHERE    PLAYERNO = NEW.PLAYERNO
```

The structure of the second trigger equals that of the first. The only difference is that we must specify OLD.PLAYERNO now.

Exercise 33.1: What is the most important difference between a stored procedure and a trigger?

Exercise 33.2: Create a trigger guaranteeing that at any time only one treasurer, one secretary, and one chairman exist.

Exercise 33.3: Create a trigger guaranteeing that the sum of all penalties of one player is not greater than $250.

Exercise 33.4: Imagine that the TEAMS table contains a column called NUMBER_OF_MATCHES. For each team, this column contains the number of matches played by that team. Create the trigger(s) required to update the values in this column automatically.

33.4 Triggers as Integrity Constraints

Triggers can be used for many purposes, including updating redundant data and securing the integrity of the data. Chapter 21, "Specifying Integrity Constraints," discussed integrity constraints and their possibilities. With triggers, a wide range of integrity constraints can be specified. To give more examples of triggers, we show how specific integrity constraints can be written as triggers.

All check integrity constraints (see Section 21.6) are easy to implement with triggers.

Example 33.11: Make sure that a player's year of birth is at least smaller than the year he or she joined the club (this integrity constraint is in line with Example 21.15).

```
CREATE TRIGGER BORN_VS_JOINED
   BEFORE INSERT, UPDATE ON PLAYERS FOR EACH ROW
   BEGIN
      IF YEAR(NEW.BIRTH_DATE) >= NEW.JOINED) THEN
         ROLLBACK WORK;
      END IF;
   END
```

Explanation: The trigger is simple and needs to be activated only for INSERT and UPDATE statements, not for DELETE statements. If the new data is incorrect, the running transaction is rolled back.

Example 33.12: The PENALTIES.PLAYERNO column is a foreign key pointing to PLAYERS.PLAYERNO; redefine this foreign key as a trigger.

We need two triggers, one for changes in the PENALTIES table and one for changes in the PLAYERS table.

```
CREATE TRIGGER FOREIGN_KEY1
   BEFORE INSERT, UPDATE ON PENALTIES FOR EACH ROW
   BEGIN
      IF (SELECT COUNT(*) FROM PLAYERS
          WHERE PLAYERNO = NEW.PLAYERNO) = 0 THEN
         ROLLBACK WORK;
      END IF;
   END
```

Explanation: With the SELECT statement, we determine whether the player number of the newly inserted or updated player appears in the PLAYERS table. If not, the variable NUMBER has a value greater than 0 and the transaction is rolled back.

The trigger on the PLAYERS table with MySQL follows:

```
CREATE TRIGGER FOREIGN_KEY2
   BEFORE DELETE, UPDATE ON PLAYERS FOR EACH ROW
   BEGIN
      DELETE
      FROM     PENALTIES
      WHERE    PLAYERNO = OLD.PLAYERNO;
   END
```

Explanation: The method chosen corresponds to the triggers, ON DELETE CASCADE and ON UPDATE CASCADE. If the player number is removed from the PLAYERS table, the related penalties are fully removed.

Of course, it is not the intention for you to implement all the integrity constraints with triggers. Indeed, doing so would not help performance. The rule is that if you can implement the integrity constraint with a CHECK or FOREIGN KEY, you should do so.

So why do we keep talking about implementing integrity constraints with triggers? This is because the functionality of triggers goes further than what is possible with the integrity constraints discussed in Chapter 21. For example, it is not possible to use one of the keys or the check integrity constraint to specify that if the penalty amounts are changed, the new amount should always be greater than the last one. Triggers, however, can do this.

33.5 Removing Triggers

As with any other database object, a DROP statement can remove triggers from the catalog.

```
<drop trigger statement> ::=
   DROP TRIGGER [ <table name> . ] <trigger name>
```

Example 33.13: Remove the BORN_VS_JOINED trigger.

```
DROP TRIGGER BORN_VS_JOINED
```

Removing triggers has no further influence, except that the trigger will no longer be activated.

The first versions of MySQL supported specifying a table name in front of the trigger name. From Version 5.10, it is possible to specify the database name (no longer the table name).

33.6 Triggers and the Catalog

In the INFORMATION_SCHEMA catalog, data on triggers is stored in the TRIGGERS table.

33.7 Answers

33.1 The most important difference between a stored procedure and a trigger is that programs and other stored procedures cannot call triggers directly.

33.2
```
CREATE TRIGGER MAX1
   AFTER INSERT, UPDATE(POSITION) OF COMMITTEE_MEMBERS
      FOR EACH ROW
   BEGIN
      SELECT   COUNT(*)
      INTO     NUMBER_MEMBERS
      FROM     COMMITTEE_MEMBERS
      WHERE    PLAYERNO IN
              (SELECT   PLAYERNO
               FROM     COMMITTEE_MEMBERS
               WHERE    CURRENT DATE BETWEEN
                        BEGIN_DATE AND END_DATE
               GROUP BY POSITION
               HAVING   COUNT(*) > 1)
```

```
      IF NUMBER_MEMBERS > 0 THEN
         ROLLBACK WORK;
      ENDIF;
   END
```

33.3
```
CREATE TRIGGER SUM_PENALTIES_250
   AFTER INSERT, UPDATE(AMOUNT) OF PENALTIES
      FOR EACH ROW
   BEGIN
      SELECT   COUNT(*)
      INTO     NUMBER_PENALTIES
      FROM     PENALTIES
      WHERE    PLAYERNO IN
              (SELECT   PLAYERNO
               FROM     PENALTIES
               GROUP BY PLAYERNO
               HAVING   SUM(AMOUNT) > 250);
      IF NUMBER_PENALTIES > 0 THEN
         ROLLBACK WORK;
      ENDIF;
   END
```

33.4
```
CREATE TRIGGER NUMBER_MATCHES_INSERT
   AFTER INSERT OF MATCHES FOR EACH ROW
   BEGIN
      UPDATE   TEAMS
      SET      NUMBER_MATCHES =
              (SELECT   COUNT(*)
               FROM     MATCHES
               WHERE    PLAYERNO = NEW.PLAYERNO)
      WHERE    PLAYERNO = NEW.PLAYERNO
   END

CREATE TRIGGER NUMBER_MATCHES_DELETE
   AFTER DELETE, UPDATE OF MATCHES FOR EACH ROW
   BEGIN
      UPDATE   TEAMS
      SET      NUMBER_MATCHES =
              (SELECT   COUNT(*)
               FROM     MATCHES
               WHERE    PLAYERNO = OLD.PLAYERNO)
      WHERE    PLAYERNO = OLD.PLAYERNO
   END
```

CHAPTER 34

Events

34.1 What Is an Event?

The MySQL database server never executes actions on the database by itself or executes a SELECT or UPDATE statement suddenly. Applications ask MySQL to execute an SQL statement or to start a stored procedure. Triggers are also started indirectly by an application; MySQL does not start the trigger on its own.

When using *events*, MySQL appears to directly access the database without the request of an application. Events are procedural database objects that MySQL invokes at the appropriate time. An event can be invoked only once—for example, on January 6, 2010, at 2 p.m. An event can also be started periodically—for example, every Sunday at 4 a.m. When events are scheduled, MySQL keeps a schedule that tells when events must be started.

Events resemble triggers—both start if something happens. Triggers start when a statement is fired on the database, and events start according to the scheduled time. Because they resemble each other, events are sometimes called *temporal triggers*.

For what purposes can we use events? Several application areas exist:

- Events can close accounts. At the end of each month or each year, for example, many accounting departments need to close their accounts. You could use an event to do this.
- Events can turn database indicators on or off. For example, consider an airline company. When a flight has departed, no more reservations can be made for that flight. The column CLOSED in the FLIGHTS table must be set to YES. You could schedule an event to automatically start 20 minutes after the flight's planned departure time to complete this task.
- Data in data warehouses is refreshed at certain intervals; for example, every Sunday or at the end of each day, data is copied from one table to another.

This periodic updating of the data warehouse tables could be done with the help of events.

- Applications do not always perform complex checks of incoming data. You could schedule these checks—for example, at the end of a day or on the weekend.

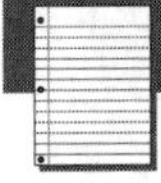

NOTE

Events have been added to MySQL in version 5.1.6. This chapter describes the features available in this version. If you are using a different version, these features might deviate.

34.2 Creating Events

A *CREATE EVENT statement* creates a new event. Each event consists of two main components. The first is the *event schedule* that indicates when and how often the event must be started and with which frequency. The second component is the *event action*. This is the code that is executed when the event is started. The event action consists of one SQL statement. This can be a simple SQL statement, such as an INSERT or UPDATE statement. It can also be the call of a stored procedure or a begin-end block—both of these allow us to execute multiple SQL statements.

In addition, with a CREATE EVENT statement you can assign certain properties to an event. We return to this topic in Section 34.3.

DEFINITION

```
<create event statement> ::=
   CREATE EVENT [ IF NOT EXISTS ]
      [ <database name> . ] <event name>
      ON SCHEDULE <event schedule>
      [ ON COMPLETION [ NOT ] PRESERVE ]
      [ ENABLE | DISABLE ]
      [ COMMENT <alphanumeric literal> ]
      DO <event action>

<event schedule> ::=
   <single schedule> | <recurring schedule>

<single schedule> ::=
   AT <timestamp expression>

<periodical schedule> ::=
   EVERY <number> <time unit>
   [ STARTS <timestamp literal> ]
   [ ENDS <timestamp literal> ]

<event action> ::=
   <declarative sql statement> |
   <begin-end block>
```

An event can be *active* (enabled) or *inactive* (disabled). Active means that the scheduler checks whether the event action must be invoked. Inactive means that the specifications of the event are stored in the catalog, but the scheduler does not check whether it should be invoked. Immediately after an event is created, it becomes active.

An active event can be executed one or more times. Execution of an event is called *invoking the event*. Each time an event is invoked, MySQL processes the event action.

The *MySQL event scheduler* is responsible for invoking the events. This module is part of the MySQL database server. This scheduler continuously monitors whether an event needs to be invoked. The scheduler must be turned on to create events. For this, we use the system variable EVENT_SCHEDULER, which is turned on with the following statement:

```
SET GLOBAL EVENT_SCHEDULER = TRUE
```

It is turned off like this:

```
SET GLOBAL EVENT_SCHEDULER = FALSE
```

When the MySQL database server starts up, the scheduler can also be turned on immediately:

```
mysqld ... -event_scheduler=1
```

To illustrate when an event is invoked, we use an additional table in the following examples. In this table, the different events write rows to the event action.

Example 34.1: Create the EVENTS_INVOKED table to register the name and timestamp of each event invocation.

```
CREATE TABLE EVENTS_INVOKED
      (EVENT_NAME       VARCHAR(20) NOT NULL,
       EVENT_STARTED    TIMESTAMP NOT NULL)
```

We begin with examples of events that have a *single schedule*—events that are invoked only once.

Example 34.2: Create an event that starts immediately.

```
CREATE EVENT DIRECT
   ON SCHEDULE AT NOW()
   DO INSERT INTO EVENTS_INVOKED VALUES ('DIRECT', NOW())
```

Explanation: The single schedule is listed behind the specification ON SCHEDULE AT. This event is invoked only once, immediately after the event is created. So after the event has been registered, the MySQL event scheduler checks whether the event must be invoked. You can show the result of this event with a SELECT statement:

```
SELECT    *
FROM      EVENTS_INVOKED
WHERE     EVENT_NAME = 'DIRECT'
```

The result is:

```
EVENT_NAME  EVENT_STARTED
----------  -------------------
DIRECT      2006-06-27 15:36:15
```

Events are stored in the current database. We may qualify the names of events with a database name. The previous CREATE EVENT statement could have been formulated as follows:

```
CREATE EVENT TENNIS.DIRECT
   ON SCHEDULE AT NOW()
   DO INSERT INTO EVENTS_INVOKED VALUES ('DIRECT', NOW())
```

Example 34.3: Create an event that starts on December 31, 2010, at 11:00 a.m.

```
CREATE EVENT END2010
   ON SCHEDULE AT '2010-12-31 11:00:00'
   DO INSERT INTO EVENTS_INVOKED VALUES ('END2010', NOW())
```

The effect on the EVENTS_INVOKED table looks like this:

```
EVENT_NAME  EVENT_STARTED
----------  -------------------
END2010     2008-12-31 11:00:00
```

In the schedule of the END2010 event, a precise timestamp is specified. Any timestamp or date expression may be used here.

Example 34.4: Create an event that starts in exactly three days.

```
CREATE EVENT THREEDAYS
   ON SCHEDULE AT NOW() + INTERVAL 3 DAY
   DO INSERT INTO EVENTS_INVOKED VALUES ('THREEDAYS', NOW())
```

The effect on the EVENTS_INVOKED table looks like this:

```
EVENT_NAME  EVENT_STARTED
----------  -------------------
THREEDAYS   2006-06-30 15:50:15
```

Explanation: The value of the timestamp expression in the schedule is calculated and stored in the catalog. Instead of using the NOW function, we can also use the CURDATE function. Note that the event is invoked on the day indicated right after midnight.

Example 34.5: Create an event that starts next Sunday.

```
CREATE EVENT NEXT_SUNDAY
   ON SCHEDULE AT
      CASE DAYNAME(NOW())
         WHEN 'Sunday'    THEN NOW() + INTERVAL 7 DAY
         WHEN 'Monday'    THEN NOW() + INTERVAL 6 DAY
         WHEN 'Tuesday'   THEN NOW() + INTERVAL 5 DAY
         WHEN 'Wednesday' THEN NOW() + INTERVAL 4 DAY
         WHEN 'Thursday'  THEN NOW() + INTERVAL 3 DAY
         WHEN 'Friday'    THEN NOW() + INTERVAL 2 DAY
         WHEN 'Saturday'  THEN NOW() + INTERVAL 1 DAY
      END
   DO INSERT INTO EVENTS_INVOKED
         VALUES ('NEXT_SUNDAY',NOW())
```

The effect on the EVENTS_INVOKED table looks like this:

```
EVENT_NAME   EVENT_STARTED
----------   ------------------
NEXT_SUNDAY  006-07-02 11:26:12
```

Explanation: With the case expression and the DAYNAME function, we can determine the current day. If it is a Monday, for example, we add six days to the current date. The result is the date of the following Sunday. This example shows that the timestamp expression can be very complex—even scalar subqueries are allowed.

We can simplify the expression used in the previous example; however, it leads to an expression that is a little harder to understand:

```
CREATE EVENT NEXT_SUNDAY
   ON SCHEDULE AT
      NOW() + INTERVAL (8 - DAYOFWEEK(NOW())) DAY
   DO INSERT INTO EVENTS_INVOKED
         VALUES ('NEXT_SUNDAY',NOW())
```

Example 34.6: Create an event that starts tomorrow at 11:00 a.m.

```
CREATE EVENT MORNING11
   ON SCHEDULE AT TIMESTAMP(CURDATE() +
                            INTERVAL 1 DAY, '11:00:00')
   DO INSERT INTO EVENTS_INVOKED VALUES ('MORNING11', NOW())
```

The effect on the EVENTS_INVOKED table looks like this:

```
EVENT_NAME  EVENT_STARTED
----------  -------------
MORNING11   2006-06-29 11:00:00
```

Explanation: The `TIMESTAMP` function concatenates today's date with the time the event must be invoked.

The previous examples are all based on a nonrecurring schedule. Next we have examples that do use a recurring schedule. These are all events with one or more invocations.

Example 34.7: Create an event that starts directly and that is invoked every two hours until 11:00 p.m.

```
CREATE EVENT EVERY2HOUR
   ON SCHEDULE EVERY 2 HOUR
      STARTS NOW() + INTERVAL 3 HOUR
      ENDS   CURDATE() + INTERVAL 23 HOUR
   DO INSERT INTO EVENTS_INVOKED VALUES ('EVERY2HOUR', NOW())
```

Explanation: The EVERY2HOUR event is first invoked three hours after the event was created (`STARTS NOW() + INTERVAL 3 HOUR`). Then it is invoked again every two hours (`EVERY 2 HOUR`) until it is one hour before midnight of the current day (`ENDS '23:00:00'`).

If this event was created at exactly 3:00 p.m., it is invoked at 6:00 p.m., 8:00 p.m., and 10:00 p.m. After that, the event is inactive. If this event was created after 8:30 p.m., it would not be invoked at all. If the event was created at exactly 5:00 p.m., it would be invoked three times: at 5:00 p.m., 8:00 p.m., and 11:00 p.m. If an event was created at exactly the same time as the timestamp of the `ENDS` specification, this event would be invoked but only once.

Example 34.8: Create an event that starts tomorrow at 12:00 p.m. and is invoked every minute for six times.

```
CREATE EVENT SIXTIMES
   ON SCHEDULE EVERY 1 MINUTE
      STARTS TIMESTAMP(CURDATE() + INTERVAL 1 DAY,'12:00:00')
      ENDS   TIMESTAMP(CURDATE() + INTERVAL 1 DAY,'12:00:00')
             + INTERVAL 5 MINUTE
   DO INSERT INTO EVENTS_INVOKED
      VALUES ('SIXTIMES', NOW())
```

Explanation: This event is invoked six times: at 12:00 p.m., 12:01 p.m., 12:02 p.m., 12:03 p.m., 12:04 p.m., and 12:05 p.m. The sixth time, the event is invoked because the timestamp belonging to the last invocation is equal to the value of the ENDS specification—12:05 p.m. (on the same day).

Example 34.9: Create an event that starts on Sunday and continues the four following Sundays.

```
CREATE EVENT FIVESUNDAYS
   ON SCHEDULE EVERY 1 WEEK
      STARTS CASE DAYNAME(NOW())
         WHEN 'Sunday'    THEN NOW()
         WHEN 'Monday'    THEN NOW() + INTERVAL 6 DAY
         WHEN 'Tuesday'   THEN NOW() + INTERVAL 5 DAY
         WHEN 'Wednesday' THEN NOW() + INTERVAL 4 DAY
         WHEN 'Thursday'  THEN NOW() + INTERVAL 3 DAY
         WHEN 'Friday'    THEN NOW() + INTERVAL 2 DAY
         WHEN 'Saturday'  THEN NOW() + INTERVAL 1 DAY
      END
      ENDS CASE DAYNAME(NOW())
         WHEN 'Sunday'    THEN NOW()
         WHEN 'Monday'    THEN NOW() + INTERVAL 6 DAY
         WHEN 'Tuesday'   THEN NOW() + INTERVAL 5 DAY
         WHEN 'Wednesday' THEN NOW() + INTERVAL 4 DAY
         WHEN 'Thursday'  THEN NOW() + INTERVAL 3 DAY
         WHEN 'Friday'    THEN NOW() + INTERVAL 2 DAY
         WHEN 'Saturday'  THEN NOW() + INTERVAL 1 DAY
      END + INTERVAL 4 WEEK
   DO INSERT INTO EVENTS_INVOKED
      VALUES ('FIVESUNDAYS',NOW())
```

Explanation: Make sure that the end date is four weeks later, not five; otherwise, the event will be invoked six times.

Example 34.10: Create an event that is invoked every Sunday at 3:00 p.m., starting next Sunday and ending on the last Sunday of the current year.

```
CREATE EVENT SUNDAYS
   ON SCHEDULE EVERY 1 WEEK
      STARTS TIMESTAMP(CASE DAYNAME(NOW())
         WHEN 'Sunday'    THEN NOW()
         WHEN 'Monday'    THEN NOW() + INTERVAL 6 DAY
         WHEN 'Tuesday'   THEN NOW() + INTERVAL 5 DAY
         WHEN 'Wednesday' THEN NOW() + INTERVAL 4 DAY
         WHEN 'Thursday'  THEN NOW() + INTERVAL 3 DAY
         WHEN 'Friday'    THEN NOW() + INTERVAL 2 DAY
         WHEN 'Saturday'  THEN NOW() + INTERVAL 1 DAY
      END, '15:00:00')
      ENDS TIMESTAMP(
         CASE DAYNAME(CONCAT(YEAR(CURDATE()),'-12-31'))
         WHEN 'Sunday'    THEN
            CONCAT(YEAR(CURDATE()),'-12-31')
         WHEN 'Monday'    THEN
            CONCAT(YEAR(CURDATE()),'-12-31') - INTERVAL 1 DAY
         WHEN 'Tuesday'   THEN
            CONCAT(YEAR(CURDATE()),'-12-31') - INTERVAL 2 DAY
         WHEN 'Wednesday' THEN
            CONCAT(YEAR(CURDATE()),'-12-31') - INTERVAL 3 DAY
         WHEN 'Thursday'  THEN
            CONCAT(YEAR(CURDATE()),'-12-31') - INTERVAL 4 DAY
         WHEN 'Friday'    THEN
            CONCAT(YEAR(CURDATE()),'-12-31') - INTERVAL 5 DAY
         WHEN 'Saturday'  THEN
            CONCAT(YEAR(CURDATE()),'-12-31') - INTERVAL 6 DAY
       END, '15:00:00')
    DO INSERT INTO EVENTS_INVOKED VALUES ('SUNDAYS', NOW())
```

Example 34.11: Create an event that starts the first day of every month, beginning next month and ending on the last month of the current year.

```
CREATE EVENT STARTMONTH
   ON SCHEDULE EVERY 1 MONTH
      STARTS CURDATE() + INTERVAL 1 MONTH -
             INTERVAL (DAYOFMONTH(CURDATE()) - 1) DAY
      ENDS   TIMESTAMP(CONCAT(YEAR(CURDATE()),'-12-31'))
   DO INSERT INTO EVENTS_INVOKED
      VALUES ('STARTMONTH', NOW())
```

Example 34.12: Create an event that starts the first day of each quarter.

```
CREATE EVENT QUARTERS
   ON SCHEDULE EVERY 3 MONTH
      STARTS (CURDATE() - INTERVAL (DAYOFMONTH(CURDATE())
      - 1) DAY) - INTERVAL (MOD(MONTH(CURDATE()
      - INTERVAL (DAYOFMONTH(CURDATE()) - 1) DAY)+2,3)) MONTH
      + INTERVAL 3 MONTH
   DO INSERT INTO EVENTS_INVOKED VALUES ('QUARTERS', NOW())
```

Explanation: The rather complex timestamp expression determines the first day of the coming quarter. An ENDS specification is missing, so the event continues to be invoked until it is dropped.

Example 34.13: Create an event that starts on the last day of the year, beginning with the current year through the year 2025.

```
CREATE EVENT END_OF_YEAR
   ON SCHEDULE EVERY 1 YEAR
      STARTS ((NOW() - INTERVAL (DAYOFYEAR(NOW()) - 1) DAY)
                     + INTERVAL 1 YEAR)
                     - INTERVAL 1 DAY
      ENDS   '2025-12-31'
   DO INSERT INTO EVENTS_INVOKED VALUES ('END_OF_YEAR', NOW())
```

We can build a check into the body of an event. For example, a certain event may be invoked only if the number of rows in a table is less than 100 or if it is not a Monday.

Example 34.14: Create an event that is invoked on the last day of the year, beginning with the current year through the year 2025 (this is the same as in the previous example). However, the year 2020 must be skipped.

```
CREATE EVENT NOT2020
   ON SCHEDULE EVERY 1 YEAR
      STARTS ((NOW() - INTERVAL (DAYOFYEAR(NOW()) - 1) DAY)
                     + INTERVAL 1 YEAR)
                     - INTERVAL 1 DAY
      ENDS   '2025-12-31'
   DO BEGIN
         IF YEAR(CURDATE()) <> 2020 THEN
            INSERT INTO EVENTS_INVOKED
               VALUES ('NOT2020', NOW());
         END IF;
      END
```

Explanation: This event is invoked every year, including the year 2020, but in that year, the INSERT statement is not executed.

Suppose that the tennis club has an additional table that records the number of matches that a player has played each year.

Example 34.15: Create the table to store this data.

```
CREATE TABLE MATCHES_ANNUALREPORT
      (PLAYERNO     INTEGER NOT NULL,
       YEAR         INTEGER NOT NULL,
       NUMBER       INTEGER NOT NULL,
       PRIMARY KEY (PLAYERNO, YEAR),
       FOREIGN KEY (PLAYERNO) REFERENCES PLAYERS (PLAYERNO))
```

Example 34.16: Create the event that updates the MATCHES_ANNUALREPORT table every year.

```
CREATE EVENT YEARBALANCING
   ON SCHEDULE EVERY 1 YEAR
      STARTS ((NOW() - INTERVAL (DAYOFYEAR(NOW()) - 1) DAY)
                     + INTERVAL 1 YEAR)
                     - INTERVAL 1 DAY
   DO INSERT INTO MATCHES_ANNUALREPORT
      SELECT   PLAYERNO, YEAR, COUNT(*)
      FROM     MATCHES
      WHERE    YEAR(DATE) = YEAR(CURDATE())
      GROUP BY PLAYERNO, YEAR
```

Several rules apply when defining events:

- If two events need to be invoked at the same time, MySQL determines the order in which they are invoked. So we cannot make any assumptions concerning which event is invoked first. If you want to determine the order, you should ensure that one of the events is invoked one second later.
- For events with recurring schedules, the end date should not fall before the start date. MySQL will not accept that.
- The start time of an event with a recurring schedule and the invocation time of a nonrecurring event must always be in the present or in the future. If these times are in the past, MySQL will not accept the event.
- SELECT statements can be included in an event body. However, the results of these statements disappear, as if they have never been executed.

34.3 Properties of Events

For each event, several additional properties can be defined. The first property defines what happens to an event when it has been invoked for the last time. If nothing is specified, MySQL automatically removes the event. We can set this explicitly by specifying ON COMPLETION NOT PRESERVE. If we specify ON COMPLETION PRESERVE, MySQL will not remove the event after the last invocation.

Example 34.17: Create the event from Example 34.2 again; however, this time it should not be removed after the last invocation.

```
CREATE EVENT DIRECT
   ON SCHEDULE AT NOW()
   ON COMPLETION PRESERVE
   DO INSERT INTO EVENTS_INVOKED VALUES ('DIRECT', NOW())
```

Explanation: This event remains until the PRESERVE property is changed or until it is removed explicitly.

As with tables, an event definition can include a comment that is registered in the catalog.

Example 34.18: Create the event from Example 34.17, but now include a comment and then show the stored comment.

```
CREATE EVENT DIRECT_WITH_COMMENT
   ON SCHEDULE AT NOW()
   ON COMPLETION PRESERVE
   COMMENT 'This event starts directly'
   DO INSERT INTO EVENTS_INVOKED
      VALUES ('DIRECT_WITH_COMMENT', NOW())
```

After an event has been created, it is immediately active (or enabled). We can disable an event during its creation.

Example 34.19: Create the following event and make it inactive.

```
CREATE EVENT DIRECT_INACTIVE
   ON SCHEDULE AT NOW()
   ON COMPLETION PRESERVE
   DISABLE
   COMMENT 'This event is inactive'
   DO INSERT INTO EVENTS_INVOKED
      VALUES ('DIRECT_INACTIVE', NOW())
```

Explanation: This event will not be invoked. In fact, the scheduler completely skips the inactive events when deciding whether an event must be invoked. The event can become active again by using an ALTER EVENT statement.

34.4 Changing Events

An *ALTER EVENT statement* can change the definitions and properties of an event.

DEFINITION

```
<alter event statement> ::=
   ALTER EVENT [ <database name> . ] <event name>
      ON SCHEDULE <event schedule>
      [ RENAME TO <event name> ]
      [ ON COMPLETION [ NOT ] PRESERVE ]
      [ ENABLE | DISABLE ]
      [ COMMENT <alphanumeric literal> ]
      DO <sql statement>

<event schedule> ::=
   <single schedule> | <recurring schedule>

<single schedule> ::=
   AT <timestamp expression>

<recurring schedule> ::=
   EVERY <number> <time unit>
   [ STARTS <timestamp literal> ]
   [ ENDS <timestamp literal> ]
```

For example, by using an ALTER EVENT statement, we can make an event inactive and then active again. We can also change the name of an existing event or the entire schedule. However, when an event that has been defined with the property ON COMPLETION NOT PRESERVE is invoked for the last time, the event can no longer be changed—it simply does not exist anymore.

Example 34.20: Change the event from Example 34.11 to end on December 31, 2025.

```
ALTER EVENT STARTMONTH
   ON SCHEDULE EVERY 1 MONTH
      STARTS CURDATE() + INTERVAL 1 MONTH -
             INTERVAL (DAYOFMONTH(CURDATE()) - 1) DAY
      ENDS   TIMESTAMP('2025-12-31')
```

Example 34.21: Change the name of this event to FIRST_OF_THE_MONTH.

```
ALTER EVENT STARTMONTH
      RENAME TO FIRST_OF_THE_MONTH
```

Example 34.22: Make the event from Example 34.19 active again.

```
ALTER EVENT DIRECT_INACTIVE
      ENABLE
```

34.5 Removing Events

If an event is no longer needed, you can remove it with a *DROP EVENT statement.* With this statement, you do not have to wait until the last event invocation.

DEFINITION

```
<drop event statement> ::=
   DROP EVENT [ IF EXISTS ] [ <database name> . ] <event name>
```

Example 34.23: Remove the event called FIRST_OF_THE_MONTH.

```
DROP EVENT FIRST_OF_THE_MONTH
```

If the specification IF EXISTS is added and the event does not exist, MySQL does not return an error message.

34.6 Events and Privileges

To create, change, or remove an event, an SQL user should have the proper privileges. A special privilege on the database and user level has been introduced for this.

DEFINITION

```
<grant statement> ::=
   <grant event privilege statement>

<grant event privilege statement> ::=
   GRANT EVENT
   ON    [ <database name> . | * . ] *
   TO    <grantees>
   [ WITH GRANT OPTION ]

<grantees> ::=
   <user specification> [ , <user specification> ]...

<user specification> ::=
   <user name> [ IDENTIFIED BY [ PASSWORD ] <password> ]

<user name> ::=
   <name> | '<name>' | '<name>'@'<host name>'
```

Example 34.24: Give SAM the privilege to create events in the TENNIS database.

```
GRANT EVENT
ON    TENNIS.*
TO    SAM
```

As mentioned earlier, the properties and definition of each event is recorded in the catalog along with the user who created the event. This SQL user should have sufficient privileges for all SQL statements that are executed by an event call. For example, if an event action executes a `DELETE` statement on the PLAYERS table, the SQL user who creates the event must have the appropriate privileges.

34.7 Events and the Catalog

Event specifications are stored in the catalog table called INFORMATION_SCHEMA.EVENTS. Table 34.1 describes the columns of this table. A `SELECT`, `SHOW EVENT`, or `SHOW CREATE EVENT` statement can retrieve information from this catalog table.

TABLE 34.1 Description of the INFORMATION_SCHEMA.EVENTS Catalog Table

COLUMN NAME	EXPLANATION
EVENT_CATALOG	This column is not in use yet, so the value is always equal to the null value.
EVENT_SCHEMA	The name of the database to which the event belongs.
EVENT_NAME	The name of the event.
DEFINER	The name of the SQL user who created the event.
EVENT_BODY	The SQL statement that must be executed.
EVENT_TYPE	This column contains the value `ONE_TIME` (single schedule) or `RECURRING`.
EXECUTE_AT	The date and time that indicates when an event with a single schedule must be invoked.
INTERVAL_VALUE	For events with a recurring schedule, the length of the interval between two invocations is indicated here.
INTERVAL_FIELD	For events with a recurring schedule, the unit of the interval between two invocations is indicated here—for example `SECOND`, `HOUR`, or `DAY`.
SQL_MODE	The value of the system variable `SQL_MODE` at the moment the event was created or changed.
STARTS	The date and time the event with a recurring schedule is invoked first.
ENDS	The date and time the event with a recurring schedule is invoked last.
STATUS	This column contains the value `ENABLED` (active) or `DISABLED` (inactive).
ON_COMPLETION	This column contains the values `NOT PRESERVE` or `PRESERVE`.
CREATED	Date and time the event is created.
LAST_ALTERED	Date and time the event was changed last with an `ALTER EVENT` statement.
LAST_EXECUTED	Date and time the event was invoked last.
EVENT_COMMENT	The comment of the event.

Example 34.25: Show the statement to create the TOMORROW11 event; see Example 34.6.

```
SHOW CREATE EVENT TOMORROW11
```

The result is:

```
Event       sql_mode  Create Event
----------  --------  ----------------------------------------
TOMORROW11         ?  CREATE EVENT 'TOMORROW11' ON SCHEDULE AT
                      '2006-06-29 09:00:00' ON COMPLETION NOT
                      PRESERVE ENABLE DO INSERT INTO
                      EVENTS_INVOKED VALUES
                      ('TOMORROW11',NOW())
```

Part V

Programming with SQL

SQL can be used in two ways: *interactively* and *preprogrammed.* Preprogrammed SQL is used primarily in programs developed for end users who do not have to learn SQL statements, but who work with easy-to-use menus and screens instead.

Previous chapters have assumed interactive use of the language. *Interactive* means that statements are processed as soon as they are entered; with preprogrammed SQL, statements are included in a program that has been written in another programming language. Most products support, among others, the languages C, C++, Java, Visual Basic, PHP, Perl, and COBOL. These languages are known as *host languages.* When using preprogrammed SQL, the user cannot immediately see the results of the SQL statements; the *enveloping* program processes them. Most of the SQL statements discussed in the earlier chapters can be used in preprogrammed SQL. Apart from a few minor additions, preprogrammed SQL is the same as interactive SQL.

As an example of preprogrammed SQL, this part starts with Chapter 35, "MySQL and PHP," which covers how SQL statements can be included into PHP programs. Chapter 36, "Dynamic SQL with Prepared Statement," discusses dynamic SQL or prepared SQL statements. Chapter 37 then explains the concepts of transactions, savepoints, isolation levels, and repeatable reads, as well as how to roll back statements.

CHAPTER 35

MySQL and PHP

35.1 Introduction

This chapter contains examples of programs written in the programming language PHP, one of the most popular host languages used with MySQL; see, for example, [ATKI04].

Initially, the abbreviation PHP stood for Personal Home Page. Some prefer to use the recursive explanation: PHP Hypertext Preprocessor. Whatever it stands for, essentially PHP is a server-side scripting language to create web pages based upon HTML.

Rasmus Lerdorf wrote the first version of PHP in fall 1994. Since then, the features have been extended considerably, and thousands of web sites have already been created with this popular language.

A PHP programmer can choose from different call level interfaces (CLIs) to access a database from a PHP program. This chapter uses a CLI that was created specifically for MySQL, called MYSQL. Alternatives also exist; for example, one is an ODBC-like CLI.

We assume that you are familiar with the PHP programming language. We have made the examples as simple as possible to stress the functions used to access MySQL. You can embellish the programs yourself. We do not discuss every MYSQL function; after all, this book is about MySQL, not PHP. For the remaining functions, we refer to the many books and manuals about PHP.

35.2 Logging On to MySQL

Each program must start by logging on to the database server. Therefore, we begin there as well.

Example 35.1: Develop a PHP program that logs on to MySQL.

```
<HTML>
<HEAD>
<TITLE>Logging on</TITLE>
</HEAD>
<BODY>
<?php
$host = "localhost";
$user = "root";
$pass = "root";
$conn = mysql_connect($host, $user, $pass)
        or die ("<p>Logging on has not succeeded.</p>");
echo "<p>Logging on has succeeded.</p>\n";
mysql_close($conn);
?>
</BODY>
</HTML>
```

Explanation: This program contains HTML, PHP, and SQL statements. How and by whom are these statements processed? Or how will this program be processed? The program does not need to be compiled first. PHP is not a compiler, but an interpreter. The program is stored in a file or a page in a certain directory. Specifying the following URL in a web browser, such as FireFox, Microsoft's Internet Explorer, or Opera, requests the PHP page:

```
http://localhost/01_Logging on.php
```

The web server receives this URL in which the name of the requested PHP page occurs. Next, the web server passes the page unchanged to the PHP processor that starts to process the program. During the processing, PHP comes across function calls of the CLI, such as `MYSQL_CONNECT()`. PHP calls these functions that, in turn, call MySQL. The answers and error messages that MySQL produces are returned to the PHP processor. Finally, the PHP processor is ready and the obtained HTML page is returned to the web server as a result. The result of the program is the following HTML page:

```
<HTML>
<HEAD>
<TITLE>Logging on</TITLE>
</HEAD>
<BODY>
<p>Logging on has succeeded.</p>
</BODY>
</HTML>
```

In turn, the web server passes the HTML page to the browser that renders the page properly. The final result looks like this:

```
Logging on has succeeded.
```

Explanation: The first five lines of code in the program and the last two are pure HTML code. The PHP processor just passes this code to the web server. After that, three variables called `$host`, `$user`, and `$pass` are declared, and each is assigned a value. With the special function `MYSQL_CONNECT`, we log on to the database server. A connection is made with the database server. If anything goes wrong, the function `DIE()` is called to stop the program. The alphanumeric value of the parameter of the `DIE` function is still printed.

If the `MYSQL_CONNECT` function works, a message is displayed and the connection with the `MYSQL_CLOSE` function is closed.

35.3 Selecting a Database

The program in the previous section does not indicate which database to use because the program does not work with the database. If we want to access tables, we must make a database current; see Section 4.5. With interactive SQL, we use the `USE` statement to perform this task; with PHP, the `MYSQL_SELECT_DB` function is called.

Example 35.2: Extend the PHP program so that we can work with the TENNIS database.

```
<HTML>
<HEAD>
<TITLE>Current database</TITLE>
</HEAD>
<BODY>
<?php
$host = "localhost";
$user = "root";
$pass = "root";
$conn = mysql_connect($host, $user, $pass)
       or die ("<p>Logging on has not succeeded.\n");
echo "<p>Logging on has succeeded.\n";
$db = mysql_select_db("TENNIS")
      or die ("<br>Database unknown.\n");
echo "<br>TENNIS is the current database now.\n";
mysql_close($conn);
?>
</BODY>
</HTML>
```

The result is:

```
Logging on has succeeded.
TENNIS is the current database now.
```

Explanation: The call for the MYSQL_SELECT_DB function has been added here. The name of an existing database is the parameter in this function.

A program may call the MYSQL_SELECT_DB function more than once. Every time that happens, the current database changes.

35.4 Creating an Index

Now it is time to let the program do something. We begin by executing the simplest SQL statements: the DDL and DCL statements.

Example 35.3: Develop a PHP program that creates an index on the PLAYERS table.

```
<HTML>
<HEAD>
<TITLE>Create Index</TITLE>
</HEAD>
<BODY>
<?php
$host = "localhost";
$user = "root";
$pass = "root";
$conn = mysql_connect($host, $user, $pass)
        or die ("<p>Logging on has not succeeded.\n");
echo "<p>Logging on has succeeded.\n";
$db = mysql_select_db("TENNIS")
      or die ("<br>Database unknown.\n");
echo "<br>TENNIS is the current database now.\n";
$result = mysql_query("CREATE UNIQUE INDEX PLAY
                       ON PLAYERS (PLAYERNO)");
if (!$result)
{
   echo "<br>Index PLAY is not created!\n";
}
else
{
   echo "<br>Index PLAY is created!\n";
};
mysql_close($conn);
?>
</BODY>
</HTML>
```

Explanation: MySQL uses the function MYSQL_QUERY to process the SQL statement. Because the statement has no variables and is not a SELECT statement, the processing is simple. The only response returned is a message stating whether it has succeeded. This message is assigned to the variable $RESULT. If this value is equal to 0, the statement has been processed correctly.

MySQL does return a response when processing some DDL and DCL statements. For example, this could be the number of rows in the table on which the index is created. You can use the MYSQL_INFO function to retrieve the response.

Example 35.4: Develop a PHP program that creates an index on the PLAYERS table and then presents the response of MySQL.

```
<HTML>
<HEAD>
<TITLE>Create Index plus response</TITLE>
</HEAD>
<BODY>
<?php
$host = "localhost";
$user = "root";
$pass = "root";
$conn = mysql_connect($host, $user, $pass)
        or die ("<p>Logging on has not succeeded.\n");
echo "<p>Logging on has succeeded.\n";
$db = mysql_select_db("TENNIS")
      or die ("<br>Database unknown.\n");
echo "<br>TENNIS is the current database now.\n";
$result = mysql_query("CREATE UNIQUE INDEX PLAY
                       ON PLAYERS (PLAYERNO)");
if (!$result)
{
   echo "<br>Index PLAY is not created!\n";
}
else
{
   echo "<br>Index PLAY is created!\n";
};
echo "<br>mysql_info=".mysql_info($conn);
mysql_close($conn);
?>
</BODY>
</HTML>
```

The result is:

```
Logging on has succeeded.
TENNIS is the current database now.
Index PLAY is created!
mysql_info=Records: 14 Duplicates: 0 Warnings: 0
```

35.5 Retrieving Error Messages

If an SQL statement has not been processed correctly, it is often useful to know what went wrong. Has the statement been formulated incorrectly, or does the table not exist? The functions MYSQL_ERRNO and MYSQL_ERROR can retrieve this type of information.

Example 35.5: Develop a PHP program that reports the problem if something goes wrong when processing the CREATE INDEX statement.

```
<HTML>
<HEAD>
<TITLE>Error messages</TITLE>
</HEAD>
<BODY>
<?php
$host = "localhost";
$user = "root";
$pass = "root";
$conn = mysql_connect($host, $user, $pass)
        or die ("<p>Logging on has not succeeded.\n");
echo "<p>Logging on has succeeded.\n";
$db = mysql_select_db("TENNIS")
      or die ("<br>Database unknown.\n");
echo "<br>TENNIS is the current database now.\n";
$result = mysql_query("CREATE UNIQUE INDEX PLAY
                       ON PLAYERS (PLAYERNO)");
if (!$result)
{
   echo "<br>Index PLAY is not created!\n";
   $error_number = mysql_errno();
   $error_message = mysql_error();
   echo "<br>Fout: $error_number: $error_message\n";
}
else
{
   echo "<br>Index PLAY is created!\n";
}
mysql_close($conn);
?>
</BODY>
</HTML>
```

If the PLAY index already exists, the following result is presented:

```
Logging on has succeeded.
TENNIS is the current database now.
Index PLAY is not created!
Fout: 1061: Duplicate key name 'PLAY'
```

Explanation: The function MYSQL_ERRNO returns the error number and MYSQL_ERROR returns the descriptive text.

35.6 Multiple Connections Within One Session

We come across the term *session* frequently. When a program starts, a so-called session is actually started. When a program logs on to MySQL, a connection is made to MySQL. In many cases, a session consists of one connection, but not always. Programs can repeatedly close connections and then open others. Within one session, a switch is made from one connection to another; see the top of Figure 35.1. In this figure, the gray block at the top indicates a session. The session starts on the left and ends on the right. In this session, connection 1 is started with MySQL first. Then it is closed again, and connection 2 is started. Finally, connection 3 is started. The last two connections access the same database server, but maybe as other SQL users with other privileges.

Multiple connections can be open within one session simultaneously. In this case, for each SQL statement that is executed, you have to specify to which connection it belongs. Figure 35.1 shows how connections can be open simultaneously. In this example, connection 2 starts even before connection 1 ends.

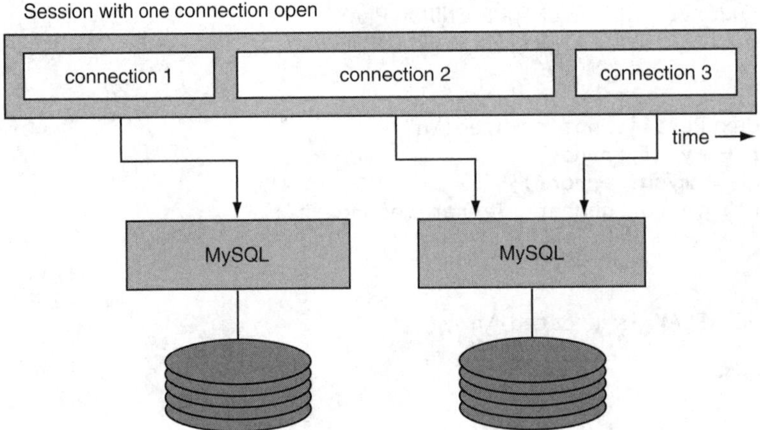

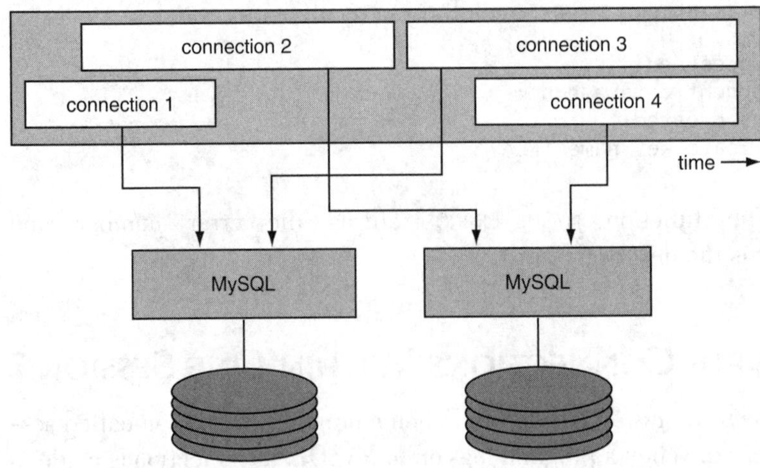

FIGURE 35.1 Sessions and connections

Example 35.6: Develop a PHP program that starts two connections.

```
<HTML>
<HEAD>
<TITLE>Two connections</TITLE>
</HEAD>
<BODY>
<?php
$host = "localhost";
$user = "root";
$pass = "root";
$conn1 = mysql_connect($host, $user, $pass)
         or die ("<p>Logging on has not succeeded.\n");
echo "<p>Logging on has succeeded.\n";
$host = "localhost";
$user = "BOOKSQL";
$pass = "BOOKSQLPW";
$conn2 = mysql_connect($host, $user, $pass)
         or die ("<p>Logging on has not succeeded.\n");
echo "<p>Logging on has succeeded.\n";
$db = mysql_select_db("TENNIS", $conn1)
      or die ("<br>Database unknown.\n");
echo "<br>Connection 1 is started.\n";
$db = mysql_select_db("TENNIS", $conn2)
      or die ("<br>Database unknown.\n");
echo "<br>Connection 2 is started.\n";
mysql_close($conn1);
mysql_close($conn2);
?>
</BODY>
</HTML>
```

Explanation: Two connections are made with the database server in this program. The first connection is for the user called root, and the second is for the user BOOKSQL. The host variables `$CONN1` and `$CONN2` contain identifiers of these connections. Because two connections are open now, we need to specify the connection for every MYSQL function, which is the last parameter for most functions. This is why we give the `MYSQL_SELECT_DB` function one of the host variables as a parameter.

35.7 SQL Statements with Parameters

Many SQL statements need parameters. Because PHP works with dynamic SQL, we could let PHP process the parameters itself, and MySQL would not be involved.

Example 35.7: Develop a PHP program that increases by 1 the number of sets won for a certain match.

```
<HTML>
<HEAD>
<TITLE>Parameters</TITLE>
</HEAD>
<BODY>
<?php
$host = "localhost";
$user = "root";
$pass = "root";
$conn = mysql_connect($host, $user, $pass)
        or die ("<p>Logging on has not succeeded.\n");
echo "<p>Logging on has succeeded.\n";
$db = mysql_select_db("TENNIS")
      or die ("<br>Database unknown.\n");
echo "<br>TENNIS is the current database now.\n";
$wnr = 22;
$result = mysql_query("UPDATE MATCHES
          SET WON = WON + 1 WHERE MATCHNO = $mno");
if (!$result)
{
   echo "<br>Update not executed!\n";
   $error_number = mysql_errno();
   $error_message = mysql_error();
   echo "<br>Error: $error_number: $error_message\n";
}
else
{
   echo "<br>WON column has increased for match $mno.\n";
}
mysql_close($conn);
?>
</BODY>
</HTML>
```

Explanation: The value 22 is assigned to the variable $MNO. PHP replaces the variable $MNO with that value. As a result, a complete SQL statement without host variables is delivered to MySQL.

35.8 SELECT Statement with One Row

When processing SELECT statements that return only one row, we use the function MYSQL_QUERY to process the statement, followed by the function MYSQL_FETCH_ASSOC to retrieve the row.

Example 35.8: Develop a PHP program that presents the number of players in the PLAYERS table.

```
<HTML>
<HEAD>
<TITLE>Query with a row</TITLE>
</HEAD>
<BODY>
<?php
$host = "localhost";
$user = "root";
$pass = "root";
$conn = mysql_connect($host, $user, $pass)
        or die ("<p>Logging on has not succeeded.\n");
echo "<p>Logging on has succeeded.\n";
$db = mysql_select_db("TENNIS")
      or die ("<br>Database unknown.\n");
echo "<br>TENNIS is the current database now.\n";
$query = "SELECT COUNT(*) AS NUMBER FROM PLAYERS";
$result = mysql_query($query)
          or die ("<br>Query is incorrect.\n");
$row = mysql_fetch_assoc($result)
       or die ("<br>Query had no result.\n");
echo "<br>The number of players ".$row['NUMBER']."\n";
mysql_close($conn);
?>
</BODY>
</HTML>
```

Explanation: After processing the MYSQL_QUERY function, MySQL stores the result of the SELECT statement somewhere. With the MYSQL_FETCH_ASSOC function, we can walk through that result row by row. The result is assigned to the variable $ROW. When we compare this process with stored procedures, the MYSQL_QUERY function is equal to the declaration and opening of a cursor. And with the MYSQL_FETCH_ASSOC function, we browse the cursor.

Because the result of a SELECT statement can contain multiple values, $ROW can have multiple values, too. $ROW is an associative array consisting of one element in which only the column name of the SELECT statement is used as the key value of the array. So to retrieve the number of players, we use the expression $row['NUMBER']. NUMBER is the name of the column; see the SELECT statement.

With the following piece of program, we create an associative array called $ROW consisting of three elements. The three elements are identified with the names NAME, TOWN, and STREET:

```
$result = mysql_query("SELECT NAME, TOWN, STREET
                       FROM PLAYERS WHERE PLAYERNO = 1");
$row = mysql_fetch_assoc($result)
```

35.9 SELECT Statement with Multiple Rows

If a SELECT statement can return multiple rows, we need to do a little more work to walk through the result row by row. We need cursors to browse the result row by row. A few different functions can be used here.

Example 35.9: Develop a PHP program that presents all player numbers sorted in descending order.

```
<HTML>
<HEAD>
<TITLE>SELECT statement with multiple rows</TITLE>
</HEAD>
<BODY>
<?php
$host = "localhost";
$user = "root";
$pass = "root";
$conn = mysql_connect($host, $user, $pass)
       or die ("<p>Logging on has not succeeded.\n");
echo "<p>Logging on has not succeeded.\n";
$db = mysql_select_db("TENNIS")
      or die ("<br>Database unknown.\n");
echo "<br>TENNIS is the current database now.\n";
$query = "SELECT PLAYERNO FROM PLAYERS ORDER BY 1 DESC";
$result = mysql_query($query)
          or die ("<br>Query is incorrect.\n");
if (mysql_num_rows($result) > 0)
{
   while ($row=mysql_fetch_assoc($result))
   {
      echo "<br>Player number ".$row['PLAYERNO']."\n";
   }
}
else
{
   echo "<br>No players found.\n";
}
mysql_free_result($result);
mysql_close($conn);
?>
</BODY>
</HTML>
```

Explanation: After the SELECT statement has been executed, we check whether the result contains rows. We use the MYSQL_NUM_ROWS function for this. This function has the host variable $RESULT as a parameter that determines the number of rows returned by the statement that are linked to that $QUERY variable. As long as rows are found, we use MYSQL_FETCH_ASSOC to walk through the result row by row. When no more rows exist, the WHILE statement stops along with the program.

As long as the PHP program runs, the result of the SELECT statement is kept in memory. If this result is no longer necessary, the MYSQL_FREE_RESULT function can release the occupied space; see the penultimate statement of the program. This is not required, but it is efficient, especially when many SELECT statements must be processed.

The function MYSQL_FETCH_ARRAY can replace MYSQL_FETCH_ASSOC, but then an additional parameter must be specified. If we specify MYSQL_ASSOC as an additional parameter, we get exactly the same result as with the MYSQL_FETCH_ASSOC function. On the other hand, if we use MYSQL_NUM, we can refer to the different values with sequence numbers. With MYSQL_BOTH, we can work with the column names and the sequence numbers.

So the following statement returns the same result as the one in the previous program:

```
while ($row=mysql_fetch_array($result, MYSQL_ASSOC))
```

The entire WHILE construct can also be written as follows:

```
while ($row=mysql_fetch_array($result, MYSQL_NUM))
{
   echo "<br>Player number ".$row[0].".\n";
}
```

Instead of using the MYSQL_FETCH_ARRAY function, you may use MYSQL_FETCH_ROW.

Example 35.10: Develop a PHP program that presents all player numbers sorted in descending order. Use the MYSQL_FETCH_ROW function.

```
<HTML>
<HEAD>
<TITLE>MYSQL_FETCH_ROW function</TITLE>
</HEAD>
<BODY>
<?php
$host = "localhost";
$user = "root";
$pass = "root";
$conn = mysql_connect($host, $user, $pass)
        or die ("<p>Logging on has not succeeded.\n");
echo "<p>Logging on has succeeded.\n";
$db = mysql_select_db("TENNIS")
      or die ("<br>Database unknown.\n");
echo "<br>TENNIS is the current database now.\n";
$query = "SELECT PLAYERNO FROM PLAYERS ORDER BY 1 DESC";
$result = mysql_query($query)
          or die ("<br>Query is incorrect.\n");
while ($row=mysql_fetch_row($result))
{
   echo "<br>Player number ".$row[0].".\n";
};
mysql_free_result($result);
mysql_close($conn);
?>
</BODY>
</HTML>
```

As with the MYSQL_FETCH_ARRAY function, we use sequence numbers (beginning at 0) to refer to the different column values. The advantage of the MYSQL_FETCH_ROW function is that we can use the MYSQL_DATA_SEEK function to jump directly to a certain row.

Example 35.11: Develop a PHP program that sorts all player numbers in descending order and presents only the fourth row.

```
<HTML>
<HEAD>
<TITLE>MYSQL_DATA_SEEK function</TITLE></HEAD>
<BODY>
<?php
$host = "localhost";
$user = "root";
$pass = "root";
$conn = mysql_connect($host, $user, $pass)
        or die ("<p>Logging on has not succeeded.\n");
echo "<p>Logging on has succeeded.\n";
```

```
$db = mysql_select_db("TENNIS")
      or die ("<br>Database unknown.\n");
echo "<br>TENNIS is the current database now.\n";
$query = "SELECT PLAYERNO FROM PLAYERS ORDER BY 1 DESC";
$result = mysql_query($query)
          or die ("<br>Query is incorrect.\n");
mysql_data_seek($result, 3);
$row=mysql_fetch_row($result);
echo "<br>Player number ".$row[0].".\n";
mysql_close($conn);
?>
</BODY>
</HTML>
```

Explanation: We invoke the MYSQL_DATA_SEEK function before the MYSQL_FETCH_ROW function. The first row contains the number 0, and the fourth row contains the number 3. If no fourth row exists, an error message is given.

The result of a SELECT statement can also be transformed to objects. In that case, we use the MYSQL_FETCH_OBJECT function.

Example 35.12: Develop a PHP program that presents all player numbers sorted in descending order. Use the MYSQL_FETCH_OBJECT function.

```
<HTML>
<HEAD>
<TITLE>Working with objects</TITLE>
</HEAD>
<BODY>
<?php
$host = "localhost";
$user = "root";
$pass = "root";
$conn = mysql_connect($host, $user, $pass)
        or die ("<p>Logging on has not succeeded.\n");
echo "<p>Logging on has succeeded.\n";
$db = mysql_select_db("TENNIS")
      or die ("<br>Database unknown.\n");
echo "<br>TENNIS is the current database now.\n";
$query = "SELECT PLAYERNO FROM PLAYERS ORDER BY 1 DESC";
$result = mysql_query($query)
          or die ("<br>Query is incorrect.\n");
while ($row=mysql_fetch_object($result))
{
   echo "<br>Player number ".$row->PLAYERNO.".\n";
};
mysql_free_result($result);
mysql_close($conn);
?>
</BODY>
</HTML>
```

35.10 SELECT Statement with Null Values

A SELECT statement can also return null values. We need to handle these null values in the PHP program separately. First, we check whether the result is a null value.

Example 35.13: Develop a PHP program that prints all league numbers and reports when a league number is equal to the null value.

```
<HTML>
<HEAD>
<TITLE>Query with null values</TITLE>
</HEAD>
<BODY>
<?php
$host = "localhost";
$user = "root";
$pass = "root";
$conn = mysql_connect($host, $user, $pass)
        or die ("<p>Logging on has not succeeded.\n");
echo "<p>Logging on has succeeded.\n";
$db = mysql_select_db("TENNIS")
      or die ("<br>Database unknown.\n");
echo "<br>TENNIS is the current database now.\n";
$query = "SELECT LEAGUENO FROM PLAYERS";
$result = mysql_query($query)
          or die ("<br>Query is incorrect.\n");
if (mysql_num_rows($result) > 0)
{
   while ($row=mysql_fetch_assoc($result))
   {
      if ($row['LEAGUENO'] === NULL)
      {
         echo "<br>Player number is unknown.\n";
      }
      else
      {
         echo "<br>Player number ".$row['LEAGUENO'].".\n";
      }
   }
}
else
{
   echo "<br>No players found.\n";
}
mysql_close($conn);
?>
</BODY>
</HTML>
```

Explanation: The condition (`$row['LEAGUENO'] === NULL`) determines whether the value of the LEAGUENO column is equal to the null value. The result looks like this:

```
Logging on has succeeded.
TENNIS is the current database now.
Player number 2411.
Player number 8467.
Player number is unknown.
Player number 2983.
Player number 2513.
Player number is unknown.
Player number is unknown.
Player number 1124.
Player number 6409.
Player number 1608.
Player number is unknown.
Player number 6524.
Player number 7060.
Player number 1319.
```

35.11 Querying Data About Expressions

You can use the `MYSQL_FETCH_FIELDS` function to query the characteristics of each expression in the `SELECT` clause of a `SELECT` statement.

Example 35.14: Develop a PHP program that retrieves the following information for each expression of a `SELECT` statement: name, data type, length, and an indication of whether the expression is a primary key.

```
<HTML>
<HEAD>
<TITLE>Characteristics of expressions</TITLE>
</HEAD>
<BODY>
<?php
$host = "localhost";
$user = "root";
$pass = "root";
$conn = mysql_connect($host, $user, $pass)
       or die ("<p>Logging on has not succeeded.\n");
echo "<p>Logging on has succeeded.\n";
$db = mysql_select_db("TENNIS")
      or die ("<br>Database unknown.\n");
echo "<br>TENNIS is the current database now.\n";
$query = "SELECT * FROM PLAYERS WHERE PLAYERNO = 27";
$result = mysql_query($query)
        or die ("<br>Query is incorrect.\n");
while ($field=mysql_fetch_field($result))
```

```
{
   echo "<br>".$field->name."  ".$field->type."  ".
        $field->max_length."  ".$field->primary_key."\n";
}
mysql_close($conn);
?>
</BODY>
</HTML>
```

Explanation: The variable `$FIELD` is an object with certain characteristics. In this example, some of these characteristics are queried; the result follows:

```
Logging on has succeeded.
TENNIS is the current database now.
PLAYERNO int 2 1
NAME string 5 0
INITIALS string 2 0
BRITH_DATE date 10 0
SEX string 1 0
JOINED int 4 0
STREET string 7 0
HOUSENO string 3 0
POSTCODE string 6 0
TOWN string 10 0
PHONENO string 10 0
LEAGUENO string 4 0
```

Special MySQL functions also can retrieve some of these characteristics.

Example 35.15: Develop a PHP program that retrieves the following information for each expression of a `SELECT` statement: name, data type, length, and table name.

```
<HTML>
<HEAD>
<TITLE>Characteristics of expressions</TITLE>
</HEAD>
<BODY>
<?php
$host = "localhost";
$user = "root";
$pass = "root";
$conn = mysql_connect($host, $user, $pass)
        or die ("<p>Logging on has not succeeded.\n");
echo "<p>Logging on has succeeded.\n";
$db = mysql_select_db("TENNIS")
       or die ("<br>Database unknown.\n");
echo "<br>TENNIS is the current database now.\n";
$query = "SELECT * FROM PLAYERS WHERE PLAYERNO = 27";
```

```
$result = mysql_query($query)
          or die ("<br>Query is incorrect.\n");
$exp = 0;
while ($field=mysql_fetch_field($result))
{
   echo "<br>Name=".mysql_field_name($result, $exp)."\n";
   echo "<br>Data type=".mysql_field_type($result, $exp)."\n";
   echo "<br>Length=".mysql_field_len($result, $exp)."\n";
   echo "<br>Table=".mysql_field_table($result, $exp)."\n";
   $exp += 1;
}
mysql_close($conn);
?>
</BODY>
</HTML>
```

Explanation: The MYSQL_FIELD_NAME function returns the name of an expression in a result, the MYSQL_FIELD_TYPE function gives the data type, the MYSQL_FIELD_LEN function supplies the maximum number of characters, and MYSQL_FIELD_NAME returns the table name. If the SELECT statement is a join, it can be useful to invoke this last function. For all these functions, the numbering of the expressions begins at 0.

35.12 Querying the Catalog

You can access catalog tables from PHP and link this data again to normal data.

Example 35.16: Develop a PHP program that returns the following information for each column of all tables from the sample database: number of different values, minimum value, and maximum value.

```
<HTML>
<HEAD>
<TITLE>Catalog tables</TITLE>
</HEAD>
<BODY>
<?php
$host = "localhost";
$user = "root";
$pass = "root";
$conn = mysql_connect($host, $user, $pass)
        or die ("<p>Logging on has not succeeded.\n");
echo "<p>Logging on has succeeded.\n";
$db = mysql_select_db("TENNIS")
      or die ("<br>Database unknown.\n");
echo "<br>TENNIS is the current database now.\n";
```

```
$query1 = "SELECT TABLE_NAME, COLUMN_NAME
           FROM   INFORMATION_SCHEMA.COLUMNS
           WHERE  TABLE_NAME IN
                  ('COMMITTEE_MEMBERS','PENALTIES','PLAYERS',
                   'TEAMS','MATCHES')
           ORDER BY TABLE_NAME, ORDINAL_POSITION";
$tables = mysql_query($query1)
          or die ("<br>Query1 is incorrect.\n");
while ($tablerow=mysql_fetch_assoc($tables))
{
   $query2 = "SELECT COUNT(DISTINCT ";
   $query2 .= $tablerow['COLUMN_NAME'].") AS A, ";
   $query2 .= "MIN( ".$tablerow['COLUMN_NAME'].") AS B, ";
   $query2 .= "MAX( ".$tablerow['COLUMN_NAME'].") AS C ";
   $query2 .= "FROM ".$tablerow['TABLE_NAME'];
   $columns = mysql_query($query2)
              or die ("<br>Query2 is incorrect.\n");
   $columnrow=mysql_fetch_assoc($columns);
   echo "<br>".$tablerow['TABLE_NAME'].".".
        $tablerow['COLUMN_NAME'].
        "  Different=".$columnrow['A'].
        "  Minimum=".$columnrow['B'].
        "  Maximum=".$columnrow['C']."\n";
   mysql_free_result($columns);
};
mysql_free_result($tables);
mysql_close($conn);
?>
</BODY>
</HTML>
```

The result is shown here:

```
Logging on has succeeded.
TENNIS is the current database now.
COMMITTEE_MEMBERS.PLAYERNO Different=7 Minimum=2 Maximum=112
COMMITTEE_MEMBERS.BEGIN_DATE Different=5 Minimum=1990-01-01 Maximum=1994-01-01

COMMITTEE_MEMBERS.END_DATE Different=4 Minimum=1990-12-31 Maximum=1993-12-31
COMMITTEE_MEMBERS.POSITION Different=4 Minimum=Chairman Maximum=Treasurer
PENALTIES.PAYMENTNO Different=8 Minimum=1 Maximum=8
PENALTIES.PLAYERNO Different=5 Minimum=6 Maximum=104
PENALTIES.PAYMENT_DATE Different=6 Minimum=1980-12-08 Maximum=1984-12-08
PENALTIES.AMOUNT Different=5 Minimum=25.00 Maximum=100.00
PLAYERS.PLAYERNO Different=14 Minimum=2 Maximum=112
PLAYERS.NAME Different=12 Minimum=Bailey Maximum=Wise
:
```

35.13 Remaining MYSQL Functions

Next we provide the descriptions of a few more MYSQL functions. Some contain pieces of code to show how they can be processed in the program.

integer mysql_affected_rows(resource connectiON): This function returns the number of rows processed with the last SQL statement belonging to the specified connection. If this is an UPDATE statement, for example, this function returns the number of rows updated.

```
$conn = mysql_connect($host, $user, $pass)
       or die ("<p>Logging on has not succeeded.\n");
echo "<p>Logging on has succeeded.\n";
$db = mysql_select_db("TENNIS")
      or die ("<br>Database unknown.\n");
echo "<br>TENNIS is the current database now.\n";
$result = mysql_query("UPDATE PENALTIES SET AMOUNT = AMOUNT + 10");
echo "<br>Number of updated rows is ".mysql_affected_rows($conn);
```

String mysql_client_encoding(resource connectiON): This function returns the character set that applies to the specified connection:

```
echo "<br>Character set=".mysql_client_encoding($conn)."\n";
```

The result is:

```
Character set=latin1_swedish_ci
```

Boolean mysql_field_seek(resource result, integer SEQUENCE NUMBER): This function makes a certain expression in the result of a SELECT statement current. It is the counterpart of the mysql_data_seek function. Next, the function mysql_fetch_field can be used to query the value of this expression.

STRING MYSQL_GET_CLIENT_INFO(): This function returns the version of the client library that is compiled to PHP:

```
echo "<br>Client info=".mysql_get_client_info()."\n";
```

The result is:

```
Client info=4.1.
```

STRING MYSQL_GET_HOST_INFO(resource connectiON): This function returns a description of the connection:

```
echo "<br>Client info=".mysql_get_host_info()."\n";
```

The result is:

```
Client info=localhost via TCP/IP
```

STRING MYSQL_GET_PROTO_INFO(resource connectiON): This function returns the version number of the protocol of the specified connection:

```
echo "<br>Protocol version=".mysql_get_proto_info()."\n";
```

The result is:

```
Protocol versie=10
```

STRING MYSQL_GET_SERVER_INFO(resource connectiON): This function returns the version number of the MySQL database server:

```
echo "<br>MySQL Version=".mysql_get_server_info()."\n";
```

The result is:

```
MySQL Version=5.0.7-beta-nt
```

INTEGER MYSQL_NUM_FIELDS(RESOURCE RESULT): This function returns the number of expressions in the result of a SELECT statement.

INTEGER MYSQL_NUM_ROWS(RESOURCE RESULT): This function returns the number of rows in the result of a SELECT statement.

CHAPTER 36

Dynamic SQL with Prepared Statement

36.1 Introduction

Since version 5.0, MySQL has supported *prepared* SQL statements (prepared SQL), sometimes called *dynamic SQL*. The opposite of dynamic SQL is, as might be expected, static SQL. This book has described static SQL so far. Each SQL statement is included in its entirety in a program or in a stored procedure or function or is entered with query tools such MySQL Query Browser, SQLyog, and WinSQL. The SQL statements are not built dynamically. For example, if we want to develop a stored procedure that has a table name as an input parameter and removes the specified table when the procedure is called, this is difficult to solve with static SQL. Of course, we could include a long and extensive `IF-THEN-ELSE` statement in the stored procedure that contains a separate `DROP TABLE` statement for each existing table, but the code of that stored procedure must be changed every time a new table is created. With dynamic SQL, we can build an SQL statement step by step, which offers new possibilities.

Three SQL statements together form dynamic SQL: `PREPARE`, `EXECUTE`, and `DEALLOCATE PREPARE`. In other words, with these statements, we can prepare SQL statements. The next sections cover their respective features.

36.2 Working with Prepared SQL Statements

If we process a static SQL statement, such as a `SELECT` statement, the following actions are performed in succession:

1. The grammar of the statement is checked for correctness.
2. The catalog is queried to check whether all the databases, tables, views, columns, and other database objects mentioned in the statement really exist.
3. Next, a check is performed to determine whether the SQL user has sufficient privileges to have the statement processed.
4. With statements such as SELECT and UPDATE, the optimizer is asked to determine the best processing strategy.
5. Finally, the SQL statement is processed.

With static SQL, these five actions form one big step. With dynamic SQL, this process can be split into two steps. With the *PREPARE statement,* we can execute actions 1, 2, 3, and 4. This is the *preparation* of the statement. Next, we use the EXECUTE statement to execute action 5; with this step, the statement is processed.

DEFINITION

```
<prepare statement> ::=
   PREPARE <statement name>
   FROM { <alphanumeric literal> | <user variable> }

<execute statement> ::=
   EXECUTE <statement name>
   [ USING <user variable> [ , <user variable> ]... ]

<deallocate prepare statement> ::=
   { DEALLOCATE | DROP } PREPARE <statement name>
```

Consider a simple example to illustrate this.

Example 36.1: Process the statement SELECT * FROM TEAMS in two steps.

```
PREPARE S1 FROM 'SELECT * FROM TEAMS'
```

Explanation: After this PREPARE statement, the SELECT statement is checked for grammar, MySQL checks whether the table TEAMS exists, and the optimizer is called to determine an efficient processing strategy. So the statement is prepared and ready to be processed. MySQL keeps all data required for that internally. Therefore, this PREPARE statement has no result. If we want to see the result of the SELECT statement, we must use an *EXECUTE statement*:

```
EXECUTE S1
```

The result is:

```
TEAMNO  PLAYERNO  DIVISION
------  --------  --------
     1         6  first
     2        27  second
```

Explanation: Multiple statements in a program or stored procedures can be prepared. For that reason, each prepared statement receives a unique name to distinguish it. To execute the final step, we only have to specify the name of the statement in the EXECUTE statement—in this case, S1.

An advantage of the two-step processing strategy is that if we want to execute a certain statement more than once, we have to execute the first four steps only once, which saves time.

The previous example used an alphanumeric literal to specify an SQL statement for the PREPARE statement. We can also specify a user variable. The previous PREPARE statement then can be built as follows:

```
SET @SQL_STATEMENT = 'SELECT * FROM TEAMS'

PREPARE S1 FROM @SQL_STATEMENT
```

This example prepared a SELECT statement, but most SQL statements may be prepared, including CREATE TABLE, DELETE, DROP INDEX, and UPDATE.

If a prepared statement will no longer be processed, it is better to remove it with a *DEALLOCATE PREPARE statement.*

Example 36.2: Remove the prepared statement S1.

```
DEALLOCATE PREPARE S1
```

Explanation: After this statement, the prepared statement S1 no longer can be processed.

Instead of using the term DEALLOCATE, you may use the term DROP to achieve the same result.

36.3 Prepared Statements with User Variables

Every time we execute the statement from Example 36.1, the same statement is processed. We can include user variables in a statement that needs to be prepared. This enables us to change the statements a little every time.

Example 36.3: Process the statement `SELECT * FROM TEAMS WHERE TEAMNO = @TNO` in two steps.

```
PREPARE S2 FROM 'SELECT * FROM TEAMS WHERE TEAMNO = @TNO'

SET @TNO = 1

EXECUTE S2
```

The result is:

```
TEAMNO  PLAYERNO  DIVISION
------  --------  --------
     1         6  first
```

In this example, if we change the value of the variable `TNO` before we use the `EXECUTE` statement, the result is different.

```
SET @TNO = 2

EXECUTE S2
```

The result is:

```
TEAMNO  PLAYERNO  DIVISION
------  --------  --------
     2        27  second
```

Of course, user variables may be used only where static SQL allows them. For example, the statement `DROP TABLE @TABLENAME` is not allowed.

36.4 Prepared Statements with Parameters

Another way to change a statement a little during the `EXECUTE` statement is to use parameters. Instead of user variables, we specify question marks, generally called *placeholders*.

Example 36.4: Process the statement SELECT * FROM TEAMS WHERE TEAMNO BETWEEN ? AND ? in two steps.

```
PREPARE S3 FROM
   'SELECT * FROM TEAMS WHERE TEAMNO BETWEEN ? AND ?'

SET @FROM_TNO = 1, @TO_TNO = 4

EXECUTE S3 USING @FROM_TNO, @TO_TNO

DEALLOCATE PREPARE S3
```

Explanation: MySQL prepares the SELECT statement first and then remembers that two parameters must be entered during the processing step. The EXECUTE statement has been extended with a USING clause in which the two user variables can be specified. To process the SELECT statement, the values of the user variables are filled in on the positions of the placeholders.

When you are working with parameters, it is important to remember that the number of question marks (or the number of placeholders) in the prepared statement must equal the number of user variables specified in the USING clause of the EXECUTE statement.

This method of working does not offer additional features over the method discussed in the previous section. However, more SQL products support this method than the one with the user variables.

36.5 Prepared Statements in Stored Procedures

As mentioned, prepared SQL statements may be used within stored procedures, stored functions, and events. Because of this, any SQL statement can be built dynamically within a stored procedure. SQL statements can even be passed as parameters. Consider examples of both.

Example 36.5: Develop a stored procedure that removes a certain table. The name of the table to remove must be passed as a parameter.

```
CREATE PROCEDURE DROP_TABLE
   (IN TABLENAME VARCHAR(64))
BEGIN
   SET @SQL_STATEMENT = CONCAT('DROP TABLE ', TABLENAME);
   PREPARE S1 FROM @SQL_STATEMENT;
   EXECUTE S1;
   DEALLOCATE PREPARE S1;
END
```

Explanation: In the SET statement, the desired DROP TABLE statement is built, the PREPARE statement is used to prepare the DROP TABLE, and the DROP TABLE is run with the EXECUTE statement. Without using prepared SQL, this stored procedure would not have been possible.

With the present implementation of prepared SQL, however, the results of prepared SELECT statements cannot be fetched row by row with a cursor. We can prepare and process a SELECT statement, but the result is sent directly to the calling program; we cannot pick it up within the stored procedure. Nevertheless, you can get around this limitation to a certain extent by using temporary tables.

Example 36.6: Develop a stored procedure that has a SELECT statement as parameter and uses a cursor to count the number of rows in the result of that SELECT statement.

```
CREATE PROCEDURE DYNAMIC_SELECT
   (IN  SELECT_STATEMENT VARCHAR(64),
    OUT NUMBER_OF_ROWS INTEGER)
BEGIN
   DECLARE FOUND BOOLEAN DEFAULT TRUE;
   DECLARE VAR1,VAR2,VAR3 VARCHAR(100);
   DECLARE C_RESULT CURSOR FOR
      SELECT * FROM SELECT_TABLE;
   DECLARE CONTINUE HANDLER FOR NOT FOUND
      SET FOUND = FALSE;
   SET @CREATE_STATEMENT =
      CONCAT('CREATE TEMPORARY TABLE SELECT_TABLE AS (',
             SELECT_STATEMENT, ')');
   PREPARE S1 FROM @CREATE_STATEMENT;
   EXECUTE S1;
   DEALLOCATE PREPARE S1;
   SET NUMBER_OF_ROWS = 0;
   OPEN C_RESULT;
   FETCH C_RESULT INTO VAR1, VAR2, VAR3;
   WHILE FOUND DO
      SET NUMBER_OF_ROWS = NUMBER_OF_ROWS + 1;
      FETCH C_RESULT INTO VAR1, VAR2, VAR3;
   END WHILE;
   CLOSE C_RESULT;
   DROP TEMPORARY TABLE SELECT_TABLE;
END

CALL DYNAMIC_SELECT('SELECT PAYMENTNO, PAYMENT_DATE, PLAYERNO
                     FROM PENALTIES', @NUMBER_OF_ROWS)

SELECT @NUMBER_OF_ROWS
```

Explanation: The first SET statement converts the SELECT statement into a CREATE TEMPORARY TABLE statement. With the PREPARE and EXECUTE statements, the new CREATE statement is processed. The result of the SELECT statement thus is assigned to the created, temporary table. Next, we have a cursor with which we can browse the rows of the temporary table. A limitation of this stored procedure is that the number of expressions in the SELECT clause of the SELECT statement must be equal to three. The reason is that three variables have been defined in the FETCH statement.

Obviously, we do not really need a cursor in this stored procedure; we could have added a COUNT function to the SELECT clause. Still, the example shows that it is possible to work with prepared statements in combination with cursors.

Prepared or dynamic SQL statements in combination with stored procedures form an interesting addition to SQL: They make it possible to develop very general stored procedures that will simplify repetitive activities. In short, prepared SQL statements are an enrichment of SQL.

CHAPTER 37

Transactions and Multiuser Usage

37.1 Introduction

So far in this book, we have assumed that you are the only user of the database. If you do the examples and exercises at home, that assumption is probably correct. But if you work with MySQL in your company, for example, the odds are good that you share the database with many other users. We call this *multiuser* usage as opposed to *single-user* usage. In a multiuser environment, you should not be aware that other users are accessing the database concurrently because MySQL hides this from you as much as possible.

The following question might arise: What happens if I access a row that is already in use by someone else? This chapter answers that question. We start with a concept that forms the basis of multiuser usage: the *transaction* (also called *unit of work*). We also discuss the concepts *savepoint, lock, deadlock,* and *isolation level,* and we consider the `LOCK TABLE` statement.

Not all storage engines support transactions; for example, `InnoDB` and `BDB` do, but `MyISAM` and `MEMORY` do not. Therefore, this chapter assumes that you created the tables with one of the storage engines that does support transactions.

This chapter looks inside MySQL. If that does not interest you, you can skip this chapter. For those who will develop real-life applications with MySQL, we recommend studying this chapter carefully.

37.2 What Is a Transaction?

What exactly is a *transaction?* This book defines a transaction as a set of SQL statements that are entered by one user and ended by specifying whether all changes are to be made permanent or rolled back (or undone). By "change," we mean each UPDATE, DELETE, and INSERT statement. SQL statements entered by different users cannot belong to the same transaction. The end of this section explains why we might want to undo changes.

Many products for interactive SQL are set up so that each SQL statement is seen as a complete transaction and each transaction (that is, individual update) is automatically made permanent. This mode of working is called *autocommit.* The user can undo changes only if he or she executes compensating changes. For example, if rows are added with an INSERT statement, this change can be undone only by executing one or more DELETE statements. However, we can turn off this automatic committing of transactions.

As an illustration, if you use WinSQL as a product for interactive SQL, you can turn off automatic commit as follows. When a new connection is created, the check mark in the Autocommit Transactions box must be removed; see Figure 37.1. The user is now responsible for ending the transactions. In other products, autocommit must be turned off in another way.

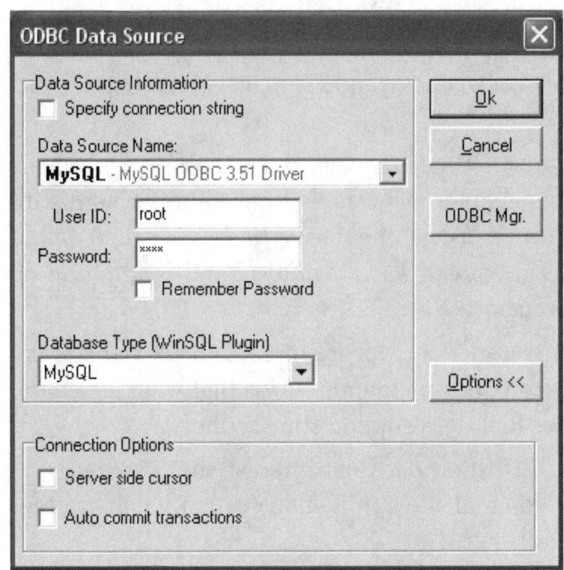

FIGURE 37.1 Turning off autocommit

However, MySQL does not settle for that. When a session is started in MySQL, the AUTOCOMMIT system variable is normally turned on. An SQL statement must be used to turn it off. The following statement turns off autocommit:

```
SET @@AUTOCOMMIT = 0
```

When autocommit must be turned on again, you issue this statement:

```
SET @@AUTOCOMMIT = 1
```

After autocommit has been turned off, a transaction can consist of multiple SQL statements, and you must indicate the end of each transaction. Two separate SQL statements accomplish this. In the next example, we illustrate how this works.

Example 37.1: Delete all penalties of player 44.

```
DELETE
FROM     PENALTIES
WHERE    PLAYERNO = 44
```

The effect of this statement becomes apparent when you issue the following SELECT statement:

```
SELECT   *
FROM     PENALTIES
```

The result is:

```
PAYMENTNO  PLAYERNO  PAYMENT_DATE  AMOUNT
---------  --------  ------------  ------
        1         6  1980-12-08    100.00
        3        27  1983-09-10    100.00
        4       104  1984-12-08     50.00
        6         8  1980-12-08     25.00
        8        27  1984-11-12     75.00
```

Three rows have been deleted from the table. However, the change is not yet permanent (even though it looks that way) because autocommit has been turned off. The user (or application) has a choice now: The change can be undone with the SQL statement *ROLLBACK* or made permanent with the *COMMIT statement.*

DEFINITION

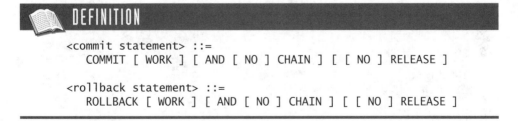

```
<commit statement> ::=
   COMMIT [ WORK ] [ AND [ NO ] CHAIN ] [ [ NO ] RELEASE ]

<rollback statement> ::=
   ROLLBACK [ WORK ] [ AND [ NO ] CHAIN ] [ [ NO ] RELEASE ]
```

Let us choose the first option and use the following statement:

```
ROLLBACK WORK
```

Explanation: If we repeat the `SELECT` statement used previously, it returns the entire PENALTIES table. The three deleted rows appear in the result again. If we wanted to make the change permanent, we should have used the `COMMIT` statement:

```
COMMIT WORK
```

This statement permanently deletes the three rows from the table. We can omit the word `WORK` because it does not affect the processing.

`COMMIT` statements make the changes permanent, and `ROLLBACK` statements undo them. Now the question is, which changes are rolled back? Is it only the last change or everything from the moment you started the application? To answer this, we return to the concept of a transaction. As previously mentioned, a transaction is a set of SQL statements. For example, the earlier `DELETE` and `SELECT` statements form a (small) transaction. `COMMIT` and `ROLLBACK` statements always relate to the so-called *current* transaction. In other words, these statements relate to all SQL statements executed during the current transaction. Now the question is, how do we mark the beginning and end of a transaction? For now, we assume that the beginning of a transaction cannot be marked explicitly (we return to this subject in Section 37.10). The first SQL statement executed in an application is considered to be the beginning of the first transaction. The end of a transaction is marked by using a `COMMIT` or `ROLLBACK` statement. Therefore, an SQL statement that follows a `COMMIT` or `ROLLBACK` statement is the first statement of the new current transaction.

Example 37.2: To illustrate these concepts, see the following series of statements that are entered consecutively. It is not important whether these statements are entered interactively (with MySQL, for example) or are embedded within a host language program:

1. `INSERT ...`
2. `DELETE ...`
3. `ROLLBACK WORK`
4. `UPDATE ...`
5. `ROLLBACK WORK`
6. `INSERT ...`
7. `DELETE ...`
8. `COMMIT WORK`
9. `UPDATE ...`
10. `end of program`

Explanation of the previous statements:

Lines 1–2	These two changes are not yet permanent.
Line 3	A ROLLBACK statement is executed. All changes of the current transaction (lines 1–2) are undone.
Line 4	This change is not yet permanent. Because this statement follows a ROLLBACK statement, a new transaction is started.
Line 5	A ROLLBACK statement is executed. All changes of the current transaction (line 4) are undone.
Lines 6–7	These two changes are not yet permanent. Because the statement on line 6 follows a ROLLBACK statement, a new transaction is started.
Line 8	A COMMIT statement is executed. All changes of the current transaction (lines 6–7) become permanent.
Line 9	This change is not yet permanent. Because this statement follows a COMMIT statement, a new transaction is started.
Line 10	Here the program is ended. All changes of the current transaction are undone—in this case, the change on line 9.

When a program stops without marking the end of a transaction, MySQL automatically executes a ROLLBACK statement. However, we advise that you always make the last SQL statement executed by a program a COMMIT or ROLLBACK statement.

Why would we want to undo transactions? This question can be formulated in another way: Why not always execute a COMMIT statement immediately after each change? Two main reasons exist. First, something can go wrong while processing SQL statements. For example, when you add new data, the database might become full, the computer may break down during the processing of an SQL statement, or a division by zero might occur during a calculation. Imagine that one of these problems occurs when you process one of the statements in the next example.

Example 37.3: Delete all data for player 6. We assume that no foreign keys have been defined.

```
DELETE FROM PLAYERS WHERE PLAYERNO = 6

DELETE FROM PENALTIES WHERE PLAYERNO = 6

DELETE FROM MATCHES WHERE PLAYERNO = 6

DELETE FROM COMMITTEE_MEMBERS WHERE PLAYERNO = 6

UPDATE TEAMS SET PLAYERNO = 83 WHERE PLAYERNO = 6
```

Five statements are required to remove all the information about a particular player: four DELETE statements and one UPDATE statement. In the last statement, player 6 is not removed from the TEAMS table, but is instead replaced by player 83 because player 6 can no longer be captain (because he no longer occurs in the PLAYERS table). A new captain must be registered as well because the PLAYERNO column in the TEAMS table is defined as NOT NULL. If you use a DELETE statement instead of an UPDATE statement, data about the team captained by player 6 will also be deleted, and that is not what you intended. These five changes together form a unit and must be handled as one transaction. Imagine that the third DELETE statement goes wrong. At that moment, two changes of the transaction have been executed and three have not. The first two changes cannot be undone. In other words, the MATCHES and TEAMS tables contain data about a player who does not exist in the PLAYERS table, which is an unwanted situation. Either all five changes must be executed or none must be. Therefore, we must be able to undo the changes that have already been carried out.

The second reason concerns the user's own mistakes. Imagine that a user changes a large amount of data in different tables about a particular player and discovers later that he chose the wrong player. He must be able to roll back these changes. Here the ROLLBACK statement can be useful.

In MySQL, statements that change the catalog, such as CREATE TABLE, ALTER FUNCTION, GRANT, and DROP INDEX, cannot be undone. Before and after processing such a statement, MySQL automatically executes a COMMIT statement. This type of statement therefore ends any current transaction. Turning autocommit on or off has no effect.

The COMMIT and ROLLBACK statements may end with the term RELEASE. This ends the transaction and also the connection with MySQL. As a result, the application can no longer access the database—a new connection must be established. Specifying NO RELEASE guarantees that the connection remains.

The system variable called *COMPLETION_TYPE* plays an important role here. This variable indicates how transactions must be ended. If its value is equal to 2, MySQL converts every COMMIT and ROLLBACK to COMMIT RELEASE and ROLLBACK RELEASE, respectively. If we do not want that, we need to add NO RELEASE to these statements. If COMPLETION_TYPE is equal to 0, then NO RELEASE is taken by default.

You can use the following SHOW statement to query the value of this system variable:

```
SHOW GLOBAL VARIABLES LIKE 'COMPLETION_TYPE'
```

As mentioned earlier, if a transaction is ended, a new transaction starts only at the next SQL statement. However, if you add AND CHAIN, the new transaction starts immediately. The new transaction also receives all the properties of the ended transaction (this is especially relevant for the isolation level; see Section 37.10). But this does not hold true for AND NO CHAIN. If the COMPLETION_TYPE system parameter is equal to 1, then AND NO CHAIN is the standard. When the value is equal to 1, then AND CHAIN is the standard.

Exercise 37.1: For the following series of statements, determine which will become permanent.

1. SELECT ...
2. INSERT ...
3. COMMIT WORK
4. ROLLBACK WORK
5. DELETE ...
6. DELETE ...
7. ROLLBACK WORK
8. INSERT ...
9. COMMIT WORK
10. end of program

37.3 Starting Transactions

The first SQL statement of an application or the first SQL statement after a COMMIT or ROLLBACK starts a new transaction. This is called an implicit start of a transaction. However, it is possible to start a transaction explicitly with the *START TRANSACTION statement.*

DEFINITION

```
<start transaction statement> ::=
   START TRANSACTION
```

Example 37.4: Rewrite Example 37.2 to explicitly start transactions.

1. START TRANSACTION
2. INSERT ...
3. DELETE ...
4. ROLLBACK WORK

5. START TRANSACTION
6. UPDATE ...
7. ROLLBACK WORK
8. START TRANSACTION
9. INSERT ...
10. DELETE ...
11. COMMIT WORK
12. START TRANSACTION
13. UPDATE ...
14. end of program

A `START TRANSACTION` statement automatically leads to a `COMMIT` of the changes that are not permanent yet. In addition, the autocommit is turned off. The `SET AUTOCOMMIT` statement is therefore not required. If the transaction is ended, the value of the `AUTOCOMMIT` variable is reset to the old value, regardless of what it was.

The statement *`BEGIN WORK`* may also be used in place of `START TRANSACTION`. However, the `START TRANSACTION` statement is preferable because many other SQL products support it.

DEFINITION

```
<begin work statement> ::=
   BEGIN WORK
```

37.4 Savepoints

In the previous sections, we discussed how to undo complete transactions. It is also possible to undo only a part of a current transaction by using *savepoints*.

DEFINITION

```
<savepoint statement> ::=
   SAVEPOINT <savepoint name>
```

To use savepoints, we must extend the definition of the `ROLLBACK` statement:

DEFINITION

```
<rollback statement> ::=
   ROLLBACK [ WORK ] [ AND [ NO ] CHAIN ] [ [ NO ] RELEASE ]
   [ TO SAVEPOINT <savepoint name> ]
```

See the next example to illustrate this functionality.

```
1.  UPDATE ...
2.  INSERT ...
3.  SAVEPOINT S1
4.  INSERT ...
5.  SAVEPOINT S2
6.  DELETE ...
7.  ROLLBACK WORK TO SAVEPOINT S2
8.  UPDATE ...
9.  ROLLBACK WORK TO SAVEPOINT S1
10. UPDATE ...
11. DELETE ...
12. COMMIT WORK
```

Explanation of the previous statements:

Lines 1–2	These two changes are not yet permanent.
Line 3	A savepoint is defined with the name `S1`.
Line 4	This change is not yet permanent.
Line 5	A savepoint is defined with the name `S2`.
Line 6	This change is not yet permanent.
Line 7	A `ROLLBACK` is issued. However, not all changes are undone—only those performed *after* savepoint `S2` (the change on line 6). The changes on lines 1 and 2 are not yet permanent but are still present.
Line 8	This change is not yet permanent.

Line 9	A ROLLBACK to savepoint S1 is entered. All changes performed *after* savepoint S1 are undone—these are the changes on lines 4 and 8.
Lines 10–11	These two changes are not yet permanent.
Line 12	All nonpermanent changes are made permanent—these are the changes on lines 1, 2, 10, and 11.

When a change is undone to a certain savepoint, only the last changes of the current transaction can be undone.

Exercise 37.2: For the following series of statements, determine which will become permanent.

1. SELECT ...
2. SAVEPOINT S1
3. INSERT ...
4. COMMIT WORK
5. INSERT ...
6. SAVEPOINT S1
7. DELETE ...
8. ROLLBACK WORK TO SAVEPOINT S1
9. DELETE ...
10. SAVEPOINT S2
11. DELETE ...
12. ROLLBACK WORK TO SAVEPOINT S1
13. COMMIT WORK
14. end of program

37.5 Stored Procedures and Transactions

Within stored procedures, all the well-known transaction-oriented statements can be used, such as COMMIT, ROLLBACK, and START TRANSACTION. A transaction does not begin with the start of a stored procedure, nor does it stop with the end of it. For transactions, MySQL does not see the difference between SQL statements delivered by the applications and those delivered by the stored procedures. This means, for example, that when certain changes of an application are not permanent yet and a stored procedure is called that also executes some changes, all changes are considered part of the current transaction. It also means that if a stored procedure sends a COMMIT statement and there are still nonpermanent changes, they also are made permanent.

Example 37.5: Develop a stored procedure that adds a new team.

```
CREATE PROCEDURE NEW_TEAM ()
BEGIN
   INSERT INTO TEAMS VALUES (100,27,'first');
END
```

Imagine that the application executes the following statements:

```
SET AUTOCOMMIT = 1

START TRANSACTION

INSERT INTO TEAMS VALUES (200,27,'first')

CALL NEW_TEAM()

ROLLBACK WORK
```

The ROLLBACK statement is now responsible for removing the row entered with the INSERT statement and also for removing the row added by the stored procedures.

37.6 Problems with Multiuser Usage

Imagine that you have removed all rows from the PENALTIES table in a transaction, but you have not yet ended the transaction. What will the other users see if they query the PENALTIES table? Will they see an empty table, or will they still see all the original rows? Are they allowed to see the changes that you have not yet made permanent? These problems are comparable to the problems of a policeman at a crossing. Whatever the policeman does and however he moves his arms, he must ensure that two cars do not use the crossing at the same time at the same place. MySQL (the policeman) must ensure that two users (the cars) do not access the same data (the crossing) simultaneously in the wrong way.

The problem described here is just one of the possible problems due to the effects of multiuser usage, but there are more. This section highlights four of the best-known problems. For more detailed descriptions and other problems, we refer to [BERN97] and [GRAY93].

37.6.1 Dirty Read or Uncommitted Read

The problem when one SQL users sees data that another user has not yet committed is called a *dirty read* or *uncommitted read.*

Example 37.6: Assume the following series of events that are entered consecutively.

1. User U_1 wants to increase the amount of the penalty with payment number 4 by $25. For this, he uses the following UPDATE statement:

```
UPDATE    PENALTIES
SET       AMOUNT = AMOUNT + 25
WHERE     PAYMENTNO = 4
```

2. Before U_1 ends the transaction with a COMMIT statement, user U_2 accesses the same penalty with the following SELECT statement and sees the updated amount:

```
SELECT    *
FROM      PENALTIES
WHERE     PAYMENTNO = 4
```

3. U_1 rolls back the UPDATE statement with a ROLLBACK statement.

The result is that U_2 has seen data that was never "committed." In other words, he saw data that never even existed. The SELECT statement that U_2 executed is called a dirty read. User U_2 has seen "dirty" data.

37.6.2 Nonrepeatable Read or Nonreproducible Read

A special version of the dirty read is the *nonrepeatable read, nonreproducible read,* or *inconsistent read.* Here a user reads partly dirty and partly clean data and combines it. The user is not aware of the fact that this result is based upon data that is only partly clean.

Example 37.7: The following events are entered consecutively.

1. With the following SELECT statement, user U_1 retrieves all players resident in Stratford and writes their player numbers on a piece of paper:

```
SELECT    PLAYERNO
FROM      PLAYERS
WHERE     TOWN = 'Stratford'
```

The result is 6, 83, 2, 7, 57, 39, and 100. Then U_1 starts a new transaction.

2. A few seconds later, user U_2 changes the address of player 7 (who lives in Stratford) with the following UPDATE statement:

```
UPDATE   PLAYERS
SET      TOWN = 'Eltham'
WHERE    PLAYERNO = 7
```

3. Next, user U_2 ends the transaction with a COMMIT statement.
4. Now user U_1 queries one by one the addresses of the players that were written on the piece of paper, using the following SELECT statement, and prints them on labels:

```
SELECT   PLAYERNO, NAME, INITIALS,
         STREET, HOUSENO, POSTCODE, TOWN
FROM     PLAYERS
WHERE    PLAYERNO IN (6, 83, 2, 7, 57, 39, 100)
```

The result of these two changes is that user U_1 also prints a label for player 7 because he assumed that player 7 still lived in Stratford. The second SELECT statement in the same transaction does not give the same picture of the database. The result of the first SELECT statement cannot be reproduced, which is not desirable, of course.

37.6.3 Phantom Read

The following problem is known as a *phantom read*.

Example 37.8: The following events are again entered consecutively.

1. With the following SELECT statement, user U_1 looks for all players residing in Stratford:

```
SELECT   PLAYERNO
FROM     PLAYERS
WHERE    TOWN = 'Stratford'
```

   The result is 6, 83, 2, 7, 57, 39, and 100. However, user U_1 does not end the transaction.
2. Sometime later, user U_2 adds a new player who lives in Stratford and ends the transaction with a COMMIT statement.
3. User U_1 sees one more row when he executes the same SELECT statement: the row user U_2 entered.

This means that the second SELECT statement in the same transaction (similar to the last example) does not present the same picture of the database. The difference between a phantom read and a nonrepeatable read is that, with the former, new data becomes available, and with the latter, data is changed.

37.6.4 Lost Update

The final problem that we discuss is called a *lost update*, in which the change of one user overwrites that of another.

Example 37.9: The following events are entered consecutively again.

1. User U_1 wants to increase the amount of the penalty with payment number 4 by $25. First, he queries the penalty amount with a SELECT statement (a transaction starts). The penalty appears to be $50.
2. A few seconds later, user U_2 wants to increase the amount of the penalty with payment number 4 by $30. He also queries the current value with a SELECT statement and sees $50. A second transaction begins here.
3. User U_1 executes the following UPDATE statement (notice the SET clause):

```
UPDATE    PENALTIES
SET       AMOUNT = AMOUNT + 25
WHERE     PAYMENTNO = 4
```

4. Next, user U_1 ends his transaction with a COMMIT statement.
5. User U_2 executes his UPDATE statement (notice the SET clause):

```
UPDATE    PENALTIES
SET       AMOUNT = AMOUNT + 30
WHERE     PAYMENTNO = 4
```

6. User U_2 also ends his transaction with a COMMIT statement.

The result of these two changes is that both users think their changes have been executed ("committed"). However, the change of user U_1 has disappeared. His change of $25 is overwritten by the change of user U_2. Losing changes, of course, is not desirable. MySQL must ensure that once changes have been "committed," they really are permanent.

All the problems described here can be solved easily by not allowing two users to run a transaction simultaneously. If the transaction of U_2 can start only if that of U_1 has ended, nothing will go wrong. In other words, the transactions are processed serially. However, imagine that you share the database with more than a hundred users. If you end a transaction, it will probably be a long time before it is your turn again. We describe the level of *concurrency* as low: No two users can work simultaneously. Therefore, it is necessary to process transactions simultaneously, or in parallel. But to do this, MySQL needs a mechanism to prevent the previously mentioned problems from occurring. This is the subject of the remaining part of the chapter.

37.7 Locking

A number of different mechanisms exist to keep the level of concurrency high and still prevent problems. This section discusses the mechanism implemented in MySQL: *locking.*

The basic principle of locking is simple. If a user accesses a certain piece of data, such as a row from the PLAYERS table, the row is locked and other users cannot access that row. Only the user who has locked the row can access it. Locks are released when the transaction ends. In other words, the life of a lock is never longer than that of the transaction in which the lock is created.

Let us see what happens with two of the problems discussed in the previous section. For the problem of the lost update (see Example 37.9), user U_1 accesses penalty number 4 first. MySQL automatically places a lock on that row. Then user U_2 tries to do the same. However, this user receives a message indicating that the row is not available. He must wait until U_1 has finished. This means that the final penalty amount is $105 (work it out for yourself). In this case, the transactions of U_1 and U_2 are processed not in parallel, but *serially.* Other users who are working with another penalty number are processed concurrently.

For the problem of the nonrepeatable read (see Example 37.7), we now have a comparable situation. Only after user U_1 has printed the labels can user U_2 change the address, which no longer causes problems.

A locking mechanism works correctly if it meets the *serializability* criterion. If the contents of the database after (concurrently) processing a set of transactions are the same as the contents of the database after processing the same set of transactions serially (order is irrelevant), the mechanism works correctly. The state of the database after problem 1 shows that the penalty amount of penalty number 4 is $80. You will never manage to get the same amount by processing the two transactions of users U_1 and U_2 serially. Whether you execute user U_1's transaction first and then user U_2's, or vice versa, the result is $105, not $80.

Where does the database store all those locks? The internal memory of the computer maintains the lock administration. Usually, a large part of the internal memory is reserved for this function. This space is called the *buffer.* Therefore, locks are not stored in the database, and users do not see locks.

We stated that the transactions of users U_1 and U_2 are processed serially after locks have been placed. This is not ideal, of course. To increase the level of concurrency, most products support two types of locks: *share* and *exclusive* (sometimes these locks are called *read* and *write,* respectively). If a user has a share lock on a row, other users can read that row but cannot change it. The advantage is that users who execute only SELECT statements in their transactions do not hold each other up. If a user has an exclusive lock, other users cannot reach the row, even to read it. The previous sections assumed that each lock was exclusive.

No separate SQL statement exists to indicate that you want to work with share locks, for example. MySQL determines the type of lock from the SQL statement. For example, if a SELECT statement is executed, a share lock is implemented. On the other hand, when you use an UPDATE statement, an exclusive lock is set.

37.8 Deadlocks

A well-known phenomenon that can occur if many users access the database simultaneously is a *deadlock*. Simply put, a deadlock arises if two users wait for each other's data. Imagine that user U_1 has a lock on row R_1 and that he or she wants to place one on row R_2. Assume also that user U_2 is the "owner" of the lock on row R_2 and wants to place a lock on R_1. These two users are waiting for each other. If we go back to the analogy of a road crossing, have you ever been at a crossroads when four cars approach at the same time? Who can drive on first? This is also deadlock.

If a deadlock arises, MySQL will *not* discover it. You must design your programs to minimize the chances of deadlocks. This requires a detailed knowledge about how MySQL handles transactions and locks. Therefore, read this chapter intently and also seek additional information about this subject.

37.9 The LOCK TABLE and UNLOCK TABLE Statements

As previously mentioned, all the data in use during a transaction is locked against other users. To keep track of which data has been locked by which application, MySQL must keep some internal administration. It is possible for a user to execute many changes on a particular table within one transaction. For example, the user might have a program that changes a column value of all rows of a table. These changes create a huge amount of internal administrative work. To avoid this, you can lock the entire table in one process at the beginning of a transaction using the *LOCK TABLE statement.*

DEFINITION

```
<lock table statement> ::=
   LOCK { TABLE | TABLES } <lock table> [ , <lock table> ]...

<lock table> ::=
   <table specification> [ AS <pseudonym> ] <lock type>

<lock type> ::= READ | READ LOCAL | WRITE | LOW_PRIORITY WRITE
```

Only base tables (tables that have been created with a CREATE TABLE statement) can be locked. At the end of a transaction, a lock is released automatically.

Example 37.10: Lock the entire PLAYERS table.

```
LOCK TABLE PLAYERS READ
```

MySQL supports the following lock types:

- **READ**—A lock of this type ensures that the application can read the table; other applications are also allowed to read the table, but they cannot change it.
- **READ LOCAL**—A lock of this type works only for tables created with the MyISAM storage engine. With this lock type, multiple users can simultaneously add rows to the table under certain conditions.
- **WRITE**— A lock of this type ensures that the application can change the table. Other applications cannot gain access to the table; they can neither read it nor change it.
- **LOW_PRIORITY WRITE**—A lock of this type ensures that the application can read the table; other applications are also allowed to read the table, but they cannot change it. An SQL user receives this lock only when all other users are finished.

With the *UNLOCK TABLE statement,* all locks that an SQL user owns are released—not just those that were created with a LOCK TABLE statement, but all of them. This is not the same as ending a transaction.

DEFINITION

```
<unlock table statement> ::=
   UNLOCK { TABLE | TABLES }
```

37.10 The Isolation Level

One further complication exists. Each transaction has a so-called *isolation level,* which defines the extent to which the users are isolated from or interfere with each other. So far, we have assumed only one isolation level. In MySQL, we find the following levels:

- **Serializable**—If the isolation level is serializable, the users are the most separated from each other.
- **Repeatable read**—If the isolation level is a repeatable read (also called read repeatability), share locks are set on all data that a user reads and exclusive locks are placed on data that is changed. These locks exist as long as the transaction runs. This means that if a user executes the same `SELECT` statement several times within the same transaction, the result will always be the same. In previous sections, we assumed that this isolation level was desirable.
- **Cursor stability or read committed**—With cursor stability, the same locks are placed as for a repeatable read. The difference is that share locks are released if the `SELECT` statement is processed. In other words, after the `SELECT` statement has been processed but before the transaction ends, data becomes available for other users. This does not apply to changes, of course. An exclusive lock is set on data that has been changed and remains there until the end of the transaction.
- **Dirty read or read uncommitted**—For reading data, a dirty read is equal to cursor stability. However, with a dirty read, a user can see the changes another user has made before that user makes them permanent with a `COMMIT` statement. In other words, the exclusive lock is released immediately after a change but before the transaction ends. This means that if you work with a dirty read, the locking mechanism does not meet the serializability criterion.

In summary, with the isolation level called serializable, users have the greatest isolation from each other, but the level of concurrency is the lowest. This is the opposite of a dirty read, in which users will definitely notice that they are not alone in using the system; they can read data that does not exist a few seconds later. However, the level of concurrency is the highest. A user will rarely need to wait for another user. Table 37.1 indicates whether each type of problem described in Section 37.6 can occur for a specific isolation level.

TABLE 37.1 Overview of Isolation Levels

Isolation Level	Dirty Read	Inconsistent Read	Nonrepeatable Read	Phantom Read	Lost Update
Dirty read/ read uncommitted	Yes	Yes	Yes	Yes	Yes
Cursor stability/ read committed	No	No	Yes	Yes	Yes
Repeatable read	No	No	No	No	Yes
Serializable	No	No	No	No	No

Only with storage engines that support transactions, such as InnoDB and BDB, can an isolation level be defined. The following statements can determine the actual isolation level:

```
SHOW GLOBAL VARIABLES LIKE 'TX_ISOLATION'

SELECT @@GLOBAL.TX_ISOLATION
```

In both cases, the result is REPEATABLE-READ if this variable still has the standard default value.

The *SET TRANSACTION statement* can change the default. However, this statement affects not the running transaction, but the next one started.

DEFINITION

```
<set transaction statement> ::=
   SET [ GLOBAL | SESSION ] TRANSACTION
      ISOLATION LEVEL <isolation level>

<isolation level> ::=
   READ UNCOMMITTED |
   READ COMMITTED   |
   REPEATABLE READ  |
   SERIALIZABLE
```

If we specify SESSION, the new isolation level applies only to the running session and connections. Other SQL users still have the same isolation level. When we specify GLOBAL, we change the system variable TX_ISOLATION, and that affects all SQL users. Of course, GLOBAL may be used only if the SQL user has enough authority.

In Section 37.3, we mentioned that you can explicitly define the beginning of a transaction with a `START TRANSACTION` statement. The `SET TRANSACTION` statement can also perform this function.

37.11 Waiting for a Lock

If a user asks for a lock on a row or table, it is possible that another user has already locked it. The former application will keep waiting until the existing lock is released. But how long will the application wait? When MySQL starts, it queries the system variable `INNODB_LOCK_WAIT_TIMEOUT`. The value of this variable holds the standard waiting time in seconds. It is not possible to adjust this variable with the `SET` statement—this must be done when the MySQL database server starts.

This variable is relevant only for table locks that were made with the storage engine `InnoDB`.

37.12 Moment of Processing Statements

We always a assume that `UPDATE`, `INSERT`, `DELETE`, `REPLACE`, and `SELECT` statements are processed immediately when there are no locks in the way. This quick way of processing can be adjusted by specifying a *processing option* in the statements. Possible processing options exist for the first four statements:

- **Delayed**—With the delayed option, the change is placed on a waiting list. The application receives the message that the statement has been processed correctly and can go on processing other statements. MySQL determines for itself, based upon the activity on the system, when the change will actually be executed.
- **Low priority**—If low priority is used, the change is performed only when no other SQL users need to read the data.
- **High priority**—MySQL ensures that no other `SELECT` statements are executed simultaneously because that could negatively affect the speed of the change. The application can temporarily use the data exclusively.

We next specify how this processing option can be included in the different SQL statements and which options can be used with which statements:

DEFINITION

```
<delete statement> ::=
   DELETE [ LOW_PRIORITY ] [ IGNORE ] ...

<insert statement> ::=
   INSERT [ DELAYED | LOW_PRIORITY | HIGH_PRIORITY ] [ IGNORE ] ...

<replace statement> ::=
   REPLACE [ DELAYED | LOW_PRIORITY] [ IGNORE ] ...

<update statement> ::=
   UPDATE [ LOW_PRIORITY ] [ IGNORE ] ...
```

We can extend the SELECT statement with a processing option in the form of a select option; see also Section 9.6. By specifying HIGH_PRIORITY in the SELECT clause of a SELECT statement, we assign this statement a higher priority. This increases the chance that this statement is processed faster. This has no effect in a single-user environment; however, it can make an impact when multiple users access the same database server concurrently. Suppose that MySQL is busy processing a SELECT statement and simultaneously other users are executing INSERT, UPDATE, or DELETE statements on the same table. Because the SELECT statement is still being processed, these updates wait in a queue. Usually, a new SELECT statement is placed at the end of this queue. By specifying HIGH_PRIORITY, this statement is placed before all other updates in the queue. This does not improve the processing speed, but the statement processing starts sooner.

37.13 Working with Application Locks

This chapter discussed only locks on rows. MySQL also supports *application locks.* These locks receive a name and are not related to a set of rows or a table. To work with these locks, four functions have been introduced: GET_LOCK, RELEASE_LOCK, IS_FREE_LOCK, and IS_USED_LOCK.

With the function GET_LOCK, we create an application lock called a *named lock.* This function has two parameters. The first is the name of the lock. If the lock is created successfully, the result of this function is equal to 1. If a lock with the name stated already exists, the system waits for the number of seconds that is specified in the second parameter. If after this number of seconds the lock is still not available, the function returns the value 0. To call this function, we use the DO statement; see Section 15.6.

Example 37.11: Create an application lock called LOCK1.

```
DO GET_LOCK('lock1',0)
```

Explanation: If the lock called LOCK1 does not exist yet, the DO statement creates it. If other applications try to create the same lock next, they will not succeed.

A SELECT statement could have achieved the same result. The difference is that the DO statement indicates whether we succeeded to call the lock.

```
SELECT GET_LOCK('lock1',0)
```

The result is:

```
GET_LOCK('lock1',0)
-------------------
                  0
```

With the *IS_FREE_LOCK function*, we can query whether a certain application lock already exists. If this lock is still available, the result is equal to 1; otherwise, it equals 0.

Example 37.12: Determine whether the application lock called LOCK1 is in use.

```
SELECT IS_FREE_LOCK('lock1')
```

The result is:

```
IS_FREE_LOCK('lock1')
---------------------
                    0
```

If an application lock is requested, we can ask for the connection identifier that has created the application lock. We use the *IS_USED_LOCK function* to do this.

Example 37.13: Determine which connection has created LOCK1.

```
SELECT IS_USED_LOCK('lock1')
```

The result is:

```
IS_USED_LOCK('lock1')
---------------------
                    2
```

The *RELEASE_LOCK function* can remove an application lock. When the function is processed correctly, the result equals 1; otherwise, it equals 0.

Example 37.14: Remove the application lock called LOCK1.

```
SELECT RELEASE_LOCK('lock1')
```

The result is:

```
RELEASE_LOCK('lock1')
---------------------
                    1
```

37.14 Answers

37.1

Line 1 A SELECT statement does not change the contents of tables; it starts a transaction.

Line 2 This change is not yet permanent.

Line 3 A COMMIT statement is executed. All changes of the current transaction become permanent. This is the change of line 2.

Line 4 A ROLLBACK statement is executed. Because this is the first SQL statement following the previous COMMIT, a new transaction starts and ends here. No changes have been executed, so no changes need to be rolled back.

Lines 5–6 These two changes are not yet permanent.

Line 7 A ROLLBACK statement is executed. All changes of the actual transaction are undone. These are the changes of lines 5 and 6.

Line 8 This change is not yet permanent.

Line 9 A COMMIT statement is executed. All changes of the current transaction become permanent. This is the change of line 8.

Line 10 Here the program is terminated. There is no current transaction, so the program can be terminated without problems.

37.2

Line 1 A SELECT statement does not change the contents of tables; it starts a transaction.

Line 2 A savepoint is defined with the name S1.

Line 3 This change is not yet permanent.

Line 4 A COMMIT statement is executed. All changes of the current transaction become permanent. This is the change of line 3.

Line 5 This change is not yet permanent.

Line 6 A savepoint is defined with the name `S1`.

Line 7 This change is not yet permanent.

Line 8 A `ROLLBACK` statement is executed. Only the change of line 7 is undone. The change of line 5 is not yet permanent.

Line 9 This change is not yet permanent.

Line 10 A savepoint is defined with the name `S2`.

Line 11 This change is not yet permanent.

Line 12 A `ROLLBACK` statement is executed. Only the changes of lines 7, 9, and 11 are undone. The change of line 5 is (still) not yet permanent.

Line 13 A `COMMIT` statement is executed. All changes of the current transaction become permanent. This is the change of line 5.

Line 14 Here the program is terminated. There is no current transaction, so the program can be terminated without problems.

APPENDIX A

Syntax of SQL

A.1 Introduction

In this appendix, we explain the notation method we have used to define the statements, present the definitions of the SQL statements discussed in this book, and show the list of reserved words.

The definitions in this appendix can differ from those in the previous chapters. The main reason for this is that, in the chapters, we explained the statements and concepts step by step. To avoid too much detail, we sometimes used simple versions of the definitions. This appendix contains the complete definitions.

A.2 The BNF Notation

In this appendix and throughout the book, we have used a formal notation method to describe the syntax of all SQL statements and the common elements. This notation is a derivative of the so-called *Backus Naur Form* (BNF), which is named after John Backus and Peter Naur. The meaning of the metasymbols that we use is based on that of the metasymbols in the SQL standard.

BNF adopts a language of *substitution rules* or *production rules,* consisting of a series of symbols. Each production rule defines one *symbol.* A symbol could be, for example, an SQL statement, a table name, or a colon. A *terminal symbol* is a special type of symbol. All symbols, apart from the terminal symbols, are defined in terms of other symbols in a production rule. Examples of terminal symbols are the word CLOSE and the semicolon.

You can compare a production rule with the definition of an element, in which the definition of that element uses elements defined elsewhere. In this case, an element equates to a symbol.

The following *metasymbols* do not form part of the SQL language, but belong to the notation technique:

```
< >
::=
|
[ ]
...
{ }
;
"
```

We now explain each of these symbols.

The Symbols < and >

Nonterminal symbols are presented in brackets (< >). A production rule exists for every nonterminal symbol. We show the names of the nonterminal symbols in lowercase letters. Two examples of nonterminal symbols are `<select statement>` and `<table reference>`.

The ::= Symbol

The `::=` symbol is used in a production rule to separate the nonterminal symbol that is defined (left) from its definition (right). The `::=` symbol should be read as "is defined as." See the following example of the production rule for the `CLOSE CURSOR` statement:

```
<close cursor statement> ::= CLOSE <cursor name>
```

Explanation: The `CLOSE CURSOR` statement consists of the terminal symbol `CLOSE` followed by the nonterminal symbol cursor name. A production rule also should exist for `<cursor name>`.

The | Symbol

Alternatives are represented by the | symbol. Here we give an example of the production rule for the element `<character>`:

```
<character> ::= <digit> | <letter> | <special symbol> | ''
```

Explanation: We can conclude from this that a character is a digit, a letter, a special symbol, or two quotation marks; it must be one of the four.

The Symbols [and]

Whatever is placed between square brackets ([ ]) *may* be used. This is the production rule for the ROLLBACK statement:

```
<rollback statement> ::= ROLLBACK [ WORK ]
```

Explanation: A ROLLBACK statement always consists of the word ROLLBACK and can optionally be followed by the word WORK.

The ... Symbol

The three dots indicate what may be repeated one or more times. Here our example is the production rule for an integer:

```
<whole number> ::= <digit>...
```

Explanation: An integer consists of a series of digits (with a minimum of one).

Combining the three points with square brackets enables us to indicate that a certain element can appear zero, one, or more times:

```
<from clause> ::=
   FROM <table reference> [ , <table reference> ]...
```

Explanation: A FROM clause begins with the terminal symbol FROM and is followed by at least one table reference. It is possible to follow this table reference with a list of elements, with each element consisting of a comma followed by a table reference. Do not forget that the comma is part of SQL and not part of the notation.

The Symbols { and }

All symbols between braces ({ }) form a group. For example, braces used with the | symbol show precisely what the alternatives are. The following example is part of the production rule for the float literal:

```
<float literal> ::=
   <mantissa> { E | e } <exponent>
```

Explanation: A float literal starts with a mantissa and ends with an exponent. In between, we can use the capital letter E or the small letter e; one must be used.

If we combine the braces with three points, we can indicate that an element should appear one or more times. This means that in the production rule A { B }..., we first have to use the element A, and it should be followed by one or more B elements.

The ; Symbol

Some symbols have the same definition. Instead of repeating them, we can use the semicolon to shorten the definitions. The following definition

```
<character literal>    ;
<varchar literal>      ;
<long varchar literal> ::= <character string>
```

is equivalent to these three definitions:

```
<character literal>    ::= <character string>
<varchar literal>      ::= <character string>
<long varchar literal> ::= <character string>
```

The " Symbol

A small number of metasymbols, such as the " symbol, are part of particular SQL statements themselves. To avoid misunderstanding, these symbols are enclosed by double quotation marks. Among other things, this means that the symbol " that is used within SQL is represented in the production rules as """.

Additional Remarks

- Whatever is presented in capital letters, along as the symbols that are not part of the notation method, must be adopted unaltered.
- The sequence of the symbols in the right part of the production rule is fixed.
- Blanks in production rules have no significance. Generally, they have been added to make the rules more readable. Therefore, the two following production rules mean the same:

  ```
  <alphanumeric literal> ::= ' [ <character>... ] '
  ```

  and

  ```
  <alphanumeric literal> ::= '[<character>...]'
  ```

A.3 Reserved Words in SQL

MySQL supports so-called *reserved words* or *keywords*, such as SELECT and CREATE. In MySQL, these reserved words may not be used as names for database objects such as tables, columns, views, and users. The following list contains reserved words as defined in the SQL3 standard, followed by the list of reserved words of MySQL itself.

- ABSOLUTE, ACTION, ADD, ALL, ALLOCATE, ALTER, AND, ANY, ARE, AS, ASC, ASSERTION, AT, AUTHORIZATION, AVG
- BEGIN, BETWEEN, BIT, BIT_LENGTH, BOTH, BY
- CASCADE, CASCADED, CASE, CAST, CATALOG, CHAR, CHARACTER, CHAR_LENGTH, CHARACTER_LENGTH, CHECK, CLOSE, COALESCE, COLLATE, COLLATION, COLUMN, COMMIT, CONNECT, CONNECTION, CONSTRAINT, CONSTRAINTS, CONTINUE, CONVERT, CORRESPONDING, COUNT, CREATE, CROSS, CURRENT, CURRENT_DATE, CURRENT_TIME, CURRENT_TIMESTAMP, CURRENT_USER, CURSOR
- DATE, DAY, DEALLOCATE, DEC, DECIMAL, DECLARE, DEFAULT, DEFERRABLE, DEFERRED, DELETE, DESC, DESCRIBE, DESCRIPTOR, DIAGNOSTICS, DISCONNECT, DISTINCT, DOMAIN, DOUBLE, DROP
- ELSE, END, END-EXEC, ESCAPE, EXCEPT, EXCEPTION, EXEC, EXECUTE, EXISTS, EXTERNAL, EXTRACT
- FALSE, FETCH, FIRST, FLOAT, FOR, FOREIGN, FOUND, FROM, FULL
- GET, GLOBAL, GO, GOTO, GRANT, GROUP
- HAVING, HOUR
- IDENTITY, IMMEDIATE, IN, INDICATOR, INITIALLY, INNER, INPUT, INSENSITIVE, INSERT, INT, INTEGER, INTERSECT, INTERVAL, INTO, IS, ISOLATION
- JOIN
- KEY
- LANGUAGE, LAST, LEADING, LEFT, LEVEL, LIKE, LOCAL, LOWER
- MATCH, MAX, MIN, MINUTE, MODULE, MONTH
- NAMES, NATIONAL, NATURAL, NCHAR, NEXT, NO, NOT, NULL, NULLIF, NUMERIC
- OCTET_LENGTH, OF, ON, ONLY, OPEN, OPTION, OR, ORDER, OUTER, OUTPUT, OVERLAPS
- PARTIAL, POSITION, PRECISION, PREPARE, PRESERVE, PRIMARY, PRIOR, PRIVILEGES, PROCEDURE, PUBLIC

- READ, REAL, REFERENCES, RELATIVE, RESTRICT, REVOKE, RIGHT, ROLLBACK, ROWS
- SCHEMA, SCROLL, SECOND, SECTION, SELECT, SESSION, SESSION_USER, SET, SIZE, SMALLINT, SOME, SQL, SQLCODE, SQLERROR, SQLSTATE, SUBSTRING, SUM, SYSTEM_USER
- TABLE, TEMPORARY, THEN, TIME, TIMESTAMP, TIMEZONE_HOUR, TIMEZONE_MINUTE, TO, TRAILING, TRANSACTION, TRANSLATE, TRANSLATION, TRIM, TRUE
- UNION, UNIQUE, UNKNOWN, UPDATE, UPPER, USAGE, USER, USING
- VALUE, VALUES, VARCHAR, VARYING, VIEW
- WHEN, WHENEVER, WHERE, WITH, WORK, WRITE
- YEAR
- ZONE

This is the list of reserved words in MySQL. The words that already appear in the previous list have been omitted.

- ANALYZE, ASENSITIVE
- BEFORE, BIGINT, BINARY, BLOB
- CALL, CHANGE, CONDITION
- DATABASE, DATABASES, DAY_HOUR, DAY_MICROSECOND, DAY_MINUTE, DAY_SECOND, DELAYED, DETERMINISTIC, DISTINCTROW, DIV, DUAL
- EACH, ELSEIF, ENCLOSED, ESCAPED, EXIT, EXPLAIN
- FLOAT4, FLOAT8, FORCE, FULLTEXT
- HIGH_PRIORITY, HOUR_MICROSECOND, HOUR_MINUTE, HOUR_SECOND
- IF, IGNORE, INDEX, INFILE, INOUT, INT1, INT2, INT3, INT4, INT8, ITERATE
- KEYS, KILL
- LABEL, LEAVE, LIMIT, LINES, LOAD, LOCALTIME, LOCALTIMESTAMP, LOCK, LONG, LONGBLOB, LONGTEXT, LOOP, LOW_PRIORITY
- MEDIUMBLOB, MEDIUMINT, MEDIUMTEXT, MIDDLEINT, MINUTE_MICROSECOND, MINUTE_SECOND, MOD, MODIFIES
- NO_WRITE_TO_BINLOG
- OPTIMIZE, OPTIONALLY, OUT, OUTFILE
- PURGE

- RAIDO, READS, REGEXP, RELEASE, RENAME, REPEAT, REPLACE, REQUIRE, RETURN, RLIKE
- SCHEMAS, SECOND_MICROSECOND, SENSITIVE, SEPARATOR, SHOW, SONAME, SPATIAL, SPECIFIC, SQLEXCEPTION, SQLWARNING, SQL_BIG_RESULT, SQL_CALC_FOUND_ROWS, SQL_SMALL_RESULT, SSL, STARTING, STRAIGHT_JOIN
- TERMINATED, TINYBLOB, TINYINT, TINYTEXT, TRIGGER
- UNDO, UNLOCK, UNSIGNED, USE, UTC_DATE, UTC_TIME, UTC_TIMESTAMP
- VARBINARY, VARCHARACTER
- WHILE
- X509, XOR
- YEAR_MONTH
- ZEROFILL

We strongly advise that you follow these recommendations when choosing the names of database objects:

- Avoid one-letter words, even if they do not occur in the list.
- Avoid words that could be seen as abbreviations of words in the list; for example, do not use DATA because the word DATABASE appears in the list.
- Avoid derivations of words in the list, such as plural and verbal forms. Therefore, do not use CURSORS (plural of CURSOR) or ORDERING (present participle of the verb ORDER).

A.4 Syntax Definitions of SQL Statements

This section contains the definitions of all the SQL statements as they are described in this book. Several statements use certain common elements, such as condition and column list. If an element belongs to only one statement, it is included in Section A.4.2 together with its statement. All others are explained in Section A.4.3. We begin with the different groups of SQL statements.

A.4.1 Groups of SQL Statements

Section 4.15 indicated that the set of SQL statements can be divided into groups, such as DDL, DML, and DCL statements. In this section, we indicate which group each statement belongs to.

SQL Statement

```
<sql statement> ::=
   <declarative statement>      |
   <procedural statement>       |
   <informative statement>      |
   <table maintenance statement>
```

Declarative Statement

```
<declarative statement> ::=
   <ddl statement> |
   <dml statement> |
   <dcl statement>
```

DDL Statement

```
<ddl statement> ::=
   <alter database statement>   |
   <alter event statement>      |
   <alter function statement>   |
   <alter procedure statement>  |
   <alter table statement>      |
   <create database statement>  |
   <create event statement>     |
   <create function statement>  |
   <create index statement>     |
   <create procedure statement> |
   <create sequence statement>  |
   <create table statement>     |
   <create trigger statement>   |
   <create view statement>      |
   <drop database statement>    |
   <drop event statement>       |
   <drop function statement>    |
   <drop index statement>       |
   <drop procedure statement>   |
   <drop table statement>       |
   <drop trigger statement>     |
   <drop view statement>        |
   <rename table statement>
```

DML Statement

```
<dml statement> ::=
   <begin work statement>              |
   <call statement>                    |
   <close cursor statement>            |
   <commit statement>                  |
   <deallocate prepare statement>      |
   <delete statement>                  |
   <do statement>                      |
   <execute statement>                 |
   <fetch cursor statement>            |
   <handler close statement>           |
   <handler open statement>            |
   <handler read statement>            |
   <insert statement>                  |
   <load statement>                    |
   <lock table statement>              |
   <open cursor statement>             |
   <prepare statement>                 |
   <replace statement>                 |
   <rollback statement>                |
   <savepoint statement>               |
   <select statement>                  |
   <select into statement>             |
   <set statement>                     |
   <set transaction statement>         |
   <start transaction statement>       |
   <truncate table statement>          |
   <unlock table statement>            |
   <update statement>
```

DCL Statement

```
<dcl statement> ::=
   <alter user statement>    |
   <create user statement>   |
   <drop user statement>     |
   <grant statement>         |
   <rename user statement>   |
   <set password statement>  |
   <revoke statement>
```

Procedural Statement

```
<procedural statement> ::=
   <begin-end block>                   |
   <call statement>                    |
   <declare condition statement>       |
   <declare cursor statement>          |
   <declare handler statement>         |
   <declare variable statement>        |
   <flow control statement>            |
   <return statement>
```

Flow-Control Statement

```
<flow control statement> ::=
   <case statement>      |
   <if statement>        |
   <iterate statement>   |
   <leave statement>     |
   <loop statement>      |
   <repeat statement>    |
   <while statement>
```

Informative Statement

```
<informative statement> ::=
   <describe statement> |
   <help statement>     |
   <show statement>
```

Table Maintenance Statement

```
<table maintenance statement> ::=
   <analyze table statement>  |
   <backup table statement>   |
   <checksum table statement> |
   <check table statement>    |
   <optimize table statement> |
   <repair table statement>   |
   <restore table statement>
```

A.4.2 Definitions of SQL Statements

Alter Database Statement

```
<alter database statement> ::=
   ALTER DATABASE [ <database name> ]
      [ <database option>... ]
```

Alter Event Statement

```
<alter event statement> ::=
   ALTER EVENT [ <database name> . ] <event name>
      ON SCHEDULE <event schedule>
      [ RENAME TO <event name> ]
      [ ON COMPLETION [ NOT ] PRESERVE ]
      [ ENABLE | DISABLE ]
      [ COMMENT <alphanumeric literal> ]
      DO <sql statement>
```

Alter Function Statement

```
<alter function statement> ::=
   ALTER FUNCTION [ <database name> . ] <stored function name>
      [ <routine characteristic>... ]
```

Alter Procedure Statement

```
<alter procedure statement> ::=
   ALTER PROCEDURE [ <database name> . ] <stored procedure name>
      [ <routine characteristic>... ]
```

Alter Table Statement

```
<alter table statement> ::=
   ALTER [ IGNORE ] TABLE <table specification>
      <table structure change>
```

Alter View Statement

```
<alter view statement> ::=
   ALTER
      [ <definer option> ]
      [ <sql security option> ]
      [ ALGORITHM = { MERGE | TEMPTABLE | UNDEFINED } ]
      VIEW <view name> [ <column list> ] AS <table expression>
      [ WITH [ CASCADED | LOCAL ] CHECK OPTION ]
```

Analyze Table Statement

```
<analyze table statement> ::=
   ANALYZE [ <analyze option> ]
      TABLE <table specification> [ , <table specification> ]...

<analyze option> ::= NO_WRITE_TO_BINLOG | LOCAL
```

Backup Table Statement

```
<backup table statement> ::=
   BACKUP TABLE <table specification>
      [ , <table specification> ]...
      TO <directory>
```

Begin Work Statement

```
<begin work statement> ::=
   BEGIN WORK
```

Call Statement

```
<call statement> ::=
   CALL [ <database name> . ] <stored procedure name>
   ( [ <scalar expression> [ , <scalar expression> ]... ] )
```

Case Statement

```
<case statement> ::=
   { CASE <scalar expression>
       WHEN <scalar expression> THEN <statement list>
       [ WHEN <scalar expression> THEN <statement list> ]...
       [ ELSE <statement list> ]
     END CASE } |
   { CASE
       WHEN <condition> THEN <statement list>
       [ WHEN <condition> THEN <statement list> ]...
       [ ELSE <statement list>
     END CASE }
```

Checksum Table Statement

```
<checksum table statement> ::=
   CHECKSUM TABLE <table specification>
      [ , <table specification> ]...
      [ <checksum option> ]

<checksum option> ::= QUICK | EXTENDED
```

Check Table Statement

```
<check table statement> ::=
   CHECK TABLE <table specification> [ , <tablespecification> ]...
      [ <check option> ]...

<check option> ::=
   FOR UPGRADE | QUICK | FAST | MEDIUM | EXTENDED | CHANGED
```

Close Cursor Statement

```
<close cursor statement> ::=
   CLOSE <cursor name>
```

Commit Statement

```
<commit statement> ::=
   COMMIT [ WORK ] [ AND [ NO ] CHAIN ] [ [ NO ] RELEASE ]
```

Create Database Statement

```
<create database statement> ::=
   CREATE DATABASE [ IF NOT EXISTS ] <database name>
      [ <database option>... ]
```

Create Event Statement

```
<create event statement> ::=
   CREATE EVENT [ IF NOT EXISTS ]
      [ <database name> . ] <event name>
      ON SCHEDULE <event schedule>
      [ ON COMPLETION [ NOT ] PRESERVE ]
      [ ENABLE | DISABLE ]
      [ COMMENT <alphanumeric literal> ]
      DO <event action>

<event action> ::=
   <declarative sql statement> |
   <begin-end block>
```

Create Function Statement

```
<create function statement> ::=
   CREATE [ <definer option> ]
      FUNCTION [ <database name> . ] <stored function name>
      ( [ <parameter list> ] )
      RETURNS <data type>
      [ <routine characteristic>... ]
      <routine body>
```

Create Index Statement

```
<create index statement> ::=
   CREATE [ <index type> ] INDEX <index name>
   [ USING { BTREE | HASH } ]
   ON <table specification>
   ( <column in index> [ , <column in index> ]... )
```

Create Procedure Statement

```
<create procedure statement> ::=
   CREATE [ <definer option> ]
      PROCEDURE <stored procedure name> ( [ <parameter list> ] )
      [ <routine characteristic>... ]
      <routine body>
```

Create Table Statement

```
<create table statement> ::=
   CREATE [ TEMPORARY ] TABLE [ IF NOT EXISTS ]
      <table specification>
      <table structure>
      [ <table option>... ]
```

Create Trigger Statement

```
<create trigger statement> ::=
   CREATE [ <definer option> ]
      TRIGGER <trigger name>
      <trigger moment>
      <trigger event>
      <trigger action>

<trigger moment> ::= BEFORE | AFTER

<trigger event> ::=
   { INSERT | DELETE | UPDATE }
      ON <table specification>
      FOR EACH ROW

<trigger action> ::= <sql statement>
```

Create User Statement

```
<create user statement> ::=
   CREATE USER <user specification>
      [ , <user specification> ]...

<user specification> ::=
   <user name> [ IDENTIFIED BY [ PASSWORD ] <password> ]
```

Create View Statement

```
<create view statement> ::=
   CREATE [ OR REPLACE ]
      [ <definer option> ]
      [ <sql security option> ]
      [ ALGORITHM = { MERGE | TEMPTABLE | UNDEFINED } ]
      VIEW <view name> [ <column list> ] AS <table expression>
      [ WITH [ CASCADED | LOCAL ] CHECK OPTION ]
```

Deallocate Prepare Statement

```
<deallocate prepare statement> ::=
   { DEALLOCATE | DROP } PREPARE <statement name>
```

Declare Condition Statement

```
<declare condition statement> ::=
   DECLARE <condition name> CONDITION FOR
   { SQLSTATE [ VALUE ] <sqlstate value> } | <mysql error code>
```

Declare Cursor Statement

```
<declare cursor statement> ::=
   DECLARE <cursor name> CURSOR FOR <table expression>
```

Declare Handler Statement

```
<declare handler statement> ::=
   DECLARE <handler type> HANDLER FOR <condition value list>
      <procedural statement>

<handler type> ::=
   CONTINUE |
   EXIT     |
   UNDO

<condition value list> ::=
   <condition value> [ , <condition value> ]...

<condition value> ::=
   SQLSTATE [ VALUE ] <sqlstate value> |
   <mysql error code>                  |
   SQLWARNING                          |
   NOT FOUND                           |
   SQLEXCEPTION                        |
   <condition name>
```

Declare Variable Statement

```
<declare variable statement> ::=
   DECLARE <variable list> <data type>
      [ DEFAULT <scalar expression> ]
```

Delete Statement

To avoid making the definition unnecessary complicated, two definitions of the DELETE statement are given here. The first deletes rows from one table; the second removes rows from multiple tables at the same time.

```
<delete statement> ::=
   DELETE [ IGNORE ]
   FROM    <table reference>
   [ <where clause> ]
   [ <order by clause> ]
   [ <limit clause> ]

<delete statement> ::=
   { DELETE [ LOW_PRIORITY ] [ IGNORE ]
     <table reference> [ , <table reference> ]...
     FROM <table reference> [ , <table reference> ]...
     [ <where clause> ] } |
   { DELETE [ LOW_PRIORITY ] [ IGNORE ]
     FROM <table reference> [ , <table reference> ]...
     USING <table reference> [ , <table reference> ]...
     [ <where clause> ] }
```

Describe Statement

```
<describe statement> ::=
   { DESCRIBE | DESC } <table specification>
      [ <column name> | <alphanumeric literal> ]
```

Do Statement

```
<do statement> ::=
   DO <scalar expression>
      [ , <scalar expression> ]...
```

Drop Database Statement

```
<drop database statement> ::=
   DROP DATABASE [ IF NOT EXISTS ] <database name>
```

Drop Event Statement

```
<drop event statement> ::=
   DROP EVENT [ IF EXISTS ] [ <database name> . ] <event name>
```

Drop Function Statement

```
<drop function statement> ::=
   DROP FUNCTION [ IF EXISTS ]
      [ <database name> . ] <stored function name>
```

Drop Index Statement

```
<drop index statement> ::=
   DROP INDEX <index name> ON <table specification>
```

Drop Procedure Statement

```
<drop procedure statement> ::=
   DROP PROCEDURE [ IF EXISTS ]
      [ <database name> . ] <stored procedure name>
```

Drop Table Statement

```
<drop table statement> ::=
   DROP [ TEMPORARY ] { TABLE | TABLES } [ IF EXISTS ]
      <table specification> [ , <table specification> ]...
      [ CASCADE | RESTRICT ]
```

Drop Trigger Statement

```
<drop trigger statement> ::=
   DROP TRIGGER [ <table name> . ] <trigger name>
```

Drop User Statement

```
<drop user statement> ::=
   DROP USER <user name> [ , <user name> ]...
```

Drop View Statement

```
<drop view statement> ::=
   DROP VIEW [ IF EXISTS ] <table specification>
      [ , <table specification> ]...
      [ RESTRICT | CASCADE ]
```

Execute Statement

```
<execute statement> ::=
   EXECUTE <statement name>
      [ USING <user variable> [ , <user variable> ]... ]
```

Fetch Cursor Statement

```
<fetch cursor statement> ::=
   FETCH <cursor name>
      INTO <local variable> [ , <local variable> ]...
```

Grant Statement

```
<grant statement> ::=
   <grant table privilege statement>    |
   <grant database privilege statement> |
   <grant user privilege statement>     |
   <grant execute privilege statement>

<grant table privilege statement> ::=
   GRANT <table privileges>
   ON    <table specification>
   TO    <grantees>
   [ WITH <grant option>... ]
```

continues

```
<grant database privilege statement> ::=
   GRANT <database privileges>
   ON    [ <database name> . ] *
   TO    <grantees>
   [ WITH <grant option>... ]

<grant user privilege statement> ::=
   GRANT <user privileges>
   ON    *.*
   TO    <grantees>
   [ WITH <grant option>... ]

<grant execute privilege statement> ::=
   GRANT EXECUTE
   ON    { PROCEDURE <stored procedure name> |
           FUNCTION <stored function name>   }
   TO    <grantees>
   [ WITH <grant option>... ]
```

Handler Close Statement

```
<handler close statement> ::=
   HANDLER <handler name> CLOSE
```

Handler Open Statement

```
<handler open statement> ::=
   HANDLER <table specification> OPEN [ AS <handler name> ]
```

Handler Read Statement

```
<handler read statement> ::=
   HANDLER <handler name> READ <read specification>
      [ <where clause> ]
      [ <limit clause> ]

<read specification> ::=
   FIRST                                              |
   NEXT                                               |
   { <index name> { FIRST | NEXT | PREV | LAST } } |
   { <index name> { = | > | >= | <= | < }
      <scalar expression list> }
```

Help Statement

```
<help statement> ::=
   HELP <alphanumeric literal>
```

If Statement

```
<if statement> ::=
   IF <condition> THEN <statement list>
      [ ELSEIF <condition> THEN <statement list> ]...
      [ ELSE <statement list> ]
   END IF
```

Insert Statement

```
<insert statement> ::=
   INSERT [ DELAYED | LOW_PRIORITY | HIGH_PRIORITY ]
      [ IGNORE ] [ INTO ] <table specification>
      <insert specification> [ <on duplicate key specification> ]

<on duplicate key specification> ::=
   ON DUPLICATE KEY UPDATE <column assignment>
      [ , <column assignment> ]...
```

Iterate Statement

```
<iterate statement> ::=
   ITERATE <label>
```

Leave Statement

```
<leave statement> ::=
   LEAVE <label>
```

Load Statement

```
<load statement> ::=
   LOAD DATA [ LOW_PRIORITY ] [ CONCURRENT ] [ LOCAL ]
      INFILE '<file name>'
      [ REPLACE | IGNORE ]
      INTO TABLE <table specification>
      [ <fields specification> ]
      [ <lines specification> ]
      [ IGNORE <whole number> LINES ]
      [ { <column name> | <user variable> }
         [ , { <column name> | <user variable> } ]... ]
      [ <set statement> ]

<fields specification> ::=
   FIELDS [ TERMINATED BY <alphanumeric literal> ]
          [ [ OPTIONALLY ] ENCLOSED BY <alphanumeric literal> ]
          [ ESCAPED BY <alphanumeric literal> ]

<lines specification> ::=
   LINES [ TERMINATED BY <alphanumeric literal> ]
         [ STARTING BY <alphanumeric literal> ]
```

Lock Table Statement

```
<lock table statement> ::=
   LOCK { TABLE | TABLES } <lock table> [ , <lock table> ]...

<lock table> ::=
   <table specification> [ AS <pseudonym> ] <lock type>

<lock type> ::= READ | READ LOCAL | WRITE | LOW_PRIORITY WRITE
```

Loop Statement

```
<loop statement> ::=
   [ <label> : ] LOOP <statement list>
   END LOOP [ <label> ]
```

Open Cursor Statement

```
<open cursor statement> ::=
   OPEN <cursor name>
```

Optimize Table Statement

```
<optimize table statement> ::=
   OPTIMIZE [ <optimize option> ]
      TABLE <table specification> [ , <table specification> ]...

<optimize option> ::= NO_WRITE_TO_BINLOG | LOCAL
```

Prepare Statement

```
<prepare statement> ::=
   PREPARE <statement name>
      FROM { <alphanumeric literal> | <user variable> }
```

Rename Table Statement

```
<rename table statement> ::=
   RENAME { TABLE | TABLES } <table name change>
      [ , <table name change> ]...

<table name change> ::= <table name> TO <table name>
```

Rename User Statement

```
<rename user statement> ::=
   RENAME USER <user name> TO <user name>
      [ , <user name> TO <user name> ]...
```

Repair Table Statement

```
<repair table statement> ::=
   REPAIR [ <repair option> ]
      TABLE <table specification> [ , <table specification> ]...
      [ QUICK ] [ EXTENDED ] [ USE_FRM ]

<repair option> ::= NO_WRITE_TO_BINLOG | LOCAL
```

Repeat Statement

```
<repeat statement> ::=
   [ <label> : ] REPEAT <statement list>
   UNTIL <condition>
   END REPEAT <label>
```

Replace Statement

```
<replace statement> ::=
   REPLACE [ DELAYED | LOW_PRIORITY] [ IGNORE ]
   [ IGNORE ] [ INTO ] <table specification>
   <insert specification>
```

Restore Table Statement

```
<restore table statement> ::=
   RESTORE TABLE <table specification>
      [ , <table specification> ]...
      FROM <directory>
```

Return Statement

```
<return statement> ::=
   RETURN <scalar expression>
```

Revoke Statement

```
<revoke statement> ::=
   <revoke table privilege statement>     |
   <revoke database privilege statement> |
   <revoke user privilege statement>      |
   <revoke execute privilege statement>  |
   <revoke event privilege statement>

<revoke table privilege statement> ::=
   REVOKE  [ <table privileges> ] [ GRANT OPTION ]
   ON      <table specification>
   FROM    <user name> [ , <user name> ]...

<revoke database privilege statement> ::=
   REVOKE  [ <database privileges> ] [ GRANT OPTION ]
   ON      [ <database name> . ] *
   FROM    <user name> [ , <user name> ]...

<revoke user privilege statement> ::=
   REVOKE  [ <user privileges> ] [ GRANT OPTION ]
   ON      *.*
   FROM    <user name> [ , <user name> ]...

<revoke execute privilege statement> ::=
   REVOKE  EXECUTE
   ON      { PROCEDURE <stored procedure name> |
             FUNCTION <stored function name>    }
   FROM    <grantees>

<revoke event privilege statement> ::=
   REVOKE  EVENT
   ON      [ <database name> . | * . ] *
   FROM     <grantees>
```

Rollback Statement

```
<rollback statement> ::=
   ROLLBACK [ WORK ] [ AND [ NO ] CHAIN ] [ [ NO ] RELEASE ]
   [ TO SAVEPOINT <savepoint name> ]
```

Savepoint Statement

```
<savepoint statement> ::=
   SAVEPOINT <savepoint name>
```

Select Statement

```
<select statement> ::=
     <table expression>
   [ <into file clause> ]
   [ FOR UPDATE | LOCK IN SHARE MODE ]
```

Select Into Statement

```
<select into statement> ::=
     <select clause>
     <into clause>
   [ <from clause>
   [ <where clause> ]
   [ <group by clause> ]
   [ <having clause> ]
   [ <select block tail> ] ]

<into clause> ::=
   INTO <local variable> [ , <local variable> ]...
```

Set Statement

To avoid making the definition unnecessary complicated, two definitions of the SET statement are given here. The first assigns values to user variables; the second assigns values to local variables of stored procedures and stored functions.

```
<set statement> ::=
   SET <user variable definition>
       [ , <user variable definition> ]...

<set statement> ::=
   SET <local variable definition>
       [ , <local variable definition> ]...

<user variable definition> ::=
   <user variable> { = | := } <scalar expression>

<local variable definition> ::=
   <local variable> { = | := } <scalar expression>
```

Set Password Statement

```
<set password statement> ::=
   SET PASSWORD [ FOR <user name> ]
      = PASSWORD( <password> )
```

Set Transaction Statement

```
<set transaction statement> ::=
   SET [ GLOBAL | SESSION ] TRANSACTION
      ISOLATION LEVEL <isolation level>

<isolation level> ::=
   READ UNCOMMITTED |
   READ COMMITTED   |
   REPEATABLE READ  |
   SERIALIZABLE
```

Show Character Set Statement

```
<show character set statement> ::=
   SHOW CHARACTER SET [ LIKE <alphanumeric literal> ]
```

Show Collation Statement

```
<show collation statement> ::=
   SHOW COLLATION [ LIKE <alphanumeric literal> ]
```

Show Column Types Statement

```
<show column types statement> ::=
   SHOW COLUMN TYPES
```

Show Columns Statement

```
<show columns statement> ::=
   SHOW [ FULL ] COLUMNS { FROM | IN } <table specification>
   [ { FROM | IN } <database name> ]
   [ LIKE <alphanumeric literal> ]
```

Show Create Database Statement

```
<show create database statement> ::=
   SHOW CREATE DATABASE [ IF NOT EXISTS ] <database name>
```

Show Create Event Statement

```
<show create event statement> ::=
   SHOW CREATE EVENT [ <database name> . ] <event name>
```

Show Create Function Statement

```
<show create function statement> ::=
   SHOW CREATE FUNCTION
      [ <database name> . ] <stored function name>
```

Show Create Procedure Statement

```
<show create procedure statement> ::=
   SHOW CREATE PROCEDURE
      [ <database name> . ] <stored procedure name>
```

Show Create Table Statement

```
<show create table statement> ::=
   SHOW CREATE TABLE <table specification>
```

Show Create View Statement

```
<show create view statement> ::=
   SHOW CREATE VIEW <table specification>
```

Show Databases Statement

```
<show databases statement> ::=
   SHOW DATABASES [ LIKE <alphanumeric literal> ]
```

Show Engine Statement

```
<show engine statement> ::=
   SHOW ENGINE <engine name> { LOGS | STATUS }
```

Show Engines Statement

```
<show engines statement> ::=
   SHOW [ STORAGE ] ENGINES
```

Show Errors Statement

```
<show errors statement> ::=
   SHOW ERRORS
      [ LIMIT [ <fetch offset> , ] <fetch number of rows> ] |
   SHOW [ COUNT(*) ] ERRORS
```

Show Events Statement

```
<show events statement> ::=
   SHOW EVENTS [ FROM <database name> ]
      [ LIKE <alphanumeric literal> ]
```

Show Function Statement

```
<show function status statement> ::=
   SHOW FUNCTION STATUS [ LIKE <alphanumeric literal> ]
```

Show Grants Statement

```
<show grants statement> ::=
   SHOW ACCOUNTS [ FOR <user name> ]
```

Show Index Statement

```
<show index statement> ::=
   SHOW { INDEX | KEY } { FROM | IN }
      <table specification> [ { FROM | IN } <database name> ]
```

Show Privileges Statement

```
<show privileges statement> ::=
   SHOW PRIVILEGES
```

Show Procedure Status Statement

```
<show procedure status statement> ::=
   SHOW PROCEDURE STATUS [ LIKE <alphanumeric literal> ]
```

Show Table Types Statement

```
<show table types statement> ::=
   SHOW TABLE TYPES
```

Show Tables Statement

```
<show tables statement> ::=
   SHOW [ FULL ] TABLES [ { FROM | IN } <database name> ]
      [ LIKE <alphanumeric literal> ]
```

Show Triggers Statement

```
<show triggers statement> ::=
   SHOW TRIGGERS [ FROM <database name> ]
      [ LIKE <alphanumeric literal> ]
```

Show Variables Statement

```
<show variables statement> ::=
   SHOW [ GLOBAL | SESSION ] VARIABLES
      [ LIKE <alphanumeric literal> ]
```

Show Warnings Statement

```
<show warnings statement> ::=
   SHOW WARNINGS
      [ LIMIT [ <fetch offset> , ] <fetch number of rows> ] |
   SHOW [ COUNT(*) ] WARNINGS
```

Start Transaction Statement

```
<start transaction statement> ::=
   START TRANSACTION
```

Truncate Table Statement

```
<truncate statement> ::=
   TRUNCATE TABLE <table specification>
```

Unlock Table Statement

```
<unlock table statement> ::=
   UNLOCK { TABLE | TABLES }
```

Update Statement

To avoid making the definition unnecessary complicated, two definitions of the UPDATE statement are given. The first changes rows in one table; the second changes rows in multiple tables at the same time.

```
<update statement> ::=
   UPDATE [ LOW_PRIORITY ] [ IGNORE ] <table reference>
   SET <column assignment> [ , <column assignment> ]...
   [ <where clause> ]
   [ <order by clause> ]
   [ <limit clause> ]

<update statement> ::=
   UPDATE [ LOW_PRIORITY ] [ IGNORE ] <table reference>
      [ , <table reference> ]...
   SET <column assignment> [ , <column assignment> ]...
   [ <where clause> ]
   [ <order by clause> ]
   [ <limit clause> ]
```

While Statement

```
<WHILE statement> ::=
   [ <label> : WHILE <condition> DO <statement list>
   END WHILE [ <label> ]
```

A.4.3 Common Elements

This section contains the general common elements used in various SQL statements. The elements that are defined as a name are all grouped at the end of this section.

```
<aggregation function> ::=
   COUNT    ( [ DISTINCT | ALL ] { * | <expression> } ) |
   MIN      ( [ DISTINCT | ALL ] <expression> )         |
   MAX      ( [ DISTINCT | ALL ] <expression> )         |
   SUM      ( [ DISTINCT | ALL ] <expression> )         |
   AVG      ( [ DISTINCT | ALL ] <expression> )         |
   STDDEV   ( [ DISTINCT | ALL ] <expression> )         |
   STD      ( [ DISTINCT | ALL ] <expression> )         |
   VARIANCE ( [ DISTINCT | ALL ] <expression> )         |
   BIT_AND  ( [ DISTINCT | ALL ] <expression> )         |
   BIT_OR   ( [ DISTINCT | ALL ] <expression> )         |
   BIT_XOR  ( [ DISTINCT | ALL ] <expression> )         |
   GROUP_CONCAT ( [ DISTINCT | ALL ] <expression> )
```

```
<alphanumeric data type> ::=
   [ NATIONAL ] CHAR [ ( <length> ) ]                |
   [ NATIONAL ] CHARACTER [ ( <length> ) ]           |
   NCHAR [ ( <length> ) ]                            |
   [ NATIONAL ] VARCHAR ( <length> )                 |
   [ NATIONAL ] CHAR VARYING ( <length> )            |
   [ NATIONAL ] CHARACTER VARYING ( <length> )       |
   NCHAR VARYING ( <length> )                        |
   TINYTEXT                                          |
   TEXT ( <length> )                                 |
   MEDIUM TEXT                                       |
   LONG VARCHAR                                      |
   LONGTEXT
```

```
<alphanumeric data type option> ::=
   CHARACTER SET <character set name> |
   COLLATE <collation name>
```

```
<alphanumeric expression list> ::=
   <alphanumeric scalar expression>
      [ , <alphanumeric scalar expression> ]...
```

```
<alphanumeric literal> ::= <character string>
```

```
<alternate key> ::=
   [ CONSTRAINT [ < constraint name > ] ]
   UNIQUE [ INDEX | KEY ] [ <index name> ]
   [ { USING | TYPE } <index type> ] <column list>
```

```
<any all operator> ::=
   <comparison operator> { ALL | ANY | SOME }
```

```
<begin-end block> ::=
   [ <label> : ] BEGIN <statement list> END [ <label> ]
```

```
<bit data type> ::=
   BIT [ ( <length> ) ]
```

```
<bit literal> ::=
   { b | B } ' { 0 | 1 }... '
```

```
<bit operator> ::= "|" | & | ^ | << | >>
```

```
<blob data type> ::=
   BINARY    [ ( <length> ) ] |
   VARBINARY ( <length> )     |
   TINYBLOB                   |
   BLOB ( <length> )          |
   MEDIUMBLOB                 |
   LONG VARBINARY             |
   LONGBLOB
```

```
<boolean literal> ::= TRUE | true | FALSE | false
```

```
<case expression> ::=
   CASE <when definition> [ ELSE <scalar expression> ] END
```

```
<character> ::= <digit> | <letter> | <special symbol> | ''
```

```
<character string> ::= ' [ <character>... ]'
```

```
<check integrity constraint> ::=
   [ CONSTRAINT [ < constraint name > ] ] CHECK ( <condition> )
```

```
<column assignment> ::=
   <column name> = <scalar expression>
```

```
<column change> ::=
   ADD [ COLUMN ] <column definition>
      [ FIRST | AFTER <column name> ]                              |
   ADD [ COLUMN ] <table schema>                                   |
   DROP [ COLUMN ] <column name> [ RESTRICT | CASCADE ]            |
   CHANGE [ COLUMN ] <column name> <column definition>
      [ FIRST | AFTER <column name> ]                              |
   MODIFY [ COLUMN ] <column definition>
      [ FIRST | AFTER <column name> ]                              |
   ALTER [ COLUMN ] { SET DEFAULT <expression> | DROP DEFAULT }
```

```
<column definition> ::=
   <column name> <data type> [ <null specification> ]
      [ <column integrity constraint> ] [ <column option>... ]
```

```
<column in index> ::= <column name> [ ASC | DESC ]
```

```
<column integrity constraint> ::=
   PRIMARY KEY                    |
   UNIQUE [ KEY ]                 |
   <check integrity constraint>
```

```
<column list> ::=
   ( <column name> [ , <column name> ]... )
```

```
<column option> ::=
   DEFAULT <literal>              |
   COMMENT <alphanumeric literal>
```

```
<column specification> ::=
   [ <table specification> . ] <column name>
```

```
<column subquery> ::= ( <table expression> )
```

```
<comparison operator> ::=
   = | <=> | < | > | <= | >= | <> | !=
```

```
<complex data type> ::=
   ENUM ( <alphanumeric expression list> ) |
   SET ( <alphanumeric expression list> )
```

```
<compound alphanumeric expression> ::=
   <scalar alphanumeric expression> "||"
      <scalar alphanumeric expression>
```

```
<compound boolean expression> ::=
   <scalar boolean expression> |
   <condition>
```

```
<compound date expression> ::=
   <scalar date expression> [ + | - ] <date interval>
```

```
<compound datetime expression> ::=
   <scalar datetime expression> [ + | - ] <timestamp interval>
```

```
<compound numeric expression> ::=
   [ + | - ] <scalar numeric expression>                        |
   ( <scalar numeric expression> )                              |
   <scalar numeric expression>
      <mathematical operator> <scalar numeric expression>       |
   ~ <scalar numeric expression>                                |
   <scalar numeric expression>
      <bit operator> <scalar numeric expression>
```

```
<compound scalar expression> ::=
   <compound numeric expression>       |
   <compound alphanumeric expression>  |
   <compound date expression>          |
   <compound time expression>          |
   <compound timestamp expression>     |
   <compound datetime expression>      |
   <compound boolean expression>       |
   <compound hexadecimal expression>
```

```
<compound table expression> ::=
   <table expression> <set operator> <table expression>
```

```
<compound time expression> ::=
   ADDTIME( <time expression> , <time interval> )
```

```
<compound timestamp expression> ::=
   <scalar timestamp expression> [ + | - ] <timestamp interval>
```

```
<condition> ::=
   <predicate>                     |
   <predicate> OR <predicate>      |
   <predicate> AND <predicate>     |
   ( <condition> )                 |
   NOT <condition>
```

```
<database privilege> ::=
   SELECT                   |
   INSERT                   |
   DELETE                   |
   UPDATE                   |
   REFERENCES               |
   CREATE                   |
   ALTER                    |
   DROP                     |
   INDEX                    |
   CREATE TEMPORARY TABLES  |
   CREATE VIEW              |
   SHOW VIEW                |
   CREATE ROUTINE           |
   ALTER ROUTINE            |
   EXECUTE ROUTINE          |
   LOCK TABLES              |
   EVENT
```

```
<database privileges> ::=
   ALL [ PRIVILEGES ] |
   <database privilege> [ , <database privilege> ]...
```

```
<database option> ::=
   [ DEFAULT ] CHARACTER SET <character set name> |
   [ DEFAULT ] COLLATE <collation name>
```

```
<data type> ::=
   <numeric data type> [ <numeric data type option>... ] |
   <alphanumeric data type>
      [ <alphanumeric data type option>... ]             |
   <temporal data type>                                  |
   <blob data type>                                      |
   <geometric data type>                                 |
   <complex data type>
```

```
<date interval> ::=
   INTERVAL <interval length> <date interval unit>
```

```
<date interval unit> ::=
   DAY | WEEK | MONTH | QUARTER | YEAR | YEAR_MONTH
```

```
<date literal> ::=
   { ' <years> - <months> - <days> ' } |
   { <years> <months> <days> }
```

```
<datetime literal> :=
   { ' <years> - <months> - <days> <space>
     [ <hours> [ : <minutes> [ : <seconds>
        [ . <microseconds>] ] ] ] ' } |
   { <years> <months> <days> <hours> <minutes> <seconds> }
```

```
<days> ::= <digit> [ <digit> ]
```

```
<decimal data type> ::=
   DEC     [ ( <precision> [ , <scale> ] ) ] |
   DECIMAL [ ( <precision> [ , <scale> ] ) ] |
   NUMERIC [ ( <precision> [ , <scale> ] ) ] |
   FIXED   [ ( <precision> [ , <scale> ] ) ]
```

```
<decimal literal> ::=
   [ + | - ] <whole number> [ .<whole number> ] |
   [ + | - ] <whole number>.                    |
   [ + | - ] .<whole number>
```

```
<definer option> ::=
   DEFINER = { <user name> | CURRENT_USER }
```

```
<directory> ::= Valid specification of a directory according to
                the rules of the operating system that is used.
```

```
<event schedule> ::=
   <single schedule>
   <recurring schedule>
```

```
<exponent> ::= <integer literal>
```

```
<export option> ::=
   FIELDS [ TERMINATED BY <alphanumeric literal> ]
          [ [ OPTIONALLY ] ENCLOSED BY <alphanumeric literal> ]
          [ ESCAPED BY <alphanumeric literal> ] |
   LINES TERMINATED BY <alphanumeric literal>
```

For each data type, a version of this expression follows.

```
<expression> ::=
   <scalar expression>      |
   <row expression>         |
   <table expression>
```

```
<expression list> ::= <expression>  [ , <expression> ]...
```

```
<fetch number of rows> ::= <whole number>
```

```
<fetch offset> ::= <whole number>
```

```
<float data type> ::=
   FLOAT [ ( <length> ) | ( <presentation width> , <scale> ) ] |
   FLOAT4 [ ( <presentation width> , <scale>) ]                 |
   REAL [ ( <presentation width> , <scale>) ]                   |
   DOUBLE [ PRECISION ] [ ( <presentation width> , <scale>) ]
```

```
<float literal> ::=
   <mantissa> { E | e } <exponent>
```

```
<foreign key> ::=
   [ CONSTRAINT [ <constraint name> ] ]
   FOREIGN KEY [ <index name> ] <column list>
   <referencing specification>
```

```
<from clause> ::=
   FROM <table reference> [ , <table reference> ]...
```

```
<geometric data type> ::=
   GEOMETRY           |
   GEOMETRYCOLLECTION |
   LINESTRING         |
   MULTILIMESTRING    |
   MULTIPOINT         |
   MULTIPOLYGON       |
   POINT              |
   POLYGON
```

```
<grantees> ::=
   <user specification> [ , <user specification> ]...
```

```
<grant option> ::=
   GRANT OPTION                               |
   MAX_CONNECTIONS_PER_HOUR <whole number>    |
   MAX_QUERIES_PER_HOUR <whole number>        |
   MAX_UPDATES_PER_HOUR <whole number>        |
   MAX_USER_CONNECTIONS <whole number>
```

```
<group by clause> ::=
   GROUP BY <group by specification list> [ WITH ROLLUP ]
```

```
<group by expression> ::= <scalar expression>
```

```
<group by specification> ::=
   <group by expression> [ <sort direction> ]
```

```
<group by specification list> ::=
   <group by specification> [ , <group by specification> ]...
```

```
<having clause> ::= HAVING <condition>
```

```
<hexadecimal character> ::=
   <digit> | A | B | C | D | E | F | a | b | c | d | e | f
```

```
<hexadecimal literal> ::=
   { X | x } <hexadecimal character>... |
   0x <hexadecimal character>...
```

```
<hours> ::= <digit> [ <digit> ]
```

```
<index change> ::=
   ADD [ <index type> ] INDEX <index name>
      [ USING { BTREE | HASH } ]
      ( <column in index> [ , <column in index> ]... ) |
   DROP { INDEX | KEY } <index name>
```

```
<index definition> ::=
   <index type> { INDEX | KEY } [ <index name> ]
   [ USING { BTREE | HASH } ]
   ( <column in index> [ , <column in index> ]... )
```

```
<index type> ::= UNIQUE | FULLTEXT | SPATIAL
```

```
<insert specification> ::=
   [ <column list> ] <values clause>                  |
   [ <column list> ] <table expression>               |
   [ <table specification> SET <column assignment>
      [ , <column assignment> ]...
```

```
<integer data type> ::=
   TINYINT   [ ( <presentation width> ) ] |
   INT1      [ ( <presentation width> ) ] |
   BOOLEAN                                |
   BIT                                    |
   SMALLINT  [ ( <presentation width> ) ] |
   INT2      [ ( <presentation width> ) ] |
   MEDIUMINT [ ( <presentation width> ) ] |
   INT3      [ ( <presentation width> ) ] |
   MIDDLEINT [ ( <presentation width> ) ] |
   INT       [ ( <presentation width> ) ] |
   INTEGER   [ ( <presentation width> ) ] |
   INT4      [ ( <presentation width> ) ] |
   BIGINT    [ ( <presentation width> ) ] |
   INT8      [ ( <presentation width> ) ]
```

```
<integer literal> ::= [ + | - ] <whole number
```

```
<integrity constraint change> ::=
   ADD <primary key>                         |
   DROP PRIMARY KEY                          |
   ADD <alternate key>                       |
   DROP FOREIGN KEY <index name>             |
   ADD <foreign key>                         |
   ADD <check integrity constraint>          |
   DROP CONSTRAINT <constraint name>
```

```
<interval length> ::= <scalar expression>
```

```
<into file clause> ::=
   INTO OUTFILE '<file name>' <export option>... |
   INTO DUMPFILE '<file name>'                   |
   INTO <user variable> [ , <user variable> ]...
```

```
<join condition> ::=
    ON <condition> | USING <column list>
```

```
<join specification> ::=
   <table reference> <join type> <table reference>
      [ <join condition> ]
```

```
<join type> ::=
   [ INNER ] JOIN                              |
   LEFT  [ OUTER ] JOIN                        |
   RIGHT [ OUTER ] JOIN                        |
   NATURAL [ LEFT | RIGHT ] [ OUTER ] JOIN     |
   CROSS JOIN
```

```
<length> ::= <whole number>
```

```
<like pattern> ::= <scalar alphanumeric expression>
```

```
<limit clause> ::=
   LIMIT [ <fetch offset> , ] <fetch number of rows>       |
   LIMIT <fetch number of rows> [ OFFSET <fetch offset> ]
```

```
<literal> ::=
   <numeric literal>        |
   <alphanumeric literal>   |
   <temporal literal>       |
   <Boolean literal>        |
   <hexadecimal literal>
```

```
<local variable> ::= <variable name>
```

```
<local variable list> ::=
   <local variable> [ , <local variable> ]...
```

```
<mantissa> ::= <decimal literal>
```

```
<mathematical operator> ::= * | / | + | - | % | DIV
```

```
<microseconds> ::= <whole number>
```

```
<minutes> ::= <digit> [ <digit> ]
```

```
<months> ::= <digit> [ <digit> ]
```

```
<null specification> ::= [ NOT ] NULL
```

```
<numeric data type> ::=
   <integer data type> |
   <decimal data type> |
   <float data type>   |
   <bit data type>
```

```
<numeric data type option> ::=
   UNSIGNED              |
   ZEROFILL              |
   AUTO_INCREMENT        |
   SERIAL DEFAULT VALUE
```

```
<numeric literal> ::=
   <integer literal> |
   <decimal literal> |
   <float literal>   |
   <bit literal>
```

```
<order by clause> ::=
   ORDER BY <sort specification> [ , <sort specification> ]...
```

```
<parameter> ::= <local variable>
```

```
<parameter list> ::=
   <parameter specification>
      [ , <parameter specification> ]...
```

Following are two definitions of parameter specification. The first applies to stored procedures; the second applies to stored functions.

```
<parameter specification> ::=
   [ IN | OUT | INOUT ] <parameter> <data type>
```

```
<parameter specification> ::= <parameter> <data type>
```

```
<password> ::= <alphanumeric literal>
```

```
<precision> ::= <whole number>
```

```
<predicate> ::=
   <predicate with comparison>    |
   <predicate without comparison> |
   <predicate with in>            |
   <predicate with between>       |
   <predicate with like>          |
   <predicate with regexp>        |
   <predicate with match>         |
   <predicate with null>          |
   <predicate with exists>        |
   <predicate with any all>
```

```
<predicate with any all> ::=
   <scalar expression> <any all operator> <column subquery>
```

```
<predicate with between> ::=
   <scalar expression> [ NOT ] BETWEEN <scalar expression>
      AND <scalar expression>
```

```
<predicate with comparison> ::=
   <scalar expression> <comparison operator>
      <scalar expression> |
   <row expression> <comparison operator> <row expression>
```

```
<predicate with exists> ::= EXISTS <table subquery>
```

```
<predicate with in> ::=
   <scalar expression> [ NOT ] IN <scalar expression list> |
   <scalar expression> [ NOT ] IN <column subquery>        |
   <row expression> [ NOT ] IN <row expression list>       |
   <row expression> [ NOT ] IN <table subquery>
```

```
<predicate with like> ::=
   <scalar expression> [ NOT ] LIKE <like pattern>
      [ ESCAPE <character> ]
```

```
<predicate with match> ::=
   MATCH ( <column specification>
      [ , <column specification> ]... )
      AGAINST ( <scalar expression> [ <search style> ] )
```

```
<predicate with null> ::=
   <scalar expression> IS [ NOT ] NULL
```

```
<predicate without comparison> ::= <scalar expression>
```

```
<predicate with regexp> ::=
   <scalar expression> [ NOT ] [ REGEXP | RLIKE ]
      <regexp pattern>
```

```
<presentation width> ::= <whole number>
```

```
<primary key> ::=
   [ CONSTRAINT [ <constraint name> ] ]
   PRIMARY KEY [ <index name> ]
   [ { USING | TYPE } <index type> ] <column list>
```

```
<recurring schedule> ::=
   EVERY <number> <time unit>
   [ STARTS <timestamp literal> ]
   [ ENDS <timestamp literal> ]
```

```
<referencing action> ::=
   ON { UPDATE | DELETE }
      { CASCADE | RESTRICT | SET NULL |
        NO ACTION | SET DEFAULT } |
   [ MATCH FULL | MATCH PARTIAL | MATCH SIMPLE ]
```

```
<referencing specification> ::=
   REFERENCES <table specification> <column list>
      [ <referencing action>... ]
```

```
<regexp pattern> ::= <scalar expression>
```

```
<routine body> ::= <begin-end block>
```

```
<routine characteristic> ::=
   LANGUAGE SQL                                   |
   [ NOT ] DETERMINISTIC                          |
   { CONTAINS SQL | NO SQL | READS SQL DATA |
     MODIFIES SQL DATA }                          |
   <sql security-option>                          |
   COMMENT <alphanumeric literal>
```

```
<row expression> ::=
   <singular row expression> |
   <row subquery>
```

```
<row expression list> ::=
   ( <scalar expression list>
      [ , <scalar expression list> ]... )
```

For each data type, a version of the scalar expression follows.

```
<scalar expression> ::=
   <singular scalar expression> |
   <compound scalar expression>
```

```
<scalar expression list> ::=
   ( <scalar expression> [ , <scalar expression> ]... )
```

```
<scalar function> ::=
   <scalar function name>
      ( <scalar expression> [ , <scalar expression> ]... )
```

```
<scale> ::= <whole number>
```

```
<search style> ::=
   IN NATURAL LANGUAGE MODE                          |
   IN NATURAL LANGUAGE MODE WITH QUERY EXPANSION     |
   IN BOOLEAN MODE                                   |
   WITH QUERY EXPANSION
```

```
<seconds> ::= <digit> [ <digit> ]
```

```
<select block head> ::=
      <select clause>
   [ <from clause>
   [ <where clause> ]
   [ <group by clause> ]
   [ <having clause> ] ]
      <limit clause>
```

```
<select block tail> ::=
   <order by clause> |
   <limit clause>    |
   <order by clause> <limit clause>
```

```
<select clause> ::=
   SELECT <select option>... <select element list>
```

```
<select element> ::=
   <scalar expression> [[ AS ] <column name> ] |
   <table specification>.*                     |
   <pseudonym>.*
```

```
<select element list> ::=
   <select element> [ , <select element> ]... |
   *
```

```
<select option> ::=
   DISTINCT | DISTINCTROW | ALL | HIGH_PRIORITY |
   SQL_BUFFER_RESULT | SQL_CACHE | SQL_NO_CACHE |
   SQL_CALC_FOUND_ROWS | SQL_SMALL_RESULT | SQL BIG_RESULT |
   STRAIGHT_JOIN
```

```
<set operator> ::= UNION | UNION DISTINCT | UNION ALL
```

```
<single schedule> ::=
   AT <timestamp expression>
```

```
<singular row expression> ::=
   ( <scalar expression> [ , <scalar expression> ]... ) |
   <row subquery>
```

For each data type, a version of the singular scalar expression follows. In addition, in a singular scalar expression, a collation may be specified only if the data type of the expression is alphanumeric.

```
<singular scalar expression> ::=
   { <literal>                                          |
     _ <character set name> <alphanumeric literal>      |
     <column specification>                             |
     <user variable>                                    |
     <system variable>                                  |
     <locale variable>                                  |
     <cast expression>                                  |
     <case expression>                                  |
     NULL                                               |
     ( <scalar expression> )                            |
     <scalar function>                                  |
     <aggregation function>                             |
     <stored function>                                  |
     <scalar subquery>                                  }
   [ COLLATE <collating_sequence_name> ]
```

```
<singular table expression> ::= <select block head>
```

```
<sort direction> ::= ASC | DESC
```

```
<sort specification> ::=
   <scalar expression> [ <sort direction> ] |
   <sequence number> [<sort direction> ]    |
   <column name> [ <sort direction> ]
```

```
<special symbol> ::=
   { \ { 0 | ' | " | b | n | r | t | z | \ | % } } |
   <any other symbol>
```

```
<sql security option> ::=
   SQL SECURITY { DEFINER | INVOKER }
```

```
<statement in body> ::=
   <declarative statement> |
   <procedural statement>
```

```
<statement list> ::= { <statement in body> ; }...
```

```
<stored function> ::=
   <stored function name>
      ( <scalar expression> [ , <scalar expression> ]... )
```

```
<subquery> ::= ( <table expression> )
```

```
<system variable> ::=
   [ @@ ] [ <variable type> . ] <variable name>
```

```
<table change> ::=
   RENAME [ TO | AS ] <table name>                                |
   <table options>...                                             |
   CONVERT TO CHARACTER SET { <character set name> | DEFAULT }
      [ COLLATE <collation name> ]                                |
   ORDER BY <sort specification>
      [ , <sort specification> ]...                               |
   { ENABLE | DISABLE } KEYS
```

```
<table contents> ::=
   [ IGNORE | REPLACE ] [ AS ] <table expression>
```

```
<table element> ::=
   <column definition>           |
   <table integrity constraint> |
   <index definition>
```

```
<table expression> ::=
   { <singular table expression > |
     ( <table expression> )         |
     <compound table expression>   }|
   [ <select block tail> ]
```

```
<table integrity constraint> ::=
   [ CONSTRAINT [ <constraint name> ] ]
   { <primary key>                     |
     <alternate key>                   |
     <foreign key>                     |
     <check integrity constraint> }
```

```
<table option> ::=
   ENGINE = <engine name>                                          |
   TYPE = <engine name>                                            |
   UNION = ( <table name> [ , <table name> ]... )                  |
   INSERT_METHOD = { NO | FIRST | LAST }                           |
   AUTO_INCREMENT = <whole number>                                 |
   COMMENT = <alphanumeric literal>                                |
   AVG_ROW_LENGTH = <whole number>                                 |
   MAX_ROWS = <whole number>                                       |
   MIN_ROWS = <whole number>                                       |
   [ DEFAULT ] CHARACTER SET
      { <character set name> | DEFAULT }                           |
   [ DEFAULT ] COLLATE
      { <collation name> | DEFAULT }                               |
   DATA DIRECTORY = <directory >                                   |
   INDEX DIRECTORY = <directory >                                  |
   CHECK_SUM = { 0 | 1 }                                           |
   DELAY_KEY_WRITE = { 0 | 1 }                                     |
   PACK_KEYS = { 0 | 1 | DEFAULT }                                 |
   PASSWORD = <alphanumeric literal>                               |
   RAID_TYPE = { 1 | STRIPED | RAID0 }                             |
   RAID_CHUNKS = <whole number>                                    |
   RAID_CHUNKSIZE = <whole number>                                 |
   ROW_FORMAT = { DEFAULT | DYNAMIC | FIXED | COMPRESSED }
```

```
<table privilege> ::=
   SELECT                          |
   INSERT                          |
   DELETE [ <column list> ]        |
   UPDATE [ <column list> ]        |
   REFERENCES [ <column list> ]    |
   CREATE                          |
   ALTER                           |
   INDEX [ <column list> ]         |
   DROP
```

```
<table privileges> ::=
   ALL [ PRIVILEGES ] |
   <table privilege> [ , <table privilege> ]...
```

```
<table reference> ::=
   { <table specification> |
     <join specification>  |
     <table subquery>       }
   [ [ AS ] <pseudonym> ]
```

```
<table schema> ::=
   ( <table element> [ , <table element> ]... )
```

```
<table specification> ::= [ <database name> . ] <table name>
```

```
<table structure> ::=
   LIKE <table specification>             |
   ( LIKE <table specification> )         |
   <table contents                        |
   <table schema> [ <table contents> ]
```

```
<table structure change> ::=
   <table change>                  |
   <column change>                 |
   <integrity constraint change> |
   <index change>
```

```
<table subquery> ::= ( <table expression> )
```

```
<temporal data type> ::=
   DATE                         |
   DATETIME                     |
   TIME                         |
   TIMESTAMP                    |
   YEAR [ ( 2 ) | ( 4 ) ]
```

```
<temporal literal> ::=
   <date literal>      |
   <time literal>      |
   <datetime literal>  |
   <timestamp literal> |
   <year literal>
```

```
<time interval> ::= <scalar time expression>
```

```
<time literal> ::=
   { ' <hours> : <minutes> [ : <seconds>
       [ . <microseconds> ] ] ' }                |
   { ' [ <hours> : <minutes> : ] <seconds> ' } |
   { <hours> <minutes> <seconds> }             |
   { [ [ <hours> ] <minutes> ] <seconds> }
```

```
<timestamp interval> ::=
   INTERVAL <interval length> <timestamp interval unit>
```

```
<timestamp interval unit> ::=
   MICROSECOND | SECOND | MINUTE | HOUR |
   DAY | WEEK | MONTH | QUARTER | YEAR |
   SECOND_MICROSECOND | MINUTE_MICROSECOND | MINUTE_SECOND |
   HOUR_MICROSECOND | HOUR_SECOND | HOUR_MINUTE |
   DAY_MICROSECOND | DAY_SECOND | DAY_MINUTE | DAY_HOUR |
   YEAR_MONTH
```

```
<timestamp literal> ::=
   { ' <years> - <months> - <days> <spacing>
     [ <hours> [ : <minutes> [ : <seconds>
        [ . <microseconds>] ] ] ] ' } |
   { <years> <months> <days> <hours> <minutes> <seconds> }
```

```
<user name> ::=
   <name> | '<name>' | '<name>'@'<host name>'
```

```
<user privilege> ::=
   SELECT                   |
   INSERT                   |
   DELETE                   |
   UPDATE                   |
   REFERENCES               |
   CREATE                   |
   ALTER                    |
   DROP                     |
   INDEX                    |
   CREATE TEMPORARY TABLES  |
   CREATE VIEW              |
   SHOW VIEW                |
   CREATE ROUTINE           |
   ALTER ROUTINE            |
   EXECUTE ROUTINE          |
   LOCK TABLES              |
   EVENT                    |
   CREATE USER              |
   SHOW DATABASES           |
   FILE                     |
   PROCESS                  |
   RELOAD                   |
   REPLICATION CLIENT       |
   REPLICATION SLAVE        |
   SHUTDOWN                 |
   SUPER                    |
   USAGE
```

```
<user privileges> ::=
   ALL [ PRIVILEGES ] |
   <user privilege> [ , <user privilege> ]...
```

```
<user specification> ::=
   <user name> [ IDENTIFIED BY [ PASSWORD ] <password> ]
```

```
<user variable> ::= @ <variable name>
```

```
<values clause> ::=
   VALUES <row expression> [ , <row expression> ]...
```

```
<variable type> ::= SESSION | GLOBAL | LOCAL
```

```
<when definition> ::= <when definition-1> | <when definition-2>
```

```
<when definition-1> ::=
   <scalar expression>
   WHEN <scalar expression> THEN <scalar expression>
   [ WHEN <scalar expression> THEN <scalar expression> ]...
```

```
<when definition-2> ::=
   WHEN <condition> THEN <scalar expression>
   [ WHEN <condition> THEN <scalar expression> ]...
```

```
<where clause> ::= WHERE <condition>
```

```
<whole number> ::= <digit>...
```

```
<year> ::= <whole number
```

```
<year literal> ::= <year>
```

```
<years> ::= <whole number
```

```
<character set name>    ;
<collation name>        ;
<column name>           ;
<condition name>        ;
<constraint name>       ;
<cursor name>           ;
<database name>         ;
<engine name>           ;
<handler name>          ;
<host name>             ;
<index name>            ;
<label>                 ;
<local variable>        ;
<pseudonym>             ;
<savepoint name>        ;
<scalar function name>  ;
<statement name>        ;
<stored function name>  ;
<stored procedure name> ;
<table name>            ;
<trigger name>          ;
<variable name>         ;
<view name>             ::= <object name>

<object name> ::= <letter> [ <letter> | <digit> | _ ]...
```

APPENDIX B

Scalar Functions

MySQL supports many scalar functions. For all functions, this appendix presents the name, a description, the data type of the result of the function, and a few examples. The functions are sorted by name.

Some functions have more than one name. To make the search easier, we have included them all, but we refer to the functions with the same name.

Note that MySQL has two data types that form a combination of a date and a time: the datetime and timestamp. If a function can work with timestamps, it can usually work with datetimes, too, and the other way round. For the sake of convenience, this appendix considers these data types to be synonyms. If you come across "timestamp" somewhere in the appendix, you actually must read "timestamp and datetime" (unless otherwise mentioned).

ABS(par1)

Description: This function returns the absolute value of a numeric expression.

Data type: Numeric

```
ABS(-25)     → 25
ABS(-25.89) → 25.89
```

ACOS(par1)

Description: This function returns, in radians, the angle size for any given arc cosine value. The value of the parameter must lie between -1 and 1 inclusive.

Data type: Numeric

```
ACOS(0)           → 1.5707963267949
ACOS(-1) - PI() → 0
ACOS(1)           → 0
ACOS(2)           → NULL
```

ADDDATE(par1, par2)

Description: This function adds an interval (the second parameter) to a datetime or timestamp expression (the first parameter). See Section 5.13.3 for specifying intervals. If the second parameter is not an interval but is a numeric value, MySQL assumes that this value represents a number of days.

Data type: Date or timestamp

```
ADDDATE('2004-01-01', INTERVAL 5 MONTH) → '2004-06-01'
ADDDATE(TIMESTAMP('2004-01-01'), INTERVAL 5 MONTH)
   → '2004-06-01 00:00:00'
ADDDATE('2004-01-01 12:00:00', INTERVAL 5 DAY)
   → '2004-01-06 12:00:00'
ADDDATE('2004-01-01', 5) → '2004-01-06'
```

AES_DECRYPT(par1, par2)

Description: This function decodes (encryption) the first parameter based upon a certain key (the second parameter); see the AES_ENCRYPT function for a description. That same AES_ENCRYPT function encodes the value.

Data type: Blob

```
AES_ENCRYPT('database','xyz') → ' ?ñ_--ZG›rN4?_ËŽš'
AES_DECRYPT(AES_ENCRYPT('database','xyz'),'xyz') → 'database'
```

AES_ENCRYPT(par1, par2)

Description: This function decodes the encoded value of the first parameter back, based upon a certain key (the second parameter). The abbreviation *AES* stands for *Advanced Encryption Standard.* Encoding is done with the help of a key that is 128 bits long; the key can be extended to 256 bits by increasing its value. Both parameters may have a numeric or alphanumeric data type. The length of the created value can be calculated as follows: `16 * (TRUNC(par1/16) + 1)`. With the AES_DECRYPT function, the encoded value is converted back to the original value.

Data type: Alphanumeric

```
AES_ENCRYPT('database','xyz') → ' ?ñ_--ZG›rN4?_ËŽš'
AES_ENCRYPT('database',12)    → 'Cn ú6•ìlí¥Ž©áÿM*'
AES_DECRYPT(AES_ENCRYPT('database','xyz'),'xyz') → 'database'
AES_DECRYPT(AES_ENCRYPT('database','xyz'),'abc') → ' à'
```

ADDTIME(par1, par2)

Description: This function adds two time expressions. The result is an interval consisting of a number of hours, minutes, and seconds. Therefore, the number of hours can be greater than 24.

Data type: Time

```
ADDTIME('12:59:00', '0:59:00')      → '13:58:00'
ADDTIME('12:00:00', '0:00:00.001') → '12:00:00.001000'
ADDTIME('100:00:00', '900:00:00')  → '1000:00:00'
```

ASCII(par1)

Description: This function returns the ASCII value of the first character of an alphanumeric expression.

Data type: Numeric

```
ASCII('Database') → 68
ASCII('database') → 100
ASCII('')         → 0
ASCII(NULL)       → NULL
```

ASIN(par1)

Description: This function returns, in radians, the angle size for any given arc sine value. The value of the parameter must lie between -1 and 1 inclusive; otherwise, the result is equal to the null value.

Data type: Numeric

```
ASIN(1)    → 1.5707963267949
ASIN(0)    → 0
ASIN(NULL) → NULL
```

ATAN(par1)

Description: This function returns, in radians, the angle size for any given arc tangent value.

Data type: Numeric

```
ATAN(0)   → 0
ATAN(100) → 1.56079666010823
ATAN(1)   → 0.78539816339745
```

ATAN(par1, par2)

Description: This function returns, in radians, the angle size for any given arc tangent value. If the ATAN function has two parameters, it is a synonym of the ATAN2 function.

Data type: Numeric

```
ATAN(30,30)          → 0.78539816339745
ATAN(8,4) - ATAN(2) → 0
```

ATAN2(par1, par2)

Description: This function returns, in radians, the angle size for any given arc tangent value.

Data type: Numeric

```
ATAN2(30,30)  →  0.78539816339745
ATAN2(-1,-1)  →  -2.3561944901923
```

ATANH(par1)

Description: This function returns the hyperbolic arc tangent value of the parameter; it must be specified in radians.

Data type: Numeric

```
ATANH(0.4)  →  0.255412811882995
```

BENCHMARK(par1, par2)

Description: This function evaluates a certain expression (the second parameter) several times (the first parameter). The result of this function is always equal to `0`. This function can be used to determine the speed of a certain expression.

Data type: Numeric

```
BENCHMARK(100, SQRT(8))  →  0
```

BIN(par1)

Description: This function transforms the numeric value of the parameter into a binary value that consists of ones and zeroes, and has the alphanumeric data type.

Data type: Alphanumeric

```
BIN(7)        →  '111'
BIN(1000000)  →  '11110100001001000000'
```

BIT_COUNT(par1)

Description: This function shows the number of bits needed to present the value of the parameter. Here, 64-bits integers are used.

Data type: Numeric

```
BIT_COUNT(3)   →  2
BIT_COUNT(-1)  →  64
```

BIT_LENGTH(par1)

Description: This function returns the length in bits of an alphanumeric value.

Data type: Numeric

```
BIT_LENGTH('database') → 64
BIT_LENGTH(BIN(2))     → 16
```

CEILING(par1)

Description: This function returns the highest whole number that is greater than or equal to the value of the parameter.

Data type: Numeric

```
CEILING(13.43)  → 14
CEILING(-13.43) → -13
CEILING(13)     → 13
```

CHAR(par1, par2, par3, ...)

Description: This function returns the alphanumeric character of each of the numeric parameters. Next, the alphanumeric characters are combined into one alphanumeric literal.

Data type: Alphanumeric

```
CHAR(80)                                    → 'P'
CHAR(82) + CHAR(105) + CHAR(99) + CHAR(107) → 'Rick'
CHAR(82, 105, 99, 107)                      → 'Rick'
```

CHARACTER_LENGTH(par1)

Description: This function returns the length of an alphanumeric expression.

Data type: Numeric

```
CHARACTER_LENGTH('database')                           → 8
CHARACTER_LENGTH((SELECT MAX(NAME) FROM PLAYERS))      → 6
CHARACTER_LENGTH('')                                   → 0
CHARACTER_LENGTH(NULL)                                 → NULL
CHARACTER_LENGTH(BIN(8))                               → 4
```

CHARSET(par1)

Description: This function returns the name of the character set of the alphanumeric parameter.

Data type: Alphanumeric

```
CHARSET('database')                       → 'latin1'
CHARSET((SELECT MAX(NAME) FROM PLAYERS))   → 'latin1'
CHARSET((SELECT MAX(TABLE_NAME)
        FROM   INFORMATION_SCHEMA.TABLES)) → 'utf8'
```

CHAR_LENGTH(par1)

Description: This function returns the length of an alphanumeric expression. See the CHARACTER_LENGTH function.

Data type: Numeric

```
CHAR_LENGTH('database')                       → 8
CHAR_LENGTH((SELECT MAX(NAME) FROM PLAYERS))  → 6
CHAR_LENGTH('')                               → 0
CHAR_LENGTH(NULL)                             → NULL
CHAR_LENGTH(BIN(8))                           → 4
```

COALESCE(par1, par2, par3, ...)

Description: This function can have a variable number of parameters. The value of the function is equal to the value of the first parameter that is not equal to null. If E_1, E_2, and E_3 are three expressions, the specification

```
COALESCE(E1, E2, E3)
```

is equivalent to the following case expression:

```
CASE
   WHEN E1 IS NOT NULL THEN E1
   WHEN E2 IS NOT NULL THEN E2
   WHEN E3 IS NOT NULL THEN E3
   ELSE NULL
END
```

Data type: Depends on the parameters

```
COALESCE('John', 'Jim', NULL)                 → 'John'
COALESCE(NULL, NULL, NULL, 'John', 'Jim')     → 'John'
```

COERCIBILITY(par1)

Description: This function determines the coercibility value of an expression.

Data type: Numeric

```
COERCIBILITY(NULL)        → 5
COERCIBILITY('Database')  → 4
```

COLLATION (par1)

Description: This function gets the name of the collation of the alphanumeric parameter.

Data type: Alphanumeric

```
COLLATION('database')
   → 'latin1_swedish_ci'
COLLATION((SELECT MAX(NAME) FROM PLAYERS))
   → 'latin1_swedish_ci'
COLLATION((SELECT MAX(TABLE_NAME)
           FROM   INFORMATION_SCHEMA.TABLES))
   → 'utf8_general_ci'
```

COMPRESS(par1)

Description: This function compresses the value of the parameter. The UNCOMPRESS function can be used to return the original value.

Data type: Alphanumeric

```
LENGTH(COMPRESS('byeeeeeeeeeeeeeeeeeee')) → 16
LENGTH('byeeeeeeeeeeeeeeeeeee'))           → 21
UNCOMPRESS(COMPRESS('database'))           → 'database'
```

CONCAT(par1, part2, par3, ...)

Description: This function combines one, two, or more alphanumeric values. You can achieve the same effect with the || operator.

Data type: Alphanumeric

```
CONCAT('Data','base')                      → 'Database'
CONCAT('MySQL ','data','base','server')    → 'MySQL databaseserver'
CONCAT('MySQL',NULL,' server')             → NULL
```

CONCAT_WS(par1, part2, par3, ...)

Description: This function combines one, two, or more alphanumeric values; however, the value of the first parameter is placed between all the others.

Data type: Alphanumeric

```
CONCAT_WS('-','a','b','c','d')  → 'a-b-c-d'
CONCAT_WS(', ','Hello','world') → 'Hello, world'
```

CONNECTION_ID()

Description: This function returns the numeric identifier of the connection.

Data type: Numeric

```
CONNECTION_ID() → 4
```

CONV(par1, part2, par3)

Description: This function converts the value (first parameter) of one number base (second parameter) to another (third parameter). The value of the two last parameters must be between 2 and 36; otherwise, the result is equal to null. Furthermore, the value of the first parameter should fit into the number base of the first parameter; otherwise, the result is 0.

Data type: Alphanumeric

```
CONV(1110, 2, 10)  → '14'
CONV(1110, 10, 2)  → '10001010110'
CONV(1110, 10, 8)  → '2126'
CONV(1110, 10, 16) → '456'
CONV(35, 10, 36)   → 'Z'
CONV(35, 10, 37)   → NULL
CONV(8, 2, 10)     → '0'
```

CONVERT(par1, par2)

Description: This function converts the data type of the first parameter. The second parameter must be equal to one of the well-known data types, including BINARY, CHAR, DATE, DATETIME, TIME, SIGNED, SIGNED INTEGER, UNSIGNED, UNSIGNED INTEGER, or VARCHAR. This specification

```
CONVERT(par1, type1)
```

is equal to:

```
CAST(par1 AS type1)
```

The following formulation may also be used:

```
CONVERT(par1 USING type1)
```

Data type: Depends on the second parameter

```
CONVERT(45, CHAR(2))                 → '45'
CONVERT('2000-01-42', DATE)          → '2000-01-01'
CONVERT(12.56, UNSIGNED INTEGER)     → 13
CONVERT(-12.56, UNSIGNED INTEGER) → 18446744073709551603
```

CONVERT_TZ(par1, part2, par3)

Description: This function determines what the timestamp value of a timestamp expression (first parameter) is when the time zone is changed. The second parameter indicates the current time zone, and the third parameter indicates the new time zone.

Date type: Timestamp

```
CONVERT_TZ('2005-05-20 09:30:40', '+00:00', '+9:00')
   → 2005-05-20 18:30:40
```

COS(par1)

Description: This function returns, in radians, the cosine value for any angle size.

Data type: Numeric

```
COS(0)        → 1
COS(PI()/2)   → 0
COS(PI())     → -1
```

COT(par1)

Description: This function returns, in radians, the cotangent value for any angle size.

Data type: Numeric

```
COT(10)       → 1.54235
COT(PI()/2)   → 0
COT(NULL)     → NULL
```

CRC32(par1)

Description: This function calculates a cyclic redundancy check beginning at the parameter.

Date type: Numeric

```
CRC32(0) → 4108050209
CRC32(1) → 2212294583
```

CURDATE()

Description: This function returns the system date with the format `YYYY-MM-DD`. If the function is regarded as a numeric expression, the system date is presented as a numeric value with the format `YYYYMMDD`. See the `CURRENT_DATE` function.

Data type: Date or double

```
CURDATE()     → '2005-02-20'
CURDATE() + 0 → 20050220
```

CURRENT_DATE()

Description: This function returns the system date with the format YYYY-MM-DD. If the function is regarded as a numeric expression, the system date is presented as a numeric value with the format YYYYMMDD. If the brackets are left out, the function changes into the system variable CURRENT_DATE. See the CURDATE function.

Data type: Date or double

```
CURRENT_DATE()     → '2005-02-20'
CURRENT_DATE() + 0 → 20050220
CURRENT_DATE       → '2005-02-20'
```

CURRENT_TIME()

Description: This function returns the system time with the format: HH:MM:SS. The abbreviation HH stands for the hours, MM for minutes, and SS for seconds. If the function is regarded as a numeric expression, the system time is presented as a numeric value with the format HHMMSS. If the brackets are left out, the function changes into the system variable CURRENT_TIME. See the CURTIME function.

Data type: Time or double

```
CURRENT_TIME()     → '16:42:24'
CURRENT_TIME() + 0 → 164224
CURRENT_TIME       → '16:42:24'
```

CURRENT_TIMESTAMP()

Description: This function returns the system date and time with the format: YYYY-MM-DD HH:MM:SS. The abbreviation YYYY stands for years, the first MM for months, DD for days, HH for hours, the second MM for minutes, and SS for seconds. If the function is regarded as a numeric expression, the system date and time are presented as a numeric value with the format YYYYMMDDHHMMSS. If the brackets are left out, the function changes into the system variable CURRENT_TIMESTAMP.

Data type: Timestamp or double

```
CURRENT_TIMESTAMP()     → '2005-10-16 20:53:45'
CURRENT_TIMESTAMP() + 0 → 20051016205345
CURRENT_TIMESTAMP       → '2005-10-16 20:53:45'
```

CURRENT_USER()

Description: This function returns the name of the SQL user.

Data type: Alphanumeric

```
CURRENT_USER() → 'root@localhost'
```

CURTIME()

Description: This function returns the system time with the following format: HH:MM:SS. The abbreviation HH stands for the hours, MM for minutes, and SS for seconds. If the function is regarded as a numeric expression, the system time is presented as a numeric value with the format HHMMSS. See the CURRENT_TIME function.

Data type: Time or interval

```
CURTIME()     → '16:42:24'
CURTIME() + 0 → 164224
```

DATABASE()

Description: This function shows the name of the current database.

Data type: Alphanumeric

```
DATABASE() → 'TENNIS'
```

DATE(par1)

Description: This function transforms the parameter into a date value. The parameter should have the format of a correct date or timestamp.

Data type: Date

```
DATE('2005-12-01')          → '2005-12-01'
DATE('2005-12-01 12:13:14') → '2005-12-01'
```

DATE_ADD(par1, par2)

Description: This function adds an interval (the second parameter) to a date or timestamp expression (the first parameter). See Section 5.13.3 for specifying intervals. See the ADDDATE function.

Date type: Date or timestamp

```
DATE_ADD('2004-01-01', INTERVAL 5 MONTH) → '2004-06-01'
DATE_ADD('2004-01-01 12:00:00', INTERVAL 5 DAY)
   → '2004-01-06 12:00:00'
```

DATEDIFF(par1, par2)

Description: This function calculates the number of days between two date or timestamp expressions.

Date type: Numeric

```
DATEDIFF('2004-01-12', '2004-01-01')                       → 11
DATEDIFF('2004-01-01', '2004-01-12')                       → -11
DATEDIFF('2004-01-12 19:00:00', '2004-01-01') )            → 11
DATEDIFF('2004-01-12 19:00:00', '2004-01-01 01:00:00') → 11
DATEDIFF('2004-01-12', CURDATE())                          → -643
```

DATE_FORMAT(par1, par2)

Description: This function transforms a date or timestamp expression (the first parameter) to an alphanumeric value. The second parameter describes the format of that alphanumeric value. Several special format strings can be used; see the following table.

Format String	Explanation
%a	Three-letter English abbreviation of the weekday (for example, Sun, Mon, or Sat)
%b	Three-letter English abbreviation of the month (for example, Jan, Feb, or Mar)
%c	Numeric code for the month (0 up to and including 12)
%D	Day of the month with an English suffix, such as 0th, 1st, and 2nd
%d	Two-digit numeric code for the day of the month (00 up to and including 31)
%e	One- or two-digit numeric code for the day of the month (0 up to and including 31)
%f	Six-digit numeric code for the number of microseconds (000000 up to and including 999999)
%H	Two-digit numeric code for the hour (00 up to and including 23)
%h	Two-digit numeric code for the hour (01 up to and including 12)
%I	Two-digit numeric code for the hour (01 up to and including 12)
%i	Two-digit numeric code for the number of minutes (00 up to and including 59)
%j	Three-digit numeric code for the day of the year (001 up to and including 366)
%k	One- or two-digit numeric code for the hour (0 up to and including 23)
%l	One- or two-digit numeric code for the hour (1 up to and including 12)

continues

Format String	Explanation
%M	English indication of the month (for example, January, February, or December)
%m	Two-digit numeric code for the month (00 up to and including 12)
%p	Indication of AM or PM
%r	Indication of the time (in 12 hours) with the format HH:MM:SS, followed by AM or PM
%S	Two-digit numeric code for the number of seconds (00 up to and including 59)
%s	Two-digit numeric code for the number of seconds (00 up to and including 59)
%T	Indication of the time (in 24 hours) with the format HH:MM:SS, followed by AM or PM
%U	Two-digit numeric code for the week in the year (00 up to and including 53), for which Sunday is considered to be the first day of the week
%u	Two-digit numeric code for the week in the year (00 up to and including 53), for which Monday is considered to be the first day of the week
%V	Two-digit numeric code for the week in the year (01 up to and including 53), for which Sunday is considered to be the first day of the week
%v	Two-digit numeric code for the week in the year (01 up to and including 53), for which Monday is considered to be the first day of the week
%W	English indication of the day in the week (for example, Sunday, Monday, or Saturday)
%w	One-digit code for the day in the week (0 up to and including 6), for which Sunday is considered to be the first day of the week
%X	Four-digit numeric code that indicates the year in which the week starts belonging to the specified date, for which Sunday is the first day of the week
%x	Four-digit numeric code that indicates the year in which the week starts belonging to the specified date, for which Monday is the first day of the week
%Y	Four-digit numeric code for the year
%y	Two-digit numeric code for the year
%%	Returns the percentage sign

Data type: Alphanumeric

```
DATE_FORMAT('2005-10-16', '%a %c %b')      → 'Sun 10 Oct'
DATE_FORMAT('2005-10-06', '%d %e %D')      → '06 6 6th'
DATE_FORMAT('2005-01-16', '%j %M %m')      → '016 January 01'
DATE_FORMAT('2005-01-09', '%U %u %V %v') → '02 01 02 01'
DATE_FORMAT('2005-12-31', '%U %u %V %v') → '52 52 52 52'
```

```
DATE_FORMAT('2005-01-09', '%W %w')          → 'Sunday 0'
DATE_FORMAT('2005-01-02', '%X %x')          → '2005 2004'
DATE_FORMAT('2005-01-09', '%Y %y')          → '2005 05'
DATE_FORMAT('2005-01-01 12:13:14.012345', '%f') → '012345'
DATE_FORMAT('2005-01-01 12:13:14', '%H %h %I %i')
   → '13 01 01 14'
DATE_FORMAT('2005-01-01 12:13:14', '%k %l %p') → '12 12 PM'
DATE_FORMAT('2005-01-01 12:13:14', '%S %s %T')
   → '14 12 12:13:14'
DATE_FORMAT('2005-01-09', 'Database')      → 'Database'
DATE_FORMAT('2005-01-09', 'It is this day %W')
   → 'This day is Sunday'
```

DATE_SUB(par1, par2)

Description: This function subtracts an interval (the second parameter) from a date or timestamp expression (the first parameter). See Section 5.13.3 for specifying intervals. See the SUBDATE function.

Data type: Date or Timestamp

```
DATE_SUB('2004-01-01', INTERVAL 5 MONTH) → '2003-08-01'
DATE_SUB('2004-01-01 12:00:00', INTERVAL 5 DAY)
   → '2003-12-27 12:00:00'
```

DAY(par1)

Description: This function returns the number of the day of the month from a date or timestamp expression. The value of the result is always a whole number between 1 and 31 inclusive. See the DAYOFMONTH function.

Date type: Numeric

```
DAY('2004-01-01')             → 1
DAY('2004-01-01 09:11:11')   → 1
DAY(CURRENT_DATE())           → 17
DAY(CURRENT_TIMESTAMP())      → 17
```

DAYNAME(par1)

Description: This function returns the name of the day of the week from a date or timestamp expression.

Data type: Alphanumeric

```
DAYNAME('2005-01-01')→ 'Saturday'
```

DAYOFMONTH(par1)

Description: This function returns the number of the day of the month from a date or timestamp expression. The value of the result is always a whole number between 1 and 31 inclusive. See the DAY function.

Data type: Numeric

```
DAYOFMONTH('2004-01-01')            → 1
DAYOFMONTH('2004-01-01 09:11:11') → 1
DAYOFMONTH(CURRENT_DATE())          → 17
DAYOFMONTH(CURRENT_TIMESTAMP())     → 17
```

DAYOFWEEK(par1)

Description: This function returns the number of the day of the week from a date or timestamp expression. The value of the result is always a whole number between 1 and 7 inclusive.

Data type: Numeric

```
DAYOFWEEK('1005-07-29')          → 2
DAYOFWEEK(CURRENT_TIMESTAMP()) → 3
```

DAYOFYEAR(par1)

Description: This function returns the number of the day of the year from a date or timestamp expression. The value of the result is always a whole number between 1 and 366 inclusive.

Data type: Numeric

```
DAYOFYEAR('2005-07-29')            → 210
DAYOFYEAR('2005-07-29 12:00:00') → 210
DAYOFYEAR(CURDATE())               → 291
```

DECODE(par1, par2)

Description: This function decodes (encryption) the first parameter based upon a certain key (the second parameter); see the DES_ENCODE function for an explanation. The value is encoded with that same ENCODE function.

Data type: Blob

```
DECODE('database','xyz') → '?2_?4b@™'
DECODE(ENCODE('database','xyz'),'xyz') → 'database'
```

DEFAULT()

Description: This function returns the default value of a certain column. See also Example 20.26.

Data type: Depends on the column

```
DEFAULT(DATE)   → '1990-01-01'
DEFAULT(AMOUNT) → 50.00
```

DEGREES(par1)

Description: This function converts a number of degrees to a value in radians.

Data type: Numeric

```
DEGREES(1.570796) → 90
DEGREES(PI())     → 180
```

DES_DECRYPT(par1, par2)

Description: This function decodes (encryption) the first parameter based upon a certain key. If a second parameter is specified, it is used as the key; otherwise, the DES key file of the server is used. See the DES_ENCRYPT function for an explanation. The value is encoded with that same DES_ENCRYPT function.

Data type: Blob

```
DES_ENCRYPT('database','xyz') → ' ?ñ_--ZG›rN4?_ËŽš'
DES_DECRYPT(AES_ENCRYPT('database','xyz'),'xyz') → 'database'
```

DES_ENCRYPT(par1, par2)

Description: This function encodes the value of the first parameter back based upon a certain key. If a second parameter is specified, it is used as the key; otherwise, the DES key file of the server is used. The abbreviation *DES* stands for *Data Encryption Standard.* Encoding is done with the help of the triple DES algorithm. The DES_DECRYPT function converts the encoded value to the original value.

Data type: Alphanumeric

```
DES_ENCRYPT('database','xyz') → 'ÿ«eµH_"Ú%__ Cûä'k'
DES_DECRYPT(DES_ENCRYPT('database','xyz'),'xyz') → 'database'
DES_DECRYPT(DES_ENCRYPT('database','xyz'),'abc') → NULL
```

ELT(par1, part2, par3, ...)

Description: This function returns the *n*th element (first parameter) from a series of values (the other parameters). If the *n*th element does not exist, the result of the function is equal to the null value.

Data type: Depends on the parameters

```
ELT(3,0,1,2,3,4)                          → 2
ELT(4,'a','b','c','d','e','f','g','i')   → 'd'
ELT(10,'a','b','c','d','e','f','g','i')  → NULL
```

ENCODE(par1, par2)

Description: This function encodes the value of the first parameter based upon a certain key (the second parameter). The DECODE function decodes the coded value to its original value.

Data type: Alphanumeric

```
DECODE('database','xyz')                     → '?2_?4b@™'
DECODE(ENCODE('database','xyz'),'xyz')  → 'database'
DECODE(ENCODE('database','xyz'),'abc')  → 'Ì?_áç'Ge'
```

EXP(par1)

Description: This function returns the result of the number e to the power of *x*, where *x* is the value of the parameter and e the basis of natural logarithms.

Data type: Numeric

```
EXP(1) → 2.718281828459
EXP(2) → 7.3890560989307
```

EXPORT_SET(par1, part2, par3, par4, par5)

Description: This function returns an alphanumeric value. The first parameter is converted to its binary representation. After that, every 1 is replaced by the value of the second parameter, and every 0 is replaced by the value of the third parameter. If a fourth parameter is specified, this value is placed between each 0 and 1. Omitting this parameter is equal to specifying a comma. If the fifth parameter is specified, it represents the maximum length of the number of values. Omitting this parameter is equal to specifying 64.

Data type: Alphanumeric

```
EXPORT_SET(9,'Y','N','', 10)                → 'YNNYNNNNNN'
EXPORT_SET(9,'Y','N','', 2)                 → 'YN'
EXPORT_SET(9,'Y','N','-', 8)                → 'Y-N-N-Y-N-N-N-N'
EXPORT_SET(CONV(111,2,10),'Y','N','-', 3) → 'Y-Y-Y'
CHAR_LENGTH(EXPORT_SET(9,'Y','N',''))       → 64
```

EXTRACT(par1 FROM par2)

Description: This function returns a component from a date or timestamp expression (the second parameter). The first parameter indicates which component. This must be one of the following values: MICROSECOND, SECOND, MINUTE, HOUR, DAY, WEEK, MONTH, QUARTER, YEAR, SECOND_MICROSECOND, MINUTE_MICROSECOND, MINUTE_SECOND, HOUR_MICROSECOND, HOUR_SECOND, HOUR_MINUTE, DAY_MICROSECOND, DAY_SECOND, DAY_MINUTE, DAY_HOUR, or YEAR_MONTH.

Data type: Numeric

```
EXTRACT(MICROSECOND FROM '2005-07-29 12:13:14.012345')   → 12345
EXTRACT(SECOND FROM '2005-07-29 12:13:14.012345')        → 14
EXTRACT(YEAR FROM '2005-07-29 12:13:14.012345')          → 2005
EXTRACT(MINUTE_SECOND FROM '2005-07-29 12:13:14.012345') → 1314
EXTRACT(DAY_HOUR FROM '2005-07-29 12:13:14.012345')      → 2912
```

FIELD(par1, par2, par3, ...)

Description: This function looks for the position of the first parameter in the series of other parameters.

Data type: Numeric

```
FIELD('e','a','b','c','d','e','f','g','i')  → 5
FIELD('k','a','b','c','d','e','f','g','i')  → 0
FIELD(NULL,'a','b','c','d','e','f','g','i') → 0
```

FIND_IN_SET(par1, par2)

Description: This function looks for the position of the first parameter in the second parameter. This second parameter should have an alphanumeric value in which commas separate individual values.

Data type: numeric

```
FIND_IN_SET('e','a,b,c,d,e,f,g,i')  → 5
FIND_IN_SET('44',(SELECT   GROUP_CONCAT(PLAYERNO)
                  FROM     PLAYERS
                  WHERE    TOWN  = 'Inglewood'
                  GROUP BY TOWN)) → 2
```

FLOOR(par1)

Description: This function returns the smallest whole number that is less than or equal to the value of the parameter.

Data type: Numeric

```
FLOOR(13.9)  → 13
FLOOR(-13.9) → -14
```

FORMAT(par1, par2)

Description: This function formats a numeric value to the pattern *nn,nnn,nnn.nnn*. The second parameter represents the number of decimals behind the comma and must be greater than or equal to 0.

Data type: Alphanumeric

```
FORMAT(123456789.123, 2) → '123,456,789.12'
FORMAT(123456789.123, 0) → '123,456,789'
```

FOUND_ROWS()

Description: This function returns the number of rows in the result of the previous SELECT statement.

Data type: Numeric

```
FOUND_ROWS() → 14
```

FROM_DAYS(par1)

Description: This function determines the date belonging to a number of days that have elapsed since the year 0. The parameter forms the number of days and must be between 366 and 3,652,424.

Data type: Date

```
FROM_DAYS(366)                      → '0001-01-01'
FROM_DAYS(366*2000)                 → '2004-02-24'
FROM_DAYS(3652424)                  → '9999-12-31'
FROM_DAYS(3652500)                  → '0000-00-00'
FROM_DAYS(3652424) - INTERVAL 5 DAY → '9999-12-26'
```

FROM_UNIXTIME(par1, par2)

Description: This function returns the date or timestamp value belonging to a UNIX timestamp that is created with the UNIX_TIMESTAMP function. If a second parameter is specified, the same format string can be specified here as in the DATE_FORMAT function.

Data type: Date, timestamp, or alphanumeric

```
FROM_UNIXTIME(UNIX_TIMESTAMP()) → '2005-12-08 10:16:41'
FROM_UNIXTIME(UNIX_TIMESTAMP(), '%Y %U') → '2005 49'
```

GET_FORMAT(par1, par2)

Description: This function returns a format that can be used in other functions, such as DATE_FORMAT, TIME_FORMAT, and STR_TO_DATE. The first parameter represents the data type. This must be equal to DATE, TIME, or DATETIME. The second parameter represents the format type. Possible values are 'EUR', 'INTERNAL', 'ISO', 'JIS', and 'USA'. The following examples reflect all the possibilities.

Data type: Alphanumeric

```
GET_FORMAT(DATE, 'EUR')             → '%d.%m.%Y'
GET_FORMAT(DATE, 'INTERNAL')        → '%Y%m%d'
GET_FORMAT(DATE, 'ISO')             → '%Y-%m-%d'
GET_FORMAT(DATE, 'JIS')             → '%Y-%m-%d'
GET_FORMAT(DATE, 'USA')             → '%m.%d.%Y'
GET_FORMAT(TIME, 'EUR')             → '%H.%i.%s'
GET_FORMAT(TIME, 'INTERNAL')        → '%H%i%s'
GET_FORMAT(TIME, 'ISO')             → '%H:%i:%s'
GET_FORMAT(TIME, 'JIS')             → '%H:%i:%s'
GET_FORMAT(TIME, 'USA')             → '%h:%i:%s %p'
GET_FORMAT(DATETIME, 'EUR')         → '%Y-%m-%d %H.%i.%s'
GET_FORMAT(DATETIME, 'INTERNAL')    → '%Y%m%d%H%i%s'
GET_FORMAT(DATETIME, 'ISO')         → '%Y-%m-%d %H:%i:%s'
GET_FORMAT(DATETIME, 'JIS')         → '%Y-%m-%d %H:%i:%s'
GET_FORMAT(DATETIME, 'USA')         → '%Y-%m-%d %H.%i.%s'

DATE_FORMAT('2005-01-01', GET_FORMAT(DATE, 'EUR'))
   → '01.01.2005'
DATE_FORMAT('2005-01-01', GET_FORMAT(DATE, 'ISO'))
   → '2005-01-01'
```

GET_LOCK(par1, par2)

Description: This function creates a *named lock*, of which the first parameter represents the name. If this succeeds, the result of this function is equal to 1. If a lock with that name has already been created, a few seconds of waiting time is observed. The second parameter represents that number of seconds. If the lock is still unavailable after this time period, the function returns the result 0.

Data type: Numeric

```
GET_LOCK('lock1',0)  → 1
GET_LOCK('lock1',10) → 0
```

GREATEST(par1, par2, ...)

Description: This function returns the greatest value from a series of parameters.

Data type: Depends on the parameters

```
GREATEST(100, 4, 80)                             → 100
GREATEST(DATE('2005-01-01'), DATE('2005-06-12')) → '2005-06-12'
```

HEX(par1)

Description: If the parameter is numeric, this function returns the hexadecimal representation of the parameter. If the parameter is alphanumeric, this function returns a two-digit code for each character.

Data type: Alphanumeric

```
HEX(11)     → 'B'
HEX(16)     → '10'
HEX(100)    → '64'
HEX(1000)   → '3E8'
HEX('3E8')  → '334538'
HEX('ç')    → 'E7'
```

HOUR(par1)

Description: This function returns the number of the hour from a time or timestamp expression. The value of the result is always a whole number between 0 and 23 inclusive.

Data type: Numeric

```
HOUR('2005-01-01 12:13:14') → 12
HOUR('12:13:14')            → 12
HOUR(CURTIME())             → 19
```

IF(par1, par2, par3)

Description: If the value of the first parameter is `true`, the result of the function is equal to the value of the second parameter; otherwise, it is equal to the value of the third parameter. The specification

```
IF(E1, E2, E3)
```

in which E_1, E_2, and E_3 are expressions, is equal to the following case expression:

```
CASE
   WHEN E1 = TRUE THEN E2
   ELSE E3
END
```

Data type: Depends on the last two parameters

```
IF((5>8), 'Jim', 'John') → 'John'
IF((SELECT COUNT(*) FROM PLAYERS) =
   (SELECT COUNT(*) FROM PENALTIES), TRUE, FALSE) → 0
```

IFNULL(par1, par2)

Description: If the value of the first parameter is equal to the null value, the result of the function is equal to the value of the second parameter; otherwise, it is equal to the value of the first parameter. The specification

```
IFNULL(E1, E2)
```

in which E_1, and E_2 are expressions, is equal to the following case expression:

```
CASE E1
   WHEN NULL THEN E2
   ELSE E1
END
```

Data type: Depends on the parameters

```
IFNULL(NULL, 'John')  → 'John'
IFNULL('John', 'Jim') → 'John'
```

INET_ATON(par1)

Description: This function returns the integer representation of an IP address.

Data type: Numeric

```
INET_ATON('127.0.0.0')  → 2130706432
INET_ATON('WWW.R20.NL') → NULL
```

INET_NTOA(par1)

Description: This function returns the IP address belonging to an integer representation.

Data type: Numeric

```
INET_NTOA(2130706432)                    → '127.0.0.0'
INET_NTOA(INET_ATON('255.255.255.255')) → '255.255.255.255'
```

INSERT(par1, par2, par3, par4)

Description: The value of the fourth parameter is placed on the part of the first parameter that starts with the position indicated with the second parameter and that is a number of characters long (the third parameter).

Data type: Alphanumeric

```
INSERT('abcdefgh',4,3,'zzz')  → 'abczzzgh'
INSERT('abcdefgh',4,2,'zzz')  → 'abczzzfgh'
INSERT('abcdefgh',4,0,'zzz')  → 'abczzzdefgh'
INSERT('abcdefgh',4,-1,'zzz') → 'abczzz'
INSERT('abcdefgh',1,5,'zzz')  → 'zzzfgh'
```

INSTR(par1, par2)

Description: This function returns the starting position of the second alphanumeric value within the first alphanumeric value. The `INSTR` function has the value `0` if the second alphanumeric value does not appear within the first.

Data type: Numeric

```
INSTR('database','bas') → 5
INSTR('system','bas')   → 0
```

INTERVAL(par, par2, par3, ...)

Description: This function determines between which two values in a list the first parameter appears. After the first parameter, the values must be specified in ascending order.

Data type: Depends on the last two parameters

```
INTERVAL(3,0,1,2,3,4,5,6,7) → 4
INTERVAL(7,0,6,11,16,21)    → 2
```

IS_FREE_LOCK(par1)

Description: This function evaluates the status of a named lock. If this lock is still available, the result is equal to `1`; otherwise, it is equal to `0`. See also the `GET_LOCK` function.

Data type: Numeric

```
IS_FREE_LOCK('lock1') → 1
```

ISNULL(par1)

Description: The value of this function is equal to 1 if the first parameter is equal to the null value; otherwise, it is equal to 0. The specification

```
ISNULL(E1)
```

in which E_1 is an expression, is equal to the following case expression:

```
CASE E1
   WHEN NULL THEN 1
   ELSE 0
END
```

Data type: Depends on the parameters

```
ISNULL((SELECT LEAGUENO FROM PLAYERS WHERE PLAYERNO=27)) → 0
ISNULL((SELECT LEAGUENO FROM PLAYERS WHERE PLAYERNO=7))  → 1
```

IS_USED_LOCK(par1)

Description: This function returns the identifier of the connection that is the owner of a named lock. If the lock does not exist, this function returns the null value. See also the GET_LOCK function.

Data type: Numeric

```
IS_USED_LOCK('lock1') → 4
```

LAST_DAY(par1)

Description: This function returns the last day of the month belonging to a date or timestamp expression.

Data type: Date

```
LAST_DAY('2004-02-01') → '2005-02-29'
LAST_DAY('2005-02-01') → '2005-02-28'
```

LAST_INSERT_ID(par1)

Description: This function returns the number that was generated last with AUTOINCREMENT.

Data type: Numeric

```
LAST_INSERT_ID() → 25
```

LEAST(par1, par2, ...)

Description: This function returns the smallest value from a series of parameters.

Data type: Depends on the parameters

```
LEAST(100, 4, 80)                              → 4
LEAST(DATE('2005-01-01'), DATE('2005-06-12')) → 2005-01-01
```

LCASE(par1)

Description: This function converts all uppercase letters of the value of the parameter to lowercase letters.

Data type: Alphanumeric

```
LCASE('RICK') → 'rick'
```

LEFT(par1, par2)

Description: This function returns the left part of an alphanumeric value (the first parameter). The second parameter indicates the length of the part used.

Data type: Alphanumeric

```
LEFT('database', 4)            → 'data'
LEFT('database', 0)            → ''
LEFT('database', 10)           → 'database'
LEFT('database', NULL)         → ''
LENGTH(LEFT('database', 0))    → 0
LENGTH(LEFT('database', 10))   → 8
LENGTH(LEFT('database', NULL)) → 0
```

LENGTH(par1)

Description: This function returns the length in bytes of an alphanumeric value.

Data type: Numeric

```
LENGTH('database')          → 8
LENGTH('data    ')          → 8
LENGTH(RTRIM('abcd    '))   → 4
LENGTH('')                  → 0
LENGTH(NULL)                → NULL
LENGTH(CONVERT('database' USING ucs2)) → 16
```

LN(par1)

Description: This function returns the logarithm to the base value e of the parameter. See the LOG function.

Data type: Numeric

```
LN(50)      → 3.9120230054281
LN(EXP(3)) → 3
LN(0)       → NULL
LN(1)       → 0
```

LOCALTIME()

Description: This function returns the system date and system time. If the function is used within a numeric expression, the result is numeric. The brackets may be omitted. See the NOW and LOCALTIMESTAMP functions.

Data type: Timestamp or double

```
LOCALTIME()     → '2005-02-20 12:26:52'
LOCALTIME() + 0 → 20050220122652
```

LOCALTIMESTAMP()

Description: This function returns the system date and system time. If the function is used within a numeric expression, the result is numeric. The brackets may be omitted. See the NOW and LOCALTIME functions.

Data type: Timestamp or double

```
LOCALTIMESTAMP()     → '2005-02-20 12:26:52'
LOCALTIMESTAMP() + 0 → 20050220122652
```

LOCATE(par1, par2, par3)

Description: This function returns the starting position of the first alphanumeric value within the second alphanumeric value. The LOCATE function has the value 0 if the first alphanumeric value does not occur within the second. A third parameter may be included to indicate a position from which the search may be started.

Data type: Numeric

```
LOCATE('bas','database')   → 5
LOCATE('bas','database',6) → 0
LOCATE('bas','system')     → 0
```

LOG(par1)

Description: This function returns the logarithm to the base value e of the parameter.

Data type: Numeric

```
LOG(50)      → 3.9120230054281
LOG(EXP(3)) → 3
LOG(0)       → NULL
LOG(1)       → 0
```

LOG(par1, par2)

Description: This function returns the logarithm of the second parameter where the first parameter forms the base value.

Data type: Numeric

```
LOG(10,1000) → 3
LOG(2,64)    → 6
```

LOG10(par1)

Description: This function returns the logarithm to the base value 10 of the parameter.

Data type: Numeric

```
LOG10(1000)          → 3
LOG10(POWER(10,5)) → 5
```

LOG2(par1)

Description: This function returns the logarithm to the base value 2 of the parameter.

Data type: Numeric

```
LOG2(2)             → 1
LOG2(64)            → 6
LOG2(POWER(2,10) → 10
```

LOWER(par1)

Description: This function converts all uppercase letters of the value of the parameter to lowercase letters. See the LCASE function.

Data type: Alphanumeric

```
LOWER('RICK') → 'rick'
```

LPAD(par1, par2, par3)

Description: The value of the first parameter is filled in the front (the left side) with the value of the third parameter just until the total length of the value is equal to that of the second parameter. If the maximum length is smaller than that of the first parameter, the first parameter is shortened on the left side.

Data type: Alphanumeric

```
LPAD('data', 16, 'base') → 'basebasebasedata'
LPAD('data', 6, 'base')  → 'badata'
LPAD('data', 2, 'base')  → 'da'
```

LTRIM(par1)

Description: This function removes all blanks that appear at the beginning of the parameter.

Data type: Alphanumeric

```
LTRIM('   database') → 'database'
```

MAKEDATE(par1, par2)

Description: The second parameter represents a number of days, and those are added to the second parameter. This second parameter must be a numeric, date, or timestamp expression.

Data type: Date

```
MAKEDATE(2005, 1)                        → '2005-01-01'
MAKEDATE(2005, 10)                       → '2005-01-10'
MAKEDATE('2005-01-01', 1)                → '2005-01-01'
MAKEDATE('2005-01-01 12:26:52', 1) → '2005-01-01'
```

MAKETIME(par1, par2, par3)

Description: This function creates a time from a number of hours (the first parameter), a number of minutes (the second parameter), and a number of seconds (the third parameter). The number of minutes and the number of seconds must be between 0 and 59 inclusive; otherwise, the function returns the null value as result.

Data type: Time

```
MAKETIME(12,13,14)  → '12:13:14'
MAKETIME(12,90,14)  → NULL
MAKETIME(120,13,14) → '120:13:14'
```

MAKE_SET(par1, par2, par3, ...)

Description: This function creates a value of the SET data type. The first parameter indicates how many values belong to the set. Parameters two and higher contain the values from which the set is created.

Data type: Alphanumeric

```
MAKE_SET(1,'a','b','c','d','e','f','g','i') → 'a'
MAKE_SET(8,'a','b','c','d','e','f','g','i') → 'd'
MAKE_SET(7,'a','b','c','d','e','f','g','i') → 'a,b,c'
MAKE_SET(CONV(111000,2,10),'a','b','c','d','e','f','g','i')
    → 'd,e,f'
```

MD5(par1)

Description: This function calculates the 128-bits checksum belonging to the value of the parameter. The result is a binary string consisting of 32 hexadecimal characters. MD5 stands for *Message-Digest Algorithm.*

Data type: Binary

```
MD5('database') → '11e0eed8d3696c0a632f822df385ab3c'
```

MICROSECOND(par1)

Description: This function returns the number of microseconds from a time or timestamp expression. The value of the result is always a whole number between 0 and 999999 inclusive.

Data type: Numeric

```
MICROSECOND('2005-01-01 12:13:14.123456') → 123456
MICROSECOND('12:13:14.1')                 → 100000
```

MID(par1, par2, par3)

Description: This function extracts part of the alphanumeric value of the first parameter. The second parameter identifies the start position, and the third parameter identifies the number of characters. See the SUBSTRING function.

Data type: Alphanumeric

```
MID('database',5)     → 'base'
MID('database',10)    → ''
MID('database',5,2)   → 'ba'
MID('database',5,10)  → 'base'
MID('database',-6)    → 'tabase'
```

MINUTE(par1)

Description: This function returns the number of minutes from a time or timestamp expression. The value of the result is always a whole number between `0` and `59` inclusive.

Data type: Numeric

```
MINUTE(CURTIME())  → 52
MINUTE('12:40:33') → 40
```

MOD(par1)

Description: This function returns the remainder from the division of two parameters.

Data type: Numeric

```
MOD(15,4)       → 3
MOD(15.4, 4.4) → 2.2
```

MONTH(par1)

Description: This function returns the number of the month from a date or timestamp expression. The value of the result is always a whole number between `1` and `12` inclusive.

Data type: Numeric

```
MONTH('1988-07-29') → 7
```

MONTHNAME

Description: This function returns the name of the month from a date or timestamp expression.

Data type: Alphanumeric

```
MONTHNAME('1988-05-20') → 'May'
MONTHNAME('1988-06-20') → 'June'
```

NOW()

Description: This function returns the system date and system time. If the function is used within a numeric expression, the result is numeric. See the `LOCALTIME` and `LOCALTIMESTAMP` functions.

Data type: Timestamp or numeric

```
NOW()     → '2005-02-20 12:26:52'
NOW() + 0 → 20050220122652
```

NULLIF(par1, par2)

Description: If the value of the first parameter is not equal to that of the second parameter, the result of the function is equal to the null value; otherwise, it is equal to the first parameter. The specification

```
NULLIF(E1, E2)
```

in which E_1 and E_2 are two expressions, is equal to the following case expression:

```
CASE
   WHEN E1 = E2 THEN NULL
   ELSE E1
END
```

Data type: Depends on the parameters

```
NULLIF(NULL, 'John')    → NULL
NULLIF('John', 'Jim')   → 'John'
NULLIF('John', 'John')  → NULL
```

OCT(par1)

Description: This function returns the decimal of the first parameter. This parameter has an octal value.

Data type: Alphanumeric

```
OCT(8)    → '10'
OCT(64)   → '100'
OCT(100)  → '144'
```

OCTET_LENGTH(par1)

Description: This function returns the length in bytes of an octal value.

Data type: Numeric

```
OCTET_LENGTH('100')     → 3
OCTET_LENGTH(OCT(64))   → 3
```

OLD_PASSWORD(par1)

Description: This function encrypts the parameter the same way as a password of a user that is stored in the catalog tables. This was the `PASSWORD` function as implemented for Version 4.1.1 of MySQL.

Data type: Alphanumeric

```
OLD_PASSWORD('database') → '30599f1725b9f8a2'
```

ORD(par1)

Description: This function returns the (ordinal) character set position of the first character of an alphanumeric expression.

Data type: Numeric

```
ORD('Database') → 68
ORD('database') → 100
ORD('')         → 0
ORD(NULL)       → NULL
```

PASSWORD(par1)

Description: This function encrypts the parameter the same way as a password of a user that is stored in the catalog tables.

Data type: Alphanumeric

```
PASSWORD('database')
   → 'A9D467528C52CF9DD63A2168DBE51A8241160241'
```

PERIOD_ADD(par1, par2)

Description: This function adds a number of months to a specific date. The date must have the format `YYYYMM` or `YYMM`. The format of the result is `YYYYMM`. Therefore, this function does not work with traditional dates.

Data type: Alphanumeric

```
PERIOD_ADD('200508', 2)  → '200510'
PERIOD_ADD('200508', -2) → '200506'
PERIOD_ADD('200508', 12) → '200608'
```

PERIOD_DIFF(par1, par2)

Description: This function determines the number of months between two dates. Both dates must have the format `YYYYMM` or `YYMM`. Therefore, this function does not work with values with the date data type.

Data type: Numeric

```
PERIOD_DIFF('200508', '200510') → -2
PERIOD_DIFF('200508', '200506') → 2
PERIOD_DIFF('200508', '200608') → -12
```

PI()

Description: This function returns the well-known number, pi.

Data type: Numeric

```
PI()         → 3.141593
PI()*100000  → 314159.265359
```

POSITION(par1 IN par2)

Description: This function returns the starting position of the first alphanumeric value within the second alphanumeric value. The LOCATE function has the value 0 if the first alphanumeric value does not appear within the second. Note that the word IN must be specified between the two parameters.

Data type: Numeric

```
POSITION('bas' IN 'database') → 5
POSITION('bas' IN 'system')   → 0
```

POW(par1, par2)

Description: The value of the first expression is raised to a specific power. The second parameter indicates the power. See the POWER function.

Data type: Numeric

```
POW(4,3)    → 64
POW(2.5,3)  → 15.625
```

POWER(par1, par2)

Description: The value of the first expression is raised to a specific power. The second parameter indicates the power.

Data type: Numeric

```
POWER(4,3)     → 64
POWER(2.5,3)   → 15.625
POWER(4, 0.3)  → 1.5157165665104
POWER(4, -2)   → 0.0625
```

QUARTER

Description: This function returns the quarter from a date or timestamp expression. The value of the result is always a whole number between 1 and 4 inclusive.

Data type: Numeric

```
QUARTER('1988-07-29') → 3
QUARTER(CURDATE())    → 1
```

QUOTE(par1)

Description: This function returns the value of an alphanumeric expression as a correct alphanumeric literal enclosed by quotation marks; if the value contains a quotation mark itself, it is also processed. The quotation marks are added to the literal itself.

Data type: Alphanumeric

```
QUOTE((SELECT MAX(NAME) FROM PLAYERS)) → 'Wise'
QUOTE('database')                      → 'database'
QUOTE("'")                             → '\''
```

RADIANS(par1)

Description: This function converts a number in degrees to a value in radians.

Data type: Numeric

```
RADIANS(90)         → 1.5707963267949
RADIANS(180) - PI() → 0
RADIANS(-360)       → -6.2831853071796
```

RAND(par1)

Description: This function returns a random number (with a float data type) between 0.0 and 1.0. The parameter indicates the starting point for the calculation of the next random value. The result is the same when this function is called repeatedly with the same parameter value. If no parameter has been specified, the next random value is calculated.

Data type: Numeric

```
RAND()                                 → 0.42908766346899
RAND(5)                                → 0.40613597483014
CAST(RAND() * 10000 AS UNSIGNED INTEGER) → 8057
```

RELEASE_LOCK(par1)

Description: This function removes a named lock. If the function is processed correctly, the result is equal to 1; otherwise, it is equal to 0. See also the GET_LOCK function.

Data type: Numeric

```
RELEASE_LOCK('lock1') → 4
```

REPEAT(par1, par2)

Description: This function repeats an alphanumeric value (the first parameter) a specified number of times. The second parameter indicates the number of times.

Data type: Alphanumeric

```
REPEAT('bla',4)  → 'blablablabla'
REPEAT('X',10)   → 'XXXXXXXXXX'
```

REPLACE(par1, par2, par3)

Description: This function replaces parts of the value of an alphanumeric expression with another value.

Data type: Alphanumeric

```
REPLACE('database','a','e')          → 'detebese'
REPLACE('database','ba','warehou') → 'datawarehouse'
REPLACE('data base',' ','')          → 'database'
```

REVERSE(par1)

Description: This function reverses the characters in an alphanumeric value.

Data type: Alphanumeric

```
REVERSE('database') → 'esabatad'
```

RIGHT(par1, par2)

Description: This function returns the right part of an alphanumeric value (the first parameter). The second parameter indicates the length of the part used.

Data type: Alphanumeric

```
RIGHT('database', 4)           → 'base'
RIGHT('database', 0)           → ''
RIGHT('database', 10)          → 'database'
RIGHT('database', NULL)        → ''
LENGTH(RIGHT('database', 0))   → 0
LENGTH(RIGHT('database', 10))  → 8
LENGTH(RIGHT('database', NULL)) → 0
```

ROUND(par1, par2)

Description: This function rounds numbers to a specified number of decimal places. If the second parameter has not been specified, it is equal to the specification of 0.

Data type: Numeric

```
ROUND(123.456,2)  → 123.46
ROUND(123.456,1)  → 123.5
ROUND(123.456,0)  → 123
ROUND(123.456,-1) → 120
ROUND(123.456,-2) → 100
ROUND(123.456)    → 123
```

ROW_COUNT()

Description: This function returns the number of rows that the previous SQL statement updated—for example, the number of rows deleted or updated. If the previous statement was a SELECT statement, the result of this function is equal to -1.

Data type: Numeric

```
ROW_COUNT() → 38
```

RPAD(par1, par2, par3)

Description: The value of the first parameter is filled in the front (the right side) with the value of the third parameter just until the total length of the value is equal to that of the second parameter. If the maximum length is smaller than that of the first parameter, the first parameter is shortened on the right side.

Data type: Alphanumeric

```
RPAD('data', 16, 'base') → 'databasebasebase'
RPAD('data', 6, 'base')  → 'databa'
RPAD('data', 2, 'base')  → 'da'
```

RTRIM(par1)

Description: This function removes all blanks from the end of the value of the parameter.

Data type: Alphanumeric

```
RTRIM('database    ')             → 'database'
CONCAT(RTRIM('data     '), 'base') → 'database'
```

SECOND(par1)

Description: This function returns the number of seconds from a time or timestamp expression. The value of the result is always a whole number between 0 and 59 inclusive.

Data type: Numeric

```
SECOND(CURTIME())  → 6
SECOND('12:40:33') → 33
```

SEC_TO_TIME(par1)

Description: This function transforms a number of seconds in a time.

Data type: Time

```
SEC_TO_TIME(1)               → '00:00:01'
SEC_TO_TIME(1000)            → '00:16:40'
SEC_TO_TIME((24*60*60)-1) → '23:59:59'
SEC_TO_TIME(24*60*60*2)      → '48:00:00'
```

SESSION_USER()

Description: This function returns the name of the SQL user.

Data type: Alphanumeric

```
SESSION_USER() → 'root@localhost'
```

SHA(par1)

Description: This function is a synonym of the SHA1 function. For an explanation, see the SHA1 function.

Data type: Binary

SHA1(par1)

Description: This function calculates the 160-bit checksum belonging to the value of the parameter. For this, the *Secure Hash Algorithm* is used. The result is a binary string consisting of 40 hexadecimal characters.

Data type: Binary

```
SHA1('database') → '6d613a1ee01eec4c0f8ca66df0db71dca0c6e1cf'
SHA1(NULL)       → NULL
```

SIGN(par1)

Description: This function returns the character of a numeric value.

Data type: Numeric

```
SIGN(50)  → 1
SIGN(0)   → 0
SIGN(-50) → -1
```

SIN(par1)

Description: This function returns, in radians, the sine value of any angle size.

Data type: Numeric

```
SIN(0)       → 0
SIN(PI()/2) → 1
SIN(PI())   → 0
```

SOUNDEX(par1)

Description: This function returns the SOUNDEX code of the alphanumeric parameter. A SOUNDEX code consists of four characters. Alphanumeric values that sound roughly the same are converted to identical SOUNDEX codes. The SOUNDEX code is specified according to the following rules:

- All blanks at the beginning of the parameter are removed.
- All the following letters are removed from the parameter, provided that they do not appear on the first position: a e h i o u w y.
- The following values are assigned to the remaining letters:

```
b f p v           = 1
c g j k q s x z   = 2
d t               = 3
l                 = 4
m n               = 5
r                 = 6
```

- If two linked letters have the same value, the second is removed.
- The code is broken after the fourth character.
- If the remaining code consists of less than four characters, it is filled with zeroes.
- Characters appearing behind a blank are skipped.
- If the value of the parameter does not begin with a letter, the result is equal to 0000.

Data type: Alphanumeric

```
SOUNDEX('Smith')      → 'S530'
SOUNDEX('Smythe')     → 'S530'
SOUNDEX('Bill')       → 'B400'
SOUNDEX(' Bill')      → 'B400'
SOUNDEX('Billy')      → 'B400'
```

SPACE(par1)

Description: This function generates a row with blanks. The number of blanks is equal to the value of the numeric parameter.

Data type: Alphanumeric

```
SPACE(1)          → ' '
SPACE(5)          → '     '
LENGTH(SPACE(8))  → 8
```

SQRT(par1)

Description: This function returns the square root of the value of the parameter.

Data type: Numeric

```
SQRT(225) → 15
SQRT(200) → 14.14
SQRT(-5)  → NULL
```

STRCMP(par1, par2)

Description: This function compares the values of two alphanumeric expressions. The result is `0` if the values of the parameters are equal, `-1` if the value of the first parameter is smaller, and `1` if the value of the right one is smaller.

Data type: Numeric

```
STRCMP(1,1) → 0
STRCMP(1,2) → -1
STRCMP(2,1) → 1
```

STR_TO_DATE(par1, par2)

Description: This function is the opposite of the `DATE_FORMAT` function. A certain alphanumeric value is converted to a date or timestamp value through a number of format strings. If the format strings do not fit in the first parameter, the function returns a null value as result.

Data type: Date or timestamp

```
STR_TO_DATE('2005 Sun Oct 1st', '%Y %a %b %D')→ '2005-10-01'
STR_TO_DATE('2005/11/10', '%Y/%c/%d')         → '2005-11-10'
```

SUBDATE(par1, par2)

Description: This function subtracts an interval (the second parameter) from a date or timestamp expression (the first parameter). See Section 5.13.3 for the specification of intervals. If the second parameter is not an interval, but a numeric number, MySQL assumes that this value represents a number of days.

Data type: Date or timestamp

```
SUBDATE('2004-01-01', INTERVAL 5 MONTH) → '2003-08-01'
SUBDATE('2004-01-01 12:00:00', INTERVAL 5 DAY)
   → '2003-12-27 12:00:00'
SUBDATE('2004-01-01', 5) → '2003-12-27'
```

SUBTIME(par1, par2)

Description: This function subtracts two time expressions and returns a new time.

Data type: Time

```
SUBTIME('12:59:00', '0:59:00')       → '12:00:00'
SUBTIME('12:00:00', '0:00:00.001') → '11:59:59.999000'
SUBTIME('100:00:00', '900:00:00')  → '-800:00:00'
```

SUBSTRING(par1, par2, par3)

Description: This function extracts part of the alphanumeric value of the first parameter. The second parameter identifies the starting position, and the third identifies its number of characters. If the third parameter is not specified, up to the last character is included.

Data type: Alphanumeric

```
SUBSTRING('database',5)     → 'base'
SUBSTRING('database',10)    → ''
SUBSTRING('database',5,2)   → 'ba'
SUBSTRING('database',5,10)  → 'base'
SUBSTRING('database',-6)    → 'tabase'
```

SUBSTRING(par1 FROM par2 FOR par3)

Description: This function extracts part of the alphanumeric value of the first parameter. The second parameter identifies the starting position, and the third identifies its number of characters. If the third parameter is not specified, up to the last character is included.

Data type: Alphanumeric

```
SUBSTRING('database' FROM 5)         → 'base'
SUBSTRING('database' FROM 10)        → ''
SUBSTRING('database' FROM 5 FOR 2)   → 'ba'
SUBSTRING('database' FROM 5 FOR 10)  → 'base'
SUBSTRING('database' FROM -6)        → 'tabase'
```

SUBSTRING_INDEX(par1, par2, par3)

Description: This function looks for the *n*th appearance of an alphanumeric value in the value of the first parameter. The second parameter shows which value must be looked for, and the third parameter returns the number *n*. If the third parameter is positive, the function looks for the *n*th appearance from the left side and returns everything that is found left from that appearance. If the third parameter is negative, the function looks for the *n*th appearance from the right and returns everything that is found right from that appearance.

Data type: Alphanumeric

```
SUBSTRING_INDEX('database', 'a', 3)      → 'datab'
SUBSTRING_INDEX('database', 'a', -3)     → 'tabase'
SUBSTRING_INDEX('database', 'data', 1)   → ''
SUBSTRING_INDEX('database', 'data', -1)  → 'base'
```

SYSDATE()

Description: This function returns the system date and system time. If the function is used within a numeric expression, the result is numeric. See the `LOCALTIME` and `LOCALTIMESTAMP` functions.

Data type: Timestamp or numeric

```
SYSDATE()      → '2005-02-20 12:26:52'
SYSDATE() + 0  → 20050220122652
```

SYSTEM_USER()

Description: This function returns the name of the SQL user.

Data type: Alphanumeric

```
SYSTEM_USER() → 'root@localhost'
```

TAN(par1)

Description: This function returns, in radians, the tangent value of any angle size.

Data type: Numeric

```
TAN(0)       → 0
TAN(PI())    → 0
TAN(PI()/4 → 1
TAN(1)       → 1.5574077246549
```

TIME()

Description: This function returns the time part of a time or timestamp expression.

Data type: Time

```
TIME('2005-12-08 12:00:00') → '12:00:00'
TIME('12:13')                → '12:13:00'
```

TIMEDIFF(par1, par2)

Description: This function returns the amount of time that has elapsed between two time expressions.

Data type: Time

```
TIMEDIFF('12:00:01','12:00:00') → '00:00:01'
TIMEDIFF('12:00:00','12:00:01') → '-00:00:01'
TIMEDIFF('23:01:01','22:00:59') → '01:00:02'
```

TIME_FORMAT(par1, par2)

Description: This function transforms a time, date, or timestamp expression (the first parameter) to an alphanumeric value. The second parameter indicates the format of that alphanumeric value; several special format strings can be used here—see the following table. This function looks like the DATE_FORMAT function; however, all time-related format strings may be used now.

FORMAT STRING	EXPLANATION
%f	Six-digit numeric code for the number of microseconds (000000 up to and including 999999)
%H	Two-digit numeric code for the hour (00 up to and including 23)
%h	Two-digit numeric code for the hour (01 up to and including 12)
%I	Two-digit numeric code for the hour (01 up to and including 12)

continues

Format String	Explanation
%i	Two-digit numeric code for the number of minutes (00 up to and including 59)
%k	One- or two-digit numeric code for the hour (0 up to and including 23)
%l	One- or two-digit numeric code for the hour (1 up to and including 12)
%p	Indication of AM or PM
%r	Indication of the time (in 12 hours) with the format HH:MM:SS, followed by AM or PM
%S	Two-digit numeric code for the number of seconds (00 up to and including 59)
%s	Two-digit numeric code for the number of seconds (00 up to and including 59)
%T	Indication of the time (in 24 hours) in the format hh:mm:ss, followed by AM or PM
%%	Returns the percentage sign

Data type: Alphanumeric

```
TIME_FORMAT('11:12:13','%h') → '11'
TIME_FORMAT('11:12:13','%f') → '000000'
TIME_FORMAT('12:00:00', 'It is now %h o''clock')
   → 'It is now 12 o'clock'
```

TIMESTAMP(par1, par2)

Description: This function transforms the first parameter into a timestamp value. If a second parameter is specified, it should be a time expression; that is added to the value of the first parameter.

Data type: Timestamp

```
TIMESTAMP('2005-12-08')          → '2005-12-08 00:00:00'
TIMESTAMP('2005-12-08 12:00:00') → '2005-12-08 12:00:00'
TIMESTAMP('2005-12-08 12:00:00', '11:12:13')
                                 → '2005-12-08 23:12:13'
TIMESTAMP('2005-12-08 12:00:00', '-11:12:00')
                                 → '2005-12-08 00:48:00'
TIMESTAMP('2005-12-08 12:00:00', '-48:00')
                                 → '2005-12-06 12:00:00'
```

TIMESTAMPADD(par1, par2, par3)

Description: This function adds a certain interval to a date or timestamp expression. The first parameter indicates the unit of the interval, such as days, months, or years; the second parameter indicates the number of days or months. The third parameter is the expression to which the interval is added. Supported interval units are YEAR, QUARTER, MONTH, WEEK, DAY, HOUR, MINUTE, SECOND, and FRAC_SECOND.

Data type: Date or timestamp

```
TIMESTAMPADD(DAY, 2, '2005-12-08')    → '2005-12-10'
TIMESTAMPADD(MONTH, 2, '2005-12-08') → '2006-02-08'
TIMESTAMPADD(YEAR, -2, '2005-12-08') → '2003-12-08'
TIMESTAMPADD(MINUTE, 3, '2005-12-08 12:00:00')
   → '2005-12-08 12:03:00'
TIMESTAMPADD(FRAC_SECOND, 3, '2005-12-08 12:00:00')
   → '2005-12-08 12:00:00.000003'
```

TIMESTAMPDIFF(par1, par2, par3)

Description: This function calculates the time between two date or timestamp expressions. The first parameter indicates the unit of the interval, such as days, months, or years; the second and third parameters form the two expressions. Supported interval units are YEAR, QUARTER, MONTH, WEEK, DAY, HOUR, MINUTE, SECOND, and FRAC_SECOND.

Data type: Numeric

```
TIMESTAMPDIFF(DAY, '2005-12-04', '2005-12-08') → 4
TIMESTAMPDIFF(DAY, '2005-12-08', '2005-12-04') → -4
TIMESTAMPDIFF(YEAR, '1960-12-08', NOW())       → 45
TIMESTAMPDIFF(MINUTE, '2005-12-08 12:00:00',
   '2005-12-08 12:03:00') → 3
TIMESTAMPDIFF(FRAC_SECOND, '2005-12-08',
   '2005-12-08 12:00:00.000003') → 43200000003
```

TIME_TO_SEC(par1)

Description: This function transforms a time into a number of seconds.

Data type: Numeric

```
TIME_TO_SEC('00:00:01') → 1
TIME_TO_SEC('00:16:40') → 1000
TIME_TO_SEC('23:59:59') → 83399
TIME_TO_SEC('48:00:00') → 172800
```

TO_DAYS(par1)

Description: This function determines how many days have elapsed between the specified date (the parameter) and the year 0.

Data type: Numeric

```
TO_DAYS('2005-12-08') → 732653
```

TRIM(par1)

Description: This function removes all blanks from the start and end of an alphanumeric value (the parameter). Blanks in the middle are not removed.

Data type: Alphanumeric

```
TRIM('database     ') → 'database'
TRIM('    da ta    ') → 'da ta'
```

TRIM(par1 FROM par2)

Description: If an alphanumeric value (the first parameter) appears at the start or end of another alphanumeric value (the second parameter), it is removed. Before the first parameter, you may specify the terms `LEADING`, `TRAILING`, or `BOTH` can be specified. Adding `BOTH` has no effect on the result. If `LEADING` is specified, only values at the start are removed; with `TRAILING`, only the values at the end are removed.

Data type: Alphanumeric

```
TRIM(' ' FROM ' data base ')                → 'data base'
TRIM('a' FROM 'database')                   → 'database'
TRIM('da' FROM 'database')                  → 'tabase'
TRIM('da' FROM 'dadadatabase')              → 'tabase'
TRIM('da' FROM 'dadadatabasedada')          → 'tabase'
TRIM(LEADING ' ' FROM ' data base ')        → 'data base '
TRIM(TRAILING 'da' FROM 'dadadatabasedada') → 'dadadatabase'
```

TRUNCATE(par1, par2)

Description: This function truncates numbers to a specified number of decimal places.

Data type: Numeric

```
TRUNCATE(123.567, -1) → 120
TRUNCATE(123.567, 1)  → 123.5
TRUNCATE(123.567, 5)  → 123.56700
```

UCASE(par1)

Description: This function converts all lowercase letters of the value of the parameter to uppercase letters. See the UPPER function.

Data type: Alphanumeric

```
UCASE('Database') → 'DATABASE'
```

UNCOMPRESS(par1)

Description: This function restores the original value belonging to the compressed value of the parameter. The COMPRESS function compresses the value.

Data type: Alphanumeric

```
UNCOMPRESS(COMPRESS('database')) → 'database'
```

UNCOMPRESS_LENGTH(par1)

Description: This function returns the length of the compressed value that has been created with the COMPRESS function.

Data type: Numeric

```
UNCOMPRESSED_LENGTH(COMPRESS('database')) → 8
```

UNHEX(par1)

Description: This function returns the hexadecimal representation of the parameter. Each pair of characters is converted to the corresponding character.

Data type: Alphanumeric

```
UNHEX('334538')    → '3E8'
UNHEX('E7')        → 'ç'
UNHEX(HEX('SQL')) → 'SQL'
```

UPPER(par1)

Description: This function converts all lowercase letters of the value of the parameter to uppercase letters.

Data type: Alphanumeric

```
UPPER ('Database') → 'DATABASE'
```

UNIX_TIMESTAMP(par1)

Description: This function returns the number of seconds since the UNIX epoch (1 January 1970 at 00:00:00). If this function has a parameter, it should be a date expression.

Data type: Numeric

```
UNIX_TIMESTAMP()             → 1134135565
UNIX_TIMESTAMP('2000-01-01') → 946681200
```

USER()

Description: This function returns the name of the SQL user.

Data type: Alphanumeric

```
USER() → 'root@localhost'
```

UTC_DATE()

Description: This function returns the actual UTC date. UTC stands for *Coordinated Universal Time,* or Zulu time, or *Greenwich Mean Time* (GMT). If the function is part of a numeric expression, the result of the function also is numeric.

Data type: Date of numeric

```
UTC_DATE()     → '2005-01-01'
UTC_DATE() + 0 → 20050101
```

UTC_TIME()

Description: This function returns the actual UTC date; see the UTC_DATE function. If the function is part of a numeric expression, the result of the function is also numeric.

Data type: Date or numeric

```
UTC_TIME()                              → '2005-01-01'
HOUR(TIMEDIFF(UTC_TIME(), TIME(NOW()))) → 1
```

UTC_TIMESTAMP()

Description: This function returns the actual UTC date and time; see the UTC_DATE function. If the function is part of a numeric expression, the result of the function is also numeric.

Data type: Date or numeric

```
UTC_TIMESTAMP() → '2005-01-01 13:56:12'
```

UUID()

Description: This function generates an 18-byte-wide unique code. The abbreviation UUID stands for *Universal Unique Identifier.* The first three parts of this code are derived from the system time. The fourth part must make sure that the codes are unique, in case duplicate values arise because of time zones. The fifth part identifies the server in a certain way. Generating unique values is not guaranteed but is likely.

Data type: Alphanumeric

```
UUID() → '2bf2aaec-bc90-1028-b6bf-cc62846e9cc5'
UUID() → '390341e3-bc90-1028-b6bf-cc62846e9cc5'
```

VERSION()

Description: This function returns an identification of the version number of MySQL.

Data type: Alphanumeric

```
VERSION() → '5.0.7-beta-nt'
VERSION() → '5.0.3-alpha-log'
```

WEEK(par1, par2)

Description: This function returns the week from a date or timestamp expression. The value of the result is always a whole number between `1` and `53` inclusive. The second parameter shows how to determine the week number; see the following table.

Code	First Day of the Week	Range of Result	Meaning
0	Sunday	0..53	Week 1 begins on the first Sunday of the year.
1	Monday	0..53	Week 1 is the first week with more than three days.
2	Sunday	1..53	Week 1 begins on the first Sunday of the year.
3	Monday	1..53	Week 1 is the first week with more than three days.
4	Sunday	0..53	Week 1 is the first week with more than three days.
5	Monday	0..53	Week 1 begins on the first Monday of the year.
6	Sunday	1..53	Week 1 is the first week with more than three days.
7	Monday	1..53	Week 1 begins on the first Monday of the year.

Data type: Numeric

```
DATE_FORMAT('2005-01-01','%W') → 'Saturday'
WEEK('2005-01-01',0)           → 0
WEEK('2005-01-01',1)           → 0
WEEK('2005-01-01',2)           → 52
WEEK('2005-01-01',3)           → 53
WEEK('2005-01-01',4)           → 0
WEEK('2005-01-01',5)           → 0
WEEK('2005-01-01',6)           → 52
WEEK('2005-01-01',7)           → 52
WEEK('2005-01-02',0)           → 1
WEEK('2005-01-02',1)           → 0
WEEK('2005-01-02',2)           → 1
WEEK('2005-01-02',3)           → 53
WEEK('2005-01-02',4)           → 1
WEEK('2005-01-02',5)           → 0
WEEK('2005-01-02',6)           → 1
WEEK('2005-01-02',7)           → 52
WEEK('2005-01-03',0)           → 1
WEEK('2005-01-03',1)           → 1
WEEK('2005-01-03',2)           → 1
WEEK('2005-01-03',3)           → 1
WEEK('2005-01-03',4)           → 1
WEEK('2005-01-03',5)           → 1
WEEK('2005-01-03',6)           → 1
WEEK('2005-01-03',7)           → 1
```

The second parameter may be omitted. In that case, MySQL uses the value of the system variable DEFAULT_WEEK_FORMAT. By default, the value is 0, but you may use a SET statement to change it to one of the previous codes.

WEEKDAY(par1)

Description: This function returns the number of the days in the week. The result is a number between 0 (Monday) and 6 (Sunday).

Data type: Numeric

```
WEEKDAY('2005-01-01') → 5
```

WEEKOFYEAR(par1)

Description: This function returns the week number belonging to a certain date expression. The result is a number between 1 and 53.

Data type: Numeric

```
WEEKOFYEAR('2005-01-01') → 53
WEEKOFYEAR('2005-01-03') → 1
```

YEAR(par1)

Description: This function returns the number of the year from a date or timestamp expression. The result is always a number greater than 1.

Data type: Numeric

```
YEAR(NOW())          → 2005
YEAR('2005-12-03') → 2005
YEAR(20051203)       → 2005
```

YEARWEEK(par1, par2)

Description: If only one parameter is specified, this function returns the year followed by the week number in the format YYYYWW from a date or timestamp expression. The week number goes from 01 to 53 inclusive. It is assumed that a week starts on Sunday. If a second parameter is specified, it must be the same code as the one used in the WEEK function.

Data type: Numeric

```
YEARWEEK('2005-12-03')    → 200548
YEARWEEK('2005-12-03',0) → 200548
YEARWEEK('2005-01-02',0) → 200501
YEARWEEK('2005-01-02',1) → 200453
```

APPENDIX C

System Variables

This appendix contains an alphabetical listing of the system variables that relate to the functioning of SQL statements; see Sections 4.14 and 5.7 for descriptions of system variables and how to change the values of system variables. For all system variables, we give the allowed values and the default value, describe the type of the system variable, and give a short description.

Autocommit

Type: Session

Values: 0 (OFF) or 1 (ON)

Default value: 0 (OFF)

Description: If this system variable is turned on (value 1), a COMMIT statement is executed after each SQL statement. Assigning the value 0 to this variable turns off this automatic committing; see Section 37.2.

Auto_increment_increment

Type: Global, session

Values: All values greater than 1

Default value: 1

Description: The number that is used to increase the values in a numeric column that is defined with the AUTO_INCREMENT option; see Section 20.4.3.

Auto_increment_offset

Type: Global, session

Values: All values greater than 1

Default value: `1`

Description: The starting value of a numeric column that has been defined with the `AUTO_INCREMENT` option; see Section 20.4.3.

Character_set_client

Type: Global, session

Values: Alls supported character sets

Default value: `latin1`

Description: The character set of the statements that are sent from the client to the server; see Section 22.8.

Character_set_connection

Type: Global, session

Values: All supported character sets

Default value: `latin1`

Description: The character set of the client/server connection; see Section 22.8.

Character_set_database

Type: Global, session

Values: All supported character sets

Default value: `latin1`

Description: The default character set of the current database. The value of this variable can change every time the `USE` statement is used to "jump" to another database. If no current database exists, this variable has the value of the `CHARACTER_SET_SERVER` variable; see Section 22.8.

Character_set_results

Type: Global, session

Values: All supported character sets

Default value: `latin1`

Description: The character set of the end results of `SELECT` statements that are sent from the server to the client; see Section 22.8.

Character_set_server

Type: Global, session

Values: All supported character sets

Default value: `latin1`

Description: The default character set of the server; see Section 22.8.

Character_set_system

Type: Global, Session

Values: `utf8`

Default value: `utf8`

Description: The character set of the system. This character set is used for the names of database objects, such as tables and columns, but also for the names of functions that are stored in the catalog tables. The value of this variable is always equal to `utf8`; see Section 22.8.

Character_sets_dir

Type: Global, session

Values: All valid directories

Default value: `C:\?\share\charactersets\`. Here, the question mark stands for the directory in which MySQL has been installed itself.

Description: The name of the directory in which the files with all character sets have been recorded; see Section 22.8.

Collation_connection

Type: Global, session

Values: All supported collations

Default value: `latin1_swedish_ci`

Description: The character set of the current connection; see Section 22.8.

Collation_database

Type: Global, session

Values: All supported collations

Default value: `latin1_swedish_ci`

Description: The default collation of the current database. The value of this variable can change every time the `USE` statement is used to "jump" to another database. If no current database exists, this variable has the value of the `COLLATION_SERVER` variable; see Section 22.8.

Collation_server

Type: Global, session

Values: All supported collations

Default value: `latin1_swedish_ci`

Description: The default collation of the server; see Section 22.8.

Default_week_format

Type: Global, session

Values: `0` up to and including `7`

Default value: `0`

Description: The default mode for the `WEEK` function; see also the description of the `WEEK` function in Appendix B, "Scalar Functions."

Foreign_key_checks

Type: Session

Values: `0` (`OFF`) or 1 (`ON`)

Default value: 1 (`ON`)

Description: If this system variable has the value `0`, the foreign keys are not checked. This applies only to the InnoDB storage engine.

Ft_boolean_syntax

Type: Global, session

Default value: `+ -><()~*:""&|`

Description: The list of operators supported by full-text searches; see Section 8.12.

Ft_max_word_len

Type: Global, session

Default value: 84

Description: The maximum length of a word that can be included within a `FULLTEXT` index; see Section 8.12.

Ft_min_word_len

Type: Global, session

Default value: `4`

Description: The minimum length of a word that can be included within a `FULL-TEXT` index; see Section 8.12.

Ft_query_expansion_limit

Type: Global, session

Default value: `20`

Description: The number of top matches that is used for searches with `WITH QUERY EXPANSION`; see Section 8.12.

Skip_show_database

Type: Global, session

Values: `0` (`OFF`) or `1` (`ON`)

Default value: `OFF`

Description: If this variable is turned `ON`, only users who are granted the SHOW `DATABASE` privilege may execute a `SHOW DATABASE` statement. Otherwise, anyone can.

Sql_auto_is_null

Type: Session

Values: `0` or `1`

Default value: `1`

Description: If the value of this variable is `1`, the next `WHERE` clause `WHERE C1 IS NULL` can be used to retrieve the latest generated value for C1, provided that C1 has the `AUTO_INCREMENT` option.

Sql_mode

Type: Global, session

Default value: Empty alphanumeric string

Description: The `SQL_MODE` variable is a complex system variable. This variable can have zero, one, or more settings. When more than one setting exists, commas must separate the settings. Table C.1 contains the allowed settings. Basically, all these settings are turned off, but they can be turned on.

TABLE C.1 Overview of the *SQL_MODE* Settings

ALLOWED SETTINGS FOR THE SQL_MODE SYSTEM VARIABLE	MEANING
`ALLOW_INVALID_DATES`	See Section 5.2.5.
`ANSI_QUOTES`	See Section 20.8.
`ERROR_FOR_DIVISION_BY_ZERO`	If this setting is turned on, MySQL returns an error message if, in an `INSERT` or `UPDATE` statement, a division by zero is taking place. If this statement has the `IGNORE` option, only a warning is given.
`HIGH_NOT_PRECEDENCE`	The condition `NOT E1 BETWEEN E2 AND E3` is processed as `NOT (E1 BETWEEN E2 AND E3)`. In older versions of MySQL, this was processed as `(NOT E1) BETWEEN E2 AND E3`. This setting simulates this old situation.
`IGNORE_SPACE`	Normally, it is not allowed to specify a blank between the name of a function and the opening bracket. This setting enables you to add spaces. In this case, the names of the functions are regarded as reserved words.
`NO_AUTO_CREATE_USER`	If privileges are assigned and the receiving user does not exist yet, he is automatically created. With this setting, you can turn off this automatic creation of new users. After that, every user must be explicitly created first.
`NO_AUTO_VALUE_ON_ZERO`	For a column with the `AUTO_INCREMENT` option, a new value is created if a `0` or a null value is entered. With this setting, this works for null values only.
`NO_BACKSLASH_ESCAPES`	The backslash (\) is seen as an escape symbol. This setting turns it off.
`NO_DIR_IN_CREATE`	If a table is created, the `INDEX DIRECTORY` and `DATA DIRECTORY` specifications are ignored if this setting is turned on.
`NO_ENGINE_SUBSTITUTION`	If a table is created that specifies a nonactive storage engine, the default storage engine is used. This setting turned switches off this behavior.

continues

TABLE C.1 Continued

Allowed Settings for the SQL_MODE System Variable	Meaning
NO_FIELD_OPTIONS	The SHOW CREATE TABLE statement shows the CREATE TABLE statement of a certain table. The column options, such as DEFAULT and COMMENT, are presented as well. Turning this setting on means these column options will not be included.
NO_KEY_OPTIONS	The SHOW CREATE TABLE statement shows the CREATE TABLE statement of a certain table. The index options are presented as well. Turning this setting on means these index options will not be included.
NO_TABLE_OPTIONS	The SHOW CREATE TABLE statement shows the CREATE TABLE statement of a certain table. The table options, such as the storage engine, are presented as well. Turning this setting on means these table options will not be included.
NO_UNSIGNED_SUBTRACTION	If this setting is turned on, the result of the subtraction of two integers is regarded as UNSIGNED.
NO_ZERO_DATE	See Section 5.2.5.
NO_ZERO_IN_DATE	See Section 5.2.5.
ONLY_FULL_GROUP_BY	If this setting is turned on, all nonaggregated columns appearing in the SELECT clause should also appear in the GROUP BY clause.
PIPES_AS_CONCAT	See Section 4.14.
REAL_AS_FLOAT	If this setting is turned on, REAL is seen as a synonym for FLOAT; otherwise, it is a synonym for DOUBLE.
STRICT_ALL_TABLES	If this setting is turned on, incorrect dates are not accepted; see Section 5.2.5.
STRICT_TRANS_TABLES	If this setting is turned on, incorrect dates are not accepted in tables that are created with storage engines that support transactions, such as InnoDB.

Because certain combinations of settings are used regularly, a combined setting can be used. In fact, these are shortened notations for writing out all the individual settings. Table C.2 contains the combined settings and their respective meanings. For example, if we give the SQL_MODE system variable the value MYSQL40 and then retrieve the value of SQL_MODE, the result is equal to NO_FIELD_OPTIONS, HIGH_NOT_PRECEDENCE.

TABLE C.2 Overview of the Combined *SQL_MODE* Settings

Combined Setting	Meaning
ANSI	REAL_AS_FLOAT, PIPES_AS_CONCAT, ANSI_QUOTES, IGNORE_SPACE
DB2	PIPES_AS_CONCAT, ANSI_QUOTES, IGNORE_SPACE, NO_KEY_OPTIONS, NO_TABLE_OPTIONS, NO_FIELD_OPTIONS
MAXDB	PIPES_AS_CONCAT, ANSI_QUOTES, IGNORE_SPACE, NO_KEY_OPTIONS, NO_TABLE_OPTIONS, NO_FIELD_OPTIONS, NO_AUTO_CREATE_USER
MSSQL	PIPES_AS_CONCAT, ANSI_QUOTES, IGNORE_SPACE, NO_KEY_OPTIONS, NO_TABLE_OPTIONS, NO_FIELD_OPTIONS
MYSQL323	NO_FIELD_OPTIONS, HIGH_NOT_PRECEDENCE
MYSQL40	NO_FIELD_OPTIONS, HIGH_NOT_PRECEDENCE
ORACLE	PIPES_AS_CONCAT, ANSI_QUOTES, IGNORE_SPACE, NO_KEY_OPTIONS, NO_TABLE_OPTIONS, NO_FIELD_OPTIONS, NO_AUTO_CREATE_USER
POSTGRESQL	PIPES_AS_CONCAT, ANSI_QUOTES, IGNORE_SPACE, NO_KEY_OPTIONS, NO_TABLE_OPTIONS, NO_FIELD_OPTIONS
TRADITIONAL	STRICT_TRANS_TABLES, STRICT_ALL_TABLES, NO_ZERO_IN_DATE, NO_ZERO_DATE, ERROR_FOR_DIVISION_BY_ZERO, NO_AUTO_CREATE_USER

Sql_select_limit

Type: Session

Values: All positive numeric values

Default value: Null

Description: Giving this system variable a value limits the maximum number of rows in the result of every SELECT statement.

Sql_quote_show_create

Type: Session

Values: 0 (OFF) or 1 (ON)

Default value: 1 (ON)

Description: Because the names of tables, columns, and other database objects may be equal to reserved words, MySQL places quotation marks before and after each name in the result of a SHOW CREATE TABLE and SHOW CREATE DATABASE statement. Turning off the system variable SQL_QUOTE_SHOW_CREATE omits these quotation marks.

Storage_engine

Type: Global, session

Values: Any supported storage engine

Default value: MyISAM

Description: This system variable contains the value of the default storage engine.

System_time_zone

Type: Global, session

Default value: W. Europe Daylight Time

Description: This is the actual time zone of the operating system; see also Section 5.2.7.

Time_zone

Type: Global, session

Default value: SYSTEM

Description: This is the actual time zone; see also Section 5.2.7.

Unique_checks

Type: Session

Values: 0 (OFF) or 1 (ON)

Default value: 1 (ON)

Description: If the system variable has the value 0, the uniqueness of columns, on which a unique index has been defined, is not checked. This does not apply to the primary key, of course.

APPENDIX D

Bibliography

[ASTR80] Astrahan, M. M., et al. "A History and Evaluation of System R." *IBM RJ 2843* (June 1980).

[ATKI04] Atkinson, L., and Suraski, Z. *Core PHP Programming*, Third Edition. Prentice Hall, 2004.

[BENZ03] Benz, B., Durant, J., and Durant, J. *XML Programming Bible.* John Wiley & Sons, 2003.

[BERN97] Bernstein, P. A., and Newcomer, E. *Principles of Transaction Processing.* Morgan Kaufmann Publishers, 1997.

[BOYC73a] Boyce, R. F., et al. "Specifying Queries as Relational Expressions: SQUARE." *IBM RJ 1291* (October 1973).

[BOYC73b] Boyce, R. F., and Chamberlin, D. D. "Using a Structured English Query Language as a Data Definition Facility." *IBM RJ 1318* (December 1973).

[CATT97] Cattell, R. G. G., et al. *The Object Database Standard: ODMG 2.0.* Morgan Kaufmann Publishers, 1997.

[CHAM76] Chamberlin, D. D., et al., "SEQUEL 2: A Unified Approach to Data Definition, Manipulation, and Control." *IBM R&D* (November 1976).

[CHAM80] Chamberlin, D. D. "A Summary of User Experience with the SQL Data Sublanguage." *IBM RJ 2767* (March 1980).

[CODD70] Codd, E. F. "A Relational Model of Data for Large Shared Data Banks." *Communications of the ACM* 13, no. 6 (June 1970).

[CODD79] Codd, E. F. "Extending the Database Relational Model to Capture More Meaning." *ACM Transactions on Database Systems* 4, no. 4 (December 1979).

[CODD82] Codd, E. F. "Relational Database: A Practical Foundation for Productivity." Turing Award Lecture in *Communications of the ACM* 25, no. 2 (February 1982).

[CODD90] Codd, E. F. *The Relational Model for Database Management, Version 2.* Addison-Wesley, 1990.

[COOP97] Cooper, R. *Object Databases, an ODMG Approach.* International Thomson Computer Press, 1997.

[DARW98] Darwen, H., and Date, C. J. *The Third Manifesto: Foundation for Object/Relational Databases.* Addison-Wesley, 1998.

[DATE95] Date, C. J. *An Introduction to Database Systems Volume I*, Sixth Edition. Addison-Wesley, 1995.

[DATE97] Date, C. J., and Darwen, H. *A Guide to the SQL Standard*, Fourth Edition. Addison-Wesley, 1997.

[DELO95] Delobel, C., Lécluse, C., and Richard, P. *Databases: From Relational to Object-Oriented Systems.* International Thomson Publishing, 1995.

[ELMA06] Elmasri, R., and Navathe, S. B. *Fundamentals of Database Systems*, Fifth Edition. Addison-Wesley, 2006.

[GEIG95] Geiger, K. *Inside ODBC.* Microsoft Press, 1995.

[GILL96] Gill, H. S., and Rao, P. C. *The Official Client/Server Computing Guide to Data Warehousing.* Que, 1996.

[GRAY93] Gray, J. and Reuter, A. *Transaction Processing: Concepts and Techniques.* Morgan Kaufmann Publishers, 1993.

[GULU99] Gulutzan, P., and Pelzer, T. *SQL-99 Complete, Really.* Miller Freeman, 1999.

[HARO04] Harold, E. R., and Means, W. S., *XML in a Nutshell*, Third Edition. O'Reilly, 2004.

[ISO87] ISO TC97/SC21/WG3 and ANSI X3H2. *ISO 9075 Database Language SQL.* International Organisation for Standardisation, 1987.

[ISO92] ISO/IEC JTC1/SC21. *ISO 9075:1992 (E) Database Language SQL.* International Organisation for Standardisation, 1992.

[KAY04] Kay, M. *Xpath 2.0 Programmer's Reference.* Wrox, 2004.

[KIM85] Kim, W., Reiner, D. S., and Batory D. S. (eds). *Query Processing in Database Systems.* Springer-Verlag, 1985.

[LANS92] van der Lans, R. F. *The SQL Guide to Oracle.* Addison-Wesley, 1992.

[LARO04] Larose, D. T. *Discovering Knowledge in Data: An Introduction to Data Mining.* Wiley-Interscience, 2004.

[MELT01] Melton, J., and Simon, A. R. *SQL:1999: Understanding Relational Language Components.* Morgan Kaufmann Publishers, 2001.

[MELT03] Melton, J., and Simon, A. R. *SQL:1999: Understanding Object-Relational and Other Advanced Features.* Morgan Kaufmann Publishers, 2003.

[SIMS04] Simsion, G. C., and Witt, G. C. *Data Modeling Essentials,* Third Edition. Morgan Kaufmann Publishers, 2004.

[STON86] Stonebraker, M. *The INGRES Papers: Anatomy of a Relational Database System.* Addison-Wesley, 1986.

[STON99] Stonebraker, M., Moore, D., and Brown, P. *Object-Relational Database Servers, the Next Great Wave.* Morgan Kaufmann Publishers, 1999.

[THOM02] Thomsen, E. *OLAP Solutions, Building Multidimensional Information Systems*, Second Edition. John Wiley & Sons, 2002.

[WIDO96] Widom, J., and Ceri, S. *Active Database Systems, Triggers and Rules for Advanced Database Processing.* Morgan Kaufmann Publishers, 1996.

[ZLOO77] Zloof, M. M. *Query By Example.* Proceedings of the NCC 44, Anaheim, Calif., May 1975 (AFIPS Press, 1977).

Index

Symbols

A

B

C

D

G

H

J-K

L

N

S

U

V

W

X

Y

Z

THIS BOOK IS SAFARI ENABLED

INCLUDES FREE 45-DAY ACCESS TO THE ONLINE EDITION

The Safari® Enabled icon on the cover of your favorite technology book means the book is available through Safari Bookshelf. When you buy this book, you get free access to the online edition for 45 days.

Safari Bookshelf is an electronic reference library that lets you easily search thousands of technical books, find code samples, download chapters, and access technical information whenever and wherever you need it.

TO GAIN 45-DAY SAFARI ENABLED ACCESS TO THIS BOOK:

- Go to **http://www.awprofessional.com/safarienabled**
- Complete the brief registration form
- Enter the coupon code found in the front of this book on the "Copyright" page

If you have difficulty registering on Safari Bookshelf or accessing the online edition, please e-mail customer-service@safaribooksonline.com.